Copyright © 2025 by Eddie Daniels

All rights reserved.

This book or any portion may not be reproduced, stored, transmitted, or used in any matter whatsoever without the express written permission of the copyright holder except for the use of brief quotations in a book review.

Published in the United States of America

ISBN 978-0-9970739-6-6

Contact the author at chrisekeedei@yahoo.com.

Table of Contents

Chapter 1: What Is a Shock Film? 10
    Why I'm Interested in Shock Films 11
    Shocks Writ Large 19
    What Makes Film So Special? 21
    A Few More Quick Notes 23

Chapter 2: The Silent Era, 1895-1929 25
    Edison 25
    Meanwhile, in France 28
    Back in the U.S. 31
    Fiction Takes Over 33
    Is Nudity Necessarily Naughty? 39
    What About Free Speech? 42
    The Birth of a Nation 44
    Griffith's Encore 47
    Content-Based vs. Message-Based Shocks 48
    Back to Content-Based Shocks 51
    The Birth of Exploitation 53
    Sex Hygiene Overseas 56
    Movies in Their Sights 59
    If the Medium is the Message, Shoot the Messenger 64
    Weird Shocker Overseas 67
    The Flap Over Flappers 68
    So Let's Go Back to Europe 70
    Exploitation on the Rise 72
    Something Old, Something New 74
    The "Don'ts and Be Carefuls" 76

    Back to Europe 80
Chapter 3: The Pre-Code Era: 1929-1934 86
    How Is It "Pre-Code"? 86
    Is the Exploitation Circuit Helping? 87
    The Production Code 89
    The Message-Based Shock of Women's Dangerous Problems . 92
    Enter Howard Hughes 100
    The Arrival of a Pre-Code Superstar 102
    Sexy Cartoons? 103
    Germany Again? 104
    Crime Time 106
    What About Horror? 110
    Let's Get Back to Sex 115
    It's Not Sinful; It's History 118
    The "Bad Girl" 119
    More Real-Life Scandal 121
    Aren't Europeans Doing Anything? 122
    Nudity Is Good for You 125
    Make Way for the Queen 127
    Joseph Breen and the Legion of Decency 129
    The Cops Break Up the Party 131
    A Final Few Shockers 134
Chapter 4: The Code Era: 1934-1948 137
    A Time of "Decency" 137
    Independence and Exploitation 142
    Overseas 146
    The Good Kind of Exploitation 150

- The Outlaw 154
- The Ultimate Sex Hygiene Film 161
- Song of the South 164
- Anger 167
- Chaplin's Last Stand 168
- Post-War Neorealism 169

Chapter 5: The Transitional Era, Part 1: 1949-1959 175
- Chocs français 175
- Freedom of Message-Based Expression..................... 178
- Tentative First Steps Toward Sex 181
- The New Exploitation 188
- Night and Fog 192
- Back in the Mainstream 193
- Sexy Imports 198
- The Code Might Bend, But It Won't Give Up Bigotry ... 203
- Preminger Again 205
- A New Frontier in Nudity 209
- Birth 211
- Wrapping Up the 1950s 212

Chapter 6: The Transitional Era, Part 2: 1960-1968 214
- The New Brutality 214
- Continental Horrors 219
- The Connection 221
- Messages That Could Still Shock 223
- Irreverence Overseas 231
- (Mostly) Real Content-Based Shocks 236
- Exploitation Gets Rough 239

Deeper Underground 245
Nudity Comes to Hollywood 250
Censor Me, Stupid 253
Sweden on the Cutting Edge 255
Blasphemy! (Probably!) 258
What About Japan? 259
Up from the Underground 260
The Spirit of '66 261
New Hollywood, New Exploitation 268
James Joyce on Fucking 271
Unseeable Shocks 273
Back to Women and Sex 277
What About Men and Sex? 280
OK Guys, You Can Defy Gender Norms, But No Sex! 281
The New Horrors 283
Time for Ratings 285

Chapter 7: The New Freedoms, 1969-1976 287
X-Rated 287
Shockbusters 291
Let's Check In with Japan 294
The Masters Dive In 296
What's Left to Exploit? 298
Make Way for the King 301
The Mainstream Attempts LGBTQ+ 302
Russ Meyer in the Mainstream? 305
Black Power 306
Time for Panic 311

- Even Weirder? ... 313
- What's Happening in Australia? ... 314
- Experimenting with Corpses ... 315
- Back in the Mainstream ... 317
- The Trilogy of Life, Then Death ... 323
- Another Peak Shocker ... 328
- Genuine Trash ... 330
- The Real Thing ... 333
- The Prudes Strike Back ... 337
- What If We Made the Core Softer? ... 342
- Bakshit Crazy ... 345
- Bloody Good Fun ... 347
- What's Left for Horror? ... 348
- The Peak of Exploitation Shocks ... 352
- The Peak of Art Film Shocks ... 359
- Best Shock Movie Ever? ... 370

Chapter 8: Post-Peak Synthesis 1978-1980 ... 372
- Horror Heyday ... 375
- The Germans Are Back ... 377
- New Hollywood Shockers Limp to the End Point ... 379
- What If Kiddie Porn Were Cutesy? ... 382
- And Now for Something Completely Different ... 386
- The Absolute Rock Bottom ... 390
- The Synthesis Is Formed ... 393

Chapter 9: The Reagan Era: 1980-1988 ... 395
- Conservatism and the Status Quo ... 395
- Ignorance and Exploitation of LGBTQ+ Identities ... 397

- New Horror Heights (or Lows, Depending on Your Perspective) 401
- Real-Life Horror 403
- Real-Life Horror of a Very Different Kind 405
- New and Old in Shock Comedy 410
- You Can See It at Home 413
- Can the Arthouse Still Shock? 420
- Pure, Distilled Gore 423
- Horror with Meaning 425
- A Shock Film About Shock Film Fans 427
- Return of the Roughie? 429
- Blackface is Back 433
- Can Horror Get More Shocking? 435
- The Last Third Rail of Cinema 440
- The UK Gets in on the Fun 443
- Let's Wrap This Chapter Up 444

Chapter 10: A Slight Swing Back Toward Freedom 448
- NC-17-Rated 448
- Do the Right Thing 451
- New Queer Cinema 454
- What About Women? 457
- Return of the Shock Auteurs 460
- Shocks Return to the Mainstream 464
- A High Rating That Worked 468
- Peter Jackson's Last, Best Shock Film 470
- More Adventures at the Borderline Between R and NC-17 470
- Let's Try That Famous 1990s Indie Scene 474
- The Internet Disrupts 483

Chapter 11: The Shock Auteurs ... 486
- The Godfather of the 21st-Century European Shock Auteurs ... 487
- Shockfathers ... 488
- Mothershockers ... 490
- The New French Extremity ... 496
- Sex Triumphs Over Censorship ... 499
- Searching for American Shock Auteurs ... 503
- Real Sex 2 ... 509
- Hard-Core Horror Returns ... 512
- Getting Political ... 514
- Mysterious Skin ... 518
- The Next Breakthrough in Shock Comedy ... 521
- Hungary Man ... 522
- The French Up the Stakes ... 523
- Your Turn, Japan ... 524
- Doc Shocks ... 524
- Upset by the Dutch ... 526
- Back to the European Shock Auteurs ... 527
- What About the Internet? ... 530
- The Last Movie ... 532

Afterword ... 536

List of Official Shock Films ... 538
- Chapter 2: The Silent Era, 1895-1929 ... 538
- Chapter 3: The Pre-Code Era, 1929-1934 ... 540
- Chapter 4: The Code Era, 1934-1948 ... 542
- Chapter 5: The Transitional Era, Part 1, 1949-1959 ... 543
- Chapter 6: The Transitional Era, Part 2, 1960-1968 ... 544

Chapter 7: The New Freedoms, 1969-1977 547

Chapter 8: Post-Peak Synthesis, 1978-1980 552

Chapter 9: The Reagan Era, 1980-1989 553

Chapter 10: A Slight Swing Back Toward Freedom, 1989-1997 554

Chapter 11: The Shock Auteurs, 1997-2010 556

Shock Film Stats 559

Directors with More than Two Shock Films 560

Index 561

Acknowledgements 590

Chapter 1: What Is a Shock Film?

Nearly every movie contains some sort of shock. A good plot twist can feel shocking. A shot of beautiful scenery can provide a jolt. In this book, I'm exploring a specific type of shock: one that breaks taboos, specifically in the realms of sex, violence, profanity, sacrilege, controversial messaging, and a few other areas that many cultures find transgressive. The films that contain these shocks often fall in the genres of horror, exploitation, or art films, but can come from anywhere.

Beyond that vague description, it's difficult to define what constitutes shocking content. It's different for everyone. One person could have no problem with nudity but avert their eyes at any sight of blood, while another can be just the opposite. Cultures are also very different. A Danish audience likely won't be bothered by a blasphemous scene that would horrify a group of Saudis.

To keep this book at a reasonable length, I have to pick one culture to focus on. And when it comes to movie history, it's hard not to at least start with the United States. The United States has produced the most films that have received widespread international viewership. Even if you focus on only the most historically significant films as chosen by the likes of critics and directors, the United States is dominant.

A French, Italian, or Japanese cinephile might disagree with that, but I have data. The website They Shoot Pictures, Don't They? compiles thousands of lists of favorites to produce a top 1,000 film list. It includes the entries of the more famous Sight and Sound poll, plus hundreds more from people in the know about movies. This larger pool makes They Shoot Pictures, Don't They?'s list more valid and less mercurial than Sight and Sound's, in my view. Of the top 1,000 in the 2025 list, the most recent at this writing, 427 are primarily from the United States. France is second with 142 and Italy and the United Kingdom are tied for third with 64.[1]

This isn't to say that American films are objectively better. It's just to say that there's some justification for putting the United States at the center of my review of shock films. Plus, I am American, and it's not easy to remove your own cultural lens.

But I won't be the typical American who ignores non-American film. Americans may have made more great films than any other country, but as you can see from the above numbers, they don't have a majority. And even the most American-centric overview of shock films wouldn't be complete without all the non-American influences.

Thus, for the most part, I'm covering the film content that has shocked American/Western audiences. Even with that focus, there is a surplus of candidates. I'll try my best to cover the films that are the most interesting and best illustrate how what shocks us has changed in the past 130 years.

Why I'm Interested in Shock Films

No one outside of my friends and family is reading this book to learn about me. But explaining why I'm interested in shock films might shed some light into why other people like them, without me indulging in the pretense of speaking for all humanity. While I'm pretty arrogant to write about myself, I think I'd be even more arrogant to try to write on behalf of everyone.

This is why I write in first person a lot. It isn't entirely out of egotism. I think that most people who write about art try too hard to universalize their own subjective reactions. Film criticism is full of over-generalizations, using phrases like "this gives the viewer the feeling that …" and "the film doesn't work because …" What the

---

[1] https://www.theyshootpictures.com/gf1000.htm, visited on 10/9/2025

writer really means is "this gives me the feeling that ..." and "the film doesn't work for me because ..."

No writer can reach into the brains of the rest of humanity. To me, attempting to speak for everyone about something as subjective as art is even more egotistical than frequently referring to yourself. Only through a consensus of many opinions can you reach anything close to a generalization about a film's quality. A single person can't decide whether a movie is objectively "good" or "bad"; they can only say if they liked it and why.

I didn't invent this perspective; a version of it dates back at least to the 1950s, with a critic named Robert Warshow. In the preface of an essay collection called "The Immediate Experience," he writes about how your average film critic concerned himself too often with "those elements which he believes to be affecting or expressing 'the audience' rather than what he himself responds to."[2] (It was the 1950s, so everything was gendered as male.)

But I understand why film critics usually don't write in the first person. It sounds presumptuous to imply that any reader would be interested in your personal opinion about a film. Moreover, you're trying to position yourself as an impartial authority, expressing objective truths. Your knowledge, experience, and capacity for insight is supposed to elevate your opinion beyond the knee-jerk reaction of an easily wowed neophyte.

There is certainly some value in expressing that you have expertise. In all activities, even watching and thinking about movies, some people have more experience than others. But you can simultaneously express the credentials behind your opinion and make it clear that it's your opinion. Many of the great film critics,

---

[2] Quoted in Harvey Shapiro. "Rediscovering 'The Immediate Experience' by Robert Warshow," *The Georgia Review*, Vol. 47, No. 4 (Winter 1993), pp. 726-732

including probably the most beloved one ever, Roger Ebert, do just that.

Telling my story might also have the personal benefit of making me seem a little less like a weird creep for being so interested in shock films. But you are free to skip to the next section if this seems too self-indulgent. I will be introducing some concepts that will come into play later, though.

As a kid, I was definitely not into shocks. I was very timid, and any disturbing imagery would plague my mind indefinitely. I had to close my eyes during the opening of "Scooby-Doo" to avoid seeing a skull with eyes that glowed. The most terrifying thing I saw as a child was at the end of "Superman III," in which a woman gets sucked into a computer and turned into a robot. This was the 1980s, mind you, when most kids were watching "Poltergeist" or "A Nightmare on Elm Street." There was no way I was going to subject myself to those. Just a poster of Freddy Krueger would give me nightmares. I did not feel the sort of sick thrill that many kids felt for scary movies. I felt only pure fear and revulsion.

I was a very prudish kid in other ways. I never said bad words, and if I thought of one I would immediately pray for forgiveness. Sex was a mystery I did not want to explore; I remember refusing to read a Trivial Pursuit question that mentioned *Playboy* and Marilyn Monroe.

I even had a vague sense that if I witnessed something extremely shocking and forbidden, my soul would be permanently warped and I would somehow be consigned to a life of misery. It was more than a bit melodramatic, but I bet I got it from some sort of Christian fall-from-grace concept, a loss of innocence leading to eternity in Hell or something like that.

It wasn't just my upbringing. We did go to church each week, but we were Presbyterian, and there's a limit to how pious you can be as a Presbyterian. It's a sect for nice, quiet people who don't overdo things. My parents were strict but not puritanical. They looked down on popular culture not because it was filthy but because they were academics, and didn't think we should waste our time with things that people did not write masters' theses about. This perspective didn't prevent me from loving Saturday morning cartoons and bad sitcoms, so I don't think it really sunk in. No, it was pure inborn anxiety that drove my extreme repulsion from anything remotely shocking.

When I got into my mid-teens, my reactions to shock media turned around 180 degrees. Shocking content was stimulating to the same degree, but the pain turned to thrills. I changed from a child who couldn't look at a picture of Freddy Krueger to a teenager who was electrified by "The Silence of the Lambs" and "The Shining."

I got some insight into how this works when I studied human emotions in graduate school. (I did nothing with my degree, by the way – the short version of the story is that academia is brutal.) Check out the circumplex model of emotion, developed by James Russell:[3]

---

[3] Reproduced from "Independence and bipolarity in the structure of current affect," by L. Feldman Barrett and J.A. Russell, 1998, *Journal of Personality and Social Psychology*, 74(4), p. 970. Copyright 1998 by the American Psychological Association.

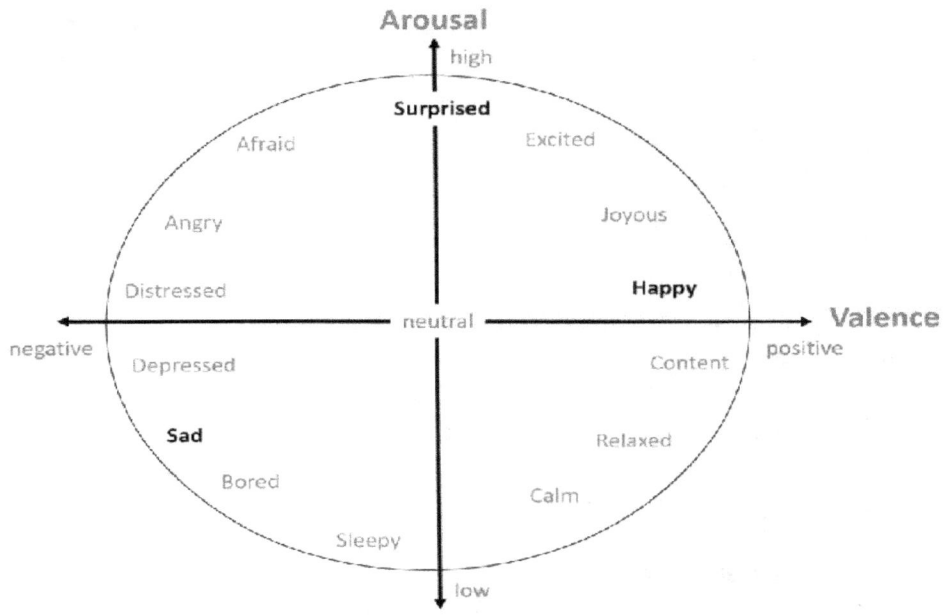

In the above figure, you see how all the most basic emotions can be organized along two axes. The vertical axis represents how much stimulation you feel, but doesn't involve whether it's positive or negative. The horizontal axis is about how positive or negative it is.

When I was a little kid, shocking images gave me high stimulation that was firmly on the negative side of the spectrum. Any disturbing sight would cause tremendous immediate distress and plague my mind for months afterwards. It was all in the "Afraid" part of the above graph.

When I was a teenager, my reactions moved rightward on the positive/negative axis, into excitement. I began to seek out the most shocking movies. In an essay, filmmaker Catherine Breillat calls this impulse a "devouring desire to see what had always terrified me."[4]

In their teenage years, human brains develop an ability to better separate reality and fantasy. As a prepubescent I felt, deep down,

---

[4] Catherine Breillat, "Pier Paolo Pasolini: Writing on Burning Paper"

that a gory image was real. When I was older, I would think it was real for a split-second, but then the rational part of my brain would quickly take over. I would feel a rush of relief that then shifted the high arousal from the "Afraid" into the "Excited" area. Then there was the rush from mastering my fear. That's part of it, anyway.

This is my experience, mind you, and probably of some other people too. It's certainly not universal. Many people don't like shock films at all. Their reactions stay on the negative side of the above model both before and after they become able to separate reality from fantasy. I could offer theories about what makes shock-seekers different from shock-avoiders, but they would be pretty half-baked. Suffice it to say, I think getting a charge out of shock films is just a personality difference and not a personal failing.

There is a general assumption, though, that watching and enjoying shocking content is, at the very least, disreputable. More stridently, many believe that if you consume shock content, you will be encouraged to do shocking things in real life.

Again, I'm not going to speak for all humanity, but I can say that it certainly hasn't happened for me. I've never been violent; in fact, I am perhaps overly conflict-avoidant. In terms of sex, let's just say I'm very far from being a swinger and leave it at that. My capacity for guilt and shame is prodigious, which forces me into a very morally upstanding life. I am a happily married father of three kids who goes to bed at 9:30 each night. As a young adult, I would occasionally try to be cool and go to bars and concerts and such, but that was about as much wildness as I've managed to experience.

Film is a gateway into a life I only want to experience vicariously, because it would be too scarring in reality. I can be thrilled by a battle scene, but I know that living through an actual battle would leave me deeply traumatized.

This gets to another aspect of fantasy and reality that is relevant to this book. In the film "The Pervert's Guide to Cinema," philosopher Slavoj Zizek talks about fantasy and reality as it is depicted in film.

There's a scene in "Vertigo," for example, where Scotty, played by Jimmy Stewart, dresses up a woman to look exactly how he wants her to. It's a realization of his fantasy, and Zizek says that "we have a name for fantasy realized -- it's called 'nightmare.'"

This might seem counter-intuitive, and without the context Zizek provides, it sounds like a gross oversimplification. He's not talking about a fantasy of falling in love or owning a home. He's talking about the darker, more elemental fantasies that should never be realized.

Zizek goes on to talk about how a screen is not some window into another reality, but an access point into a separate part of our minds, that of fantasy. In his definition, fantasy is not a wish about what could happen. It is instead an illusion that you need to conjure the motivation, in the form of emotion, to accomplish something difficult. In "Vertigo," Scotty's sexual fantasy was so powerful that it compelled him to do a horrible, manipulative thing that ran contrary to his values and even his self-interest.

Zizek didn't mention violence, but you can see the fantasy version of violence in almost every film. It's portrayed as a heroic, manly triumph over an immediate threat. Meanwhile, real-life violence tends to be much more of a grubby, sad victimization of the weak. The fantasy of noble violence gives people the emotional motivation to go to war, start a fight, or commit other acts that they would deem not worth the risk in any calm, rational assessment.

I believe that many human beings are saddled with fantasies that would be hell to carry out. In a moment of rage, I could fantasize about assaulting someone. If I actually did it, though, it would be a horrible experience and I would regret it for the rest of my life. My fantasy brain doesn't know me very well. Moreover, it doesn't have a conscience. It only understands lizard-brain drives that it channels into dramatic imagined actions.

In human beings, there are several layers of brain on top of the lizard brain, and thank goodness for them. These layers prevent the lizard brain from acting out its impulses except in acceptable contexts. It can release its sexual urges only when with a willing partner. It can release its violent impulses only when participating in a sport like boxing. Society teaches these upper layers what the acceptable contexts are, and then these layers restrain the lizard brain unless those contexts are manifested. That's how it works most of the time, anyway. When this system fails, you get crime.

If you're so disposed, you could make the same argument in Freudian terms. Usually, the id is controlled by the ego and superego. When watching movies, the superego and ego permit the id a little vicarious fulfillment. I'm sure I'm missing subtle differences between these frameworks, but I think the basic idea is the same.

The main appeal of shock films for me is the temporary release for those unacceptable fantasies that are rightly tucked away in my id / lizard brain / Zizek-style "fantasy" realm. It isn't a case of Victorian-style inhibitions that need to be loosened so I can realize my true self. We're talking about the good kind of inhibitions, the ones that prevent me from doing something that will hurt someone else and saddle me with regret.

Again, I'm mentioning this in case my story connects with readers. I'm by no means suggesting this is a universal human trait. If you don't identify with any of this, consider yourself lucky. There's no valid use for shock-loving lizard-brain impulses that I can see. Maybe if I were thrown into a situation where I were forced to do something violent, I could do it more readily than would someone who lacks or is not in touch with any capacity for sick thrills. I could summon the motivation for action by plumbing the depths of Zizek-style "fantasy" (and then be saddled with guilt forever). It seems unlikely that will come up in my life though, and I sure don't want it to.

Shocks Writ Large

So I believe the story of shock films is largely about safely indulging justly forbidden impulses. But there's more to the story than that. There are many films that shocked audiences decades ago, but no longer do because societal mores have changed. A loving kiss between two men would have been unthinkable in 1930s Hollywood, but now it happens regularly in "Star Trek" episodes. As a straight man who grew up in the 1980s, I'm sure I was shocked to see a romantic gay kiss for the first time. Now I've internalized that there's nothing wrong with it, and it doesn't affect me.

Meanwhile, many 1930s Hollywood films contain racial stereotypes that while acceptable then would be shockingly offensive today. The changes over time in what constitutes a shock will be another running thread throughout this book.

And then there is the fact that the impact of film shocks weakens rapidly the more you see them. The first time most Americans saw a bloody death on screen, in 1967's "Bonnie and Clyde," they were shocked beyond measure. The average grown-up seeing it now will not be affected much. The rate at which film shocks subside will be another running thread throughout this book.

You can call it desensitization, and maybe it is. People often worry that viewing film violence leads to desensitization to real-life violence. From what I've seen, the desensitization is confined to the screen experience. A real-life act of violence will feel a hundred times more disturbing than a typical death scene in a horror film, even if the real one is one hundredth as graphic.

I'm re-opening the can of worms here that I tried to close before by retreating into my "it's just my experience" stance. Before I retreat again, though, I can't resist noting that there is no evidence that shocking media has made the world more violent. Japan has probably the most disturbing films in the world, but has a miniscule murder rate. Almost every other developed nation is similarly libertine in its media and surprisingly free of violence.

Even the United States, which is an outlier in terms of violence levels, has seen a dramatic drop in the violent crime rate since the 1990s. Violent crime was indeed on the rise in the United States until 1992, but then it started dropping off. FBI statistics show a historic low in 2023.[5] Media has not gotten less violent in that time. Shock media can't cause real-life violence when they don't even correlate. The popular book and documentary "Freakonomics" go through some of the possible reasons for the historic improvement in violent crime rates; movie content does not come up one way or another.

Now when it comes to sex, or blasphemy, or bad words ... maybe. It's certainly possible that the societal rules concerning those have changed in part due to movies. Sex outside of marriage has probably increased in the last few decades, but I'm not sure that's necessarily a bad thing for society. It becomes a problem when teenagers get pregnant, and there has also been dramatic improvement there since the 1990s. In 1991, 61.8 out of every 1000 females aged 15-19 got pregnant; in 2023 that number was down 78% to 13.6.[6]

We can explore these ideas more throughout the book. But this book is not primarily an exploration of real-world problems. We're staying in the realm of fantasy here, specifically in the release of unacceptable fantasy through watching films.

---

[5] FBI Crime Data Explorer, https://cde.ucr.cjis.gov/LATEST/webapp/#/pages/explorer/crime/query
[6] Trends in Teen Pregnancy and Childbearing, Office of Population and Child Affairs, U.S. Department of Health and Human Services, https://opa.hhs.gov/adolescent-health/adolescent-sexual-and-reproductive-health/trends-teen-pregnancy-and-childbearing

What Makes Film So Special?

Among all types of media, film is especially adept at delivering shocks. But don't take my word for it; read the views of perhaps the greatest novelist of all time, Leo Tolstoy. In a 1908 interview, Tolstoy effused about film's possibilities:

> [Film] is a direct attack on the old methods of literary art. We shall have to adapt ourselves to the shadowy screen and to the cold machine. A new form of writing will be necessary. I have thought of that and I can feel what is coming.
>
> But I rather like it. This swift change of scene, this blending of motion and experience – it is much better than heavy, long-drawn-out kind of writing to which we are accustomed. It is closer to life. In life, too, changes and transitions flash by before our eyes, and emotions of the soul are like a hurricane. The cinema has divined the mystery of motion. And that is greatness.
>
> When I was writing 'The Living Corpse,' I tore my hair and chewed my fingers because I could not give enough scenes, enough pictures, because I could not pass rapidly enough from one event to another. The accursed stage was like a halter choking the throat of the dramatist; and I had to cut the life and swing of the work according to the dimensions and requirements of the stage. I remember when I was told that some clever person had devised a scheme for a revolving stage, on which a number of scenes could be prepared in advance. I rejoiced like a child, and allowed myself to write ten scenes into my play. Even then I was afraid the play would be killed.
>
> But the films! They are wonderful! Drr! and a scene is ready! Drr! and we have another! We have the sea, the coast, the city, the palace – and in the palace there is tragedy (there is always tragedy in palaces, as we see in Shakespeare).

> I am seriously thinking of writing a play for the screen. I have a subject for it. It is a terrible and bloody theme. I am not afraid of bloody themes. Take Homer or the Bible, for instance. How many bloodthirsty passages there are in them -- murders, wars. And yet these are the sacred books, and they ennoble and uplift the people. It is not the subject itself that is so terrible. It is the propagation of bloodshed, and the justification for it, that is really terrible! Some friends of mine returned from Kursk recently and told me a shocking incident. It is a story for the films. You couldn't write it in fiction or for the stage. But on the screen it would be good.[7]

Because films mimic seeing and hearing real-life experiences so well, their stories shoot through the human nervous system and deliver a visceral impact more easily than literature or theater can. In Tolstoy's words, films are "closer to life. In life, too, changes and transitions flash by before our eyes, and emotions of the soul are like a hurricane."

I'm not saying theater and literature are in all ways inferior to film. I doubt Tolstoy is either. A well-written novel can deliver a deep, disturbing shock that rocks your foundation. But it needs thousands of words to do it, and that takes time. Speed is the key here.

Stage plays also "could not pass rapidly enough from one event to another," in Tolstoy's words. The "bloody themes" he cites as being fundamental to everything from Homer to the Bible are well-served by the immediacy of film. Any crappy film can provide a shallow shock in a split-second. Also, a well-made film can take a little longer to provide a novel-style shock.

This is true in terms of sex. Romance novels can be very erotic, but they need time to do so, and are heavily dependent on the context: the characters, the situation, etc. Film can be erotic in a shallow way with a quick shot of a naked attractive person arching an eyebrow. A

---

[7] David Bernstein (trans.), 'Tolstoy on the Cinema', *New York Times*, 31 January 1937, p. 158, quoting Leo Tolstoy in conversation August 1908

good film can also take a little more time to spin a more complex, novelistic eroticism.

This is also true in terms of violence. If you read that 1,000 people were killed in a landslide in Asia, you would be disturbed. But if you watched a film of the same 1,000 people dying, the impact would be exponentially larger. A picture is worth a thousand words, and a film is 24 pictures per second.

The visceral power of film often proves too much for some people. This underlies many calls for censorship. We'll see examples of this throughout the following pages.

A Few More Quick Notes

When I describe movies in the book, I try not to ruin their endings. There are times, though, when it can't be helped. I will put any blatant spoilers in HTML-style tags, like this: <SPOILER ALERT> blatant spoiler </SPOILER ALERT>.

Also, I realize that you're probably more interested in reading about "The Exorcist" than, say, the 1908 film "The James Boys in Missouri," which you can't even watch because no copies of it survive. Still, I encourage you to read this book in order. It's a history, not a compilation of movie reviews, and I try to develop themes and shape it into a narrative as much as possible. If I start relating "The Exorcist" to "Häxan" or the "Miracle" decision, you'll thank me for this warning.

That said, although this is a history, it's not an academic text. An advantage of not being in academia is that I have no colleagues I have to impress with a deadly serious tone, a personality-free voice, and long, overstuffed sentences. Honestly, I don't even know why academics write so dryly and impenetrably. Maybe if you're discussing hard science, you want to sound as fact-based and unbiased as possible. But if you're writing about the arts? What is art if not beautifully messy, emotional subjectivity? Anyone who chronicles and analyzes artistic achievements as if they were a dispassionate truth-dispensing machine is trying to fool both themselves and their readers. Anyway, my point is that I feel fully justified in trying to make this book at least a little bit entertaining.

Along the same lines, I sometimes throw in tangents that I think will be of interest. When a movie makes me think of an interesting story or fact, I can't resist including it. This book is mostly for fun, after all. Let's get to it already.

Chapter 2: The Silent Era, 1895-1929

Edison

There were earlier collections of images that could be called films, but the ones generally recognized as being the first mass-produced for public consumption were created by German inventor Ottomar Anschütz. Few of these survive, and his achievement was quickly eclipsed by similar movies made by Thomas Edison's company. This was Edison's m.o.: Co-opt some emerging technology, order an underling to make a few tweaks, and claim it as his own invention.

Edison's films were not projected for crowds. To see them, you had to go to a business that had machines called kinetoscopes. After plugging a coin into the kinetoscope, a single person could watch very short films through a peephole. Films were more like carnival novelties, like strength tests or whack-a-mole, than anything approaching a narrative art form.

Edison's first offerings were mostly filmed vaudeville acts, shot from the perspective of an audience member. They caused a craze that peaked in 1895. Some were shots of women dancing, and were of course meant for men. One called "**Carmencita**" is credited with being the first film portraying a woman. (I'm putting all my official shock films in bold the first time they come up, by the way. Non-shock films do not get the honor of being bolded.) It was pulled from an Asbury Park, New Jersey exhibitor's lineup after the town's founder, James A. Bradley, saw it and "was so shocked by the glimpse of Carmencita's ankles and lace that he complained to Mayor Ten Broeck."[8]

---

[8] Quoted in David Robinson, "[Carmencita description]," in Mannoni et al., *Light and Movement*

Otherwise, there is not much record of scandal over these films. As with real-life Victorian-era shows involving dancing women, the patrons probably didn't talk about them much in mixed company.

The novelty quickly wore off. After seeing a few soundless, black-and-white versions of the same acts they could catch a few doors down in real life (often at the same price), people understandably lost interest. The draw was really about watching pictures move for the first time. It's a bit like those View-Master toys that could be very fun for a minute or two, but after you see the Grand Canyon in 3D a few times, you set them aside to collect dust.

One 1895 Edison film that broke this mold, and may have given people a shock of the type I'm interested in, was "**The Execution of Mary Stuart**." This odd little film is credited as being the first to use actors. It might be a stretch to call it the first fiction film; at only 18 seconds, there isn't time for a narrative. A male actor dressed as Mary, Queen of Scots puts his head on a stump. An executioner lifts his ax, and then a jump cut replaces the actor playing Mary with a dummy. This "stop trick" is the first known special effect in a film. The executioner then brings down his axe and chops off the dummy's head.

"The Execution of Mary Stuart" of course looks primitive and clumsy today. Children upload better-produced films to YouTube every second. But for someone who had never seen the stop trick before, it could have provided a sick thrill for at least a split-second, analogous to seeing a real execution. Surely that was the point at least. It's hard to imagine it being made for any other reason.

After the kinetoscope fad faded, Edison kept diversifying his offerings. In 1896, he released **"The May Irwin Kiss."** It's less than a minute long, and (spoiler alert) depicts a woman named May Irwin kissing. Specifically, two middle-aged people nuzzle a bit and then have a quick mouth-to-mouth peck. It was a huge hit.

Many viewers were disgusted by "The May Irwin Kiss." One critic bellowed "Such things demand police interference. Our cities from time to time have spasms of morality, when they arrest people for displaying lithographs of ballet-girls; yet they permit, night after night, a performance which is infinitely more degrading ... While we tolerate such things, what avails all the talk of American Puritanism and the filthiness of imported English and French stage shows?"[9]

"The May Irwin Kiss" is of course not shocking nowadays. In 1896, though, kissing in public was illegal in many places. Plus, the movie is one medium shot, where you see just the performers' shoulders and heads, instead of being filmed from the then-standard perspective of an audience member at a vaudeville show. In this movie you could clearly see the people's faces for a change. And because the scene no longer appeared to be on a stage, it felt more like it was really happening, that you were really a voyeur watching this couple in an intimate moment.

The shock people felt watching "The May Irwin Kiss" is hard for us to fathom, since we've all been raised on screens. We learn both consciously and unconsciously where we stand in relation to the people we are watching. From birth, we are slowly eased into the deep-seated understanding that everything on a screen is fake, first through viewing bright colors and shapes in YouTube videos, then through cartoons, then through cartoonish live-action kids' shows, and eventually to realism.

But the people of 1896 had only seen actual, living people or people in photographs. They'd seen people on stage, so the filmed vaudeville acts fit into that context. But when seeing a medium shot of people kissing, their only point of reference was actually watching real people kiss.

Around this time, the Roman Catholic Church made their first-ever call for censorship of films. It didn't happen, but the conversation

---

[9] Quoted in Frank Miller, "Censored Hollywood: Sex Sin & Violence on Screen," p.24

began. Censorship will of course be a major theme in this book. It is the best indicator of how shocking something was in its own era.

From 1897 on, Edison produced mainly what he called "actuality films," very short depictions of real events. Some were newsworthy, like footage of William McKinley's inauguration, while others were shots of tourist sites. They were essentially bits of newsreel.

Edison was not overly interested in artistic innovation with this new medium. His chief interest was in selling kinetoscopes; the films were secondary. The films existed to keep repeat customers coming back to the kinetoscopes, which justified the expense of shopkeepers buying and maintaining them.

With kinetoscopes at the center of the business, Edison did not want movies exhibited to roomfuls of people. This kept films in the realm of barroom novelties that respectable types would never deign to partake of. As with many other cultural breakthroughs throughout history, the middle and upper classes turned up their blue noses to something newfangled that appealed to working folk.

Meanwhile, in France

Soon after Edison's first kinetoscope films, brothers Auguste and Louis Lumière brought the medium to a different audience. They created a film recorder and projector that they called a cinematograph. Their factory produced photography equipment, and the brothers were respectable businessmen. In 1895, they screened a single film, "Workers Leaving the Lumière Factory" for an audience at the Society for the Development of the National Industry. Their aim was to demonstrate their invention to their peers. Unlike Edison's grubby little peep shows, this was a respectable event.

Later that year, the brothers toured France with a cinematograph and 10 films, each less than a minute long. Apart from some exhibitions by Ottomar Anschütz and maybe a few others, it was the first time that groups of people paid to see what we think of as movies projected onto a screen. The success of the tour demonstrated that people liked company while watching films. The Lumière brothers then brought their show all over the world and reached people of all social classes.

None of the Lumière brothers' films could be said to contain shocks beyond the basic thrill of seeing photographs move for the first time. Most were just static single shots of some ordinary thing occurring in real life. Perhaps "The Arrival of a Train" (1896) really did make some people jump out of their seats, terrified that the train on screen was going to hit them. I don't think that makes it a shock film by my definition -- that's more about people adjusting to a new medium than anything that breaks taboos.

After a few years of sending cameramen all over the world to capture real-life scenes, the Lumière brothers didn't see anywhere else to go with the medium. They were reported as saying "The cinema is an invention without any future."[10] They refused to even sell a cinematograph to anyone, insisting that they were only interested in the scientific principles it demonstrated.

It didn't take long for other people to make their own versions of cinematographs. And they quickly figured out a future for cinema: pornography. "**Le Coucher de la Mariée**" ("**Bedtime for the Bride**" or "**The Bridegroom's Dilemma**") was first shown publicly in November 1896. It depicts a woman getting undressed for her wedding night. This being the Victorian era, she has to remove dozens of articles of clothing, and her husband is relegated to behind a screen the whole time (but keeps peeking at her, cheekily). Only a minute and half survives from the original seven-minute running time. It struck me as footage of a rather spirited, slightly saucy stage show with no actual nudity.

---

[10] Quoted in James Naremore, "An Invention without a Future: Essays on Cinema," p. 1

"Le Coucher de la Mariée" was a huge hit in Paris, and became the first stag film. Thus it opens up a path that I'm mostly not going to follow in this book. Pornography is a worthy topic of discussion, but it is outside my scope. I'm interested in how shocking scenes in films developed in films that entertain general audiences. Pornography exists on a different track, for a different purpose (which I presumably don't have to inform you of).

For decades, it was illegal to make, own, or watch pornography. Pornos were mostly secreted away in men's clubs, for packs of drunk guys to whoop and holler at. I'm sure men watched it when alone too. I haven't studied early pornography to any real extent, but I imagine it's always been pretty repetitive stuff. People meet, have sex, the end. Sorry if I'm offending any porn cineastes who might be reading.

Granted, the pornographic and mainstream tracks cross sometimes, and when they do, I'll write about it. Segregating pornography from the rest of film can be a bit subjective sometimes, because a huge percentage of mainstream film shocks involve sex and nudity. United States Supreme Court Justice Potter Stewart became famous for the ultimate legal cop-out, saying that he can't define pornography, but "I know it when I see it."

A better definition is given by Slavoj Zizek in "The Pervert's Guide to Cinema." He describes pornography as a "deeply conservative genre" in which you can see everything, but narrative is sacrificed. Emotional engagement is thus cut off, which removes the fantasy that drives full-fledged eroticism. This definition might not establish a clear line between porn and non-porn, but it at least provides some guidelines for making assessments of individual films.

In writing this book, I try to detect the line between films that exist only to provoke sexual arousal and those that contain erotic or titillating scenes while also serving other, non-masturbatory purposes. It may be a fuzzy line, and there may be subjective calls in putting films on one side or the other. But the line exists, and my interests lie on the non-pornography side of it.

Let's move on to someone else who charted a cinematic future that the Lumiere brothers were too high-minded to fathom. Georges Méliès was a stage magician who often used a magic lantern in his shows. After seeing a Lumière brothers screening, he was inspired to seek out a camera. He did not have the brothers' highfalutin predisposition, so his films were wacky spectacles full of surprises. Many hold up well to this day, in my opinion, thanks to fast pacing, expert comedic timing, and an infectious sense of fun. Méliès' company clearly had a ball making movies.

Méliès' hundreds of films spanned every existing genre, including pornography. The 1897 film "**After the Ball**" simulates nudity by showing a woman in a body stocking. Méliès had an admirable tendency to throw everything at the wall with this new medium to see what stuck. There were plenty of societal mores that may have constrained him, but there were none prescribed specifically for film.

The most enduring films of Méliès' are those in the genre of the *féerie*, which was a blend of fantasy, science fiction and horror. "**House of the Devil**" (1896) is a féerie credited by some as being the first horror film. It's mostly a showcase for Méliès' favorite technique, the stop trick, in which one thing immediately changes to another through the magic of editing. To a non-1896 audience, "House of the Devil" is a pretty darn goofy procession of devils, bats, skeletons, etc. suddenly appearing to scare the protagonist. But if you try very hard to put yourself in the perspective of someone who has seen very few films, you can imagine getting some shocks out of it.

Back in the U.S.

1897 saw the release of "**Orange Blossoms**" in the United States. No copies of the film survive, so I can't verify what it's like. I also can't verify that it was a rip-off of "Le Coucher de la Mariée," but the description of it makes it sound suspiciously similar. Newlyweds come to their bedroom for their first night together. The man is sent out while the woman strips down and puts on a nightgown. She gets into bed, turns out the light, and says the French word "*entrez.*" Apparently, "in removing her clothing, however, she skillfully limits the exposure of her person."[11]

That line is from court documents, because a man was arrested in New York for exhibiting "Orange Blossoms." The court found him guilty, condemning the film for its ability to "outrage public morals."[12] This very vague definition effectively meant that cops and judges could punish anyone for whatever movie made them feel icky.

This may have been the first known case of someone being arrested for showing a film, and many other later cases rested on the same dubious, subjective legal basis. Filmmakers and exhibitors became hesitant to present anything too racy. Thus self-censorship preceded the more direct kind.

Edison's company responded to the success of the Lumière brothers' screening tour by creating the Vitascope, which could project films for crowds. It did not respond to Georges Méliès' innovations, instead sticking with relatively safe actuality films for several years. Most actuality films are pretty dull to modern eyes, but occasionally one could provide a real shock (no pun intended).

The story of "**Electrocuting an Elephant**" (1903) is a grim one. At Luna Park on Coney Island, an elephant named Topsy killed a drunken circusgoer who had burnt her trunk with a lit cigar. Several previous violent incidents by Topsy were probably provoked by abuse from her handlers. The Luna Park owners concluded that Topsy was a liability. Being sleazy circus owners, they decided to hang Topsy and charge admission to watch.

---

[11] Quoted in Edward de Grazia and Roger K. Newman, "Banned Films: Movies, Censors, and the First Amendment," p. 9
[12] Ibid

The American Society for the Prevention of Cruelty to Animals (ASPCA) was not happy with this plan. In that more brutal time for animals, the ASPCA was not only active; it had been around since 1866. Their power was more limited in those days, however. They protested the idea of making the hanging of an elephant into a public spectacle.

The only concession the ASPCA got was that the execution would be open to only invited guests and members of the press, and that poison and electricity would be used along with hanging.[13] The Edison film of Topsy's execution lasts a little more than a minute, and, as with "The May Irwin Kiss," the title says it all.

Perhaps surprisingly to people nowadays, "Electrocuting an Elephant" was not as controversial in 1903 as "The May Irwin Kiss" was in 1896. Most people, particularly the working-class people who watched movies, were very accustomed to seeing animals die. In the days before supermarkets, ordinary people regularly killed animals for food. Elephants were unusual, of course, which is why it was a spectacle. But it was more like a gonzo version of a normal occurrence than the bizarre horror it looks like now.

This demonstrates one central principle we will see throughout this book. For the most part, what we can see on a screen has expanded over time. What was unacceptable in 1896 would be unremarkable in a PG-rated movie today. But there are a few types of content that have taken an opposite trajectory, becoming more shocking over time. Animal cruelty is certainly one; racist depictions is another. We will get into plenty of examples later.

Fiction Takes Over

By 1903, Edison may have been getting a bit desperate to retain viewers. Competitors were cropping up everywhere. An employee of

---

[13] This story is taken from Michael Daly's book "Topsy: The Startling Story of the Crooked-tailed Elephant, P.T. Barnum, and the American Wizard, Thomas Edison."

the Edison company, Edwin S. Porter, was inspired by Georges Méliès' flights of fancy to push for more fiction films.

His persistence worked, and in 1903, Porter directed "**The Great Train Robbery**." It was such a blockbuster that it firmly established the predominance of fiction over actuality films. The film wasn't out of the ordinary for its time -- it was just the most effective western anyone had ever seen. And it had a great final shot (no pun intended).

This final shot, which I won't spoil (even though the film is 120 years old), is startling because it breaks dramatically from the rest of the film. "The Great Train Robbery" is mostly composed of long takes of wide shots that can feel pretty tedious to modern eyes. The final shot is as different as possible to maximize its effect.

I have not discovered many cries for censorship of "The Great Train Robbery," though. In the early 1900s, sex was more scandalous than violence, and the violence in "The Great Train Robbery" is not graphic. If you wanted to leave it out of your personal list of shock films, I guess I couldn't object. But it is only 10 minutes long, it's in the public domain, and it's very important in film history. You might as well see it.

And at the time, a general objection to movies about crime was bubbling up among the middle and upper classes. It was the Progressive Era, which resulted in both vital reforms, like women's suffrage, and misguided moralistic crusades, like Prohibition. The latter strain became manifest in a lot of especially condescending hand-wringing over movies. In their invaluable book "Banned Films: Movies, Censors, and the First Amendment," Edward de Grazia and Roger K. Newman write:

> "No sooner were the silent 'photoplays' publicly shown than the guardians of culture began to fear the social effects of films and to denounce the irresponsibility of the

moviemakers. Immigrants and children were of special concern."[14]

Most people would agree, then and now, that children should be shielded from strong content. But the fact the crusaders lumped immigrants in with children speaks to their paternalistic, xenophobic motivations. The Progressive Era was a time of massive immigration to the United States, particularly from Italy, Russia, and the Slavic countries. These countries were poor, and few of the arrivals had formal education. U.S.-born citizens were very concerned about what these people might do in the few hours when they weren't toiling in hellish factories. Again from de Grazia and Newman:

> "People who formerly had spent their spare time in poolrooms, dance halls, and, especially, saloons, now flocked to new and converted movie houses, which shortly became the *bête noire* of progressives."[15]

You might think that the people campaigning ardently against immigrants frequenting saloons would welcome a non-alcoholic alternative, but no. This strand of progressivism had more than a bit of Victorianism, in that, in the words of de Grazia and Newman, "leisure time was not intended to be socializing with peers in settings that might threaten the traditional authority of home, church, and school."[16]

It wasn't just progressives starting to agitate, though. "The counterforce was provided by attacks from what were to become the American cinema's two arch-antagonists: organized religion and the political Right," writes David A. Cook in "A History of Narrative Film." "These institutions had tolerated 'living pictures' so long as they promised to be a short-lived novelty, but when it became clear that the cinema was well on its way to becoming a major social and

---

[14] de Grazia and Newman, p. 7
[15] Ibid
[16] de Grazia and Newman, p. 8

economic force in the nation, they took the offensive."[17] If you have organized religion, the political Right and progressives arrayed against you, you don't have much of a chance.

The legal system would occasionally punish someone for showing a racy film. But at that point, in the view of the reformers, the cat was out of the bag. They wanted something to stop the offending material before it went public.

The first film censorship law was passed by the Chicago City Council in 1907. It decreed that any movie had to get a permit from the police department before it could be shown. The police would determine which films were "immoral or obscene" and unfit for public viewing.[18]

Immediately, the Chicago police clamped down on "**The James Boys in Missouri**" and "**Night Riders**" (both 1908). It's hard to judge whether these two shorts really were immoral or obscene, since no known copies have survived. This is true of about 75% of all silent films, according to Library of Congress film historian and archivist David Pierce.[19]

People weren't preserving films in the early days, by the way, because movies were considered disposable entertainment for the great unwashed. Films were usually printed on cheap stock that was very flammable. Most films would be shown for a few days, and then the stock would be melted down and recycled. Even the films that people thought were worth saving were often later lost in fires at studios.

I don't know if there's any analog in present-day culture for what film was in its early days. Maybe TikTok videos? For anything tangible,

---

[17] David A. Cook, "A History of Narrative Film." p. 34
[18] de Grazia and Newman, p. 178
[19] "The Survival of American Silent Films: 1912-1929." Library Of Congress. Council on Library and Information Resources and the Library of Congress.

even the most seemingly throwaway bits of culture now have some stalwart guardians who collect them in plastic sleeves for permanent preservation. If you lived in the 1940s, you would know how the world saw comic books and dime-store novels. Nowadays those items are often million-dollar treasures, but at the time, they were "low culture" trash that people consumed and then threw in the garbage.

"The Great Train Robbery" might give us a hint as to what Chicago authorities found offensive about "The James Boys in Missouri" and "Night Riders": simply depicting murders and crime was shocking at the time. After the Chicago police refused to issue permits for the two movies, an exhibitor sued. He argued that the ordinance deprived him of "rights under the Constitution" and objected to the concept of the police being the arbiters of what could and could not be shown.[20] The case went to the Supreme Court of Illinois, which declared that since the films showed crimes being committed, the police should be in charge of whether they can be seen.

It boggles the mind to think about what movies would be like now if they couldn't show someone doing something illegal, or if your local police department decided what you could see. But it's also interesting to try to put yourself in the shoes of people at the time. People who had not watched films had probably seen very few major crimes committed in their lives, and likely no murders. We of course watch them on screen all the time now, but in those days it might have delivered a shock like we feel when we see someone shoot heroin in a movie.

On the other hand, the people of 1908 were watching characters commit crimes on stage all the time. In court, the exhibitor made sure to point out that "The James Boys in Missouri" and "Night Riders" were based on stage plays. The Supreme Court of Illinois had a response to that too: that movies need special restrictions because they attract a different audience, "those of limited

---

[20] Dawn B. Sova, "Forbidden Films: Censorship Histories of 125 Motion Pictures," p. 161

means."[21] In other words, the lowly rabble who watched movies could not be trusted with grown-up ideas the way you can trust middle-class theatergoers. This sort of nakedly condescending classism will characterize justifications for censorship throughout this book.

As more and more films were produced, police departments were mostly replaced by boards of censors who could commit more of their time to editing and banning films. Soon censorship boards were cropping up in cities and states across the country, with each board having its own ideas about what films were acceptable. Kansas was a dry state and its board cut all scenes of drinking. For a while the Maryland board was led by a druggist, who would not permit any scenes involving poisoning.[22] Even if filmmakers genuinely tried to not cross the line, they would put out their films and discover that there were hundreds of lines, and all of them were invisible until you crossed them.

Exhibitors responded by trying to regulate themselves. They established a non-governmental organization to screen every movie before it could be shown. The National Board of Censorship of Motion Pictures, later the National Board of Review of Motion Pictures, was born. (It still exists, but is now basically a film fan club in New York City.)

As you might expect from any attempt at self-regulation, the National Board was pretty weak. It simply labeled films as "passed," "passed with changes as specified," or "condemned." Exhibitors could act on this information or ignore it. The National Board didn't replace local censorship boards, but often the local boards' decisions would be based on National Board judgments.[23]

---

[21] Ibid
[22] Miller, p. 42
[23] de Grazia and Newman, p. 10-13

Is Nudity Necessarily Naughty?

A film that demonstrates the weakness of the National Board was "**Hypocrites**," directed by Lois Weber in 1915. Weber was the most successful American auteur of the era apart from D.W. Griffith, and one of many powerful female directors. (Once corporations took over the movie industry in the 1920s, by the way, women were pushed out of positions of power. By the 1930s, there was only one female film director at the studios. More on her later.) Lois Weber made entertaining, popular films with a strong sense of moral outrage.

"Hypocrites" has moral outrage in spades. It's the story of a mordantly pious preacher who tries to confront hypocritical people with the naked truth, which is personified by an actual naked young woman. The woman appears nude in a good portion of the film, but is never regarded as a sex object. Instead, in a ghostly form, she holds a literal mirror up to the politicians, rich people, wild youths, etc., to expose their hypocrisy.

The film passed the National Board with no apparent controversy. But the real-life politicians, rich people, etc. of 1915 were outraged by the naked woman in "Hypocrites." It was banned in Ohio and caused riots in New York. The Boston mayor demanded that the negatives be painted over to clothe the nude woman.[24] This is the sort of thing the National Board was supposed to prevent.

In response to the controversy, Weber said "'Hypocrites' is not a slap at any church or creed – it is a slap at hypocrites, and its effectiveness is shown by the outcry amongst those it hits hardest, to have the film stopped."[25] I'd like to think that this was all part of her plan from the beginning, that she knew powerful people would

---

[24] Kitty Lindsay, "Forgotten Women of Film History: Lois Weber," *Ms. Magazine*, 11/6/2014
[25] Quoted in ibid

exhibit the same hypocrisy in their reactions to the film that the film itself portrays.

Granted, that sort of clever irony is nowhere to be found in the film. "Hypocrites" is over-the-top preachy, in my opinion – if you're curious about Lois Weber, try "The Blot" first. But I did find it wild to see so much full-frontal female nudity in a silent film that is explicitly religious. Look for a version that is 50 minutes or longer and produced by Kino Lorber, as it has the correct continuity and a sharper picture. Hopefully the version I saw, posted to YouTube by Women's Film Classics, is still there as you read this.

There were other films of the 1910s that featured non-sexual nudity. A 1911 Italian film of "The Divine Comedy" showed naked people being tortured in Hell. An actress named Audrey Munson appeared nude as an artist's model in 1916's **Inspiration,** another lost film. A contemporary review of it said:

> "Miss Munson's classic beauty and her remarkable poise absolutely remove every suggestion of the objectionable ... George Foster Platt, who directed the picture, has used the utmost delicacy producing the picture, and it would have to be a very prudish person who could find any serious objection to the film."[26]

It might be hard to fathom how full nudity could have been treated in such a contemporary-sounding way in the pseudo-Victorian 1910s. Of course, not everyone was as sophisticated as the above reviewer. "Inspiration" also caused great controversy. In 1916, the National Board announced that it would allow nudity in films only if it was "an essential element of a drama the nature of which warrants such presentation."[27]

---

[26] Quoted in Q. David Bowers, "Inspiration". Thanhouser Films: An Encyclopedia and History.
[27] Cynthia Chris, "Censoring Purity". *Camera Obscura*. 27 (1 (79))

I think of this book as being about movies that broke taboos, but really, at this early stage, the taboos for film were still being worked out. The points of reference for establishing film's taboos varied. Nudity was strictly forbidden on stage, but paintings had been packed with nude figures since the Renaissance. While many films were based on plays, Lois Weber was inspired to make "Hypocrites" by seeing Jules Joseph Lefebvre's 1870 painting "La Vérité."[28] Film occupied some amorphous space in between theater and painting. You were not looking at a real live person, as you would in a play. But at the same time, it was an image of a real person moving as they would in real life. Is theater or painting more analogous?

The decision was effectively made by the likes of the rioters in New York over "Hypocrites." I think they and many others had a gut feeling that watching a movie was a lot more like seeing a play than looking at a painting. It speaks to the immediacy of film that I talked about in the "What Makes Film So Special?" part of the first chapter. Seeing a naked person move in a film brings a visceral punch that, for most people, isn't provided by a static painted image.

After "Hypocrites," societal conditioning took over to firmly stigmatize nudity in film. Now, in the United States at least, there is effectively no such thing as non-sexual film nudity of the kind attempted in "Hypocrites" and "Inspiration." All nudity is now presumed to be a source of arousal, regardless of context. It's at the point where any non-arousing nudity is interpreted as horrifying. Seeing a naked person with an older or imperfect body, as you do in "It Follows" and "Hereditary," brings a visual shock on par with watching a beheading. If you've been to a European beach or even a park, you'll know this is less true outside the United States.

I'm tempted to conclude that movies are responsible for making nudity more taboo, but that might be a stretch. More likely, people stopped encountering non-sexual nudity in real life. The working class in the 1910s lived in cramped urban tenements with lots of

---

[28] "Hypocrites" at the AFI Catalog of Feature Films

other people. Their only options for bathing were public bathhouses. In such conditions, you can't avoid seeing your parents, uncles, grandparents, etc. naked from time to time. You would certainly witness your mother and other relatives breastfeeding.

Middle- and upper-class folks each had their own rooms, so they could afford to be more modest. They were able to adopt the Victorian/religious prudishness that eventually led to blanket bans on certain body parts being visible. It seems so set in stone nowadays that a female nipple is forbidden for kids to see on screen, but that was something that had to be hammered out in the 1910s.

What About Free Speech?

Throughout the battles over film content, the First Amendment cast doubt on the legality of censorship boards. If movies are a form of speech, what right does a state or city have to arrest someone for making or showing one just because some powerful person deems it "immoral"? There are limits to free speech, but saying subjectively immoral things in public does not breach any of them.

The question came to the U.S. Supreme Court in the 1915 case *Mutual Film Corporation v. Industrial Commission of Ohio*. Ohio's state government had empowered a censor board with approving all movies to be shown in the state. If anyone showed an unapproved film, they could be arrested. The Mutual Film Corporation sued, arguing this was a violation of free speech.

The Supreme Court ruled 9-0 that free speech did not extend to movies. In the case opinion, Justice Joseph McKenna wrote:

> "... the exhibition of moving pictures is a business, pure and simple, originated and conducted for profit ... not to be regarded, nor intended to be regarded by the Ohio

Constitution, we think, as part of the press of the country, or as organs of public opinion."[29]

This decision dealt a major blow to the film industry. It meant their productions would continue to be controlled by a confusing, haphazard patchwork of censorship boards across the country. And it sealed the fate of anyone who wanted to make shock films: Best not to try.

The *Mutual v. Ohio* decision raised a lot of questions that would later lead to more court cases. So wait, all of a sudden free speech doesn't apply to profit-making enterprises? The "press of the country" of the 1910s was the newspaper business, which made profits. What not-for-profit press of the country was there? There was no public radio or TV at the time. Government propaganda, I suppose?

If you read between the lines of the decision, you can detect the real message. Movies are just dumb swill that people crank out to entertain the great unwashed, so they're not deserving of constitutional protection.

Just four days before the decision, Chief Justice Edward Douglass White was asked if the court would watch a film. He responded "Moving picture! It's absurd, sir. I never saw one in my life and I haven't the slightest curiosity to see one."[30]

White changed his mind when he heard that the film on offer was a sympathetic portrait of the Ku Klux Klan, of which he had been a member. He and the other eight justices conceded to watch one the most controversial films of all time.

---

[29] Quoted in de Grazia and Newman, p. 5
[30] Quoted in de Grazia and Newman, p. 4

The Birth of a Nation

Unfortunately, a comprehensive review of any facet of the history of film has to include D.W. Griffith's "**The Birth of a Nation**." It was important in many ways, not the least of which was that it was the first wildly popular feature-length American film. Europeans had been making longer films for a few years, but they were often stagey "filmed plays." "The Birth of a Nation" was more what we now recognize as "cinematic."

Even middle-class people flocked to "The Birth of a Nation." They were hungering for something similar to serious theater in terms of length and intricacy of plot. As Harry M. Geduld writes in "Focus on D.W. Griffith," "People who had previously dismissed the movies as nothing more than a crude entertainment suddenly realized that they had become the century's most potent and provocative medium of expression."[31]

"The Birth of a Nation" is also unwatchable today, in my view. This is a film where the Ku Klux Klan are the heroes. The Black characters, usually portrayed by white men in blackface, are cartoonish, primitive monsters whose only interests are lazing about and trying to rape virginal white women.

Even in 1915, "The Birth of a Nation" was offensive to many. It barely passed the National Board of Censorship of Motion Pictures after a furious internal argument that was well-publicized. Thomas J. Dixon, Jr., who wrote the novel "The Clansman" that formed the basis of the film, was worried "The Birth of a Nation" would be suppressed.

To head off government intervention, Dixon arranged for a private showing for his old college buddy, President Woodrow Wilson. Wilson reportedly extolled the film as "like writing history with

---

[31] Quoted in Cook, p. 84

lightning" and said, "My only regret is that it is all so terribly true."[32] Wilson was a history professor before he became president, and his book "History of the American People" was a major source for Dixon's book.[33]

With Wilson's approval, theaters across the nation began showing "The Birth of a Nation." The National Association for the Advancement of Colored People (NAACP) quickly launched a major protest. Historians and prominent progressives lambasted the film's wild distortions and malevolent racism.

A riot at the Boston premiere of "The Birth of a Nation" compelled Massachusetts' governor to ban it across the state. Eventually six other states and many cities refused to permit its exhibition. In "Banned Films," de Grazia and Newman declare that "Birth of a Nation" "has been banned more often than any other film in motion picture history."[34] President Wilson had to walk back his previous praise and state that it had used great technique for specious ends.

People often think that the whole country was as racist as "The Birth of a Nation" in 1915. A huge majority was, but it's important to know that there were some non-racists and even a few anti-racists fighting to be heard. Black people were segregated and suppressed but not completely voiceless. It took much too long, but their perspective eventually became widespread. Positive social change usually takes decades of hard, grinding, seemingly hopeless work before finally reaching a tipping point.

And sometimes a major event will set progress back decades. Where "The Birth of a Nation" was shown, it caused great damage. The original Ku Klux Klan had effectively died out after the creation of the federal Department of Justice in 1870 and the Enforcement

---

[32] Quoted in de Grazia and Newman, p. 4
[33] Mark Benbow, "Birth of a Quotation: Woodrow Wilson and 'Like Writing History with Lightning'". *The Journal of the Gilded Age and Progressive Era.* **9** (4): 509–533.
[34] de Grazia and Newman, p. 5

Act of 1871. In 1915, "The Birth of a Nation" inspired a new iteration of the Klan based on the version shown in the film.[35] Thomas Dixon.'s book "The Clansman" invented the white hoods and burning crosses that the film popularized. The first mass parade of hooded Klansmen was to a theater showing "The Birth of a Nation."[36]

Previously, I puzzled at the moralists decrying films like "The May Irwin Kiss." They were scared that such films might compel viewers to do "horrible" things, like, presumably, kissing in public. But "The Birth of a Nation" did compel viewers to do things that actually were horrible. Granted, racial hatred was rampant throughout the United States before the film was ever shown. If not for "The Birth of a Nation," it likely would have found a different outlet. But it may not have found such an organized and violent outlet as the Klan if the film had not galvanized so many people to unify in one evil organization.

It goes to show that the story of shock films is not a simple trajectory in which the Western world slowly discovers that greater permissiveness has benign effects. It is more of a gradual sorting out of which types of shocking content are harmless and which are not. All shock cinema mines the depths of humanity's darkest impulses. We have mostly learned that adults indulging vicariously in sex and violence by watching them in film is not as warping as many believed. We have also learned that endorsing racist animus on screen the way "The Birth of a Nation" does is extremely harmful, and therefore such depictions are now rightly considered unacceptable.

---

[35] John Hope Franklin, "The Birth of a Nation: Propaganda as History". *Massachusetts Review*. 20 (3): 417–434.
[36] "A 1905 Silent Movie Revolutionizes American Film – and Radicalizes American Nationalists". Southern Hollows podcast.

Griffith's Encore

The outcry against "The Birth of a Nation" was by all accounts a surprise to director D.W. Griffith. People talk about being in echo chambers or media bubbles now -- it was even more so in the days before national radio and television broadcasts. Griffith had grown up in the South and ingested racist ideology from birth. In seeing the response to "The Birth of a Nation," he was blown away to discover that not everyone thought Black people were subhuman monsters incapable of governing themselves.

Did he learn from this experience? Well, if you've ever been on social media, you can probably predict what happened next. You've likely seen someone post something offensive, followed by people responding angrily. Does the original poster ever say "Hm, I never knew that could cause offense. Thank you for teaching me something new." Not likely; the time-honored tradition is for that person to blast their critics for being "intolerant." "It can't be my fault that I said something that hurt people," this reasoning goes, "because I'm not evil or dumb. It must be someone else's fault, like the people who were offended. Yeah, their 'intolerance' of my views is the real problem. You know who else was intolerant: the Nazis!"

Because Facebook had not been invented yet, Griffith responded with a massive film called "**Intolerance**." It weaves together four historical stories that exemplify the terrible consequences of intolerance, in Griffith's extremely amorphous definition. As David A. Cook writes in "A History of Narrative Film," "Griffith seems hardly to have known what he meant by the term 'intolerance,' except that he associated it with the bitter outcry against 'The Birth of a Nation.' In the context of the film itself, 'intolerance' is simply an omnibus word encapsulating any form of human evil."[37]

One of Griffith's four stories is about Jesus Christ. Thus D.W. Griffith equated criticism over his racist film with the persecution and

---

[37] Cook, p. 93

crucifixion of Jesus. Thank God the film was made before World War II, or he definitely would have set a story in a Nazi concentration camp.

But if you can somehow set aside all this context (and Griffith's purple prose in the intertitles), "Intolerance" is actually kind of good, in my opinion. It has no Black characters, so no outlets for Griffith's racism. The story of the Babylonian king Belshazzar has a kick-ass female protagonist, the so-called "Mountain Girl," whose strength and self-assurance stand in welcome contrast to Griffith's typical virginal damsels desperate for rescue. The ending to this story is a wild, huge-scale battle that was very dangerous to shoot.

In this battle there are some genuine shocks that qualify "Intolerance" for this book. I don't want to spoil anything by giving specifics, but suffice to say the level of violence was more graphic than would be permitted in later years. Also, in an earlier harem scene there is some female nudity that was justified as being historically relevant – again, context could make for exceptions in those days. "Intolerance" might qualify for a PG-13 rating nowadays.

Because of its importance to film history, "The Birth of a Nation" used to appear on best-films-ever lists, such as the 1998 version of American Film Institute's 100 Greatest American Movies of All Time." The 2007 version of the same list replaced "The Birth of a Nation" with "Intolerance." It seems a wise move to me. "Intolerance" may not have been the first to use many of the cinematic techniques that Griffith pioneered, but it is in many ways a more impressive spectacle. Plus, it carries the big advantage of being endurable by non-racists.

Content-Based vs. Message-Based Shocks

Note that while "Intolerance" had shocking visuals, the shock content of "The Birth of a Nation" is more about the message of the film. There's no nudity or gore in the latter. There is instead a malevolent ideology being pushed in blatant terms. Let's call this kind of shock "message-based."

For lack of a better term, I'll call the "Intolerance"-style shocks "content-based." Content-based shocks came from obvious sources: women's nipples, a bloody stabbing, a curse word, etc. These are relatively easy to censor.

Message-based shocks are more ambiguous. They're based on what the film is trying to say, at least according to the viewer. You usually can't just cut a few scenes or shots to suppress a message. If the whole message of the film raised the hackles of a censorship board, they would ban it.

When a film is cut for content, it can still be shown and the producers can still make money (if perhaps less than they would have if the shocking content remained). When a film is banned outright, the producers get nothing. That creates a big disincentive toward making message-based shockers.

The story of "The Birth of a Nation" might leave you wondering whether message-based censorship might not be so bad. But a counterpoint is provided by a very different message-based shock film, the 1917 polemic "**Birth Control**." It was produced by and starred Margaret Sanger, an early birth control advocate whose organizations later evolved into Planned Parenthood.

Sanger was already well-known for her monthly newsletter *The Woman Rebel*. In it, she made a strong case for contraception, but against abortion. The very existence of the newsletter constituted a bold stand for free speech, as it plainly broke federal Comstock laws prohibiting the distribution of any information about contraception. Sanger was indicted for sending her newsletter through the mail and escaped to England.[38] In 1916, she returned to the States and

---

[38] Emily Douglas. "Margaret Sanger: Pioneer of the Future". p. 57

opened the country's first birth control clinic. "Birth Control" was about it and her career.

"Birth Control" is a lost film, unfortunately. But we do have plenty of court documents describing it, because it was the first film to test the *Mutual v. Ohio* decision declaring that films don't constitute free speech.

"Birth Control" re-created the incident that Sanger credited with inspiring her lifelong work. A woman is about to give birth, surrounded by her many malnourished children. Her doctor pleads with her to not have any more, but refuses to give her any information about birth control, because doing so would be illegal. The woman then "resort[s] to malpractice [i.e., a self-induced abortion] to avoid the birth of a child, from which she dies."[39] The film concludes with Sanger herself proselytizing about the need for birth control and then being thrown in jail.

The film evidently didn't have any content-based shocks; there is no mention of portrayals of sex or abortion, or even description of contraception methods. But because it dramatized the need for birth control, the New York City License Commissioner threatened to revoke the license of a theater that planned to show it. The Commissioner's decision was also based on his concern that it would "raise a class issue"[40] because it pointed out the differences experienced by poor and wealthy people. Again, class was central to a powerful person's attempt at suppression. Word quickly spread among exhibitors and the film was effectively banned.

In court, the distributor of "Birth Control" argued that it had "a constitutional right to agitate"[41] against the law prohibiting the dissemination of birth control information. Unlike "The James Boys in Missouri," "Birth Control" has an explicitly political message, akin to an editorial in a newspaper. This argument won the day, but was

---

[39] Quoted in de Grazia and Newman, p. 186
[40] Quoted in de Grazia and Newman, p. 187
[41] Quoted in ibid

overturned on appeal. All the appellate court did was refer to the Supreme Court's *Mutual v. Ohio* decision of 1915. Films were "a business, pure and simple ... not part of the press of the country" and unworthy of free speech protection.

Back to Content-Based Shocks

1917 also saw the peak of the career of the then-queen of content-based shocks, Theda Bara. She was famous for her "vamp" characters, who seduced men and was coded as "exotic" (i.e., non-white, so white men could be titillated without being offended by the notion of a white woman pursuing sex). Her studio cooked up a story that she was an Egyptian woman involved in the occult. Press releases frequently noted that Theda Bara was an anagram for "Arab death."[42] She was actually Theodosia Burr Goodman from Cincinnati. She loved to read and lived quietly with her parents and siblings.

Bara's 1917 film "**Cleopatra**" was a huge hit. In it, she wore all sorts of revealing costumes. Once again, it's a lost film, but you can at least get a sense for what shocked people by looking up some stills and the few scenes that have survived. It's not full nudity, but it's much more than what was allowed later. Under the Motion Picture Production Code (aka "Hays Code") of the 1930s and 1940s, "Cleopatra" was deemed obscene and banned from exhibition.[43]

In 1917, it was just chopped to bits by local censors. The Chicago Board of Censors had such a long list of cuts that it's a wonder there was any film left to show. But as I said before, an edited film can still make money. As long as it's not banned, it can sell.

In fact, as Karina Longworth proposes in episode 17 of her podcast *You Must Remember This*, all the cuts may have helped the bottom

---

[42] Garza, Janiss (2008). "Cleopatra (1917)". Movies & TV Dept. *The New York Times*.
[43] "Why Cleopatra continues to fascinate more than 2000 years later," sbs.com.au

line. The publicity created by one town's censorship board cutting a bunch of scenes would convince people in other towns to go see the film. By 1917, filmmakers had caught on to this and intentionally exploited gray areas. The perverse incentives set up by the patchwork of local censorship boards inadvertently encouraged pushing the envelope in terms of content-based shocks, if not message-based ones.

What about violence? As we saw with "Electrocuting an Elephant" vs. "The May Irwin Kiss," violence was not as taboo as sex. And unless actual violence was depicted, it never looked graphic. Special effects were unsophisticated, to put it kindly. To get in trouble for violent content, you needed some unusual circumstances.

"Spirit of '76" was another lost film released in 1917. It dramatizes the Revolutionary War, and as you might expect, the British don't come across well. In one battle scene, a British soldier spears a baby with a bayonet and twirls it around his head.[44]

The problem was not that a baby was bayoneted; it was that a British soldier did it. The Americans had just joined World War I on the United Kingdom's side. Chicago's censorship board told the film's director, Robert Goldstein, to remove this and other battle scenes because they would generate hostility towards the country's new allies. Mind you, there was nothing in the film about World War I; it just shows evil redcoats. Goldstein complied with the Chicago censorship board's order, but then sneakily put the scenes back in for the film's Los Angeles run.[45] I can't see the film, of course, but I would have to imagine a war film without battle scenes would seem a bit anticlimactic.

The federal government intervened, and didn't just ban the film: It put Goldstein on trial for violating the Espionage Act of 1917. The charge was that "Spirit of '76" constituted "aiding and abetting the

---

[44] Hans J. Wollstein, "Spirit of '76 (1917)". *The New York Times*.
[45] "The Unluckiest Man in Hollywood, Part 2". Slate.com, June 30, 2000)

German enemy." Goldstein argued that a Hessian soldier was the one bayoneting the baby, but it did not help his case. He was sentenced to 10 years in federal prison. Goldstein was one of many Americans prosecuted for expressing anti-British views during the war.[46]

The Birth of Exploitation

"Exploitation film" is a tough term to pin down. It's usually thought of as a low-budget movie that blatantly caters to people's prurient instincts. We've already covered films that someone could consider exploitative of lust, of bloodthirst, etc. Are "The May Irwin Kiss" or "The Execution of Mary Stuart" exploitation films? They both had low budgets and no apparent purposes besides providing transgressive thrills.

Luckily, I don't have to make these kinds of decisions, because Eric Schaefer does a great job of it in his book "Bold! Daring! Shocking! True! A History of Exploitation Films, 1919-1959." Schaefer pins the origin of exploitation film to the lost 1918 movie "**Fit to Fight**," aka "**Fit to Win**." It was part of a trend of didactic sex hygiene films that warned people about venereal disease.

Before "Fit to Fight," sex hygiene films were very formulaic. They were mostly copies of a very successful non-shock film from 1913 called "Traffic in Souls." In these movies, an innocent young person is always lured into illicit sex by an evil person, which leads to prostitution, venereal disease, or both. The innocent one is always saved by a crusading doctor, teacher, reporter, or other professional who pushes for greater awareness of the societal problems relating to sex. These films never have a hint of nudity, much less intercourse.[47]

---

[46] de Grazia and Newman, p. 20, 193-194
[47] Schaefer, p. 30-31

A key theme of a conventional sex hygiene film is that the innocent is a middle-class person and the evil tempter is of a lower class.[48] This message catered to the eugenics movement that was popular at the time. Eugenics held that the middle class was suffering "race suicide" because the lower classes were outbreeding them. Among eugenicists, a primary solution to this "problem" was forcibly sterilizing people whom the eugenicists deemed unfit to procreate. At the height of the movement, more than 30 states had compulsory sterilization laws on the books. From 1907 to 1963, courts sentenced more than 64,000 Americans to be sterilized, disproportionately working-class women, people with disabilities, and people of color.[49] Adolf Hitler got many of his ideas from eugenics.

"Fit to Fight" broke the mold of sex hygiene films by showing venereal disease as a threat to everyone, not just middle-class people. It also provided the genre's first content-based shocks: shots of infected genitalia covered with sores. When it was released to the general public, it played to capacity crowds for weeks. Children under 16 were strictly forbidden, and many screenings were open only to men.[50]

You might predict that "Fit to Fight" was made by some enterprising, forward-thinking schlockmeister. It was actually produced by the federal government to be shown to soldiers fighting in World War I. The military was a class leveler, with both middle- and lower-class people working together against the same threats, including venereal disease. "Fit to Fight" reflected that reality.[51]

Unlike previous sex hygiene films, "Fit to Fight" had to work. It had to demonstrably reduce the incidence of venereal disease in the military. If that took scaring people straight with the sight of real

---

[48] Schaefer, p. 23
[49] Paul Lombardo; "Eugenic Sterilization Laws", Eugenics Archive
[50] Schaefer, p. 27-29
[51] Schaefer, p. 32

syphilitic sores, then so be it. The film also endorsed prophylactics, pragmatically proposing "If you can't be moral, be careful."[52]

Moralists did not allow for the option of being immoral. In reaction to "Fit to Fight" and its follow-up films, protectors of the middle class turned against all sex hygiene films. Condemnations filled the newspapers. Medical organizations that had previously endorsed the genre publicly reversed their stances. Connecticut passed a law mandating that all sex hygiene films had to be approved by the state commissioner of health. Pennsylvania's censorship board banned any films dealing with venereal disease.[53]

Film studios got the message. They had plenty of other problems to deal with, as we'll see in the next chapter. Sex hygiene films were not a big enough hill to die on. They abandoned the genre, leaving a lot of demand unmet. In the United States, demand does not stay unmet for long.

A few independent producers arose to fill demand, showing sex hygiene films outside the normal system. Because the big studios had established contracts with most theaters, these independent producers had to hustle across the country to find screens open to their movies. They'd haul film cans from town to town or contract with distributors in each state where the movies were legal.[54] Each showing was like the circus coming to town, or at least a circus that consisted only of the sideshow. The exploitation circuit was born.

I admit, I'm not thrilled to explore exploitation films in this book. Most of them are quite dull, not even amusingly terrible in a "so bad it's good" sort of way. A main characteristic of exploitation is that the marketing is more important than the film. It's all about "ballyhoo," the ads and other wild attention-getting tactics borrowed from circus sideshows and carnival barkers that hype up the wild stuff you'll see

---

[52] Quoted in ibid
[53] Schaefer, p. 36
[54] "Shlock! The Secret History of American Movies," 2001 film directed by Ray Greene

in the movie. Whether the film actually delivers on the promises made by the marketing is secondary at best. Even if it does deliver nudity or some other forbidden footage, the film is usually padded out to full length by depressingly cheap-looking nonsense. But if viewers are disappointed, who cares? By the time you've fleeced the rubes, you move to the next town.

A book about shock films would not be complete without covering the genre that promises little else. Exploitation films are basically shock delivery systems. I'll try to hit on the ones that had the biggest impact.

Sex Hygiene Overseas

The graphic sex hygiene film was a step too far for the United States film studios, but not for Germany's. After losing World War I, the country threw the door open to experimentation. A revolutionary fervor swept the arts, the likes of which I've never experienced personally. Maybe the late 1960s was similar, but that was before my time.

The well-known result of this broad embrace of the avant-garde was Expressionism. If you've seen "The Cabinet of Dr. Caligari," you can appreciate how radical this change was. That film is more startling in its form and artistry than in breaking societal taboos, so I'm not counting it as a shock film. I'm focused on dumber stuff: boobs, blood, etc. If you want the smart stuff, there is no shortage of other sources.

And there were plenty of dumb film shocks in 1918-1919 German film, largely because national censorship was abolished in 1918. It was a bold societal experiment. It had a perhaps predictable result: pornography.

At least, that's the word that a scholarly source, "A History of Narrative Film," uses for most of the "Aufklärungsfilme," aka "films of elucidation" or "films about the facts of life."[55] I can't confirm that the Aufklärungsfilme cited by the book are pornographic, because there is little information about these films, much less footage. Beyond even the typical neglect that doomed a lot of silent films, the Aufklärungsfilme were later targeted by the Nazis, who burned all copies for being decadent.

Dozens of Aufklärungsfilme were produced from 1918 to 1919. They were relatively mainstream, full-length, high-budget sex hygiene films. Some earnestly tried to examine a pressing societal issue involving sex, a la "Fit to Fight." Most apparently exploited the fig leaf of "educational content" to throw lots of sex scenes on the screen. This would become a primary tactic used by exploitation films.

Many of the Aufklärungsfilme were popular enough to get sequels. "Prostitution," which warned of the dangers of sex work, was followed by "Prostitution II" in the same year. Of course, plenty of people were not pleased about the popularity of these films, and lobbied for reinstatement of censorship.

The film that purportedly proved to be the last straw for Germany's brief censor-free experiment was called "**Anders als die Andern**," or "**Different From the Others**." It has no hint of pornography, and only a few shots of nudity that are decidedly non-sexual. What it has is a sympathetic portrayal of homosexuality. Like Margaret Sanger's "Birth Control," it is a polemic against a law that criminalized victimless behavior. In this case, it was Paragraph 175 of Germany's Penal Code, which made gay sex illegal.

No full copy of "Anders als die Andern" survived the Nazis, but some scenes were preserved by being cut into a different movie. You can see a 50-minute version online with intertitles and stills substituting for the lost scenes. It seems like a typical Victorian-style morality play, with the crucial distinction that the gay men are the heroes.

---

[55] Cook, p. 104-105

To me, the most interesting parts of "Anders als die Andern" are the speeches by Dr. Magnus Hirschfeld, the real-life leader of the movement protesting the criminalization of homosexuality. He co-wrote the film and played himself in it, giving himself quite a few lines, via intertitles, that are pleasantly surprising to see in a 1919 film:

"You mustn't think poorly of your son because he is a homosexual. He is not at all to blame for his orientation. It is neither a vice nor a crime, indeed, not even an illness, but instead a variation, one of the borderline cases that occur frequently in nature."

"Your son suffers not from this condition, but rather from the false judgment of it. This is the legal and social condemnation of his feelings, along with widespread misconceptions about their expression."

"Love for one's own sex can be just as pure and noble as that for the opposite sex. This orientation is to be found among many respectable people in all levels of society."

Dr. Hirschfeld also talks a lot about how homosexuality represents some sort of "intermediary" between male and female, so his conception doesn't perfectly match the current one. But still, it's a remarkably progressive view that unfortunately failed to gain wide purchase. As we saw with the blowback to "The Birth of a Nation," there were some people 100 years ago who believed in a tolerance that we think of as modern. There just weren't enough of them then.

"Anders als die Andern" was initially successful, but screenings quickly attracted protests and disruptions by both Christian and explicitly antisemitic groups. Both Dr. Hirschfeld and the film's director, Richard Oswald, were Jewish, and homosexuality was portrayed as a "Jewish vice" by conservative groups.[56]

---

[56] "Anders als die Andern," website for the Deutsche Kinemathek Museum fur Film und Fernsehen,

The conservative groups' primary argument was the more predictable one, that "Anders als die Andern" was a threat to children. Specifically, they said it would recruit young people into becoming homosexual.[57] What I saw was not at all homoerotic, but they apparently felt that just broaching the idea will convert people. Apparently, that's how sexy homosexuality is in the minds of homophobes.

Conservatives also objected that the film was too one-sided, which is a typical criticism for anything that expresses a viewpoint. Considering that the "other side" in this case is that homosexuality is evil and scary and must be punished, I'm not sure how both views could be included equally in a comprehensible narrative.

In 1920, censorship was reinstated in Germany, and the first meeting of the new censorship board outlawed "Anders als die Andern." It could only be screened among doctors, and after the Nazis took power, not even among them.[58] Plenty of other films were banned and edited, and Germany's censorship-free experiment was dead.

Movies in Their Sights

Moralist reformers were making big strides in the United States as well. On January 17, 1920, Prohibition went into effect. It was the culmination of decades of agitation by churches, women's groups, and progressive organizations. Its effects are debatable and beyond the scope of this book. (If you're interested, I strongly recommend Daniel Okrent's book "Last Call.") But Prohibition certainly did a number on the American production of alcoholic beverages, which was the country's fifth-largest industry before 1920.

---

https://www.schwulesmuseum.de/ausstellung/anders-als-die-anderen-100-jahre-schwule-filmgeschichte/

[57] Beachy, Robert, Gay Berlin: Birthplace of a Modern Identity

[58] Hans-Michael Bock, "Richard Oswald - Regisseur, Autor, Produzent" in "CineGraph - Lexikon zum deutschsprachigen Film," Lieferung 23, 1993

The same reform groups then took aim at the U.S.'s fourth-largest industry: movies. Prohibition leader Wilbur F. Crafts said that movies should be the next target because their main objective was a "sex thrill," and besides, it was a business controlled by, in his words, "the devil and 500 non-Christian Jews."[59]

Along with antisemitism, classism was intertwined in the furor over revealing costumes on the likes of Theda Bara. In episode 5 of the "Fake News: Fact-Checking 'Hollywood Babylon'" series of her podcast *You Must Remember This*, Karina Longworth discusses how the wild success of movies in the 1910s made a lot of working-class people rich. Reformers asserted that this brought money to people who didn't know what to do with it. In Longworth's assessment, the movie reform movement was largely about powerful people not wanting wealth in the hands of the types they were bred to look down on.

Reformers backed up this condescension by citing sensationalized news stories of dangerously wild Hollywood parties and hedonism. These stories fit their conception that working-class people were like a bunch of wild teenagers who needed more discipline.

In 1920, charming 25-year-old star Olive Thomas accidentally drank something poisonous while drunk. As she lay in a hospital dying, newspapers printed every rumor: that she had attempted suicide over her husband's infidelities, that she was addicted to drugs, that the couple was involved in "champagne and cocaine orgies,"[60] etc.

1920 was past the peak of "yellow journalism," but it was still pervasive. William Randolph Hearst, later the unstated (but obvious) inspiration for "Citizen Kane," was the primary newspaper mogul

---

[59] Quoted in Karina Longworth, "Roscoe 'Fatty' Arbuckle and Virginia Rappe: Fake News: Fact-checking 'Hollywood Babylon'" *You Must Remember This* podcast, episode 3

[60] Quoted in Deborah Blum, "The Poisoner's Handbook Murder and the Birth of Forensic Medicine in Jazz Age New York," p. 107

producing sensationalist stories that sold lots of papers but had little connection to reality.

Hearst enthusiastically publicized the really big scandal: Roscoe "Fatty" Arbuckle was a very popular comedy star, second only to Charlie Chaplin in 1921. Over Labor Day weekend of that year, he had a party at a hotel in San Francisco. One of the women at the party, Virginia Rappe, fell ill in Arbuckle's bedroom. She started screaming and writhing in pain. The hotel doctor gave Rappe morphine to calm her down. Two days later, she was admitted to a hospital for a ruptured bladder, which caused peritonitis. After a day in the hospital, she died.[61]

Rappe's friend accused Arbuckle of rape. A doctor found no evidence of rape, but the police ran with it anyway, concluding that Arbuckle's large body must have caused Rappe's bladder to burst. Never mind that that is not how the human body works – bladders are not balloons that pop when you squeeze them – and that doctors exist to make medical conclusions based on actual medical knowledge. Doctors later learned that Rappe had chronic urinary tract infections, which are irritated by alcohol consumption.[62]

Arbuckle may have tried to seduce or sexually assault Rappe, but there's no evidence he was in any way successful. We do know that once Rappe started screaming and writhing, he and his friends put her in an ice bath to try to alleviate her pain. Rumors transformed this into Arbuckle inserting ice into Rappe's vagina, and then to inserting a bottle. Hearst was thrilled to print every rumor, and most of the public swallowed it all and called for Arbuckle's execution.

Arbuckle was arrested for manslaughter. After two mistrials, he was found not guilty, and the jury took the unusual step of writing a

---

[61] Denise Noe, "Fatty Arbuckle and the Death of Virginia Rappe". Crime Library at truTV
[62] "Testify Regarding Early Life of Virginia Rappe". *The Lewiston Daily Sun*. October 31, 1921.

formal apology for the ordeal he had undergone.[63] But Arbuckle's career was over.

Film studios panicked. Something had to be done, and quick, to preserve their business. They certainly didn't want the press digging into the actual drug abuse and debauchery going on.

Moreover, Hollywood was terrified that the Arbuckle controversy would lead to more government regulation. The studios were already hampered by seven state censorship boards, which influenced around 90 municipal boards. After the Arbuckle incident, Massachusetts voted to start an eighth. Then a referendum was scheduled to approve federally mandated censorship in Massachusetts.[64] This would open the door to every state having a board controlled by the federal government. Hollywood's worst nightmare was imminent.

All of Arbuckle's films were banned, but that wasn't enough. The crisis came at a vulnerable time for the film business. People were wary of crowding in theaters because of the flu pandemic of 1918-1920. The new medium of radio was keeping people entertained at home.[65] Hollywood needed a big, dramatic change.

The studio heads looked to the example of the 1919 Black Sox scandal, which had threatened the survival of major-league baseball. Baseball owners had responded by hiring the first commissioner, Judge Kenesaw Mountain Landis, who acted and looked like a vengeful Old-Testament-style God. Landis handed out lifetime bans to the eight White Sox players accused of throwing the World Series without any regard to their culpability. Fans were mollified, and baseball continued to thrive.

---

[63] "OPINION | OLD NEWS: Fatty Arbuckle found innocent after three trials; judgment came too late for his career". Arkansas Online. September 27, 2021.
[64] de Grazia and Newman, p. 26
[65] Miller, p. 28

The studios approached a member of the recently elected Warren G. Harding administration, Will Hays, to become their Judge Landis. Hays looked more like a character in a Warner Brothers cartoon than a vengeful God, but no matter: He was a respectable Presbyterian deacon with close connections to the most powerful people in the country. It looked like the government and the church were taking charge, even if neither actually were.

The major studios founded the Motion Picture Producers and Distributors of America (MPPDA), later MPAA and then MPA) and installed Hays as chairman. As with the commissioner of baseball, Hays was touted as an impartial arbiter, even though he was in the full employ of the owners and served only their interests. It was largely a P.R. move to placate the reformers.

But Hays couldn't be the sort of autocrat that Landis was in baseball. He had no power over the morass of censorship boards that still controlled what people could see. His new job was mostly about trying to save the studios money. It was expensive to go through the rigmarole of shooting all these scenes that would just be excised anyway. Then there was the expense of having to print different versions for each market. Also, many state laws required the studios to pay the censorship boards for each foot of film cut. This made the clever calculation of the Theda Bara movies, in which news reports of censored scenes in one market seemed to juice business elsewhere, no longer add up.

Hays earned his salary ($100,000 a year, or $1.8 million in 2023 dollars) by pushing enough propaganda to ensure the defeat of the Massachusetts referendum that would have led to federal oversight of all movies.[66] Then he began work as an advisor on individual films, making suggestions to forestall censorship expenses. He also lobbied with censorship boards to pass films. All the while, he kept making sanctimonious pronouncements for public consumption. It

---

[66] Frank Miller, "Censored Hollywood: Sex Sin & Violence on Screen,", p. 34

would be several years before Will Hays attempted to install any set of guidelines laying out what was and wasn't acceptable content.

If the Medium is the Message, Shoot the Messenger

Amidst all the censorship hullabaloo from 1920-1922, I couldn't find any unequivocal American shock films, perhaps ironically. And the only films that led to court cases in the first half of the 1920s were newsreels, which were compilations of real footage of current events. In 1921, the New York legislature passed a law declaring that any newsreels had to pass through censorship boards. Pathé, a French film giant that produced newsreels, filed a lawsuit asserting that this was a violation of free speech. (All quotes and information in this section are from de Grazia and Newman, p. 201-203.)

Pathé's lawyers argued that their footage was "in principle the same as any ordinary newspaper" and thus deserved the same first-amendment protections. "[N]o logical or reasonable distinction can be made between the two media of expression," they stated, adding "it is the news that is [constitutionally] privileged, not the medium of expression."

This again threw into question the 1915 *Mutual v. Ohio* case establishing that films were "a business, pure and simple, not to be regarded ... as part of the press of the country, or as organs of public opinion." As in the previous tests of this decision, New York's top court shot Pathé's free-speech argument down with dubious logic.

The court declared that movies are a "a spectacle or show," unlike newspapers. Such a "spectacle or show" could not be considered a "medium of opinion." In reality, newsreels were more sober and truthful than newspapers at the time. As you saw, William Randolph Hearst's papers were filled with sensationalized lies of a magnitude that newsreels could not even approach. No one invented newsreel footage of Roscoe Arbuckle inserting a bottle into Virginia Rappe's vagina, for example.

The court offered more rationalization for their icky feeling about movies: Again, it was about protecting children and lower-class adults. Instead of patronizingly worrying that immigrants might be tainted, they cited "illiterates" as being especially vulnerable to newsreels. "The picture creates its own atmosphere so vividly, so attractively, that even the child and illiterate may see and learn," the court declared. Somehow, in their minds, a medium that encourages illiterate people to "see and learn" was a bad thing. Shouldn't we welcome, not repress, a medium that informs adults who can't get news through the written word?

You can make a valid case that children should be protected from especially violent or sexual news footage. But apparently protecting children wasn't sufficient justification, so they had to throw in illiterate people. The court was transparently grasping for some distinction between newspapers and newsreels, and the best they could come up with was that some adults could absorb information from the latter but not the former. So because they can't read newspapers … they can't be trusted with uncensored news reports of any kind, I guess?

By my interpretation, what this court and the others we've reviewed were really saying was "But movies just feel wrong!" It's an example of what I call "Grumpy Old Man Syndrome," or GOMS. People with Grumpy Old Man Syndrome get scared of anything that's new and want to stop it. In the words of Grandpa Abe Simpson from "The Simpsons," "I used to be with 'it', but then they changed what 'it' was. Now what I'm with isn't 'it' anymore and what's 'it' seems weird and scary."

Grumpy Old Men can be women or even young people – all that matters is that they're old at heart. Most Grumpy Old Men were formed by the ways of their childhoods. Any new invention or trend that doesn't fit those old ways intimidates them. They fight off that irrational fear by turning it into anger, which is a standard defense mechanism for emotionally immature people. They conjure up reasons why the new thing will destroy the world, usually using slippery-slope arguments and other specious tactics. "Gay people are getting married now? That makes me feel icky," a Grumpy Old Man might think. "Therefore, it must portend the collapse of society somehow ... uh, I know, because it will lead to people marrying their dogs!"

I grant that the basic thought pattern underlying GOMS sophistry is used by all human beings in almost every decision: You have an emotional reaction to something, and then work backwards to justify that reaction with logical arguments. It's usually innocuous. For example, you might make vague but fervent declarations about why your childhood hero Roger Maris belongs in the Hall of Fame even though his stats aren't even close to measuring up. It's nonsense, but no one is getting hurt, so who cares?

It becomes dangerous when powerful people use such thought patterns to decide matters of great consequence. Perhaps more than any other people in the world besides scientists, Supreme Court justices undergo extensive training and experience in using critical thinking, the skill of basing decisions on principles and rationality instead of personal feelings. Sometimes it seems like all that training and experience only goes to fabricating more complex rationalizations.

The gut feelings driving Grumpy Old Men arise from the toxic manipulations of nostalgia. Nostalgia paints the past in rose colors while obscuring its negative aspects. Current-day Grumpy Old Men think of the 1950s and early 1960s as being just like "Leave it to Beaver," a bunch of happy families suffering no real problems. They forget things like the Cold War and its imminent fear of nuclear destruction, not to mention that it was a brutal time for anyone who wasn't a straight white conservative man. In the 1920s, the Grumpy Old Men tried to force the clock back to a time before these newfangled moving pictures were making all these whippersnappers go crazy.

Anyway, you can take or leave that rant. The upshot was that some frightened, elitist old men closed the door to even the most objective and informative cinema being protected speech.

Weird Shocker Overseas

Even if no fun shock films can be drawn from the United States from 1920-1922, one came out of Denmark. **Häxan** is a pseudo-documentary presenting old tales of witchcraft. It stages enactments of many of these tales, which involve plenty of nudity, torture and gore. It was a hit in Sweden and Denmark, but elsewhere the censors cut it to pieces and it wasn't successful.[67]

The standards were laxer in Europe. For example, nudity was more common. Short films of Josephine Baker dancing topless were quite popular. Fritz Lang's 1922 film "Dr. Mabuse, the Gambler" has a scene in which a nearly naked woman is on stage at a bizarre night club.

The shock content of "Häxan" is of a level above all that, though still below a typical post-1960s horror movie. To me, one of the more interesting things about it is that it doesn't seem like an exploitation film. Exploitation is kind of in the eye of the beholder, but to my eye at least, the film is an earnest attempt to explore the history of witchcraft.

You have to be an eccentric to film such a thing in 1922, and director Benjamin Christensen apparently was just that. He was such a geek for the subject that I doubt he fully considered how shocking most people would find it. Because of Christensen's

---

[67] Chris Fujiwara, "Häxan: The Real Unreal". The Criterion Collection: https://www.criterion.com/current/posts/147-haxan-the-real-unreal

enthusiasm for the history of witchcraft, "Häxan" struck me as about the most charming exploration of Satanic torture possible.

"Häxan" also brings up a theme that we'll see again: The stories that make up traditional lore are filled with sex and violence. For centuries people have relished telling them to each other and putting them in books. Sometimes the books are repressed, but often not. When you put those stories on screen, they take on a viscerality that many people find overwhelming. As was also demonstrated by the censorship of newsreels but not newspapers, that viscerality often compels powerful old scaredy cats to invent reasons to shut it down.

The Flap Over Flappers

Back in the United States, the public scandals that fueled most of the furor over censorship kept coming. Actor Wallace Reid was known as "the screen's perfect lover": an athletic, handsome exemplar of American manhood. In his off hours he was a champion race car driver. It's hard not to be reminded of Paul Newman. In 1923, the world learned Reid was also a morphine addict when he died trying to kick the habit in a sanitorium.[68]

People were seeing Hollywood-style wildness closer to home, as young people were busy creating a new culture with a new morality. A 1923 film called "**Flaming Youth**" brought flappers to the masses. No less an expert than F. Scott Fitzgerald, in his essay "Echoes of the Jazz Age," cited "Flaming Youth" as the only film that truly captured the new sexual freedoms of the 1920s. In his words, the movie showed that women could be "seduced without being ruined."

Only a portion of "Flaming Youth" survives, and it provides barely a hint of what caused controversy. The advertising for "Flaming Youth" talked up its "pleasure mad daughters" and a skinny-dipping

---

[68] Mary Lynn Anderson, "Twilight of the Idols: Hollywood and the Human Sciences in 1920s America" p. 15

sequence that was shot in silhouette.[69] Mostly the film delivered message-based shock, especially in the context of its time. This was still an era of Victorian-style drama, as exemplified by the films of D.W. Griffith. The women in Victorian stories were usually ineffectual, delicate victims who exist only to be rescued by macho, violent men. Their worth was based on their virginity. Flappers, however, were the heroes of their own stories. They partied and pursued men for their own pleasure. This was not OK with the Grumpy Old Man Syndrome crowd.

Grumpy Old Men were also not OK with the ultimate source of flapper culture: the Black community. In her book "Wayward Lives, Beautiful Experiments: Intimate Histories of Social Upheaval," historian Saidiya Hartman lays out how Black women invented flapper fashion and behavior after World War I. The movement centered on the exciting new music of the time, jazz, which of course was invented by Black musicians. As would happen with rock 'n' roll in the 1950s and rap in the 1980s, white kids listened to Black music and mimicked Black culture, which caused white parents to panic.

"Flaming Youth" was banned in Canada, but it passed Will Hays' Motion Picture Producers and Distributors of America (MPPDA). After it became a huge success, many imitators followed. Reformers began to wonder if Will Hays and the MPPDA were really protecting the public or just protecting filmmakers' profits.

In 1924, Hays got serious about policing movie content. He put in place the "Hays Formula," in which studios had to send scripts to readers employed by the MPPDA before any shooting could start. No less than 67 treatments were rejected outright in the first year. Producers learned what would and wouldn't pass muster and planned accordingly. The system worked for a few years, and no major American shock films were released in the mid-1920s.[70]

---

[69] Jon Savage, "Teenage: The Creation of Youth Culture," p. 205
[70] Miller, p. 38-39

So Let's Go Back to Europe

… or more like Eurasia, as we're now diving into the films of the USSR. During World War I, Russia suffered an estimated 9,150,000 casualties,[71] more than any other country. The Russian Revolution pulled them out of World War I but immediately led to the Russian Civil War. This massive, messy conflict resulted in another 9 million deaths,[72] almost all Russians and members of other ethnic groups that would be swallowed up into the USSR. As in Germany, all the societal devastation led the newly dubbed USSR to embrace avant-garde artistic ideas.

In the early 1920s, Dziga Vertov and Lev Kuleshov developed a new approach to film based on what they called "montage theory." The idea was that meaning comes from the juxtaposition between shots, not just within individual shots. Editing was paramount. Insert a shot of a beautiful woman before a shot of a man with a blank expression and people will think the man looks lusty, while a shot of a child in a coffin before the same shot of the man will make him look stricken with grief.[73] This was a radical departure from previous film technique, which was still inching away from being mere filmed theater. Montage theory was the first approach to filmmaking that was based on the unique properties of film.

While form and style could get radical in the USSR, content and message were a different story. The Russian Revolution and Civil War had established communism as the only acceptable mode of thought. By Lenin's and then Stalin's orders, all movies had to be communist propaganda. Almost every plot had to entail a group of proletarians overthrowing a group of evil capitalists. Shocking

---

[71] "World War I: Killed, wounded, and missing." Encyclopedia Brittanica: https://www.britannica.com/event/World-War-I/Killed-wounded-and-missing
[72] Matthew White, "Atrocities: The 100 Deadliest Episodes in Human History," p. 359
[73] Cook, p. 135-137

images, at least in the mid-1920s, could fly as long as they served the ideology.

After the Cultural Revolution, which started in 1928 according to most historians, even this degree of freedom evaporated. Stalin's desire for propaganda to dominate all media quickly overwhelmed his tolerance for avant-garde filmmaking ideas. If any aspect of a film, including the editing, overshadowed its message, Stalin would accuse the filmmaker of the "formalist error." Being too "formalist" could mean a literal death sentence.[74]

During the brief window of time when formal experimentation wouldn't get you killed, Sergei Eisenstein made a few classics. His two 1925 films, "**Strike**" and "**Battleship Potemkin**," use some shocking imagery to make viewers feel the horrors wrought by the enemies of the proletariat. "Strike" ends with a barrage of edits, at accelerating speed, some of them close-ups of actual cattle being slaughtered.

"Battleship Potemkin" is the one that makes all the lists of best films ever. The highlight is the famous sequence in which a baby in a carriage is accidentally released down the Odessa steps. This slow fall is intercut with people panicking and killing each other. The point of the scene is to shock, both through editing and violent imagery, and I think it succeeds.

But if you decide to watch either of these films, I'll warn you: They can be hard to connect with, in my opinion. You can't get invested in the characters, because there basically aren't any. "Strike" and "Battleship Potemkin" feature groups of people fighting other groups of people, with no clear leaders or even standouts. This conforms to communist dogma, in which individuals are subservient to their classes. I think the imagery, action, and fast pace still make these films enjoyable, but your mileage may vary.

---

[74] David Bordwell, "The Cinema of Eisenstein"

The Soviet Union's brief window of artistic freedom also allowed a very different shock film to sneak through: "**Bed and Sofa**" (1927). Instead of a grand battle between classes, this is a small-scale domestic drama about a love triangle. Plus, it's all message-based shocks instead of quick cuts through violent shots.

<SPOILER ALERT>

The love triangle of "Bed and Sofa" is resolved with the trio essentially becoming a throuple. This arrangement comes to a head when the woman gets pregnant, and the husbands insist on an abortion. The movie is not pro-abortion, though; the wife can't go through with it and the throuple collapses as a result.

</SPOILER ALERT>

"Bed and Sofa" was made to dramatize the dangers of the sexual freedom of the age. But just by bringing up the issues, it caused a firestorm. Several powerful Soviet organizations launched a campaign against it, calling it "psychopathological," an "apology for adultery," and a "Western European adulterous romance." Western Europe wanted nothing to do with the movie, though; it was banned throughout Europe and the U.S. "Bed and Sofa" was screened publicly only in the USSR.[75] It's the old Grumpy Old Man Syndrome pattern: The rage people feel from seeing a shocking movie latches onto whatever reasons they can conjure to repress it. Often this involves blaming whatever people they don't like.

Exploitation on the Rise

Nudity remained the main point of contention in American film in the late 1920s. The most popular female star, Clara Bow, has a nude bathing scene in the 1927 movie "Hula." There is also some nudity in "Wings," a blockbuster that would become the first-ever winner of

---

[75] Tretia Meshchanskaia, filmreference.com,
http://www.filmreference.com/Films-Thr-Tur/Tretia-Meshchanskaia.html

the Best Picture Academy Award. Flashes of partial nudity were relatively mainstream.

Exploitation films took things further. "**Is Your Daughter Safe?**" was a sex hygiene film that warned young people about being lured into illegal sex work. Since it's a lost film, I can't opine on whether it was earnestly trying to address an important issue. It allegedly contained lots of nudity.

Being in the exploitation realm meant that "Is Your Daughter Safe? " relied on ballyhoo tactics borrowed from circus sideshows. Supposedly, women reportedly stood in glass cases outside some theaters showing the film to provide "a flash for the boobs."[76]

The screenings were accompanied by alleged sexual education experts who showed slides depicting the genitalia of people with venereal diseases. There is some anecdotal evidence that "Is Your Daughter Safe?" really did scare some kids away from sex. Seeing penises covered with pustules can do that.

The movie was widely decried, banned and censored. It only passed the Chicago censorship board because the mayor had been given a role in the film. San Diego demanded that the title be changed from "Is Your Daughter Safe?" to "The Octopus" so that it would not call into question the effectiveness of the police.[77]

The Hays Office had no power over "Is Your Daughter Safe?" because it was independently produced and distributed. The studios still viewed it as a threat, because most people didn't make a distinction between independent and mainstream. People just heard about this crazy movie that shows genital warts and concluded that movies in general needed to be cleaned up.

The studios couldn't go too hard against independents because the independents might accuse them of restraint of trade and unfair

---

[76] Schaefer, p. 145
[77] Schaefer, p. 59

competition. And neither side dared utter anything that hinted at censorship of any kind.[78]

The Hays Office tried more subtle tactics. They gathered a focus group of women to review "Is Your Daughter Safe?," hoping the group would condemn it. Instead, in the words of the Hays Office's Jason Joy, the women said that the movie "teaches a very splendid lesson and that every girl over sixteen years of age ought to be compelled to see it."[79] (Of course, boys did not have any lessons to learn about sex.) Other Hays Office strategies were about as successful. Hollywood was in a bind.

Something Old, Something New

Meanwhile, the watershed moment of 1927 was the release of the first film with extended stretches of synced sound: "The Jazz Singer." Hearing someone on screen talk for the first time was a shock, but not the kind we're talking about. To a modern audience, it will be much more shocking, and not in a fun way, to see the protagonist perform in blackface.

This is a hazard of watching old movies. "Swing Time" (1936) and "Holiday Inn" (1942). just to name a few, seem like perfectly delightful musicals until a white protagonist puts on blackface and begins a horrifyingly insulting pantomime. It was considered normal at the time, part of the tradition of minstrel shows that came into prominence in the 1830s.

As in the case of "The Birth of a Nation," though, "normal" does not mean "universally accepted." Frederick Douglass called blackface performers "the filthy scum of white society, who have stolen from

---

[78] Schaefer, p. 146
[79] Quoted in Schaefer, p. 145

us a complexion denied them by nature, in which to make money, and pander to the corrupt taste of their white fellow citizens."[80]

Minstrel shows involved more than just putting on blackface and singing. There was a range of stock characters with names like Gombo Chaff, Mammy, Zip Coon, and Jim Crow (which would lend its name to racist laws after the Civil War). Each character personified a stereotype of Black people that persists in the imaginations of racists to this day. The characters were all dehumanized objects of ridicule.

Minstrel characters were so popular that sometimes Black performers put on blackface to portray them. Even when no blackface was involved, minstrel tropes dominated the imagination of white people. You could argue that the only film roles available to Black actors in the first half of the 1900s were essentially minstrel roles. Some actors, like Stepin Fetchit, became famous for playing a variation on a minstrel character. Often just a scene or two will mar an otherwise perfect film. A few brief cuts to the W.C. Fields movie "The Bank Dick" (1940) or Preston Sturges' "The Palm Beach Story" (1942) could make them unimpeachable classics.

Minstrel shows and blackface are a huge, complicated topic that I'm not qualified to describe much further. But I wanted to at least mention it to illustrate my point about the ways shock media has changed over the years. While sex and violence have become more acceptable on screen, some things have become less so. Most of us learned that adults seeing naked people in movies does not cause great societal damage. We also learned that ridiculing and dehumanizing ethnic groups does.

---

[80] Quoted in Ken Padgett, "Blackface! Minstrel Shows," p. 1, https://web.archive.org/web/20140927230547/http://black-face.com/minstrel-shows.htm

The "Don'ts and Be Carefuls"

In different ways, "Is Your Daughter Safe?" and "The Jazz Singer" both made it clear that the Hays Office needed to make some rules for content. "Is Your Daughter Safe?" brought the threat of federal government censorship frighteningly close. The advent of sound made it harder to make cuts to film prints. Chopping a scene out of a silent film was easy (if expensive), but the sound-on-disc technology of early talkies made doing so nearly impossible.[81] It would be much cheaper to not include the offending material from the start.

Pressure came from above. By this time, New York investors owned most film companies. This enabled studios to own theaters and gobble up competitors, but it also meant carefully protecting the bottom line. As Leonard J. Leff and Jerold L. Simmons say in their book "Dame in the Kimono: Hollywood, Censorship, and the Production Code," "expansion meant capital, capital meant Wall Street, and Wall Street meant conservative business practices."[82]

Will Hays urged the studio heads to create a set of guidelines, which were later nicknamed the "Don'ts and Be Carefuls." Here they are verbatim:

> Resolved, That those things which are included in the following list shall not appear in pictures produced by the members of this Association, irrespective of the manner in which they are treated:
>
> > 1. Pointed profanity-by either title or lip-this includes the words "God," "Lord," "Jesus," "Christ" (unless they be used reverently in connection with proper religious ceremonies), "hell," " damn," "Gawd," and every other

---

[81] Cook, p. 262
[82] Leonard J. Leff and Jerold L. Simmons, "Dame in the Kimono: Hollywood, Censorship, and the Production Code**Error! Bookmark not defined.**," p. 4

profane and vulgar expression however it may be spelled;

2. Any licentious or suggestive nudity-in fact or in silhouette; and any lecherous or licentious notice thereof by other characters in the picture;

3. The illegal traffic in drugs;

4. Any inference of sex perversion;

5. White slavery; [ED's note: This is a racist's way of referring to sex trafficking.]

6. Miscegenation (sex relationships between the white and black races);

7. Sex hygiene and venereal diseases;

8. Scenes of actual childbirth-in fact or in silhouette;

9. Children's sex organs;

10. Ridicule of the clergy;

11. Willful offense to any nation, race or creed;

And be it further resolved, That special care be exercised in the manner in which the following subjects are treated, to the end that vulgarity and suggestiveness may be eliminated and that good taste may be emphasized:

1. The use of the flag;

2. International relations (avoiding picturizing in an unfavorable light another country's religion, history, institutions, prominent people, and citizenry);

3. Arson;

4. The use of firearms;

5. Theft, robbery, safe-cracking, and dynamiting of trains, mines, buildings, etc. (having in mind the effect which a too-detailed description of these may have upon the moron);

6. Brutality and possible gruesomeness;

7. Technique of committing murder by whatever method;

8. Methods of smuggling;

9. Third-degree methods;

10. Actual hangings or electrocutions as legal punishment for crime;

11. Sympathy for criminals;

12. Attitude toward public characters and institutions;

13. Sedition;

14. Apparent cruelty to children and animals;

15. Branding of people or animals;

16. The sale of women, or of a woman selling her virtue;

17. Rape or attempted rape;

18. First-night scenes;

19. Man and woman in bed together;

20. Deliberate seduction of girls;

21. The institution of marriage;

22. Surgical operations;

23. The use of drugs;

24. Titles or scenes having to do with law enforcement or law-enforcing officers;

25. Excessive or lustful kissing, particularly when one character or the other is a "heavy."

There's a lot I could try to unpack here. For instance, you might notice that you merely had to be careful about how you depicted rape, but you were strictly forbidden from revealing a loving relationship between a Black man and a white woman, or vice-versa.

I'm mainly including the full list so you can get an idea of what hot topics the Hays Office was trying to avoid. It compiled the "Don'ts" based on experience. These were the issues that most frequently resulted in cut scenes and protests. As Eric Schaefer points out in "Bold! Daring! Shocking! True!," the list doesn't cover sexual intercourse, graphic violence, sadomasochism, or necrophilia because no one, even the exploitationeers, was approaching those.[83]

Seven of the eleven "Don'ts" were a direct response to sex hygiene films: 2, 3, 4, 5, 7, 8, and 9. These seven would continue to be exploitation's stock in trade. The circuit would come to be defined by their willingness to break the "Don'ts." In fact, they were often inspired by them. Number 6, mixed-race relationships, only became a major topic in the 1930s.

Studio films would not always follow the "Don'ts and Be Carefuls" either, as we will see. But at least the existence of the list drew a line between mainstream and exploitation. It could make some people realize that mainstream films usually didn't address these

---

[83] Schaefer, p. 198

topics. If someone got offended by a film that did, they hopefully wouldn't blame Hollywood.

Hays established a Studio Relations Committee to make recommendations on both scripts and finished films based on the "Don'ts and Be Carefuls." Since Hays worked out of New York City, he appointed an underling in Los Angeles, Jason Joy, to lead it.

Joy wasn't given much power. All he could do was "forecast the censor boards' cuts and trims; he sent the predictions to the studios as suggestions, in dire cases warnings, but never demands."[84] Hays' and Joy's employers, the studios, did not want strict enforcement that might threaten profits. The real point was that now, five years after pretending to tackle the problem, they could point to a system of self-regulation that, they declared, obviated the need for more of the governmental kind.

It worked for a couple of years. As the American film world transitioned to sound, it would not produce more major shock films that I could find. To get our fix, we need to go …

Back to Europe

In Germany, the Aufklärungsfilme were long dead, but the sexual liberation of the Weimar Republic lived on. "**Pandora's Box**" (1929) is, in my experience, the best surviving filmic distillation of flapper womanhood from any country. Louise Brooks plays Lulu, a charming, cheerful woman who displays no shame about having many simultaneous sexual relationships. One of her admirers is a lesbian, but nothing comes of that. The film gets the most transgressive when Lulu is sold into a brothel on a gambling ship.

Lulu meets a grim end, which you could interpret as saying that free sexuality inevitably results in ruin. But Brooks plays the role as such a lovable innocent that I found it hard to see "Pandora's Box" as a

---

[84] Leff and Simmons, p. 13

cautionary tale. I felt like the film was always on her side, and that the villains were the idiotic, overly emotional men in her orbit.

"Pandora's Box" was despised by pearl-clutching critics and heavily censored throughout the world. In most countries, the ending was changed so that Lulu joined the Salvation Army, which apparently made little sense.[85] In the United States, the film was butchered by various censorship boards, in one cut going from 132 minutes to 66.[86]

While "Pandora's Box" arose from the trends of popular culture, "**Un chien andalou**" (1929) was like a transmission from another planet. Surrealist Spaniards Salvador Dali and Luis Buñuel wrote down their dreams and other weird ideas and then Buñuel filmed them. Dali and Buñuel worked on the principle that "No idea or image that might lend itself to a rational explanation of any kind would be accepted"[87] and "nothing, in the film, symbolizes anything. The only method of investigation of the symbols would be, perhaps, psychoanalysis."[88] The resulting short film eschews character, narrative, and all rules about what can be shown on screen.

"Un chien andalou" is as pure a representation of surrealism as has ever been achieved in film. Surrealism arose from Freudian psychoanalysis, with a focus on removing all inhibitions to allow the subconscious mind to express itself with complete freedom. In his 1974 book "Film as a Subversive Art," Amos Vogel sums up the aim of the surrealists: "to destroy all censors and liberate man's libidinal, anarchist, and 'marvelous' impulses from all restraint."[89]

---

[85] J. Hoberman, "Opening Pandora's Box." The Criterion Collection, https://www.criterion.com/current/posts/458-opening-pandora-s-box
[86] Jack Harrower, "Louise Brooks in 'Pandora's Box' (Silent)", review, *The Film Daily.* December 8, 1929
[87] Luis Buñuel, "My Last Sigh", p. 104
[88] Quoted in P. Adams Sitney, "Visionary Film: The American Avant-Garde"
[89] Amos Vogel, "Film as a Subversive Art," p. 46

This approach to art-making opens the door to shocking stuff. Per Vogel, "these 'irrational' associations [resulting from surrealist methods] constitute the primary surrealist weapon, the use of 'shock.'"[90] Shock was a virtue for the surrealists, who were furiously opposed to every convention favored by the bourgeoisie and polite society. In the documentary "Luis Buñuel: The Journey of a Surrealist," filmmaker (and Luis's son) Juan Luis Buñuel described a main principle of surrealism as "mala leche," which he loosely translated in this context as "a nasty way of thinking that's meant to disturb people, to make people question their very values in society."

One scene in "Un chien andalou" is a good candidate for the most shocking scene of all time. If you've seen the film, you know what I mean. If you haven't, you will probably find out about it accidentally before you turn it on. I won't spoil it, but be forewarned. Just thinking about it causes me physical pain.

"Un chien andalou" was first screened in Paris for a bunch of Dali's and Buñuel's artist friends, including Pablo Picasso, Jean Cocteau, Le Corbusier, and surrealist godfather André Breton. The crowd loved it. That was a relief to Buñuel, who had filled his pockets with rocks in case a riot broke out. Dali later said he was disappointed there was no violence at the screening[91] (but take that with a grain of salt, as he was a notorious self-mythologizer).

The film toured and became a success. Buñuel expressed exasperation, writing "What can I do about the people who adore all that is new, even when it goes against their deepest convictions, or about the insincere, corrupt press, and the inane herd that saw beauty or poetry in something which was basically no more than a desperate impassioned call for murder?"[92] The surrealists were the

---

[90] Vogel, p. 48
[91] "Un Chien Andalou". Close-Up Film Centre.
[92] "Preface to the script for Un Chien Andalou". *La Révolution Surréaliste*. no. 12.

punk rockers of their time, trying to assault the audience and provoke them into a fury.

While Dali and Buñuel chafed in the glow of the success of "Un chien andalou," they gained some influential fans. Among them were French nobles and art patrons Marie-Laurie and Charles de Noailles. Charles financed the next Dali/Buñuel collabo as a gift to Marie-Laurie.

A fight between Dali and Buñuel began almost immediately. They could at least agree that the next film needed to take Christianity down a peg. Buñuel was a lapsed Catholic and Dali was raised atheist. But Buñuel also wanted the film to rake the bourgeoisie over the coals, while Dali was a closet elitist who would eventually support fascist leader Francisco Franco and the aristocracy.[93] Dali left the film project, and their friendship collapsed.

Luis Buñuel's "**L'Age d'Or**" (1930) became a 63-minute compilation of short films. The first is a documentary about scorpions. Then some poverty-stricken men sit around. I was quite bored by this, and if you feel the same, don't worry, keep watching. The next short film, making up a majority of the running time, depicts a couple who is repeatedly frustrated from having sex. This part has plenty of surrealistic touches and random acts of violence that I found hilarious. It's scandalous enough by 1930 standards, but the last part is the real shocker. I won't spoil it, but let's just say that if you're a devout Christian, you might not enjoy it.

Dali told the press that the film was an attack on Catholicism, which got the scandal started. One early screening was overtaken by the Anti-Jewish Youth Group and a fascist organization called the League of Patriots. They hurled ink at the screen and set off smoke bombs and firecrackers. Then they ran to the lobby and destroyed surrealist artwork by Dali, Man Ray, Joan Miró, Yves Tanguy, and

---

[93] "Marxism – European Cinema Before and After World War II," filmreference.com

others.[94] Buñuel got the blowback he thought he wanted for "Un chien andalou."

A review in a right-wing Spanish newspaper condemned "L'Age d'Or" as "the most repulsive corruption of our age ... the new poison which Judaism, Masonry, and rabid, revolutionary sectarianism want to use in order to corrupt the people."[95] (You might notice how often Judaism gets implicated in these pre-World War II film scandals regardless of whether any Jewish people were involved. Anti-Semitism was well established in the years before Hitler came to power.)

Paris' Prefect of Police strongly encouraged the French Board of Censors, which had passed "L'Age d'Or" initially, to review it again. The Board then banned it from further exhibition.[96] Marie-Laurie and Charles de Noailles, both Catholics, were threatened with excommunication by the Vatican. The couple pulled all prints of "L'Age d'Or" from distribution, and no one would see it again until 1979.

Sometimes, shock films can change a culture, or at least make it more tolerant of unsettling images on screen. At the very least, controversy can sell tickets. For "L'Age d'Or," the scandal was so overwhelming that the film didn't get the opportunity to do much of anything. Very few people saw it until Western culture was finished with the massive media liberalization of the 1960s and 1970s.

In that sense, the impact of "L'Age d'Or" is minimal. But the story of the scandal demonstrated that if you take shock content too far, too fast, it can backfire. It also made clear that the third rail of film was sacrilege. Attitudes on portraying sex and violence would ebb and flow in the first half of the 1900s, but making fun of Christianity was

---

[94] "L'Age d'Or," moviediva.com
[95] Quoted in C. B. Morris, "This Loving Darkness: The Cinema and Spanish Writers 1920–1936," p. 28–9.
[96] "L'Age d'Or," moviediva.com

always a suicide mission. It would rarely be attempted again until the 1960s.

Chapter 3: The Pre-Code Era: 1929-1934

How Is It "Pre-Code"?

"The Pre-Code Era" is a rather confusing term for the period of American film history from 1929 to 1934 (more often cited as 1930 to 1934; not many of the era's favorites are from 1929). After all, the whole silent era was "pre-Code," literally speaking. People cite 1929 or 1930 as the beginning of the Pre-Code Era because it's when enough theaters had been adjusted to play sound films, which made silent movies disappear. Understandably, people like us who grew up on sound films tend to be more interested in them than in the silents, so we separate them into two eras.

Some enjoy the Pre-Code Era because it was the peak of transgressive American film until the 1960s. But as you saw in the previous chapter, the "Don'ts and Be Carefuls" were established three years before, in 1927. Those rules supposedly meant Will Hays was clamping down on the naughty stuff.

Will Hays' underling Jason Joy had been trying his darnedest, sending recommendations for cleaning up both scripts and finished movies. But studios often ignored him because there was no enforcement mechanism.

Also, the sound-on-disc technology of the earliest talkies was replaced by sound-on-film, which made it much easier and cheaper to cut footage out of a film. Even if state and local censorship boards cut a few scenes, the movies infused with naughtiness tended to be more profitable than those without.

This was demonstrated by "**The Cock-Eyed World**" (1929), one of the first movies with wall-to-wall sound. It was also one of the first to use sound to offend people. The movie's soldier characters tell a bunch of off-color jokes, mostly concerning women who they have had sex with or are trying to. There are no sex scenes, of course – in 1929 that would get a filmmaker arrested. But it does show several women in revealing costumes and in the bath. The principal trait of all these women is that they are very eager to seduce the soldiers.

For me, it all felt like juvenile male fantasy. It turned especially sour when the two main soldiers made a bet on who would "make" a certain woman first. At that point the movie reached the depths of those misogynistic 1980s teen sex comedies. Mostly it's a load of corny gags and men insulting each other. I recommend you skip it.

Audiences in October 1929 loved "The Cock-Eyed World" and it made a ton of money. Religious leaders were not as enthused. Controversy over the movie and other saucy talkies rattled the investors in film studios.[97] Simultaneously, the stock market was crashing, starting the series of events that would result in the Great Depression. To top it off, a bill was introduced to establish federal censorship of movies. Will Hays came under pressure to make changes once again.

Is the Exploitation Circuit Helping?

The exploitation circuit, per usual, was not helping. "**Ingagi**" (1930) was cobbled together from some 15-year-old footage of a real African safari and some ridiculous newer scenes of actors pretending to be on safari. The real safari footage is upsetting in that it shows the shooting and killing of a hippo, lion, elephant, and other now-protected species. The faked safari footage is upsetting because it spins a racist fantasy about an African tribe that sacrifices a topless virgin to a gorilla. I only enjoyed one scene, a ludicrous attempt to pass off a tortoise with wings glued to its back

---

[97] Mark A. Vieira, "Sin in Soft Focus: Pre-Code Hollywood," p. 12-13

as a new animal called a "tortadillo." You can watch the movie on YouTube, but I recommend you don't.

Censorship battles concentrated on the nudity in "Ingagi," of course. But there was also a public outcry over what was real and what was fabricated. It is hard for me to fathom that anyone was fooled by any of the faked scenes, but I suppose faking documentary footage was a new concept to many people. Eventually the Federal Trade Commission launched an investigation and uncovered that the fabricated footage was filmed at the Los Angeles Zoo. It also discovered that the two explorers listed in the credits and often mentioned in the narration never existed.[98]

The various controversies only boosted the box office business for "Ingagi." It was not only successful for an exploitation film; some sources say it was among the top twenty money makers among all American movies of the 1930s. It bred a subgenre of so-called "exotic" exploitation films that instilled a racist version of Africa in the minds of white people. In "Bold! Daring! Shocking! True!," Eric Schaefer discusses how the "exotic" movies created a kind of "ur-jungle ... of the middle-class American imagination." All Black people in this ur-jungle were "either lazy, childlike innocents ... or prehistoric savages, displaced in time for the sole purpose of reminding us how 'civilized' our culture is."[99]

The construction of Africa as a land of half-naked cannibals was perpetuated by everything from mainstream films ("King Kong" was reportedly inspired by "Ingagi") to children's books ("Babar" comes to mind). As with minstrel characters, this twisted vision of Africa persists in the minds of many Americans to this day.

---

[98] Schaefer, p. 267
[99] Schaefer, p. 269

The Production Code

After "The Cock-Eyed World" and "Ingagi" became hits, an editor of a Catholic youth magazine with an appropriately Biblical name, Father Daniel Lord, picked the right time to act. In 1930, he wrote and circulated an expansion of the Don'ts and Be Carefuls. Will Hays committed his board to turning them into a new set of rules for self-regulation.[100] Hays was up for anything that would forestall more government action.

Catholic leaders were also ideologically opposed to government intervention, so they were willing to play ball. MGM production chief Irving Thalberg worked with Father Lord and other prominent Catholics to hammer out the Production Code.[101] It's so long that I'm not going to reproduce it here.

I should note one thing about the text of the Production Code: It made clear that the moralists weren't only interested in protecting kids from adult content. They were also out to prevent adults whom they looked down on from getting any wild ideas. In the "Reasons Supporting Preamble of Code," the Production Code authors spell out their elitist, condescending intentions. Here are some of their justifications for the rules establishing that "no picture shall be produced which will lower the moral standards of those who see it" and "law, natural or human, shall not be ridiculed":

> "Most arts appeal to the mature. This art [i.e., film] appeals at once to every class, mature, immature, developed, undeveloped, law abiding, criminal. Music has its grades for different classes; so has literature and drama. The art of the motion picture, combining as it does the two fundamental appeals of looking at a picture and listening to a story, at once reaches every class of society."

---

[100] Vieira, p. 17
[101] Vieira, p. 17-18

> "... it is difficult to produce films intended for only certain classes of people. The exhibitors' theatres are built for the masses, for the cultivated and the rude ..."

Upper- and middle-class people weren't just concerned about immigrants or illiterates being dangerously impressionable; they were frightened that the whole working class would be propelled into psychopathy by film depictions of violence and sexuality. In their minds, this was less of a problem with music, literature, and drama, which all have different "grades" for "different classes." Presumably the music, literature, and drama of the elite had adult content that the ignorant rabble couldn't be trusted with. I don't know how they maintained this segregation; what would stop some prole from getting their grubby hands on Shakespeare's "Titus Andronicus" or hearing Mozart's "The Abduction from the Seraglio"? I guess it was assumed the lower classes wouldn't be interested? Our ancestors had decided that Shakespeare and Mozart are High Art, so they get to have sex and violence; meanwhile no movie gets an elite status.

Beyond elitism, I detect a Grumpy Old Man Syndrome subtext: Movies are new and scary, but books and drama aren't, because we grew up with the latter and feel comfortable with them. Indeed, the Code later says "A book describes, a film vividly presents. One presents on a cold page; the other by apparently living people." The viscerality of film makes it too much for the lower classes to handle.

You might be wondering: Why didn't they just focus on protecting children? It wasn't a foreign concept at the time. Exploitation films like "Fit to Fight" only admitted adults.

The Code responds to this idea by stating that putting an age restriction in place was "not completely satisfactory and is only partially effective." Maybe they genuinely believed that, but there was also a financial consideration. Barring kids from your movie meant turning away paying customers, both children and their parents. Producers felt that only movies open to everyone could be guaranteed profit-makers.

At first, all this was mostly moot, because the Code was ineffective for several years. Establishing the Production Code in early 1930 did not start the "Code Era" – it started the "Pre-Code Era."

The Code did have an actual enforcement mechanism, but it quickly proved toothless. Jason Joy was given the power to reject films that did not live up to the Code. Initially, this caused studios to take him seriously. But if you look at the fine print, the studios didn't really give up control. While Joy was the presiding judge over movie content, there was also an appeals court, a rotating committee of three Hollywood producers. When a filmmaker disagreed with one of Joy's rulings, he would appeal to the committee. The producers on the committee knew that if they sided with Joy, they'd get on the bad side with a rival producer. When that angry producer got his turn on the committee, there would be hell to pay. The committee almost always sided with the filmmaker.[102]

Another key to the initial failure of the Production Code was a rule slipped in by MGM's Irving Thalberg. It says that you can present evil deeds as long as "throughout, the audience feels sure that evil is wrong and good is right." Later this became known as "compensating moral values."[103] It provided a squishy gray area that filmmakers could easily exploit. In practice, without a strong Production Code administrator at the helm, it meant people could sin throughout a film provided that they repent and/or get punished for it in the end. This allows you plenty of screen time for sinning.

The upshot is that filmmakers were not intimidated by the Code for long before the naughty films started gaining steam again. Self-regulation tends to get put aside when there's money to be made.

And studios got increasingly desperate when the Great Depression caused a major drop-off in box office receipts. The sea of red ink gave producers a powerful argument to get their films approved by the Hays Office: that a controversial film could save the studio from

---

[102] Leff and Simmons, p. 13-14
[103] Vieira, p. 17, 149

collapse. Because the Hays Office was employed by the studios, it was hard to deny them their shots to avoid bankruptcy.

From 1930 on, studios made incrementally more racy films each year. Every time they pushed the limits a bit more, they got more profits, until it all came crashing down in 1934.

Until 1934 at least, the Production Code was a bit like Prohibition. Both were rules pushed into place by religious groups and other moralists, and both were flouted with impunity by the rest of the country. As in so many other periods of United States history, the country was split between the fervently devout and the people who take religion less seriously or not at all.

The Message-Based Shock of Women's Dangerous Problems

Less than a month after the Code was announced, Irving Thalberg's MGM released "**The Divorcee**." Based on a best-selling and controversial novel, it portrays a high-society woman getting even with her philandering husband by having an affair of her own. I found it quite satisfying when she turns around on him his off-repeated excuse "But it didn't mean a thing!" Of course, the husband can't handle the turnabout and reacts like a lunatic.

"The Divorcee" has no nudity or curse words and refers to sex as obliquely as possible. Instead, it delivers a good kind of message-based shock, by my reckoning. To me, most of the movie was surprisingly proto-feminist in critiquing the sexist double standard in society's perception of marital infidelity. Unfortunately, the movie's ending abruptly undercuts all this. It provides an example of Irving Thalberg's "compensating moral values" in action.

Moralists were not mollified, though. Many were shocked to see its normally squeaky-clean star, Norma Shearer, playing a so-called "loose woman." "The Divorcee" subverts the "Madonna/whore dichotomy," which is a terrible name for many reasons. "Madonna" here refers to the Virgin Mary, not the singer who I'd say has taken over the name. And "whore" is just not a nice word -- let's go with "sex worker." The idea of what I will call the saint/sex worker dichotomy is that women in fiction are permitted to embody only one of two archetypes: They can be pure, faithful, self-sacrificing saints, or they can be sex workers who men use and throw away without feeling any guilt.

Married men who frequented brothels, a very large cohort in the 1930s, were especially protective of the saint/sex worker dichotomy because it psychologically justified their behavior. When the saint reveals interest in sex, or the sex worker reveals vulnerability or unwillingness to be solely a sex object, it threatens to breach men's flimsy justification and expose them to guilt. This results in anger, because few things make men angrier than a suggestion that they might have done something wrong.

Despite or perhaps because of the provocation, moviegoers flocked to "The Divorcee." It was nominated for Best Picture and Shearer won the Best Actress Oscar for her performance. The success of "The Divorcee" launched a spate of serious, high-minded investigations into sexual politics that skirt on the edge of feminism. These movies are not about titillation. Usually they end on compensating moral values that undercut their messages, but at least they pose some interesting questions.

Of course, they were questions that Father Daniel Lord and other moralist crusaders did not want posed. About such movies, Lord complained,

> "The stories are concerned with problems. They discuss morals, divorce, free love, unborn children, relationships outside of marriage, single and double standards, the relationship of sex to religion, marriage and its effects upon

the freedom of women. These subjects are fundamentally dangerous."[104]

This broad set of "fundamentally dangerous subjects" covered just about everything interesting a woman could do in a 1930s film besides fall in love. "Possessed" (1931), starring Joan Crawford, was an early film that broke from these restrictive roles. It isn't really a shock film, but its plot, of an ambitious small-town girl turned "kept woman," caused controversy. "Possessed" lays out its thesis statement in early dialogue of Joan Crawford's character Marian, as she turns down a marriage proposal from a small-town yokel:

- Marian: "All I've got is my looks and my youth ... do you think I'm going to trade that in on a chance that'll never come? ... My life belongs to me."

- Marian's mother: "You frighten me when you talk like that."

- Marian: "If I were a man it wouldn't frighten you. You'd think it was right for me to go out and get anything I could out of life, and use anything I had to get it. Why should men be so different?"

Marian's ambition depended on wooing a rich man, so it's not exactly Gloria Steinem-level feminism we're talking about here. But in the 1930s, opportunities for women in the workplace were scarce at best. Joan Crawford's character had plenty of intelligence but knew that the only way she could use it to her advantage was by conniving ways to get her pretty face in front of a wealthy young playboy.

A more sinful example of message-based sex shocker is "**Merrily We Go to Hell**" (1932). A young woman from a wealthy family falls for a witty, alcoholic reporter. They marry, but he keeps holding a torch for an old flame. Their solution is to try an open marriage. He

---

[104] Quoted in Vieira, p. 55

messes with the old flame, and she tries a pre-superstardom Cary Grant on for size. It's the kind of plot that would have been rejected at the script stage after 1934.

"Merrily We Go to Hell" was a big moneymaker in 1932 even though at least one major newspaper refused to print its advertisements because of the H-E-double-hockey-sticks in the title.[105] Moralists of course decried the creative marital arrangement. I think it's a brilliant film with fully-fledged characters struggling with realistic problems.

"Merrily We Go to Hell" was directed by Dorothy Arzner, the only female director employed by American film studios in the 1930s. I find her story fascinating, so I hope you'll agree it's worth a digression.

Arzner got her start in writing and editing, which were the behind-the-scenes roles open to women at the time. After she proved herself invaluable, Arzner went to the bosses at Paramount and asked for a chance to direct. They refused, so she accepted a deal from then-"poverty row" studio Columbia to write and direct. Rather than lose her, Paramount begrudgingly tossed her a script called "The Best Dressed Woman in Paris."[106] She agreed to stay.

It was a laughably bad fit: Female fashion was not a subject Dorothy Arzner cared about. She wore pants, ties, and suit jackets at a time when it was nearly illegal for women to wear anything besides dresses. Either the bosses were setting her up to fail or didn't think beyond "female director = movie about fashion." Regardless, Arzner turned the script into the hit 1927 film "Fashions for Women" and went on to a successful career. She was integral in the transition to sound films. One of her main innovations was inventing the boom mic by attaching a microphone to a fishing pole.

---

[105] "Merrily We Go to Hell" at the AFI Catalog of Feature Films
[106] Karyn Kay and Gerald Peary, "Interview with Dorothy Arzner", agnès films, July 16, 2011, https://agnesfilms.com/interviews/interview-with-dorothy-arzner/

In case you were wondering, Dorothy Arzner was in a committed relationship for 40 years with a female dancer and choreographer named Marion Morgan. A 1983 documentary called "Longing for Women: Dorothy Arzner" examines their relationship. It reveals that after Morgan died, Arzner retreated from the world in grief.

The documentary also features an interview with Arzner's lifelong friend, longtime next-door neighbor, and authorized biographer, Evelyn Scott. In it, Scott pushes aside the suggestion that Arzner and Morgan were lesbians, instead spinning a long and elaborate set of other reasons that the two women lived together for so long. I got the impression that Scott was self-deluded, and that Arzner was very good at keeping her private life private. Those of us of a certain age can all remember uncles, aunts, or other acquaintances who never married but lived with a person of the same sex for decades. The friends of these couples who were capable of facing reality knew they were LGBTQ+, while the bigoted ones somehow lived their lives in deep denial.

I realize it's not my place to come to conclusions about the sexual preferences of people who never publicly declared anything. At the same time, I would imagine stories like Arzner's could be inspirational to queer people today. It demonstrates that there were always people who refused to conform to traditional gender roles. Even the severe repression of the time could not force them to live conventional lives.

Speaking of women pushing against heteronormativity, "**Queen Christina**," starring Greta Garbo, was released in 1933. Garbo used the power she had at the height of her fame to force this film into production. She was fascinated by the real-life Queen Christina, who ruled Sweden from 1632-1654.

Queen Christina was famous for her gender nonconformity and probable lesbianism. In her autobiography, she revealed "an insurmountable distaste for marriage" and "for all the things that females talked about and did."[107] She often wore men's clothes and apparently had a romantic relationship with a woman named Ebba Sparre. Despite leading a country that was fighting the Thirty Years' War to preserve Protestantism, she was attracted to Catholicism and its vows of celibacy. Christina made it clear throughout her life that she never wanted to have sex with a man. Her reign ended when she abdicated the throne to convert to Catholicism and explore Europe, engaging in her true passions of arts and academics.

Garbo was able to get some of Christina's life on screen, but much of the movie concerns a love affair with a Spanish man who was invented by the screenwriters. Garbo was unhappy with this, telling friends, "Just imagine Christina abdicating for the sake of a little Spaniard."[108] Because of this grafted-on hetero love plot, "Queen Christina" is borderline as a shock movie. It still caused some fuss in 1933 and had to be heavily edited to be re-released after 1934.[109]

"**Ann Vickers**" is another story centered on a woman forging her own path. It's based on a novel by Sinclair Lewis, a fact that is hammered home in the title sequence: A hand takes Lewis' novel from a bookshelf, where it shares space with other respectable literature. The message I received was "Hey, this is classy, smart-people stuff, so be a grown-up about it."

Indeed, it's telling that content-based shock films tend to be based on books and plays. In the 1930s it was more acceptable, if still controversial, to deal with adult themes in literature and theater. As the Production Code made clear, the assumption was that these media were more for adults – higher-class adults in particular.

---

[107] Quoted in Una Birch, "Maxims of a Queen," p. 33.
[108] Quoted in Sarah Waters, "'A Girton Girl on a Throne': Queen Christina and Versions of Lesbianism, 1906-1933," *Feminist Review*, No. 46, Sexualities: Challenge & Change, p. 41-60
[109] Vieira, p. 153-154, 196

Literature also had more free-speech protection than movies did. In 1933, the same year "Ann Vickers" was released, the New York case *United States v. One Book Called Ulysses* (presumably given that title to clarify that the U.S. wasn't suing a pile of books called "Ulysses") established that a book was not obscene if it did not promote lust.[110] At issue was a description of masturbation in James Joyce's "Ulysses." Faced with the prospect of banning one of the great works of literature over one scene, the judges were forced into making a legal breakthrough.

Even an allusion to masturbation would never appear in a 1933 movie, of course. It would be many years before movies would get the freedom of subject matter that *United States v. One Book Called Ulysses* gave literature. As we saw in previous chapters, the elites, including the highest courts in the land, thought movies were dangerously attractive to lower-class people. Upper- and middle-class people felt the grown-ups they infantilized couldn't handle discussions of adult issues.

The adult issue that "Ann Vickers" covers is abortion. Ann Vickers is a thoroughly noble heroine devoting her considerable intelligence to helping the less fortunate. She has a weakness for ballsy men, though, and one manages to sweep her off her feet and impregnate her. When his true, caddish colors come out, she confides in a high-society friend, who brings her to Cuba for the abortion.

It's handled subtly enough that adults can understand what's going on while kids can conclude that the baby died for some unknown reason. Ambiguity was necessary to get it past the Hays Office, much less the censorship boards.

The plot of "Ann Vickers" involves both (off-screen) premarital and extramarital sex, so it caused fights with the Hays Office throughout production. Vickers gets married to a dull drip and then has an affair with a more dynamic fellow. She loses everything because of this

---

[110] *United States v. One Book Entitled Ulysses by James Joyce*, 72 F.2d 705, 706 (2d Cir. 1934), p. 708-709.

affair, but that wasn't enough for the Hays Office's Studio Relations Board. It "made further demands that the film include 'a definitive affirmative announcement' of the character's transgressions 'made by a 'spokesman for accepted morality.'"[111] Presumably they wanted the pope to jump into frame and list all the sins that Vickers had committed. RKO, the studio behind "Ann Vickers," shot this idea down hard, and the Hays Office backed down.

Because it was made in the Pre-Code era when studios could fight the censors, "Ann Vickers" was able to sneak some proto-feminism into a woman-centered story. Vickers becomes a very successful activist for prison reform and then a warden running a progressive prison. The ending, though, is so heavy on "compensating moral values" that it wrecks a lot of that message, for me at least. I don't necessarily recommend "Ann Vickers" – it also rushed to move through its story in under 80 minutes -- but it is interesting.

A much rougher story is found in "**The Story of Temple Drake**." It also has a strong literary pedigree, this time from William Faulkner's extremely controversial novel "Sanctuary." When Paramount began converting it into a film, Will Hays said to his staff, "We simply must not allow the production of a picture which will offend every right-thinking person who sees it."[112] The appeals board of film producers above Hays approved the treatment and pre-production began.[113]

The makers of "The Story of Temple Drake" were still forced to sand down some of "Sanctuary"'s rough edges. In the novel's most disturbing incident, the protagonist, Temple Drake, is raped by an impotent man with a corn cob. In the movie, the man traps her in a barn full of corn, and the picture fades out while she screams. The man then forces her to work in a brothel, which the movie unconvincingly calls a boarding house.

---

[111] Sova, p. 25
[112] Quoted in Vieira, p. 149
[113] Mille, p. 77

The rest of the film deals with her trauma and how the stigma attached to it prevents her from seeking help or pursuing justice. Maybe there were compensating moral values at the end, but I usually only notice them when they undercut the rest of the movie. For what it's worth, I found "The Story of Temple Drake" to be a sensitive, powerful, and emotionally complex treatment of a very fraught topic. But I recognize that as a straight male, my opinion on any work of art exploring rape is not the most relevant.

Many straight males in 1933 had strong opinions about "The Story of Temple Drake" and the other serious dramas I've covered in this section. Films that honestly interrogated issues involving women and sex were considered a huge threat. Mark A. Vieira, whose book "Sin in Soft Focus: Pre-Code Hollywood" is my main source for this chapter, cites "The Story of Temple Drake," "Ann Vickers," and "Possessed" among the ten movies most responsible for the institution of a strong Production Code in 1934.[114] But we have plenty of other movies to discuss before we get into all that.

Enter Howard Hughes

Let's go back to 1930. Independent film producer Howard Hughes had been making "**Hell's Angels**," a story about World War I flying aces, since 1927. It's mainly a showcase for aerial battles, which did look startling to me because they're mostly made of footage of real planes.

Hughes pushed the action so far that three stunt pilots and one mechanic were killed.[115] After pilots refused to do one especially dangerous stunt, Hughes performed it himself. He crashed, suffering a fractured skull and needing facial surgery.[116] Some say this crash caused his later mental difficulties. It certainly could have

---

[114] Vieira, p. 210

[115] James H. Farmer, "Howard & Hell's Angels". *Air Classics*. Volume 26, Number 12, December 1990, p. 20

[116] Peter Harry Brown and Pat H. Broeske, "Howard Hughes: The Untold Story", p. 63

been a contributing factor, but Howard Hughes had never been exactly stable.

All of "Hell's Angels"'s less interesting scenes, of people interacting on land, had been filmed in 1927 and 1928 as silent footage. While Hughes was spending years and millions of dollars shooting the action, sound took over the film world. By 1930, silence would no longer fly. (Ha. Pun.)

Hughes reshot all the land-bound scenes with sound. He quickly decided the actress playing his femme fatale, Norwegian-American Greta Nissen, had too much of an accent to play a British socialite. He replaced her with starlet Jean Harlow, who could only do an American accent.[117] But that was no problem, since almost all of the British characters spoke in American accents. Harlow was put in a bunch of low-cut outfits and tried her best to portray an evil vamp. She was unconvincing, to me at least, because she had such a naturally cheerful demeanor. I think Harlow could have been great in a role as a sweet-faced ingénue, a sort of Judy Garland type. But because she was curvaceous, Hughes and then Hollywood were determined to make her a "bad girl."

Along with Harlow's exposed skin, "Hell's Angels" features the content-based shocks of soldiers making out with and otherwise consorting with sex workers. There are also a few mild curse words that shocked 1930 audiences. The whole package made for a box-office triumph, but it had cost so much to film that it lost money.[118] It was still a success for Howard Hughes in that it established him as a mogul and allowed him to make more shocking films. And while its dogfights were the main draw, the movie showed once again that film audiences are up for titillation.

---

[117] Donald L. Barlett and James B. Steele, "Empire: The Life, Legend and Madness of Howard Hughes", p. 66
[118] Eyman, Scott. "The Speed of Sound: Hollywood and the Talkie Revolution, 1926–1930", p. 253

The Arrival of a Pre-Code Superstar

While "The Divorcee" and its progeny intelligently critiqued sexual mores, "Hell's Angels"'s shocks were more about showing a hot lady in skimpy costumes. You get both in the 1930 German film "**The Blue Angel**." Directed by Joseph von Sternberg, it established Marlene Dietrich as a powerhouse: smart, strong, seductive, and in control. She was no damsel in distress. She was a grown woman who used what she had to get what she wanted. If that meant making a fool out of some dumb, horny old toad, well, that was his fault.

"The Blue Angel" is a brilliant film, in my opinion. It made me feel loads of empathy for the dumb, horny old toad, played by silent film legend Emil Jannings, who falls for Dietrich and then suffers. I was also captivated by Dietrich's character, who is the film's true protagonist (a fact Jannings realized during filming and was not happy about). The film seems to revel in her charisma. She may be a femme fatale, but she's not a villain.

This is no simplistic cautionary tale about the dangers of consorting with fast women. It presents a complex morality that is not only light-years away from D.W. Griffith-style sexual mores; it makes "Pandora's Box" seem old-fashioned. "The Blue Angel" was scandalous in 1930, and heck, maybe it would trigger some incels today.

Before "The Blue Angel" was even allowed to reach American theaters, Dietrich and von Sternberg were lured to Hollywood to make "**Morocco**." To me, "Morocco" represents a step backward, because it makes Dietrich's character more beholden to a man. Apparently, Hollywood couldn't yet bring itself to depict a sexually active woman with as much agency as her "Blue Angel" character. Granted, the man in "Morocco" is hunky, swoon-worthy Gary Cooper instead of Emil Jannings with a silly beard. And at least she makes him the object of desire, reversing the typical Hollywood sexual dynamic.

"Morocco" qualifies as a shock film primarily because of one scene that Dietrich devised. Dietrich's character delivers a sexy performance at a cabaret bar wearing a top hat, white tie, and man's tailcoat. This alone was plenty alarming in 1930. Dietrich clinches the shock value by approaching a woman in the crowd and kissing her on the mouth.

After the success of "Morocco," "The Blue Angel" was permitted to be screened in the States in 1931. It was usually so butchered by censors that it was rendered nonsensical.[119] It was also an apparently inferior English-language version that had been filmed simultaneously with the German-language one.[120] In the first few years of sound films, there was no good way to dub dialogue or overlay subtitles. If you wanted your film to play in other countries, you had to make it several times in different languages. This forced actors to muddle through lines in languages they didn't speak well or at all.

Thus "The Blue Angel" didn't have the impact in the United States that "Morocco" had. It didn't matter; Marlene Dietrich and Joseph von Sternberg were firmly established as leading filmmakers of the era, and would turn out several more classics together.

Sexy Cartoons?

This might not be the ideal spot, but I need to mention Betty Boop at some point in this chapter. Betty Boop was a popular character who wore very little clothing and danced suggestively in short cartoons. In the early 1930s, animation was not entirely the domain of kids, so a cartoon sex symbol wasn't as strange at the time. It was still plenty disturbing to moralists.

The most shocking Betty Boop short that I've seen is "**Barnacle Bill**" from 1930. It's mainly about seaman Bill, who sneaks off his

---

[119] Vieira, p. 26
[120] James Travers, "Der Blaue Engel (1930)", Films de France (2005)

ship to visit a female dog who is an early prototype of Betty Boop. She's clearly a sex worker, and the movie makes us think we're going to catch her in the act with Bill before it does a switcheroo gag. Throughout she reveals a surprising amount of skin. After 1934, Betty would be fully clothed and much less popular.

Germany Again?

I'm sorry I haven't covered many of the great films from France, Italy, etc. It's just that even with the Aufklärungsfilme banned, Weimar-era Germany was the place for the best European shock films.

"**Mädchen in Uniform**" (1931) is a sort of sanitized Aufklärungsfilm. It's the story of lesbian desire in an all-girl's boarding school, but it's not nearly as prurient as that may sound. Apart from a quick kiss on the lips, there are no content-based shocks. It's more about pronouncements of love and looks of deep longing. I found it to be a quite sensitive and affecting portrayal of homoerotic desire.

"Mädchen in Uniform" was a big success across the world, but not without controversy. It only played in the United States after First Lady Eleanor Roosevelt pushed for and got it a limited American release. Within Germany it inspired several imitators. This mini-trend was killed when the Nazis took over and burned all copies of films about homosexuality. Thankfully, plenty of copies of "Mädchen in Uniform" survived worldwide.[121]

Another time Nazis got upset was over one of Fritz Lang's planned projects. In 1930, the Nazis were not yet in charge, but many of them had enough power to cause trouble. They were triggered when Lang stated in a newspaper ad that his next film would be called "Mörder unter uns," or "Murderer Among Us." Threatening

---

[121] Amanda Lee Koe, "The Femme Solidarity and Queer Allyship of 'Mädchen in Uniform,'" Criterion.com.
https://www.criterion.com/current/posts/7429-the-femme-solidarity-and-queer-allyship-of-m-dchen-in-uniform

letters poured in and his studio refused to give him space to shoot the film. When Lang asked why, the studio chief said that the Nazis assumed from the title that the movie was going to be about them.[122] Lang informed him that it was actually about a child rapist and murderer. That was much more acceptable to the Nazis, who allowed Lang to shoot his film.[123]

The title of Lang's film became "**M**," and it is a shocker. It's all message-based shock, but any film about a man raping and killing children is going to be disturbing. This culminates in an ending with a level of moral complexity that even pre-Code Hollywood wouldn't touch.

<SPOILER ALERT>

At the end of "M," the murderer, played by Peter Lorre, makes his plea for mercy. In front of a kangaroo court of gangsters, he argues,

> "What right have you to speak? Criminals! Perhaps you are even proud of yourselves! Proud of being able to crack into safes, or climb into buildings or cheat at cards. All of which, it seems to me, you could just as easily give up, if you had learned something useful, or if you had jobs, or if you were not such lazy pigs. I can not help myself! I have no control over this evil thing that is inside me—the fire, the voices, the torment!"

At that moment, I felt real empathy for a man who habitually committed the worst crimes imaginable -- not enough empathy to want him ever set free, of course, but some nonetheless. It takes genuine courage to allow a child rapist and murderer to reveal a soul. Lang meant it as a message against capital punishment, showing how even the worst criminal doesn't deserve death.

---

[122] Paul M. Jensen, "The Cinema of Fritz Lang," p. 93
[123] John Wakeman, "World Film Directors," p. 614

</SPOILER ALERT>

Fritz Lang said "M" arose from the stories of real-life German serial killers and a general tension about urban crime. "M" is credited as one of the first films noir, a term that was applied much later to dark films about criminals. I've seen plenty of American noirs made during and after World War II, many of which are terrific, but none of which I'd classify as a shock film by my definition. Some caused controversy, but not a lot of it. They almost all work within the strictures of the then-powerful American censorship system.

In fact, one of the few peak-period noirs that got into trouble was a 1951 American remake of "M." The Ohio censorship board banned it, saying it "creates sympathy rather than a constructive plan for dealing with perversion."[124] The U.S. Supreme Court overturned the decision in one of its many anti-censorship rulings after World War II. But that's a story for a later chapter.

Crime Time

Hollywood was also exploiting the public fascination with criminals in the early 1930s. Soon after Prohibition began in 1920, newspapers were packed with stories of the gangsters who took advantage of a boom market in the illegal transportation of liquor. The movie world took notice and cranked out gangster films.

The very existence of films with gangsters as protagonists was shocking to many. I don't know if there's a modern analogue -- maybe if "American Psycho" were rated PG and kids wandered into it on their own. Thomas Doherty, author of "Pre-Code Hollywood: Sex, Immorality, and Insurrection in American Cinema; 1930-1934," wrote:

> "No motion picture genre of the Pre-Code era was more incendiary than the gangster film; neither preachment yarns

---

[124] Quoted in de Grazia and Newman, p. 235

nor vice films so outraged the moral guardians or unnerved the city fathers as the high caliber scenarios that made screen heroes out of stone killers."[125]

Moral guardians were not pleased with newspaper stories about gangsters, but when those stories turned into movies, the outrage hit a much higher pitch. This demonstrates again the greater viscerality of film as a medium, how it is "closer to life," in Tolstoy's terms.

The first big gangster film was "Little Caesar." It has no hint of sex or graphic violence and ends on some big-time "compensating moral values." The New York and Pennsylvania censorship boards still demanded extensive cuts.[126]

"Little Caesar" made money anyway, so **The Public Enemy** (1931) upped the ante. It features Jean Harlow as a sexy moll and scenes of a couple canoodling in bed, which were cut by every censor. The most famous scene is of Jimmy Cagney shoving a grapefruit half in his girlfriend's face for little reason. This was the most shocking scene to my eyes, but was only cut by a few boards.[127] In 1931, the unsimulated physical abuse of a woman was not considered as disturbing as a fully clothed couple making innuendos in bed.

"The Public Enemy" brought in even more money than "Little Caesar," but it also brought Will Hays angry letters from everyone from The United Presbyterian Church to the Veterans of Foreign Wars.[128] Even Al Capone was quoted saying "these gang pictures are making a lot of kids want to be tough guys, and they don't serve

---

[125] Thomas Patrick Doherty, "Pre-Code Hollywood: Sex, Immorality, and Insurrection in American Cinema, 1930-1934", p. 139
[126] Vieira, p. 30
[127] Vieira, p. 33
[128] Ibid

any useful purpose."[129] Will Hays declared a ban on any more gangster films from the studios.

Howard Hughes did not belong to a studio, so he started production on "**Scarface**." The script got into the hands of Will Hays' loyal sidekick Jason Joy. After Joy's first few polite entreaties were ignored, he sent Hughes a letter saying "Gangsterism must not be mentioned in the cinema. If you should be foolhardy enough to make 'Scarface,' this office will make certain it is never released."[130]

Hughes ignored the threat, telling "Scarface"'s director, Howard Hawks, "Screw the Hays Office. Start the picture and make it as realistic, as grisly, and as exciting as possible."[131] Hawks did exactly that, and Hughes showed Jason Joy a rough cut. Joy gave some of his trademark polite suggestions and was pleasantly surprised to see Hughes agree to several of them. That put Joy on Hughes' side, and Joy went off to lobby the censorship boards to pass "Scarface."[132]

Meanwhile, Hughes arranged press screenings of the movie, which resulted in rave reviews. Hughes then opened it in New Orleans, the place with the laxest censorship board. "Scarface" was a hit with both critics and audiences and created a nationwide buzz.[133]

The northern censorship boards were not moved. "Scarface" was passed by the Ohio board but not by the all-important New York, Pennsylvania, or Chicago ones. Hughes was understandably furious – this was the sort of outcome that the Hays Office was designed to prevent. After months-long fights in public and private, Hughes consented to allow a toned-down version to be screened in New York. (If you wanted to see the regular version, you just had to hop a train to New Jersey.) Disgusted by all the struggle, Hughes

---

[129] Quoted in Vieira, p. 38
[130] Quoted in Vieira, p. 69
[131] Quoted in ibid
[132] Ibid
[133] Vieira, p. 70

retreated from filmmaking and committed himself to his airplane business.[134] "Scarface" was pulled from distribution in 1932 and not released again until 1979.[135] It marked the end of gangster films until after World War II.

After all that buildup, you might be expecting "Scarface" to be some Eli Roth gore-fest, or at least something similar to the loose 1983 remake. Temper your expectations: The version you can see still passed the Hays Office. It's now rated PG, which shows how much times have changed. Granted, we're talking about a 1979 version of PG; as I write this in 2025, PG is for kids' films and G is reserved for footage of babies smiling and not much else. (If the baby starts crying, it's a PG for sure.) If "Scarface" were remade shot-for-shot today, they'd throw in a single f-bomb to guarantee a PG-13.

"Scarface" does have a rawer and more brutal feel than any other film of the 1930s, in my estimation. It's reminiscent of gangster films from the 1970s in that the protagonist, brilliantly played by Paul Muni, is a straight-up thug: uneducated, fearless, psychotic, and positively thrilled by violence. Muni will likely remind you of Robert De Niro, Al Pacino, Joe Pesci, etc. There's no blood in the film but there are so many shootings that at several points I lost track of who was shooting whom.

I thought it was great, with one demerit brought by some ham-handed "compensating moral values" shtick. Halfway through the movie, it suddenly cuts to a bunch of randos arguing about the issue of gangsters. They blame newspapers, blame the government, propose changing specific laws, fuss and scream, etc. It's as if a classroom filmstrip about the gangster problem accidentally got spliced in. Luckily, this interlude is short, and then it cuts back to people being shot.

---

[134] Ibid
[135] Ian Brookes, ed., "Howard Hawks: New Perspectives", p. 27

What About Horror?

Besides "Häxan," I haven't designated any horror films as shockers yet. All horror is shocking; that's the point. They all explore death in some disturbing way. To stand out from the horror pack, you have to show something truly transgressive. "Nosferatu," "The Phantom of the Opera," etc. have plenty of terrifying images, but do they violate the "Don'ts and Be Carefuls"? Possibly a few of the Be Carefuls, but what doesn't?

Nothing in "Dracula" comes close either. In fact, it carefully cuts away before Dracula can even bite a neck. **Frankenstein** has one scene that qualifies, I think. A little girl is sitting by a lake when up stumbles Frankenstein.

A pedant might tell you he's actually called "Frankenstein's monster." But that's a mouthful, and "The Monster" is too vague. Besides, fictional characters regularly have shortened or colloquial names. If you can call the Warner Brothers character the Tasmanian Devil "Taz," then you can call Frankenstein's monster "Frankenstein." Unless a real Frankenstein's monster gives a press conference to say he prefers being called "Frankenstein's monster," I think you can keep referring to him as "Frankenstein."

Back to the point: The little girl is the first person who isn't horrified by Frankenstein's appearance. She plays a game with him throwing flowers into a lake. When he runs out of flowers, Frankenstein gets confused and throws the girl into the lake, where she drowns.

The version you see probably won't include the shot that makes clear the girl has drowned, which was removed by most censors. The rest of the scene barely survived: It was cut from the negative in 1934 and a copy wasn't rediscovered until the 1980s.[136] I still found it disturbing, especially after learning what went into getting the shot.

---

[136] Robert Horton, "Frankenstein", p.24

Boris Karloff was a genuinely sensitive soul and had a terrible time throwing a little girl. He wanted to gently place the girl in the water and show that she survived. Director James Whale insisted it had to look like the girl died. Karloff tried but could not throw her very far. The young actress's mother was on set, yelling "Throw her in again! Farther!" Whale got two technicians to throw the girl, but they threw her too far. He ended up going with Karloff's attempt.[137]

"Frankenstein" was released when the Great Depression was hitting the industry hard. The movie was so popular it was credited as saving several theaters.[138] It of course caused lots of consternation and spawned many other shockers.

1932 brought a similar story in "**Island of Lost Souls**." The great Charles Laughton plays mad scientist Dr. Moreau, who perverts the principles of evolution to create mutant animal-human hybrids. The censorship boards that didn't ban the movie cut it to pieces. Attempts to re-release it in 1935 and 1941 were denied by the Hays Office. The office's response in 1941 said:

> "[T]he blasphemous suggestion of the character, played by Charles Laughton, wherein he presumes to create human beings out of animals; the obnoxious suggestion of the attempt of these animals to mate with human beings, and the ... excessive gruesomeness and horror ... all these tend to make the picture quite definitely repulsive and not suitable for screen entertainment before mixed audiences."[139]

Many countries banned "Island of Lost Souls" outright. The British Board of Film Censors "refused a certificate" to the film (which is an

---

[137] Vieira, p. 43
[138] Ibid
[139] Gregory William Mank, "Angels and Ministers of Grace Defend Us!", p. 44

appropriately British-y way to put it), describing its plot as being "against nature."[140]

"Island of Lost Souls" may have been too much for most people of the 1930s, but as with almost all the movies we've covered so far, people nowadays won't find it too rough. In her essay accompanying Criterion's 2011 re-release of the film, Christine Smallwood says, "'Island of Lost Souls' no longer has the brute power to shock. That sensation – the violence of the mind's assimilating a totally new piece of information or feeling – can't be ours here."

While I agree with the general thrust of that statement, I think "Island of Lost Souls" retains some small amount of shock power. I found several shots of the animal-human hybrids genuinely disturbing. And then there's the leopard woman who tries to seduce a man, with all the bestiality that implies. Plus, unrelated to shocks, if you're a fan of the band Devo, you'll discover the origin of one of their main catchphrases. I recommend you watch it.

Finally, we have to cover one of the most controversial films in American history. After the runaway success of "Dracula," its director, Tod Browning, got a blank check from MGM's Irving Thalberg. Thalberg also gave him the instruction to make a film "even more horrible" than "Dracula" and "Frankenstein."[141] Browning harkened back into his roots working in a traveling carnival, where he had developed genuine affection for the sideshow performers. He hired little people, conjoined twins, a man with no legs, another with no limbs, people with microcephaly (called "pinheads" in the credits), and others with physical differences to star in "**Freaks**."

---

[140] Quoted in Christine Smallwood, "'Island of Lost Souls': The Beast Flesh Creeping Back", Criterion.com;
https://www.criterion.com/current/posts/2034-island-of-lost-souls-the-beast-flesh-creeping-back
[141] Quoted in Vieira, p. 85

When the sideshow performers appeared on the MGM lot, people were horrified. Studio supervisor Harry Rapf complained to Thalberg that people were running out of the commissary and throwing up. Thalberg relegated most of the group to a tent, but refused to shut the film down, saying "If it's a mistake, I'll take the blame."[142]

Especially considering all the fuss, the fascinating thing about the film this group produced is that its so-called "freaks" are the good guys. They are shown as a happy, cohesive chosen family. The bad guys are the ordinary people who ridicule them and worse. Tellingly, the two main villains are a woman known for her beauty and a man known for his strength, each fulfilling gender ideals that signal virtue in most movies. When the good guys dispense justice on the normies at the end, they get rough. But until then, the "freaks" don't do anything shocking.

Well, I suppose their very existence constitutes content-based shock for most people. I admit that the first time I saw "Freaks" I was disturbed to watch the limbless man light a cigarette and to see the microcephalic people at all. But nothing the carnival performers do approaches the Be Carefuls, much less the Don'ts, until the violent ending. These are just people who look unusual living their lives. My initial response was ableism, obviously.

Perhaps there is exploitation involved in the very fact that the performers are in a carnival sideshow, which entails displaying their unusual characteristics for gawking crowds. They do some carnival shtick in the film, which you could argue makes "Freaks" exploitative too. But I imagine the carnival performers themselves would take exception to that assessment. "Freaks" was the best job they ever got, in probably the only field in which they could make a living at the time. And they got to play sympathetic characters who may have changed a few viewers' minds about people who look different.

Of course, the main reaction to "Freaks" was shock and revulsion. A 90-minute version, which had already been cut down significantly,

---

[142] Ibid

was received very poorly in test screenings. One woman threatened to sue MGM because she said watching the film made her miscarry.[143]

Irving Thalberg responded by cutting out huge chunks of the film. He removed most of the final confrontation, including the castration of one especially macho character. So much was cut that, to get it back up to 64 minutes, Thalberg had to pad it out with some extra footage and a lame epilogue.[144] This final scene awkwardly absolves the main heroes for the purpose of compensating moral values. Thalberg's cut is the version that survives. The other footage is lost.

"Freaks" was cut further by various censorship boards and released sporadically throughout the United States. The censorship boards of Atlanta and San Francisco banned it. It would become the only MGM movie pulled from theaters before it completed its engagements.[145] The British Board of Film Censors refused a certificate to "Freaks" and only allowed it to be shown thirty years later, with an X rating.[146] Like "L'Age d'Or," it apparently took shock content too far, too fast to make a real impact.

It may not have made a big impact in the mainstream, but the world of exploitation was a different story. Having lost a bundle of money on the movie, Thalberg sold "Freaks" to producer Dwain Esper, who retitled it "Forbidden Love" and kept it on the exploitation circuit for years.[147]

Reviews in 1932 were mixed. Some critics recognized how Tod Browning had allowed the carnival performers' humanity to shine through. Others couldn't: A review in *Variety* said "it is impossible for

---

[143] Angela Smith, "Hideous Progeny: Disability, Eugenics, and Classic Horror Cinema", p. 93
[144] Devin Faraci, "The Unseen 'Freaks'". Birth.Movies.Death.com. Alamo Drafthouse Cinema.
[145] Vieira, p. 85
[146] "Freaks", AFI Catalog of Feature Films, American Film Institute.
[147] Schaefer, p. 60

the normal man or woman to sympathize with the aspiring midget." I think that's a terrible thing to say, but it shows how some people couldn't get past the shock of watching people who look so different from themselves.

Let's Get Back to Sex

Until movies got gory in the 1960s, sex was usually the main point of controversy in American film. It's a weird country. The United States is probably the most individualistic country in history; its people tend to assert they should be able to do whatever they want whenever they want. What human beings often want to do is have sex. This makes sense when you consider that it's the impulse that's responsible for the survival of the species. If sex didn't feel really good, our prehistoric ancestors would have been too exhausted from scrounging for food to bother with it.

But in the first half of the 1900s at least, the United States also tried to maintain the kinds of strict sex rules that are more characteristic of collectivist countries. Perhaps it's no surprise that movies became a primary outlet for pent-up sexual desire.

In 1931, this took the form of watching ladies disrobe down to bras and slips. You get a lot of that in the beginning of "**Night Nurse,**" a 72-minute exemplar of everything that made pre-Code movies different than post-Code ones. The first part is mostly about nurses played by Barbara Stanwyck and Joan Blondell changing clothes and engaging in hijinks at a hospital. Then it takes a drastic turn into a very grim story of two little girls starving to death while their wealthy, negligent mother drinks and parties in the next room. Plus, the love interest is a bootlegger who gets someone murdered, an act that is tossed off as if it's a fun lark. I found "Night Nurse" to be a pretty enjoyable curiosity.

When a man is the star, the movies take a very different tack. Paramount had a series of films in which Maurice Chevalier plays an irresistible hunk that drives every woman who lays eyes on him into a sexual frenzy. Personally, I find Chevalier to be a charmer, but also a grinning, mugging goofball who seems implausible as a walking aphrodisiac for the ladies. He ain't Brando in "A Streetcar Named Desire," that's for sure.

I admit that as a heterosexual man, I'm not exactly qualified to judge which men are attractive. But similarly unqualified heterosexual men at Paramount were making the decisions on who the ladies should be told to swoon over. I wonder if Chevalier was chosen because he best enabled men to indulge in a fantasy of being a ladies' man. If he were too clearly studly, men would be resentful. But if he's a bit more ordinary-looking, men could identify with him. This strategy would later be used in much more disreputable sex comedies like "Alvin Purple" (1973) and "Confessions of a Driving Instructor" (1976).

Anyway, the Chevalier films consistently find ways to have women show off their legs, but otherwise deliver message-based shocks. Chevalier always has sex with a series of women off-camera. These encounters are portrayed as slightly naughty fun in the context of light comedy. Even when Chevalier's affairs are extramarital, it doesn't prove problematic for long.

"Love Me Tonight" is considered the best of the bunch, but the most shocking for me was "**One Hour with You**" (1932). Chevalier's character, Andre, is happily married to Colette, played by Jeanette MacDonald. They are best friends with a couple in an unhappy marriage, and these friends want to have affairs with Andre and Colette. And the crazy thing is ...

<SPOILER ALERT>

Andre does it. He hems and haws but ends up having sex with his wife's best friend. Colette, meanwhile, rebuffs the guy. And then after a tiny bit of consternation, Colette shrugs off Andre's infidelity. Then the two of them sing a merry song and Colette looks into the camera and says "Can you blame me? Just look at him! He could bang the whole world twice, but since he's the hottest chunk of beefcake in history, I can't stay mad! La la la ..." (I'm paraphrasing.) Point is, I found it insane.

</SPOILER ALERT>

Pre-Code American movies with this sort of free and easy sexuality were often set in France. This let Americans (well, American males, mostly) indulge in fantasies of consequence-free sex without thinking it reflected on their own society.

The director of "One Hour with You," Ernst Lubitsch, was masterful at making sexual freedom overseas look classy. In his film "**Design for Living**" (1933), an American woman in Paris has trouble choosing between two men, who happen to be best friends. She expresses her dilemma:

> "You see, a man can meet two, three, or even four women and fall in love with all of them, and then by a process of interesting elimination, he is able to decide which he prefers. But a woman must decide purely on instinct—guesswork—if she wants to be considered nice."

After a complicated series of events, she chooses ...

<SPOILER ALERT>

Both. And they roll with it, resolving to live as a throuple. It's all done in a light and comedic way, but it still felt like a message-based shock to me. I wonder if Ernst Lubitsch was one of the few Westerners to see "Bed and Sofa," the Soviet film with a similar plot.

</SPOILER ALERT>

Because "Design for Living" portrays a woman having multiple sexual partners outside of marriage, it was the Lubitsch film that moralist reformers really hated. The Hays Office passed it reluctantly, but after the Code really started being enforced in 1934, it was banned from re-release.[148]

It's Not Sinful; It's History

We've covered sex and violence in pre-Code film -- how about a movie with both? **"The Sign of the Cross"** (1932) is one of Cecil B. DeMille's big bombastic epics. Being set in ancient Rome meant it could justify showing a lot of naughty stuff. It features Claudette Colbert bobbing up and down in a milk bath that was filled to the exact height that would cover her nipples. Later a woman does a sexy dance to convert a Christian woman to the ways of the flesh.

The movie's ending at the gladiatorial arena Circus Maximus gives DeMille an opportunity to roll out a sizzle reel of brutal confrontations, each more twisted than the last. Perhaps the most bizarre involves a woman tied to a stake, while a gorilla is let loose to do God knows what to her. These parts were easily cuttable by censorship boards so that a version could play in every market.

In keeping with the deeply entrenched homophobia of the 1930s, implied gorilla-on-girl brutality wasn't considered as shocking as a woman behaving seductively to another woman. The so-called "lesbian dance" proved the most offensive. Go-along-to-get-along guy Jason Joy let it pass the Hays Office because, in his words, "the director obviously used the dancing to show the conflict between paganism and Christianity."[149] Before the film was even released, Catholic publications disagreed vehemently with Joy, this time joined by Protestant and Jewish leaders. Will Hays asked DeMille what he was going to do about it, and DeMille said, "Not a damn

---

[148] Kim Morgan, "'Design for Living': It Takes Three", Criterion.com, https://www.criterion.com/current/posts/2084-design-for-living-it-takes-three
[149] Quoted in Vieira, p. 107

thing." No censorship boards ended up cutting the scene.[150] Likely by no coincidence, "The Sign of the Cross" was a blockbuster.

The compensating moral values are woven throughout "The Sign of the Cross" in the form of Christian characters covertly carrying on the faith in Rome soon after Jesus's crucifixion. They are 100% noble and pious, and Christianity is portrayed in the most positive possible light. I don't think it will surprise you or even count as a spoiler to say that Christian values win at the end.

This affirmation of Christianity did not provide enough moral value compensation for Catholic leaders. Father Daniel Lord, whose rewrite of the Don'ts and Be Carefuls led to the Production Code, threw up his hands. He and other prominent Catholics started creating an organization to fight back. More on that later.

The "Bad Girl"

"The Sign of the Cross" set up a clear saint/sex worker dichotomy: Claudette Colbert and the other Romans were evil and sexually active while the Christian girl they try to seduce is the saintly, virginal protagonist. **Red-Headed Woman** (1932) messed with the dichotomy by making the woman in the "sex worker" category pretty darn charming.

Jean Harlow plays Lilian, a striver who is more of a shameless figure of fun than the protagonist of "The Divorcee." After a montage that shows as much of Harlow's body as was permitted at the time, the movie draws you into Lilian's cheerful connivances to land a rich married man, played by Chester Morris. Hollywood finally managed to merge Harlow's natural sweet-faced charm with the saucy sex symbol persona it required of her, thanks in part to shaving her eyebrows and drawing on two thin arches that would make a drag queen proud.

---

[150] Ibid

Chester Morris's character is a stand-up guy, but Lilian persists until he gives in. Surprisingly, we then switch to the devastation felt by his wife, which I found genuinely moving. The movie pulls you back and forth between reveling in the sexual hijinks of Harlow's character and showing the genuine pain that they cause. It's as if a sex comedy and a heart-rending melodrama got chopped up and mixed together. I won't give away more, but it's hard to say that compensating moral values were fully realized. The United Kingdom banned "Red-Headed Woman" and American censorship boards put it through extensive edits.[151]

Baby Face" (1933) took the "bad girl" subgenre a step further. Barbara Stanwyck plays Lily Powers, a young woman who opens the film fending off grubby factory workers in her father's cheap speakeasy. When the drunks stumble out, her father tries to pimp her out to a politico who has the power to shut his place down. She forcibly rebuffs the guy's sexual assaults, which infuriates her father. Then you get this exchange:

- Her father: "You little tramp, you!"
- Lily Powers: "Yeah, I'm a tramp, and who's to blame? My father. A swell start you gave me. Ever since I was fourteen, what's it been? Nothing but men! Dirty rotten men! And you're lower than any of them. I'll hate you as long as I live!"

As with "Scarface," "Baby Face" felt a lot more like a raw 1970s drama to me than anything I'd seen from the 1930s. Lily's saving grace is the one man who's not trying to have sex with her: An irascible old cobbler encourages her to read Nietzsche and be inspired to "Exploit yourself! Go to some big city where you will find opportunities. Use men! Be strong! Defiant! Use men to get the things you want."

That sets the stage for Lily to climb the ranks of a giant New York bank, one sexual conquest at a time. I was with her every step of the way, cheering each time her feminine wiles and smarts

---

[151] Vieira, p. 91

overpowered another horndog. As with Marlene Dietrich's character in "The Blue Angel," Lily is both the femme fatale and the clear hero. She uses the only power society allows her, her sexuality, to get what she wants. There are no cutaways to sympathetic wives in "Baby Face." Even a kind of lame ending didn't compensate for all the moral values.

"Baby Face" underwent cuts but played in all states except Ohio and Virginia. After 1934, it joined "Red-Headed Woman" and "Design for Living" as one of the films that could not be re-released.[152]

More Real-Life Scandal

Meanwhile, Hollywood scandals in the newspapers kept adding fuel to the fire. William Haines was a handsome leading man whom film exhibitors had rated as the top box-office draw in the country in 1930. He was openly gay – that is, openly only to the people of Hollywood, not the general public. In 1933, Haines was arrested in a YMCA with a sailor he had picked up. His studio, MGM, demanded that he marry a woman to kill the publicity. He refused, and MGM terminated his contract. After a few more roles in small films, his career was over.[153]

Usually these sorts of Hollywood stories end in alcoholism and early death. When performers can't perform any more, they usually collapse. They are dramatic people by nature. But William Haines started a new career as an interior designer and became wildly successful at it. His business partner was also his life partner, and they had a committed relationship for the rest of their lives. Their good friend Joan Crawford called them "the happiest married couple

---

[152] Sova, p. 32
[153] Stacie Stukin, "Gentlemen preferred Haines", *The Advocate*, Feb. 5, 2002, p. 58.

in Hollywood."[154] Maybe this story wasn't critical to include in this book, but sometimes I can't resist a happy ending.

Aren't Europeans Doing Anything?

Luis Buñuel's film career was down in the dumps after "L'Age d'Or" proved too hot for 1930. Then he got a lucky break when one of his friends won the lottery and used his winnings to finance another Buñuel shocker.[155]

Buñuel was very excited about left-wing politics, even briefly joining the Communist Party of Spain. Urban Spain had undergone a drastic modernization in the 1920s, but many rural areas remained desperately poor. Buñuel saw great hypocrisy in the self-congratulatory ways that the establishment bragged about rising living standards.[156]

He read about an impoverished remote Spanish region called Las Hurdes that only made money by taking in orphans. Buñuel took a film crew there and filmed what he saw. Sometimes he couldn't get clear shots of the most shocking events. So he staged some footage by pushing a goat off a mountain, covering a sick donkey with honey so it would be attacked by bees, etc. These were re-creations of things that really happened in Las Hurdes, so it's not like he was inventing shock scenes out of whole cloth. Luis Buñuel was a lifelong animal lover, but he loved provocation even more.

Buñuel put it all together into a short called "**Las Hurdes: Tierra Sin Pan**," or "**Land Without Bread**" (1932). It was made as a silent film, but Buñuel added narration that parodied the travelogue documentaries that were popular at the time. His point was that you didn't need to leave Spain to see people living in the depths of

---

[154] Quoted in Eve Golden, "Golden Images: 41 Essays on Silent Film Stars", p. 45
[155] David Weir, "Anarchy & Culture: The Aesthetic Politics of Modernism", p. 253
[156] "Luis Buñuel: The Journey of a Surrealist," documentary

poverty. After concentrating his previous films on pissing off the establishment in as many ways as possible, Buñuel channeled his love of provocation into a specific altruistic aim.

Once again, though, Buñuel had taken the shock content too far, and "Land Without Bread" didn't reach many people. During the movie's premiere, a fight erupted between Buñuel and the government official in charge of improving conditions in Las Hurdes. Further uproar led Spanish conservatives to ban the film.[157]

Of course, I missed all this context the first time I watched "Land Without Bread" on YouTube. I saw some disturbing animal cruelty paired with some genuine righteous indignation over the squalid living conditions endured by the people of Las Hurdes. The combination of shock content and genuine societal critique constitutes much of what I love about Luis Buñuel, one of my favorite filmmakers ever. Later Buñuel films would center on surreal humor and be lots more fun. I can't say I'm a huge fan of "Land Without Bread," but the film sets the template for his future masterpieces.

On the other side of the continent, Czech director Gustav Machatý had a wild idea. He decided to make a slow, nearly silent art film with full female nudity and a sex scene in which you see a young woman (from the neck up only) having an orgasm.

It wasn't just the obvious content-based shocks that made "**Ecstasy**" (1933) verboten. The young female character, played by Hedy Lamarr (then Hedy Kiesler), marries a rich old guy who cannot perform in bed. The relationship sours, and she seeks her first sexual experience elsewhere. The young, virile hunk she chooses represents the noble working class, contrasting strongly with her unmanly capitalist husband. A bizarre final sequence drives this communist messaging home with the subtlety of a sledgehammer, trumpeting that proles who work with their hands are perfect ideals

---

[157] Iker Jiménez Elizari, "El paraíso maldito"

of humanity. Czechoslovakia was an independent democracy at the time, but "Ecstasy" sure feels Soviet.

Another odd thing about "Ecstasy" is that it has very little dialogue. What lines it does have were filmed in three languages because dubbing and subtitles were still not feasible options. Having so little dialogue means only a handful of shots need to be reshot in different languages. For me, the paucity of dialogue gives "Ecstasy" a dreamy quality that is supported by gorgeous cinematography.

Of course, people in 1933 were more interested in the nudity and the orgasm. The film played in Czechoslovakia and Austria in early 1933 but only made it to German theaters in 1935 with major cuts. Mussolini made an exception to Italy's censorship laws to get "Ecstasy" in the Venice Film Festival, but the Vatican denounced it. Hedy Lamarr's then-husband tried to buy every print and production still to destroy them.[158]

Even sending a print of "Ecstasy" to the United States sparked a legal battle. The U.S. Customs Bureau seized it on arrival and a judge and jury ruled it was obscene. While the decision was on appeal, a federal marshal burned the print. This lunkheaded move made the court lose jurisdiction. The distributor got a new print, cut out some offending material, and it passed through Customs.[159]

The legal problems didn't end there. The New York censorship board banned "Ecstasy" because of the orgasm scene. State law held that a film had to be passed "unless such film or a part thereof is obscene, indecent, [or] immoral." The film's distributor sued, saying that the board could just cut the offending scene and then approve it. The court upheld the censorship board's decision, stating that "Ecstasy" "unduly emphasizes the carnal side of the sex relationship."[160] That is, you can't make a movie that reveals that sex is a big part of marriage. If a young woman discovers her new

---

[158] Miller, p. 102
[159] de Grazia and Newman, p. 210
[160] Quoted in de Grazia and Newman, p. 211

husband is impotent, she should be happy to live out the rest of her life as a virgin.

Just to cap off the rejection, the newly formed Catholic Legion of Decency condemned "Ecstasy" in 1934. The film's distributors lobbied for Production Code approval as late as 1935, which of course it had zero chance of achieving.

The exploitation circuit remained an option, if not a good one. By the early 1930s, movie studios had bought a huge majority of the country's movie theaters. Thus most theaters were open only to studio product that had passed the Hays Office and censorship boards. This arrangement let the studios maintain an oligopoly and choke off competition from independents. Even if "Ecstasy" had great potential, it could earn money only in the few independent theaters still scattered around the United States.

Exploitation mogul Samuel Cummins took on the film. The version he used was re-edited so that the rich old husband died midway through the film and Lamarr married the hunky young prole before having sex with him.[161] This killed the plot's potency, but oh well. Cummins was happy to showcase "Ecstasy"'s nudity and orgasm, but couldn't let it happen extramaritally.

An odd thing about exploitation films was that even though their raison d'etre was content-based shocks, they avoided message-based ones. After wallowing in naughtiness, they would revert to conservative values. Exploitation producers had to at least pretend to promote positive messages to placate reformers who might prevent nude scenes from getting in front of people's eyes.

Nudity Is Good for You

The pump had already been primed for "Ecstasy"'s nude scenes to succeed in the exploitation circuit. A few years before the film came

---

[161] de Grazia and Newman, p. 210

to the few exploitation-friendly U.S. screens, they were packed with the message that nudity was the healthiest thing since water. Nudist colonies became a trend in Europe in the 1920s and reached the States in the early 1930s. Soon after the first newspaper stories publicized the phenomenon, "**Elysia (Valley of the Nude)**" (1933) was slapped together.

"Elysia" is a 45-minute film about a reporter going to a nudist colony and learning about nudism. That's pretty much it. There's no conflict; to me it came across as an earnest attempt to proselytize about the health benefits of being naked outdoors. The diseases purportedly cured by nudity ranged from rickets to the common cold.

Of course, the primary purpose of the film was to show naked people, specifically young, thin women. I don't know if the women were genuine nudists or were imported by the filmmakers, but they certainly get the lion's share of the screen time. Meanwhile, the few male nudists are carefully filmed to obscure their penises. One walks past the camera with a bunch of tools awkwardly held in front of his crotch. "Elysia" may have been written by true believers in nudism, but it was filmed and edited by exploitationeers.

"Elysia" also finds a way to sneak in some racism. Early on, a doctor shows the reporter some films of people in Africa and the South Pacific. The doctor drones on about how the so-called "savages" have strong physiques because they are often nude outdoors. You get the idea. As usual with exploitation films, beware.

Censors in Maryland, New York, and many cities tried their best to stop "Elysia" from being screened. Los Angeles police interfered with screenings until the movie's producer got an injunction to stop them. After more local censorship laws were passed and another federal censorship bill was introduced in 1933, the major film studios blamed it all on nudist movies and other exploitation films.[162]

---

[162] Schaefer, p. 151

None of this prevented "Elysia" from starting a wave of nudist movies that became a staple of the exploitation circuit throughout the 1930s. They would fall out of fashion in the 1940s but come back in a big way in the 1950s. To their credit, they were probably the least sleazy ways to see naked women at the time. And because the standard practice was to allow only adults into exploitation films, no one could say children were being corrupted.

Make Way for the Queen

Back in the mainstream, the likes of Jean Harlow and Barbara Stanwyck had set the stage for the arrival of the supreme pot-stirrer: Mae West. West had been perfecting sexual provocation for years on Broadway. In 1926 she wrote, produced, directed, and starred in a play called "Sex." Tickets sold well but it earned her a ten-day jail sentence for "corrupting the morals of youth."[163]

Her next play, "The Drag," was about homosexuality. A strong supporter of gay rights, West hired a cast of gay actors and let them improvise a script. The result didn't even hit the stage before The New York Society for the Prevention of Vice succeeded in shutting it down.[164] Undaunted, West continued writing plays and provoking controversy until Hollywood came calling.

It took a while. Will Hays did not want Mae West in movies, under any circumstances. He succeeded in keeping her away for a few years.[165] But when box office receipts plummeted in the depths of the Great Depression, Paramount decided to take the risk.

In 1932, Paramount gave West a supporting part in the movie "Night After Night." She rewrote her lines and stole the show. It was clear to everyone that West needed a starring role. The Hays Office was

---

[163] Patrick Bunyan, "All Around the Town: Amazing Manhattan Facts and Curiosities," p. 317
[164] George Eells and Stanley Musgrove, "Mae West: A Biography", p. 66–68
[165] Leff and Simmons, p. 21

nervous, but conceded on the condition that no one attempted to adapt her banned play "Diamond Lil."[166]

Paramount began producing an adaptation of "Diamond Lil." The Hays Office fought it, and the dispute went to the MPPDA appeals board, which was as always full of producers obsessed with the bottom line. Will Hays thought the producers would be scared off by potential protests, but they were swayed by Paramount's argument that the movie would rescue the company from imminent financial collapse.[167]

"Diamond Lil" was toned down a bit to become "**She Done Him Wrong**" (1933). It's filled with the double entendres that became West's trademark, but the shocker was her persona: She enjoys sex, pursues it, and enthusiastically lets everyone know. This sets her apart from the more mercenary characters of "Red-Headed Woman" or "Baby Face," who use sex to get ahead. West takes on the stereotypically male role of an unabashed sexual adventurer.

Mae West was 40 years old in 1933, stood 5' 0," and did not have the rail-thin body that Hollywood preferred even in the 1930s. She was not the perfect physical manifestation of male sexual fantasy that Jean Harlow was. But West told everyone she was a sex goddess so convincingly that she made it true.

"She Done Him Wrong" made so much money that it did indeed help save Paramount from bankruptcy.[168] The studio rushed a follow-up into production. The opening credits of "**I'm No Angel**" (1933) trumpet "Story, Screen-Play [sic] and All Dialogue by MAE WEST." Precious few women have had comparable levels of creative input into Hollywood films before or since. Many women have been successful screenwriters, but, outside of the silent era, I

---

[166] Vieira, p. 112
[167] Miller, p. 72
[168] Vieira, p. 116

can't think of any other woman whose writing was a selling point to audiences until perhaps Nora Ephron.

Throughout "I'm No Angel," West's character Tira celebrates having had affairs with many men. Later this is turned against her in a court case full of what would now be called "slut-shaming," with ex-lovers taking the stand to impugn her character. Tira acts in her own defense and grills each ex about his own sexual history: how many times he was married, the fact that he was engaged to someone else during their tryst, etc. Like "The Divorcee," "I'm No Angel" turns the tables on men who live by a double standard.

The movie was an even bigger hit than "She Done Him Wrong." It doesn't really have content-based shocks, just a high-spirited celebration of sex. About "I'm No Angel," influential Catholic leader Martin Quigley wrote "its sportive wisecracking tends to create tolerance if not acceptance of things essentially evil."[169] That quote comes from Mark A. Vieira's "Sin in Soft Focus: Pre-Code Hollywood," which goes on to quote a Louisiana exhibitor's pithy response to such criticisms: "The church people clamor for clean pictures, but they all come out to see Mae West."[170]

Joseph Breen and the Legion of Decency

The tremendous success of Mae West movies provoked many reform-minded Catholics into action, including a man named Joseph Breen. Breen had worked in the Hays Office for years, as probably the only strict moralist on the payroll. He would regularly communicate on the sly with Father Daniel Lord and other influential Catholics about the moral rot surrounding him. In one letter he wrote that "nobody out here cares a damn for the Code or any of its provisions."[171] In another he wrote that movie producers were "a foul

---

[169] Quoted in Vieira, p. 128-130
[170] Quoted in Vieira, p. 130
[171] Quoted in Vieira, p. 148

bunch, crazed with sex, dirty-minded and ignorant in all matters having to do with sound morals."[172]

Breen also frequently said that Will Hays was a weak leader who was frightened by the studios. In late 1933, Hays got the studios to assure Breen and a group of Catholic leaders that something would be done about the latest spate of immoral films.[173] Nobody believed Hays and the moguls. They'd been burned by them enough.

Simultaneously, popular books trotted out statistics and anecdotes "proving" that children were being destroyed by racy films.[174] As the Great Depression deepened, the country was turning away from flapper culture and towards conservative social values. The Depression was also reducing ordinary people's disposable income, and the film studios could not afford to lose many patrons.

A lost film called "**Convention City**" (1933) allegedly provided the last straw. It was apparently a wacky sex farce set in Atlantic City. Censors tore into it with the most cuts for any film since 1929, and its producer would later claim it "brought on the whole Code."[175]

On November 15, 1933, Breen and a pack of archbishops, bishops, and other prominent Catholics officially founded the Catholic Legion of Decency. Churches pushed parishioners to join. All they had to do was sign a pledge to "remain away from all motion pictures except those which do not offend decency and Christian morality."[176]

The Catholic Legion of Decency relied on each priest or bishop to decide for himself which movies offended decency and Christian morality. Reportedly, when some churches handed out lists of disreputable films, those films would get a boost in business. Other

---

[172] Ibid
[173] Vieira, p. 152
[174] Vieira, p. 152-153
[175] Quoted in Vieira, p. 151
[176] Quoted in "Religion: Legion of Decency". *Time*. June 11, 1934

priests decided to make lists of acceptable films instead, lest they give free publicity to the unacceptable ones.[177] Neither approach proved very effective. The Catholic Legion of Decency had some kinks to work out.

Soon after the founding of the Catholic Legion of Decency in late 1933, Joseph Breen took over the top spot at the Hays Office's Studio Relations Board. Now the reformers had a leader on the inside. Unlike his predecessor Jason Joy, Breen was no pushover. He could scream and pound the table just as well as any studio representative. It took a little time for him to bend Hollywood to his and the Legion's will, but he would succeed.

The Cops Break Up the Party

In early 1934, Hollywood didn't yet know whether Joseph Breen and the Catholic Legion of Decency were genuine threats. Going by previous attempts at reform, it seemed a safe bet that nothing much would change. Business proceeded as usual, and several films pushed boundaries further.

I have not covered musical comedies, but have seriously considered doing so. "Gold Diggers of 1933" and "Dames" I found to be great fun, highlighted by wild, psychedelic dance sequences choreographed by Busby Berkeley. "Gold Diggers of 1933" is closer to qualifying as a shock film, with more ladies in skimpy clothes. I didn't feel like it quite got there. Meanwhile, "Dames," in my opinion, has a better plot. In the end, though, neither could compare in terms of shock value to "**Murder at the Vanities**."

That's a shame, because I found "Murder of the Vanities" to be a far inferior film. Its plot is the most slipshod mystery I've ever seen. I'd say the only reason to watch the movie is for two shocking musical numbers. One features a parade of women with bizarre outfits and other arrangements of objects that strategically cover their nipples

---

[177] "Catholics Differ Over Film Listing". *The New York Times*. December 12, 1934

and crotches. The outfits and arrangements get so baroque that it started feeling kind of twisted to me.

The other wild number extols the virtues of marijuana. Marijuana was legal in 1934 and there wasn't much public awareness about it. The singer of the marijuana number, Kitty Carlisle, reportedly thought that marijuana was the name of a Mexican musical instrument. If you can find a clip of "Sweet Marijuana" online, maybe watch that instead of the whole movie. I found it to be quite a sight to see such a song in a movie from 1934. (But then, as I write this, marijuana is being legalized most everywhere. I can foresee it losing much of its stigma, and this scene losing much of its shock value.)

Joseph Breen tried to stop "Murder at the Vanities" and many other films in early 1934, but kept being stymied by the studios. In May 1934 he brought out the big guns. He told Cardinal Dennis Dougherty of Philadelphia to unleash the Catholic Legion of Decency, for real this time. Dougherty raged at the pulpit that all Catholics should boycott all movies, not just the sinful ones. Box-office business immediately dropped 40 percent in the city.[178]

This put the fear of God in the studios. After years of bloviating, the moralists had finally demonstrated in dollar terms what they were capable of. Father Daniel Lord started his own campaign, and Protestant churches signaled they were ready to join the effort. The Federal Council of Churches of Christ announced plans to bring its 24 million members into the Catholic Legion of Decency and push for a federal censorship law.[179] Hays called Joseph Breen and pleaded "For the love of God, come over here! What can you do?" Breen coolly responded, "I've been telling you guys it's coming."[180]

The new order was pounded out by Breen and Catholic leaders. The Hays Office's Studio Relations Board was replaced by the Production Code Administration, with Breen at the head. The

---

[178] Vieira, p. 181
[179] Miller, p. 82
[180] Quoted in Vieira, p. 182

appeals court of three film producers was replaced by the New York Board of Directors, who were money men, not filmmakers. They may not have been moralists like Breen, but didn't care about artistic freedom the way the producers did. The Board of Directors was seeing very good evidence that censorship would keep their industry financially stable, so they wanted censorship.[181]

Under the new system, Joseph Breen would have to approve every script. Then he would watch the finished film before anyone else. If he approved, he would give the movie a seal. Only movies with that seal could be shown at the theaters owned by the studios, which was almost all of them. If your movie didn't get that seal, good luck getting it seen.

In mid-1934, Breen's first major test came with the latest Mae West film. He had already read the script for "It Ain't No Sin" in February and decried it as a "glorification of prostitution and violent crime without compensating moral values of any kind"[182] – in other words, a typical Mae West movie. West and her collaborators ignored him and made the movie they wanted.

When Breen saw the finished film, now as the head of the Production Code Administration, he demanded extensive cuts. A shouting match with Paramount's production chief didn't change his position. Meanwhile, a promotional poster for the film was put up in New York and drew pickets by priests. Paramount backed down and made Breen's suggested edits, which resulted in a film riddled with continuity errors. Breen didn't like that version either, so it had to be reworked again.[183] The title was also changed to the less provocative "Belle of the Nineties."

"Belle of the Nineties" was watered down into a non-shock film. It proved much less successful at the box office than "She Done Him

---

[181] Vieira, p. 191
[182] Quoted in Vieira, p. 194
[183] Leff and Simmons, p. 51-52

Wrong" or "I'm No Angel."[184] The message was clear to Hollywood: If Joseph Breen was willing to ruin the guaranteed cash cow that a 1934 Mae West film was bound to be, he did not care about the bottom line. He would sink a studio rather than pass a sinful film. This was something new.

If you'll permit me a quick homily, there's a lesson here about private corporations in American-style capitalism. American corporations talk about being in business to make the world better and such, and many businesspeople genuinely believe it. But history shows that if you want them to change their behavior, it works best to put your demands in concrete monetary terms. Otherwise, they'll probably just fob you off with promises of self-regulation that will be conveniently ignored when restrictions stand in the way of profits.

A Final Few Shockers

For the most part, Joseph Breen's new system worked. American film studios made very few shockers from 1935 to the 1950s. You'll see that the movies in the next chapter are almost all foreign or exploitation films. But before the age of true censorship began, 1934 saw a couple more shock films squeeze through.

One was a big hit. Cecil B. DeMille returned to the template that had worked in "The Sign of the Cross": a historical story in a non-Christian era starring Claudette Colbert wearing very little. "**Cleopatra**" (1934) has more than just Colbert in skimpy costumes; its first hour is packed to the gills with women in revealing outfits. There is even a lot of cleavage, which I mention not to be a 1930s version of Mr. Skin but because cleavage was a big no-no after 1934. The very first shot of the film is of a naked woman lit from the back so you can't see everything, but you can see a lot more than

---

[184] Marybeth Hamilton, "'When I'm Bad, I'm Better': Mae West, Sex, and American Entertainment", p. 217

you might expect. Later in the film you get some violence of a level that would be disallowed soon afterwards.

"Cleopatra" also carries message-based shock throughout: Colbert's Cleopatra pursues sex and is the clear heroine of the film. I was rooting her on as she seduced men to feed her ambition, a la Barbara Stanwyck's character in "Baby Face." But at the end, I felt whiplashed by some dreadful compensating moral values. Patriarchy is restored in a big, ugly, misogynistic way. "Cleopatra" is sometimes quite a spectacle, in my view, but maybe turn it off ten minutes early. Regardless, people loved it in 1934 and it set a record for first-week admissions for a Paramount movie.[185]

Another late-1934 shocker was barely seen, but is a much better movie from where I stand. Joseph von Sternberg and Marlene Dietrich profiled another powerful woman from history who reportedly enjoyed sex, Catherine the Great. "**The Scarlet Empress**" is a wild film beginning with a series of quick torture scenes, some of which feature female toplessness. It's one of very few mainstream 1930s films with the kind of nudity that would have to be cut for basic cable.

The rest of "The Scarlet Empress" offers the message-based shock of a woman who develops a vibrant sexual appetite, one that is mostly incidental to her struggle for power. There are no compensating moral values that I could see, unless we're talking about Peter III getting what's coming to him for being an idiot. Another non-shock-related asset of the film is some of the most wonderfully bizarre choices I've ever seen for set decoration. If you have any interest in 1930s movies, put this one on the top of your list.

Joseph Breen saw "The Scarlet Empress" in April 1934 and was horrified. He called an emergency meeting with Joseph von Sternberg and Paramount executives. But before he could lay down

---

[185] "110,383 See "Cleopatra" in First Week". *The Film Daily*. LXVI (47): 1. August 25, 1934

the law, he was pulled away to a confab with some Catholic leaders. While the cat was away, one of Breen's underlings was intimidated into passing the film. Later Breen was too busy to revisit the movie and assumed the necessary cuts were made. They weren't, but it didn't matter much, because "The Scarlet Empress" proved too weird for audiences in 1934. It flopped and disappeared.[186]

Thus the American Pre-Code Era ended with a whimper, with possibly its best and most transgressive film making little to no impact. Hollywood would have to find other ways besides provocation to make money. It would succeed.

---

[186] Vieira, p. 207

Chapter 4: The Code Era: 1934-1948

A Time of "Decency"

From 1934-1948, the Production Code was held firmly in place by Joseph Breen, in partnership with the Catholic Legion of Decency. The Legion rated films "A," "B," or "C," with A being acceptable for anyone and C being condemned. The idea spread to Protestant churches, so the group changed its name to the National League of Decency. It became a unified army of millions that could mobilize against any film.

In other eras, having your movie marked as condemned by religious groups would likely boost your box office. Quite the opposite was true during the Code Era. The Legion would organize boycotts of C films, and the large contingent who were trying to avoid shock films would know to stay away.

It took only a year or two for Hollywood to learn the power of the Legion of Decency. By 1936, filmmakers would change a film rather than allow it to be released with a C. The list of C films from 1936 on is composed almost entirely of exploitation movies and foreign imports.

Film studios couldn't manipulate or ignore the Legion the way it had with the Hays Office, because the Legion wasn't employed by the film studios. The Legion provided the independent censorship that the studios had feared all along; it was just religious groups doing the censoring instead of the government.

With the Legion of Decency's firepower backing him up, Joseph Breen took full control of keeping movies clean from conception to release. You couldn't even buy the film rights to a book or play without Breen's say-so. If you tried adapting something shocking, you'd better adapt the shocks right out of it.

Lillian Hellman's play "The Children's Hour" was a big hit on Broadway in 1934, which meant a film adaptation was nearly inevitable. The problem, from Joseph Breen's perspective, was that it was about two women being accused of a lesbian affair. Even if there was no actual affair in the play, just mentioning lesbianism at all broke the "sexual perversion" rule in the Production Code. The solution was to scrub away all queerness by changing the fateful rumor into one woman sleeping with the other's fiancée. Breen also wouldn't allow the title "The Children's Hour," because it would connect the film to the play. It was renamed "These Three" and was a success.[187]

With precious few exceptions, there were no shocks, as I'm defining the term, in Hollywood movies from 1934 to 1948. What controversies existed were over issues so minor as to be beyond the comprehension of modern viewers.

For example, there was a huge behind-the-scenes fight over the famous "damn" in the line "Frankly my dear, I don't give a damn" from "Gone with the Wind." Joseph Breen eventually allowed it, but made clear that it would not set a precedent.[188]

An even more baffling example came in the 1937 screwball comedy "The Awful Truth." It has a silly recurring fantasy bit involving a man and a woman coming out of opposite sides of a cuckoo clock. Several times, they walk out of their own doors and walk back in their own doors. At the end, the man follows the woman into her door. To be clear, they are fully clothed and don't touch each other, say anything, or behave suggestively in any way. Still, this moment and other seemingly innocuous ones only survived the cutting room floor because Joseph Breen felt the movie and its stars were high-class.[189]

---

[187] Miller, p. 104-105
[188] Leff and Simmons, p. 100
[189] Leff and Simmons, p. 64

If this sort of thing didn't satisfy a person's itch to be shocked, they would be hard pressed to find alternatives. Hollywood essentially owned the entire movie system from top to bottom, including the theaters. Per an article by the National Constitution Center:

> "The major studios had a near-monopoly on the movie business in the United States. Each studio had exclusive contracts with actors and directors; owned the theaters where their movies played; worked with each other to control how movies were shown in independent theaters; and, in some cases, owned the companies that processed the film.
>
> "The system of "vertical integration" was expensive to maintain, but it was lucrative when the movie business was booming."[190]

And the movie business boomed after 1934. Check out the percentage of the U.S. population that went to the movies weekly, by year:[191]

---

[190] Scott Bomboy, "The day the Supreme Court killed Hollywood's studio system," https://constitutioncenter.org/blog/the-day-the-supreme-court-killed-hollywoods-studio-system, May 4, 2023

[191] Taken from "The Decline in Average Weekly Cinema Attendance, 1930-2000," Michelle C. Pautz, Issues in Political Economy, 2002, Vol. 11

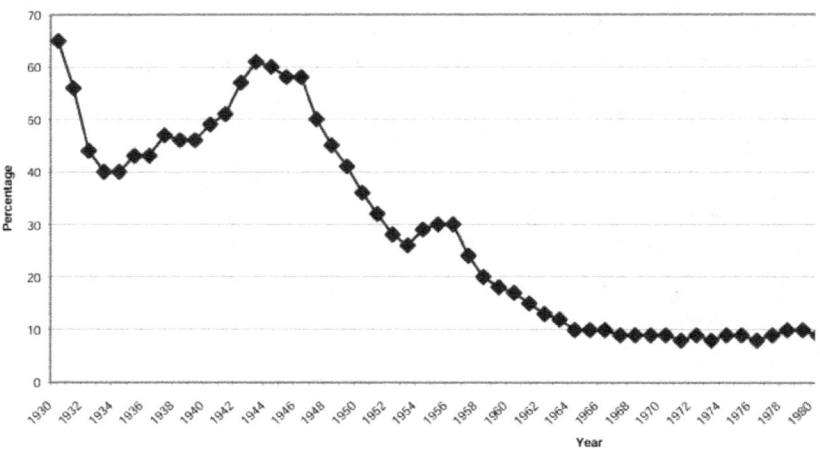

You can see why the industry was panicking in 1933 and 1934. The percentage of Americans going to the movies dropped from around 66% in 1930 to 40% in 1934. After 1934, things gradually improved each year until a new peak during the U.S. involvement in World War II.

This turnaround was not caused by vertical integration, which was completed by 1930. That wouldn't make much sense anyway. People don't go to movies more often because they want to support oligopolies. Studios may have taken over almost the whole pie, but that's no reason for the pie to get bigger.

Correlation is not causation, but there is at least correlation between Joseph Breen taking charge and audiences growing. At the very least, the masses were not turned off by clean films. And some classic clean films came out of the main Code era from 1934-1948: "Citizen Kane," "Casablanca," "Gone with the Wind," "The Wizard of Oz," etc.

How does this jibe with what we saw in the previous chapter? Individual Pre-Code films brought big business through scandal. Shockers like "Frankenstein" and "She Done Him Wrong" were so popular that they saved their studios from bankruptcy. Individual producers saw these returns and were incentivized to make saucy films.

But these films may have also scared a significant percentage of the population away from going to any movies at all. After 1934, families could trust movies to be wholesome, and their increased patronage outweighed the loss of shock fans. Especially in the 1930s, when people married young, there were more families than there were thrill-seekers.

It's perhaps similar to what happened in Las Vegas and Times Square. In the mid-1900s, they were legendary places for vice. When they were cleaned up, many businesses went under. And then families started streaming in and overall profits rose.

This illustrates what economists call the "fallacy of composition." People assume that what's good for an individual is good for the group, but that's not necessarily true. If you stand up at a baseball game, it will help you see better. But it will not help anyone else enjoy the game, especially the people behind you. The same applies to businesses: What brings your firm profits might bring down your industry. You might make money from "She Done Him Wrong," but it also might turn off a large sector of the population from movies altogether.

Mind you, this doesn't really apply to movies today. In the 1930s, there weren't thousands of streaming options. The media landscape then was very monocultural; any given week, people had a handful of movies to choose from, at most. You might prefer a western or a musical, and maybe look at some reviews. Mainly you just went to what was playing and assumed it would be fine for everyone. It's a setup best suited for the tastes of the majority, which was families. There wasn't much opportunity to split the audience into sectors.

As with every historical question, there are a zillion possible reasons for the recovery of the film business in the late 1930s, and scholars can spend careers debating the relative contributions of each. For the purposes of this book, I've already spent enough time on the topic. The upshot is that the money men were happy, so Joseph Breen remained in power and the mainstream stayed clean.

Independence and Exploitation

With the studios controlling so many theaters, very few venues exhibited independent films. What little money there was to be made was hard-won by films that appealed to the shock-seekers who were not served by the mainstream.

Dwain Esper was the man for the job. I mentioned him once before as the independent producer who took "Freaks" off MGM's hands, retitled it "Forbidden Love," and toured it on the exploitation circuit. He also made his own movies, such as the 1934 oddity "**Maniac**."

"Maniac" is often cited as one of the worst films of all time. That typically means it's fun to watch. Bad movies with long, dull stretches, like "Ingagi," are a dime a dozen; they don't stand out as notably bad the way "Maniac" does. If you think you've seen it all, I recommend "Maniac." It's one of the most bizarre movies I've ever seen.

Be forewarned that animal abuse and sexual assault constitute two of the biggest shocks in "Maniac." There is also nudity, which is startling in the context of a 1930s movie.

Previous exploitation films had some grounding in dispensing education. "Fit to Fight" and "Is Your Daughter Safe?" reportedly provided valuable information about sex that the rest of society was too prude to broach. At least some people behind "Elysia" were motivated by a genuine desire to proselytize about nudism. Even "Ingagi" was mostly real footage of an African safari.

"Maniac" brings only the barest pretense of offering anything but shocks. There is scrolling text at the beginning asserting that fear can cause psychological disorders. In the exploitation trade, these opening messages, called "square-ups," were tacked on to hammer home the educational value of the movies. But as vague as

"Maniac"'s square-up is, it doesn't have much to do with the movie's parade of bizarre behavior. Brief pseudo-square-ups pop up amidst the action to define disorders that are allegedly being portrayed, but those also test the bounds of plausibility. "Maniac" represents a new step in the evolution of exploitation film, in which there is almost no pretext of enlightening the public.

"Maniac" was originally released before it became clear that Joseph Breen would succeed in cleaning up movies. After 1934, you didn't have to go to "Maniac"'s extremes to stand out as a shocker. Dwain Esper's 1936 movie "**Marihuana**" is much tamer. It squeezes in some female nudity with a skinny-dipping scene. Otherwise, it follows the "kids smoke pot and their lives collapse" plot of "Reefer Madness" (1938) and other drug polemics of the time.

These movies capitalized on a spate of lurid news articles about the scary new drug marijuana. Despite what you may have heard from your stoner friend, George Washington did not smoke a bowl each night. The practice of smoking marijuana entered the country via Mexican day laborers in the 1920s. When the Great Depression took hold, their labor was no longer in demand, and racist fears took over. As Eric Schaefer states in "Bold! Daring! Shocking! True!," "the plant had not changed, but the name and the cultural Otherness associated with its minority users served to create a threat."[192]

Many news stories argued for criminalization of marijuana because of widespread beliefs about "its potential to induce violent behavior, which eventually terminated in irreversible insanity."[193] The pervasiveness of this myth speaks both to the lack of experience people had with the drug and their capacity for indulging in hysteria. Middle-aged middle-class people read these falsehoods about marijuana and did what they always do: panic about their children. Films like "Marihuana" constituted one outlet for panic, as it strenuously warned parents that pot was coming for their teens. In reality, as Schaefer writes, "all indications are that marijuana use

---

[192] Schaefer, p. 228
[193] Schaefer, p. 230

prior to the 1960s was neither large-scale nor prevalent among adolescents."[194]

Any movie that mentioned drugs at all was breaking the Production Code. I'm choosing Esper's "Marihuana" as the representative of the drug polemic movie because it has the most shocks. It was capitalizing on a trend rather than being an earnest, lunkheaded cautionary tale like "Reefer Madness." So don't watch it expecting unintentional laughs. No one in it gets high and then dances wildly or mugs hyperactively as in "Reefer Madness"'s famous scenes.

Actually, I was pleasantly surprised by "Marihuana." I thought the lead actress was charming and the melodramatic plot wasn't completely inept. It's very far from a must-see, but if you're curious about 1930s exploitation cinema, you could do worse.

For instance, you could watch another 1936 film that exploited sensationalistic news stories, "**Lash of the Penitentes**." Newspapers were abuzz about a religious cult in a remote area of New Mexico. One of the cult's ceremonies involved men reenacting Jesus's final moments by carrying crosses up a mountain while other members of the community whipped them. The movie takes footage of the real ceremonies and cuts them into a dramatization of a reporter trying to document it all.

The plot is similar to that of "Ingagi," the inscrutably popular 1930 exploitation movie about an African safari. "Land of the Penitentes" similarly overlays the documentary footage with condescending, racist narration, which is only entertaining when its pomposity is punctured by a flubbed line. It also shoehorns in female nudity, staging a scene in which a woman is stripped bare and whipped. There is some real animal cruelty too. Steer clear if any of this sounds too unsavory.

As was typical with exploitation films, there were many different versions of "Lash of the Penitentes." The cut I saw was only 48

---

[194] Schaefer, p. 231

minutes long. Shorter versions excised the gratuitous female nudity. Longer versions inserted irrelevant scenes about religions in India and Africa, including a scene of a naked African being thrown into a volcano.[195] Exploitationeers knew what they could get away with in each market, and modified their movies accordingly.

The director who added the fictional footage to "Lash of the Penitentes," Harry Revier, went on to direct probably the most disturbing film of the era, **"Child Bride"** (1938). It capitalized on the national frenzy over a news story about a 22-year-old Tennessee farmer marrying his 9-year-old neighbor. Tennessee had no minimum age for marriage at the time.[196] In other states, the minimum age was ten; in Delaware it was 7.[197]

After the Tennessee farmer scandal, many states quickly reworked their laws. "Child Bride" dramatizes an effort to change the laws in one backwoods town. Of course, it wouldn't be 1930s exploitation if it didn't contradict its own message with prurient content. In "Child Bride," this takes the form of sexualizing a 12-year-old girl, particularly in a gratuitous nude bathing scene.

I saw an edited version, but I saw plenty enough to turn my stomach. "Child Bride" provided one of the most unpleasant movie-watching experiences of my life. It's one of the few films we've encountered that went over my personal line from shocking to repellent. It wasn't classified as pornography, which was illegal at the time, because no genitalia are exposed and there is no sex. Today I don't think it could get on any screens.

"Child Bride" serves as another illustration of how for a few types of content, what we can see on screen has rightfully become more restrictive, not less. Pubescent nudity was certainly not permitted in Hollywood films in the 1930s, but it carried less stigma than the kind of adult sex scenes and graphic violence that are now

---

[195] Schaefer, p. 284
[196] "Frontline: Married Young: The Fight Over Child Marriage in America"
[197] Schaefer, p. 283

commonplace. Even as most film content has liberalized since the 1930s, American society has become more aware that anything potentially arousing to pedophiles is unacceptable.

Overseas

Under the Production Code, American filmmakers couldn't even refer to sex workers. In China, a sex worker was the very sympathetic protagonist of "**The Goddess**" (1934). The film opens with the following text laid over a painting of a naked woman breastfeeding a baby, while her hands are tied behind her back:

"The Goddess, struggling within the vortex of life: On the nighttime streets, she is a cheap prostitute. When she holds her child in her arms, she is a divine and pure mother. In both lives, she shows great moral character."

As that intro indicates, the protagonist of "The Goddess" is neither an object of the film's scorn or a clichéd "hooker with a heart of gold" who exists to deflower a young man, impart a few nuggets of wisdom, and then be forgotten. Instead, this is a woman with no other means to support her child, at the mercy of an evil criminal. The film constitutes an earnest plea for empathy for sex workers.

Probably because of the current conception of China as a very socially conservative place, I was quite surprised to see such a progressive-minded examination of sex work in any Chinese film, much less one from the mid-1930s. But then I learned that sex work was legal in Chinese cities until after World War II. According to "Regulating Prostitution in China: Gender and Local Statebuilding, 1900-1937," by Elizabeth J. Remick,

> "Prostitution was a huge business in China during the first four decades of the twentieth century. Tens of thousands of women worked in brothels as courtesans and in public venues as streetwalkers. In many cities, going to brothels for banquets, entertainment, gambling, alcohol, opium, and sex

was one of the most popular forms of recreation for men with even only a little money, and brothels were one of the most important places to conduct business, along with teahouses and restaurants. Famous prostitutes were important leaders of fashion and culture in many cities."

This was not unique to China. Most countries have gone through alternating periods of tolerance and repression of prostitution. In the 1800s, most American cities had areas in which brothels were legally protected. Brothels were legal throughout France until 1946. In Germany, sex workers were tolerated as long as they were registered with the government. (Germans tend to be OK with anything they can organize.)

Still, "The Goddess" was not a typical movie in 1930s China. Director Wu Yonggang had made many "fallen woman" films, in which a woman has sex outside of marriage and is punished for it. With "The Goddess," he sought to paint a picture of the realities of sex work. His new approach made the authorities nervous. During the filming, Wu noticed an unusual number of government officials checking in to make sure nothing offensive was happening.[198]

The result didn't have anything censors could object to. "The Goddess" conformed to China's Film Censorship Law of 1930 by avoiding any sexual imagery and having the protagonist fully embody Confucian values of self-sacrifice and discipline. She does so to such an extent that I could imagine a modern viewer feeling she is too saintly to be human. Personally, I found "The Goddess" to be a moving melodrama, if not an exemplar of realism.

Meanwhile, the primary European country for shock films, Germany, was overtaken by the Nazis in 1933. Both Hitler and his minister of propaganda, Joseph Goebbels, were big film fans. They seized control of the industry and destroyed films they deemed

---

[198] Harris, Kristine (2008). "The Goddess: Fallen Woman of Shanghai". Chinese Films in Focus II. Bloomsbury. pp. 128–136.

"subversive," which encompassed most of the German films I've discussed.

No new film could be made that contradicted Nazi ideology. Of the 1200 German feature films produced from 1933 to 1945, 300 were later banned by the Allies for being Nazi propaganda, according to the documentary "Forbidden Films" (2014). Forty films are still restricted from general distribution in Germany and Austria.

I won't be reviewing any of these 40 films for this book. It would feel more than a bit facile and insulting to rummage through Nazi propaganda for shocks. Nazis represent the height of evil, and scouring their most virulent films for cheap thrills minimizes and trivializes that evil. I don't want to appear glib in any way about a movie like "Jud Suss" (1940), the infamous anti-Semitic drama that neo-Nazis still use to recruit impressionable teens.

Then again, I did cover "The Birth of a Nation," which espoused racism and the American slavery system responsible for massive intergenerational trauma and 15 million deaths, per a United Nations estimate. The film also inspired a revival of the Ku Klux Klan. If "The Birth of a Nation," why not "Jud Suss"?

"The Birth of a Nation" looms so large in American film history, particularly in terms of censorship, that I found it impossible to ignore. No Nazi-era films have a comparable level of importance. They were immensely popular in Germany, but little seen elsewhere. While I try to cover world cinema, this book's primary focus is the United States.

And at this point in the book, it should be clear that I'm mostly focused on the kind of shocks that are enjoyable, "The Birth of a Nation" and a few other examples notwithstanding. Even message-based shocks can be fun in a way, if, like "Birth Control" or "Anders als die Andern," they take bold stands against harmful, outdated ideas. But there's no fun to be had when the message is abhorrent.

I'm willing to risk occasionally coming across a monstrosity like "Child Bride" if it means potentially discovering another "Maniac." I'm not willing to look for a diamond in the rough among the 40 banned Nazi movies. Life is too short.

Instead, I recommend watching the documentary "**Forbidden Films**." It covers the most important Nazi films and shows modern Germans debating whether the films should continue to be repressed. A major topic is the context in which Nazi films should be seen. For example, as part of a history class, the movies can be accompanied by discussion about how they manipulate people. "Forbidden Films" itself provides intelligent, thoughtful context, in my opinion. If you see it and then want to explore Nazi cinema further, that's your choice.

Outside of the banned 40, there is one Nazi film that I feel compelled to cover because it has pervaded the canon of world cinema. The documentary "Triumph of the Will" (1935) does deliver some unpleasant shocks by lionizing Hitler. I found it very unsettling to watch history's worst human being smile at adoring crowds while happy music plays in the background.

If that qualifies as a reason to watch "Triumph of the Will," it's about the only one I can see. There's no story, and not even much information. It's mostly a series of rallies and parades that I found increasingly dull. As reviewer "ciara" on Letterboxd said, "Great, now we have to add being boring to the list of Hitler's crimes."

"Triumph of the Will" is often cited as great, or at least important, because it's skillfully directed by Leni Riefenstahl. Students of documentary technique might have to see it to appreciate her innovations. As for the rest of you, try her film "**Olympia**" (1938) instead. While it has some disturbing Hitler adulation, it mostly reviews the action of the 1936 Olympic Games in Berlin.

Some of "Olympia" felt very tedious to me; you don't know boredom until you've watched several minutes of a single, static, black-and-white shot of a field hockey match taken at ground level from about

50 feet away. But "Olympia" also has some oddly beautiful sequences of athletes posing and twirling around. Sometimes these people are naked, which is of course a shock in a 1930s movie. If you're not afraid to make liberal use of the fast-forward button, you might get something out of "Olympia."

As German film became isolated, France took over as the premier European country for shock movies. Throughout the late 1930s, many French films got the dreaded C for "condemned" by the Legion of Decency. All-time classics "Pépé le Moko" (1937) and "**La Bête humaine**" (1938) were among those banned from United States distribution for many years. Neither have content-based shocks; they just have dark, grown-up themes that constituted message-based shocks at the time.

"La Bête humaine," directed by the legendary Jean Renoir (son of Impressionist painter Pierre-Auguste Renoir), is the one that still packed a punch for me, shock-wise. Everyman par excellence Jean Gabin plays a protagonist who at first seems like a working-class hero. Then you discover that he is plagued by powerful homicidal impulses. It's a bit like if, 20 minutes into "Captain Phillips," Tom Hanks's character turned out to be Dexter from the TV show of the same name. "La Bête humaine" has the kind of complex anti-hero that you might see in a 1970s New Hollywood film, but never within the strict moral universe carefully constructed by the Production Code. I don't want to give away anything else, as you should see it and many other Renoir masterpieces ("The Rules of the Game," "The Grand Illusion," "The Crime of Monsieur Lange," and "The River" are personal favorites). You deserve a palate cleanser after all the exploitation and Nazi films.

The Good Kind of Exploitation

You might recall that the first exploitation film, 1918's "Fit to Fight," was not intentionally exploitative. It wasn't made just to provide content-based shocks that people couldn't get in the mainstream. The U.S. military produced it to give soldiers the truth about venereal disease. "Fit to Fight" became a huge success among civilians largely because it provided shocking sights, like penises with genital warts. But it also provided a great service, dispensing information about venereal diseases and condoms that people couldn't get anywhere else. It was the only sex education available outside of brothels.

In 1938, "**The Birth of a Baby**" played a similar role. It tells the story of a married woman getting important information about her pregnancy and then giving birth. The film broaches plenty of topics that were verboten in 1938 Hollywood, but that any worthwhile doctor would discuss with their patients. It's even a bit conservative by modern standards, especially in a scene where the doctor comes down hard on a woman seeking an abortion.

"The Birth of a Baby" provides the template for the sex education films that you may have seen in junior high school, complete with poor editing, bland characters, and awkward, didactic dialogue. Unlike most sex education films, however, it has almost no content-based shocks. The big exception comes when you see a real baby coming out of a real vagina. Even this is presented as demurely as possible: Towels are placed around the vaginal opening to obscure all genitalia. I still found it bracing, because the sight of one human being being pushed out of another will always do that to me. Childbirth is miraculous, wonderful, etc., but I'm sorry, the newborn always comes out looking so lifeless and rubbery.

The makers of "The Birth of a Baby" had no designs on the exploitation circuit. They didn't even intend it for theaters; it was "planned as a nontheatrical presentation for medical conventions and physician training."[199] After it was made, a group called the American Committee on Maternal Welfare, Inc. tried to get it wider distribution. The group was a collaboration of respectable organizations like the American College of Surgeons and the U.S.

---

[199] Schaefer, p. 188

Public Health Service. Even First Lady Eleanor Roosevelt lent her support.

The American Committee on Maternal Welfare tried to get a special dispensation to show "The Birth of a Baby" in regular theaters. It circumvented the Production Code Administration and made its case to state censorship boards. New York's board shot them down, calling the movie "indecent" and "immoral" and saying it "would tend to corrupt morals."[200] "The Birth of a Baby" is actually one of the most morally upstanding movies I've ever seen, without an iota of violence or sexually provocative material. It's hard to imagine who would leap into sin because they learned what it's like to be pregnant and give birth within wedlock. I have to assume what the New York board was really saying was "Ew, this lady stuff makes us feel icky."

The case came to the New York Appellate Division. In upholding the censors' decision, Appellate Court Justice Gilbert V. Schenk wrote "Undoubtedly, this picture may have its scientific value. It is not indecent in the ordinary accepted sense of the word, but it becomes indecent when presented in places of amusement."[201] It's unclear how a change of venue can turn a movie indecent, but I assume they were thinking of the children and/or illiterates and/or immigrants who the courts usually tried to protect from movies. (To be fair, two judges wrote a dissent that praised the film's educational value.)

The court's decision sealed the deal in New York, and "The Birth of a Baby" didn't fare well with other censorship boards. The only outlet remaining was the exploitation circuit. There it became a massive hit that played for twenty years.[202] Unquestionably, many people bought tickets expecting titillation, and some distributors probably spliced in a few lurid scenes to keep them happy. Other patrons went to it with a genuine desire to learn. Regardless, everyone who saw "The Birth of a Baby" gained valuable knowledge

---

[200] Quoted in de Grazia and Newman, P. 218
[201] Quoted in de Grazia and Newman, p. 218
[202] Shaefer, p. 191

about pregnancy and birth that the rest of American popular culture was too prudish to provide. The exploitation circuit may have been disreputable, but sometimes it provided real benefits to society.

Meanwhile, Dwain Esper was less concerned with benefiting the American public. "**Sex Madness**" (1938) was his version of sex education. It follows the more traditional exploitation formula of a cautionary tale about venereal disease. It's not as nakedly exploitative as "Maniac" or "Marihuana," as it imparts some important information about a genuinely dangerous affliction.

As far as shocks are concerned, it depends on which version you see. The cut you can easily catch on YouTube omits most of the disturbing footage. I saw it first and didn't think it needed to be in this book. Then I saw "Sex Madness Revealed" (2018), a mockumentary that overlays a longer cut of "Sex Madness" with audio of Patton Oswalt and Rob Zabrecky playing a podcast host and guest, respectively. "Sex Madness Revealed" has a much crisper print of "Sex Madness" than the one on YouTube or anywhere else I've looked. And crucially, it does not omit any shock material.

Both versions broach the topic of lesbianism through two female characters, but that storyline is abandoned. What qualifies the "Sex Madness Revealed" version as a shock film is its medical footage of real people with syphilis. I found the shots of adults covered with sores and missing body parts plenty disturbing, but the real stomach-churning stuff was of babies born with syphilis. To my eyes, it could scare a person into thinking twice before diving into unprotected sex. It's exploitative, but possibly also beneficial.

In "Sex Madness Revealed," Oswalt and the other actors talk over much of "Sex Madness"'s dialogue, but that's not a huge loss. I can be a purist when it comes to good films; I'm the type who will shush people who talk during a serious drama. But a movie like "Sex Madness" can only be improved by chatter, especially if it's by a comedic genius like Patton Oswalt. I'd recommend watching "Sex Madness Revealed" and counting it as having seen "Sex Madness."

The Outlaw

Exploitation film in the 1930s should perhaps be referred to as independent film instead. While Dwain Esper and his ilk were exploiting the public's desire for shocks, the altruistic doctors behind "The Birth of a Baby" were genuinely trying to educate people. What these movies shared was that they were independent of the studios.

Also, they both operated on a shoestring. They didn't have the money to hire good actors, directors, cinematographers, etc. There were no film schools in the 1930s, so you couldn't scoop up recent graduates who were cheap, inexperienced, and knowledgeable, as Roger Corman would decades later. The only training grounds for filmmaking were the studios, and they locked up their employees in ironclad contracts. Even if professionals wanted to do an indie, studios wouldn't let them.

There was one independent producer who had enough money to make a professional-looking film: Howard Hughes. But his frustrating conflicts with censors over "Scarface" in 1932 had sent him off to sulk in his airplane business. It wasn't until 1939 that he caught the movie bug again. (My primary source for the following section is episode 18 of Karina Longworth's podcast "You Must Remember This," entitled "The Many Loves of Howard Hughes, Chapter 4: Jane Russell")

Hughes wanted to make a western about Billy the Kid. Most of his attention went to casting a female star. He was inspired by a publicity campaign orchestrated by Russell Birdwell for "Gone with the Wind," in which an open casting call for the part of Scarlett O'Hara lasted for years and generated acres of ink. Hughes hired Birdwell and told him his western, "**The Outlaw**," would be full of sex and violence.

Quickly, Hughes's office filled up with headshots of young actresses. His process proved much simpler than that of "Gone with the Wind": He homed in on a picture of a 19-year-old woman with a 38-inch bust. Jane Russell was brought in for a test and got the part.

Russell was not needed for the first few days of the shoot, so Birdwell invited magazines to photograph her in costume. She had no idea these pictures would cover magazines and movie posters for years, making her a major sex symbol before anyone had seen her on screen. An early promotion for the movie accompanied a picture of Russell in a tight shirt with the words "Two good reasons for seeing 'The Outlaw.'"

With Howard Hawks directing, Hughes turned his extensive engineering experience to Jane Russell's breasts. He wanted it to look like Russell was perky without wearing a bra, even though that was impossible for a woman of her bust size. Hughes invented a bra that he thought would do the trick. He proudly presented it to Russell, who put it on and realized it made her look ridiculous. When Hughes wasn't looking, she junked his invention, put on one of her custom-made bras, and used tissues to cover any visible seams. Despite his pathologically obsessive attention to detail, and to breasts, Hughes was never the wiser.

Early in the filming of "The Outlaw," Hughes complained to Howard Hawks that there weren't enough clouds in the exterior footage. This was one of Hughes' many obsessions; he had the same complaint in previous films. Rather than undergo reshoots to get more clouds, Hawks quit.

After months of delay, Hughes took over as director. He micromanaged actors' performances and often required dozens of takes for each shot to achieve exactly the look he wanted. Shooting finally wrapped in 1941.

Russell was immediately put back to work posing for photographs. Under Birdwell's supervision, she sat for sexy pictures from 9 to 5, Monday through Friday, for two whole years. The more than 40,000 photos that resulted showed up everywhere. Russell became a bona fide movie star despite having never appeared in a movie.

The Production Code Administration was not amused by all this. Apart from all the sex-drenched publicity, they were disturbed by the script. Its hero, Billy the Kid, was an unrepentant mass murderer who rapes Jane Russell's character at their first encounter.

The Administration did not get to see the film for two years. Hughes' perfectionism slowed the editing process to a crawl. As Karina Longworth notes in Episode 18 of her "You Must Remember This" podcast, Hughes' mental health was rapidly deteriorating.

In December 1941, the United States entered World War II. As his contribution to the war effort, Hughes promised to make the largest plane in history, entirely out of wood. What Hughes called "The Hercules" the newspapers dubbed "The Spruce Goose." There was no way he could deliver it by his self-imposed one-year deadline, but he tried to anyway. "The Outlaw" was on the back burner.

The Production Code Administration finally saw "The Outlaw" in 1943, and found more to object to. Joseph Breen cited the implied extramarital relationships between Rio and both Billy the Kid and Doc Holliday, the many shots in which Rio's breasts were not fully covered, and an especially baffling scene that suggests sleeping next to a naked Jane Russell causes you to recover from illness.

The exposed flesh was the biggest sticking point. Breen demanded that Hughes delete every shot with even a hint of cleavage, which made up the lion's share of his 108 requested cuts. Hughes responded by locking the film in a vault. He told Birdwell to make the film's failure to get a Production Code seal into big news.

Meanwhile, the boys fighting overseas loved Jane Russell (who still had never been seen in a film), sending her 10,000 fan letters a week. Birdwell spun this into an appeal to patriotism. Russell became a symbol of defiance, of the freedoms that the soldiers were trying to preserve. Hughes wasn't a horny film dilettante in this version; he was a hero, trying to liberate poor Jane from the oppression of the censors.

Bridwell represented Hughes at an appeal of the Production Code Administration's ruling. He brought a professional mathematician whose job was to measure the portion of Russell's bosoms that were exposed in "The Outlaw" and compare the percentages to those of other actresses in movies that the board had passed. It worked, and the requested cuts dropped from 108 to 3.

Hughes still refused to release "The Outlaw." Then, for unknown reasons, he changed his mind, made the three cuts, and got the approval of the Production Code Administration. He premiered the movie in a San Francisco theater and plastered sexy billboards throughout the city. Terrible reviews didn't prevent "The Outlaw" from selling out for nine straight weeks.

The Legion of Decency gave "The Outlaw" their C rating, for "condemned." The Catholic Church threatened to excommunicate anyone who saw it. Sermons across all denominations thundered condemnations of this "wanton woman," as if Jane Russell was the problem. Few people knew that she was a devout Christian who was faithful to her longtime boyfriend. The many Hollywood bigwigs who tried to seduce her, including Howard Hughes, got shot down without equivocation. No one could make Jane Russell do something she didn't want to do.

Russell introduced every San Francisco showing of "The Outlaw" in person. After the run ended, she zoomed down to Los Angeles and demanded that her boyfriend finally marry her. They went to Las Vegas and got hitched.

Then Hughes canceled the planned rollout of "The Outlaw" to other cities. There is plenty of speculation about why he did this, but no one knows for sure. It might have been because Hughes was angry that Russell got married, but he probably just had bigger fish to fry. As the Spruce Goose became more of a public laughingstock, he spent the next two years restoring his aviation business. "The Outlaw" remained in the can the whole time.

Russell was under contract to Hughes, meaning he was in full control of her career. Since he wasn't making other movies, Russell wasn't working. After five years of national fame, she had only been in one movie that had shown in one theater. Finally, in 1946, Hughes loaned her out to star in "Young Widow."

"Young Widow" and "The Outlaw" were then packaged together for nationwide release. In an unprecedented move, the Production Code Administration rescinded its previous approval of "The Outlaw." Hughes sued the Motion Picture Producers and Distributors of America (MPPDA), the trade organization that oversaw the Production Code Administration. He then offered the movie to any theater bold enough to show it without the required seal of approval. Every theater that did so made money hand over fist.

There were still other roadblocks. New York's state censorship board approved "The Outlaw," and three New York City theaters booked it. But after the city's police commissioner and commissioner of licenses saw it, they threatened to arrest any exhibitor who showed it on obscenity charges and revoke their license.

Hughes sued, asserting that the censorship board was supposed to be the sole authority on whether a film could be exhibited. The state court bent over backwards to support the police and license commissioners. It dismissed the suit, stating that the censorship laws and obscenity laws could be enforced "side by side."[203] It makes me wonder what the point of a censorship board would be if the police and license commissioners could just ignore its decisions and do whatever they want. I leave it to you to imagine what other abuses could occur if something could be approved by one governmental body but then prosecuted because the police

---

[203] de Grazia and Newman, p. 226

commissioner had a different view. It gives one person de facto veto power over virtually everything.

Through it all, "The Outlaw" put the first big crack in the Production Code since 1934. You might be tempted to see it because of its importance to film history. Just don't expect a good film. I found it to be downright offensive. It wasn't cleavage that bothered me; it was the brutal misogyny. Jane Russell's character Rio starts as an ass-kicker but becomes more submissive after being raped by our "hero," Billy the Kid. Later she is ordered to nurse her rapist back to health, and she acts as a mother figure while also falling for him.

Rape, you may remember from the "Don'ts and Be Carefuls," was not a totally forbidden plot point under the censorship of the time – unlike, say, showing a Black woman and a white man holding hands. The guidance for using both rape and seduction as plot points were the same: They "should never be more than suggested, only when essential for the plot, and even then never shown by explicit method. They are never the proper subject for comedy."[204]

In fact, censors sometimes found rape less offensive than seduction. To appease the Production Code Administration, the writers of the film version of "The Fountainhead" (1949) changed a one-night stand to a rape.[205] The censors thought making a male hero a rapist was more family-friendly than a heroine who had sex outside marriage.

In the twisted reasoning of the Production Code Administration, there is nothing positive about a consensual so-called "first-night scene," but something good can come out of rape. In an article in *Cinema Journal*, University of Utah professor Sarah Projansky says that often, "narratives depicted rape as a woman's punishment for

---

[204] Richard Maltby, ed., "Documents on the Genesis of the Production Code," *Quarterly Review of Film and Video* 15, no. 4; 1995: 62
[205] Miller, p. 144

inappropriate action."[206] For example, Joseph Breen called Stanley's rape of Blanche in "A Streetcar Named Desire" (1951) "justified"[207] by her erratic behavior. Sometimes the sociopathic misogyny of the past boggles the mind.

The only female director in Hollywood at the time, Ida Lupino, fought back against this ignorant toxicity in a message film called "Outrage" (1950). It sought to convince the American public that rape is a horrible act of violence that ruins the lives of its victims. Many, many more women had to speak out before men started to understand. As we will see in future chapters, it took decades for movies to treat rape with the appropriate level of seriousness. As with the gradual reduction of racist depictions, this is an example of how movies have become more restrictive over time for some topics, and rightly so.

Speaking of racism, in "The Outlaw," Jane Russell plays a Latina for no reason except that, at the time, it was one of the "exotic" ethnicities that were allowed to exude sexuality on screen. Honestly, it's hard to find many good things about this movie.

Rio nurses and then consents to sex with Billy the Kid, an unlikeable character played poorly by Jack Buetel. After this she is pushed into the background of the movie. She becomes wholly subservient to the men while weathering their belittling insults, which are spun as "comedy." In one hi-LAR-ious scene, Billy the Kid and Doc Holliday bicker over who gets her and who gets the horse they both claim. They both choose the horse. Get it? Women you've already had sex with are commodities that are worth less than animals! Ha! What could be funnier?

Rio is perturbed by this horrific mistreatment but doesn't put up much of a fight. While her personality is squashed into oblivion, her

---

[206] Sarah Projansky. "The Elusive/Ubiquitous Representation of Rape: A Historical Survey of Rape in U.S. Film, 1903-1972", *Cinema Journal*, Vol. 41, No. 1 (Autumn, 2001), p. 63-90
[207] Miller, p. 154

body remains on display. In one telling shot, she serves the men lunch in a framing that cuts off her head while highlighting her bust. She is now just a pair of boobs providing food and titillation on demand. After being "tamed" through rape, Rio becomes a mixture of every dehumanizing fantasy in the minds of insecure, sociopathic men.

I shouldn't psychoanalyze people I have only read about, but Howard Hughes makes it so easy. He was a spoiled rich kid who never grew past getting enraged when he didn't get exactly what he wanted. He probably wanted Jane Russell more than any of the many other women he chased, but she refused him. "The Outlaw" enabled Hughes to live out fantasies of dominating her. He put Russell's character on a pedestal only to break her spirit through force and then brutalize her for not complying faster. The movie clearly acts out the sociopathic, misogynistic impulses raging in Hughes' childish, over-entitled psyche. Through "The Outlaw" he could punish Jane Russell for the power she exerted over him because of his own lust.

The Ultimate Sex Hygiene Film

"The Outlaw" sold sex and delivered it, along with misogyny. The independent film "**Mom and Dad**" (1945) sold sex along with a lot of other shocking sights. It delivered on the shocks, if not the sex.

"Mom and Dad" begins as a standard sex hygiene film, even a rather square one. A squeaky-clean high-school girl is seduced by a slickster and impregnated. This is handled as demurely as possible, with no hint of nudity. The movie doesn't even use the word "pregnant," instead referring to "being in trouble." Sex is mentioned once or twice, but sex education is usually called "personal hygiene."

The girl's mother is an excessively prude crusader who fights any mention of sex in the schools. After people discover her daughter is pregnant, all blame is placed squarely on the mother's shoulders, repeatedly. It was a message I could thoroughly get behind, that parents should not prevent young people from learning the facts of life. But in retrospect, it seemed to me that its true purpose is to justify the footage of the final half-hour.

Once everyone is convinced of the need for sex education, a classroom of teens watch some filmstrips. These films-within-the-film trot out every shock that was legal to show at the time. You get the same sort of childbirth scene as in "The Birth of a Baby," plus a Caesarian section in grisly detail. You get people suffering from venereal disease, as in "Sex Madness Revealed," but more of them. Anyone expecting sexiness would be horribly disappointed.

As with many exploitation films of the time, attendees got more than just the movie. At around 55 minutes in, a title card introduces "the famous hygiene commentator Mr. Elliot Forbes." In the theater, a man professing to be Forbes would then stop the film, answer questions, and sell booklets about sex. As there were as many as 15 separate tours of "Mom and Dad" happening simultaneously, many men pretended to be the A-list "hygiene commentator" Mr. Elliott Forbes. Women dressed as nurses were also in attendance, purportedly to help anyone who fainted from shock. Really, they were there to "run the aisles and make transactions for the booklets."[208]

"Mom and Dad" was a massive hit. Filmsite.org estimates it was the all-time 5th-biggest moneymaker originally released in the 1940s, after, ironically, four Disney films: "Bambi," "Pinocchio," "Fantasia," and "Song of the South." All these films earned their millions from multiple theater runs, as each new generation of the target audience came of age. "Mom and Dad" kept touring the country through the 1950s and played drive-in theaters as late as 1975.[209] Estimates have the total take around $100 million, including booklet sales.

---

[208] Schaefer, p. 129
[209] Schaefer, p. 198

The movie had great timing. In 1948, Alfred Kinsey's landmark book "Sexual Behavior in the Human Male" sat on the *New York Times* bestseller list for 27 straight weeks. People were eager to read dry, scientific text revealing that masturbation was nearly universal and that most American men had sex before marriage. In 1953, Kinsey stunned the nation again with "Sexual Behavior in the Human Female." This one presented American men with the revelation that clitorises exist and are very important for female sexual stimulation. The post-war baby boom was booming, and people hungered for information.

Also in 1948, the case *United States v. Paramount* opened many theaters up to independent fare like "Mom and Dad." In the decision, the U.S. Supreme Court ruled that studios were violating antitrust laws by owning every aspect of the film business, from the actors to the theaters. The "vertical integration" that was both expensive and lucrative was over. Studios sold off their theaters, and the new theater owners could show whatever movies they wanted.[210] That made a lot more screens available for "Mom and Dad" and other non-Hollywood product.

Still, of all the independent sex hygiene films competing in the late 1940s, "Mom and Dad" was the one that became a blockbuster. The success wasn't solely due to the movie; producer Kroger Babb was a brilliant promoter. Before the movie came to a town, he would swamp the surrounding area with advertisements and other marketing schemes. One was to hire people to pretend to protest the film, handing out leaflets that included fake letters from nearby towns' mayors denouncing the movie. Babb knew that controversy drove attendance, and if controversy wasn't already there, he would manufacture it.

There was of course real controversy over "Mom and Dad." It was condemned by the Legion of Decency, but that had little effect. More impactful were the legal wranglings. In 1948, the Newark, New

---

[210] "The day the Supreme Court killed Hollywood's studio system," The National Constitution Center

Jersey city director of public safety tried to revoke a theater's operating license for showing "Mom and Dad." A court ruled that he had no power to do so. Eight years later, in 1956, the New York censorship board refused to license the movie and also lost in court.[211]

After World War II, courts no longer bent themselves into pretzels to justify authorities' attempts to suppress movies. That didn't stop the authorities from trying; exploitation producer David F. Friedman estimated that Babb appeared in court more than 400 times over the movie.[212]

Song of the South

I try my hardest to make good segues between the films in this book. When I'm arranging them chronologically, though, it can get challenging. It's hard to think of two more dissimilar movies than "Mom and Dad" and "**Song of the South**" (1946).

As I mentioned before, both were huge financial successes because of re-releases. "Song of the South" was only the 37th biggest grosser in 1946, but re-releases in 1956, 1972, 1980, and 1986 brought it into the all-time top 5 of movies made in the 1940s.

Otherwise, the movies are opposites. "Mom and Dad" is an independent feature meant to shock and educate about sex; "Song of the South" is a family film made by Disney. "Mom and Dad" was a big taboo-buster in its time but an obscure curio today; "Song of the South" elicited only minor controversy in the 1940s but is now infamous. It now sits in the deepest depths of the Disney vault, having never been released on video, DVD, or streaming in the United States. I found it on Internet Archive.

---

[211] de Grazia and Newman, p. 229
[212] David Chute, "Wages of Sin: An Interview with David F. Friedman". *Film Comment*. July-August 1986, p. 42

"Song of the South" depicts a plantation in the 1870s as a happy place full of singing Black people who are only too pleased to serve a white family. They embody archetypes straight from minstrel shows, most clearly in a "mammy" character played by Hattie McDaniel. The primary Black character is Uncle Remus, a kindly old man who can't resist telling children stories about Brer Rabbit, Brer Fox, and Brer Bear.

In one revealing line, Uncle Remus speaks wistfully about the past, saying that things were better all around in the old days. Considering that "the old days" in this movie was clearly before the Civil War, the message is clear: Black people were better off enslaved. Southern whites in the 1800s often wrote that Black people were so inherently inferior that enslavement was a blessing for them. These Southern whites thought enslavers should be congratulated for their altruism in having slaves.

Karina Longworth's wonderful podcast *You Must Remember This* is the best resource I've found for this film. In episode 146, she details how not everyone in 1946 was pleased with "Song of the South." The United Negro Congress protested it, though the NAACP decided to save their energy for more egregious examples of racism. In his contemporary review, influential movie critic Bosley Crowther wondered if Disney would have preferred if Abraham Lincoln hadn't freed the slaves.

Just like D.W. Griffith after the blowback to "The Birth of a Nation," Walt Disney was stunned by the negative press. His studio protested that Uncle Remus was a sympathetic character, and that "Song of the South" depicted a Black boy and a white boy playing together.

Privately, Walt Disney was convinced that communists must have infiltrated Black organizations. Because of a past strike by his animators, he was paranoid about communism. This again revealed Disney's patronizing, paternalistic attitude toward Black people:

Apparently, it didn't occur to him that they could come to critical conclusions on their own.

Then the controversy, such as it was, died down. Disney was sufficiently untroubled by "Song of the South" to release it four more times, as I mentioned. The 1972 re-release was a huge hit, bigger than the original run. In episode 150 of *You Must Remember This*, Karina Longworth cites film historian Ed Guerrero's explanation for the movie's success in 1972: Many white filmgoers were indulging in nostalgia for a time before the civil rights movement. At least on screen, they could suppress the Black revolt. They longed for a time when Black people "knew their place," i.e., a place of subservience.

I suppose I can congratulate myself for not enjoying "Song of the South" on any level. Granted, I am a middle-aged American white man, so my opinion on this movie is not the most relevant. For what it's worth, I felt the offensive stereotypes robbed the movie of any joy it was meant to impart.

"Song of the South" is also not as painful as I expected. It certainly isn't nearly as malevolent as "The Birth of a Nation." The Black characters in the "Song of the South" are not villains. They are instead neutered and cheerfully subservient, embodying an oppressor's idealized version of how an underclass should behave. It's awful, but at least it's a step up from "The Birth of a Nation" (which is faint praise indeed). It's also sadly in line with other films of the era; the Black characters in the 1953 John Ford film "The Sun Shines Bright" were even more disturbing to me. In that movie, all the Black characters are dim-witted objects of ridicule. Uncle Remus at least possesses some shreds of dignity.

But "The Sun Shines Bright" was not re-released to huge crowds in 1972, 1980, and 1986, after the civil rights movement had given white America a wake-up call about offensive stereotypes. And "The Sun Shines Bright" is not a Disney family film, and thus is not meant to be consumed by the most impressionable, uncritical audience in existence. Kids will not be able to contextualize "Song of the South" within the history of American racism. They will only see preternaturally cheery Black people who live to serve whites. The fact that Disney made "Song of the South" qualifies it as a shock film for me. It's not shocking in a fun way; it's one I feel compelled to include because of its infamy. As with "The Birth of a Nation," non-racists won't enjoy it.

Anger

Here's another whiplash-inducing topic switch for you: Outside both the 1940s mainstream and exploitation circuits was film prodigy Kenneth Anger. His earliest surviving work is a short art film called "**Fireworks**" (1947). It depicts a dream in which a young gay man, played by Anger, attempts to pick up a sailor and is beaten to a pulp. The movie has plenty of homoerotic imagery but not much nudity. It originally featured a brief shot of Anger's genitals, but Anger scratched any hint of them out of the print. He was afraid that, if he shipped the movie, he would be arrested for sending pornography through the mail.[213]

"Fireworks" was only seen publicly a few times in the 1940s and 1950s, so it couldn't make much of an impact. Screening it was dangerous; in 1957 an exhibitor was arrested on obscenity charges for showing it in one Los Angeles theater.[214] It's still notable as a very early work of bold defiance at a time when gay sex was illegal. Kenneth Anger would unfortunately become better known for his book "Hollywood Babylon," a terrible compilation of salacious, untrue rumors about Hollywood figures. He deserves to be remembered as the godfather of gay film in the United States.

---

[213] Bill Landis, "Anger: The Unauthorized Biography of Kenneth Anger," p. 46

[214] Whitney Strub, "The Clearly Obscene and the Queerly Obscene: Heteronormativity and Obscenity in Cold War Los Angeles", *American Quarterly*, 60 (2), June 2008

Chaplin's Last Stand

Meanwhile, to mainstream Americans in 1947, simply watching a movie with an anti-hero could be too shocking to take. Since becoming financially independent from the studios by co-founding United Artists in 1919, Charlie Chaplin had become very selective about his film projects. He went against type in "**Monsieur Verdoux**" (1947), casting himself as a con artist who woos rich women and then kills them for their money.

Joseph Breen did not find this premise funny. At the script stage, he objected to the moral ambiguity of Chaplin's character, which was encapsulated in lines like "Who knows what sin is … who knows what mysterious destiny it serves?" Breen firmly believed he knew what sin was, and his destiny was to prevent movies from endorsing it. Chaplin countered Breen's criticisms by saying that Plato had wrestled with gray areas between good and evil. Breen's associate Jack Vizzard was later quoted as saying "With such arguments did Chaplin dig his grave as a would-be intellectual."[215] In 1947, would-be intellectuals arguing moral ambiguities were prime targets for paranoia about communism.

Chaplin got his movie past Breen and on screens, but his troubles were only beginning. The American Legion called "Monsieur Verdoux" "un-American" and sent letters to theaters threatening boycotts if they showed it. Picket lines formed outside those that did.[216]

Around the same time, Chaplin was subpoenaed by the House Un-American Activities Committee in part because he had joined anti-fascist organizations before the war.[217] You might think that being anti-fascist would be considered pretty darn pro-American right after the country defeated the Nazis. But in the insanity of the immediate

---

[215] Quoted in Miller, p. 124-125
[216] Ibid
[217] Ibid

post-war era, the key was <u>when</u> you became anti-fascist. If you came out too hard against Nazis too early in the 1930s, people would suspect you of being a communist.

"Monsieur Verdoux" didn't do well in theaters; not enough Americans were in the mood for an anti-hero in 1947. It was Chaplin's first flop and ended up capping his career in the United States. The day after he began a trip to London in 1952, Attorney General James P. McGranery revoked his permission to re-enter the country. McGranery insisted he had a strong case against Chaplin, but a later analysis of the FBI files revealed there was no real evidence.[218] Chaplin, thoroughly soured on the United States, didn't fight it. He remained in Europe for the rest of his life.

Post-War Neorealism

The paranoid persecutions by the post-war American government constitute one example of how people spent the late 1940s reeling from the trauma of World War II, probably history's worst event. In his book "Atrocities: The 100 Deadliest Episodes in Human History," aka "The Great Big Book of Horrible Things," Matthew White estimates that World War II was responsible for 66 million deaths. He ranks it as the deadliest human-caused event in history.

After the epoch-making devastation of World War II, many Europeans were happy to return to escapist entertainment. But some hungered for films that reflected the brutal reality of the age. Italian neorealism arose as a radical departure from the glossy, cheerful romps that had dominated Italian cinema.

Neorealist films were dark depictions of desperately poor people scrabbling to survive. Their actors were amateurs who looked and acted like real people instead of like movie stars. The filmmaking was quick and dirty, seldom working to capture beautiful shots.

---

[218] Charles J. Maland, "Chaplin and American Culture". p. 280-287

If you watch an Italian neorealist movie now, you might be put off by how shabby and amateurish it seems. That was the point; it was a depiction of unvarnished reality that contrasted with immaculate studio products. Before Italian neorealism came along, there was basically one set-in-stone film style. Nowadays, in large part because of Italian neorealism, you can see a wide range of film styles, from found-footage horror to micromanaged big-budget spectacle.

Roberto Rossellini was one of the primary standard-bearers of Italian neorealism. His 1946 film "Rome, Open City" brought the movement to the world, winning the Gran Prix at the Cannes Film Festival. It's startling in parts, but the most shocking Rossellini film is probably "**Germany, Year Zero**" (1948). In the bombed-out wasteland of post-war Berlin, a boy in his early teens struggles to scrounge up money to feed his family. The many message-based shocks include a thirteen-year-old girl prostituting herself and being called "a mattress with cigarettes" by teen boys. The ending is also shockingly violent, but not gory.

"Germany, Year Zero" was not well-received in its time. Contemporary reviews made some valid criticisms while also revealing their squeamishness about the film's negativity. Austrian critic Hans Habe said it was "a terrifying film ... not artistically, but because it would be terrifying if the world saw the new Germany as Rossellini does."[219]

To me, that sounds like either denial or a need to cover up the truth. From what I've read about post-war conditions, and considering that Rossellini had a well-established devotion to pulling his stories from reality, I'm willing to believe at least some of the "new Germany" was a lot like "Germany, Year Zero." I think Habe and others couldn't handle the idea that conditions had gotten that bad in some cities. German audiences certainly weren't interested: The movie

---

[219] Quoted in Tag Gallagher, "The Adventures of Roberto Rossellini". p. 245

was shown once in a German film club and never again in the country until 1978.

"Germany, Year Zero" didn't do well in the United States either. It failed to live up to the success of "Rome, Open City," which had been such a hit on the arthouse circuit that it opened up an American market for neorealist films.

The next arthouse phenomenon proved to be the Vittorio De Sica masterpiece "Bicycle Thieves" (1949). Its American distributor, Joseph Burstyn, thought it could make money in mainstream theaters, so he applied for the Production Code seal. Note that I did not put "Bicycle Thieves" in bold type. I refuse to count it as a shock film, even when considering the context of its time, because only Joseph Breen thought it was untoward.

Breen demanded cuts in two scenes. In one, a little boy pauses as if he's about to relieve himself against a wall but is stopped by his father. In the other, the father chases a thief into a house of fully clothed women eating a meal. Breen surmised that this house of women was a bordello.

Neither of these moments broke Code rules, and the Legion of Decency passed "Bicycle Thieves" with a B rating. The film had already toured the world without incident. De Sica and Burstyn refused to cut a frame to appease Joseph Breen.

The ensuing fight spilled into the newspapers, which mostly took the perspective that the Production Code Administration was being ridiculous. Paranoid that it was all an attempt to weaken the Production Code, Breen dug in his heels and refused to grant a seal.

But the Production Code seal wasn't as important as it once was. The 1948 *United States v. Paramount* case had made theaters independent from the studios. Many theaters could show whatever they wanted, seal or no seal. The controversy over censorship of "Bicycle Thieves" was only creating buzz, making it seem like forbidden fruit. Simultaneously, "The Outlaw" was generating big box office returns.

Five major theater chains arose after the *United States v. Paramount* ruling, and three decided to screen "Bicycle Thieves." It had been many years since so many theaters showed a film that didn't have a Production Code seal. Local censorship boards did not interfere; the powerful boards in New York, Pennsylvania, and Ohio all passed the movie without cuts.[220] "Bicycle Thieves" became a minor hit.

Thus a decidedly non-shock film became an early test case for defying Joseph Breen and the Production Code. It didn't break the system; the seal still had meaning to many people, and censorship boards always loomed. But the blowback was severe, and the Code was increasingly perceived as outdated. Anyone who saw "Bicycle Thieves," a heartbreakingly beautiful work of art that is universally regarded as one of the top 20 films of all time, would have to conclude that Joseph Breen was off his rocker. A major crack had formed in the wall that Breen worked so hard to maintain.

An even bigger crack came from another Roberto Rossellini movie. "**The Miracle**" (1948) is the story of a mentally unstable, fervently religious woman who is impregnated by a passing stranger (played by a young Federico Fellini, who also wrote the script). Because the woman believes the stranger was Saint Joseph, she is convinced she is carrying the Christ child.

There are only message-based shocks in "The Miracle," and the message was not even considered shocking by most people. It was controversial in Italy but was not subject to any legal action, and didn't attract much business.[221] It passed the powerful New York Board of Censors without any trouble. But after news of its showings hit papers in 1950, the Legion of Decency condemned it as a

---

[220] All information about "Bicycle Thieves" is from Leff and Simmons, Chapter 7
[221] Miller, 149

"sacrilegious and blasphemous mockery of Christian religious truth."[222]

Pickets formed outside the New York theater showing "The Miracle" and two screenings were canceled because of bomb threats.[223] Few of those protesting had seen the movie – I imagine if they had, they would have been much less triggered. But the controversy attracted big crowds and "The Miracle" became a hit.[224]

The theater showing "The Miracle" was independent of the Motion Picture Association of America (MPAA) (renamed from the MPPDA in 1945) or any censorship board, so authorities cast about to find a governmental body that could repress it. A first attempt by New York City's commissioner of licenses to revoke the theater's license was shot down by the New York Supreme Court. Then the New York Board of Regents, which controlled the state education department, stepped in. It determined that because the film was sacrilegious, the Board could revoke just the license to show "The Miracle." Distributor Joseph Burstyn fought the case to the U.S. Supreme Court, where he got more than he could have bargained for.

In 1953, the U.S. Supreme Court not only affirmed the right to show "The Miracle" publicly, regardless whether it seemed sacrilegious to some. It also decided that all movies were "a significant medium for the communication of ideas," and therefore constituted speech worthy of protection by the First Amendment. Justice Tom C. Clark wrote that "The importance of motion pictures as an organ of public opinion is not lessened by the fact that they are designed to entertain as well as inform. Nor should film be subject to censorship because it is an industry conducted for profit, as such a category would also include the press."[225] This overturned the 1915 *Mutual v. Ohio* decision, which had declared films were "a business, pure and simple, originated and conducted for profit ... not to be regarded, nor

---

[222] de Grazia and Newman, p. 232
[223] Miller, p. 149
[224] Miller, p. 149-150
[225] Quoted in de Grazia and Newman, p. 232

intended to be regarded by the Ohio Constitution, we think, as part of the press of the country, or as organs of public opinion."

The so-called "Miracle" decision would prove monumental for American film. Mind you, granting free-speech protection didn't mean abolishing censorship overnight. The decision applied most clearly to movies expressing views about religion in New York. Later cases would expand the scope of permissible messages and content. It became no longer possible to ban a movie for being "immoral." Only "obscenity" would be grounds for censorship.

The Production Code Administration, the Legion of Decency, and the censorship boards certainly did not give up without a fight. But after the "Miracle" decision, they would find themselves fighting with less weaponry.

Chapter 5: The Transitional Era, Part 1: 1949-1959

Chocs français

Before the "Miracle" decision was finalized in 1953, France was the spot for shock movies. One is "**Le sang des bêtes**," or "**Blood of the Beasts**" (1949), a short French documentary. It is a very matter-of-fact and graphic depiction of what happens in slaughterhouses. Much the same way seeing real people with syphilitic sores in "Mom and Dad" might make you think twice about unprotected sex, watching "Blood of the Beasts" could turn you vegetarian.

That wasn't director Georges Franju's intention, however. In an excerpt from French television accompanying "Blood of the Beasts" in the Criterion Channel, Franju explains that his motivation was to depict reality through surrealistic means. The film didn't seem terribly surrealistic to me, except in its willingness to shock. It certainly reminded me of the animal abuse in the Luis Buñuel films "Un chien andalou" and "Land without Bread."

On the other side of the spectrum of short French shock films is "**Un chant d'amour**" (1950), writer Jean Genet's only movie. It shows a series of men in prison bursting with homoerotic desire. I wouldn't call "Un chant d'amour" pornographic as much as a celebration of gay love and an indictment of its repression. The sheer number of exposed penises would still earn it an NC-17 rating if released today.

That's not to say that "Un chant d'amour" was ever released unedited, at least not for decades. Instead it traveled around the gay subculture, inspiring Andy Warhol, Derek Jarman, Paul Morrissey, and other later filmmakers. You still can't watch it on streaming services or YouTube; I found it through a site called rarefilmm.com.

As a heterosexual man, I am not the intended audience for "Un chant d'amour," and not the best judge of its effectiveness as a movie. I can only imagine how revelatory it must have felt to see your sexuality depicted on screen when it was literally illegal to engage in it. I marvel at the courage it took to make such a strong taboo-buster in 1950. Its entry in the Oxford Dictionary of World Cinema credits "Un chant d'amour" with "inspir[ing] a new 'cinema of transgression.'"[226]

Even sixteen years later, "Un chant d'amour" could get you in legal trouble. In 1966, an exhibitor in Berkeley, California tried to show the movie publicly. The police threatened to arrest him and confiscate his copy of the film. The exhibitor sued, but was shot down at every level of appeal, including the U.S. Supreme Court. Each court called the movie pornographic and framed gay sex as inherently perverse. The "Miracle" decision may have been 15 years old, but progress was incremental.

In their opinions, the judges deciding against "Un chant d'amour" revealed how their feelings of shock drove their decisions, in true Grumpy Old Man style. Most were unmoved by the argument that Jean Genet had similar scenes in his written works, which were widely celebrated instead of being suppressed. The District Court of Appeal of California wrote in its decision "Because of the nature of this medium, we think a motion picture of sexual scenes may transcend the bounds of the constitutional guarantee long before a frank description of such scenes in the written word."[227] Translation: Movies make us feel more icky about homosexual behavior than books do, so no one should see them.

Mainstream French films of the early 1950s did not go nearly as far as "Un chant d'amour," but they were still too hot for most Americans. The French attitude toward sex is exemplified by "**La ronde**" (1951), directed by Max Ophüls. "La ronde" is a playful, nudity-free glorification of extramarital affairs, simultaneously

---

[226] Quoted in Sova, p. 79
[227] Quoted in Sova, p. 80

naughty and sophisticated in that uniquely French way. Max Ophüls made many such films, often with the kind of strong, multi-faceted female protagonists that were all too rare.

Max Ophüls is one of my favorite directors. "The earrings of Madame de ..." and "Lola Montes" are the places to start if you're interested in his French films; he also made some great American ones. (I have to sneak in a plug for his American film "Caught," in which Robert Ryan plays a megalomaniac clearly based on Howard Hughes. Ryan's character brutally oppresses a woman played by Barbara bel Geddes, who had been fired by the real Hughes because he didn't think she was sexy enough.) "La ronde" is a sort of anthology film, and since each episode centers on another affair, it packs in the most sauciness of Ophüls' many masterpieces.

"La ronde" proved too much for the New York censorship board, which denied it a license because it was "immoral" and "would tend to corrupt morals."[228] This was the first test of the "Miracle" decision. The U.S. Supreme Court stood by its earlier ruling and overturned the censorship board's ban of "La ronde." You can't ban a movie because you find it "immoral" any more. Justice William O. Douglas concluded his argument with the remarkable statement that "In this nation, every writer, actor, or producer, no matter what medium of expression he may use, should be freed from the censor."[229]

Soon afterwards, an American remake of "M" would test the "Miracle" decision once more. Again, the U.S. Supreme Court shot down censors' attempts to suppress it.[230] In the 1950s, the Supreme Court was fully committed to a 180-degree shift on movies being protected speech. Rather than bending over backwards to support the authorities' attempts to suppress movies, they bent over forwards, to coin a phrase, into permitting free expression. Still, it

---

[228] Quoted in de Grazia and Newman, p. 233
[229] Ibid
[230] de Grazia and Newman, p. 235-236

would be many years before William O. Douglas' vision of censorship-free cinema came close to reality.

Freedom of Message-Based Expression

American censors weren't just trying to suppress the freedom to watch naughty French people in movies. They were also explicitly preventing certain progressive ideas from being expressed in the century's most dynamic "organ of public opinion." You couldn't portray queer love. And it was explicitly forbidden to show mixed-race couples.

Europe was the place for ideas that the Production Code wouldn't allow. "**Olivia**" (1951) is a French film about lesbian desire in an all-girls school. Though its story is very similar to that of the 1931 German film "Mädchen in Uniform," it is not a remake. I feel that both tell their stories effectively without ever being preachy. In her review of "Olivia," Beatrice Loayza said:

> "Olivia is never punished with tragic moral payback for her yearning over Miss Julie, and while the extremity of her emotions is acknowledged and understood by those around her, she's never deemed an outcast or punished for them."[231]

Over in the United Kingdom, "**Pool of London**" (1951) broached the topic of race. It's less subtle than "Olivia," but still avoids being a polemic about racism, in my view. I was reminded of 1960s Sidney Poitier films: An essentially flawless Black man tries to navigate a white world that pretends to be accepting while making his existence impossible. It's only a shock film in the context of its time,

---

[231] Beatrice Loayza, "On Jacqueline Audry's Newly Restored Lost Queer Cinema Classic, Olivia," RogerEbert,com, August 20, 2019, https://www.rogerebert.com/features/on-jacqueline-audrys-newly-restored-lost-queer-cinema-classic-olivia

in that it was the first British film to show a romantic relationship between a Black person and a white person.

"Pool of London" might not seem like a shocker today, but it was well beyond the capacity of American cinema at the time. The 1949 drama "Pinky" tries its hardest to expose the effects of racism through the struggles of a Black woman who sometimes passes as white. But because the character falls in love with a white man, Hollywood rules dictated she be played by a white actress. "Pinky" was still banned in one Texas city – which was overturned by the U.S. Supreme Court post-"Miracle" decision – but its casting keeps it from being a full-fledged shock film in the context of its time, I'd say. Still, it was a pretty bold story at a time when people thought "Song of the South" and "The Sun Shines Bright" were acceptable. I found it surprisingly affecting.

The contemporary story that was the most incisive about racism was the 1940 novel "Native Son," by Richard Wright. In it, a young Black chauffeur, Bigger Thomas, accidentally kills a young white woman and goes on the lam. It's a shocking noir-ish plot that Richard Wright, a huge movie buff, wanted to see on screen.

The book was wildly successful and influential, the first novel to reveal the truth of 20th-century American racism to a wide, white audience. A Broadway version directed by Orson Welles was also a huge hit. Still, getting a film adaptation off the ground was a major struggle. MGM's offer to make a "Native Son" movie hinged on having an all-white cast. The sheer absurdity of a "Native Son" adaptation without any Black characters speaks volumes about the systemic racism of the time. Another producer thought he was meeting Richard Wright halfway by making Bigger Thomas "into 'an oppressed minority white man,' specifically a 'Pole or Italian.'"[232] Wright understandably declined both offers.

---

[232] This quote and most of the other information about "Native Son" is from "'Native Son' and the Cinematic Aspirations of Richard Wright," Anna Shechtman's article in the April 4, 2019 edition of T*he New Yorker*.

With no chance to make a sensical "Native Son" movie on American soil, Wright looked overseas. Both France and Italy refused permits for filming because they didn't want to get on the bad side of the United States government, which was dead set against the project. Eventually, the Argentine government financed the film and it was shot in Buenos Aires.

It proved difficult to find an actress to play the young white woman because very few wanted to be on film in the arms of a Black man. The actor who had played Bigger Thomas on Broadway, Canada Lee, was slated to reprise the role. But the U.S. refused his visa to enter Argentina because of his alleged communist sympathies. At the last minute, Richard Wright stepped in to play Thomas himself.

The 1951 film version of "**Native Son**" sanitizes the book's content. American censors were still terrified of the message-based shocks inherent to the story. Many chopped it into incomprehensibility, turning Bigger Thomas into an unsympathetic villain rather than a victim of circumstance who made some critical mistakes. The movie's distributor billed it as a "Dynamite Loaded Story of a Negro and White Girl!" In her article in the April 4, 2019 edition of *The New Yorker*, Anna Shechtman states "Reviewers and theatre owners were encouraged to receive it as tawdry entertainment, and most did." One of the great landmarks of American literature was reduced to a racist exploitation film.

"Native Son" also ran into legal issues. The Ohio censorship board refused to issue a license to show it, even after several rounds of cuts. The board stated that the movie "contributes to racial misunderstanding, presenting situations undesirable to the mutual interests of both races … undermining confidence that justice can be carried out [and presenting] racial frictions at a time when all groups should be united against everything that is subversive."[233] In other words, exposing systemic racism might make people angry about it.

---

[233] de Grazia and Newman, p. 242

The Supreme Court of Ohio upheld the board's ban, but the U.S. Supreme Court reversed it. As with "La ronde," all they had to do was point to the "Miracle" decision. If novels and other forms of speech could freely investigate racism, along with religion, extramarital affairs, etc., movies could too. Slowly, message-based shock films were being freed from the censors.

If only "Native Son" were a better movie, it might be considered a landmark achievement. Even the uncut version of "Native Son" has its flaws, in my opinion. A key problem is that Richard Wright was a much, much, much better writer than actor. I think it's still worth seeing, to appreciate the boldness of the story in the context of a time when "Song of the South" constituted family entertainment. The book, as you might expect, is better.

Tentative First Steps Toward Sex

Hollywood may not have wanted to explore racism in the early 1950s, but it was up for re-engaging with sex. American society had changed since a peak of social conservatism in the mid-1930s. Men's magazines featuring pictures of Jane Russell and others became wildly popular during and after World War II. Starting in 1953, *Playboy* would bring cheesecake to the masses. Alfred Kinsey's dry academic texts were flying off of bookstore shelves. "Mom and Dad" sold more tickets than anyone could have predicted.

With the young men back from the war, America was releasing pent-up sexual frustration. Predictably, the needs of heterosexual men were virtually the only focus. The country was gratefully indulging the desires of the young men who had risked their lives for freedom.

Hollywood was slow to join the party. It finally did so as one of many strategies to turn business around. Let's bring back that chart of film attendance from the chapter about the full implementation of the Production Code in 1934:

Percent of people who went to the movies weekly, by year:

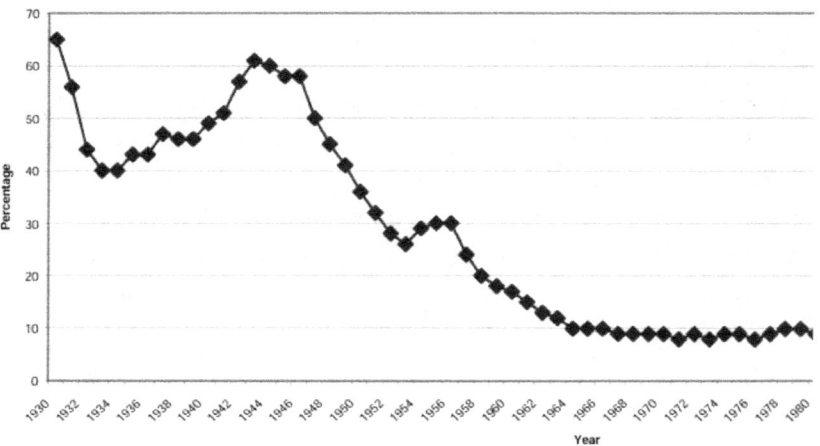

You can see how bad the numbers got in the post-war years. Granted, the percentages were artificially high during the war, when a large section of the population was overseas. Movies were one of the few entertainments not heavily stifled by wartime restrictions; Will Hays managed to get filmmaking designated an "essential industry" by the federal government in exchange for producing propaganda films.[234] Once the boys returned from the war, the percentage of people going to the movies every week was bound to drop. But then it kept dropping each year, until rates got well below those of the 1930s.

The main culprit was television, which delivered entertainment to tired young parents of baby-boom kids in the comfort of their homes. Hollywood's primary initial reaction was to hamper the new medium by preventing their talent from working in TV. By 1952, it was clear they needed a new strategy. Film studios started launching every

---

[234] Miller, p. 123

gimmick that television couldn't deliver: color films, widescreen, 3D, etc.[235]

Movies could try delivering sex, but it wouldn't be easy. The "Miracle" decision may have weakened the Production Code Administration and censorship boards, but they still ruled. After fifteen years of ironclad enforcement of the Production Code, mainstream directors and producers were gun-shy. As Leff and Simmons say in "Dame in the Kimono," "Inertia, the looming presence of the Legion of Decency, and the memory of outraged pickets and boycotts caused most exhibitors to avoid pictures that ventured beyond the manners and mores of the Code."[236] They would need a sex symbol powerful enough to overcome their hesitations.

Like Jane Russell, Marilyn Monroe became a star through pinup photos for soldiers. The army newspaper *Stars and Stripes* anointed her "Miss Cheesecake Photo 1951."[237] Simultaneously, she was gaining popularity for small roles in films, usually playing ditzy sexpots.

In March 1952, news hit that Monroe had posed for nude calendar photos in 1949. This sort of story would ruin a career in the late 1930s. Her studio did damage control, saying she desperately needed the money at the time. Surprising everyone in Hollywood, the public was mostly sympathetic, and the story provoked more excitement about Monroe.[238] Producers took notice, realizing they needed not only to get her starring roles, but also to make them more sexually provocative than the Production Code typically allowed.

The 1953 film "**Niagara**" serves as a film-length advertisement for Marilyn Monroe's body (as well as for the song "Kiss" and for

---

[235] Cook, p. 458-463
[236] Leff and Simmons, p. 192
[237] Donald Spoto, "Marilyn Monroe: The Biography," p. 192
[238] Spoto, p. 210-213

Niagara Falls as a vacation destination). In the process, it breaks several Production Code rules about how the female form can be represented. For example, Monroe is shown nude behind a semi-transparent shower door, revealing all of her curves if not all the details. She oozes sex appeal in every scene, in a way that no woman had in mainstream American films since the Pre-Code era. (I'm counting "The Outlaw" as being outside the mainstream, though it served as a template for what "Niagara" tried to get away with.)

Surprisingly, "Niagara" didn't cause too much of a stir. The Production Code Administration didn't object; after his major defeat with "Bicycle Thieves," Joseph Breen was quietly relaxing some Code restrictions.[239] More importantly, audiences loved it. It thus provided a valuable test case for Hollywood, setting the boundaries for what they could show in later bombshell-centered films starring Monroe, Jane Russell, Jayne Mansfield, etc.

The Production Code Administration may have relaxed a few rules about content-based sex shocks, but refused to budge on message-based ones. "Niagara" proved much less objectionable to the Production Code Administration than "**The Moon Is Blue**" (1953), a silly sex farce with no titillation. What it has instead was open discussions of sexual mores. If you've heard of it, it might be from an episode of "M*A*S*H*" called "The Moon Is Not Blue." Hawkeye and the gang get a copy of "The Moon Is Blue" expecting "Niagara"-style sexiness and are very disappointed.

The primary joke of "The Moon Is Blue" is that the young female love interest, played by Maggie McNamara, proudly proclaims her virginity while blithely asking impolitic questions about other people's sex lives. The male characters try to use the sly, sideways language about sex that could get past the Production Code Administration, but she refuses to pull any punches. She is a guileless innocent, a twentysomething acting like a bubbly 12-year-old girl who has lots of questions and no filter.

---

[239] Leff and Simmons, p. 192

For me, the childishness of McNamara's character makes her a poor love interest. I didn't enjoy wondering what she represented in the fantasies of her creator. More charitably, you could consider her character an attempt to wrestle with the cult of virginity amidst the post-war sexual awakening.

These were topics that the Production Code allowed to be discussed very obliquely, if at all. An initial script for "The Moon Is Blue" was rejected by the Production Code Administration in 1951. Joseph Breen said "This unacceptability arises from the fact that the humor in this play stems, almost entirely, from a light and gay treatment of the subject of illicit sex and seduction. While there is no actual seduction in the story, the general attitude towards illicit sex seems to violate that Code clause which states: 'Pictures shall not infer that low forms of sex relationship are the accepted or common thing.'"[240] A second draft got a similar response.

Director Otto Preminger decided to film the script anyway. Preminger was an Austrian who had been a successful director in Hollywood since 1937. His studio, United Artists, gave him the freedom to do whatever he wanted for six months. What he wanted to do was mess with the Code. United Artists backed him to the hilt and released "The Moon Is Blue" without the Production Code seal. It was the first time a major studio had done so since the Production Code was established.[241]

It was a gamble, but not a crazy one. "Bicycle Thieves" and "The Outlaw" had proven that movies without the Production Code seal could do well in the newly independent theater chains, especially if they'd been hyped up by controversy. But "The Moon Is Blue" ran into another gatekeeper: state censorship boards.

The Ohio, Kansas, and Maryland boards all banned the film. Preminger and United Artists sued, and pushed the case all the way

---

[240] Quoted in "The Moon Is Blue (1953)". Catalog of Feature Films. American Film Institute: https://catalog.afi.com/Catalog/moviedetails/50950
[241] Ibid

to the U.S. Supreme Court. Once again, the highest court in the land ruled against censorship of message-based shocks.[242] "The Moon Is Blue" got widespread distribution, became a financial success, and garnered three Oscar nominations. As with "Bicycle Thieves," Joseph Breen had stood firm and lost.

Howard Hughes smelled blood in the water. By 1953, he had bought a major studio, RKO, and was busy running it into the ground. Amidst the turmoil, he pushed out a few films starring Jane Russell. One, called "**The French Line**," was deemed too sexy by the Production Code Administration.

Specifically, they objected to one scene at the end of the movie. In it, Jane Russell sings and dances on stage in a revealing outfit that comes close to being a bikini. "The French Line" was in the newfangled technology of 3D, and an early ad emphasized Russell's breasts and sported the tagline "J.R. in 3D. It'll knock both of your eyes out!"[243]

When Joseph Breen refused to give "The French Line" a Production Code seal, Hughes opened it anyway in St. Louis. Breen may not have had any direct power over theaters, but he could still fine RKO $25,000 for releasing a film without a seal. The movie did good business in St. Louis, but as soon as ticket sales started to flag, Hughes unexpectedly pulled it.[244]

Hughes calculated that the strong showing in St. Louis and accompanying publicity had weakened Joseph Breen's hand. He submitted "The French Line" for a Production Code seal again, but it got another rejection. The Legion of Decency followed up with a C rating. Censors banned it, and, most critically, theater chains

---

[242] de Grazia and Newman, p. 240-241
[243] Leff and Simmons, p. 208
[244] "The French Line (1954)". Catalog of Feature Films. American Film Institute: https://catalog.afi.com/Catalog/moviedetails/51207#1

decided it wasn't worth the risk.[245] Hughes was backed into a corner.

What Hughes didn't understand, and Breen did, was that "The French Line" was a different beast than "The Moon Is Blue" and "Bicycle Thieves." Exhibitors were willing to rebel for an urbane modern comedy and one of the best films of all time, respectively. They weren't willing to stick their necks out for a crass Howard Hughes movie that was only a step or two above a burlesque show. As one unnamed exhibitor told Variety, "The Code has been defied before … but for the most part there was some principle involved. In the Hughes matter I fail to see how principle enters into it."[246]

Hughes gave in. While he did not try again for a seal, he did cut the offending scene out entirely and release "The French Line" to a few markets. Another 2D version with that scene trimmed down apparently made Jane Russell's breasts seem less provocative.[247] In the final tally, the box office receipts from "The French Line" were good, but not good enough to arrest the decline of RKO. Hughes sold the studio in 1954 and was done with the movie business. RKO collapsed in 1957.[248]

As for the merits of "The French Line," it is certainly better than "The Outlaw," in my opinion. Jane Russell gets to be her ass-kicking self throughout this one. But the movie is still loaded with 1950s-style sexism. Its plot is also pretty dumb; Howard Hughes was a much better provocateur than filmmaker. I'd skip "The French Line" and stick with "Gentlemen Prefer Blondes" and "The Revolt of Mamie Stover" if you want to revel in all that Jane Russell could offer.

After protecting the Code from Howard Hughes, Joseph Breen went out on a relative high note. He was exhausted by a tough,

---

[245] Leff and Simmons, p. 214
[246] Quoted in Leff and Simmons, p. 213
[247] Gerard R. Butters Jr., "Banned in Kansas: Motion Picture Censorship, 1915-1966", p. 267
[248] Richard B. Jewell with Vernon Harbin, "The RKO Story", p. 245, 290

demanding job that had only become harder of late. Breen retired as head of the Production Code Administration and was replaced by the more flexible, liberal-minded Geoffrey Shurlock.[249]

In 1953, the year the "Miracle" decision was handed down, the Production Code bent but didn't break. It made room for a few content-based shocks in "Niagara" but held the line against the ones in "The French Line." "The Moon Is Blue" forced the Code to reckon with message-based shocks. It might not sound like much, but change can be slow. And remember that the "Miracle" decision didn't declare that anything goes; it ruled that movies were protected as free speech. If you had a message you wanted to get across about race, sexual mores, etc., you could make it in a major film. If what you're trying to say is just "check out her boobs," you might still be relegated to the exploitation circuit.

The New Exploitation

With theaters now able to choose what they showed, many more screens opened up for exploitation producers. Also, the proliferation of drive-in theaters in the mid-1950s offered safer spaces for shock films. Being located in the boonies meant that prudes were less likely to start "not in my backyard" campaigns against them.

As always, exploitationeers scoured the newspapers for inspiration. In 1952, Christine Jorgensen made headlines for having sex reassignment surgery. It was the first time most Americans had heard of transgender people. Independent producer George Weiss wasted no time in contacting Jorgensen about starring in an exploitation film about her experience. Jorgensen, always a smart cookie, declined.[250]

A neophyte named Ed Wood managed to convince Weiss that he was qualified to make a movie capitalizing on the Jorgensen story

---

[249] Leff and Simmons, p. 216-218
[250] Gary D. Rhodes, "Lugosi: His Life in Films, on Stage, and, in the Hearts of Horror Lovers", p. 142.

because he was a transvestite. Never mind that transvestism and transgender identity are two very different things; Weiss either wasn't aware of the difference or had no better options.

Wood shot "**Glen or Glenda**" (1953) in four days. He roped in heroin-addicted Bela Lugosi to play a small part that is completely unnecessary. In fact, the majority of the film has nothing to do with transgender identity or sex reassignment surgery; most of its running time is devoted to an earnest, if poorly executed, plea for tolerance of transvestism. Wood awkwardly grafted a quick story about sex reassignment surgery to the end in order to fulfill his obligations.

George Weiss was not happy with the result, but he didn't have the luxury of junking it and starting over. He stuffed in a few scenes from his personal collection of bondage films and released "Glen or Glenda." The thoroughly bizarre end product made it to a few drive-in screens and not many others.

Ed Wood is popularly known as history's worst director. By my reckoning, he's the worst director whose movies are watchable, which means he's definitely not history's worst director. Wood may have been incompetent at almost every aspect of filmmaking, but he knew how to move a story along. Coleman Francis, Ray Dennis Steckler, and many others made painfully slow and depressing movies that offer no enjoyment, ironic or otherwise. A film that doesn't entertain at all is much worse, in my view, than one that entertains through daffiness.

"Glen or Glenda" is by far my favorite Ed Wood movie. As with "Maniac," processing its weird curveballs evokes a certain giddiness in me. Unlike "Maniac," "Glen or Glenda" is oddly touching at times. It genuinely tries to make viewers understand that transvestites are people too. The movie, and Wood, deserve some measure of unironic respect for that.

Undeterred by the failure of "Glen or Glenda," Ed Wood made a few other movies for drive-ins, none of them shockers by my definition, all of them wildly incompetent. The 1994 biopic "Ed Wood," directed by Tim Burton and starring Johnny Depp, is a delightful introduction to this part of Wood's career. The rest of Wood's life was a sad descent into alcoholism.[251]

With more screens available to them, most of the independent filmmaking world took a step toward professionalism. In 1954, Sam Z. Arkoff and Jim Nicholson founded American Releasing, later called American International Pictures. Roger Corman would become American International's most famous producer/director. The company targeted an audience that the major studios mostly ignored: the growing cohort of teenagers with cars and disposable income. Rather than employing middle-aged white guys to imagine what teens wanted to see, American International would ask the teens for ideas.[252] Most of the movies that American International produced were relatively clean, at least at first. A separation grew between drive-ins catering to teens and the true grindhouses of yore.[253]

On those grindhouse screens, one old-fashioned exploitation genre made a comeback. "**Garden of Eden**" (1954) is a nudist camp movie, a la "Elysia" and its imitators. "Garden of Eden" was also made by a nudist organization as a proselytizing tool, but is less explicitly polemical than "Elysia." It has no introductory "square-up" or dull ersatz intellectual lecturing on the health benefits of nudism. This lack of pseudo-educational window dressing no doubt made the copious nudity more shocking to 1950s audiences. There is still no sex or exposed genitalia, and the story is cheesy and benign.

The New York censorship board banned "Garden of Eden" because it was "indecent." The board demanded all scenes with nudity cut, which would of course make for a strange (and very short) movie

---

[251] Rudolph Grey, "Nightmare of Ecstasy: The Life and Art of Edward D. Wood, Jr.," pp. 144–145.
[252] Karina Longworth, "Boris and Roger Corman", *You Must Remember This* podcast, episode 120
[253] "Schlock! The Secret History of American Movies," 2001 documentary

about nudism. This case didn't have to go to the U.S. Supreme Court; the highest New York court reversed the decision. Judge Charles S. Desmond wrote "Nothing sexually impure is shown or suggested ... so there is no legal basis for censorship."[254] Nudism films were officially back after a wartime hiatus.

Titillation got more forthright with a trend of burlesque movies. Short films of strippers had spread underground for many years, but not until 1949's "Midnight Frolics" did anyone try to release a feature-length compilation to theaters.[255] In it and the movies that followed, there is no pretense of providing education of any kind. Even "Maniac," you may recall, threw in a few "facts" about mental illnesses. After the "Miracle" decision, exploitation films could be honest about their intentions.

"**Teaserama**" (1955) is probably the most shocking of the bunch. Most of its content is relatively tame, if clearly forbidden by the Production Code: Bettie Page, Tempest Storm, etc. strip and dance in skimpy outfits. No one gets completely naked. The acts are more provocative than Jane Russell in "The French Line" but less so than strippers on stage. A few vaudeville-style comedy bits are interspersed to make it all feel a little less pornographic.

No doubt viewers of burlesque films wanted the dances to end with full female nudity, but that would get exhibitors arrested on obscenity charges. Outside of nudist colony movies, which got a special dispensation, it was very dangerous to show the key areas: genitalia, rear ends, and women's nipples.

<SPOILER ALERT>

Only one dancer in "Teaserama" goes fully topless. When Vicki Lynn finishes her striptease and takes off her bra, it's revealed that

---

[254] Quoted in de Grazia and Newman, p. 247
[255] Schaefer, p. 306-308

she's a man in drag. Laughs erupt on the soundtrack for the first and only time, including during the comedy bits.

I mention the dubbed laughs because I have to assume they were inserted to deflate any anger that arose among heterosexual male viewers. Vicki Lynn's dance is as erotic as those of the other dancers, and no doubt heterosexual men were turned on at first. Then she finishes her act by doing what no other dancer did, what many heterosexual men were eagerly awaiting, only to be hit with the realization that they had been aroused by a man. It's a courageous act, one that I imagine could lead to violence in a real 1950s burlesque club. The dubbed laughs, I think, try to place the act in the context of the drag acts that Milton Berle and others were famous for. If so, the ploy succeeds only partially. Milton Berle never turned on many straight guys, to my knowledge.

</SPOILER ALERT>

Night and Fog

There is no good way to transition from just about any of the movies I've mentioned in this book to "**Night and Fog**," (1955) a harrowing documentary about the Holocaust. Most shocks we've encountered are frivolous, even when they are within films that address serious issues. Including "Night and Fog" in this context could be construed as minimizing the film.

That is of course not my intention. I felt I had to discuss "Night and Fog" to demonstrate a different role for shock content in film. By showing horrific sights like piles of emaciated corpses, "Night and Fog" uses the power of filmic imagery to elicit profound repulsion over the brutality of the Nazis. The film provides a vital service to humanity by making viewers feel in their cores the monstrous crimes that result from genocidal bigotry.

Several other films documented the Holocaust soon after World War II. "Camps of the Dead" (1947) is a short documentary produced by the United States military, and "Distant Journey" (1949) is a Polish drama about a Jewish family destroyed by the Nazis. Both are worthwhile, but "Night and Fog" is universally regarded as the seminal document of the Holocaust of the post-war era. If everyone saw it, we would have a better chance of not repeating history. Please watch it.

Back in the Mainstream

Joseph Breen may have slapped down Howard Hughes for good in 1953, but a new rebel was emboldened that year. Otto Preminger, director of "The Moon Is Blue," decided to tackle another Production Code taboo: the depiction of illicit drug use. Stories about drugs filled the newspapers but were absent from mainstream films. The exploitation circuit was still offering drug polemics in the vein of "Reefer Madness" and "Marihuana." White, middle-class parents were terrified that their kids were using narcotics, even though most users were "poor, Black, and concentrated in New York, Los Angeles, and Chicago."[256]

Nelson Algren's 1949 novel "The Man with the Golden Arm" was a bestseller and won the first National Book Award. That sort of pedigree usually led straight to a movie adaptation in the so-called Golden Age of Hollywood, even more so than today. Hollywood always favored basing movies on "intellectual property" that had proven successful in another, less expensively produced medium. The difference is that in the past, the IP was plays and novels rather than comic books.

But Joseph Breen shot down every attempt at adapting "The Man with the Golden Arm" because the story involved drug addiction and trafficking. Breen not only threatened to withhold the Production Code seal and guaranteed a C rating from the Legion of Decency; he also promised condemnation from the United States Treasury

---

[256] Schaefer, p. 246

Department, the Bureau of Narcotics and "state and municipal censor boards, both in this country and abroad."[257]

After Breen retired, Otto Preminger took up "The Man with the Golden Arm." Rather than toning down the drug-related content of the novel, Preminger's rewrite emphasized it further. Frank Sinatra, at the time arguably the most popular American entertainer, enthusiastically signed on to star.

The result is a pretty solid drama, to my eyes, that deals capably with drug addiction. Sinatra's character shooting up provides the main shock scene, in the context of the time, though you don't see a needle piercing flesh. Unlike, say, "Trainspotting," **"The Man with the Golden Arm"** (1955) doesn't depict the pleasure of drug use; it only reveals the terrible consequences. It's unambiguously a cautionary tale, essentially a much more professional version of a drug polemic.

Knowing that any drug use in a film explicitly contravened the Production Code, United Artists did not even submit "The Man with the Golden Arm" for a seal before scheduling its distribution, which was a first. The studio then submitted the movie to the Production Code Administration and got rejected. United Artists responded by resigning from the Motion Picture Association of America, which controlled the Production Code office.[258]

After Preminger deleted the scene of Sinatra shooting up, the Legion of Decency passed the movie with a B rating. As with "Bicycle Thieves," the religious pressure group looked more rational than the industry's self-regulatory body. Preminger had succeeded in dividing the once-impenetrable united front against adult themes in movies. Every theater chain screened "The Man with the Golden Arm," and it was a huge hit with both audiences and critics, earning

---

[257] Quoted in "The Man With The Golden Arm", American Film Institute website. https://catalog.afi.com/Film/51583-THE-MANWITHTHEGOLDENARM
[258] Ibid

three Oscar nominations.[259] Theater owners were quoted in newspapers as saying they didn't care much about the Production Code seal anymore.[260]

Reportedly, this clinched it for the MPAA: The Production Code needed to be revised.[261] A new version completed in 1956 permitted treatments of drug use, abortion, kidnapping, and prostitution "within the limits of good taste."[262] The ban on miscegenation, or mixed-race couples, was quietly omitted.[263] Remaining taboos included full nudity, venereal disease, and "sexual perversion," which included any reference to homosexuality.[264]

"The Man with the Golden Arm" didn't get a Production Code seal until 1961, but it didn't matter. Otto Preminger had demonstrated the right way to change the Code in the 1950s. You don't go the crass route, as Howard Hughes did. You go the classy route, making a good movie that examines a serious issue and appeals to critics and urban liberals. Both Hughes and Preminger cribbed from exploitation films: Jane Russell's final dance in "The French Line" is toned-down burlesque, while Preminger made a high-tone drug polemic. Preminger had the good sense to choose the exploitation genre that the mainstream was ready for. He picked at the weak spot of the Code, the message-based rules that American courts had already adjudicated as contravening free speech.

The next big mainstream controversy came from another powerful director: Elia Kazan. Kazan had arisen from the cutting-edge post-war New York theater scene, along with Marlon Brando and the new Method style of acting. In 1951, Kazan and Brando joined forces

---

[259] de Grazia and Newman, p. 91
[260] Miller, p. 168
[261] The Man With The Golden Arm", American Film Institute website. https://catalog.afi.com/Film/51583-THE-MANWITHTHEGOLDENARM
[262] "Motion Picture Code Made 'More Flexible'". *Eugene Register Guard.* December 17, 1956.
[263] de Grazia and Newman, p. 92
[264] Leff and Simmons, p. 224

with superstar Southern playwright Tennessee Williams and rocked the movie world with "A Streetcar Named Desire."

Before its release, The Legion of Decency had forced cuts to "A Streetcar Named Desire", without Elia Kazan's approval. The result is not quite a shock film, but the Legion still called it "morally objectionable in part for all."[265] All of the country loved the movie, in no small part due to Brando's era-defining performance. "A Streetcar Named Desire" became the fifth-biggest earner of the year[266] and won four Oscars (including awards for all the four main actors except Brando – the Academy was a step behind the times, per usual). The film established Kazan and his New York-based compatriots as a source for that precious, rare animal: artistically challenging drama that makes lots of money. Again, if you want to push the boundaries of the mainstream, do it with art, not schlock.

After further success with "On the Waterfront" and "East of Eden," Kazan got final cut rights for his next movie.[267] That meant the Legion of Decency couldn't force any edits. In 1956, he returned to the Tennessee Williams well with "**Baby Doll**." "Baby Doll" was based on a Tennessee Williams one-act play, but Kazan made major rewrites and Williams was mostly uninvolved in the screenplay.[268]

The resulting film's main content-based shock is the introduction of the character of Baby Doll: She is a 19-year-old sleeping in a crib and sucking her thumb while her middle-aged husband peeps at her lasciviously through a hole in the wall. The rest of the film features a few attempts to seduce her, but nothing too graphic. It's more about a pervasive atmosphere of grubby sordidness and desperation.

---

[265] Quoted in de Grazia and Newman, p. 93
[266] "The Top Box Office Hits of 1951", *Variety*, January 2, 1952
[267] de Grazia and Newman, p. 93
[268] Courtney Reed, "In the galleries: The productive, but complicated, relationship between Tennessee Williams and Elia Kazan". *Cultural Compass*, March 17, 2011

In my opinion, "Baby Doll" is Southern Gothic melodrama pushed to the point of unintentional camp. Elia Kazan later defended it by saying that "I did the best I could to get on film what I felt in the South."[269] I bet the film would have had more emotional depth if it were more about what the characters felt in the South than what Kazan felt. Tennessee Williams should have been more involved.

The Legion of Decency was much more concerned with "Baby Doll"'s sleaziness than its one-dimensional portrayal of the South. In a public statement, the Legion declared the movie to be "morally repellent in theme and treatment," dwelling "almost without variation or relief upon carnal suggestiveness in action, dialog, and costuming."[270]

Meanwhile, the Production Code Administration had already awarded a seal to "Baby Doll." No doubt the MPAA was excited at the prospect of another Elia Kazan/Tennessee Williams collaboration, especially if it reminded anyone of "A Streetcar Named Desire." Back in the days when Joseph Breen led the Production Code Administration, he and the Legion of Decency worked in lockstep. After his retirement, that teamwork collapsed. The Legion of Decency called the awarding of a seal to "Baby Doll" "an open disregard of the Code by its administrators."[271] The enemies of shock films were publicly divided again.

Catholics across the country took a stand. The nationally famous and influential Cardinal Francis Spellman took to the pulpit of New York's St. Patrick's Cathedral for the first time in more than seven years to command Catholics to avoid "Baby Doll" "under pain of sin." Other Catholic leaders told parishioners to boycott for six months any theater that screened the movie. The threats worked, and many theater chains canceled their bookings. "Baby Doll" ended up on

---

[269] Quoted in de Grazia and Newman, p. 93
[270] Ibid
[271] Ibid

around 4,000 screens instead of the 20,000 originally planned, and profits were disappointing.[272]

The "Baby Doll" controversy reasserted the power of the Legion of Decency, independent of the Production Code Administration. "The Man with the Golden Arm" and "A Streetcar Named Desire" were able to become envelope-pushing hits because their producers played ball with the Legion, while "Baby Doll" defied the organization and lost. The rules may have become a bit malleable, and the rulers may have been at odds, but they still ruled.

Sexy Imports

While mainstream American film changed incrementally, European film was quickly becoming more open-minded. Swedish director Ingmar Bergman is known for slow, poetic explorations of spirituality. You might not think of him as a crusader for sexuality on screen, and he probably didn't either. Still, his "**Summer with Monika**" (1952 in Europe, 1955 in the U.S.) was a breakthrough.

"Summer with Monika" tells the story of a young woman, played by Harriet Andersson, who uses her attractiveness to get what she wants. Andersson's character is sex-positive in a similar way to Mae West, except that it's played for drama instead of comedy. "Summer with Monika" confronts sexual mores instead of ridiculing them. For me, this makes it more shocking in the context of the times. In a key shot, Harriet Andersson stares into the camera for an extended period, as if to say, "You got a problem?" The male heterosexual viewer, who is likely judging her while also being turned on by her, is forced to examine himself.

Stateside, "Summer with Monika" made inroads everywhere except mainstream theaters. Kroger Babb, the exploitationeer responsible for "Mom and Dad," bought the rights to "Summer with Monika." He then dubbed it in what he called "American English," cut it down to

---

[272] de Grazia and Newman, p. 94

62 minutes (leaving in all the partial nudity), and released it as "Monika, the Story of a Bad Girl." As Babb's version played the drive-ins, an unedited, subtitled version arrived in arthouse theaters.[273] You could see two very different versions of the same movie the same day in both lowbrow and highfalutin venues.

"Summer with Monika" cemented progressive Sweden in the minds of Americans and Brits as the place for open sexuality. It also initiated a trend of both exploitation and arthouse venues profiting from sexy foreign films.

On the heels of "Summer with Monika" came "**And God Created Woman**" (1956). Brigitte Bardot plays a similarly attractive woman whose sexuality is front and center. The movie communicates some criticism of sexist double standards: Bardot's character pursues sex just like the men do but people vilify her for it. "And God Created Woman" is not the artistic achievement that "Summer with Monika" is, in my view; I found it surprisingly gloomy and dull in stretches. Regardless, it's no exploitation film, even if it never misses an opportunity to make Bardot look seductive. It was another movie that could play in both arthouse and exploitation theaters.

"And God Created Woman" was a huge hit in its native France and throughout Europe. Even in the stodgy United Kingdom, which had censorship standards as strict or stricter than the United States in many respects, the movie was one of the ten most popular of the year.[274]

In the States, "And God Created Woman" was denied a Production Code seal. The Legion of Decency concurred, giving it a C. There were still plenty of theaters that wouldn't screen a C movie, so the rating usually limited box-office potential. But "And God Created Woman" was such a phenomenon that it didn't matter. One Columbia spokesman insisted that, if the movie had earned a B, it

---

[273] Schaefer, p. 335
[274] "Most Popular Film of the Year". *The Times (London, England)*, Thursday, 12 Dec 1957; p. 3

would have shown in twice as many theaters but made half as much money.[275] Even if that spokesman exaggerated a tad, it was clear that a Legion of Decency C was not always the kiss of death it was supposed to be. "And God Created Woman" ended up setting a box-office record for foreign films in the States.[276]

The Production Code Administration and the Legion of Decency had been weakened once again. Even though the censors remained united this time, demand was just too great. There were lots of Americans who were unashamed to buy tickets to a sexually provocative film that has the trappings of sophisticated, European art. American film studios of course wanted to respond to this demand and make similar films. It would take some time though.

In the meantime, foreign films would have a heyday in the States. In 1958, another European film about a sexually liberated woman came out: "**The Lovers**," directed by Louis Malle. Jeanne Moreau stars as a woman who frequently swaps suitors. While I found it easy to feel for Brigitte Bardot's character's struggles to navigate a sexist society in "And God Created Woman," Moreau's character complicated my sympathies in a fascinating way.

The controversy over "The Lovers" was primarily about a sex scene that goes beyond that of "Summer with Monika" or "And God Created Woman." Again, I don't want to sound like Mr. Skin, but it is relevant in this case that Moreau appears topless. French films would increasingly show female breasts at this time, which was still strictly forbidden in the States.

"The Lovers" was banned and cut in many jurisdictions throughout the United States, and people who exhibited it were jailed. The resulting court cases culminated in a U.S. Supreme Court decision. In siding with the film's exhibitors, Justice William Brennan stated that "material dealing with sex in a manner that advocates ideas, or

---

[275] Tino Balio, "The Foreign Film Renaissance on American Screens, 1946–1973", pp. 114–115
[276] "Top Grossers of 1958". *Variety*. 7 January 1959. p. 48.

that has literary or scientific or artistic value or any other form of social importance, may not be branded as obscenity" and therefore could not be banned. Justice Potter Stewart wrote that only "hardcore pornography" qualified as obscenity. As to what qualifies as pornography, Stewart gave his famous line "I know it when I see it."[277]

This was a drastic re-interpretation of what constitutes obscenity. Things had come a long way since "Ecstasy," the Czech film that was banned in the 1930s for being obscene. "The Lovers" shares many traits with "Ecstasy": Both are art films with nude scenes, and both center on women following their sexual desires. What had changed was the courts. The "Miracle" decision had led to more message-based shocks in movies, and now content-based shocks had a chance of getting widely seen.

"**Lady Chatterley's Lover**" (1955 in France, 1959 in the States) was a clear analogue to "Ecstasy" in a different way. Both films are about wealthy women who have impotent husbands and find sexual satisfaction with working-class men. Both explore the message-based shock that marital infidelity could be a good thing.

But "Lady Chatterley's Lover" is more chaste than "Ecstasy" or any of the other films in this section. Lady Chatterley does not begin the film as a young woman exploring her sexuality. She is a saintly, self-sacrificing wife devoted to taking care of her husband, who was paralyzed from the waist down by a war injury. The pompous Lord Chatterley is the one who pushes her into an extramarital affair, because it's the only way he can have a male heir.

The movie has no nudity. While there are certainly some erotic scenes, they depict a couple's tender, private moments, as opposed to the more exhibitionistic tone of the above films. On its face, "Lady Chatterley's Lover" might seem no more or less shocking than "La

---

[277] de Grazia and Newman, p. 264-265

ronde" and the many similar French films in which extramarital affairs are handled blithely.

"Lady Chatterley's Lover" came with a pedigree, though. It's based on a 1928 D.H. Lawrence novel that is one of the most controversial of all time. Sexuality is integral to the story, because it hinges on Lady Chatterley's revelation that her mind and her body could feel integrated with the right partner. To illustrate the power of sexual pleasure within a loving relationship, you have to get somewhat explicit. The novel also has some grade-A expletives.

Lawrence printed a few thousand copies on his own. A censored version was published after he died. The unedited version was unavailable in the United Kingdom until a landmark 1960 court case. It was also banned in the United States until after the film version roused controversy.

By this time, the Production Code Administration and the Legion of Decency were irrelevant for foreign films. The arthouse and exploitation circuits were large enough to provide profits outside of the mainstream, especially after "And God Created Woman" had been such a success. According to Leff and Simmons, "One distributor told Congress that because the seal cost a minimum of $500, fewer than five percent of the independents sought one."[278]

If anyone was going to stop the film version of "Lady Chatterley's Lover," it would have to be the state and local censors. In 1957, The New York censorship board refused to issue a license to the movie. On appeal, the state's board of regents concurred, saying that the "whole theme ... is the presentation of adultery as a desirable, acceptable and proper behavior."[279] This made it clear that the dispute was about ideas concerning sex, not obscenity or content-based shocks.

---

[278] Leff and Simmons, p. 229
[279] de Grazia and Newman, p. 253

The case wound through the system until it hit the U.S. Supreme Court. The Court handed down a unanimous decision against the censorship of messages. Our friend Potter Stewart said "What New York has done ... is to prevent the exhibition of a motion picture because that picture advocates an idea – that adultery under proper circumstances may be proper behavior. Yet the First Amendment's basic guarantee is of freedom to advocate ideas. The State, quite simply, has thus struck at the very heart of constitutionally protected liberty."[280]

This decision was a critical blow to the suppression of message-based shocks in the United States. While previous decisions had freed messages about specific topics: religion in the "Miracle" case, race in the "Native Son" case, etc., the "Lady Chatterley's Lover" decision most clearly defined all messages as legitimate topics for movies. Filmmakers came much closer to being "freed from the censor," per Supreme Court Justice William O. Douglas' stated vision. Authorities would not stop trying to ban message-based shocks, but they would do so without a legal leg to stand on.

The Code Might Bend, But It Won't Give Up Bigotry

With the Supreme Court firmly establishing the freedom to make movies about whatever you want, the Production Code Administration realized it had to be more flexible on message-based shocks. Better that than become totally obsolete. Administration president Geoffrey Shurlock told a colleague "In trying to hew to the classic tradition, the Code may often seem cumbersome and, to use a word which is by now becoming hackneyed, 'hackneyed.' We will still have to struggle along and do our best to make the pictures (in our favorite escape-hatch phrase) reasonably acceptable to the reasonable members of the modern-day audience."[281]

---

[280] Quoted in ibid
[281] Quoted in Leff and Simmons, p. 232

Does that mean acknowledging the existence of homosexuality? In the Production Code, homosexuality was referred to as "sexual perversion" and was still a forbidden topic, even after the 1956 Code revisions. No character could be overtly acknowledged as LGBTQ+. Characters could only be coded as queer, to make them villains and/or objects of ridicule. For example, in "The Maltese Falcon" (1941), Peter Lorre's character Joel Cairo has a calling card scented with gardenia, which indicates that he's a villainous gay man. An adult would catch the "gay" part, while a kid would just understand that he's some sort of "lesser" man to be despised because of his feminine qualities.

Since World War II, many directors had been shot down trying to film stories touching more overtly on LGBTQ+ identities. For example, the 1956 film "Tea And Sympathy" was supposed to be about a boy who was worried he might be gay and impotent. The Production Code Administration forced the filmmakers to make him merely impotent, at least explicitly, and to stuff any gayness into a coding of vague unmasculineness. "Tea and Sympathy" star Deborah Kerr said the Administration was "very difficult about the homosexual angle … Adultery is OK, impotence is OK, but perversion is their bête noire."[282]

The 1959 film "**Suddenly, Last Summer**" was the first Hollywood film that was allowed to openly broach the topic of homosexuality. The Production Code Administration could hardly say no to the crowd behind it: Katherine Hepburn and Elizabeth Taylor starring, "All About Eve" director Joseph L. Mankiewicz at the helm, and a basis in a Tennessee Williams play. Its producer made clear that he was going to let Mankiewicz film what he wanted, regardless of what the Production Code said.[283] "Suddenly, Last Summer" got its seal, which the Administration justified by saying that "since the film

---

[282] Leff and Simmons, p. 231
[283] Miller, p. 187-188

illustrates the horrors of such a lifestyle, it can be considered moral in theme even though it deals with sexual perversion."[284]

"Suddenly, Last Summer" does indeed make queerness seem like a horrific disease. The gay character is often spoken of but never seen or heard, so the audience is never able to empathize with him. He's essentially a faceless monster whose homosexuality causes the destruction of his family. It's hard to think of a more insulting debut for acknowledged LGBTQ+ characters in Hollywood movies. Maybe if they had also made him a Nazi?

The rule may have been broken on never openly admitting a character was queer, but "Suddenly, Last Summer"'s message of demonizing LGBTQ+ people was far from revolutionary. Many previous films, such as Alfred Hitchcock's "Rope," had done so while coding characters as queer a bit more opaquely.

I'm begrudgingly including "Suddenly, Last Summer" as a shock film after a long internal debate. The movie did at least speak of "the love that dare not speak its name," even if it spoke of it in bigoted terms. It's also such an overheated and melodramatic movie, in my opinion, with such a ludicrous final reveal, that many people have interpreted it as camp. If you can watch "Suddenly, Last Summer" with that lens, maybe you can get something out of it.

Preminger Again

After his successes with "The Moon Is Blue" and "The Man with the Golden Arm," Otto Preminger found another way to chip away at the Production Code. "**Anatomy of a Murder**" (1959) is a serious courtroom drama about a violent sex crime. Today, the movie feels like an especially realistic and sober episode of "Law and Order." Most episodes of "Law and Order: SVU" are much more shocking.

---

[284] Quoted in B. Hadleigh, "The Lavender Screen: The Gay and Lesbian Films—Their Stars, Makers, Characters, and Critics (Rev. ed.)", p. 23

In the 1950s, though, "Anatomy of a Murder" intentionally broke some rules.

The weak spot in the Code that Preminger targeted this time was the blanket ban on certain words. They're probably not the words you're thinking of: "Anatomy of a Murder" uses words like "rape," "sperm," "contraceptive," "penetration" and "panties," all of which the Production Code Administration had always disallowed. The movie uses these words within the serious context of a trial about rape and murder. The screenplay drives home that the context makes the words acceptable and necessary. In one scene, attorney Paul Biegler, played by Jimmy Stewart, is interviewing policeman James Durgo on the witness stand:

- Durgo: "We also looked for a -- uh -- a certain undergarment of Mrs. Manion's, but we didn't find it."

- Judge Weaver: "Will the attorneys from both sides approach the bench please?"

    Paul, Dancer and Mitch [the attorneys] come to the Judge's bench. The Judge leans over to look down at them and their conversation is conducted in a low monotone.

- Judge Weaver: "Mr. Biegler, you finally got your rape into the case and I think all the details should be made very clear to the jury. Do you agree, Mr. Lodwick?"

- Mitch: "Absolutely."

- Judge Weaver: "What exactly was the undergarment just referred to?"

- Paul: "Panties, your honor."

- Judge Weaver: "Do you expect this subject to come up again?"

- Paul: "Yes sir."

- Judge Weaver: "There is a certain light connotation attached to the word 'panties.' Can we find another name for them?"

- Mitch: "I never heard my wife call 'em anything else."

- Judge Weaver: "Mr. Biegler?"

- Paul: "I'm a bachelor, your honor."

- Judge Weaver: "That is a great help. Mr. Dancer?"

- Dancer: "When I was overseas during the war, Your Honor, I learned a French word but it might be slightly suggestive."

- Judge Weaver: "Most French words are. All right, go back to your places."

The attorneys return to their tables.

- Judge Weaver: "For the benefit of the jury, but more especially for the spectators, the undergarment referred to in the testimony was, to be exact, Mrs. Manion's panties."

A snicker goes through the room. Judge Weaver waits for quiet again.

- Judge Weaver: "I wanted you to get your snickering over and done with. This pair of panties will be mentioned again in the course of the trial and when that happens there will not be one laugh, one snicker, one giggle or even one smirk, in my courtroom. There isn't anything comic about a pair of panties which figure in the violent death of one man and in the possible incarceration of another."

A long pause, a pin drop can be heard.

As I watched this scene, I imagined Judge Weaver's speech being directed to the Production Code Administration and the viewing public. At the very least, I bet Otto Preminger underlined and circled these passages in any script he submitted. "Look, you idiots," the exchange seems to be saying. "They're called 'panties.' We are not talking about them to be naughty. We are talking about them because they are relevant to a serious crime. Get over it."

The Production Code Administration and Legion of Decency got the message and did not put up much of a fight over "Anatomy of a Murder." They got a few choice words removed, but most stayed.[285] The censors had already fought Otto Preminger twice, with "The Moon Is Blue" and "The Man with the Golden Arm," and lost each time. And this movie was the most non-obscene of the bunch, with clear-as-crystal reasons why the very mild forbidden words must be allowed. "Anatomy of a Murder" demonstrated that the gatekeepers had learned to be flexible. They weren't going to make a mistake again like Joseph Breen had with "Bicycle Thieves." Thus Preminger had succeeded in making another small change to Code enforcement, this time without a public battle.

The Production Code Administration was picking its battles carefully, because it didn't have much firepower left. It couldn't fine a studio for releasing a film without a seal anymore, and could even be sued and lose if it failed to grant one.[286] Their main tactic became hurting the bottom line of little movies that didn't have the money to fight back.

Meanwhile, the Legion of Decency was adapting to a more tolerant nation. In 1957, it opened up its staff in charge of evaluating movies to lay people and more liberal-minded priests. The Legion was also responding to the changes in theaters, as many that used to only screen A- and B-rated movies would increasingly show Cs.[287]

---

[285] Miller, p. 186
[286] Leff and Simmons, p. 231
[287] Leff and Simmons, p. 238

There were still local censors, and "Anatomy of a Murder" experienced one minor skirmish with one of those. The Chicago censorship board refused to license it, which led to a lawsuit. A higher Illinois court quickly swatted down the board, citing a U.S. Supreme Court decision that something can't be obscene if "its diction or episodes are so slight or infrequent as not to convey an obscene savor to the entire book or play."[288] In other words, "Anatomy of a Murder" is clearly not titillating, so grow up.

A New Frontier in Nudity

If you wanted clear titillation in 1959, the exploitation circuit had an exciting new offering. Exploitation had seen many of their favorite subjects overtaken by mainstream films: drug abuse, racial relations, etc. The topic with the greatest money making potential, female nudity, was relegated to lame nudist movies until 1957.

That year, the U.S. Supreme Court decision *Roth v. United States* established that material about sex was not necessarily obscene. Samuel Roth was not a filmmaker; he was arrested on obscenity charges for running a store that sold adult books.[289] In siding with him, the Court established that art with "redeeming social importance" was not obscene.[290] Among other things, this meant that you could get away with showing the long-forbidden areas of women's nipples and rear ends in movies.

In 1959, director Russ Meyer was the first to take full advantage of the new standards. He released "**The Immoral Mr. Teas**," which inaugurated a trend of "nudie cuties." Unlike burlesque films, this was a movie with a narrative, of sorts. Mr. Teas is a door-to-door salesman who gains some sort of magical ability to see women

---

[288] Quoted in de Grazia and Newman, p. 258
[289] Richard Jr. Pacelle, "*Roth v. United States*". First Amendment Encyclopedia.
[290] Quoted in Miller, p. 263

naked. It's nominally a comedy, but mostly a showcase for cheesecake-style female nudity.

"The Immoral Mr. Teas" has the light-hearted tone of a burlesque movie. But because it at least pretends to have a story, it might have seemed less seamy. I could imagine men going to see it who would be embarrassed to buy a ticket for a burlesque title.

At the same time, "The Immoral Mr. Teas" is a celebration of voyeurism. Mr. Teas leers at female characters who are unaware they are being objectified, at least within the world of the movie. Meanwhile, burlesque dancers were always presented as willing performers looking straight into the camera. Despite packaging itself as more legitimate than burlesque movies, "The Immoral Mr. Teas" is more exploitative.

Of course, the operative reason for the success of "The Immoral Mr. Teas" was that it showed body parts that burlesque movies did not. Nudist movies always did too, and they featured (thin) stories. But they always pushed nudity as the cure for all the world's problems. "The Immoral Mr. Teas" dispenses with all that boring proselytizing, delivering titillation in a seemingly whimsical package. In its eccentric way, it is the progenitor of teen sex comedies.

Other nudie cuties followed "The Immoral Mr. Teas" and the genre quickly overtook burlesque and nudist films to become the primary method for sexually arousing straight guys in movie theaters. Many arthouse theaters converted to showing nudie cuties. Because these movies were made outside the MPAA, theaters and filmmakers didn't have to worry about the Production Code. They only had to adhere to the new legal landscape established by the *Roth* decision. The MPAA studios that did have to play by the Production Code rules were unhappy that this source of easy revenue was denied them. They started pushing for relaxing restrictions.[291]

---

[291] Sova, p. 103

The nudie cutie trend would last a few years, until other subgenres would up the ante in shock value. More on that later.

Birth

I want to squeeze out one more 1950s film that presages the significantly more shocking 1960s. "**Window Water Baby Moving**" (1959) is a short made by the godfather of underground art film, Stan Brakhage. It depicts his wife giving birth in graphic detail. The 1938 movie "The Birth of a Baby" showed a baby coming out of a vagina from a distance, but "Window Water Baby Moving" has many extreme close-ups before, during, and after the delivery. You see all the bleeding, crowning, afterbirth, etc.

These were very bracing sights for me. At the same time, I was thinking "This is a regular day in the life of a midwife or Ob-Gyn." Everything in "Window Water Baby Moving" comprises a very normal and healthy event that happens thousands of times a day and is responsible for the survival of our species. For those of us who are parents, it marks the beginning of a deep and powerful love that we spend the rest of our lives devoted to. I can't think of any other human experience that mixes such extreme and usually diametrically opposed emotions.

Unlike the much more clinical and drab "The Birth of a Baby," "Window Water Baby Moving" also reveals the life-changing beauty inherent in the birthing process. We see the affection between Brakhage and his wife and the touching first moments of a mother with her newborn. This is no exploitation film; it is a moving document of one of the most essential and important human activities.

Brakhage had trouble getting it made. His initial plan to film it in a hospital was dashed when the hospital changed its mind and refused to allow it. He then moved the birth to his home, which was unusual and expensive at the time.[292]

In those days you had to send film away to be processed. After Brakhage did so, Kodak sent him a letter saying that if he didn't consent to them destroying the footage, they would turn it over to the police. Brakhage had to get a doctor to send Kodak a letter before they would return his film.[293]

Kodak was no doubt reacting to the visceral shocks of an entire screen filled with a vulva expelling a child. Any footage of female genitalia was assumed to be pornographic, even though that is an unspeakably perverse assumption when applied to a birth. Brakhage was aware of the risk he was taking, saying later "you could definitely go to jail for showing not only sexuality but nudity of any kind – though the idea of childbirth being somehow pornographic has always been offensive and disgusting to me."[294] This demonstrates once again that the sort of cut-and-dried rules that made up the Production Code are never adequate for an art form; context is always key.

Wrapping Up the 1950s

The 1950s had several movies that punched holes in oversimplified censorship rules. The Supreme Court made it possible by establishing and maintaining that free speech applied to movies. Roberto Rossellini, Ingmar Bergman, Otto Preminger, Elia Kazan, and others then demonstrated how forbidden topics could be valid subjects for movies when presented in artistically credible contexts. Meanwhile, exploitation producers were monitoring the gradual broadening of what they could get away with and capitalizing on it.

---

[292] Scott MacDonald, "A critical cinema: interviews with independent filmmakers," p. 64-66
[293] Ibid
[294] Quoted in ibid

For both, the rate of change was slow in the 1950s. Perhaps if it weren't a politically conservative time in the United States, censorship would have decayed faster. Regardless, the liberal societal experimentation that characterized the 1960s throughout the Western world would change things in a hurry.

Chapter 6: The Transitional Era, Part 2: 1960-1968

The New Brutality

If you ask a typical movie buff what the most shocking film of all time might be, there's a good chance they'll say "**Psycho**" (1960), especially if you're talking to a baby boomer. "Psycho" has several scenes which are world-famous for inducing shock, such as the iconic one in the shower.

For our purposes, "Psycho" is not the most shocking film of all time. It played ball with the censors, getting a Production Code seal and earning a B from the Legion of Decency. American state and local censors did not pitch a fit over "Psycho," so there were no court cases over its content. If you use censorship scuffle as a primary yardstick for shock value, as I usually do, "Psycho" is less shocking than the dour, straight-laced courtroom procedural "Anatomy of a Murder."

Granted, American censors were so discombobulated after all their defeats in the 1950s that their activity might no longer provide the best indicator of shock. The Legion of Decency and the state and local censorship boards were rapidly fading away. On page 251 of "Dame in the Kimono," Leff and Simmons note:

> "Screenwriters knew that state and municipal boards – the raison d'etre for the Production Code – no longer threatened Hollywood. The censor boards had gradually drifted into backwaters ... By the late 1950s, pluralism had moved American from a religious to a secular base, from a common notion of evil to one more relative. One landmark case after another demonstrated that the mainstream currents were too swift for the censor boards or even the church. ... The attrition of Catholic Alumnae, and the addition of young

professionals, both laity and priests, to the reviewing staff continued to diminish the zealousness of the Legion."

The Production Code Administration was still trying to do its job, but it was acting a bit punch-drunk after losing several rounds to Otto Preminger. The stories of their evaluation process for "Psycho" do not make the organization sound like it was operating on all cylinders. Reportedly, some of the reviewers in the Production Code Administration thought they saw a flash of Janet Leigh's breasts in the shower scene. A few days later, director Alfred Hitchcock brought the exact same print back to the reviewers, without having changed a frame. This time, the ones who thought they saw a breast didn't see it and those who didn't see it before now did. Ultimately, they were all pacified when Hitchcock cut a shot showing buttocks.[295]

The Production Code Administration also didn't like the opening scene of an unmarried couple in bed. Hitchcock promised that if they let him keep the shower scene intact, he would reshoot the opening scene and invite Administration reviewers on set to watch. The reviewers didn't show up to the reshoot, so Hitchcock abandoned it and the opening scene stayed in the film.[296]

Foreign censors demanded other cuts, many of them baffling. For example, the censor for Ireland wanted fewer stabs in the first murder scene, saying "One stab is surely enough."[297] I get the sense that the intensity of "Psycho" made censors think they had to do something to tone it down, even if they didn't know what. They all found different nits to pick so they could feel like they'd done their jobs.

---

[295] Christopher Nickens and Janet Leigh, "Psycho: Behind the Scenes of the Classic Thriller," p. 112
[296] Nickens and Leigh, p. 112
[297] Quoted in Kevin Rockett, "Irish Film Censorship: A Cultural Journey from Silent Cinema to Internet Pornography," p. 171-3

The censors couldn't edit out the whole plot of "Psycho," which was what made it truly shocking in 1960. The film is based on a novel which was inspired by the true story of Ed Gein. Gein was a small-town farmer who murdered women and exhumed corpses. He would then turn human bones and skin into a wide range of objects, such as bowls and lampshades. Always mentally disturbed, Gein became especially pathological after the death of his oppressive mother, who had taught him that all women were evil. The parts of Gein's life that were too grotesque for "Psycho" later inspired "The Texas Chain Saw Massacre" and "The Silence of the Lambs."[298]

Before production began on "Psycho," Alfred Hitchcock's studio, Paramount, had warned him that the novel he wanted to base it on was "too repulsive"[299] and "impossible for films."[300] Paramount offered him a drastically reduced budget. Hitchcock rejected it and used his own production company instead. The deal worked out for him; instead of his typical $250,000 director's fee, he took 60% ownership of "Psycho"'s negative.[301] That earned him more than $15 million from the eventual profits.[302]

It was no small thing for a studio to say no to Alfred Hitchcock in 1960. He had 35 years of successful films behind him, most recently "North by Northwest" in 1959. Film directors were almost never celebrities at the time, but Hitchcock made himself one by hosting the hit TV show "Alfred Hitchcock Presents" (1955-1961). He alone had the kind of clout that allowed him to push the boundaries of subject matter into the realm of psychosexual violence.

The most likely reason the Production Code Administration could only nibble at the edges of "Psycho" was that it didn't dare deny Hitchcock a seal outright. Remember that the Code was overseen by the MPAA, which was mostly concerned about making money

---

[298] Robert H. Gollmar, "Edward Gein: America's Most Bizarre Murderer"
[299] Stephen Rebello, "Alfred Hitchcock and the Making of Psycho", p. 13
[300] Nickens and Leigh, p. 6
[301] Rebello, p. 29
[302] Rebello, p. 181

from movies. Overall film viewership was still falling (see the graph at the beginning of Chapter 5), and Hitchcock was a pillar of the industry, a world-famous auteur with a huge public following. Hitchcock could have released "Psycho" without a seal and theaters would have still lined up to exhibit it. That would have delivered yet another blow to the censors.

Maybe the Production Code Administration would have gathered the courage to deny a seal if Hitchcock had given them something like, say, "The Exorcist," which would have gone too far for 1960 audiences. But "Psycho" pushed the envelope just the right amount. Americans gave it the second-largest box-office returns of 1960, after only "Spartacus."[303] Throughout the rest of the world, "Psycho" set box-office records. People were ready for rougher stuff.

Hitchcock hit on just the perfect level of shock content for 1960, but Michael Powell was not so lucky. Powell was also a superstar director with decades of critical and box-office successes behind him. His 1960 film "**Peeping Tom**" profiles a serial killer who films his victims so he can make compilations of their dying expressions. The fact that the victims are young, attractive women strongly suggests that the killer has twisted psychosexual motivations.

While the reviews of "Psycho" were mixed, they were brutal for "Peeping Tom." "Peeping Tom" is a British film, and the British critics had a field day expressing revulsion about it. One wrote "It's a long time [sic] since a film disgusted me as much as 'Peeping Tom'" and another quipped "The only really satisfactory way to dispose of 'Peeping Tom' would be to shovel it up and flush it swiftly down the nearest sewer."[304] The film didn't reach much of an audience in the

---

[303] Tom Brueggemann, "'Psycho' Turns 60 This Week: How the 1960 Release Created an Iconic Film". *Indiewire*, June 14, 2020
[304] Quoted in Felicia Feaster, "Peeping Tom: Articles and Reviews", Turner Classic Movies website, https://www.tcm.com/tcmdb/title/86435/peeping-tom

United Kingdom or overseas. After finishing one more movie, Michael Powell was demoted to TV work for several years.

To my eyes, "Psycho" and "Peeping Tom" seem pretty comparable, shock-wise. "Peeping Tom" seems to empathize more with the killer; certainly he gets more screen time than Norman Bates does. We see killings from his perspective, especially the first one. That first murder is of a sex worker; in the British version of the film she exposes her breast, which was a first for a British film. Maybe these elements proved too much?

This is one instance where hindsight isn't a benefit. It's hard to put myself in the perspective of a 1960 audience and judge what would push a movie over the line from thrills into disgust. Regardless, both "Psycho" and "Peeping Tom" are now considered classics, and I highly recommend both.

"Psycho" and "Peeping Tom" represent a turning point in film horror. Classic horror was the "creature features" of "Dracula," "Frankenstein," and other movies based on old Gothic novels. They were about mythical beings with clearly defined supernatural powers and weaknesses. Set in creepy old castles in old-time-y European settings, these movies were all quite distant from contemporary life.

By the 1950s, the shock of classic horror had thoroughly worn off for most people. The old monsters remained popular on TV, but were increasingly seen as kids' stuff. There were some variations on the old formulas that worked -- "Creature from the Black Lagoon," "Invasion of the Body Snatchers," the 1958 Hammer Films version of "Dracula," etc. – but most 1950s horror was low-budget schlock made for teens.

"Psycho" and "Peeping Tom" were drastically different from classic horror. They were inspired by real-life serial killers, not old novels. These killers looked like ordinary people who lived in our world. They had homicidal psychosexual pathologies rather than supernatural abilities. "Psycho" and "Peeping Tom" not only birthed modern horror, with its slashers and psychopaths; they also inaugurated a new era of brutality in all film. While the 1950s shock films were almost all about sex, you'll see a lot more violent films to come.

Continental Horrors

I shouldn't give all the credit for the brutality of 1960s films to "Psycho" and "Peeping Tom." In the same year, director Georges Franju's "**Les yeux sans visage**," aka "**Eyes Without a Face**," hit theaters in France. It's not quite as much of a departure from traditional horror as "Psycho" and "Peeping Tom," as it is about a mad scientist. But it is grounded in reality and deals with genuine despair in a more grown-up way than almost all 1950s horror.

"Les yeux sans visage" also has a few shots of gruesome gore that qualify it for this book. These shots share a similar ick factor with most of Franju's 1949 slaughterhouse documentary "Blood of the Beasts." That short film and others we've covered show mutilated animals, but I'm not aware of any feature film before "Les yeux sans visage" that takes human gore to a comparable level.

British critics were scandalized once again. One called "Les yeux sans visage" "the sickest film since I started film criticism"[305] and another was nearly fired for liking it.[306] The offending scenes were cut from the American version, which made little impact.

French critics expressed disdain that Franju should take a step down from documentaries to horror, which one called a "minor genre, quite unworthy of his abilities." Franju responded that he was trying to elevate the genre.[307] History would agree with Franju: "Les yeux sans visage" is now regarded as one of the best horror films of all time. Don't go into it expecting a typical horror film, though;

---

[305] Quoted in Justine Ashby and Andrew Higson, "British Cinema: Past and Present," p. 222
[306] "Eyes Without a Face" booklet for The Criterion Collection edition
[307] Kate Ince, "Georges Franju," p. 52

prepare yourself for more of a somber, slow art film with a few shocks.

The kind of horror movie that French critics looked down upon was made by the likes of Mario Bava. His first credited directorial effort, **"Black Sunday,"** (1960) is traditional in many ways: creepy castle, old-timey European setting, supernatural beings, etc. I personally found it melodramatic and clichéd, so I guess I'm siding with the snooty French critics on this one at least.

I'm mentioning "Black Sunday" because it has a handful of gory scenes that made it notorious. It was banned in the United Kingdom until a censored version was released in 1968.[308] In 1960, an edited version was brought to the United States by American International Pictures, the independent outfit that employed Roger Corman and made cheap drive-in movies for teens. "Black Sunday" proved a huge moneymaker, indicating that there might be a market for gory movies.

"Black Sunday" also jump-started Italian horror. Most were similarly Gothic in theme until Dario Argento's "The Bird with the Crystal Plumage" (1970) initiated the dominance of what is known in the English-speaking world as "giallo" films. (Italians call them "giallo all'italiana" to distinguish them from other uses of the word.) They're especially bloody mysteries that use wild, wide color palettes. Like "Psycho" and "Peeping Tom," gialli involve real-life killers in contemporary settings. They are meant to be shocking but are not exceptionally transgressive by the very high standards of 1970s horror.

There were gialli in the 1960s, but they weren't popular enough to start a trend. One of the first true gialli, **"Blood and Black Lace"** (1964), I think, has a luridness that stands out in the context of its time. It shows a series of professional models being picked off in gory ways.

---

[308] Tim Lucas, "Mario Bava - All the Colors of the Dark" (2nd ed.), p. 317

Otherwise, Italian horror films of the 1960s and 1970s knew exactly how much to push the boundaries of acceptable content without busting through them. As I mentioned back in the chapter about the Pre-Code Era, horror is a genre based on shocks; to stand out you have to really break the rules and cause a public fuss.

For instance, a 1962 movie called "The Horrible Dr. Hichcock" broaches the topic of necrophilia, which you'd think would break ground at that time. But the movie takes great pains to prevent the necrophiliac from doing anything too shocking. Any shot of sexual contact with a dead body could have led to protests and censorship, which would threaten box office returns. Italian horror filmmakers were in the business of delivering shocks just strong enough to get butts in seats but not so strong as to affect the bottom line.

The Connection

American director Shirley Clarke did not care about the bottom line. In 1962, she pronounced "I'm revolting against the conventions of movies. Who says a film has to cost a million dollars and be safe and innocuous enough to satisfy every 12-year-old in America?"[309] Since 1934, the MPAA had been saying just that. So Clarke remained outside the mainstream her entire career. She became a foundational figure of American independent film.

Outside the mainstream was where Clarke found her inspiration anyway. As an ambitious woman in the early 1960s, she felt like an outcast. When asked about her groundbreaking treatments of racism, she said:

> "I identified with Black people because I couldn't deal with the woman question and I transposed it. I could understand very easily the Black problems, and I somehow equated

---

[309] Quoted in Lawrence Van Gelder. "Shirley Clarke Is Dead at 77; Maker of Oscar-Winning Film". *The New York Times*. September 26, 1997, p. D.18.

them to how I felt. When I did 'The Connection,' which was about junkies, I knew nothing about junk and cared less. It was a symbol – people who are on the outside. I always felt alone, and on the outside of the culture that I was in. I grew up in a time when women weren't running things. They still aren't."[310]

Clarke's first feature, "**The Connection**" (1961), demonstrates her approach very clearly. It's about a group of heroin addicts sitting in an apartment and waiting for a fix. "The Connection" is probably the first "found footage" film; the audience is told all footage was taken by a documentarian, who shows up in the movie and becomes a primary character. Seasoned movie watchers will be able to tell it's actually based on a play. The less savvy viewers of 1961 who bought that it's a true documentary would experience some serious shocks.

"The Connection" goes much farther than "The Man with the Golden Arm" had in depicting the realities of heroin addiction. In 1961, though, authorities were most offended by its characters saying "shit" and the camera catching glimpses of nudie mags.

Clarke was trying to make a movie that would test New York's censorship rules, and she succeeded. New York's censorship board refused to grant a license to screen "The Connection." Interestingly, the board cited only the use of the word "shit." Legal wrangling went back and forth until a court of appeals decided that because "shit" was being used as slang for heroin instead of for feces, it wasn't obscene.[311]

I don't know about you, but to me the appeals court's decision sounds a bit like parents inventing new rules on the fly so they don't have to punish a kid who missed curfew for some minor reason. It's

---

[310] Dee Dee Halleck, "Shirley Clarke Interview". The Early Video Project. https://davidsonsfiles.org/shirleyclarkeinterview.html
[311] Sova, p. 84

another example of how post-World War II courts bent over forwards to allow freedom of expression.

I'm sure the New York censorship board based their entire case on "shit" because they realized they had the deck stacked against them from the beginning. For scenes depicting drug use or nudity there is always a gray area: Who is to say what goes too far and what doesn't? But curse words are unambiguous. People either say them or they don't. If the rule is that you can't say "shit," then censors can pop you for saying "shit." It's an open and shut case – at least, you'd think so. The court of appeals still found a way to weasel out of cracking down on "The Connection." Clarke had succeeded in making the censors weaker than ever.

Curse words have a strange power that I don't intend to unpack much further. They are certainly part of the shock content landscape but not central; they tended to make their way into movies as a sort of afterthought to sex and violence. If you were hoping for more about curse words, I'm sorry to disappoint. It is a fascinating and strange topic. Comedian George Carlin's classic monologue "Seven Words You Can Never Say on Television" is a great place to start exploring the illogic of the whole realm.

Messages That Could Still Shock

Central to freedom of expression afforded to films after World War II was that the United States should be open to any message-based shock. The "Lady Chatterley's Lover" decision in particular was supposed to make every idea acceptable for a film. Most ideas involving sexuality were now fair game, and Hollywood saw opportunities to make money from them. As Frank Miller writes in "Censored Hollywood," "increased sexuality was viewed as a practical solution to competition not just from foreign films but from the more heavily censored television medium."[312]

---

[312] Miller, p. 184

What about the idea that queerness might not be evil? "Suddenly, Last Summer" may have mentioned homosexuality in 1959, but that movie hewed closely to the Production Code Administration's dogma that it constituted "sex perversion" and was inherently monstrous.

Director William Wyler decided to take a page from Otto Preminger's playbook and chip away at a Production Code rule by adapting a hit play. Wyler had been a powerful, prestigious director since the 1930s. His 1959 epic "Ben-Hur" had just won the Oscars for Best Picture and Best Director and was the biggest box-office hit of the year.

At the peak of his power, Wyler could have taken on another huge-budget epic. Instead he wanted to make a proper adaptation of the Lillian Hellman play "The Children's Hour." I mentioned this play in Chapter 4; it's about two women who run a girls' school. When one brat spreads the rumor that they're lovers, all hell breaks loose.

In 1936, Wyler had directed the aforementioned film adaptation of "The Children's Hour" that was stripped of any mention of queerness and turned into a regular heterosexual love triangle. Joseph Breen didn't even allow the movie to keep the same name as the play, so it was called "These Three."

In 1961, Wyler saw his chance to do "The Children's Hour" right. He signed on Shirley MacLaine and Audrey Hepburn, both big stars that American moviegoers were eager to see. The film's distributor made clear it was willing to release "The Children's Hour" without a seal.[313] The Production Code Administration was cornered. If it tried to stand firm, such formidable opponents would surely fight back and win. That would weaken the Production Code once again.

The Administration amended the Code to say "In keeping with the culture, the mores, and values of our time, homosexuality and other sexual aberrations may now be treated with care, discretion and

---

[313] Miller, p. 189

restraint."[314] Wyler got to make "**The Children's Hour**" (1961) how he wanted. He insisted he wasn't doing a remake of "These Three," saying, "This time, I have actually filmed Lillian Hellman's play, which we were not able to do twenty-five years ago."[315]

The heroism of Wyler's achievement is tempered by the fact that even the faithful version of "The Children's Hour" is problematic. In his essay on Criterion.com, "Neither Here nor There: The Conflicted Queerness of 'These Three' and 'The Children's Hour,'" Michael Koresky explains the problems better than I could. I'll mention just one thing:

<SPOILER ALERT>

Shirley MacLaine's character admits to her romantic feelings for Audrey Hepburn's character as if confessing to an unpardonable sin. Then she hangs herself. This exemplifies the "bury your gays" trope, where the only cure for queerness is death. It's clearly a terrible message to send to any LGBTQ+ viewer.

</SPOILER ALERT>

The Production Code Administration could still justify giving "The Children's Hour" a seal because its ending "illustrates the horror of such a lifestyle," in the bigoted words it used to justify "Suddenly Last Summer." Still, "The Children's Hour" made viewers feel at least some empathy for a character who felt homosexual love. That love is not subtext; it is spelled out very clearly. That counted as a message-based shock in 1961.

Soon after "The Children's Hour" came the British movie "**Victim**" (1961 in the United Kingdom, 1962 in the United States). It is a so-called "social problem film" that examines the criminalization of homosexuality. Dirk Bogarde plays a successful attorney whose

---

[314] Quoted in Vito Russo, "The Celluloid Closet: Homosexuality in the Movies", p. 121-122
[315] Quoted in Miller, p. 188

career is threatened when his past romance with a man threatens to surface. This makes him vulnerable to blackmail.

Dirk Bogarde, by the way, might sound like a name for a square-jawed, cigar-chomping action star, but he was a lot more interesting than that. He was groomed as a swoon-worthy matinee idol because he was handsome, much the same way Jean Harlow was pushed into being a vamp because she was curvy. It was a bad fit for his personality; dreamboats are supposed to smile a lot, and Bogarde often smiled like it hurt his face to do so.

Bogarde jumped at the chance to star in "Victim," which was a significantly smaller film than his typical fare. He strove to push the movie further into then-controversial ideas: He insisted his character should still be attracted to men, rather than sticking with the script's idea that the affair was a one-time experiment.[316] Later he said "For the first time I was playing my own age. At [his previous studio] Rank, the fixed rule was that I had to look pretty. 'Victim' ended all that nonsense."[317] Bogarde would go on to become an arthouse legend, lending a fascinatingly dark, secretive demeanor to classics like "The Servant" and "Death in Venice."

"Victim" has a similar plot to "Anders als die Andern," the 1919 German film that advocated decriminalization of homosexual relationships. Even more than "Anders als die Andern," "Victim" is as chaste as a movie can be, with no nudity and not even a reference to sex. It's entirely focused on showing in stark, realistic terms how treating gay people like criminals destroys innocent lives. It's not a flawless movie, but it holds up much better than I expected, because it focuses on the drama of the situation without much speechifying or theorizing.

Homosexual activity was illegal in the United Kingdom in 1961, but attitudes were changing. In 1967, the Sexual Offences Act

---

[316] Geoff Mayer and Brian McDonnell, "Encyclopedia of Film Noir", p. 433
[317] Quoted in Aljean Harmetz, "Dirk Bogarde, 78, Matinee Idol Turned Serious Actor, Dies". *New York Times*. May 9, 1999

decriminalized queer sex among adults. "Victim" gets some credit for turning the tide. The primary advocate of the Sexual Offences Act, Conservative politician Lord Arran, wrote Dirk Bogarde to tell him that after "Victim" came out, support for decriminalization of homosexuality rose from 48 to 63 percent.[318]

In 1961, British censors gave "Victim" an X rating, which was defined at the time as "For exhibition when no child under 16 is present." There could be no reason for turning children away from "Victim" besides paranoia that empathizing with a gay person might turn them queer. The board gave some nonsense justifications; for example, they cited a blackmailer in the film who launches a brutal tirade against homosexuality as being too unsympathetic.[319] It's the same both-sides-ism that detractors of "Anders als die Andern" used: In this movie about how gay people are innocent victims of malevolent bigotry, why didn't you make the bigots seem nicer? And in "Faust," why does Satan come across as such a villain?

At least the British Board of Film Censors passed "Victim." In the States, the Production Code Administration refused to grant it a seal. In the Administration's words, the problem was that "Victim" was "an overtly expressed plea for an acceptance of homosexuality, almost to the point of suggesting that it be made socially tolerable."[320] I'm sure it was also easy for the censors to pick on the little British movie that couldn't fight back.

The distributor of "Victim" did not sue. There were enough theaters that would exhibit it without a seal, and it's not like a serious, low-budget, British "social problem film" was destined to be a 20,000-screen blockbuster. Still, it would have been very revealing to see whether the U.S. Supreme Court would have followed through on its

---

[318] Tobias Grey, "Out of the closet, on to the screen: the legacy of 'Victim'". *Financial Times.* July 14, 2017
[319] John Trevelyan, "PG Tips". *Harper's Magazine.* July 2012. p. 17.
[320] Quoted in Kim Luperi, "The Celluloid Closet", Turner Classic Movies, https://www.tcm.com/articles/Programming-Article/021783/the-celluloid-closet/

guarantee of the "freedom to advocate ideas," per the "Lady Chatterley's Lover" decision. A message of marital infidelity being acceptable is one thing, but would the Court have balked at a message suggesting a homosexual relationship might not actually be perverse?

After "The Children's Hour" and other movies, major American movie studios got the message that they could keep pushing the envelope. It was time to attempt a film version of one of the most popular and shocking books of the century.

The novel "Lolita" was the most controversial of its time. Only a disreputable French publisher would put it out in 1955, and the first version was filled with typos. British Customs agents were ordered to seize any copies entering the country.[321] In 1958 it finally found a publisher in the United States and sold like gangbusters.[322]

Hollywood was reluctant to touch "Lolita," but in the end couldn't resist adapting a book that stayed on the *New York Times* bestseller list for 56 weeks.[323] Young Stanley Kubrick took the job. Kubrick had some successes behind him – "The Killing" and "Paths of Glory" were low-budget marvels and "Spartacus" was a huge-budget blockbuster – but he was not yet a director who could do whatever he wanted. For him, getting the necessary financing hinged on keeping the Production Code Administration happy.[324]

Kubrick toned down the content of the novel, hinting at many of the more shocking scenes instead of showing them. He also cast a 14-year-old girl as Lolita instead of a 12-year-old. Fourteen is still of course ridiculously young, but an actress any older would negate the crux of the story. I'm not endorsing pedophilia, but it is what

---

[321] Felicity Capon and Catherine Scott, "Top 20 books they tried to ban". *The Telegraph*, October 20, 2014
[322] "Culture Shock: Flashpoints: Vladimir Nabokov's Lolita", PBS.org: https://www.pbs.org/wgbh/cultureshock/flashpoints/literature/lolita.html
[323] Miller, p. 190
[324] Leff and Simmons, p. 225-226

"Lolita" is all about. If Kubrick had cast, say, a 20-year-old woman and a middle-aged man, it would just be a depiction of most powerful men's second marriages.

The finished film went first to the Production Code Administration and then to the Legion of Decency, both of which ordered cuts here and there. Neither dared ban the film outright. The Production Code Administration's newly broadened rule about "sex perversion" allowed it to give the "**Lolita**" film a seal in early 1962.[325] The Legion of Decency demanded and got veto power over all advertising for the movie. One of its goals was to ensure that the caption "For persons over 18 only" would be on every ad.

This sort of caveat was becoming more common, even though it was not enforceable. Nothing could stop a child from buying a ticket to "Lolita." Recognizing this, religious leaders started insisting that the MPAA start an enforceable ratings system. Many filmmakers, tired of fighting with the Production Code Administration, were warming to the idea.[326] The Legion of Decency and other organizations had made ratings for ages; The Legion not only condemned movies as C but also divided the acceptable ones among A and B. The British Board of Film Censors instituted a movie rating system in 1951. Why not have the Production Code Administration do the same thing?

The MPAA, and thus the Production Code Administration, was dead set against the idea, and not for ideological reasons. When a movie was labeled "For persons over 18 only," it would only play in the downtown theaters. That meant less money, and the MPAA's job was to make money from movies.[327] Exploitation films provided dozens of test cases, catering only to adults and receiving limited returns.

---

[325] Leff and Simmons, p. 241
[326] Leff and Simmons, p. 242
[327] Leff and Simmons, p. 245

But the MPAA was losing its rationalizations for one-size-fits-all censorship. You may remember that before World War II, authorities would cite not only children as needing protection from naughty films; they would also throw illiterates, immigrants, or some other ignominious group of adults into the mix. After World War II, in which both poor and rich boys were killed fighting fascism, such blatant classism became more gauche. It also helped that the GI Bill and postwar prosperity created a huge, educated middle class. Immigration was also at historic lows.[328] There simply weren't as many illiterates and immigrants in the United States to infantilize.

Also, from 1946 to 1962, the world had seen 16 years of brilliant movies catering specifically to grown-ups, from "Bicycle Thieves" to "The Virgin Spring," Ingmar Bergman's brutal film about rape, murder, and revenge. All the arthouse theaters springing up in the United States were helping film be seen as a true art form. Those theaters may have made their money on "And God Created Woman," but they also exposed intellectuals to the likes of Jean-Luc Godard's "Breathless." I haven't even mentioned the French New Wave, which was in full swing by 1962, and was really getting eggheads excited. When intellectuals latch on to a medium, they want it free to be challenging.

Most importantly, most of the country had grown up watching movies. That meant they went through the same change I and many other people go through vis-a-vis film shocks. I talked in the first chapter about how I was very averse to any disturbing content as a kid, but when I became a teenager I started to be thrilled by it. At that point, the emotional overstimulation of those moments would be quickly overcome by waves of relief, as my brain reassured itself that it's all fake. The memories of those moments then end up being more pleasurable than painful. At that point I had developed a

---

[328] "U.S. Immigrant Population and Share over Time, 1850-Present", Migration Policy Institute, https://www.migrationpolicy.org/programs/data-hub/charts/immigrant-population-over-time

stronger psychological and emotional separation between what happens on the screen and what happens in real life.

By the early 1960s, most of the country had gone through some similar process in their youths. People had grown up with movies and thus developed a healthy psychological and emotional distance from their content.

No longer were Grumpy Old Men saying things like "Moving picture! It's absurd, sir. I never saw one in my life and I haven't the slightest curiosity to see one," as Supreme Court justice Edward Douglass White sniffed before watching "Birth of a Nation." Grumpy Old Man Syndrome is always focused on whatever cultural movement didn't exist when the Grumpy Old Men were kids. Almost all of the film-o-phobic Grumpy Old Men had died off by 1962. The new crop of Grumpy Old Men were concentrating their irrational anxieties on rock 'n' roll. Most American adults were not scared of movies, and wanted to see some that addressed grown-up issues.

"Lolita" was a story that grown-up Americans were very interested in; the book kept selling like crazy and libraries couldn't keep copies on the shelves. The movie was also a hit despite mixed reviews. Moviegoers wanted to learn the answer to the question on the movie poster: "How did they ever make a movie of 'Lolita'?" Many critics decried how much the movie had sanitized the book.[329] When people pack theaters for a movie about pedophilia, and critics slam it for being too tame, it's clear that the country is ready for shock content.

Irreverence Overseas

American movies may have been growing up, but European films remained ahead of them. Europeans looked upon American puritanism with bemusement. There's a fun moment in the 1960 Francois Truffaut movie "Shoot the Piano Player" when the

---

[329] Leff and Simmons, p. 244

protagonist sits in bed with a sex worker, who is topless. The protagonist takes the sheet and covers her breasts, joking "This is how you do it in movies." It's a great little throwaway meta gag, lampooning the awkward, unrealistic staging Hollywood films still undertook to avoid showing some parts of the body.

The European films that hit the States did a lot more than show naked breasts, of course. Many showed Americans how to grapple with adult themes in sophisticated, incisive ways.

In 1960, Federico Fellini was well-established as one of the top directors in the world. His films "La Strada" and "Nights of Cabiria" won Oscars for Best Foreign Film in 1957 and 1958, respectively. In 1960 he topped even those with "**La Dolce Vita.**"

"La Dolce Vita" is a series of episodes in the life of a journalist who covers entertainment figures in Rome. He lives a glamorous life of parties and sex, quite different from the struggles of the underclass in Fellini's previous movies, not to mention "Bicycle Thieves" and Roberto Rossellini films. Italy experienced an economic miracle in the 1950s, and neorealism became passe. By the early 1960s, "Bicycle Thieves" director Vittorio De Sica was still making movies about people in poverty, but now his films' dominant messages boiled down to "man, Sophia Loren is hot."

In "La Dolce Vita," Fellini revealed some uneasiness underneath the sudden upsurge in Italian wealth. In depicting the decadence of the new Rome, Fellini gets a little shocking by 1960 standards. One of the movie's parties features a failed attempt at an orgy, abuse of women, and openly gay characters dancing in drag. It was all too much by Production Code Administration standards, but that didn't matter. "La Dolce Vita" was a box-office hit.

It helped that the Legion of Decency was basically on board with "La Dolce Vita." Worried that it was falling behind the times, the Legion was busy revising its ratings. In 1957 and 1963, it created four levels of A movies: A-1 (morally unobjectionable for all), A-2 (morally unobjectionable for adults and adolescents), A-3 (morally unobjectionable for adults), and A-4 (morally unobjectionable for adults with some reservations). "La Dolce Vita" got an A-4.[330]

In Europe, the concern was mostly about how "La Dolce Vita" treated Christianity. The film has one sequence in which children report having seen the face of the Virgin Mary. A media circus ensues, which quickly turns into a farce. The Catholic Church banned "La Dolce Vita" in some countries because it perceived criticisms of the faith. But many European religious authorities felt "La Dolce Vita" affirmed religious faith by showing the emptiness of debauchery and false piety.[331]

In 1960, Luis Buñuel returned to Europe to test the limits of religious tolerance. He had spent the 1950s in Mexico, building an international reputation with a series of artistic and commercial successes. His native Spain owned a paltry film industry and was eager to reclaim him. After the Spanish Civil War ended in 1939, the country had become a right-wing dictatorship, which never creates a good climate for artistic expression. But under American pressure in the late 1950s, the country was beginning to modernize somewhat.[332]

Buñuel's first Spanish film since the 1930s was "**Viridiana**" (1961). In it, a novice nun tries to practice Christian values of charity and generosity and is stymied at every turn. One shot spoofing Leonardo da Vinci's "The Last Supper" is the most overt example of the fun the film has at the expense of Christianity.

"Viridiana" is a lot more than just jabs at Christian idealism. It's a masterpiece of wry cynicism, both in my opinion and that of the Cannes Film Festival, which awarded it the Palme D'Or in 1961. The Spanish government had submitted it to Cannes before almost

---

[330] Ibid
[331] Sova, p. 103
[332] Martín García Óscar, "Soft Power, Modernization, and Security: US Educational Foreign Policy Toward Authoritarian Spain in the Cold War". *History of Education Quarterly*, May 2023, 63 (2): 198–220

anyone had seen it. After Cannes, Vatican officials caught a showing and were scandalized. They launched a campaign against "Viridiana" and threatened Buñuel and the other main contributors with excommunication.[333] When asked for his reaction, Buñuel quipped "I didn't deliberately set out to be blasphemous, but then Pope John XXIII is a better judge of such things than I am."[334]

The Spanish government official who had sent "Viridiana" to Cannes was fired and the movie was banned from the country.[335] The film's negative barely escaped being burned by Spanish authorities.[336] It would not be publicly screened in Spain until 1977. Buñuel returned to Mexico for his next film, "The Exterminating Angel," and spent most of the rest of his career in France.

Pier Paolo Pasolini was another established European filmmaker who had criticisms of modern Christianity. Pasolini was an Italian poet and Marxist intellectual who thrived on depicting the struggles of marginalized people. His films "Accattone" (1961) and "Mamma Roma" (1962) stirred controversy and were banned in some areas for sympathetically portraying sex workers and thieves.

Pasolini's short film "**La ricotta,**" released as part of the 1963 anthology film "Ro.Go.Pa.G.", proved much more shocking to religious authorities. It's the story of a man who works as an extra on a movie set and desperately needs a meal. The film being made within the film is about Jesus' crucifixion, but no one acts with Christian charity to the poor starving man. The ending makes the parallel to Jesus Christ very clear.

The Vatican was not pleased. It understood that the cruel, uncharitable film crew depicted in "La ricotta" represented the

---

[333] "A propósito de Buñuel," 2000 documentary about Buñuel directed by José Luis López-Linares and Javier Rioyo
[334] Quoted in Michael Wood, "Viridiana: The Human Comedy," Criterion.com: https://www.criterion.com/current/posts/423
[335] Ibid
[336] Javier Zurro, "Interview with Pere Portabella", eldiario.es, April 8, 2022

Catholic establishment. This time, public outrage and suppression of the film was not enough. Pasolini was arrested and tried for "contempt of the state religion." He was sentenced to four months' imprisonment but was able to pay a fine instead. Years later, the conviction was overturned.[337]

Pasolini was no stranger to the courtroom. As a queer man in the post-war era, he risked criminal prosecution every time he had sex. (Pasolini's sexuality was complicated – he might not have appreciated being called "gay" – but he definitely preferred male lovers.) He was also very outspoken about his atheism and left-wing politics, which made him lots of powerful enemies. His films became easy targets because they often pushed boundaries in exploring sexuality. Throughout his life, Pasolini underwent 33 trials for "pornography," "foul language," "public disgrace," "obscenity," "contempt of the state," etc. These are the sorts of vague charges that authorities levy when they want to shut someone up. Pasolini was eventually acquitted in almost every case.[338]

Pasolini's next fiction film was a dramatic departure from the irreverent rabble-rousing of "La ricotta." "The Gospel According to St. Matthew" (1964) faithfully adapts the Book of Matthew – much too faithfully, in my opinion. It films exactly what the Bible says with no added dialogue, which I felt made it bizarre and difficult to follow. The Book of Matthew may be one of history's greatest works of the written word, but that doesn't make it a shooting script. Adaptations are supposed to adapt their source material for a different medium. I got the feeling that Pasolini was scared straight after the "La ricotta" prosecution, and wanted to make the most unimpeachable film possible. You can't be arrested for "contempt for state religion" when you just film the Bible.

Granted, this is not what Pasolini himself said about the "The Gospel According to St. Matthew." He dedicated the film to Pope

---

[337] Erminia Passannanti, "La ricotta. Il sacro trasgredito."
[338] Pier Paolo Pasolini and the White Book of Persecutions, Rewriters, https://rewriters.it/pier-paolo-pasolini-e-il-libro-bianco-delle-persecuzioni/

John XXIII and talked about wanting to "consecrate things again"[339] and being an "unbeliever who has a nostalgia for belief."[340] And it remains Pasolini's most beloved film. So maybe it's just me.

I'm probably digressing too much here, especially since "The Gospel According to St. Matthew" is a sort of anti-shock movie, seemingly created with the express purpose of offending no one. The larger point is that after this brief detour into extreme piety, Pasolini would return to political critique and scandalous subject matter throughout the late 1960s and early 1970s. If you've only seen "The Gospel According to St. Matthew," you have a warped view of Pasolini. We'll encounter him again.

(Mostly) Real Content-Based Shocks

Criticism of Catholicism was off the table in Italy, but real animal mutilation was A-OK. The Italian exploitation film "**Mondo Cane**" (1962) strings together shocking (to Westerners) cultural practices from around the world. Some involve nudity and many feature people killing or harming animals. It's a pseudo-documentary, meaning that some scenes are made of genuine documentary footage, while others are staged events passed off as real.

The ostensible point of "Mondo Cane" is to take Western elitism down a peg by making parallels between sexual and violent behavior by Westerners and that of people in Africa, Asia, and the South Pacific. In true exploitation tradition, though, the filmmakers undercut their own message with narration that is condescending at best and blatantly racist at worst. At one point, the smug narrator declares that while Chinese people are "untiring in their studies of endless ways of making money, they are at the same time also known for their physical laziness … Between one snack and

---

[339] Quoted in Luigi Martellini, "Pier Paolo Pasolini; Retrato de un intelectual," pp. 117–118
[340] "Interview with Pier Paolo Pasolini," *Film Culture*, no. 42 (1966), p. 101

another, the Chinese find time to fill their houses with dozens of legitimate and illegitimate children."

"Mondo Cane" might not play well to a contemporary audience, but in 1962 it was a massive international success everywhere -- except the United Kingdom, where it was banned because of the British Board of Film Censors' rule about animal abuse in films.[341] I can conjecture as to why it was popular. Compared to any other exploitation film before it, "Mondo Cane" packs in the most shocks per minute. The people of 1962 had been raised on film and were ready for the increase in intensity. Also, "Mondo Cane" has actual production values, in contrast to its exploitation predecessors. It doesn't look like the sort of shoddy, grainy film you'd have to go to the bad part of town to see.

Well-filmed shocks enabled "Mondo Cane" to penetrate the mainstream more than any exploitation film before it. "Mom and Dad" may have eventually made tons of money, but it did so by plodding year after year through a small circuit of grindhouses and circus-like small-town showings. "Mondo Cane" couldn't play everywhere, but it found plenty of conventional theaters. It was even nominated for the Palme d'Or at Cannes, while one of its songs was nominated for an Oscar. "Mondo Cane" thus represents a landmark for bringing exploitation shocks into mainstream culture.

"Mondo Cane" was so popular that it birthed a subgenre of mondo films, most of which have titles starting with "Mondo." They're all variations of a theme, so we don't need to go into detail on each one. "Mondo Cane 2" compiles unused footage made for the first film, "Women of the World" focuses on belittling and objectifying women, etc. If you get through "Mondo Cane" and want to see more, you have plenty of options. The important point is that throughout the 1960s, moviegoers worldwide were indulging in very

---

[341] The first sequence of "Mondo Cane 2" (1964) talks about the ban, while showing English dogs whose vocal cords have been cut by surgeons who practice vivisection on them.

strong content-based shocks in mondo movies. Those kinds of shocks would soon seep into fiction films.

I've talked about how documentaries (and pseudo-documentaries) could always show things that fiction features couldn't, and for good reason. For every dozen movies that exploit documentary footage as a loophole to elicit sick thrills, there is one masterpiece, like "Night and Fog," that uses shock to express an important truth.

The Iranian film "**The House Is Black**" (1963) is another short documentary that uses shocking imagery for altruistic ends. It opens with narration saying, "On this screen will appear an image of ugliness, a vision of pain that no caring human being should ignore. To cure this ugliness, to aid to ease the pain, and to relieve the victims is the motive behind making this film."

Then you see people living in a leper colony, many of whom have been severely mutilated by the disease. But unlike sex hygiene films that speed through shots of people disfigured by syphilis, "The House Is Black" stays long enough to reveal the humanity of the afflicted. The people despair, but they also thank Allah for creating them, play games, take care of their children, and undergo the treatments that can cure them. "The House Is Black" asks its audience to move beyond the shock they feel at these people's appearances to a position of compassion and a desire to help. Forugh Farrokhzad, a feminist poet who directed only this film, also walked the walk, adopting a child from the leper colony.

"The House Is Black" reached a tiny percentage of the audience enjoyed by "Mondo Cane." But nowadays "The House Is Black" is widely seen, imparting compassion to people across the world. It is also credited with helping launch the Iranian New Wave,[342] which jump-started one of the world's greatest cinematic traditions. Iranian films reveal the true complexities of a nation that Westerners often think of as uniformly villainous. Because Iran is a very religious

---

[342] Eric Henderson, "The House Is Black", SlantMagazine.com. https://www.slantmagazine.com/film/the-house-is-black/

place, it doesn't make shock films, so Iranian cinema won't come up again in this book. But I have to squeeze in plugs for "Close-Up" (1990) and "A Moment of Innocence" (1996), two of my all-time favorite films. Both are filled with warmth and a singular sort of gentle, unflashy meta-humor.

Exploitation Gets Rough

On the heels of "Mondo Cane"'s success, American exploitation filmmakers started looking for a new thrill. Nudie cuties copying Russ Meyer's "The Immoral Mr. Teas" were flagging in popularity. Director Herschell Gordon Lewis remembered how he reacted to seeing "Psycho": that he thought it should have been much gorier.[343]

Lewis' **Blood Feast** (1963) is a huge leap forward in goriness, becoming the first splatter film. Just a few years after "Black Sunday" and "Les yeux sans visage" shocked moviegoers with mere glimpses of blood and guts, "Blood Feast"'s camera lingers on bloody mutilations to a near-farcical extent. As this is a low-budget exploitation movie made before gore effects became professionalized, it looks quite amateurish. But it's still brutal, even by today's standards. The most notorious scene involves the killer cutting out a young woman's tongue. I found it quite disturbing, especially in the context of a 1960s movie.

In the documentary "Herschell Gordon Lewis: The Godfather of Gore" (2010), Lewis reveals himself to be a charming, intelligent fellow who knew exactly what he was doing. His explicit goal was to bring movies into a new realm of shock. He compares "Blood Feast" to Walt Whitman's poetry, and doesn't mean it as a compliment. In his view, both aren't any good, but they're the first of their kind. I would agree about "Blood Feast" at least; I found it to be more like an experiment in the on-screen depiction of violence than anything

---

[343] Jason Zinoman, "Shock Value: How a Few Eccentric Outsiders Gave Us Nightmares, Conquered Hollywood, and Invented Modern Horror," p. 33-34

coherent or enjoyable on any level. But because it broke new ground, it was a big moneymaker, earning $4 million on a $24,000 budget.[344]

Lewis was much prouder of his follow-up splatter film, "**2,000 Maniacs!**" (1964). This one is more obviously satirical. It's about a remote Southern town that lures in Northerners for a violent centennial commemoration of the end of the Civil War. The villains are broad hillbilly caricatures who whoop and holler as they maim and kill people. I was reminded of movies by John Waters, who is a big Herschell Gordon Lewis fan. The broad tone of "2,000 Maniacs!" made it more palatable to me personally. I'd recommend watching it and then deciding if you want to try "Blood Feast."

Not long after the splatter film was established, along came the "roughie," an exploitation subgenre that combined sex and violence. The movie sometimes credited as the first roughie is Russ Meyer's "**Lorna**" (1964). Lorna is dissatisfied with her husband, who is a bad lover and otherwise coded as insufficiently manly. After a nude swim alone, Lorna is sexually assaulted by an escaped convict. Lorna struggles for a while, but soon is overcome by passion and gives in. Then she falls head over heels for the new man, becoming excessively submissive to his macho, domineering treatment.

This idea that sexually assaulting a woman will awaken her sexuality and make her love you is unfortunately not an uncommon trope in old movies. It even shows up in a Jean Renoir film called "Boudu Saved From Drowning." I don't think I'm taking a bold stand when I say that movies should never promote this idea. How many boys have watched movies like "Lorna" and then tried attacking women? How many rapes resulted?

"Lorna" epitomizes toxic masculinity in many other ways as well. In case it wasn't clear, it joins "Child Bride" and "The Birth of a Nation" among movies that cross my personal line. Roger Ebert would give

---

[344] "Blood Feast (1963) - Financial Information", The-Numbers.com, https://www.the-numbers.com/movie/Blood-Feast-(1963)#tab=summary

zero stars to movies that weren't just bad; they were morally abhorrent. Zero stars to "Lorna" from me.

The Maryland censorship board did not have a high opinion of "Lorna" either, and denied it a license to be shown in the state.[345] As the resulting lawsuit wound through the courts, another case effectively killed off all state and local censorship.

In 1964, an exhibitor in Maryland screened a film called "Revenge at Daybreak," aka "Desperate Decision," without having first submitted it to the censorship board. This broke state law. "Revenge at Daybreak" is not a shock film in any way and would have been passed on the nod. The exhibitor was deliberately creating a test case to get the whole concept of state and local censorship before the Supreme Court.[346]

The exhibitor was arrested and convicted, and duly appealed his arrest all the way to the U.S. Supreme Court. The Court ruled in his favor, declaring that it's a violation of free speech to force someone to submit a film to a censorship board before it can be shown publicly. All boards were thus guilty of "prior restraint," suppressing speech before anyone can judge whether it breaks the law. Prior restraint is a bit like arresting someone carrying a diamond and then checking to see if there was a heist in town. There should at least be evidence that a crime has been committed before you can take any legal action.

Therefore, all governmental movie censorship systems were based on unconstitutional practices. After this decision, if a censorship board objected to a film, it was the board's responsibility to sue to suppress it. Justice William O. Douglas, who previously said he wanted to see all films "freed from the censor," put a pin in this historic decision: "Movies are entitled to the same degree and kind

---

[345] de Grazia and Newman, p. 276
[346] de Grazia and Newman, p. 277

of protection under the First Amendment as other forms of expression."[347]

Within a few years of this ruling, most censorship boards disappeared. All governmental bodies were left with was to combat hard-core pornography. Very few filmmakers were in that business at the time. Authorities successfully suppressed art films with strong sexual content, like the 1950 Jean Genet film "Un chant d'amour," but not a lot else.

Remember that the Production Code Administration was created to appease the censorship boards, and then strengthened to placate the Legion of Decency. With the boards effectively neutered, and the Legion voluntarily shrugging off its previous mandate, the Production Code Administration really had little reason to exist.

I'll return to the foundering Production Code Administration later; now I'll begrudgingly finish the story of "roughies." I've spent much of this book giving cheers to movies that pushed the envelope and jeers to the Grumpy Old Male authorities who suppressed them. With free speech triumphing for good in 1964, I now have mixed feelings, because it meant "Lorna" and other roughies could proliferate.

As awful as "Lorna" is, it doesn't involve trapping and beating a woman, which is a hallmark of roughies. The first of this type could be "Body of a Female" (1964), which is most likely a lost film. (I don't think anyone's looking too hard for it.) "**The Defilers**" (1965) is the movie cited as the first true roughie by one source, the documentary "Schlock! The Secret History of American Movies" (2001).

In "The Defilers," two young men spend their lives on the hunt for what they repeatedly call "kicks." This culminates in imprisoning a young woman in a basement to beat and rape her at will. The movie always cuts away before any rape, but there are lots of beatings. It's another zero-star movie, even more foul in my opinion than "Lorna."

---

[347] Quoted in de Grazia and Newman, p. 278-279

I'm torn about whether I should even mention it and give it whatever minute publicity this book will provide.

"The Defilers" is not about BDSM because what it depicts is not consensual. It's just straight sadism. The female characters not only don't get any agency; they don't even get much personality. They are just sex objects on which men take out psychopathic frustrations. I don't think there's anything like "The Defilers" in contemporary cinema, apart from, I assume, the junk in the dark corners of the internet.

Later we'll encounter famous and beloved movies that have even more brutal scenes than what is shown in "The Defilers." But in the later movies, the brutality is framed as being perpetrated by a great evil, and is not meant to be sexually arousing. "The Defilers" and other roughies suggest straight male viewers will be turned on by a woman being assaulted. This demonstrates that what matters is not necessarily the content of a movie, but the perspective the movie takes on that content.

In the mid-1960s, exploitation filmmakers were apparently unconcerned with perspective. They were focused on one-upping each other to keep achieving the next level of shock. It took the character of what drug addicts call "chasing the dragon." After the initial shock wears off, later similar doses have less effect. You have to keep increasing the dose to get the same feeling. After you see enough nudie cuties, you want something stronger, so you try a gore film. Then you get used to gore films and need a new fix. If the movies were well-made, you'd have emotional investment in all the shocks. But cheap thrills attenuate quickly, so you're always on the hunt for a stronger jolt.

In this race to keep upping the shock ante, maybe it was inevitable that someone would try showing rapes and beatings. Sexual violence has always been rampant, before and after the 1960s. I just don't know why putting it on screen proved successful enough to make roughies a subgenre.

I bet roughies appealed to the infantile frustrations of unattractive, unpleasant losers who had been indoctrinated by the sexual revolution into believing they were entitled to sex with beautiful women. When women proved unwilling, they blamed the women and wanted to punish them. This was easier for men than examining their behavior and trying to improve themselves. That's a classic recipe for violent misogyny that is far from unique to the 1960s, though.

In "Schlock! The Secret History of American Movies," film historian Michael Bowen conjectures that because people weren't allowed to see sex in roughies, violence took its place as the "eruptive" physical act permissible. That feels like a poor excuse to me, though I admit I don't really understand how sex and violence get intertwined in people's minds. I may have already wandered too far into a minefield.

Anyway, roughies may have had a brief period of success, but they disappeared in the early 1970s. They are less than a footnote today. "The Defilers" doesn't even have a Wikipedia page. I found it on Amazon Streaming, but it was under the title "The Defilers: Classic Thriller." It was mislabeled as a 2016 release, and its thumbnail image had nothing to do with the movie; it was a clearly recent photograph of a random woman holding a chain. It's a bait-and-switch altogether fitting for a deplorable old exploitation movie that no one wants to see on purpose.

The only roughies anyone watches now are the ones made by exploitation legend Doris Wishman. I have seen two of those, and in each she manages to squeeze in some defiance by the women. They are also just generally very strange movies. Wishman would film the backs of people's heads and then write dialogue to dub in during post-production, so you very seldom see people talking. If for some reason you have to see a roughie, try Wishman's **"Bad Girls Go to Hell"** (1965).

I might be writing more about roughies than anyone wants, including me. I'm wrestling with their existence, in part, because it contradicts a primary theme of this book: that applying freedom of speech to movies is a good thing. This theme is best supported by films like "Birth Control" or "Victim" that espouse political views that were revolutionary when they were made but are now prevalent. I suppose it's also important to at least acknowledge the other end of the spectrum, the movies that shocked because they put forth horrible ideas, by both older and current standards.

It's like freedom of speech in any other realm. If you let anyone say whatever they want in a public forum, you have to accept that the hate groups get to do so too. After the hate groups speak freely, your job as a decent human being is to speak freely in response, contradicting what they say, even louder. The hateful people might then respond with "What happened to free speech?" They never seem to understand that free speech does not mean consequence-free speech. Free speech only means you can't be thrown in jail for what you say. It does not mean you can't be publicly shamed, banned from privately owned organizations, or even fired for what you say.

And granted, there are some things you can be thrown in jail for saying. You can't make terroristic threats, you can't yell "Fire!" in a crowded theater if there isn't a fire, etc. It's complicated, and it's always subject to revisions. But it's the best system we've come up with so far.

Deeper Underground

Let's abandon roughies and dive into the even more underground world of short art films. Kenneth Anger, the director of the 1947 film "Fireworks," kept making provocative shorts. His most celebrated film, "**Scorpio Rising**" (1963), came right at the right time.

The movie follows a real-life biker nicknamed Scorpio and his buddies as they hang out, moon each other, initiate a newbie by spreading mustard on his genitals, etc. Anger also includes clips from a religious movie and plenty of homoerotic undertones. The New York underground/independent film scene founded by Shirley Clarke and others was thriving, and "Scorpio Rising" became a big success there.

When "Scorpio Rising" was screened in Los Angeles, the American Nazi Party launched protests outside the theater because the movie contained desecrations of their flag. No one was too sympathetic, but it did bring the police to the scene. The cops arrested the theater manager for public obscenity and canceled the rest of "Scorpio Rising"'s run.[348]

In court, the prosecutor argued that "Scorpio Rising" contained a "depiction of certain degenerate activity" (i.e., homoeroticism) and that a few frames showed a penis. The case hinged on that last point, even though no one was really sure about it. "I cannot even identify it as a penis by magnification," said one witness on the stand. "I see a blob of something there ... might be a potato."[349] On this sort of ironclad evidence, the theater manager was convicted. The verdict was an obvious attempt to suppress free speech about homosexuality. It clearly went against precedent and the verdict was rapidly overturned by the California Supreme Court.[350]

While "Scorpio Rising" was becoming a cause célèbre in Los Angeles, "**Flaming Creatures**" (1963) was doing the same in New York City. It's a collection of campy scenes enacted mostly by drag performers. Plenty of penises are on display, none of which could be mistaken for potatoes. I have not read that John Waters was inspired by it, but I would not be surprised.

---

[348] R. Serge Denisoff and William D. Romanowski, "Risky Business: Rock in Film", p. 168
[349] Quoted in Whitney Strub, "The Clearly Obscene and the Queerly Obscene: Heteronormativity and Obscenity in Cold War Los Angeles". *American Quarterly*, Vol. 60, No. 2 (Jun., 2008), p. 385
[350] Ibid

"Scorpio Rising" and other underground films were celebrating homoeroticism, but "Flaming Creatures" went beyond them. Susan Sontag was quoted as saying "The truth is that 'Flaming Creatures' is much more about intersexuality than about homosexuality."[351] In an article in *Film Comment*, critic J. Hoberman states it projected "intersexuality, monosexuality, homosexuality, no sexuality, just sexuality."[352]

To me, "Flaming Creatures" feels like a student film made by someone who really wants to shock their classmates. But that was revelatory in 1963, particularly for LGBTQ+ viewers who had never experienced true representation in movies. Again, as a straight man, I may not be the target market, but I'm awed by the courage it takes to make this kind of movie in such a hostile environment.

"Flaming Creatures" was enough of a hit in New York's underground film scene to win an Independent Film Award from *Film Culture*, an avant-garde cinema magazine published by impresarios Jonas and Adolfas Mekas. *Film Culture* planned to show it at a theater known for sexploitation movies, but the theater manager canceled the event after seeing it. Hundreds of people gathered to protest. The resulting publicity brought "Flaming Creatures" mainstream attention.[353]

Mainstream attention meant suppression. A March 1964 screening arranged by Jonas Mekas was busted up by the police, who seized the projection equipment and the prints of both "Flaming Creatures" and an Andy Warhol movie. It was the only copy of the Warhol film, and it's believed to still be somewhere in the New York City police

---

[351] Quoted in J. Hoberman, "Treasures of the Mummy's Tomb: The Lost Films of Jack Smith", *Film Comment*, Vol. 33, No. 6, p. 44
[352] Ibid
[353] Callie Angell, "Batman and Dracula: The Collaborations of Jack Smith and Andy Warhol", *Criticism*. 56 (2), p. 163-164

evidence rooms. The police arrested Mekas, the projectionist, the ticket seller, and the ticket taker for obscenity.[354]

Mekas tried to raise funds for his legal defense through a public showing of the 1950 Jean Genet film "Un chant d'amour." It was an interesting choice because, as you may recall, that movie also showcases lots of penises. Mekas was arrested again. These charges were dismissed on the condition that he not show "Flaming Creatures" until the California courts finished deciding whether "Un chant d'amour" violated obscenity laws.[355] (This is the case I referred to back in the section on "Un chant d'amour.")

A civil rights attorney took on the "Flaming Creatures" case with the intention of getting it before the U.S. Supreme Court. He was no doubt encouraged by the Court's decade-plus of favorable rulings for free speech in films. But "Flaming Creatures" proved too transgressive for the Supreme Court, which dismissed the appeal.[356]

Within the text of the dismissal, the lone sentence "MR. JUSTICE FORTAS would reverse the judgment of the lower court" (i.e., let Mekas and co. go free) got Abe Fortas in trouble when he was later nominated for Chief Justice. Fortas' liberal leanings made him an enemy of Senator Strom Thurmond. To smear Fortas, Thurmond screened "Flaming Creatures" and other underground films in the Senate chambers after hours and called it the "Abe Fortas Film Festival."[357] It proved to be one of the reasons Fortas' nomination failed.

"Flaming Creatures" kept causing trouble on college campuses throughout the 1960s. Students would screen it, the police would

---

[354] Callie Angell, "Batman and Dracula: The Collaborations of Jack Smith and Andy Warhol", *Criticism*. 56 (2), p. 165
[355] Lawrence Witchel and Ernest Leogrande, "The Gamey Tastemakers". *New York Daily News*. June 11, 1967, p. 25-26
[356] *Jacobs v. New York*, 388 U.S. 431 (U.S. 1967),
[357] J. Hoberman, "Treasures of the Mummy's Tomb: The Lost Films of Jack Smith", *Film*, Vol. 33, No. 6, p. 46

raid the venue and confiscate the print, and things would sometimes get violent. "Flaming Creatures" was the "L'Age d'Or" of its time, with the big difference that in the 1960s there were more people fighting for the right to watch shocking films.

Meanwhile, back in Europe, an avant-garde art movement devoted itself to exploring shock. The Viennese Actionists staged proto-performance-art rituals that mixed together sexual acts, animal blood, urine, feces, and anything else that could elicit disgust. Actionists often ended up in jail for their performances.

Experimental filmmaker Kurt Kren took footage of the "Actions" and made shorts out of them. One you can find on YouTube is called "**Mama and Papa**" (1964). It's four minutes of a naked woman being covered in dirt, paint, and other substances while a man kisses her and performs other sexual acts, not including intercourse.

"Mama and Papa" has no sound and is composed of hundreds of quick cuts that jumble the performance chronologically. This makes the film feel more like a work of art itself than mere documentary footage, though I personally would have just preferred the documentary footage. I'm not sure whether the manic editing makes for a more shocking experience or less.

I'm including the Actionists in this book not because I'm convinced they had a big influence on film history. They do show up in one movie I'll cover later, but I'm not aware of any other direct links. I mention them because they embody the spirit of shock for shock's sake that was pervading the artistic culture.

In previous film history, the only analogs to the Actionist movies are the early Buñuel movies and the sequences in exploitation films like "Mom and Dad" that existed mainly to make people gasp and retch. The latter were disreputable and low-class, of course, while the Actionists were avant-garde art. In the mid-1960s, even smarty-pants artsy people were discovering that it's kinda fun to be grossed out.

Nudity Comes to Hollywood

As underground movies and avant-garde art rapidly got more graphic, Hollywood was changing much more slowly. Its next frontier, predictably, was more female nudity.

It had become quite normal to put women's bodies on display since "Niagara" showed how it's done in 1953. The huge-budget epic "Cleopatra" (1963) forces Elizabeth Taylor into an array of poses that seem meticulously choreographed to reveal every inch of her body except the strictly forbidden areas: nipples, genitalia, and most of the buttocks. Movies starring Marilyn Monroe and Jayne Mansfield relied on the same contrivances.

Mansfield was the first to break through with toplessness in **"Promises ... Promises"** (1963). Apart from the shots of nudity, the movie is a knock-off of her comedies "The Girl Can't Help It" (1956) and "Will Success Spoil Rock Hunter?" (1957). "Promises ... Promises" has such a goofy tone, so thoroughly "1950s" in almost every way, that the nude scenes seemed oddly discordant to me. It felt as if they were cut in from a different movie made much later. They certainly were not necessary for the plot.

That also made the scenes easy to cut out, which some jurisdictions insisted on. Many areas of the United States still banned nudity on screen and had no exploitation theaters. "Promises ... Promises" was a low-budget independent movie outside the purview of the Production Code Administration, but it was still no nudie cutie. Nudity makes up a few minutes of runtime at most. A censored version would still constitute a film.

"Promises ... Promises" was really more of a marketing scheme than a film. It was heavily promoted by *Playboy* magazine, which also published some behind-the-scenes nudes. The cross-promotion made it a hit. The movie was banned in Cleveland, but that was a minor blow. "Promises ... Promises"'s producers didn't bother seeking a Production Code seal but still found enough screens to make a sizable profit.

The next major American film to have female toplessness could not be more different than "Promises ... Promises." **"The Pawnbroker"** (1964) is a very serious drama about a Holocaust survivor who runs a pawn shop in New York City. Rod Steiger gives a brilliant Method performance as the main character. The director, Sidney Lumet, had established himself as a superior adapter of plays into film, especially with "12 Angry Men" (1957) and "Long Day's Journey Into Night" (1962).

"The Pawnbroker" was based on a book, but to me it had the feeling of the many movies adapted from plays in the 1950s and 1960s: naturalistic acting, few settings, complex characters you don't normally see in movies, etc. It's the type of film you would expect to earn several Oscar nominations, but not sweep the awards.

As the first American film with non-documentary scenes in a Nazi concentration camp, "The Pawnbroker" boldly ventured into very powerful, very sensitive territory. Many people alive in 1964 had lived through the horrors. Anything less than the most deft handling of the story and character would spell disaster. "The Pawnbroker" premiered at the Berlin Film Festival and received an extended ovation. Rod Steiger won the festival's Best Actor prize.[358]

Throughout the film, the titular pawnbroker maintains a facade of emotional detachment. But his defenses break down when he sees something that floods his mind with a traumatic memory. At one point he sees a woman's breasts, which makes him flash back to seeing his wife at a concentration camp, in the bed of a Nazi, about to be raped. It's a powerful and pivotal scene.

In stark contrast to "Promises ... Promises," no sane person could watch "The Pawnbroker" and conclude that the nudity is gratuitous

---

[358] Mark Harris, "Pictures at a Revolution: Five Movies and the Birth of the New Hollywood", p. 175

titillation. It still got a C from the Legion of Decency, which stated that the film was "not in itself obscene, but because the Legion has a principle according to which nudity, for whatever reason, will not be accepted in motion picture treatment – and this for the common good."[359]

Allied Artists proved to be the only distributor willing to take on "The Pawnbroker," and would not release it without a Production Code seal. The Production Code Administration rejected the film for being "unacceptably sex suggestive and lustful," both because of the bare breasts and another scene of a couple in bed. The producers of "The Pawnbroker" appealed the decision to the MPAA appeals board.[360]

Allied Artists changed their tune and threatened to release "The Pawnbroker" without a seal, if need be. The New York censorship board, the nation's most powerful, licensed the film without any cuts. These developments put pressure on the MPAA to overturn the Production Code Administration's decision. After a vigorous debate, the appeals board approved "The Pawnbroker" for a seal.

But the board made it clear it wasn't going to roll over without a few conditions: The producers had to reduce some offending scenes and keep any mention of nudity out of advertising. The board declared that this was a special exception to the rules, and should not set a precedent.[361]

Of course, that was a ridiculous hope, and "The Pawnbroker" did set a precedent that nudity can be used in artistic ways in films. There was no immediate flood of similar films, but in a few years there would be.

---

[359] Quoted in Leff and Simmons, p. 249
[360] Leonard J. Leff, "Hollywood and the Holocaust: Remembering The Pawnbroker", *American Jewish History*, Vol. 84, No. 4, SPECIAL ISSUE: Defining Jewish Identity in America, Part One (December 1996), p 369
[361] Leff, p. 370

"The Pawnbroker" also marked the end of the Legion of Decency's strict approach. The organization got so much flak for giving the movie a C that it began relaxing its rating system.[362] It would never again be as doctrinaire about minor offenses like flashes of nudity in otherwise exemplary films.

Beyond depiction of nudity, "The Pawnbroker" was also a landmark in the expression of Jewish identity, according to my main source for this segment, Leonard J. Leff's article "Hollywood and the Holocaust: Remembering 'The Pawnbroker'" from the journal *American Jewish History*. Leff reveals that, in the 1950s, narratives that came from distinctly Jewish sources were scrubbed of their "Jewishness" to make them more "universal." When "The Diary of Anne Frank" was adapted for the stage, its producer declared "The fact in this play the symbols of persecution and oppression are Jews is incidental." The play and the 1959 film that followed "touched on the war but tiptoed around the Holocaust," in Leff's words.

In the 1950s, Hollywood didn't want to tell any stories that didn't speak directly to Christian white people. When "The Pawnbroker" novel was being shopped around Hollywood, producers wanted the main character made into a gentile and all references to the Holocaust removed.[363] I don't think you need me to tell you that that would have cut the heart out of the film. But those producers were out of touch; Leff notes that "both the 'general American' and the 'minority' audience of the 1960s were more curious about others' heritage and history." "The Pawnbroker" deserves credit for being unabashedly about the experience of a minority group, in a way that we take for granted today.

Censor Me, Stupid

For several years, Billy Wilder had refused to consult with the Production Code Administration on screenplays or anything else

---

[362] Miller, p. 199
[363] Leff and Simmons, p. 256

during production. He would just hand the Administration finished films and let it tangle with the Legion of Decency and local censors. The results were movies that bent Code rules but scored big, such as "Some Like it Hot" in 1959 and "The Apartment" in 1960.[364]

Other directors took notice and also shut out the Production Code Administration until the money was spent and the film was done. This made Production Code Administration leader Geoffrey Shurlock miserable. His bosses, the studio heads, were only too willing to make Shurlock's job harder if it meant Wilder was free to crank out profitable hits. Shurlock approved Wilder's saucy 1964 movie "**Kiss Me, Stupid**" knowing it would cause a fuss. He calculated that it would "precipitate a crisis" that would lead to either a revision of the Code or tougher enforcement during film production.[365]

"Kiss Me, Stupid" is a light farce that has no nudity but smiles on extramarital sex. The Legion of Decency was not amused and slapped it with a C rating, the first for a Hollywood film since "Baby Doll." ("The Pawnbroker" was released later that year.) Reviews were negative, and not just because of the off-screen sexual couplings. It also wasn't deemed very funny. Box office was disappointing.[366]

Billy Wilder lost this round, but Geoffrey Shurlock didn't exactly come out victorious. "Kiss Me, Stupid" didn't precipitate the crisis he wanted. It was only naughty enough to cause some minor dissension. And because it didn't last long in theaters, everyone quickly forgot about it. Wilder may have come out a bit chastened, but the Code kept creaking along. Both sides wanted change, but "Kiss Me, Stupid" was the wrong catalyst.

---

[364] Miller, p. 194
[365] Miller, p. 194-195
[366] Miller, p. 195

Sweden on the Cutting Edge

After "Summer with Monika," Ingmar Bergman directed a string of international successes – "Smiles of a Summer Night," "The Seventh Seal," "Wild Strawberries," "The Virgin Spring" – that established him as one of the world's most important directors. In the early 1960s, he put out three especially dark films that some people insist make up a sort of thematic trilogy: "Through a Glass Darkly," "Winter Light," and "**The Silence**" (1963).

This pseudo-trilogy gets progressively gloomier, with "The Silence" being so restrained and plotless that I wasn't sure what to make of it. One prevalent interpretation is that the title refers to the gnawing void left when you stop believing in God, though I didn't catch that personally. Regardless, it's not an easy watch. Bergman later recounted that before it was released, he told a producer "You might as well realize, this isn't a film that will have people storming the theaters."[367]

"The Silence" was a big hit across the world. This surprised Bergman and probably not many other people who saw it, as the movie features a lot of nudity and the most explicit sex scene in any non-pornographic feature film up to that time, as far as I know. I don't know what it says about Bergman that he was blissfully unaware that this content would bring in lookie-loos.

Maybe it was just a Swedish thing, as the Swedish censorship board passed "The Silence" without any cuts. Then again, Swedish censors would have been even more scared to go against Bergman than American ones would have been about crossing swords with Alfred Hitchcock or William Wyler. There are other great Swedish film directors, but Bergman is the alpha and omega. The 2024 version of They Shoot Pictures, Don't They?'s top 1000 movies of

---

[367] Quoted in Jonas Simas, Stig Björkman, and Torsten Manns, "Bergman om Bergman", p. 195

all time contains 14 films directed by Ingmar Bergman and 5 from all the other Swedish directors in history combined.

And Sweden may have been the world's most progressive country in 1963, but "The Silence" still caused a lot of controversy there. In plenty of other countries the sex and nudity was cut down, but not all.[368] Once again, an arty film made by a star director was able to push the boundaries of acceptable content. In his book "Swedish Sensationsfilms: A Clandestine History of Sex, Thrillers, and Kicker Cinema," Daniel Ekeroth wrote:

> "'Tystnaden' ['The Silence'] is the production, and marks the exact moment, when sex and nudity became normal in Swedish film. If an internationally acknowledged director like Ingmar Bergman could portray sex in such an explicit way, the last border had been crossed. Hordes of less serious filmmakers immediately abandoned all remaining inhibition about depicting whatever crazed and depraved ideas they thought would attract and scandalize a paying audience."[369]

For example, there was "**491**" (1964). This story of a group of young criminals contains several rapes, including one involving bestiality. The Swedish censorship board drew the line. It insisted that the movie be recut so that the rapes are suggested instead of shown. When the censored version of "491" was imported to the United States, it was seized by U.S. Customs agents and a federal court adjudicated it as obscene. Predictably, the biggest sticking point for American authorities was nudity and not rape. On appeal, the conviction was overturned and "491" was deemed "constitutionally protected and not obscene."[370]

---

[368] Jerry **Vermilye**, "Ingmar Bergman: His Life and Films", p. 28
[369] Daniel Ekeroth, "SWEDISH SENSATIONSFILMS: A Clandestine History of Sex, Thrillers, and Kicker Cinema",
[370] Sova, p. 124-125

To this day "491" is still banned in the United Kingdom.[371] I'm sure that if there were enough public interest, they would review it and pass it. There is no graphic content and almost all of the horrors are off-camera. While "491" is a serious drama and not an exploitation film, I doubt many people would really clamor to see it. I thought it was competent but not essential.

The films of Mai Zetterling, on the other hand, should be better known, if you ask me. Her debut fiction feature "**Loving Couples**" (1964) intertwines several stories by feminist author Agnes von Krusen. The film doesn't shy away from homosexuality, blasphemy, and childbirth in telling authentic-feeling stories about women in the 1910s. It's the rare women-centered film from the days before the women's liberation movement. As such, it was often dismissed at the time by male critics but plays well today.

In 1966, Ingmar Bergman decided to be much more blatant with his shocks. The opening sequence of "**Persona**" feels to me like intentional provocation, almost as a prank on the audience. It speeds through all the bases of shock cinema: bloody violence, animal mutilation, sacrilege, and so-called "graphic" nudity. It's like a compressed version of "Un chien andalou," the 1929 Luis Buñuel/Salvador Dali surrealist short.

Then "Persona" settles into an odd, haunting story of two women interacting at a remote retreat – at least, that's one theory of what it's about. "Persona" is as important to film history as it is ambiguous and complex. It's known among film scholars to be the second-most analyzed film ever, after "Citizen Kane." I doubt I'll be able to add anything to the discussion, so I'll leave it there. See it if you haven't already.

The same year, Mai Zetterling's second feature film, "**Night Games**" (1966), caused a firestorm at the Venice Film Festival. It was deemed too provocative to show publicly, and was only seen by

---

[371] "491". BBFC.co.uk: https://www.bbfc.co.uk/release/491-q29sbgvjdglvbjpwwc0ynjy4ndy

festival jurors at a private screening. One juror, Shirley Temple (38 years old at the time, in case you were wondering), was especially disturbed. Later, when she learned "Night Games" would be part of the San Francisco International Film Festival, she resigned her positions as director and program chair.[372]

Temple called "Night Games" "pornography for profit,"[373] which was either meant hyperbolically or revealed how little she knew about pornography. There is certainly some disturbing sexual content of an incestual nature, but it's not presented erotically. "Night Games" is a pretty Freudian movie, perhaps a bit overly so, but I found it to be an interesting portrayal of a wounded man trying to move past a troubled childhood.

Blasphemy! (Probably!)

The biggest European movie controversy of the mid-1960s arose over a film that had no incestual themes or content-based shocks. **"The Nun"** is the story of a woman whose family pushes her into a convent against her will. She then suffers a series of abuses by an uncaring and repressive establishment.

"The Nun" is no sleazy nunsploitation film. It's based on a novel by Enlightenment philosopher Denis Diderot and directed by the serious French New Wave auteur Jacques Rivette. I found it to be a realistic, austere portrayal of a woman forced into a life she hates. There is no nudity, and it has only sly allusions to lesbianism.

The mere news that Diderot's novel was being filmed caused religious authorities to panic in 1965. Letters of protest poured into the French Ministry of Information. Rivette struggled to find

---

[372] Bosley Crowther, "'Night Games' on View at Festival Theater:Mai Zetterling's Movie a Deliberate Shocker", *The New York Times*, December 20, 1966
[373] Quoted in "Shirley Temple - obituary", *The Telegraph*, February 11, 2014

churches that would allow him to film inside.[374] The Ministry of Information demanded and got a number of cuts. Then it banned "The Nun" anyway in 1966, insisting it would incite violence if released. This only heightened public interest, which was stoked further by a "Free 'The Nun'" speaking tour by Rivette and fellow French New Wave director Claude Chabrol.[375]

When "The Nun" finally hit theaters in 1967, audiences were reportedly disappointed to find most of the salacious material of Diderot's novel absent from the film.[376] The whole mess served to make the Ministry of Information look ridiculous. It had taken its big stand on a rather slow and chaste period drama while the floodgates were opening to genuinely scandalous film content throughout the world.

What About Japan?

It's strange that a book about shock movies hasn't mentioned Japan yet. Nowadays, Japan is probably the nation that produces the most shocking films per capita. Before the 1960s, though, it was busy with sober artistic triumphs directed by Akira Kurosawa, Kenji Mizoguchi, Yasujirō Ozu, etc. I'm sure many of those movies could've broken Production Code rules, but that's true of probably half of films made overseas in the 1950s.

Things got more clearly transgressive in the Japanese New Wave of the 1960s. As in Europe, female nudity became relatively common. Director Shohei Imamura's films stood out as especially lurid; they were treated like soft-core exploitation within Japan.[377] But his 1966

---

[374] Benoit Pavan, "The day Jacques Rivette came face to face with censorship," https://www.festival-cannes.com/en/2018/the-day-jacques-rivette-came-face-to-face-with-censorship/
[375] Thomas Delapa, "'The Nun' Review," *Cinéaste*, Vol. 44, No. 4 (Fall 2019), p. 60-62
[376] Ibid
[377] J. Hoberman, "The Pornographers," Criterion.com, Aug 4, 2003: https://www.criterion.com/current/posts/294-the-pornographers

film "**The Pornographers**" is less concerned with gratuitous nudity than it is with the message-based shocks of people talking about taboo sexual arrangements. "The Pornographers" is a black comedy that lampoons sexual obsessions, not an exploitation film. Along with the aforementioned Swedish movies, "The Pornographers" was ahead of the curve in intelligently exploring unconventional sexuality.

Up from the Underground

In the United States, unconventional sexuality was confined to the New York underground film scene that spawned "Flaming Creatures." The scene got a bit more notice in 1966 thanks to Andy Warhol's worldwide fame. He made dozens of films in the mid-1960s which tended to be heavy on concept but simple in execution.

Among many other labels, Warhol was a conceptual artist. Conceptual art presumes that you'll go beyond merely enjoying how a piece looks, that you'll want to pontificate on the ideas behind it too. For Warhol, it was about the concept behind painting a Campbell's soup can and putting it in a museum, not just about the beauty of the painting itself. You can give a mass-produced object the same degree of artistic analysis that you give a Monet.

Warhol's film efforts came from a similar place. The concept behind "Empire" (1964), which is just one static eight-hour-long shot of the Empire State Building, is to observe the building the way you would observe the soup can. Whether you can really observe one building for eight straight hours and get something out of it I don't know; I have not tried and I don't intend to. I can appreciate slowcore films – I've seen all seven hours and 19 minutes of the Bela Tarr film "Sátántangó," which only has around 150 shots (for comparison, your average 90-minute movie will contain about 1,000 shots) – but I have my limits.

I have seen the Warhol movie that was a relative hit, "**Chelsea Girls**" (1966), and did not find it easy to get through. The concept behind it was to film scenes of Warhol's friends improvising and then show two scenes simultaneously, side by side. You would only hear audio from one of the scenes at a time. When a scene on one side ends, another follows. Every showing would feature a different arrangement of these scenes and their audio.

To show "Chelsea Girls" in most theaters, Warhol got his friend Paul Morrissey to choose the best scenes and put them in the most engaging possible arrangement. Whatever entertainment value the movie has is due to Morrissey's work and some strong shock content, such as full-frontal male nudity and intravenous drug use. I don't recommend "Chelsea Girls" necessarily, but it deserves mention for bringing 1960s underground film and its attendant shocks to a wider audience.

The Spirit of '66

What we think of as "the spirit of the '60s": protests, hippies, sex, drugs, rock 'n' roll, etc., finally hit movie screens in 1966. As Peter Biskind writes in "Easy Riders, Raging Bulls," "Because movies are expensive and time-consuming to make, Hollywood is always the last to know, the slowest to respond, and in those years it was at least half a decade behind the other popular arts."[378]

The 1966 British film "**Blow-Up**" is an iconic filmic depiction of the 1960s, both good and (in my opinion) bad. The first half of the film follows fashion photographer Thomas as he tools around London and abuses people of lower status. I found all this to be a slog; my repulsion for the supremely arrogant Thomas and his artistic pretensions overwhelmed all other concerns. It's unclear to me whether he's meant to be a hero or an anti-hero. Many men of the time found his persona and lifestyle alluring.

---

[378] Peter Biskind, "Easy Riders, Raging Bulls," p. 14

The movie is often cited as controversial because of one scene with explicit nudity. In it, two women flirt with Thomas to try to get work as models. He rudely ignores them until he attacks them, which perfectly sums up his personality. This scene is often described as an orgy but looked more like sexual assault to me.

"Blow-Up" provides an early example of a problem I have with how film opened up to shock content in the late 1960s and 1970s. For the most part, it was a welcome change. Filmmakers were finally able to fully address adult themes in realistic ways. They could ditch the obvious contrivances that kept the censors happy, such as bedsheets carefully situated to cover breasts and the false endings that upheld "compensating moral values."

But relieving restrictions also led immediately to movies where we are meant to identify with misogynistic, self-pitying, over-privileged white men. A comparison to roughies is unfair – "Blow-Up" is several leagues above "The Defilers" – but a strain of sociopathic male entitlement runs through it all.

My distaste for "Blow-Up" is far from universal, as it's widely considered one of the best movies in history. Even I got something from the second half, when it finally discovers a plot.

Like most foreign films, "Blow-Up" didn't bother seeking a Production Code seal. The Legion of Decency condemned it. None of that mattered, and it was a big hit in the States and elsewhere. This was a surprise even to its distributor, which had planned to relegate it to the art-house circuit.[379] "Blow-Up" provided one of the final nails in the coffin of the American censorship system.

Roger Corman and American International Pictures jumped on the sociopathic, entitled white male bandwagon. Corman had already churned out dozens of independent movies for teens without ever getting too controversial. In 1966, he and young film geek Peter Bogdanovich decided to go bolder by gathering stories from the

---

[379] Miller, p. 205

Hells [sic] Angels biker gang and adding them to a boilerplate script to make "**The Wild Angels**."

In it, the Wild Angels gang parties and brawls while covered in swastikas and other Nazi symbols – so you have to assume they are either genocidal bigots or such childish provocateurs that they are willing to trivialize history's greatest horror just to look tough. One gang member is injured and eventually dies. The rest of the movie is devoted mostly to the grief felt by the leader of the gang. Relegated to a sideshow, at best, is the grief felt by the dead man's girlfriend.

<SPOILER ALERT>

Specifically, the gang leader expresses his grief by abusing his own girlfriend and having sex with someone else right in front of her. All this is happening while his gang knocks out an innocent preacher and trashes a church for no reason except that it's all too square for their tastes.

How does the dead man's girlfriend grieve? She doesn't get much of a chance, because during her boyfriend's funeral, gang members pin her down and rape her repeatedly in the church. If "The Wild Angels" had an ounce of humanity in it, the story would then center on that horrific act and its aftermath. Instead, the rest is about the gang leader honoring his fallen friend with a stupid self-sacrifice. We're supposed to feel for this psychopath and forget about the gang rape. My reaction was (and there's no better way to say it) "Fuck this guy and fuck this movie."

</SPOILER ALERT>

Another problem with "The Wild Angels" is that the swastika-covered biker gang's pointless mayhem is framed as being in the name of "freedom." Mind you, this was 1966, when the civil rights movement was at the crest of an epic struggle to gain freedom for people who were actually oppressed. The American women's liberation movement was underway, and soon large campaigns for

LGBTQ+ people and American Indians would launch. In an era filled with genuine freedom movements, the gang leader of "The Wild Angels" articulates his rallying cry:

> "We wanna be free! We wanna be free to do what we wanna do. We wanna be free to ride! We wanna be free to ride our machines without being hassled by The Man. And we wanna get loaded. And we wanna have a good time."

It's not exactly Dr. Martin Luther King Jr.'s "Letter from Birmingham Jail." That's an unfair comparison, of course; no one is calling "The Wild Angels" a thesis for a reform movement. But I think the movie does illustrate how sociopathic, entitled white men exploited the revolutionary spirit of the time. Granted, some white men fought on behalf of genuine causes, like the Vietnam War. But the sociopathic ones rebelled for the freedom to get loaded and abuse women and squares.

"The Wild Angels" writer Peter Bogdanovich would later criticize a primary manifestation of sociopathic, entitled male "freedom": the sexual revolution. In his book "The Killing of the Unicorn," he takes on the main propaganda arm of the sexual revolution, *Playboy*. The magazine billed itself as freeing everyone from puritanism, says Bogdanovich, but it really was just about making it easier for guys to get laid. *Playboy* told women they should be sexually liberated, but then pushed them to fulfill submissive roles that catered to male desires. The culture it created resulted in "myriad cases of manic depression, anorexia, and suicides of women trying to make these visions real."[380]

Bogdanovich spoke from experience, as he was a regular at the *Playboy* mansion in the 1970s. He experienced the dark underbelly of sociopathic male sexual entitlement first-hand when the *Playboy* Playmate he fell in love with, Dorothy Stratten, was murdered by a jealous ex-boyfriend.

---

[380] Peter Bogdanovich, "The Killing of the Unicorn," p. 176

Even before that tragedy, Bogdanovich's career was hurt by his own libertinism. After achieving his dream of becoming a successful director, he ditched his better half (and I do mean *better*) Polly Platt for pretty young starlet Cybill Shepherd. Platt was Bogdanovich's close collaborator, and after they stopped working together, he stopped making good movies. She went on to be instrumental in many more great films, from "Broadcast News" to Wes Anderson's debut, "Bottle Rocket." In a more just world, Polly Platt would have been the celebrated director and Bogdanovich would have been the support system. Listen to episodes 160-169 of Karina Longworth's podcast *You Must Remember This* for more about Platt.

Anyway, I guess I have to get back to "The Wild Angels." Whatever the movie's appeal, it certainly did tap into something. It was the most financially successful low-budget film to that point, earning $15.5 million on a budget of $360,000.[381] A legion of brutal biker films followed, almost all of which involved sexual assault.

With foreign and independent movies making lots of money from shocks, Hollywood knew it had to start following suit. But it couldn't alienate families, who still bought tickets to safe movies. The MPAA remained steadfastly opposed to dividing its audience with a rating system.

Instead, in the wake of "The Pawnbroker," the MPAA was considering another overhaul to the Production Code. They wanted something "more in line with present-day thinking."[382] This was no easy task; "present-day thinking" was all over the place in 1966. Most of the country was as conservative as ever, but young people were busy exploring LSD, eastern mysticism, sexual freedom, and just about anything else you can imagine. Hollywood was losing the young adults who had plenty of time and disposable income for movies. They were going to art films like "Blow-Up" and exploitation

---

[381] "The Wild Angels, Box Office Information". The Numbers website, https://www.the-numbers.com/movie/Wild-Angels-The
[382] Quoted in Leff and Simmons, p. 260

movies like "The Wild Angels" because there was so little in the mainstream that spoke to them.

As before, a big spark for change came from Hollywood trying to adapt a hit Broadway play. When it opened in 1962, Edward Albee's "Who's Afraid of Virginia Woolf?" scandalized theater audiences with utterances of "goddamn," "screw you," "hump the hostess," and other mild expletives. It was a Broadway smash, but everyone thought it was too dirty to ever become a movie.[383]

Warner Brothers decided to give it a try in 1965. It signed on actors guaranteed to gin up excitement: married couple Elizabeth Taylor and Richard Burton. Just a few years before, they made headlines for having an affair during the legendarily chaotic production of "Cleopatra." Taylor and Burton pushed Warner Brothers to hire top theater director Mike Nichols for his first film.

The Production Code Administration promised to deny a seal if they left in all the bad words. Warner Brothers played ball for a while, but Nichols insisted on keeping the dialogue intact. He went to the media with his concerns that the Production Code Administration would screw up a story that had already won the Tony Award for Best Play.[384] It was another open defiance of the Production Code of the type that filmmakers made regularly in the Pre-Code Era.

The final cut of **"Who's Afraid of Virginia Woolf?"** was rejected for a seal, as promised. Warner Brothers appealed to the MPAA, and insisted that anyone under 18 should be prevented from seeing it. This was a first; studios do not tend to propose that theaters turn sectors of the audience away from their movies. The idea was to force the MPAA into adopting a rating system.[385]

---

[383] Nick Clooney, "The Movies That Changed Us: Reflections on the Screen", p. 81-82
[384] Leff and Simmons, p. 249-256
[385] Leff and Simmons, p. 261

In this, Warner Brothers had an ally in the Legion of Decency, which had renamed itself the National Catholic Office for Motion Pictures, or NCOMP (opening up its members to the nickname NCOMPoops). Chastened by its mistake with "The Pawnbroker," NCOMP was now more focused on pushing for an MPAA rating system similar to their own than in launching public battles over individual films. As the MPAA appeal for it was being considered, "Who's Afraid of Virginia Woolf?" was narrowly approved by NCOMP with an A-4 rating (morally unobjectionable for adults, with reservations). NCOMP did not request any cuts.[386]

Even beyond a lack of support from the Catholics, the MPAA appeals board had the deck stacked against them with "Who's Afraid of Virginia Woolf?" Appeals board members recognized that this was an artistic triumph that would probably earn lots of Oscar nominations. With big, controversial stars, it would likely be a box-office hit.[387] Warner Brothers was an MPAA charter member and was counting on both acclaim and returns, as it had invested a ton of money in the movie. If a film on this scale didn't get a seal, this could prove the tipping point into making the Production Code Administration truly irrelevant.

The MPAA had just hired a new president, Jack Valenti. He convinced the appeals board to make a special exception for "Who's Afraid of Virginia Woolf?" As they had with "The Pawnbroker," the MPAA issued a statement saying that this was a one-time thing, that "[t]his Exemption [sic] means exactly that – approval of material in a specific, important film which would not be approved for a film of lesser quality, or a film determined to exploit language for language's sake."[388]

Most importantly for the future, the MPAA gave the Production Code Administration the power to label a movie "Suggested for Mature

---

[386] Leff and Simmons, p. 263
[387] Leff and Simmons, p. 266
[388] Quoted in Miller, p. 203

Audiences."[389] The label served as a signal to parents that this might not be one for the kids. It was essentially an oversimplified, half-hearted rating system, but it opened the door for more adult-oriented content.

"Who's Afraid of Virginia Woolf?" would prove a good test case of the new label. It became the third-highest grosser of 1966[390] and garnered 13 Academy Award nominations. Not every theater could resist the temptation to sell tickets to unaccompanied children, though.[391] The vague "Suggested for Mature Audiences" label wasn't made to last.

New Hollywood, New Exploitation

In 1967, "**Bonnie and Clyde**" was the mainstream film "suggested for mature audiences" that shocked the country. Its writers originally conceived it as a French New Wave-style crime film, with "a more complex morality, more ambiguous characters, more sophisticated relationships"[392] than seen in Hollywood movies. After Jean-Luc Godard and Francois Truffaut declined offers to direct, Warren Beatty expressed interest in producing it.[393]

The "complex morality" of "Bonnie and Clyde" was that of the gangster film, which had so disturbed people in the early 1930s that the entire genre was banned. The attractive young protagonists are criminals and the bad guys are police and other members of the establishment. "Bonnie and Clyde"'s script would have been shot down at conception if anyone really wanted to enforce the Production Code in 1967.

In addition, producer/star Beatty and director Arthur Penn made "Bonnie and Clyde" the most violent Hollywood movie to date. They

---

[389] Ibid
[390] Joel Waldo Finler. "The Hollywood Story". p. 358–359
[391] Leff and Simmons, p. 271
[392] Biskind, p. 27
[393] Ibid

decided that the "bullets should hurt not only the characters, but the audience as well."[394] One climactic gunshot to the head was meant to evoke John F. Kennedy's assassination, which had traumatized the country just four years before.[395] The film's studio, Warner Brothers, was disgusted and buried it in a small-scale release.

After "Bonnie and Clyde" did unexpectedly well in London and generated a lot of attention, Warren Beatty threatened to sue Warner Brothers for not opening it up to a wider audience. The studio backed down and re-released it across the country. On the first day of the re-release, it won 10 Oscar nominations.[396] Warner Brothers was stunned to find itself with the third-highest grossing movie of the year.[397]

Alongside the number one moneymaker of the year, "The Graduate," "Bonnie and Clyde" ushered in the period known as the New Hollywood Era. This is the era of Martin Scorsese and Francis Ford Coppola, of gritty realism and tragic endings, that American male cinephiles in particular tend to love most. Like never before, the blockbusters were artistically challenging movies that examined adult issues. It was a boon time for high-quality shock films.

Peter Biskind's book "Easy Riders, Raging Bulls" gives an authoritative (if a bit gossipy) account of New Hollywood. In the introduction, Siskind discusses how it was an era of directors having unprecedented levels of power. The traditional driving force for movies, old white male studio executives, had no idea what young people wanted to see. By 1967, they had felt out to sea for several years. But when the number one and number three box-office champs of the year are incomprehensible to you, it can really hit home. The executives didn't give up power easily, of course – no

---

[394] Biskind, p. 34
[395] Luke Buckmaster, "How Bonnie and Clyde's final scene changed Hollywood", BBC.com, https://www.bbc.com/culture/article/20170814-how-bonnie-and-clydes-final-scene-changed-hollywood
[396] Biskind, p. 46
[397] Finler, p. 358–359

one ever does. But the suits who bet on the young, rabble-rousing directors made money while the ones relying on old formulas or on their own tastes lost money.

Roger Corman didn't have such a difficult time transitioning to shock films. He relied on old formulas, but he never made decisions based on his own tastes, which leaned towards the movies of Fellini, Bergman and Michaelangelo Antonioni, the director of "Blow-Up." Corman distributed the movies of these European masters, but he was always too afraid of financial disaster to make art films of his own.[398]

Roger Corman was a businessman first, filmmaker second. He was a soft-spoken and humble guy, but would often boast that he never lost money on a film. His career provides a great test case for treating the creation of art like any other business by operating according to pure capitalist principles. Corman kept costs to a minimum, mastered marketing techniques, and supplied products that he knew would satisfy adequate demand to yield profits. And almost all of his movies are terrible. That's how the weird business of making art often goes.

The undercapitalized demand that Corman supplied had always been the movies teenagers asked for. After the success of "The Wild Angels," his new resource became young adults trying to make it in Hollywood: "The Wild Angels" stars Peter Fonda and Bruce Dern, plus Dennis Hopper, Jack Nicholson, etc.

Nicholson wrote a script based on his own experience with LSD. Against his agent's wishes, Fonda jumped at the chance to star.[399] **"The Trip"** became the first major film that celebrated an illegal drug rather than being a polemic against one. Its shock value comes

---

[398] "Corman's World: Exploits of a Hollywood Rebel," 2011 documentary directed by Alex Stapleton
[399] "The Trip, AFI.com
https://catalog.afi.com/Film/21511-THE-TRIP?sid=0e2e1e81-5100-434f-bf1e-3c2913ef18c6&sr=6.4892507&cp=1&pos=1

mainly from that fact and some nudity, so it won't disturb anyone who has seen a modern drug comedy. It's still a pretty fun movie, in my estimation, especially if you're a fan of psychedelic imagery.

"The Trip" ran afoul of the rather ineffectual censors that still existed. The National Association of Broadcasters told its members to refuse to run any advertisements for the movie. Its justification was that the ads were "an affront to good taste, community attitudes and responsibility to children":[400] i.e., the typically vague dressing-up of "this stuff scares us." "The Trip" didn't play in the United Kingdom at all because The British Board of Film Censors refused to grant it a license. It was all irrelevant, of course, as it did so well in the States that it launched a mini-genre of drug movies.

James Joyce on Fucking

The British Board of Film Censors also took issue with "**Ulysses**" (1967), an adaptation of the James Joyce novel. I can't comment on how well the film adapts the book, which I've never been able to get through. I do know that it is one naughty novel; "Lady Chatterley's Lover" author D.H. Lawrence blasted its final section as "the dirtiest, most indecent, obscene thing ever written."[401]

As I mentioned in passing before, the novel changed American censorship law forever. The 1933 case *United States v. One Book Called Ulysses* opened the written word to shock content that never would've flown for a second in movies.

The film "Ulysses" is loaded with frank and honest talk about sex, though it doesn't show any, not really. It closes with a long stream-of-consciousness monologue by Molly Bloom, in which she rather casually talks about her own desires, her sexual experiences, men's

---

[400] Quoted in Ibid
[401] Quted in Jeffrey Meyers, "Joyce and Lawrence: Virtuous Immoralists," *Style*, Vol. 55, No. 2 (2021), p. 161-171

penises, and the like. Crucially, she also throws out the words "fuck" and "shit." It was the first utterance of "fuck" in a major film.

At the Cannes Film Festival, these and other words were censored, which director Joseph Strick discovered during the screening. He stormed into the projection booth to shut it down. Before he could, he was grabbed and thrown down a flight of stairs by "festival goons."[402]

The British Board of Film Censors insisted that the naughty talk be cut before "Ulysses" could be passed with an X. Strick responded by replacing the offending dialogue with screeches and other annoying noises. He then brought the fight to the press and convinced a few local authorities to show the film uncut.[403] These local authorities used to work in lockstep with the Board. As in the United States, the main censor of the U.K. was seeing its power wane in the face of changing mores.

It helped Strick's case that he was touting a faithful adaptation of a classic work of literature. That's a surefire way to get liberal intellectuals on your side. Literature professors who otherwise raise their noses at contemporary movies love to show their classes film versions of what they're reading.

All this was happening in the United Kingdom, which was not technically the home turf of "Ulysses." The novel is a crown jewel in the cultural history of Ireland, a country of only 7 million people (fewer than in Arizona) that punches well above its weight literature-wise. The book's subject matter could hardly be more Irish, as it's

---

[402] Dennis McLellan, "Joseph Strick dies at 86; independent filmmaker brought 'Ulysses' to big screen", *Los Angeles Times*, https://www.latimes.com/local/obituaries/la-me-joseph-strick-20100604-story.html

[403] Mike Hally, "Local Authorities and film censorship: a historical account of the 'Naughty Pictures Committees' in Sale and Manchester", *Entertainment and Sports Law Journal* 11, 4, 2016

about ordinary people wandering around Dublin. Regardless, the movie was banned outright in Ireland until 2000.

"Ulysses" the movie was seen in enough places by enough people to become a relative success and break ground in terms of shocks. I personally doubt it would have gotten that far if not for its literary pedigree. Judging it solely as a film, I don't think it works. Keeping faithful to a novel full of characters' streams of consciousness means violating the old movie maxim "show, don't tell" for very, very long stretches. At least it's easier to watch than the novel is to read.

Unseeable Shocks

In 1967, "**Titicut Follies**" joined the subgenre of documentaries that use shock for altruistic ends. It immerses viewers in the world of a maximum-security Massachusetts prison for the criminally insane through a "direct cinema" style, meaning that it strings together footage with no narration. With no voice leading you to conclusions, direct cinema makes a documentary feel as much like unconstructed reality as possible. It's harder to accuse such a film of being biased or polemical, which makes direct cinema ideal for an exposé of disturbing behavior. "Titicut Follies" exposes the reality of insane asylums of the 1960s, which entailed force-feeding, naked inmates in bare cells, and bullying by staff members.

Right before the first scheduled screening of "Titicut Follies" at the 1967 New York Film Festival, the Commonwealth of Massachusetts filed suit to stop it. Massachusetts argued that the film's producer/director, Frederick Wiseman, had not gotten adequate permissions from the participants.[404] Wiseman insisted he got permission from all relevant authorities; filming for months in a maximum-security prison with no hidden cameras would have been impossible if he hadn't. Inmates and their keepers gave consent as situations arose. Wiseman had shown the finished film to the prison superintendent and the Massachusetts attorney general and gotten

---

[404] de Grazia and Newman, p. 313

their approval. Both thought the film would help them get funding for better guards, social workers, and psychiatrists.[405] Later, they both testified that they had brought up privacy concerns, but they did not claim they withheld consent.[406] As Carolyn Anderson wrote in her article "The Conundrum of Competing Rights in 'Titicut Follies," "The dispute came down to the state's word against Wiseman's."

According to Wiseman, Massachusetts only took legal action after its governor got a letter from a social worker who objected to "Titicut Follies" because she'd read it featured naked men. She hadn't seen the movie. The governor got nervous the film would jeopardize his career and filed suit.[407]

Note that the on-screen participants of "Titicut Follies" were not the ones suing to have it suppressed, even though their rights were the ones presumably being violated. One inmate was roped into the lawsuit, but the prison superintendent acted as his guardian and he never spoke on his own behalf.[408] Since the inmates depicted were "incapacitated," according to the state's lawyers, the state felt it had jurisdiction to act in their stead.[409]

The New York Film Festival showing of "Titicut Follies" went ahead, but the Massachusetts government successfully prevented any further public screenings. To do so, a Massachusetts judge invented a specific privacy right that was not in state law. He also ordered all copies of the film destroyed.[410]

---

[405] Jesse Pearson, "The Follies Of Documentary Filmmaking". *Vice Magazine*, September 1, 2007, https://www.vice.com/da/article/doc-v14n9/
[406] Carolyn Anderson, "The Conundrum of Competing Rights in TITICUT FOLLIES". *Journal of the University Film Association*, Vol. 33, No. 1, CRITICAL APPROACHES (Winter 1981), p. 15-22
[407] Pearson, "The Follies Of Documentary Filmmaking."
[408] Anderson, "The Conundrum of Competing Rights in TITICUT FOLLIES"
[409] Wendy Lesser, "Unwise Restrictions". *The Threepenny Review* (48): 25, 1992
[410] Anderson, "The Conundrum of Competing Rights in TITICUT FOLLIES"

On appeal, the Massachusetts Supreme Court dialed things back a bit. It reversed the decision to destroy all copies. It also allowed "Titicut Follies" to be shown, but only to doctors, lawyers, legislators, psychiatrists, and other professionals with a vested interest in the conditions at state prisons. This meant that anyone who wanted to see it had to go through a complicated application process days in advance.[411]

The U.S. Supreme Court refused to take up an appeal. Its brief denial included the following telling sentence:

> "['Titicut Follies']'s stark portrayal of patient-routine and treatment of the inmates is at once a scathing indictment of the inhumane conditions that prevailed at the time of the film and an undeniable infringement of the [398 U.S. 960 , 961] privacy of the inmates filmed, who are shown nude and engaged in acts that would unquestionably embarrass an individual of normal sensitivity."[412]

So the decision hinged on the shock of seeing men naked. It also mentions the very vague and subjective "acts that would unquestionably embarrass an individual of normal sensitivity." I can only guess what that refers to: maybe being force-fed, or being humiliated while naked – which brings us back to full-frontal male nudity. If Wiseman had superimposed black bars over the inmates' privates, perhaps "Titicut Follies" would have survived the court challenge.

Wiseman would have never considered that, of course, as it would lessen the horror of the inmates' treatment. And the horror is what makes the "scathing indictment" so scathing; the shock is necessary to compel people to demand change. As in "The House Is Black," "Titicut Follies" elicits empathy for people who have been hidden from public view and ignored. I think the greater good of exposing systematic dehumanization outweighs the presumption that some

---

[411] Ibid
[412] *Wiseman v. Massachusetts*, 398 U.S. 960 (1970).

content could "embarrass an individual of normal sensitivity." If the inmates or prison staff had spearheaded the lawsuit, I would weigh it quite differently. But it sure looks to me like the Massachusetts government was covering its own ass at the expense of a film that could have led to the improvement of many people's lives.

"Titicut Follies" was not cleared for public screening until 1991, when a judge determined that enough inmates had died, so their privacy concerns were no longer paramount.[413] You can see "Titicut Follies" on YouTube now, and I recommend doing so. It's a sobering demonstration of what can happen when an institution is allowed to operate without public oversight.

"Titicut Follies" also demonstrates the weirdly powerful effect that seeing penises on screen has on straight men (who were the only people with power in the 1960s, in case you weren't aware). "Un chant d'amour" and "Flaming Creatures" were also deemed unworthy of free-speech protection by the highest courts in the land in the 1960s, largely because they prominently feature this especially anxiety-producing body part. Unlike in those films, though, the nudity in "Titicut Follies" is not remotely sexual or titillating; it evokes only vulnerability and humiliation.

Academic theses could be and probably have been written about why penises on film cause so much disturbance among straight men. Women regularly expose their private parts on film, and their worthiness as screen idols is judged partially on how those parts look. Granted, women seldom expose their genitalia, so it's not a perfect analogy; still, it seems like men are excessively triggered by the sight of a body part they all own. I could make guesses about deep-seated fears of inadequacy or public exposure, but that requires more training in psychology that I've had. It's enough for my purposes to establish that shots of male genitalia occupy the apex of shock content.

---

[413] Anderson, "The Conundrum of Competing Rights in TITICUT FOLLIES"

Back to Women and Sex

The mere sight of a male sexual organ on screen could justify legal suppression in the mid-1960s, but plenty of films were free to explore unconventional aspects of female sexuality. In 1967, Luis Buñuel dove into unusual sexual practices with "**Belle de Jour**." Catherine Deneuve plays a bored housewife who becomes a sex worker during the day. She participates in and fantasizes about all sorts of kinks, ranging from cuckolding her husband to having mud thrown on her while she's tied to a stake.

"Belle de Jour" is not my favorite Buñuel film – throughout, I can't help wondering "Are these the erotic fantasies a woman would have or the fantasies a man would want a woman to have?" – but it certainly gets into areas of subversive erotica that would have been unthinkable in a film just a few years before. Its release led to relatively little blowback.

The world had caught up with Luis Buñuel. In 1967 he was 67 years old, and he was just beginning the most celebrated part of his career. From this point on, he'd regularly win Oscar nominations and other markers of mainstream acceptance. Not that Buñuel cared – he never attended award ceremonies. When his most beloved movie, "The Discreet Charm of the Bourgeoisie," won the Academy Award for Best Foreign Language Film, he conceded only to posing for a picture with the award, and insisted on doing so in big silly glasses and a wig.

Meanwhile, lesbianism was becoming the type of queer love that straight men would permit in movies. The small-scale Canadian film "**The Fox**" (1967) is reminiscent of "The Children's Hour," with a similarly problematic ending. It has a more accepting view of lesbianism, but not by a ton. Like "Lady Chatterley's Lover," it's an adaptation of a long-banned D.H. Lawrence story. Unlike both of the previous films, "The Fox" has nudity and (mild) sex scenes, allowing it to delve into its characters' sexual feelings. Some people were shocked, but the movie was a hit, earning $25 million on a budget of

$1 million.[414] It was sufficiently accepted by the mainstream to win a Golden Globe for Best English-Language Foreign Film and an Oscar nomination for Best Score.

The British film "**The Killing of Sister George**" (1968) was groundbreaking in that even though all of its main characters are lesbians, it's not really about lesbianism. You could recast two of the female characters as men and the plot wouldn't change much (though you would have to sacrifice the best scene of the movie, set in a real-life lesbian bar).

"The Killing of Sister George" is more about the ups and downs of showbiz, embodied in a main character who careens out of control when her career starts to sour. Actually, she is out of control throughout, to the point of being a campy villain. This made it hard for me to empathize with her during the dramatic moments. I think the movie should have been either a serious drama or black comedy instead of an awkward mash-up of both.

Predictably, "The Killing of Sister George" also includes a few dated conceptions of queerness. Sapphic Underground's YouTube video "Let's discuss the disturbing lesbianism of 'The Killing of Sister George'" gives perspective on this that I'm not qualified to provide.

Regardless of whether it's a great film, "The Killing of Sister George" deserves mention because it dared to show queer people living the same sorts of lives that straight people do. This would be extremely rare for decades afterwards. When the movie came to the United States after the ratings system was established, director Robert Aldrich offered to cut the lone scene of sex and nudity to secure an R rating. He was told not to bother. Because "The Killing of Sister George" was entirely about a lesbian subculture, it would get an X regardless.[415]

---

[414] Miller, p. 208
[415] Miller, p. 218

"**Therese and Isabelle**" (1968) exists in the odd confluence of art films and exploitation movies that grew out of "And God Created Woman." It's set in an all-girls school, like "Mädchen in Uniform" and "Olivia," but includes nudity and lesbian sex. To my eyes, it genuinely attempts to depict eroticism and not just provide masturbation fodder for straight men. Whether it depicts eroticism successfully is debatable: The sex scenes are saddled with a voice-over that ladles on purple prose straight out of a romance novel (one example: "With my jeweler's tongue I dropped glistening gems into her mouth"). "Therese and Isabelle"'s slow, gloomy style, possibly in emulation of Ingmar Bergman, makes it work somewhat on a dramatic level, I feel. It helps that it does not portray lesbian love as anything but valid and wonderful.

Local censorship boards may have been mostly dead by 1968, but cops and judges would still try to unilaterally declare movies obscene. The legal systems in Jackson, Mississippi and Allegheny County, Pennsylvania shut down screenings of "The Fox" and "Therese and Isabelle," respectively. In both cases local officials were overstepping their authority and ignoring the law. They got away with it in Mississippi but the injunction against "Therese and Isabelle" was overturned on appeal.[416]

The Allegheny County district attorney trying to ban "Therese and Isabelle" had an interesting (losing) argument. He said that "because of the more vivid impact that movies have, the test of its obscenity should be different from that applicable to books."[417] It's the viscerality of the medium of film that Tolstoy talked about and that pre-World War II courts used to justify censoring everything from exploitation films to newsreels. In 1968, many people still felt film shocks so negatively that they felt spurred to take legal action. The higher courts were not playing along any more, but the offended people wouldn't stop trying.

---

[416] de Grazia and Newman, p. 309-312
[417] Quoted in de Grazia and Newman, p. 312

The Ohio Supreme Court successfully banned Russ Meyer's 1968 movie "**Vixen!**," which proved easier to brand as obscenity than "Therese and Isabelle." "Vixen!" has no artsy pretensions, though it is skillfully directed. And thankfully, Meyer abandons the toxic masculinity of "Lorna" and makes his protagonist a woman who aggressively pursues sex for her own pleasure, a la Mae West. The big differences from Mae West movies are that "Vixen!" shows all the sex scenes and offers tongue-in-cheek outlandishness instead of one-liners. Meyer admirer (and later collaborator) Roger Ebert referred to "Vixen!" in saying "Meyer's ability to keep his movies light and farcical took the edge off the sex for people seeing their first skin flick."[418] Meyer insisted that "Vixen!"'s success was due in large part to attracting a female audience.[419]

What About Men and Sex?

If you wanted to see an attractive naked man being sexual in 1968, you had to tap into that aforementioned New York underground film scene. Paul Morrissey, who had made "Chelsea Girls" as entertaining as possible for distribution, got $4,000 from Andy Warhol and directed "**Flesh**." Young bisexual hunk Joe Dallesandro plays a street hustler trying to make enough money to get his wife's girlfriend an abortion.

It might sound like a premise for a John Waters movie, but it's not high camp. Everyone underplays their roles, and the humor comes from how blasé everyone behaves in shocking situations. Like "Chelsea Girls," it's mostly improvised conversations among a couple of people at a time. But there is some narrative structure, and Morrissey uses jump cuts to remove the most boring bits. "Flesh" still drags fairly often, in my opinion, but it's much more watchable than "Chelsea Girls."

---

[418] Roger Ebert, "Russ Meyer: King of the Nudies." *Film Comment*, Vol. 9, Iss. 1, (Jan/Feb 1973): 35-46.
[419] Roger Ebert, "Russ Meyer: Ten Years After the 'Beyond'." *Film Comment,* Vol. 16, Iss. 4, (Jul/Aug 1980): 43-48, 80.

The British Board of Film Censors refused to grant "Flesh" a certificate, banning it from theaters. The head censor told the film's distributor that the movie could be screened in private film clubs, though. One such screening caused someone to complain to the police. Then 32 policemen raided the venue and confiscated the film, the screen, parts of the projector, and the club's membership register. They also took down all attendees' names and addresses.[420]

The distributor of "Flesh" staged a public protest. The controversy even reached the floor of the House of Commons. No prosecutions resulted, and soon after, the censors lifted the ban on "Flesh" by giving the uncut version an X rating. It marked the first time that the notoriously stodgy British Board of Film Censors sided with the anti-censorship crowd.[421] It was clear that the United Kingdom was opening up to shock content.

West Germany was certainly open to "Flesh." There it was taken up by a major distribution company and became one of the top five box office champions of the year.[422] In the States, however, "Flesh" could not get on many screens.

OK Guys, You Can Defy Gender Norms, But No Sex!

If you weren't one of the few Americans able to catch "Flesh" in 1968, maybe you lived near a theater showing "**The Queen**." In the direct cinema style also used by "Titicut Follies," "The Queen" chronicles the drama surrounding the 1967 Miss All-America Camp Beauty Contest. We see drag queens talk about their lives and their sexualities, get dressed up, and strut their stuff for a crowd that includes Andy Warhol and George Plimpton. Drag had long been a

---

[420] "The Flesh Raid," ScreenOnline.Org.uk, http://www.screenonline.org.uk/film/id/591940/index.html
[421] Ibid
[422] "Flesh (1968)," https://warholstars.org/

butt of jokes in movies; it took a documentary to give it an honest and respectful treatment.

In 1968, "The Queen" was a revelation to both queer people who were thrilled to see it on a big screen and straight people who never imagined such a thing existed. Drag balls date back at least to the 1880s, when formerly enslaved person William Dorsey Swann held a series of them in Washington D.C. When he was arrested for impersonating a woman, Swann was defiant. He became the first American to launch a legal fight for LGBTQ+ rights.

Thanks to Swann and the many drag queens who followed, drag balls are now part of popular culture. To a contemporary viewer, "The Queen" will feel like a typical episode of "Ru-Paul's Drag Race." But watch it anyway, because the ending is legendary.

<SPOILER ALERT>

At the end of "The Queen," Crystal LaBeija expresses in no uncertain terms her displeasure with finishing fourth. She declares loud and clear for all to hear that she looks better than the winner. I don't pretend to be an expert at drag ball judging, but honestly, it's hard to disagree with LaBeija.

There was a subtext that LaBeija, even in all her fury, did not touch on. LaBeija was Black and the winner was white and blond. Apparently Black contestants almost always lost to blondes.

After this loss, LaBeija was done with the main drag scene. In 1968, she founded the House of LaBeija, which is credited with launching the New York ball culture that was immortalized by "Paris Is Burning." If you've seen that documentary, you know that it's a vibrant scene that has provided a haven for queer people of color ever since. Watch "The Queen" if you want to witness a seminal moment in LGBTQ+ history unfold.

</SPOILER ALERT>

The New Horrors

For whatever reason, "Psycho" and "Peeping Tom" did not lead to an immediate run of horror movies about realistic psychopaths. Instead, Gothic tales in creepy castles kept on truckin' through the 1960s. Roger Corman produced one adaptation of a public-domain Edgar Allan Poe story after another. They're often fun, but they're not very shocking, especially not compared to Herschell Gordon Lewis's campy splatter movies.

In 1968, horror grew up. **"Night of the Living Dead"** (1968) brought Herschell Gordon Lewis-style gore into a serious, well-written story. It was made by amateurs, but it does not have the campy amateurishness of Lewis's movies. Being grounded in reality makes "Night of the Living Dead" more shocking. It also features the message-based shock, in the context of 1968, of a Black hero who takes charge, overpowers a white middle-aged blowhard, and smacks a white woman. These were all unheard of in the carefully proscribed roles that Hollywood permitted Black people to play.

The 1968 Roger Corman-produced **"Targets"** was more deliberate in contrasting old horror with something newer and more realistically unnerving. Its scares come from a whitebread insurance agent who starts shooting random people. It was inspired by Charles Whitman, a gunman who had done the same from a University of Texas clock tower in 1966.

Most horror movies, up to and including "Psycho," provide an explanation for the killer's actions. This gives audiences some level of reassurance. "Targets" has no interest in doing anything of the kind.

The movie's real-life monster ripped from the headlines is contrasted with an old-time horror star (Boris Karloff playing a version of himself) who feels increasingly irrelevant. "Targets" is not an especially gory movie; it's more interested in the message-based shock of bringing the threats of real late-1960s life into horror.

"Targets" was a small-scale release; **Rosemary's Baby** was the movie that brought realistic horror to mainstream America. Its director, Roman Polanski, had roots in theater and serious drama. He was picked to direct over William Castle, who was an old hand at silly, simple horror movies for teens like "House on Haunted Hill" (1959) and "The Tingler" (1959).[423] Polanski crafted "Rosemary's Baby" to be even more naturalistic and grounded in reality than "Night of the Living Dead" and "Targets."

You probably know the basic idea of "Rosemary's Baby" even if you haven't seen it, but to be safe, I'll just say that religion plays a role. NCOMP gave it a C because of its "perverted use" of Christian beliefs.[424] The objections had little effect: "Rosemary's Baby" earned ten times its budget and a few Oscar nominations.

I wouldn't say "Rosemary's Baby" is particularly sacrilegious, but regardless, its success made clear that you could now push boundaries on that third rail of shock content, religion. There were very few taboos left that mainstream American audiences had not embraced on the big screen.

Apart from impiety, "Rosemary's Baby" offers the more abstract content-based shock of a horror movie with moral ambiguity. One contemporary critic thought he was taking the movie down a peg when he said "Traditional horror films turn on an agreed dichotomy of angel and devil, right and wrong. ['Rosemary's Baby''s] surfaces are too accurate and Miss Farrow's anguish too real to let us be comfortable in some never-never land of escape."[425]

---

[423] Jason Zinoman, "Shock Value: How a Few Eccentric Outsiders Gave Us Nightmares, Conquered Hollywood, and Invented Modern Horror". p. 15-16

[424] Tim Dirks, "The 100+ Most Controversial Films of All-Time," FilmSite.org, https://www.filmsite.org/controversialfilms.html

[425] Quoted in Zinoman, p. 26

"Rosemary's Baby" is not intended to make you comfortable in any way. It was definitively grown-up horror for a generation that had thoroughly aged out of William Castle movies.

Time for Ratings

The success of "Rosemary's Baby" proved once again that many Americans were hungering for "suggested for mature audiences" movies. Plenty of other people still did not approve. But whatever plans they may have had for blanket legal repression were shut down by the 1968 U.S. Supreme Court decisions *Ginsberg v. New York* and *Interstate Circuit v. Dallas*, which involved *Playboy* magazine and the non-shock film "Viva Maria!" (1965), respectively. These cases established "variable obscenity," the principle that material can be deemed legally obscene for kids but not for adults.[426]

This meant local governments couldn't block grown-ups from shock movies any more. But municipalities could start their own rating systems that would bar children from whatever movies they deemed inappropriate. Thus the studios faced the prospect of another national patchwork of conflicting standards, just like when local and state censorship boards sprung up in the 1910s.

MPAA head Jack Valenti convinced Hollywood to head this off by finally initiating a system that would apply to the whole country.[427] In November 1968, they rolled it out:

- Rated G: Suggested for general audiences.
- Rated M: Suggested for mature audiences – Parental discretion advised.
- Rated R: Restricted – Persons under 16 not admitted, unless accompanied by parent or adult guardian.
- Rated X: Persons under 16 not admitted.

---

[426] Miller, p. 210
[427] Miller, p. 211-212

"M" would later be renamed "GP" and then "PG," and what was permissible within each rating would always be in flux. But the basic structure of these ratings would not change until PG-13 was added in 1984.

The Production Code was dead. The old guiding principle that "no picture shall be produced which lowers the moral standards of those who see it" was replaced by the goal that movies "keep in close harmony with the mores, culture, the moral sense and change of our society,"[428] per the announcement of the rating system. The concept of strictly adhering to a film Ten Commandments was gone; now the goal was to adapt with the times.

With this new approach, Hollywood officially opened the door to shocks. Even the most cautious producer could now confidently greenlight movies about sex and violence. They would do so enthusiastically throughout the next era of film.

---

[428] Quoted in Miller, p. 212

Chapter 7: The New Freedoms, 1969-1976

X-Rated

With the creation of the rating system in late 1968, the floodgates opened to shock movies. The flood didn't hit its peak immediately, but wouldn't take long.

The new X rating was not meant for porn movies, which would not get any official ratings. The first film that the MPAA rated X was "Greetings," a comedy directed by Brian De Palma and starring Robert De Niro. It's mostly about young men chasing women, but there's little nudity and just one sex scene, which is sped up for comedic effect (and possibly to make it less erotic). Many films with much stronger sexual content have received R ratings since. Before November 1968, "Greetings" would have counted as a shock film, but after, it was nothing special.

A movie has to go a step farther to be a shocker in this era, like the Swedish film "**I Am Curious (Yellow)**" did. It was released in Sweden in 1967 and finally hit stateside screens in March 1969 after a prolonged legal battle.

I had heard about "I Am Curious (Yellow)" long before I saw it and always assumed it was a soft-core porno with a plot, a "young woman's journey of sexual discovery," etc., etc. I was surprised to discover it's mostly a political film, a young woman's journey through late-1960s activism, if you will. A good chunk of it is devoted to real people expounding on politics, including Martin Luther King Jr. and the then-Minister of Transportation of Sweden Olof Palme, who would soon after become one of the country's most consequential prime ministers. Those two are worth seeing of course, but other interviews bored me. I'm interested in the social issues of the 1960s, but not enough to enjoy large sections of "I Am Curious (Yellow)."

More relevantly to this book, "I Am Curious (Yellow)" is also about the protagonist's romantic life, and it does not cut away from the sex. You see penises in "I Am Curious (Yellow)," including one being kissed. This tipped the movie into "Un chant d'amour" territory, enabling legal authorities to declare it obscene and ban it. The first attempt to import the film into the United States in 1968 led to Customs seizing the film reels. The government requested a jury trial, which adjudicated that "I Am Curious (Yellow)" was obscene. An appeals court reversed that verdict, and permitted the movie to enter the United States.[429]

The appeals court was going by a legal standard set in the 1966 *Memoirs v. Massachusetts* U.S. Supreme Court decision, which concerned the book "Memoirs of a Woman of Pleasure," aka "Fanny Hill." In this decision, Justice William Brennan had established a "three-fold test" for determining if a movie was legally obscene. One of the "folds" was that "the dominant theme of the material taken as a whole appeals to the prurient interest in sex" and another was that "the material is utterly without redeeming social value."[430] The idea was to ban pornos but allow art films that involved sex.

Because "I Am Curious (Yellow)" is primarily about politics, it should have been clear in the initial jury trial that the movie had "redeeming social value" at the very least. As for sex being the movie's "dominant theme," you can argue it is the most potent one (especially if you find the politics a bit dull), but there's no way sex takes up a lion's share of screen time.

But as we've seen before, exposed penises can cause such distress that rational evaluation goes out the window. Now that "I Am Curious (Yellow)" was in the country, it had to contend with every local censorship board coming to its own decision about whether it constituted pornography. It hit a crazy quilt of bans and restrictions throughout the United States. "I Am Curious (Yellow)" was shown in 125 communities, while being blocked in many others, including

---

[429] de Grazia and Newman, p. 298-299
[430] Quoted in Miller, p. 265

Boston, Baltimore, Kansas City, Phoenix, and Spokane.[431] The U.S. Supreme Court was no help, resolving nothing with a 4-4 decision. (William O. Douglas, the judge who wanted movies "freed from the censor," abstained.)

The lone survivor of state censorship boards, Maryland's, banned "I Am Curious (Yellow)" statewide. The Maryland Supreme Court upheld the board's decision by saying the movie had no "redeeming social value" because its engagement with political issues was "patently strained and contrived."

So to determine whether an entire state of people could exercise their First Amendment rights and experience a piece of art, a handful of judges went by their feelings on how effectively a movie explored politics. Imagine if actual qualified movie critics got to decide what you were allowed to watch. Now imagine that instead of movie critics, it was a few Grumpy Old Men without any particular interest in or knowledge about film. The absurdity of this situation and similar ones enabled "I Am Curious (Yellow)" to deal a blow to the whole concept of legally banning a film for obscenity. In practice, doing so requires so much subjectivity that it's a fool's errand.

Much of the American public was on board with "I Am Curious (Yellow)." On "The Tonight Show," Johnny Carson talked about having seen the movie. Jacqueline Kennedy Onassis was caught leaving a theater showing it by a reporter (whom she slammed to the ground with a karate move).[432] "I Am Curious (Yellow)" earned the 12th-highest gross of all 1969 releases in the United States and Canada, and set a record for foreign film earnings.[433] The market had spoken, and in the United States, when the market speaks, everyone listens.

As moviegoers were flocking to "I Am Curious (Yellow)," the 1969 Supreme Court decision *Stanley v. Georgia* made it legal for people

---

[431] de Grazia and Newman, p. 300
[432] "She Was Furious". *San Francisco Chronicle*. October 6, 1969
[433] "Variety's B.O. Charts' 1969 Results". *Variety*. April 29, 1970. p. 26.

to have pornographic movies and other obscene materials in their own homes. It didn't apply to public theaters, but it destroyed the idea at the heart of obscenity law, that the government should control what media adults could consume. This decision paved the way for hard-core pornography to become widespread.

"I Am Curious (Yellow)" didn't go so far as having an unsimulated sex scene, but "**Blue Movie**," aka "**Fuck**" (1969) did. As he had with "Chelsea Girls," Andy Warhol filmed his friends for a few hours, cut out some of it, and called it a film. "Blue Movie" is 105 minutes of just one couple in their apartment, discussing the Vietnam War, puttering around, and having sex for 10 minutes.

Warhol described the inspiration for the movie: ""I'd always wanted to do a movie that was pure fucking, nothing else, the way 'Eat' had been just eating and 'Sleep' had been just sleeping. So in October '68 I shot a movie of Viva having sex with Louis Waldon. I called it just 'Fuck.'"[434]

"Eat," by the way, is just silent footage of artist Robert Indiana eating a mushroom for 45 minutes. "Sleep" shows Warhol's lover sleeping for 5 hours and 21 minutes, with most of the footage repeated many times. These preceded the aforementioned "Empire," the slowed-down static shot of the Empire State Building that lasts eight hours. As you might surmise, "Blue Movie" is not a thrill ride.

But because it was a reasonable length and directed by Andy Warhol, "Blue Movie" got into a few theaters. It thus marked the first time real sexual intercourse was shown on above-board American movie screens. The New Andy Warhol Garrick Theater in New York was a friendly venue, as you might expect – that is, until police busted in and arrested the manager, projectionist, and ticket-taker for obscenity. The charges against the projectionist and ticket-taker were dropped, but the manager was convicted. His conviction was

---

[434] "Blue Movie (1968)", WarholStars.org, https://www.warholstars.org/andy-warhol-blue-movie.html

upheld on appeal all the way to the U.S. Supreme Court.[435] A scene of actual people having actual sex made adjudicating obscenity a lot easier than "I Am Curious (Yellow)" had.

Shockbusters

Sex could still be barred from American screens in 1969, but violence could make for a mainstream blockbuster. Director Sam Peckinpah was a combative, hard-drinking tyrant who specialized in westerns. With "**The Wild Bunch**," he achieved a new level of brutality in film. The movie has long sequences of bloody gun violence that are so masterfully composed that they are frequently referred to as "balletic." They expand upon the much briefer shootouts of "Bonnie and Clyde" that were meant to "hurt not only the characters, but the audience as well."

Peckinpah was motivated by his disgust with how traditional Westerns glamorized violence by making it seem clean and bloodless. David Weddle's biography of Peckinpah, "If They Move … Kill Em!", quotes him as saying:

> "The point of ["The Wild Bunch"] is to take this façade of movie violence and open it up, get people involved in it so that they are starting to go in the Hollywood television predictable reaction syndrome, and then twist it so that it's not fun anymore, just a wave of sickness in the gut … it's ugly, brutalizing, and bloody awful; it's not fun and games and cowboys and Indians. It's a terrible, ugly thing, and yet there's a certain response that you get from it, an excitement, because we're all violent people." (p. 334)

"The Wild Bunch" was controversial, "praised and condemned with equal vehemence, like 'Pulp Fiction,'"[436] in Roger Ebert's words.

---

[435] de Grazia and Newman, p. 316-318
[436] Roger Ebert, "The Wild Bunch: The Director's Cut," March 17, 1995, RogerEbert.com, https://www.rogerebert.com/reviews/the-wild-bunch-the-directors-cut-1995

Enough people loved it to make it a touchstone for screen violence. Afterwards, movie gunplay was much less likely to be sanitized.

The violence in "The Wild Bunch" isn't gore, exactly – at least it isn't the sort of fetishistic mutilation you'd see in the Herschell Gordon Lewis movies "Blood Feast" and "2,000 Maniacs!." "The Wild Bunch" didn't break ground in portraying blood and guts as much as it shocked by showing violence realistically, in a well-made, mainstream movie. It has no irony or camp value to distance the viewer from the bloodshed.

It didn't take long for another mainstream western to get gorier. "**Soldier Blue**" (1970) depicts the Sand Creek massacre of 1864, in which American cavalry slaughtered a Cheyenne and Arapaho village, killing mostly women and children. The intended parallel with the My Lai massacre was not lost on the audience in 1970.

The massacre is shown in gory detail, but was intended to be much longer. Test audiences who saw the full massacre were so horrified that the scene was chopped down dramatically. The cut footage was lost. Even that footage likely didn't compare to accounts of the real-life Sand Creek massacre, in which soldiers made trophies of fetuses and children's genitals.[437]

I still found the released version of the massacre quite shocking, especially in the context of the rest of the film, which is a rather boilerplate romantic action/comedy in a "Romancing the Stone" vein. "Soldier Blue" was a big hit overseas but didn't do well in the United States. Americans raised on westerns might not have been quite ready to watch the calvary ride in to kill, maim, and rape.

American audiences were very ready for "**Easy Rider**" in 1969, much to the surprise of almost everyone. "Easy Rider" is an independent film about drug-using hippies that stars most of the

---

[437] Graham Fuller, "All Violent on the Western Frontier: Reassessing Two Revisionist Native American Westerns," *Cinéaste*, Vol. 46, No. 1, Winter 2020

New Hollywood wunderkinds behind "The Trip": Peter Fonda, Dennis Hopper, and Jack Nicholson. "The Trip" may have broken ground in celebrating illegal drug use, but "Easy Rider" goes further in making drug dealers the peaceful heroes who are victimized by violent squares.

If anyone in 1969 wasn't sure whether New Hollywood was here to stay, "Easy Rider" convinced them. It was massively popular and influential, epitomizing 1960s counterculture like no other movie. As such, it feels a bit dated to me – but granted, I'm a Gen-Xer who by his teenage years had had his fill of baby boomers lionizing their youths. Either way, "Easy Rider" is a must-see for anyone interested in American film history.

While we're on the topic of blockbuster shock films from 1969, I should at least mention "Midnight Cowboy." Famously, it was the only X-rated movie to win a Best Picture Oscar. But it was going to be released with an R rating until a psychologist advised its studio, United Artists, to go with a self-imposed X rating instead. The film has some drug use, sex scenes and a rape scene, but none of that was the issue. No, the psychologist was concerned with its "homosexual frame of reference" and its "possible influence on youngsters."[438] By that he meant that the movie has gay characters who aren't monsters, and therefore might convert some kids to homosexuality. The specter of "sex perversion" lived on.

In 1971, "Midnight Cowboy" was re-rated R, after an adjustment to the rating system. I wish I could say that this was a corrective measure to the ridiculous homophobia behind its initial X rating, but that wasn't the real reason. The X rating was already failing its mission in 1971. Despite X being intended for non-pornographic but thoroughly adult fare, porn producers were happily labeling their movies X-rated. They could do this because it was the only rating in the new system that wasn't copyrighted. You could not label your movie with a G, PG or R unless it had received that rating from the

---

[438] Quoted in Tino Balio, "United Artists: The Company That Changed the Film Industry," p. 292

MPAA, but you could call your movie "X-rated" to your heart's content. So many pornos did so that they gave the rating its current definition.

With X representing porn in most moviegoers' minds, non-pornographic X-rated films suffered by association. By 1972, newspapers were refusing ads for any film rated X, and 47% of theaters wouldn't show them.[439] An X rating for a non-porno meant 50% less revenue.[440] Almost all producers of non-pornos did whatever they could to avoid an X rating. "Midnight Cowboy" retaining its 1969 rating would have crippled its chances for re-release.

Regardless of its rating, "Midnight Cowboy" is not a shock film for me because it's more on the "Greetings" level of shocks: high for the previous era, but not unusual after 1968. Perhaps seeing gay characters did constitute a big shock in 1969; after all, "The Killing of Sister George" was rated X because it was entirely about lesbians. But it seems like "Midnight Cowboy"'s X rating was mostly a fluke driven by one homophobic psychologist. So fuck that guy – he doesn't tell me what to do. (It's 1969, so I get to curse now.)

Let's Check In with Japan

When we last checked in with Japan, its movies had lots of female nudity and even touched on taboo sexual practices with "The Pornographers." **"Funeral Parade of Roses"** (1969) took on topics that were taboo at the time but are less so now: gay and transgender identities. The movie struck me as an honest depiction of the lives of its LGBTQ+ characters, neither mocking them nor turning them into martyrs. "Funeral Parade of Roses" is also an avant-garde trip, so don't expect to always understand what's going on.

---

[439] Miller, p. 222
[440] Miller, p. 223

Also in 1969, the Godfather of Manga, Osamu Tezuka, decided to bring adult content into anime. He produced "**A Thousand and One Nights**" (1969), which interprets some of the folk tales from "One Thousand and One Nights" as a world populated by loads of busty, topless women. It also throws in a couple of psychedelic sex scenes. Cartoons like Betty Boop shorts had alluded to sex before, but I'm not aware of an earlier non-pornographic animated movie that is so clearly inappropriate for children.

While seeing a sexualized cartoon can feel discordant, at least the characters of "A Thousand and One Nights" don't look like they're from cute Disney cartoons. Thus it doesn't make me as queasy about mixing sexuality with the iconography of childhood as later American movies do. Sometimes, though, the characters of "A Thousand and One Nights" react in the big, comically exaggerated ways characteristic of Looney Tunes. It might not have birthed adult animation fully formed, but "A Thousand and One Nights" established a concept that anime would refine later.

"A Thousand and One Nights" was a big success in Japan but was ignored by the rest of the world. Two more adaptations of old stories followed. There are no recurring characters or plotlines connecting the three movies, but they make a thematic trilogy called "Animerama." "Cleopatra" (1970) doesn't move things forward much, so we can skip it. "**Belladonna of Sadness**" (1973) is the really bonkers one.

None of these movies portray women in a good light, but they get progressively better. "Belladonna of Sadness" at least attempts to be feminist in telling a tale of a woman who gets revenge on a town that wronged her. It's also the weirdest of the bunch, which is saying something. Though it struck me as the least gratuitous, "Belladonna of Sadness" is the Animerama movie most loaded with sexual imagery (again, that's saying something). Watching it is a wild experience that I recommend for anyone with adventurous movie tastes.

The Masters Dive In

Back in the West in 1969, many of the world's greatest living directors were jumping at the chance to dive into shock material. Michael Powell, whose once-dominant career had collapsed after making "Peeping Tom," went to Australia to film "**Age of Consent**" (1969). Helen Mirren plays an underage girl who poses nude and explores her burgeoning sexuality. Mirren was 24 at the time, but it's still a pretty icky movie in my opinion; at one point a cry of "I was raped!" is used as a punchline. It's another example of the new freedoms being taken too far in the direction of indulging sociopathic straight male fantasy.

If there was any established master who was more ready to make shock films than Pier Paolo Pasolini, I'm not sure who it would be. Pasolini, you may remember, was convicted for "offense to the Italian state and religion" for directing the short film "La ricotta." His "Teorema" (1968) could probably qualify as a shock film, as it's about a young Terence Stamp seducing every member of a middle-class household, women and men. But it pales in comparison to "**Porcile**," aka "**Pigsty**" (1969), which alternates between philosophical arguments and cannibalism, references to bestiality, etc.

Federico Fellini was another great candidate to embrace the new film freedoms. In 1960 he had pushed the boundaries with "La Dolce Vita" and in 1969 he blew them apart with "**Fellini Satyricon**." (Fellini's name was put in the title to distinguish it from another film called "Satyricon" put out the same year.) It's a catalog of stories set in ancient Rome that revel in sex and violence. Pulling them all from a classic text, Petronius' first-century fiction "The Satyricon," underlines the fact that narrative art has always trucked in shock content. The wild, grotesque visuals of "Fellini Satyricon" make it a thrilling experience for me, but if you're less devoted to filmic weirdness you might not love it.

An internationally beloved director that probably no one could predict would delve into shock material was Luchino Visconti. He got his start in Italian neorealism but also specialized in big, ornate, high-toned dramas about European aristocrats, sort of like especially operatic Merchant/Ivory films. His 1969 film "**The Damned**" is about another extremely wealthy European family. However, this family gets mixed up with Nazis and some extreme moral decadence, including child molestation, incest, and more. It got an X rating in the States but was cut down to earn an R. Already, distributors were doing what they had to do to avoid X ratings.

Michaelangelo Antonioni took four years to produce his follow-up to "Blow-Up," "**Zabriskie Point**" (1970). Both are very much products of the 1960s, with "Zabriskie Point" being more explicitly political. Because of Antonioni's left-wing stances, its production in California attracted attention from law enforcement, including the FBI. Throughout the 1960s, FBI director J. Edgar Hoover covertly persecuted many left-leaning public figures who had committed no federal crimes, ranging from Martin Luther King Jr. to actress Jean Seberg.

The feds found their opportunity to crack down after hearing a rumor that Antonioni would film an orgy of 10,000 extras in the desert of Zabriskie Point. The U.S. Department of Justice stood ready to charge the production with violating the Mann Act,[441] which made it a federal offense to transport "any woman or girl for the purpose of prostitution or debauchery, or for any other immoral purpose."

That's a preposterously broad statute. Thus the Mann Act was one of the FBI's favorite tools of repression: It could be invoked any time it wanted to punish a man who traveled across state lines with a woman who wasn't his wife. The Mann Act was passe in response to the same panic about prostitution that inspired the earliest sex hygiene films. Its first high-profile use had nothing to do with

---

[441] "Zabriskie Point: Trivia," TCM.com, https://www.tcm.com/tcmdb/title/96629/zabriskie-point#trivia

prostitution: In 1913, Jack Johnson, the first Black heavyweight boxing champion, was arrested for driving across state lines with his girlfriend, who was white. (Congress amended the Mann Act in 1978 and 1986 to limit it to cases involving prostitution and underage sex.)[442]

No doubt the Justice Department was disappointed to learn that Zabriskie Point was in California, so no state line would be crossed. And more importantly, the orgy scene was actually carried out by a bunch of carefully choreographed actors. It's still a pretty shocking scene, as is the stridently anti-establishment thrust of the whole film. "Zabriskie Point" is a bit like "Easy Rider," except that the hippies are on offense instead of being peaceful victims, and their opponents are rich capitalists instead of backwoods yokels. You can see why establishment types would be more disturbed by "Zabriskie Point." The film took politics a bit too far for most people's comfort, and bombed among audiences and critics. I found it to be powerful and fascinating, and its reputation has grown since the 1970s.

What's Left to Exploit?

With mainstream films, including ones made by some of the greatest directors in history, taking shocks so much farther, what was left for exploitation? Did exploitation film collapse in the 1970s?

Quite the opposite. It turned out there was plenty of demand for all kinds of shocks in all forms. Mainstream, foreign, exploitation, underground – every type of movie was filled with nudity and violence.

Exploitationeers didn't even have to push the envelope that hard to make money. In 1970 Roger Corman established New World Pictures to crank out movies featuring just enough shock content to stay within the R rating. New World's first effort was an

---

[442] Eric Weiner, "The Long, Colorful History of the Mann Act," NPR.org, https://www.npr.org/2008/03/11/88104308/the-long-colorful-history-of-the-mann-act

unremarkable biker film, and then it hit pay dirt with "**The Student Nurses**." Corman laid out the formula behind the movie:

> "Took shape out of a formula I had been working on for some time: contemporary dramas with a liberal to left-wing viewpoint and some R-rated sex and humor. But they were not to be comedies. I frankly doubt the left-wing bent, or message, was crucial to the success of the films we would do. But it was important to the filmmakers and me that we have something to say within the films ... I insisted each [nurse] had to work out her problems without relying on a boyfriend."[443]

This odd combination of feminism and exploitation was directed by Stephanie Rothman, who said:

> "[W]e were free to develop the story of the nurses as we wished, as long as there was enough nudity and violence distributed throughout it. Please notice, I did not say sex, I said nudity. This freedom, once I paid my debt to the requirements of the genre, allowed me to address what interested me... political and social conflicts and the changes they produce."[444]

Apart from the nudity, "The Student Nurses" offers bold message-based shocks that make it stand out. It advocates for abortion, which was still illegal nationwide in 1970, and sides with armed left-wing revolutionaries. It's not very well acted, and one of the plots is quite sexist. But if you want a taste of what exploitation film was like in 1970, you could do much worse.

The only other 1970s exploitation movies I will cover go beyond the level of "The Student Nurses" into X-rated territory. Corman and his

---

[443] Roger Corman and Jim Jerome, "How I Made a Hundred Movies in Hollywood and Never Lost a Dime," p. 181

[444] Henry Jenkins, "Exploiting Feminism: An Interview with Stephanie Rothman (Part One)," https://henryjenkins.org/2007/10/stephanie_rothman.html

ilk found the formula that worked and stuck with it as long as it kept making money. They had no need to keep upping the shock ante to turn profits the way Herschell Gordon Lewis and Russ Meyer had in the 1960s. The exploitationeers of the 1970s might sometimes hit on a subgenre that worked well – "The Big Doll House," for example, sparked a spate of women-in-prison movies – but for our purposes, those are variations on a theme rather than anything groundbreaking.

The central element of the 1970s exploitation formula was nudity. These movies would reliably show all of their young female stars topless, at least once every half-hour. Roger Corman made this a formal mandate for all his directors. When he found a formula that worked, he stuck with it until it didn't.

Nudity was enough to sell tickets because the sight of beautiful naked women was not as easy to come by then as it is now. This was before the internet, VCRs, and even pay cable stations. Few people had film projectors, and few of those who did had naughty filmstrips. There were *Playboys* and other nudie mags, but to see a naked woman in motion before the 1970s, your only option had been to visit the scary part of town – that's assuming your town even had a scary part. Suddenly, with drive-ins and relatively safe movie theaters showing the likes of "The Student Nurses," the less adventurous types could indulge.

Of course, if you were interested in male nudity, you were still mostly out of luck. Stephanie Rothman snuck some into "The Student Nurses," but other directors didn't bother. For a hot naked guy, you had to live in a big enough city to screen a movie like Paul Morrissey's "**Trash**." (1970) (aka "Andy Warhol's Trash": Like most of Morrissey's films, Warhol's name is attached to it for marketing purposes, but he just provided some financing and little else.)

I don't know if Joe Dallesandro is at his sexiest in this one, though, as the main thrust (no pun intended) is that he can't get an erection because he is addicted to heroin. "Trash" feels like a parody of a porn film: Dallesandro meets several women who want to have sex with him, but instead he chooses to shoot up. It's the most shocking and also the funniest Morrissey film I've seen. Transgender actress Holly Woodlawn steals the show as Dallesandro's girlfriend, giving a big, broad performance that feels very John Waters-y.

Make Way for the King

Speaking of John Waters, it's now time to delve into the king of shock film. By 1970, Waters had directed several shorts and one feature, "Mondo Trasho," that he has since said should have been a short. His first film to get any significant attention was "**Multiple Maniacs**" (1970).

"Multiple Maniacs" is charmingly amateurish. It feels like some guy filming his friends being crazy, because it basically is. It's not Waters' best, but the basic formula is in place: Drag queen Divine does a series of outrageous things, which I won't describe because that would ruin the shocks. It's all delivered in a spirit of high camp, of course, which makes it go down easier than if it had been gritty and realistic (not that most scenes would make any sense in that context).

You might notice that underground shock films of this era tended to be directed by gay men. As a straight man, it's not my place to conjecture why shocks carried such an appeal for queer people at the time. But I can at least try to empathize. I can try to imagine what it would be like if who I loved and how I loved them was considered by almost everyone in my country to be shockingly horrific. I could internalize that hate, deny my sexuality, refuse to experience true love, and live a tortured life. Or I could go the other direction, and say "Yes, my very existence is shocking, and I love it!" I could commiserate with other outcasts and boldly give the middle finger to every rule of propriety. The latter seems like a much healthier way to go.

The Mainstream Attempts LGBTQ+

A few years after lesbian protagonists hit the mainstream, gay men got a starring role in "**The Boys in the Band**" (1970). It represented a major step forward only a year after "Midnight Cowboy" was bumped to an X rating just for exhibiting a "homosexual frame of reference" through a couple of gay characters. "The Boys in the Band" has no sex or nudity but is 99% gay characters exhibiting a "homosexual frame of reference," and was rated R.

Per Hollywood's m.o., this groundbreaker was based on a successful play by the same name, which played off-Broadway in 1968. In it, a group of seven gay friends get together for a birthday party and lay bare their anguish over living in a homophobic world. In June 1969, the Stonewall riots kicked off the gay rights movement, and many LGBTQ+ people declared themselves out and proud. By the time the movie version of "The Boys in the Band" was released in 1970, some gay men found the movie's self-hating characters already dated and stereotypical.[445] Nowadays, I imagine it's best seen as an attempt to encapsulate a range of archetypes struggling with the homophobia of the late 1960s.

Its studio was counting on "The Boys in the Band" shocking the squares into buying tickets. Beyond exposing the straight world to the previously forbidden thoughts and feelings of gay men, the movie squeezes in every curse word. Its poster depicts only the birthday boy and a male sex worker whose services constituted one of his gifts, along with the tagline "Today's Harold's birthday. This is his present." The sex worker is a minor part in the movie; it wouldn't be much different if you cut him out entirely. The marketing team was spotlighting the behavior that it deemed most shocking.

Hollywood studios knew that shocks brought in bucks in 1970; sometimes they were so overeager that they didn't plan well. The

---

[445] Edward Guthmann, "'70s Gay Film Has Low Esteem". *The San Francisco Chronicle*, January 15, 1999

Gore Vidal novel "Myra Breckinridge" was a surprise best-seller in 1968. In a very campy style, it sends up American masculinity through a transgender protagonist who is out to "re-create the sexes."

20th Century Fox rushed a film version into production. To direct, they homed in on 29-year-old British pop singer Michael Sarne, whose movie resume consisted of one short and one low-budget feature, neither of which were successful. Despite being eager to work within a Hollywood studio, he was reluctant to direct "Myra Breckinridge." Sarne didn't actually like Vidal's novel and threw it away after reading a particularly shocking scene. He was a swinging playboy full of machismo, the exact type that the novel attacks ruthlessly.

The producers interviewed Sarne, liked him, and offered him money he couldn't refuse. They thought he was young and hip, and therefore could direct something cutting-edge.[446] I'm reminded of how Ed Wood got the job to direct a movie about transgender identity because he was a transvestite; yes, both are subjects that old white men don't know anything about, but that doesn't make them the same thing.

It's worse than that, really. Unlike Sarne, Wood was at least part of a repressed identity group, which could help him identify on some level with the premise of his movie. I bet the old straight white producers of "Myra Breckinridge" just picked a young straight white guy who reminded them of themselves or embodied the confident stud they wished they were, regardless of qualifications. They probably thought they were "going by their gut," when they were really going by their prejudices. Decisions like these are responsible for maintaining white-dominated patriarchy.

Granted, there were very few experienced film directors in 1970 who weren't old straight white men. This demonstrates the problem with establishing an old boys' club. Once you face a job that an old boy

---

[446] Steven Daly, "Swinging Into Disaster". *Vanity Fair*, April 2001

wouldn't be great at, you're SOL. Sarne may not have been qualified to direct "Myra Breckinridge," but the candidates with significant directing experience were too old to understand the young people at all. John Waters could've done a bang-up job, but he was still many years away from being trusted with a budget.

Production on "Myra Breckinridge" was troubled from the start. At one point George Cukor ("Gaslight," "The Philadelphia Story," "My Fair Lady," and probably the only gay member of the old-boys' club) had the inside track on replacing Sarne mid-production. It didn't happen, but maybe it should have. Cukor might have had the sense to say no to Mae West's demands. West had a supporting role in "Myra Breckinridge," her first appearance in a movie since 1943. She insisted on writing her own dialogue, singing two songs, and never appearing in a shot with star Raquel Welch. There were doubts that she had read the whole script.[447] I still found West pretty entertaining in "Myra Breckinridge," but her scenes felt like they were spliced in from another movie.

Cukor certainly knew how to handle a large-scale production, which Sarne apparently did not. The film "**Myra Breckinridge**" is a bizarre mishmash of some very good scenes, in my opinion, and some very bad ones. Apparently Sarne wasted a lot of time during filming and editors had to cobble together what he was able to get done.[448] The plot felt incomplete to me and I absolutely hated the ending, which undercuts the whole point and was Sarne's addition.

"Myra Breckinridge" has plenty of shocking parts, but many critics were most offended by cutaways to classic Hollywood clips starring the likes of Laurel and Hardy. Leonard Maltin's review is one that decries the insertion of these clips as if the old stars were permanently stained just by proximity to all the queer camp transgression.

---

[447] Ibid
[448] Ibid

One scene of fellatio originally cut to young Shirley Temple squeezing a cow udder; President Richard Nixon himself called and demanded this clip be removed.[449] By that time Temple was a conservative Republican politician who had served as a delegate to the United Nations General Assembly.

The newspapers were filled with reports about "Myra Breckinridge"'s troubled production, and the publicity ensured a big opening weekend. After critics savaged the movie, it tanked. It has since been tarred as one of the worst movies of all time. To me, that's a preposterous notion. I could name 10 worse 1930s exploitation movies off the top of my head.

The people who called "Myra Breckinridge" one of the worst ever were using different criteria than I am, though. In their reviews, they reveal being deeply disturbed by the sight of a confident trans character brutalizing traditional masculinity. One infamous rape scene does take the theme too far. If that sounds triggering to you, then by all means avoid "Myra Breckinridge." It's not a must-see either way, but I think it's kinda fascinating.

Russ Meyer in the Mainstream?

"**Beyond the Valley of the Dolls**" (1970) was a more successful attempt by Hollywood to create a shock film for young people. The trashy "Valley of the Dolls" had been a blockbuster in 1967, and plans for a sequel were kicked around for years. Finally, the project was handed to Russ Meyer, who had just made a ton of money with "Vixen!" Meyer hired young film critic Roger Ebert to help him write the screenplay.

Told to "make an R film smashing against an X rating,"[450] Meyer and Ebert packed in everything they thought would appeal to the young people of 1970, from sex and violence to a psychedelic party full of

---

[449] Ibid
[450] Kevin Thomas, "King of the Nudies on Biggest Film Caper Yet". *Los Angeles Times*, November 30, 1969.

drugs and oddballs. Ebert later talked about how he was aiming for a campy satire, but because the actors played it straight, many square viewers thought it was all meant earnestly. Meyer was upset that the movie ended up with an X rating, as he had much steamier material he would have included if he weren't shooting for an R.[451]

Meyer would go on to make the unambiguously X-rated movies "Supervixens," "Up!," and "Beneath the Valley of the Supervixens," usually with Ebert's assistance. All have broad, colorful tones and strong violence and sex. They're all shockers but I don't think we need to go into each one. If you like "Beyond the Valley of the Dolls," give them a try.

Black Power

American movie producers were throwing doors open to all sorts of stories in the early 1970s, desperately trying to cash in on the latest shocking things that would get young people into theaters. It was still an old boys' club, though, so their imagination was limited.

Specifically, it was a white old boys' club. Even would-be shockers about Black people and racism had to come from white guys. After listening to his liberal white friends say racist things, writer Herman Raucher wrote a script about a racist white man waking up one morning as a Black man. Columbia picked it up and wanted to hire Alan Arkin or Jack Lemmon to play the man – which would of course have required a lot of blackface.[452]

The studio at least realized that hiring an old white guy to direct would bring blowback. They went with Melvin Van Peebles, who had to go to France in the 1960s to establish a film career. Van Peebles

---

[451] Roger Ebert and Russ Meyer, "Russ Meyer: Ten Years After the 'Beyond'". *Film Comment*, Vol. 16, No. 4, p. 43-48
[452] Melvin Van Peebles in the introduction to the 2004 DVD of "Watermelon Man."

insisted on hiring a Black man, comedian Godfrey Cambridge, to play the lead.

Throughout production, Van Peebles battled with Columbia about the story. Raucher's ending was that it was all a dream: The protagonist wakes up as white again. Van Peebles did not like the implication that being Black is like living a bad dream. Mid-production, he refused to work another day until Columbia let him shoot an ending that was less insulting.[453]

"**Watermelon Man**" (1970) ended up a rather awkward combination of both perspectives, in my opinion. There are loads of jokes based on racial stereotypes that seem like hacky stand-up to me, but I suppose they could have been groundbreaking at the time. Some of the satire felt incisive, though, and I liked where Van Peebles took the story in the end.

"Watermelon Man" confronted racial issues from a Black perspective more boldly than any Hollywood film ever had before. To Hollywood's surprise, this translated to box-office success. The proto-blaxploitation crime film "Cotton Comes to Harlem" was released the same day as "Watermelon Man." It was also directed by a Black director, Ossie Davis, and also contained some pro-Black politics. It was also a hit. Hollywood was forced to recognize that Black directors could make profitable movies.

Columbia offered Van Peebles a three-picture deal. By most people's measures, Van Peebles had made the big time, the way no Black director ever had before. Black people had made independent films for decades, but the first Black film director employed by a major Hollywood studio was Gordon Parks only a year earlier.[454]

---

[453] Benjamin Wiggins, "'You Talkin' Revolution, Sweetback': On Sweet Sweetback's Baadasssss Song and Revolutionary Filmmaking," *Black Camera*, Vol. 4, No. 1, p. 28-52

[454] A.O. Scott, "We Are Family, Chapter 1: Heirs and Alumni, The Directors," *The New York Times*,

But Van Peebles didn't want to make any more compromises. He rejected Columbia's deal and made his own independent movie, **"Sweet Sweetback's Baadasssss Song**" (1971). It's the story of male sex worker Sweetback, played by Van Peebles, who fights the cops and goes on the lam. It breaks every rule in Hollywood's book about what Black people were allowed to do on screen.

Hollywood's rules for Black characters were legion. I already talked about how for decades Black characters weren't allowed to stray far from demeaning stereotypes derived from minstrel shows. Only in the 1960s did Sidney Poitier break free and play dignified protagonists with inner lives. But soon enough, his roles as essentially flawless human beings started feeling restrictive too. In "Guess Who's Coming to Dinner" (1967), he had to be a respectful, kind, humble, brilliant, handsome, well-dressed, world-famous doctor all to justify him marrying some rather ordinary white girl. And even that required a movie's worth of conversation.

Van Peebles blew away all that. Sweetback is a powerful hero, having sex, killing people, and generally being a badass. It was a power fantasy for people who really needed one, with a stridently political bent. Sweetback is fighting against "the Man," i.e. the white power structure. And he's not doing it the Sidney Poitier way, the way the white liberals preferred, to say nothing of what white conservatives wanted.

Van Peebles could throw up a middle finger to what white people wanted because "Sweet Sweetback's Baadasssss Song" was made outside every conceivable Hollywood stricture. He pretended it was a porn film so he could hire a non-union crew, which was cheaper and allowed him to employ 50% people of color. It wasn't a total fabrication on his part; many sex scenes were unsimulated. Van Peebles said that during one scene he contracted gonorrhea, for which he got workers' compensation from the Director's Guild for

---

https://www.nytimes.com/interactive/2020/04/13/t-magazine/gordon-parks.html

being "hurt on the job."[455] He used the money from workers' comp to buy desperately needed film stock. The biopic "Baadasssss!" (2003), directed by and starring Melvin's son Mario, is a very fun and mostly accurate telling of the herculean task of making "Sweet Sweetback's Baadasssss Song."

What with the many hardships during production and severely limited budget, it's a miracle any movie got made. That said, "Sweet Sweetback's Baadasssss Song" has its flaws, in my opinion, for whatever my opinion is worth. The pacing is odd; I don't think it needed nearly so many shots of Sweetback running in the desert in the second half. Van Peebles' filmmaking roots were in the French New Wave, so the movie's unclear plotting could have been a choice – but it also could have been a case of not getting all the necessary footage. And there is a very problematic scene of young Sweetback (played by 13-year-old Mario Van Peebles) losing his virginity. But "Sweet Sweetback's Baadasssss Song" has its moments, and it's monumentally important in film history for its raw, unfiltered expression of African-American rage.

"Sweet Sweetback's Baadasssss Song" got an X rating from the MPAA in March 1971. Van Peebles objected at first, knowing it would severely limit its chance of being seen. (Later the movie poster proudly proclaimed "Rated X by an All-White Jury.")[456] Because of its rating and its politics, it got into only two independent theaters, one in Detroit and one in Atlanta. In the Detroit theater, "Sweet Sweetback's Baadasssss Song" set box-office records. Word spread, and it ended up in 140 theaters across the country. By 1972, it had grossed at least 20 times its budget.[457]

"Sweet Sweetback's Baadasssss Song" is often called an early blaxploitation movie. That's partially because people tend to

---

[455] Melvin Van Peebles, The Real Deal: What It Was...Is!. Sweet Sweetback's Baadasssss Song DVD, Xenon Entertainment Group, 2003
[456] "Sweet Sweetback's Baadasssss Song," AFI Catalog, https://catalog.afi.com/Catalog/moviedetails/54130
[457] Ibid

presume that every 1970s movie centering on Black people is automatically blaxploitation. This is reductive and probably a bit racist. In the 1970s, Black actors filled the top of the call sheets for comedies (e.g., "Uptown Saturday Night" (1974)), teen dramas (e.g. "Cooley High" (1975)), romantic comedies (e.g., "Claudine" (1974)), political dramas (e.g., "The Spook Who Sat by the Door" (1973)), musical biopics (e.g., "Lady Sings the Blues" (1972)), westerns (e.g., "Buck and the Preacher" (1972)), and much more.

Granted, "Sweet Sweetback's Baadasssss Song" has more in common with blaxploitation than any of those movies. It does show powerful Black characters reveling in the sex and violence typical of exploitation. But the film's revolutionary politics are front and center in a way that exploitation filmmakers usually wouldn't risk doing, Stephanie Rothman notwithstanding. Exploitation is about delivering boobs and blood in formulaic packages that don't offend anyone with messages they might disagree with.

In the documentary "How to Eat Your Watermelon in White Company (And Enjoy It)" (2005), Van Peebles says that, for him, the message was first, the medium second. He started in painting and sculpture but found he could better reach the people he wanted to reach through film.

The true blaxploitation films that followed "Sweet Sweetback's Baadasssss Song" would not be so committed to political messaging. They might include subplots about Black Panthers-style groups, but would mainly focus on drugs, crime, or some other topic more palatable to a wide (i.e., white) audience.

Just a few months after "Sweet Sweetback's Baadasssss Song" made its mark, the first full-fledged blaxploitation film, "**Shaft**," was released. It was based on a novel about Black detective John Shaft, but Hollywood being Hollywood, the original script called for Shaft to be white. Director Gordon Parks insisted on casting Black man

Richard Roundtree.[458] Parks had a similar idea to Van Peebles', of giving the Black community a powerful hero who fought back against white people and was a sexual dynamo.

"Shaft" is not as transgressive as "Sweet Sweetback's Baadasssss Song"; it's an R-rated movie made by a major studio. It still breaks a lot of Hollywood rules about how Black people are supposed to behave on screen. Coming just after "Sweet Sweetback's Baadasssss Song" meant "Shaft" wasn't the first to do so, but it was a more conventionally structured Hollywood film that ultimately reached a bigger audience. That is, it shocked a lot more white people.

And "Shaft" made a lot of money: $13 million on a $500,000 budget. It was one of only three profitable films for MGM the whole year.[459] Its success inspired the blaxploitation films that followed – "Super Fly," "The Mack," "Foxy Brown," etc. These movies would keep delivering shocks, both of the sex-and-violence variety and of defying the neutered and non-threatening screen stereotypes descended from minstrel caricatures. (Blaxploitation arguably gave rise to other stereotypes, but that's a conversation best left to other people.)

Time for Panic

The late 1960s and early 1970s was a heyday not only for shock content, in movies and other aspects of popular culture; it was also a boon time for weirdness. LSD-inspired psychedelia, as shown in "The Trip," provides the most obvious example.

It was a time when weirdos like Alejandro Jodorowsky and Fernando Arrabal could make inroads into popular culture. They made up most of a French performance art collective called the Panic Movement that aimed to give surrealism a jolt through

---

[458] Howard Hughes, "Crime Wave: The Filmgoers' Guide to Great Crime Movies," p. 106
[459] "Show Business: Black Market," *Time*, April 10, 1972

Viennese Actionists-style shocks. According to a *New York Times* biography of Jodorowsky, "One four-hour ephemera starred a leather-clad Jodorowsky and featured the slaughter of geese, naked women covered in honey, a crucified chicken, the staged murder of a rabbi, a giant vagina, the throwing of live turtles into the audience, and canned apricots."[460]

Working in Mexico, Jodorowsky ventured into film by adapting Arrabal's play "Fando & Lis" (1968). A couple proceed through a series of violent, sacrilegious, and strange horrors to reach a promised land. Its premiere in the Acapulco Film Festival inspired a riot, which led to an outright ban throughout Mexico.[461] A heavily edited version was shown in a New York theater and nowhere else until 1971. As such, it could make little impact until after the next Jodorowsky movie became a relative hit. "Fando & Lis" is certainly shocking, but it's a lesser effort that I don't think I need to include in the shock film list. If you see the other Panic Movement movies and love them, go for it.

"**El Topo**" (1970) marks the true beginning of the Panic Movement's series of filmic freakouts. Alejandro Jodorowsky directs and stars as a gunslinger undergoing a series of bizarre adventures. It was too weird to get any sort of conventional release in 1970, but it became the first "midnight movie." At New York's Elgin Theater, "El Topo" played every night at midnight for seven straight months. John Lennon saw it there and prompted his manager, Allan Klein, to bring it to other midnight showings around the country.[462] Thus began the midnight movie phenomenon that survived through the 1970s. It led to "Pink Flamingos," "The Rocky Horror Picture Show," and other bizarre films finding audiences they wouldn't have otherwise.

---

[460] Keith Phipps, "Alejandro Jodorowsky - Biography". *The New York Times*. Baseline & All Movie Guide, 18 November 2007
[461] Virginie Selavy, "Fando y Lis: The Savage Surrealism of the First Panic Movement Film," liner notes of Alejandro Jodorowsky DVD box set
[462] Michael Atkinson,"El Topo,, Once Upon a Time at Midnight," liner notes for Blu-Ray release

Along with the shocking sights within "El Topo," Jodorowsky set up shocks in the promotion. He told whoever would listen that a scene in which he rapes his co-star shows a real rape. If you see the film, you realize that this is preposterous. Jodorowsky has since admitted it was a lie to drum up publicity. It still casts a pall on the film, I feel.

Even if you are able to dismiss Jodorowsky's lie as early-1970s "anything goes" attitudes taken too far, you still have to contend with the fact the fictional rape is shown as giving the female character her first orgasm and opening her up to sexuality. This is the same toxic idea that made "Lorna" unwatchable and likely resulted in many real sexual assaults. At least in "El Topo," the woman eventually abandons the man for another woman – but still, the endorsement of rape remains.

A much better option for the first-time Jodorowsky viewer is "**The Holy Mountain**" (1973). This movie mixes together a stew of religious symbols, bizarre imagery, anti-establishment rage, and even some humor. The plot stops dead halfway through for a series of mostly irrelevant character introductions, but you have to just roll with it. It's all meant to be an overwhelming experience that evokes some sort of ill-defined spiritual feeling. I love weird movies even more than I love shock movies, and "The Holy Mountain" is the ultimate weird movie. It's certainly not for everyone.

Jodorowsky's Panic Movement compatriot Fernando Arrabal was less interested in spirituality, but also thrived on revolutionary politics and shocks. "**Viva la Muerte**" (1971) is surreal but relatively plot-driven compared to "**I Will Walk Like a Crazy Horse**" (1973), which is essentially a series of disturbing vignettes strung along a thin premise. Neither is a masterpiece, in my opinion, but a shock film fan might enjoy them.

Even Weirder?

Outside of the Panic Movement, and indeed outside of any framework that even most cineastes had heard of, came

Yugoslavian director Dušan Makavejev. He had gained some renown for the interesting but relatively uncontroversial films "Man Is Not a Bird" and "Innocence Unprotected." In 1971 he threw the world a dramatic curveball with "**W.R.: Mysteries of the Organism**."

The "W.R." of the title refers to both "World Revolution" and Wilhelm Reich, a psychoanalyst who started as a protege of Sigmund Freud. Reich theorized that sexual inhibition was a primary means of societal repression. Eventually he came to believe that life was composed of "orgone energy," the word "orgone" arising from "orgasm" and "organism." He built orgone accumulators, metal boxes you could sit in to keep your orgone from flying away. Reich claimed that doing so could cure cancer. In 1947, the U.S. government cracked down on him for selling orgone accumulators, which it argued "could have deleterious effects on one's health." After Reich refused to appear in court, he went to jail, where he died in 1956.[463]

"W.R.: Mysteries of the Organism" covers orgone, but it is mostly concerned with sex. Sex can cure just about everything, it would seem, even communism. The movie shifts wildly between fiction and non-fiction sequences to get this thesis across. It's not pornography, but if it were ever rated, I'm confident it would get an NC-17. The scene of Cynthia Plaster Caster making her art would ensure that.

What's Happening in Australia?

If Yugoslavia can spawn a wild movie in the early 1970s, then surely Australia can too. Australia had little film industry to speak of until the government established the Australian Film Development Corporation in 1970. It then enacted extremely generous tax incentives, with deductions for up to 150% of film production costs.

---

[463] James Roy MacBean, "Sex and Politics: Wilhelm Reich, World Revolution, and Makavejev's WR," *Film Quarterly*, Vol. 25, No. 3 (Spring, 1972), p. 2-13

(My main source for this section is the documentary "Not Quite Hollywood: The Wild, Untold Story of Ozploitation!" (2008), which I recommend.)

The next key step was to relax very strict censorship laws in 1971 and create an R rating. The resulting Australian New Wave was lauded for art films like "Picnic at Hanging Rock" (1975).

It was less beloved internationally for a surge of shock films. Australian audiences relished the new homegrown movies full of sex and violence. The biggest success of the early years was "Alvin Purple" (1973), an alleged comedy that purports that sexual assault is endlessly hilarious. Sex on the screen peaked with "Fantasm" (1976), a soft-core porno that was released to regular theaters and stayed there for months. These and other early hits have not aged well. Later violent movies, such as "Mad Max" (1979), are much more enduring.

To represent the Australian New Wave, I'm going with a movie that actually was not well-received in Australia, "**Wake in Fright**" (1971). It was unpopular in part because it portrays Australians as overbearing, violent, hard-drinking, amoral yahoos. Also, its shocks were too much for many people, even by Australian New Wave standards. Specifically, an extended scene of animal slaughter proved so brutal that producers felt the need to tack a disclaimer about it at the end.

This scene makes "Wake in Fright" stand out in terms of shocks. It also has a fascinatingly unique tone; I've never seen another horror movie in which the antagonists are motivated by friendliness. I recommend you check it out.

Experimenting with Corpses

Experimental film godfather Stan Brakhage was not the type to jump on any international trend, even one that was about freeing filmmakers to show previously forbidden sights. He was already very free anyway, since he worked completely independently. With no financial backers or employees, he did not need to make money from his movies. He would just get an idea and put it on film. He didn't have to worry too much about whatever rules or conventions he might be breaking. In 1959's "Window Water Baby Moving," Brakhage had revealed childbirth up close – sights that were forbidden on film but everyday for the midwives, Ob-Gyns, etc. who facilitate this vital and normal practice.

In 1971, Brakhage decided to make short silent films capturing the everyday lives of public workers in Pittsburgh. One is about the police, one is about a hospital, and "**The Act of Seeing with One's Own Eyes**" shows forensic pathologists putting human corpses through autopsies. For someone like me who has never seen a real dead body outside of a casket in a funeral home, it is deeply unsettling to see a brain being cut out of a skull while the scalp is folded over the face, or layers of knobbly fat bursting forth when a body is sliced down the middle, etc. Often the real-life gore looks downright surreal; if some of these shots were faithfully duplicated in a feature film, I bet people wouldn't buy them.

These surreal manipulations of dead flesh reminded me of "Blood of the Beasts," the 1949 Georges Franju documentary short about a slaughterhouse. Neither movie focuses on the people doing the gory work. In "The Act of Seeing with One's Own Eyes," you see living people's hands but very rarely their faces. You also don't see any of the corpses' faces, which was a condition of being allowed to film. Brakhage trained his camera almost exclusively on the dead bodies being examined and cut apart.

"Blood of the Beasts" and "The Act of Seeing with One's Own Eyes," are also similar in how matter-of-factly they document the extreme gore that they reveal to be part of the normal workings of almost every human society. Still, I had to ask myself several times while watching "The Act of Seeing with One's Own Eyes" whether it was exploitative, in effect if not intent. Pseudo-documentaries like "Mondo Cane" will cut suddenly to rotting corpses to deliver quick and dirty shocks. "The Act of Seeing with One's Own Eyes" is never that blatant, but I was left wondering if it needed to be 32 minutes long. It certainly doesn't have the heart that "Window Water Baby Moving" does (though it may show an actual human heart). Like most experiments, "The Act of Seeing with One's Own Eyes" can yield some interesting results, but it might not provide much entertainment value.

Back in the Mainstream

In the early 1970s, every studio was looking for a director with a proven ability to make a profitable shock film. British director Ken Russell scored an international smash hit in 1969 with "Women In Love," a rather talky period drama based on a D.H. Lawrence novel. It's about couples in 1920s England who yearn for more creative marital arrangements than the typical one man/one woman thing. Its main selling point was a nude wrestling match between the two male leads. The homoeroticism doesn't quite transition into gay sex, but the men talk about love a lot. "Women In Love" could maybe qualify as a shock film for the exposed penises alone, but meh.

United Artists decided Ken Russell was the man to adapt Aldous Huxley's 1952 non-fiction book "The Devils of Loudun" into another period shocker. The book tells the story of a French priest in the 1600s who got in the way of Cardinal Richelieu's power plays. Richelieu managed to get the priest accused of seducing an entire convent. The nuns claimed the priest made a pact with the Devil, which led to them becoming possessed. To prove it, they ranted and raved at regular intervals, which became a tourist attraction.

Russell had read "The Devils of Loudun" after seeing a theatrical adaptation of it. He was later quoted as saying "when I first read the story, I was knocked out by it – it was just so shocking – and I wanted others to be knocked out by it, too. I felt I had to make it."[464]

---

[464] Quoted in Mark Kermode, "The Devil Himself: Ken Russell". *Video Watchdog*. No. 35, 1996, p. 53–58

After reading Russell's shocking screenplay, United Artists was so knocked out they decided they did not have to make it. Warner Brothers took it on.

No one thought the finished film would get anything lower than an X rating from the British Board of Film Censors. The British X rating meant that no one under 18 could see it, but it wasn't applied to pornography the way the American X rating was. The Brits were smart enough to copyright their X rating. You had to qualify for a British X, and Ken Russell's original cut of **The Devils** (1971) went too far for that. Russell was threatened with violating the Obscene Publications Act, which would have exposed him to criminal prosecution.[465] He was forced to chop down several scenes of torture and cut two scenes entirely. One cut scene involved a character masturbating with a human bone, and the other came to be known as "The Rape of Christ."[466]

The latter provides a climax to a large and important section of the movie, and in my opinion, the film suffers for not having it. It has never been re-inserted into any official release, but in 2002 film critic Mark Kermode found it in the Warner Brothers vaults and put it in a director's cut of "The Devils." Warner Brothers fought him tooth and nail because it found the scene "distasteful." The studio has a long history of turning down offers to release "The Devils" on home media.[467] As I write this, it's not streaming anywhere. Every few years it will pop up on the Criterion Channel and then disappear a month later.

This is unusual for an infamous movie that was a hit, as "The Devils" was in 1971. It did well throughout Europe, but only got a limited release in the United States. The movie was cut further for

---

[465] Mark Kermode, "Hell on Earth: The Desecration and Resurrection of 'The Devils,'" documentary
[466] Ibid
[467] "Kermode Uncut: What To Do About The Devils", https://www.youtube.com/watch?v=hAY6TFTAmQg

American audiences, apparently to the point of incomprehensibility, and was still rated X.

Even young, hip critics thought "The Devils" went too far. One who was thoroughly offended was that frequent writer of X-rated Russ Meyer movies, Roger Ebert. His zero-star review is all childish sarcasm, mostly along the lines of "[Russell] has stripped the lid of respectability off the Ursuline convent in Louden, France. He has exposed Cardinal Richelieu as a political schemer. He has destroyed our illusions about Louis XIII."[468] Ebert wasn't a dumb guy; he knew that stories about historical events can communicate truths beyond their settings. No one reads "The Crucible" for a hard-hitting expose of 1690s Salem. Ebert feints at larger ideas that "The Devils" might touch on, but stops at "violence" and "political atrocities" instead of the obvious messages about the perversity of sexual repression and how powerful people destroy lives to amass more power. As a former altar boy, Ebert may have been blinded by his rage over the movie's portrayal of the Catholic Church.

Religion can have that kind of effect. In 1971 on-screen sex and violence was becoming commonplace, but mixing in blasphemy put a movie over the top. It's as if it had a multiplicative effect instead of just an additive one. "The Devils" hits all the bases of shock content in big, bold, operatic terms. As a non-believer, I think it's a very good movie, but if you're religious, it might be too much for you.

"The Devils" has sex and violence but no sexual violence. ("The Rape of Christ" involves an inanimate object.) In 1971, rape was common in mainstream cinema. Rape is of course a very tricky area that I don't have much license to pontificate on. I'll try my best to cover the following movies sensitively, but if you have no intention of watching movies with rape scenes, skip the rest of this section.

In December 1971, two films centering on rape got widespread releases in the United States: "**Straw Dogs**" and "**A Clockwork**

---

[468] Roger Ebert, "The Devils". RogerEbert.com, Jan. 1, 1971, https://www.rogerebert.com/reviews/the-devils

Orange." "The Wild Bunch" director Sam Peckinpah was responsible for "Straw Dogs," which has a long rape scene. A major controversy developed over this scene, not only because of its brutality but also because of its ambiguity. The full version of the scene makes clear that the victim is thoroughly traumatized. To secure an R rating in the United States, the scene was cut down, but in such a way as to make it seem like the victim eventually came to enjoy the rape. This wasn't the effect that the censors intended, but still, they let it pass.

Susan George, who played the victim, speaks about this scene in a video called "Susan George interviewed on Sam Peckinpah's STRAW DOGS" that you can find on her YouTube channel. If you're interested in investigating this scene, watch that. I have nothing to add, nor do I feel it's my place to do so. I'll gladly excoriate "Lorna" and "El Topo" for their clear pro-rape messaging. But for the very complicated rape scene in "Straw Dogs," I'll let people who are affected by and vulnerable to sexual violence do the talking.

The ambiguity of the rape scene in "A Clockwork Orange" comes from whether you think it's meant to be comedic, or whether you've been identifying at all with the rapist, who has been the movie's narrator and ostensible protagonist. Like the whole movie, the scene has a very precise tone of cold-blooded, jeering psychopathy that makes it uniquely disturbing.

"A Clockwork Orange" is set in a near future that is an exaggeration of the early 1970s and all its worries: of decadence, amorality, rampant violence, uncontrollable youth, etc. I suppose those are the worries that middle-aged people always have, but they were especially justified in the 1970s. Crime rates really were going up at the time, and the young people were especially wild compared to their parents.

Anthony Burgess' novel "A Clockwork Orange" was published in 1962. In 1964, Mick Jagger campaigned to star in a film version, with Ken Russell to direct, but British censors made clear that they would never allow an adaptation of such a shocking story.[469] After it was finally made by Stanley Kubrick in 1971, it earned an X rating in both the United Kingdom and the United States. NCOMP gave it a C. Critics were split on it much the way they were with "The Wild Bunch," with some calling it the best of the year and others saying it was abhorrent. It was wildly popular with audiences everywhere.

"A Clockwork Orange" is largely a critique of operant conditioning, a psychological concept championed by B. F. Skinner. The basic idea is that you can change behaviors by pairing them with immediate rewards or punishments. Burgess' version of operant conditioning was injecting his main character Alex with a drug that induces fear while forcing him to watch footage of shocking events. This treatment makes Alex averse to sex and violence.

It's an interesting twist on the presumption that people have always had about on-screen sex and violence, that seeing too much of it must warp your mind and moral compass, especially if you're a young person. I gave my view on this presumption in the first chapter, which is essentially "maybe in theory, but not in practice." It might feel like a logical worry, and maybe in the 1970s there was a correlation, if not proof of causation. But since the 1990s, rates of violent crime and teenage pregnancies have dropped dramatically, while shock content has not.

Ironically, the movie "A Clockwork Orange" got caught in a controversy over it influencing young people to do terrible things. Several violent crimes committed by youths were blamed on the movie, with varying degrees of plausibility. Pickets formed outside director Stanley Kubrick's home. His family received so many death threats that Kubrick asked Warner Brothers to pull "A Clockwork Orange" from distribution in the United Kingdom.[470] Warner Brothers

---

[469] "A Clockwork Orange," AFL Catalog, https://catalog.afi.com/Catalog/moviedetails/54041

[470] Henry Barnes and Xan Brooks, "Cannes 2011: Re-winding A Clockwork Orange with Malcolm McDowell – video". *The Guardian*, May 20, 2011

did so, and it did not show up in theaters, on VHS, or on DVD in the U.K. until after Kubrick's death in 1999.

There is some striking irony in people threatening real-life violence to protest screen violence's alleged effect on real-life violence. It would have fit well in a movie exposing hypocrisy about how societies deal with violence, such as, say, "A Clockwork Orange."

With "A Clockwork Orange," Stanley Kubrick joined the club of well-established master filmmakers who dove headfirst into the new freedoms. Arguably the best director of all time, Alfred Hitchcock, was also a natural to do so. He had eagerly gone to very dark and brutal places throughout his filmography, most obviously in "Psycho." But he always did so within the restraints of censorship; remember that "Psycho," as groundbreaking as it was, didn't cover the most disturbing aspects of Ed Gein's story. Those would be left for "The Texas Chain Saw Massacre" and "The Silence of the Lambs."

A few other Hitchcock films could maybe qualify for the shock film list — I'm especially torn on "Marnie" (1964) — but **Frenzy**" (1972) is the clearest exemplar of Alfred Hitchcock unbound. It's the story of a rapist/murderer, and the brutality is front and center. About one rape scene, Jason Zinoman wrote in the book "Shock Value: How a Few Eccentric Outsiders Gave Us Nightmares, Conquered Hollywood, and Invented Modern Horror":

> "The camera pauses on the woman's face as you wait for Hitchcock to turn it away, to shift to a quick-cutting sequence as in the shower scene in 'Psycho.' It never happens. Instead of building suspense through indirection and clever pacing, he plants the camera in front of a brutal act of violence and then gets closer and waits. The tenor of the horror film changed. It wasn't enough to titillate or direct the audience. Now you had to assault them." (p. 32)

"Frenzy" is thus less artful than previous Hitchcock movies, and, like "Straw Dogs" and "A Clockwork Orange," not recommended for people who do not want to endure rape scenes. It's second-tier Hitchcock, if not third-tier, so if you skip it you won't be missing that much. At the very least it gives an indication of how his pre-1968 movies could have been different.

Yet another mainstream film centered on rape was released in 1972: "**Deliverance**." In this one, there is no ambiguity about the rape, which is portrayed as an unimaginable crime inflicted by evil lunatics. By no coincidence, the rape is man-on-man. Perhaps seeing "Deliverance" made men understand the true horror of rape, or perhaps it just firmed up entrenched homophobia. Either way, it was certainly a shock.

The Trilogy of Life, Then Death

Pier Paolo Pasolini had a field day with the new freedoms. In 1971, Pasolini filmed the most sexual and scatological stories from one of the foundational texts of Western literature, Boccaccio's 14th-century anthology "The Decameron." As had "Fellini Satyricon," Pasolini's "**The Decameron**" demonstrated that those intimidating centuries-old canonical works, the ones that literature professors dissect endlessly but no one else reads, were as obsessed with sex as were the people of the supposedly especially naughty 1970s.

But Pasolini's interests weren't in the "free love" ethos of the 1960s and 1970s. In episode 125 of the podcast *Criterion Reflections*, film professor Daniel Humphrey discusses how Pasolini was yearning for the pansexuality of the pre-capitalism, pre-Victorian times. Sexuality was more fluid in the Middle Ages, he says; Michel Foucault reveals in "The History of Sexuality" that there was no concept of a "homosexual" before the mid-1800s. If you had same-sex relations, you were a sodomite, which was seen as a temporary condition. Sodomy was still a crime, granted – the Middle Ages was not a queer-affirming time. It's just that society wasn't as interested in categorizing people according to their sexual practices. That interest came along in the Victorian era, which suppressed sex but also obsessively analyzed it. I doubt life in the Middle Ages was better for a queer person than it is now, but it was probably better than what Pasolini grew up with in the 1930s.

In the Middle Ages, the Catholic Church may have tried to police people's bedrooms, but it could not have much success at it. Policing in general was haphazard at best; if no one raised a big stink with the few authorities who existed within walking distance, you could get away with anything. With a predominantly rural population, little transportation, and no mass communication, each country was more disunited than anything we can imagine. What happened within a farmhouse or small town mostly stayed within that farmhouse or small town.

Pasolini's "The Decameron" delights in the freedom afforded by disunity by showing people breaking the church's sex laws and suffering no consequences. Several of the sexy stories occur in convents, with lusty nuns jumping on whatever men they could find. In 1971, Pasolini could rest easy that no one would arrest him for "contempt of the state religion."

"The Decameron" was a gigantic hit, especially in Italy. Pasolini followed it up with two more adaptations of bawdy old pillars of literature, "**The Canterbury Tales**" (1972) and "**Arabian Nights**" (1974). He dubbed these the three films "The Life Trilogy,"

While there are lots of sex scenes in The Life Trilogy, Pasolini made sure that they didn't conform to pornographic tropes. There's no woozy music playing over slow-motion thrusts and cries of ecstasy. Very few of the participants are young hotties with taut, unblemished bodies. Pasolini sought out actors with crooked teeth, because that was more realistic for the medieval settings. The environments and people in these films are as grungy as they would have been before indoor plumbing and sanitation systems. Pasolini wasn't making neorealist movies any more, but he still favored the earthiness of amateur actors and quick-and-dirty filmmaking.

A wave of movies that copied The Life Trilogy did not have such scruples. They put well-scrubbed, beautiful people in lame period costumes and watched them screw. Pasolini was so disgusted by these movies that he started a very different series of films.

Pasolini's "Death Trilogy" began with "**Salò, or the 120 Days of Sodom**" (1975). Rather than drawing from delightfully naughty stories from old anthologies, this one brought Marquis de Sade's violent psychopathy to the screen. "120 Days of Sodom" is de Sade's most repellent novel, which means it's probably the most repellent novel ever. He didn't finish it, and the last half is just a series of creative tortures and humiliations that he planned to sketch out later.[471] The word "sadism" derives from de Sade's name, and it's an apt description of his work and Pasolini's adaptation.

Several publications have put out lists of the most disturbing films of all time, and "Salò, or the 120 Days of Sodom" often tops them. The plot is simple: In Northern Italy during the end of World War II, four powerful fascists trap a group of young men and women and then rape them, kill them, force them to eat feces, and on and on. It is a stomach-churning catalog of horrors like nothing else I've ever seen.

Perhaps a few other movies are as relentlessly transgressive as "Salò, or the 120 Days of Sodom." I've seen a few that might qualify, and we will get into them later. But those other ones aren't very well made. Thus it's easier for me to distance myself from them; I can get distracted thinking about how they pulled off an especially gory effect rather than being fully immersed in the horror. "Salò" really twists the knife in my gut because it has the style of a typical neorealist film. It feels like I'm watching ordinary people doing horrific things for their own amusement.

"Salò, or the 120 Days of Sodom" is also included on lists of the greatest movies of all time – not towards the top, but still in the mix. On the They Shoot Pictures, Don't They? list that I prefer, "Salò" hovers around number 200 of the top 1,000 year after year. I wouldn't put it in the top 1,000 personally, and not just because it's

---

[471] Vincent Canby, "Film Festival: 'Salo' Is Disturbing..." *The New York Times*. October 1, 1977

so disturbing. It's essentially a well-made exploitation film, with messaging I find very dubious.

"Salò" is clearly about absolute power corrupting absolutely, which I of course agree with. That was especially relevant for people like Pasolini who had survived a fascist regime. But it's a message that I can grasp after one or two atrocities. The twentieth feels gratuitous.

In interviews, Pasolini made clear that he also meant "Salò" as a metaphor about traditional rural Italian cultures being overtaken by homogenizing consumerism. Ugh. Hey, I don't like consumerism either, but c'mon, man. Equating consumerism with fascism and Marquis de Sade is more than a bit over the top. Pasolini seems to me like a typical Grumpy Old Man here, turning his distaste for societal change into a big, overblown, apocalyptic rant. My disagreement is not enough to make me give "Salò" zero stars, but it's my second-least favorite Pasolini film, above only the very, very different "The Gospel According to St. Matthew."

Controversy started churning well before "Salò"'s release date in 1975. Pasolini kept busy giving interviews and planning his next Death Trilogy movie, a biopic of Gilles des Rais, a 15th-century French war hero who confessed to being a serial killer of children. Then three weeks before "Salò"'s premiere, Pasolini was murdered. A 17-year-old boy named Pino Pelosi was caught with Pasolini's car and confessed. Pelosi said Pasolini had picked him up, driven him to a beach, and made sexual advances. This allegedly provoked Pelosi to beat Pasolini to a pulp, breaking his bones and crushing his testicles, and then run over him several times with a car and set him on fire.[472] There were doubts about his story, but the case was considered closed.

In 2005, Pasolini's frequent collaborator Sergio Citti revealed that several reels of "Salò" had been stolen days before Pasolini's death. Pasolini was supposed to meet with the thieves on the night of the murder. Later investigations of Pasolini's clothes revealed DNA

---

[472] Ibid

traces from many people, none of whom were Pelosi. That same year, Pelosi admitted that three other men beat and killed Pasolini.[473] Pelosi said he had claimed he acted alone in 1975 so that gangsters wouldn't kill his family.[474]

In 2022, a former member of Banda della Magliana, a Roman gang with ties to neo-fascist terrorist groups, testified that Pelosi's role was to act as a mediator between Pasolini and three men who had the stolen reels of film.[475] There has been plenty of speculation about whether Pasolini was killed for political reasons, possibly by far-right groups that had always hated him. Some have implicated more respected members of the political establishment, but no one knows for sure.

What people knew in 1975 was that "Salò, or the 120 Days of Sodom" was the most disturbing movie anyone had ever seen, and its director had just been murdered. The movie was widely banned and still is in many countries. The British Board of Film Censors refused it a certificate "on the legal grounds of gross obscenity."[476] When a London cinema club screened it in 1977, it was raided by the police.[477] "Salò" was banned in Australia until 1993, but then re-banned in 1997.[478]

In probably the most tolerant period for film shocks, Pier Paolo Pasolini succeeded in making a movie that most everyone thought went too far. "Salò, or the 120 Days of Sodom" represents the peak of shock film. I suppose it's required viewing for anyone interested in the topic. Just don't say I didn't warn you.

---

[473] "Asesinato de Pasolini, nueva investigación". *La Razón*, July 2, 2012
[474] "Who really murdered Pier Paolo Pasolini?". *Financial Times*, 2024.
[475] Ibid
[476] "Case Studies: "Salo/100 Days of Sodom," The British Board of Film Censorship History website, https://www.bbfc.co.uk/education/case-studies/salo-120-days-of-sodom
[477] Ibid
[478] Rachel Browne, "Sadistic sex movie ban 'attacks art expression'". *Brisbane Times*, July 20, 2008

Another Peak Shocker

You could argue that the peak of shock film happened a few years before "Salò," in 1972. That was the year that John Waters' magnum opus **"Pink Flamingos"** premiered in Baltimore. There is a scene in "Salò" in which characters eat human feces, but of course the actors aren't eating the real stuff. An actor in "Pink Flamingos" eats real dog feces.

One "Pink Flamingos" scene involving a man, a woman, and a chicken got so twisted that John Waters later said he had regrets about it.[479] If John Waters thinks a movie went too far, you know it's in the running for the most shocking film of all time.

Waters was very intentional about pushing shocks farther to grab attention. About the dog-poop eating scene, he said:

> "I had to get people's attention some way. I figured if I did that, no one would ever be able to forget it, and that it would be a first and last in film history. It was the first idea I had for the whole movie. I had $10,000 and I knew I had to compete with regular movies. You have to go way out on a limb and give 'em something that the studios would never want to give them."[480]

On the midnight-movie circuit created by "El Topo," "Pink Flamingos" was a massive hit. It ran continuously for 95 weeks in New York City and 10 years in Los Angeles.[481] Its success meant worldwide distribution, which of course brought dozens of bans and edits for content. "Pink Flamingos" is too disturbing even for the

---

[479] Keaton Bell, "John Waters on Pink Flamingos, Divine, and 50 Years of Filth," *Vogue*, June 30, 2022
[480] Quoted in Scott McDonald, "John Waters' Divine Comedy." Artforum.com, https://www.artforum.com/features/john-waters-divine-comedy-208458/
[481] Gus Van Sant, "Timeless trash". *The Advocate*. April 15, 1997, No. 731. p. 40–41

people of today; in 2024 it was "refused classification," i.e. banned, in New Zealand.[482]

Like "The Devils," "Pink Flamingos" was too much for X-rated-film writer Roger Ebert, who gave it zero stars. Mark Kermode, the critic who made a crusade of restoring "The Devils" to its full transgressiveness, said "Pink Flamingos" is one of the few movies he ever walked out of.[483]

Meanwhile, queer audiences reveled in "Pink Flamingos"'s balls-out defiance of the "good taste" standards that had classified their identities as unspeakably repulsive. In 1997, director Gus Van Sant called it "early gay agitprop filmmaking" and Waters "a new Buñuel distorting the suburban status quo."[484] It's a "piss off the squares" act of intentional provocation, similar in spirit to punk rock except delivered with a wry smile instead of a sneer.

I should warn any potential viewers that John Waters movies regularly contain rapes. Like everything else, they are delivered as over-the-top, outlandish atrocities to laugh at in shock. I do not see them as endorsements of rape, like in "Lorna" and "El Topo." Still, I recognize that not everyone can endure rape scenes, regardless of the tone in which they are packaged.

Waters followed up "Pink Flamingos" with "**Female Trouble**" (1974) and "**Desperate Living**" (1977), which complete his so-called "Trash Trilogy." The latter two don't top the shocks of "Pink Flamingos," but still certainly earn their X ratings. I find them to be loads of campy fun. Despite "Pink Flamingos" being the most important John Waters film, maybe try one of the later movies first to make sure you're ready for the peak shocker.

---

[482] Film and Video Labeling Body, https://www.fvlb.org.nz/film-detail?id=57946

[483] "Cult Movies". Mark Kermode's Secrets Of Cinema, Season 3, Episode 3. January 25, 2021

[484] Van Sant, "Timeless trash"

Genuine Trash

A fan of John Waters is not someone who offends easily. So when I say that "**Last Tango in Paris**" (1972) is deeply offensive to me, I hope you'll take it seriously.

"Last Tango in Paris" is the story of a middle-aged man, played by Marlon Brando, who often has sex with a 19-year-old woman, played by Maria Schneider. Why in the world this gorgeous woman would be seduced by this mean, mumbly, disheveled, overweight old fart within minutes of meeting him is unclear to me. I think we're expected to go with it because we know this man is Marlon Brando.

In 1972, most people did go with it, and reviews, especially Pauline Kael's, called "Last Tango in Paris" a masterpiece. Even more than now, moviegoers then were heavily conditioned into sympathizing with white male protagonists, regardless of how they behaved. Almost every previous movie was about a middle-aged straight white man defeating some bad guys and winning a beautiful young white woman. Nowadays, stories from people besides middle-aged straight white men are increasingly asserting themselves, and I think viewers are better able to be objective about whether a straight white male character is worthy of their sympathies.

Not only did I find Brando's character unsympathetic; I didn't even find him interesting enough to be an anti-hero. I simply could not care what happened to him one way or another. Eventually the reason for his pain is revealed, and it did pull at least a couple of my heartstrings. It was too little too late to get me really invested in his fate.

I'm sure that Brando's character was especially relatable to rich, famous, powerful guys like Brando, "Last Tango in Paris" director Bernardo Bertolucci, and others in their circle. Many of them undoubtedly had affairs with gorgeous young women and thus did not find the movie's premise to be farfetched. If so, "Last Tango in Paris" is missing a key element: the dramatic power imbalance at play in those situations. Brando's character is not some celebrity who can abuse his power to have sex with young models; he's just some schlub.

Meanwhile, Maria Schneider's character is not well fleshed out, in my opinion. The movie makes a feeble attempt to justify her attraction to Brando's character by showing that her fiancee is a pretentious ass. But you'd think a woman who looks like Maria Schneider would have plenty of better options than these two losers. I don't believe "Last Tango in Paris" has any real interest in what's going on in the woman's head. She is just a beautiful object that Brando's character uses to salve his emotional wounds.

I grant that my take is subjective; many other people have felt the characters' relationship made sense on some level beyond middle-aged male wish fulfillment. The much more important strike against "Last Tango in Paris" concerns an especially controversial scene that shows Marlon Brando forcibly pushing butter between Maria Schneider's buttocks. Schneider did not consent to this and had no idea it was going to happen. It wasn't in the script because director Bernardo Bertolucci wanted to get an unsimulated "reaction of frustration and rage."[485] This is unconscionable, and I don't think any movie could be worth this kind of violation.

Schneider was permanently scarred not only by the assault but also by footage of it being replayed for millions of people across the world, many of whom found it arousing. She later said:

> "I should have called my agent or had my lawyer come to the set because you can't force someone to do something that isn't in the script, but at the time, I didn't know that. Marlon said to me: 'Maria, don't worry, it's just a movie,' but during the scene, even though what Marlon was doing wasn't real, I

---

[485] Geoffrey Macnab, "Bernardo Bertolucci: 'I thought I couldn't make any more movies'". *The Guardian*, February 1, 2013

was crying real tears ... I felt humiliated and to be honest, I felt a little raped, both by Marlon and by Bertolucci."[486]

The experience of starring in "Last Tango in Paris" sent Schneider into a spiral of depression, alcoholism, and suicide attempts.[487] She made a few more movies but developed a reputation for being unreliable and disobedient, in part because she refused to ever do another nude scene. Later in life she became a strong advocate for improving the representation of women in film.

Rape scenes may be a tricky area, but I think I'm safe in condemning a movie that tries to sell an actual sexual assault as an erotic scene. "Last Tango in Paris" brings the endorsement of rape into real life.

It seems clear to me that Bertolucci and Brando committed a felony in making "Last Tango in Paris." The Italian government did charge Bertolucci with a crime, but one of obscenity. He was acquitted, but the government still revoked his civil rights for five years and handed him a suspended prison sentence.[488] The movie was adjudicated as "esasperato pansessualismo fine a se stesso," which translates as "aggravated, gratuitous pansexualism." It was banned from Italy and all copies were ordered destroyed.[489]

I think "Last Tango in Paris" is mostly a pornographic fantasy dressed in art-film clothing. Maybe if you don't know about the real-life consequences of the movie and watch only the first 20 minutes,

---

[486] Quoted in Bonnie Malkin, "Last Tango in Paris director suggests Maria Schneider 'butter rape' scene not consensual". *The Guardian*, December 4, 2016

[487] Dennis McLellan, "Maria Schneider dies at 58; actress in 'Last Tango in Paris'". *Los Angeles Times*, February 4, 2011

[488] Ariston Anderson, "Hollywood Reacts With Disgust, Outrage Over 'Last Tango in Paris' Director's Resurfaced Rape Scene Confession". *The Hollywood Reporter*, December 3, 2016

[489] Silvia Donati, "Italy's Treasures: Bernardo Bertolucci". Italy Magazine, Nov. 30, 2018, https://www.italymagazine.com/featured-story/italys-treasures-bernardo-bertolucci

you could enjoy it as a porno with high production values: A hot young woman and a man who's basically a duller version of Ron Jeremy meet in an empty apartment and have sex almost immediately. The rest of "Last Tango in Paris" does explore some ideas that no porn film would ever approach, but I found it difficult to engage with them in light of the abuse. I think it's a zero-star exemplar of sociopathic men taking the new freedoms too far.

The people who loved "Last Tango in Paris" hoped it would lead to a rush of non-pornographic dramas dealing frankly with sex. It didn't, especially not in the States. "Don't Look Now" (1973), directed by a Brit and produced in Italy, does show a married couple in a very realistic sex scene. A few other movies we'll cover later might qualify. But as "Last Tango in Paris" was turning on sophisticates, an even more explicit movie was taking screen sex in a much less artsy direction.

The Real Thing

Hard-core pornography was widely available in 1972, and you could justify seeing it under the guise of being a hip connoisseur of cutting-edge cinema. Instead of going to "Last Tango in Paris," you could probably catch "**Deep Throat**" somewhere nearby.

"Deep Throat" was not the first feature-length porn film. It wasn't even very successful until it got free publicity from New York City mayor John Lindsay. He announced he was cleaning up Times Square by shutting down a theater that was showing "Deep Throat." Across the country, people flocked to see it, eager to discover what all the fuss was about. Newspapers reviewed it as if it were any other film, and their critical takedowns only fanned the flames.[490]

"Deep Throat" was banned in many places but got into hundreds of theaters and earned tens of millions of dollars (though certainly not $600 million, as many sources have attested. That claim is likely a

---

[490] Karina Longworth, "Erotic '80s: Porno Chic and The Brief Heyday of X Ratings," *You Must Remember This* podcast, episode 188

cover for money laundering by the mafiosos who funded the movie).[491] Its fame was only enhanced when "Deep Throat" became the code name of the secret source for Bob Woodward's and Carl Bernstein's reporting of the Watergate scandal.

Before seeing the actual movie, I watched a documentary about it, "Inside Deep Throat" (2005). and a dramatization of the events surrounding it, "Lovelace" (2013). Both made clear that star Linda Lovelace was forced to star in "Deep Throat" by her sadistic husband, who physically and psychologically abused her. This made me loath to see it, but I figured I had to for this book.

Watching the movie confirmed my disgust. "Deep Throat" is a string of grimy, ugly hard-core sex scenes interspersed with feeble stabs at broad comedy. Maybe if you squint really hard, you can see it as encouraging women to seek sexual fulfillment: Lovelace's character pursues new sexual experiences because she has never had a genuine orgasm. But the solution, that her clitoris is located in the back of her throat, is ridiculous male wish fulfillment. It means that instead of merely being willing to perform fellatio, she needs to. This fantasy can tamp down the knowledge in the back of every man's head that giving a blow job is almost no woman's idea of a good time.

For whatever reason, "Deep Throat" inspired a wave of "porno chic." People from all walks of life started going to see porn movies. Newspaper reviews and stories about the scandals kept them in the zeitgeist, and people wanted to be part of the national conversation.

The moviegoers of 1972 were hungry for the next level of shock. I think they were "chasing the dragon" the same way exploitation fans were in the 1960s. I can imagine that if you loved "The Wild Bunch" and "A Clockwork Orange," you might want to catch the latest height of transgressive thrill.

---

[491] Michael Hiltzik, "'Deep Throat' Numbers Just Don't Add Up". *Los Angeles Times*, February 24, 2005

To shock-seeking filmgoers at the time, hard-core pornography seemed like the logical next step. Graphic violence, nudity, etc. had all been strict taboos until a few years before. No one ever thought we could see those in a theater, yet here we are. Simulated sex scenes had already become commonplace; why not the real thing? After all, you're just watching people engage in a victimless act that most adults do regularly.

The next big pornographic hit was "**Behind the Green Door**" (1972). In it, a woman is kidnapped and hypnotized into going on stage to perform various sex acts for an exclusive crowd. The whole room eventually becomes host to an orgy.

Instead of trying to be a comedy like "Deep Throat" does, "Behind the Green Door" tries to be an art film. No doubt its directors noticed that smarty-pants people were a growing market for pornos. You might as well target them; the regular porn fans will show up for anything that has sex.

"Behind the Green Door" is much less grimy than "Deep Throat," and I'm not aware of any real-life coercion behind the scenes. The on-screen coercion still ruined the movie for me, though. It's unclear why the female character had to be kidnapped and hypnotized to star in the sex show. Why couldn't she have done so willingly? I have to assume the filmmakers thought that would be less erotic somehow. It's reminiscent of how the Production Code Administration forced the producers of "The Fountainhead" to change a consensual one-night stand into a rape by the protagonist. A rapist hero, or a woman who was kidnapped and hypnotized, was easier for men to accept than a woman who enjoys sex.

The next major mainstream pornographic blockbuster tried to be a fantasy/drama. "**The Devil in Miss Jones**" (1973) is about a virginal woman who dies by suicide. When an angel gives her a second chance at life, she devotes it to having sex. It's supposedly inspired by Jean-Paul Sartre's "No Exit" and is not a parody of the 1941 comedy "The Devil and Miss Jones."

"The Devil in Miss Jones" is the least disturbing one of this trio, to my eyes. The female protagonist pursues sex for her own pleasure. The movie still has the typical problem of pornography, that it caters to male wish fulfillment much more than female. (Again, women act orgasmic about performing fellatio in "The Devil in Miss Jones," while no man returns the favor.) The sex acts get freaky in parts, but I don't want to kink-shame.

"The Devil in Miss Jones" made even more money than "Deep Throat" and "Behind the Green Door." *Variety* reported that it was the sixth highest-grossing movie of any kind in 1973, ranking between Best Picture nominee "Paper Moon" and the James Bond film "Live and Let Die."[492] "Deep Throat" ranked 11th on the same list.

There were zero hard-core pornography films in *Variety*'s top 25 for 1974 or any year thereafter. As quickly as it had arisen, the porno chic trend petered out (no pun intended). Pornography certainly didn't disappear, but it found its place was underground.

I suspect it's a case of the shock wearing off. Most people might have been curious to see one or two screenings of hard-core porn films, but then felt no need to check out another. It turns out that unless you want to masturbate in public, it's not really that much fun to watch pornography in a theater. One problem is that you have to be among masturbating strangers. Beyond that, it gets boring. As Donald Richie writes in a Criterion.com article, "Most porn narratives are quite empty and are designed to be so. Any consideration of narrative consequences, of character, detracts from the recognized aim of titillation."[493] Masturbating while watching a movie and engaging in a filmic narrative are simply at cross purposes.

---

[492] Syd Silverman, "Variety Chart Summary For 1973". *Variety*. May 8, 1974, p. 68

[493] Donald Richie, "In the Realm of the Senses: Some Notes on Oshima and Pornography," Criterion.com,
April 30, 2009: https://www.criterion.com/current/posts/1108-in-the-realm-of-the-senses-some-notes-on-oshima-and-pornography

Non-pornographic films of course often have sex scenes too, but seldom long enough ones to allow for masturbation to completion. Unless it communicates some character or plot point, a sex scene lasting more than a minute becomes a sideshow that kills any dramatic thrust. (No pun intended, sigh. It's difficult to avoid inadvertent innuendos when seemingly half of the words in the English language can be interpreted as sexual euphemisms.)

There is a place for pornography, and that place is a private one. Porn is now consumed in short online clips behind closed doors, which works much better for its purpose. In the 1970s, pornos were in theaters and lasted more than an hour only because that's how all movies that were inappropriate for children were consumed.

The Prudes Strike Back

Also, a significant backlash in the mid-1970s had some effect on driving pornography back out of mainstream culture. The hipsters and porn fiends in the big cities did not represent the whole nation. Protests eventually succeeded in getting major newspapers to stop carrying ads or reviews of X-rated movies. In a world where newspapers dominated the dissemination of information, that pushed pornography firmly underground. Movie theaters stopped screening anything rated X, scared both of controversy and lower profits from the lack of advertising.

The few non-pornographic X-rated films of the time suffered collateral damage from the retrenchment. Newspapers and theaters found it much easier to maintain a blanket ban on anything with an X rating than to make exceptions that would probably cause more controversy than they were worth. Studios became even more firm about filmmakers producing movies that received an R rating or lower. Soon after "Last Tango in Paris" left theaters, its type became an endangered species. Those who predicted a flood of X-rated art films were disappointed.

Meanwhile, authorities were working overtime to suppress the handful of surprisingly popular porn films. "Deep Throat" proved easy to charge with violating obscenity laws, and many, many state and local jurisdictions did so. In "Banned Films," de Grazia and Newman note, "prosecutors around the country brought more actions against this film than against any previous film except 'The Birth of a Nation'."[494]

Convictions were not so easy to get, though. The existing legal standard for obscenity, established in 1966 by Justice William Brennan, defined an obscene work as being "utterly without redeeming social value." Juries often decided that "Deep Throat"'s meager jokes and veneer of female sexual empowerment constituted enough "social value" to warrant acquittals.

In practice, Brennan's legal standard meant finding almost nothing obscene. This was predictable; in response to the "I Am Curious (Yellow)" controversy, Massachusetts Chief Justice G. Joseph Tauro observed that "Few, if any, works will be found where some expert testimony cannot be elicited in support of some bare minimum of social value which would, according to the Brennan doctrine, preempt the court from [convicting]."[495]

After "I Am Curious (Yellow)" and the *Stanley v. Georgia* case that made porn legal, President Lyndon Johnson commissioned a major study on the effects of obscenity and pornography. "The Report of the Commission on Obscenity and Pornography" was released in 1970. It concluded that while explicit sexual material should certainly be kept from children, it didn't cause significant problems in adults. This was not the result lawmakers were looking for, and most denounced it.

In 1972, Richard Nixon was president, and he did not care what a bunch of knowledgeable, rigorous researchers said about something that made him and his friends feel icky. After he replaced

---

[494] de Grazia and Newman, p. 141
[495] Quoted in de Grazia and Newman, p. 135

two U.S. Supreme Court justices, the newly conservative-majority Court was primed to rewrite the federal obscenity standard.

The 1973 case *Miller v. California* gave the new court its chance. Their decision established a new doctrine that changed the definition of obscenity from "utterly without redeeming social value" to "lacking serious literary, artistic, political, or scientific value." The latter is more broad, ensuring that more works of art could be judged obscene.

The new obscenity standard sent the movie industry reeling. Now they had to somehow divine exactly how much "serious literary, artistic, political, or scientific value" (whatever that means exactly) they had to put in their movies. Who knew what these judges would deem "serious"? Some filmmakers toned things down to avoid courting trouble.

Studios saw their worst fears realized when "Carnal Knowledge" (1971) was charged with obscenity by a court in Albany, Georgia. "Carnal Knowledge" deals frankly with sex but doesn't show any, and isn't a shock film by the standards of its time. The U.S. Supreme Court unanimously overturned the verdict, saying that only hard-core pornography counted as obscene.[496] The studios breathed a sigh of relief.

Even for pornography, though, there was no big wave of crackdowns. "[After the *Miller v. California* decision,] fewer obscenity prosecutions were brought nationally," say de Grazia and Newman, "and the conviction rate remained constant."[497] All kinds of crime were on the rise in 1973, and the legal system was busy prioritizing the more serious ones.

One large-scale attempt to prosecute pornography proved to be a farce. In 1974, Assistant United States Attorney Larry Parrish charged 12 people and five corporations connected to "Deep

---

[496] Miller, p. 228
[497] de Grazia and Newman, p. 143

Throat" with conspiracy to transport obscenity across state lines.[498] It's not as if all these people and corporations were in a big bus hauling film cans around the country. Parrish could levy this charge on anyone who was ever involved in an obscene movie that was showing in more than one state. You might remember from the "Zabriskie Point" affair that when the feds were determined to bust someone, they conjured a way to pop them for crossing state lines.

Larry Parrish was an evangelical Christian but insisted that his religious beliefs didn't influence his work. He also told the Adult Film Association of America "If you want to know why I am a prosecutor, you can read Romans 13."[499] That chapter starts with "Let everyone be subject to the governing authorities, for there is no authority except that which God has established. The authorities that exist have been established by God. Consequently, whoever rebels against the authority is rebelling against what God has instituted, and those who do so will bring judgment on themselves." Clearly, Parrish saw himself as one of those authorities established by God to bring judgement on rebels (or in the words of Scripture, make sure they bring it on themselves, which is a clever turn of phrase that displaces culpability).

In Parrish's mind, the rebels against God's institutions included projectionists from theaters that screened "Deep Throat," a ticket taker at a Vermont theater, and actor Harry Reems. Reems had been hired to work in the movie's lighting crew but stepped in to act (i.e., have sex twice, say a few lines) for one day. That was the total extent of his involvement with "Deep Throat." He didn't edit it, produce it, or promote it, and certainly didn't transport it across state lines. In 1976, Reems was convicted, becoming the first federal felon for appearing in a film.[500]

Reems' case became a cause célèbre in Hollywood. Jack Nicholson, Warren Beatty, Richard Dreyfuss, Shirley MacLaine,

---

[498] de Grazia and Newman, p. 142
[499] Quoted in ibid
[500] de Grazia and Newman, p. 141-143

Mike Nichols, and many others contributed to his defense. Nicholson, Beatty and Louise Fletcher offered to testify on his behalf.[501] The injustice may have motivated them, but I bet they also did not like the precedent that actors could be thrown into federal prison just for doing perfectly legal things that directors told them to do.

Reems was able to hire attorney Alan Dershowitz. Dershowitz assembled a host of strong arguments. One was that "Deep Throat" was made before the *Miller* decision, which meant that the new, tougher obscenity standard didn't apply to it. Somehow this hadn't been established in Reems' first trial. Dershowitz succeeded in getting Reems a new trial, but the government decided not to schedule one. Reems was free.[502]

Harry Reems became one of the most famous porn stars in history. But the reward that comes from that tends to be even more fleeting than it is for Hollywood stars. If a porn star doesn't cross over into the mainstream – and almost none do – the latter half of their life will often be characterized by drug abuse and poverty. Porn tends to be an especially ugly and brutal business. There's something about putting actual sex on film that necessitates the creation of this disreputable, separate cinematic world that gets sadder the more you look at it.

And the two cinematic worlds had been firmly separated by the time Reems was convicted in 1976. Mainstream America had tried hard-core pornography, decided it belonged underground, and moved on. As long as pornos weren't making headlines and screening in the suburbs, most people had bigger fish to fry. We will see later how a perceived connection to violence put the nail in the coffin of mainstream pornography.

Thus porno chic represents the first time since 1968 that a new type of shock content hit a dead end. Violence, nudity, etc. had all

---

[501] "Inside Deep Throat," documentary, 2005
[502] de Grazia and Newman, p. 143

worked like gangbusters and remain in movies today. But with very few exceptions, narrative cinema retreated from hard-core sex. At least in this one area, a more conservative and restrictive stance was restored.

What If We Made the Core Softer?

The French eventually started using the new freedoms to make erotic movies, of course. And being French, they were not so gauche as to stitch together some long hard-core scenes and call it *un film*. Even their sex films had to look professional, use attractive and capable actors, and feature long stretches of men trying to indoctrinate attractive young women with pseudo-philosophical horseshit.

"**Emmanuelle**" was the most successful of the 128 erotic movies released to French theaters in 1974.[503] It's far from the first movie that could be called "soft-core porn," but it's probably the most famous. It spawned six sequels and dozens of imitators with titles that incorporated variant spellings of the name "Emmanuelle" to avoid copyright infringement. The original "Emmanuelle" movie is "soft-core" in that it shows no penetration, but it is still overloaded with sex. No sex scene lasts so long that it brings the narrative to a standstill, so don't expect the Shannon-Tweed/late-night-Cinemax version of soft-core that is just porn without penises.

I tried and failed to convince myself that I didn't need to watch "Emmanuelle" for this book. I'm not against erotica; I just don't trust 1970s male filmmakers with it. As we've seen above, even when a movie tries to explore the era's new sexual freedoms, it ends up "freeing" women only to fulfill male sexual demands. This is the scam of the sexual revolution that Peter Bogdanovich talked about in "The Killing of the Unicorn."

---

[503] Daniel Bird. "Introduction by Borowczyk expert Daniel Bird," "Immoral Tales" Dual Format Blu-ray - Arrow Films UK.

While watching the first two-thirds of "Emmanuelle," I was frankly shocked to witness a mostly feminist, sex-positive story of a woman discovering what she desires. Emmanuelle is a young woman in an open marriage with an older man who tells her "You're not my possession." He encourages her to practice free love with their circle of idle, wealthy French expats in Bangkok.

Emmanuelle falls for someone outside the circle, the only French woman she knows who has a career. Then her husband's mask of mellow libertinism slips off. As he rages, his friend calls him out on his hypocrisy; clearly the "freedom" he wants for Emmanuelle is defined on his terms, and therefore is not freedom at all.

<SPOILER ALERT>

Emmanuelle's husband defines love as a never-ending search for pleasure. But when Emmanuelle is with this other woman, she starts to feel a deeper love she has never felt before. The woman doesn't feel the same way, though, and Emmanuelle comes home heartbroken.

Throughout the movie, Emmanuelle's husband and his circle of libertines push her to get with an old lothario named Marco. She is repulsed by Marco, but in her grief over the rejection, she finally relents. Marco spends their date indoctrinating her on what he calls "true eroticism," which he defines in flowery, pseudo-philosophical terms.

In practice, Marco's "true eroticism" turns out to be the kind of abuse a pimp puts a woman through to "turn her out," i.e., make her one of the sex workers in his "stable." Marco gets Emmanuelle high on opium and then traps her into being raped by two men. Then they go to a Thai boxing match, where he expects her to allow the winner to take her from behind in front of the whole crowd. In the final scene, Emmanuelle shows she has become a robotic, subservient sex doll dreaming only of how to gratify Marco and her husband.

If all this were portrayed as a horror, "Emmanuelle" could have been quite an indictment of the sadistic man's version of "true eroticism." Instead, it's shown as the proper path for Emmanuelle. I don't have much doubt about my interpretation here, especially after reading what star Sylvia Kristel had to say about the rape scene: "I couldn't see how a rape would be pleasurable. These two Thai people were not actors. I really had to fight for my life there." Kristel was told that her character was supposed to enjoy the rape, but she winced and struggled through the lone take of the scene that she could endure.[504]

</SPOILER ALERT>

If you didn't read the spoilers, I want to make sure you know that "Emmanuelle" is not a tale of female sexual empowerment. It pretends to be one and then pulls the rug out from under you. In terms of the plot alone, it is even more regressive and misogynistic than "Deep Throat." It is not too different from "The Outlaw."

In 1974, "Emmanuelle" was seen as a refreshing new take on sex in cinema. Roger Ebert's review said "Now that hardcore porno has become passe, it's a relief to see a movie that drops the gynecology and returns to a certain amount of sexy sophistication."[505] Columbia Pictures made it the first X-rated movie it distributed in the United States because in France, more women were lining up to see it than men.[506] (Hopefully the women left early.) Despite having been held from release for several months by French censors, "Emmanuelle" sold more movie tickets in France than any other 1974 movie of any kind by a huge margin: 8,894,132 to the second-place 6,475,758 sold for Disney's "Robin Hood."[507] In the United Kingdom, an edited

---

[504] Danny Shipka, "Perverse Titillation: The Exploitation Cinema of Italy, Spain and France, 1960-1980," p. 299
[505] Roger Ebert, "Emmanuelle". RogerEbert.com, Jan. 1, 1975, https://www.rogerebert.com/reviews/emmanuelle-1975
[506] Matthew Bernstein, ed. "The Stigma of X. Controlling Hollywood: Censorship and Regulation in the Studio Era," p. 257
[507] CBO Box Office, La référence des professionnels du cinéma, https://www.cbo-boxoffice.com/

version became, in the words of censor James Ferman, "the first film of its genre that didn't play to the raincoat brigade."[508]

"Emmanuelle" initiated a trend of European soft-core with higher production values and greater acceptability than hard-core pornography. These were movies that women could feel safe going to, and everyone could expect to not sit next to some creep masturbating. Like all pornography, the style switched to videotape in the 1980s and became integrated into the mad stew available online in the 1990s and beyond.

Bakshit Crazy

What if we combined "Emmanuelle" and "Robin Hood"? To Americans, almost none of whom had seen Japan's Animerama movies, **Fritz the Cat** (1972) was their first introduction to animated characters having sex. Ralph Bakshi took a few comics by R. Crumb and animated them for the big screen. Bakshi also added a story of his own to the end that is more brutal and humorless than Crumb's typical stew of satire and sex.

Even if it weren't animated, "Fritz the Cat"'s content would earn its X rating. But it's all the more disturbing to watch cute cartoon characters pull out their penises and shoot intravenous drugs. Being derived from R. Crumb's drawing style meant creating a stronger association between kiddie cartoons and sex than I feel comfortable with personally.

Ralph Bakshi's lifetime artistic goal was to bring adult themes into animation. I think he accomplished this better in later films by using the sort of grown-up-looking character designs that you see in

---

[508] Quoted in "Just Jaeckin, photographer and director who titillated the world with his hit film Emmanuelle – obituary," *The Telegraph*, September 21, 2022 https://www.telegraph.co.uk/obituaries/2022/09/21/just-jaeckin-photographer-director-who-titillated-world-hit/?msockid=0d214cc3ab4c64700e505d46aaaa658a

anime. Granted, "Fritz the Cat" was the Bakshi movie that was a huge worldwide hit.

"Fritz the Cat" was also frustrating to me at times. Sometimes Bakshi tries to make a genuinely interesting statement, but then finds a way to ruin it. For one sequence, Bakshi gathered audio of regular Black people discussing serious issues. It's the type of honest, unfiltered conversation that white people never heard in the 1970s and seldom do now. Bakshi animated it, but he couldn't leave well enough alone. In the middle of a normal conversation, one animated character reaches over and grabs the genitals of another. Nothing anyone is saying signals that this act makes sense in any way. Clearly Bakshi just got bored with not having anything sexual happen for more than a minute.

Bakshi spun the spirit of this scene into the full-length film "**Coonskin**" (1975). It takes characters from the Uncle Remus stories, which were well-known from "Song of the South," and turns them into blaxploitation heroes. It's all meant to be a satire of minstrel characters, but Bakshi's compulsion to shock keeps undercutting his messaging, in my view. I am obviously a fan of film shocks, but there's a time and a place for everything.

Occasionally a statement about American hypocrisy and brutality toward Black people would hit the mark for me, but even then I would be thinking "man, I wish a Black person directed this instead." I don't think it's impossible for white people to make valid political art about the struggles of Black people. But because white people don't live the struggles 24/7, it's much, much more difficult for them to get it right. To put it kindly, Ralph Bakshi did not strike me as possessing a full and nuanced understanding of the Black experience in the United States. I think he dove head-first into a deep, wide pool despite only knowing how to doggy-paddle. But Black people would be a better judge of this than me.

The Congress of Racial Equality (CORE) agreed with my position, except they expressed it more assertively. CORE's protests led

Paramount to postpone the release of "Coonskin" for months, and eventually bury it in a limited release.[509] It made a tiny fraction of the gross that "Fritz the Cat" had. Ralph Bakshi then retreated into PG-rated fantasy material with "Wizards" (1977) and "The Lord of the Rings" (1978).

The success of "Fritz the Cat" had inspired a few imitators, but the mini-trend of X- or R-rated American animation was over by the time of "Coonskin"'s release. It proved to be almost as much of a dead end as mainstream hard-core pornography. Independently, Japan would continue to create a strong tradition of animation for adults that has proven much more influential worldwide.

Bloody Good Fun

In the mid-1970s, the gore pioneered by Herschell Gordon Lewis and brought to the mainstream by "Soldier Blue" pervaded all sorts of movies across the globe. Paul Morrissey, the director of "Flesh" and "Trash," added extreme gore to his bag of shock tricks. His **"Flesh for Frankenstein"** (1973) offers lots of people being ripped apart and some very subversive sex. It was rated X in the United States and was heavily edited elsewhere. I think it's a pretty fun movie if you approach it with the tongue-in-cheek irony that was intended; I could see more literal-minded people thinking it's just poorly acted trash. The far inferior (in my opinion) "Blood for Dracula" followed in 1974.

On the other side of the world, martial arts movies were getting bloodier. The epicenter was Hong Kong, which was officially part of the United Kingdom at the time. There the dominant Shaw Brothers studio made increasingly violent wuxia and kung fu films. "The One-Armed Swordsman" (1967) was a groundbreaker, and then the Shaw Brothers went further with "Vengeance!" (1970), and then "Five Fingers of Death" (1972). Each of these movies feature a

---

[509] James Craig Holte, "Ethnicity and the Popular Imagination: Ralph Bakshi and the American Dream," *MELUS*, Vol. 8, No. 4, p. 105-113

handful of mutilations but none get that transgressive by worldwide movie standards.

In 1974, the Japanese movie "**The Street Fighter**" topped them all. It was the first movie to get an X rating in the United States for violence alone. "The Street Fighter" certainly contains lots of brutality, but the gore effects are only a little bit more sophisticated than the "slather drippy red paint over people" technique of Herschell Gordon Lewis.

What makes "The Street Fighter" genuinely shocking to me is its protagonist, played by Sonny Chiba. Chiba's character is a psychopathic thug who kills for money and has little or no sense of honor. Early on, a likeable, wholesome brother and sister ask for more time to pay him for services rendered. He assaults the brother, who dies in the scuffle, and then he sells the sister to a brothel. It's not the kind of thing people expected from Asian martial arts movies, which typically had traditional moral compasses.

What's Left for Horror?

With Herschell Gordon Lewis-style gore proliferating in everything from "Soldier Blue" to Asian martial arts, horror movies in the 1970s couldn't just be bloody to stand out. Low-budget horror films would try: "Mark of the Devil" (1970) shows some medieval tortures and "I Drink Your Blood" (1971) portrays a violent hippie gang terrorizing a town. Both try to get perverse, but I found it hard to get too shocked by either. Gore lives or dies by the quality of its special effects, and the effects in these movies look pretty goofy. The first time you see poor gore effects, it's disturbing; the third or fourth time it just looks like actors yelling with red paint on them. "Mark of the Devil" shows what's supposed to be a naked bottom sitting on a bed of nails, but it looks like someone's trying to torture a Muppet.

To make horror feel extreme in this era, you had to take after "Rosemary's Baby" and do it well. "**The Last House on the Left**" (1972), I think, is an amazing achievement in shock film. Like "The

Night of the Living Dead," it is a very-low-budget independent movie made by unknowns. Its more graphic shock content demonstrated how much things had changed in just four years. "The Last House on the Left" is based on the Ingmar Bergman film "The Virgin Spring," which itself could qualify for this book. "The Last House on the Left" has much more harrowing scenes of rape and violence and a darker ending. Its gritty, realistic, documentary-esque style made the horrific acts seem very real to me.

Occasionally a couple of bumbling police officers try to provide some lame comic relief in "The Last House on the Left," but for me they were neither comic nor relief. Their scenes felt imported from a cheap early-1960s teen movie, which provided wild cognitive dissonance next to all the early-1970s-style brutality. In an odd way, their antics heightened the shocks.

"The Last House on the Left" felt like a new level of horror to contemporary audiences too. In the United States, government and industry censorship was basically dead, so people took it upon themselves to censor it. So many viewers were complaining to theater management that projectionists started cutting the most offensive parts out of their prints.[510] The movie's producer, Sean S. Cunningham, also took it upon himself to remove some shots, over the objections of director Wes Craven.[511] Cunningham was no prude; he would go on to produce "Friday the 13th."

"The Last House on the Left" was banned in the United Kingdom until a 2002 DVD release, and even then 31 seconds were removed.[512] No one even tried submitting it to the Australian board until 1987, when it was rejected. It wasn't seen in Australia until 2004. In the 1970s, the United States had become more permissive

---

[510] Alexander Wooley, "A reprisal of 'The Last House on the Left' shows 35mm film is not dead yet," the New Statesman, September 8, 2014
[511] Zinoman, p. 81
[512] "The Last House on the Left, BBFC.co.uk, https://www.bbfc.co.uk/release/the-last-house-on-the-left-q29sbgvjdglvbjpwwc0yodgznda

than the countries that had national government censorship boards. Now that the shambolic, overcomplicated system of the Production Code, the Legion of Decency, and state and local censorship boards had collapsed, the United States had become the prime spot for grade-A shock films.

Because it was made so cheaply, "The Last House on the Left" was highly profitable. It was still nowhere near the cultural phenomenon that "**The Exorcist**" became in 1973 and 1974. Warner Brothers didn't expect much from a horror movie with no stars, but it stayed in theaters for two years. It became one of three biggest hits of the decade, along with "Jaws" and "Star Wars." To this day it owns the ninth-highest domestic gross of all time and the highest for an R-rated movie, when you adjust for inflation (which is the only way all-time box office should be measured, I say – if you don't adjust for inflation, then your list is more about inflation than about movies).[513] "Pink Flamingos" and "Salò, or the 120 Days of Sodom" may be the most shocking films ever, but "The Exorcist" brought peak shock material to the masses.

If you're reading this book, you've probably seen "The Exorcist," so you know what's shocking about it. Sex, violence, blasphemy, profanity – it's all there. Having a little girl do and say all those things heightened it further. What puts it over the top is that it's all delivered with well-made realism, just like "Rosemary's Baby." As Jason Zinoman states in his book "Shock Value," "The Exorcist" "inverted the old exploitation formula. Instead of selling the shocks and delivering the same old tricks, 'The Exorcist' sold tasteful, moody drama, and hit you over the head with brutalizing special effects."[514]

The impact of "The Exorcist"'s shocks is best illustrated by the extensive coverage of audiences' violent reactions. People running

---

[513] Top Lifetime Adjusted Grosses, Boxofficemojo.com, https://www.boxofficemojo.com/chart/top_lifetime_gross_adjusted/?adjust_gross_to=2019
[514] Zimonan, p.102

out of the theater to vomit was commonplace. "We've practically got a plumber living here now," said the manager of a Toronto theater showing the film. "The smell in the bathrooms is awful. People are rushing in and they're missing the toilet seat by inches."[515] The same theater manager reported having called an ambulance four times in one night because people kept fainting and having epileptic seizures. Newspapers and magazines were packed with stories like these, followed by the de rigeur thinkpieces full of worry and fury about what it all meant. At least one commentator was concerned that the discussion of "The Exorcist" was crowding out news about Watergate.[516]

One thing people were worried and furious about was that "The Exorcist" had been rated R instead of X, which meant children could be brought to see it. Police and courts tried to keep kids out, but couldn't do much. Everyone knew that "The Exorcist" got an R because Warner Brothers spent a lot on it, and it wouldn't recoup with an X.[517] The X rating had already become useless for anything but pornography. MPAA president Jack Valenti justified the R rating by saying the film had "unwavering morality,"[518] i.e. the old "compensating moral values" shtick. No one bought that having clear good guys and bad guys makes what Regan does with the crucifix acceptable for family viewing. Valenti's response was to hire a new chairman of the MPAA, Richard Heffner, who would crack down on extreme violence.[519]

The next great achievement in horror doesn't have much extreme violence, but still manages to be deeply disturbing. "**The Texas Chain Saw [sic] Massacre**" (1974) has a lot less gore than you might remember. Mostly you just see the results of the twisted

---

[515] Quoted in "From the crypt: How a Halloween film classic possessed Toronto". *Toronto Star*, October 31, 2019
[516] William Paul, "Laughing Screaming: Modern Hollywood Horror and Comedy." p. 288
[517] Zinoman, p. 107
[518] Ibid
[519] Zinoman, p. 108

backwoods family's monstrosity. The movie just feels like it must have been gory because it so effectively creates an intense mood of inhuman perversity. It also wallows in an especially disturbing subject, cannibalism, while mining the Ed Gein story for the butchery of human beings and the wearing of their skin.

Believe it or don't, "The Texas Chain Saw Massacre" director Tobe Hooper went light on gore because he was shooting for a PG rating.[520] The MPAA gave it an X. Hooper cut out a few minutes to get an R. The distributor then reinserted the cut material for at least some showings that were advertised as R-rated.[521] This was fairly common practice.

"The Texas Chain Saw Massacre" had a successful run in London for a year until the British Board of Film Censors banned it. It wasn't approved until 1999.[522] The movie was also banned in Australia, Brazil, Chile, Iceland, Ireland, Norway, Singapore, Sweden, and West Germany.[523] Again, Americans were free to see what people couldn't in countries with national government censorship boards.

The Peak of Exploitation Shocks

You could argue that "The Last House on the Left" and "The Texas Chain Saw Massacre" were essentially exploitation movies. They were cheaply made by independent outfits to deliver transgressive thrills. But they're not really considered exploitation because they're too good. After some cuts to earn R ratings, these movies could go beyond the exploitation circuit into mainstream theaters.

---

[520] Zinoman, p. 142
[521] Stephen Vaughn, "Freedom and Entertainment: Rating the Movies in an Age of New Media". p. 58
[522] "Case Studies: The Texas Chainsaw Massacre", BBFC.co.uk: https://www.bbfc.co.uk/education/case-studies/the-texas-chain-saw-massacre
[523] Laura Davis. "BANNED: The most controversial films". *The Independent*, October 5, 2010

The Swedish movie "**Thriller: A Cruel Picture**" (1973) maybe could have gone mainstream, if it were better. It's a very grim story of a young woman who is forced into sex slavery and then takes her bloody revenge. Uncut it's a surefire X, but it has a few very obvious choices for shots to remove to get an R. The most controversial one shows a knife going into a very sensitive body part. It's extremely realistic, as it was reportedly achieved by stabbing a fresh corpse.[524]

"Thriller: A Cruel Picture" also includes several very removable close-ups of hard-core sexual penetration which were not performed by the actors. Obviously director Bo Arne Vibenius was not shooting for mainstream success – or maybe he was. He said he added them to achieve what he called "the most commercial film ever made." At the time, hard-core porn was as popular in Sweden as it was in the United States.[525] The 1973 cinematic landscape was a confusing place.

Vibenius may have misinterpreted the climate, as the very lax Swedish film censorship board banned "Thriller: A Cruel Picture." The movie was cut from 107 minutes to 102, then to 86, and finally to 82 before it was accepted.[526] The 82-minute version made it to the United States, but it did not break out of the exploitation circuit.

No one could have envisioned anything but the exploitation circuit for "**Ilsa: She Wolf of the SS**" (1975). In it, large-chested female Nazis torture women and have sex with men in a prison camp. At least it has no pretensions of being art. "Ilsa: She Wolf of the SS" is exploitation in its purest, most repulsive form.

---

[524] Jan Lumholdt. "Christina Lindberg Interview". DBCult.com, January 21, 2012:
https://web.archive.org/web/20120216003737/http://www.dbcult.com/printed-media/christina-lindberg-interview/
[525] Alexandra Heller-Nicholas. "Rape-Revenge Films: A Critical Study". p. 41
[526] Rob Craig. "American International Pictures: A Comprehensive Filmography". p. 371–372

I can't think of any reason to combine titillation and Nazis except to exploit strong feelings about the Nazis for an extra layer of frisson. I worry that "Ilsa: She Wolf of the SS" lessened those strong feelings for some people by mixing them with cheap thrills. Hatred of Nazis is a strong feeling that I don't think should be lessened. Much the same way you should not trivialize Nazis by dressing as one for Halloween, I don't believe you should make or watch a movie that fetishizes them as sex objects.

The exploitation fans of 1975 were up for any new shock, and "Ilsa: She Wolf of the SS" did very good business. It wasn't the first so-called "Nazisploitation" film, but it jump-started a trend that didn't die down until the end of the decade. "Ilsa: She Wolf of the SS" was filmed in the United States (in the former set of the TV show "Hogan's Heroes") but Nazisploitation became an Italian phenomenon, for whatever reason. Perhaps Fellini, Pasolini, Visconti, etc. had created fertile ground for Italian shock films in the 1970s. I doubt any of them would appreciate this idea, but Pasolini's "Salò, or the 120 Days of Sodom" and Visconti's "The Damned" each have some commonalities with Nazisploitation.

I admit, I have not seen any Nazisploitation movies besides "Ilsa: She Wolf of the SS" and I don't plan to. I did watch the 2019 documentary "Fascism on a Thread: The Strange Story of Nazisploitation Cinema," which provided all the information I'll ever need to know on the topic. It discusses how these films never allowed any Nazi characters to be sympathetic and shied away from any mention of the Holocaust, the Final Solution, or other real atrocities or concepts. Nazisploitation movies are not political; they are essentially roughies in Nazi uniforms, with women sometimes doing the victimizing.

There's cowardice in using the Nazis' iconography while ignoring the effects of their evil. At the same time, I wouldn't trust these directors to engage with such a complex and fraught topic. It would probably make for more examples of exploitationeers undermining their own messages, as in "Mondo Cane," "Child Bride," etc.

Let's move on to something more pleasant: snuff films. Throughout the 1970s, rumors flew that people were being lured into acting in movies and then killed with the cameras rolling. A snuff film isn't footage of someone killed by accident or executed for a crime, and it isn't a video for a murderer's private use. The term only applies to real homicide committed to be filmed and included in a movie that people pay to see. Snuff films were supposedly so common that an entire network formed to produce them.

It's all nonsense; no actual snuff film has ever been found. A comprehensive Snopes article on the topic points out that even if people get some sick thrill from talking about them, very few actually want to see one. Certainly, the real demand for snuff films has never been high enough for producers to take the massive risk of making them. If you're going to murder someone, it's a very dumb idea to film it and distribute copies widely. That tends to provide good evidence against you.[527]

There have been plenty of misunderstandings and hoaxes, including the 1976 movie "**Snuff**." Independent sexploitation producer Allen Shackleton got his hands on a low-budget movie that was so poorly made that distributors deemed it unreleasable. He tacked on an ending that purported to show the real director of the movie seducing and then killing a woman in front of the cameras.[528] Neither the director or the woman had appeared in the footage that preceded this scene. Unless you're very unfamiliar with movies, it's pretty easy to tell the scene isn't real from the way it's cut together. It's like something from an especially bleak Herschell Gordon Lewis movie.

Shackleton drummed up publicity by hiring people to picket theaters showing "Snuff." Some believe he planted stories about snuff films

---

[527] Barbara Mikkelson, "Snuff Films," Snopes.com; https://www.snopes.com/fact-check/a-pinch-of-snuff/
[528] Eithne Johnson, Eric Schaefer, "Soft Core/Hard Gore: Snuff as a Crisis in Meaning," *Journal of Film and Video*, Vol. 45, No. 2/3, Pornography and Sexual Representation (Summer-Fall 1993), p. 40-59

in the newspapers months before the release date. The movie advertising didn't explicitly say it was an actual snuff film, which could have constituted false advertising. Instead "Snuff"'s poster suggested that it was with the xenophobic tagline "The film that could only be made in South America... where Life is CHEAP!" The footage Shackleton bought was filmed in South America, which he clearly saw as an asset in suggesting that it might be a real snuff film. As had "Ingagi" and other "exotic" exploitation movies, "Snuff" capitalized on Americans' fear and ignorance of countries not dominated by people of Northern European ancestry. The whole set of tactics was in the tradition of those 1930s and 1940s exploitation movies that enticed customers with "ballyhoo" about forbidden thrills that the movie wouldn't actually deliver.

Not only did "Snuff" not deliver in being a snuff film; it was not even over-the-top shocking. As a Mann Theaters executive said at the time in response to criticism for screening it, "The reason [the distributors of 'Snuff'] haven't submitted it to the rating board is because they thought it would only get an R. This isn't hardcore. We don't play hardcore. It's a self-imposed X."[529]

Soon the fake protestors hired by Shackleton were joined by real ones, and a media frenzy ensued. New York District Attorney Robert M. Morgenthau was compelled to investigate "Snuff," no doubt by people who hadn't seen it. You can feel his disdain for this assignment in his conclusion that the alleged snuff scene is "nothing more than conventional trick photography – as is evident to anyone who sees the movie." He tracked down the actress depicted as being murdered, whom he described as "alive and well."[530]

Because "Snuff" was labeled as rated X, rumors spread that the adult film industry was behind the movie and other snuff films. Fellow pornographers excoriated Shackleton for misapplying the X rating. The Adult Film Association of America (AFAA) expelled

---

[529] Quoted in ibid
[530] Quoted in ibid

Shackleton from the organization and banned "Snuff" from all adult movie theaters.[531]

This response backfired. Because "Snuff" was screened only in mainstream theaters, it got the attention of people who would never know about hard-core films. The self-imposed X rating ensured that "Snuff" would remain linked with pornography anyway, and in fact tainted the genre by association.

"Snuff" served to boost a critical reassessment of hard-core pornography. The usual crowd of right-wing moralists were being joined by feminists who asserted that pornography is a gateway to real-life sexual violence. In 1976, Women Against Violence Against Women (WAVAW) and Women Against Violence in Pornography and Media (WAVPM) were formed and began agitating for antipornography laws. They rallied behind a slogan from feminist leader Robin Morgan: "Pornography is the theory; rape is the practice."

The final scene of "Snuff," of a man pushing a woman into sex and then killing her, represents an apotheosis of this idea. As Eithne Johnson and Eric Schaefer say in the *Journal of Film and Video* article "Soft Core/Hard Gore: 'Snuff' as a Crisis in Meaning," "among these antipornography feminists, the snuff film is continually invoked as the archetypal sexualization of murder toward which all pornography tends."

By 1976, hip urban cineastes had moved on from hard-core pornography, at least openly. As I mentioned before, they tried it in 1972 and 1973, discovered that long sex scenes kill narratives, and then relegated it back to underground "low culture." Because of "Snuff," they were forced to reckon with the idea that pornography was misogynistic too. The occasional nods toward female sexual empowerment in "Deep Throat" and "The Devil in Miss Jones" seemed quite distant. Johnson and Schaefer write:

---

[531] Ibid

> "'Snuff' and the mythic snuff film were deployed to shift the definition of pornography from sexual representation to a literal inscription of male dominance over women. In doing so, antipornography feminism joined a larger discursive formation regulating low culture by indicting audiences for 'unhealthy' appetites, lobbying for social protectionism, policing morally suspect material, and segregating it through combat zone rhetoric."

Once the hoax of "Snuff" was thoroughly exposed, write Johnson and Schaefer, public rebuke trained on the people who paid money to see it. Johnson and Schaefer quote University of California, Berkeley film professor Linda Williams saying "For many, the horror shifted from the sadistic content of the film to the sadism of viewers who would pay to see what they thought was the ultimate orgasm." The 1970s filmgoers who thought they wanted the next level of shock were thoroughly shamed. And for what? To be tricked into paying for a movie that did not deliver what it promised, or even a basic level of competence. Along with feeling guilt, they no doubt felt like suckers.

I'm spending time on quite possibly the worst and most cynically manipulative movie of the 1970s because I think it represents a turning point in shock film. The boundaries had been pushed to a breaking point. Just the concept of an actual murder being masturbatory fodder, even if no one had ever actually done it, made many 1970s filmic shock seekers reassess their interests.

Shock film didn't go away after "Snuff," of course. But the "chasing the dragon"-esque trajectory toward more and more disturbing combinations of sex and violence hit an endpoint. People liked seeing filmic violence, sex, even hard-core sex in certain contexts – but real, sexualized murders represented a bridge too far.

The Peak of Art Film Shocks

Like snuff films, bestiality is a shocking practice that people might get sick thrills from talking about but don't actually want to see. This was confirmed by "**Vase de Noces**," aka "**Wedding Trough**" or "**The Pig Fucking Movie**" (1974). It offers (simulated) sex scenes between a man and a pig, plus other atrocities.

"Vase de Noces" has no dialogue and only one human character. It reinforces the negative stereotype of art films by being alternately dull and confusing, in my opinion. Despite its attention-grabbing premise, it did not win distribution anywhere and was only screened in a few film festivals. I mention it because a shock film fan might hear about it and be curious; I don't think it's worth seeking out for any reason.

Also, "Vase de Noces" demonstrates that art films were sometimes in the same business as exploitation films. Both often searched for new material to explore for shocks. Art films usually did so more artfully, as you might expect. They incorporated other ideas besides a sort of "check out this crazy shit!" circus-sideshow mentality.

For instance, "**Sweet Movie**" (1974) has messages about capitalism and communism. This was Yugoslavian director Dušan Makavejev's follow up to "W.R.: Mysteries of the Organism," the eccentric celebration of psychologist Wilhelm Reich's theories about sex and "orgone."

The original plan for "Sweet Movie" was just to lampoon capitalism through the story of a woman who wins a beauty contest for being "most virgin." The woman then undergoes a series of increasingly shocking adventures. It all eventually became too much for the actress playing the woman, Carole Laure. She endured a long shoot among real-life Viennese Actionist Otto Muehl and his troupe doing all kinds of disgusting things with bodily fluids. After having to manipulate a man's penis, Laure quit the movie.[532]

Makavejev was left with only half a movie's worth of footage. He added a second narrative about a different woman, played by Polish actress Anna Prucnal, floating through the canals of Amsterdam in a boat that has a giant sculpture of Karl Marx's head on the front. This woman commits her own atrocities which get progressively worse, culminating in her attempted seduction of prepubescent boys.

The movie cuts back and forth between the two stories, neither of which have a lot of narrative thrust. "Sweet Movie" is based on a continual heightening of shock level rather than a conventional narrative arc of rising action. The earlier scenes might show up in an R-rated movie today, while the later ones would not be allowed.

"Sweet Movie" is directed with real flair in its surreal visual style, so it's hard to brush it off as a cheap and worthless exploitation film. And as I said, there are some messages about capitalism and communism that you can pull out if you try. I have a lot of mixed feelings about it personally. Carole Laure's humiliation did not infuriate me as much as Maria Schneider's in "Last Tango in Paris," but I bet I could be convinced that it should have.

The moviegoing world of 1974 thoroughly rejected "Sweet Movie." It was banned or heavily cut in most countries. The Polish government exiled actress Anna Prucnal for seven years, which meant she couldn't visit her home.[533] Makavejev's career tanked, and he didn't make another movie until 1981.

Much of what made "Sweet Movie" unacceptable to most people was its footage of Otto Muehl's Viennese Actionists offshoot group just being themselves. The movie is essentially an attempt to bring

---

[532] Sarah Hamblin, "A Cinema of Revolt: Black Wave Revolution and Dušan Makavejev's Politics of Disgust", *Cinema Journal*, Vol. 53, No. 4 (Summer 2014), pp. 28-52

[533] Nina Power, "Blood and Sugar: The Films of Dušan Makavejev", *Film Quarterly*, Vol. 63, No. 3 (Spring 2010), pp. 42-51

Actionists' "shock for shock's sake" attitude to the big screen. The fact that most of the world rejected it demonstrates the limits of this attitude's appeal.

The exploitation analogue to "Sweet Movie" might be "Thriller: A Cruel Picture." Both had some solidly X-rated content that could be cut, but they were still too beyond the pale for even 1970s audiences. It's not a perfect comparison, but I'm segueing into a better one.

"The Night Porter" (1974) is much more clearly an art-film analogue to "Ilsa: She Wolf of the SS." "The Night Porter" offers my beloved Dirk Bogarde as a former SS officer trying to get by in 1957 as a humble hotel employee. One day a wealthy woman, played by Charlotte Rampling, checks into the hotel. Bogarde's character recognizes her as the same woman whom he made into a sadomasochistic sex slave during the war.

Rampling's character voluntarily begins a sadomasochistic affair with Bogarde's in 1957. This gets into lots of tricky issues. Is the movie implying that she somehow enjoyed being a sex slave to a Nazi? Maybe she delved into sadomasochism as a coping mechanism? Can BDSM really work that way? I was left unsure what to think, which is perhaps the intention. Maybe I should have the same reaction as I did to "Ilsa: She Wolf of the SS," but I felt that "The Night Porter" had a lot more on its mind.

Contemporary critics spoke of "The Night Porter" like it was Nazisploitation. Roger Ebert called it "a despicable attempt to titillate us by exploiting memories of persecution and suffering,"[534] In *The New York Times*, Vincent Canby said it was a "piece of junk" in review titled "'The Night Porter' Is Romantic Pornography.'"[535] Opinions have since softened, perhaps as attitudes toward BDSM

---

[534] Roger Ebert, "The Night Porter," Rogerebert.com, Feb. 10, 1975, https://www.rogerebert.com/reviews/the-night-porter-1975
[535] Vincent Canby, "'The Night Porter' Is Romantic Pornography," *The New York Times*, October 13, 1974

have liberalized. But combining Nazis and BDSM will always be problematic, to say the least.

Plus, feelings toward shock films usually soften over the decades. Changing mores are the main reason, but there are others. Viewers can distance themselves a bit more from older shock films by framing them as artifacts of a past time. You can approach "Pink Flamingos" as an outgrowth of those crazy 1970s, especially since John Waters' films have become tamer. Some old shock films, like "A Clockwork Orange," are now part of the canon, with all the respectability and intellectual remove that that implies. "A Clockwork Orange" has been so enmeshed within popular culture that droogs show up in the audience in "Space Jam: A New Legacy" (2021).

This isn't true for every shock movie; I doubt "**The Beast**" would be any less shocking to a viewer now than it was in 1975. That's because it centers on a female character's fantasy of sexual assault by a wolf/bear monster. This scene is played as outlandish comedy, in which the woman begins to revel in the assault. It's another endorsement of rape, with bestiality thrown in.

Attitudes toward "The Beast" have not softened since 1975, as far as I'm aware. Since then, social mores on depictions of sexual assault have become more restrictive, and rightly so. And "The Beast" has never warranted being added to the film canon, besides that of the "monster-erotica culture," which I've just read apparently exists. (No kink-shaming intended; I'm just saying I'm no expert on the topic and I would rather not research it further.)

The documentary "Love Express: The Disappearance of Walerian Borowczyk" opens with "The Beast" director Walerian Borowczyk insisting that he was just putting on screen what everyone was thinking. As demonstrated by the highly critical public reaction to "The Beast," sexual assault by a beast was not by any stretch of the imagination what everyone was thinking. Maybe a few people were, as evidenced by its apparent importance to "monster-erotica culture." But that's a very small niche compared to the people who think about conventional, consensual human-on-human sexual couplings. And even those thoughts were being sequestered into the separate cinematic universe of pornography.

Before "The Beast," cineastes thought Borowczyk would join the canon of legendary art film directors. He had gained acclaim for his surreal animated shorts and then made a successful jump to live-action drama with 1969's "Goto: Island of Love." But after the public outcry over "The Beast," he was relegated to Eurotrash-y erotica for the rest of his career. After leaving the set of "Emmanuelle 5" in disgust, he mostly gave up on live-action filmmaking.

As with so many mid-1970s shock films, both of the art and exploitation varieties, "The Beast" represents an endpoint of the trajectory toward greater film freedom. Freedom in general was very salient to Borowczyk. He chafed under the strictures of his upbringing in communist Poland. As soon as he got the chance, he moved to France for its culture of free self-expression. "Love Express: The Disappearance of Walerian Borowczyk" quotes Borowczyk saying that he wasn't a pornographer – he used sex to express the desire for freedom.

But whose "desire for freedom" is expressed in "The Beast"? The freedom of beasts to rape women? At the very least, the movie expresses a freedom to spread the lie that women will find rape enjoyable. I think this is the concept of freedom taken too far. All freedoms must have boundaries, in order to prevent harm to other people. Like the old saying goes, your freedom to swing your fist ends at the tip of my nose. By indulging in rape fantasies, Borowczyk was hitting people, metaphorically speaking.

To be clear, I'm not saying that every rape scene constitutes an assault on viewers and should be disallowed. I am saying that if they broach the topic of rape, filmmakers have a responsibility to show it as an act of brutal violence, not sex. They should not propagate the extremely harmful myth that a woman will eventually enjoy being raped, even in the context of a fantastical daydream.

"Love Express: The Disappearance of Walerian Borowczyk" also contains an interview with Cherry Potter, a psychoanalyst and film professor who is a big Borowczyk fan. She says that "The Beast" was much more of a male fantasy of female sexuality than it was a woman's own experience of her sexuality. This was a fundamental blind spot of 1970s filmmaking: Men saying what women wanted, and doing so poorly.

And when a woman tried to express her vision of female sexuality, no one got to see it. French director Catherine Breillat is now one of the premier explorers of the dark side of human sexual behavior. At age 17 in 1965, she wrote a book that was published with an 18-plus designation. This meant that she was not legally permitted to buy a copy of her own book.

In 1976, Breillat adapted her autobiographical fourth novel for the screen. **A Real Young Girl** is about a teenager exploring her sexual feelings while on summer break. It gets very graphic, but never indulges in the sadism and male fantasy fulfillment of "Emmanuelle," "The Beast" and so many other male visions of female sexuality. To me, "A Real Young Girl" seemed very authentic, if a bit amateurishly assembled. It was a first attempt; Breillat's movies would get better.

"A Real Young Girl" was financed by a producer who was hoping for another "Emmanuelle." When he saw what Breillat had made, he refused to release it. He said he was afraid of losing money because France had just instituted a tax on movies rated X. Then his company went bankrupt, and the lab kept the negative. No one risked buying it until after Breillat's 1999 arthouse hit "Romance." "A Real Young Girl" was finally released in 2000.[536]

It's too bad that no one got to see "A Real Young Girl" in 1976 and get furious about it. I would have loved to read the reactions of all

---

[536] Maria San Filippo, "'A Real Young Girl': Catherine Breillat's Adolescent Wonderland" *Senses of Cinema*, https://www.sensesofcinema.com/2016/cteq/a-real-young-girl/

the critics who gushed over "Last Tango in Paris." From a historical perspective, "A Real Young Girl" can only represent what could have been, if someone with money and power had taken a chance on it the way they had for zillions of films about sexuality from a male perspective.

Granted, the unsimulated intercourse and copious genitalia of "A Real Young Girl" would make it a hard sell to non-pornographic theaters in any era. Even in 1976, "**In the Realm of the Senses**" was the exception that proved the rule. Its real sex scenes mean that it has never been screened uncensored in Japan, the country of its origin. To film it, director Nagisa Ôshima had to register it as a French production. He also had to ship the negative to France for processing and editing.

"In the Realm of the Senses" is based on the real-life story of Sada Abe, a woman whose affair with a married man in 1936 got very out of hand. The couple cut themselves off from the world and wallowed in sex, going to extremes to keep it going until it ended in tragedy. It's a famous true-crime story in Japan, and other directors have made non-X-rated versions of it.

Despite many hard-core sex scenes, "In the Realm of the Senses" is not pornography. In an essay called "'In the Realm of the Senses': Some Notes on Ôshima and Pornography," film historian Donald Richie lays out why:

> "This wasn't two actors trying to titillate us, as in the pink film [i.e., Japanese erotic movies]; the hard-core film Ôshima was inventing would be about two real people who are titillating each other. He wanted a politicized eroticism rather than a pornographic performance."[537]

---

[537] Donald Richie, "In the Realm of the Senses: Some Notes on Oshima and Pornography," Criterion.com,
April 30, 2009: https://www.criterion.com/current/posts/1108-in-the-realm-of-the-senses-some-notes-on-oshima-and-pornography

Richie goes on to describe the many rules that pornos follow but "In the Realm of the Senses" does not. For instance, in pornography, the camera zooms in on genitalia and other body parts so that the viewer can imagine himself in the action. Ôshima films his actors in long shots and long takes so that "we are given the view that sees them whole, as other human beings engaged in pleasure. We are not encouraged to see them as chopped-up body parts that we can in our imagination take the place of."

People made these sorts of distinctions in some parts of the world in 1976, but not in Japan. There Ôshima was charged with obscenity. The case went to trial, giving Ôshima a platform for questioning the whole concept of obscenity. Even more than in the United States, "obscenity" was poorly defined in Japan. According to Richie:

> "[T]he only 'law' against it is the law of custom, where it is perceived as 'disturbing to society.' This is true of the entire concept of pornography as well. Ôshima wrote that 'pornography probably was invented as a way to avoid thinking about sex directly.' … Pornography, he continued, should be encouraged, since through its exposure the idea of the obscene would be revealed as essentially meaningless. This concept of the obscene, far from being criminal, should not even exist in a democracy."

Ôshima was acquitted in 1982. His larger goal of societal encouragement of pornography was of course not realized. As we've seen before, most people preferred pornography separate from conventional cinema, and firmly sequestered underground.

Even trying a bit of crossover between the two cinematic universes didn't really pan out. "In the Realm of the Senses" tested the idea that unsimulated sex scenes could be in a genuine, engaging narrative. It may have worked in that film, but did not launch a trend. People wanted an easy way to separate conventional and pornographic movies, and a real sex scene makes for a great dividing line.

This makes sense, if just for the sake of efficiency. Imagine if, for every movie involving sex, we had to go through the sort of exhaustive filmic analysis that Donald Richie goes through to demonstrate that "In the Realm of the Senses" is not porn. I don't think pornographers would want that either; they tend to be very clear about what they are selling. They don't give their movies titles like "Anal Nurses 3" to be ambiguous.

And really, simulated sex works just fine for the purposes that narrative films have for sex scenes. They might function to give us a brief thrill, or to reveal something about a relationship or a character. We don't actually need to see penises entering vaginas for that. And most importantly, asking actors to have actual sex is a very big ask.

So even though "In the Realm of the Senses" was a critical and commercial success, its groundbreaking combination of real sexual penetration and an engaging narrative proved to be another cinematic dead end. What about more unusual sexual practices?

"**Maîtresse**" (1976) is the realistic, grounded story of a macho bumpkin who comes to Paris and falls in love with a dominatrix. Early scenes of him being roped into her work evoked a fascinating mixture of emotions in me, including cringe humor, transgressive shock, the tension of changing power dynamics, and the warmth of witnessing a developing love. Later scenes felt more gratuitous, such as one in a slaughterhouse and another showing the real piercing of a very sensitive body part (i.e., not an earlobe). These scenes pushed "Maîtresse" into peak shock territory, so I suppose I wouldn't be talking about it without them.

"Maîtresse" was rated X in the United States and rejected for a certificate in the United Kingdom. The British Board of Film Classification acknowledged that it was not the trashy exploitation fare that usually got rejections, but noted "the actual scenes of fetishism are miles in excess of anything we have ever passed in this field."[538] An edited version got an X from the Board in 1981 and played elsewhere in the world.

Despite being of equivalent artistic value to "In the Realm of the Senses," by my estimation at least, "Maîtresse" did not make as big of a splash and is lesser known to this day. There is simply a much smaller market for movies about hard-core BDSM than for movies about hard-core heterosexual penetration.

Every time one of these movies tries to push shocks further, it hits a dead end. Is the whole arthouse shock film movement starting to run its course? "**Fellini's Casanova**" (1976) would suggest so.

Producer Dino De Laurentiis really wanted Federico Fellini to film the life of Giacomo Casanova. It seemed like a surefire winner: "Fellini Satyricon" had launched the trend of adapting sex-filled centuries-old literature for the screen. Pier Paolo Pasolini had then run wild with the idea, directing "The Decameron," "The Canterbury Tales," and "Arabian Nights" to great critical and popular acclaim. These movies appealed to both sophisticated cineastes eager for the latest masterwork and the average Giuseppe looking to be shocked and titillated. Producers get rich by backing projects that attract audiences as disparate as those.

The problem was that the more Fellini learned about the real Giacomo Casanova, the more he hated him. Casanova was a minor personality in 1700s Europe whose salacious memoir was published posthumously. Fellini found the book "boring, self-indulgent, and repetitive, and liken[ed] [Casanova] to a vulgar Fascist, an aged *vitellone*."[539] "Vitellone" refers to one of Fellini's earliest films, "I Vitelloni," which is about a group of immature and lazy young men who chase women and don't do anything worthwhile.

---

[538] "BBFC examiners' report," 14 October 1976, PDF included on British Film Institute DVD of "Maîtresse."
[539] Alberto Zamabenedetti, "Fellini's Cinematic Music Box," booklet accompanying KinoLorber Blu-Ray of "Fellini's Casanova"

Presuming the movie would be a sexy romp, De Laurentiis and his American backers pushed Fellini to cast Robert Redford as Casanova. Instead, Fellini went with Donald Sutherland, who was a great actor but has never been viewed as a dreamboat. Fellini then uglied Sutherland up by shaving his eyebrows and the front of his head and plastering on a long prosthetic nose and chin. Fellini clearly did not plan to make the ladies in the audience swoon. De Laurentiis bailed on the production, but it was eventually rescued by another producer.[540]

"Fellini's Casanova" is a visual marvel, with perhaps the best production design I've ever seen. Underneath all the spectacle, though, there is little if any warmth or human connection among the characters. This is not what you expect from one of Fellini's films, which often showcase collections of feisty oddballs who exude strong bonds of communal love. Casanova's perverse, cartoonish sexual exploits get progressively more empty and pathetic. Fellini made the movie cold by design, to communicate the emotional void in the center of his protagonist's useless life. Fellini said it shows that "the absence of love is the worst suffering anyone can endure."[541]

As an R-rated movie that did not cause a moralistic firestorm, "Fellini's Casanova" is an outlier in this section. It has many subversive sex scenes, but I'm mainly including it because I think it brilliantly dramatizes why the shock content trajectory hit an endpoint in the mid-1970s. It shows how a life spent pursuing cheap thrills eventually gets to feeling quite empty.

"Fellini's Casanova" is like a eulogy for the end of the true shock art films. After 1976, acclaimed filmmakers would seldom attempt "shock for shock's sake" the way "Sweet Movie" and "Salò, or the 120 Days of Sodom" had. Instead they would integrate disturbing

---

[540] Ibid
[541] Quoted in "'Pinocchio-in-The-Uterus' or 'A walking Sperm Bank': What Fellini Thought About 'Casanova'" Flashbak.com: https://flashbak.com/fellini-casanova-sutherland-movie-419642/

material into more balanced stories. The series of experiments with disgust originated by the Viennese Actionists were complete, and the experimental findings were subsumed into the artistic landscape.

That doesn't mean there aren't plenty more shock films to cover from the following few years. Some will inventively integrate shock content into conventional narratives. Others will be exploitation movies that feel, to me at least, like someone who has chased the dragon for too long and is hitting rock bottom.

Best Shock Movie Ever?

Before we take a deep sigh and slouch into the post-peak shockers, let's touch on probably the best shock film of all time. Among all the movies I've chosen for this book, "**Taxi Driver**" (1976) ranks the highest in the They Shoot Pictures, Don't They? rankings. It doesn't lead by much: At this writing it's just one spot above "Persona" and not much higher than "Psycho," "Battleship Potemkin," and "La Dolce Vita." But those four came out before shock movies hit their peak. "Taxi Driver" is the best movie from the best time to be thrilled by filmic transgression. If you love "Taxi Driver," you're a good candidate to like other movies in this book.

"Taxi Driver" wallows in possibly the scuzziest demimonde that the 20th century had to offer, 1970s Times Square. Its anti-hero protagonist, Travis Bickle, is a product of the sleaze: His idea of a date is bringing Cybill Shepherd's character to a porn theater. But he also despises it all and sees himself as an angel of destruction, "a man who stood up against the scum, the cunts, the dogs, the filth, the shit."

Travis Bickle is not very bright, but he is deeply lonely and very scared. Perhaps the most fundamentally disturbing thing about "Taxi Driver" is how relevant it is to any era and place, even those without child prostitutes around the corner. There are always incel-type guys who want to punish the world because they don't know how to talk to girls. This personality type rarely shows up in films, and "Taxi Driver" nails it with frightening accuracy.

Bickle's messianic complex is also an extreme embodiment of the backlash to debauchery. In the years after "Taxi Driver," the United States would restrict shock-film content in a much less furious way.

Chapter 8: Post-Peak Synthesis 1978-1980

Is Hegelian dialectics a too-grandiose topic for a book about boobs and blood in movies? Perhaps, but I don't think it's as fancy as the name makes it sound. I've tried to learn many philosophical concepts, and this is one of the few that has stuck in my head and I use often.

In a version of dialectics promoted by philosopher Georg Wilhelm Friedrich Hegel, ideas go through three stages: the thesis, the antithesis, and the synthesis. First you have the initial concept, the thesis. When this thesis proves inadequate, the antithesis counters it with the opposite idea. The antithesis is tested and proven to also be flawed. So then the synthesis merges the two ideas.

In his "Philosophy of History," Hegel's example of a thesis is "People must live according to customary morality," as he says the ancient Greeks did before Socrates. Then Socrates brought the antithesis: "People must be free to question traditional ways and think independently." The result was Greek philosophy, which revolutionized civilization.

But taking this antithesis to its extreme doesn't work either; the chaos of the French Revolution shows how there must be some order and custom in a society. The synthesis, to Hegel, was 1800s Germany: There is structure and law, but there are also freedoms, and those freedoms can lead to changes in the structure and law. A synthesis is not a perfect resolution, and indeed 1800s Germany would not prove perfect. A synthesis will just become a new thesis, and the whole dialectical process will start again.[542]

---

[542] Antonio Panovski, "What Is Hegel's Dialectic Method?" TheCollector.com https://www.thecollector.com/hegel-dialectic-method/

I propose that the history of shock films worked along an admittedly much less monumental dialectic. The thesis, going back to the origin of film, was "We need to restrict what people see on screen. They will be damaged by watching sex, violence, etc." This predominated among at least the powerful people of the first half of the 20th century. Beginning in the 1960s, people successfully realized the antithesis: "People need to be free to watch sex, violence, and whatever they want." As we saw in the last chapter, the early- to mid-1970s was filled with filmic experiments testing this approach. Some were successful, and others were less so.

The trial and error of those years forced a larger synthesis in the movie landscape. Some previously forbidden content – nudity, bloody violence, curse words – remained in R-rated movies. Other acts, like unsimulated sex, were relegated to X-rated fare that only adults were allowed to see in certain places. Bestiality and snuff films were acceptable nowhere.

Throughout the 1970s, individual mainstream movies were themselves syntheses: traditional, morally centered stories combined with shock content. "Jaws" (1975) is a relatable story of an upstanding family man defending his community. It is also peppered with a handful of bloody scenes that would have been unthinkable just 20 years earlier. "Jaws" is the essential bridge between early-1970s New Hollywood cinema and the popular crowd pleasers of the late 1970s and beyond.

As is well documented by Peter Biskind's book "Easy Riders, Raging Bulls" and elsewhere, the massive success of "Jaws" showed the way forward for the modern blockbuster. It's a horror movie, which had always been a B-movie genre, like action and sci-fi. "Jaws" and its descendants pushed the traditional B-movie genres into becoming the stuff of true A films. This includes everything from "Star Wars" to today's superhero epics.

These later movies would shed almost all shock material to target kids as well as adults, and win great financial returns. Critically acclaimed grown-up dramas like "The Godfather" and "The Graduate" would no longer become yearly box-office champs. After the release of "Star Wars" in 1977 you see the bifurcation we see now, with Oscar contenders and blockbusters occupying mostly separate worlds. From 1967-1977, the biggest domestic earner each year was nominated for the Best Picture Oscar 9 out of 11 times. In the 11 years that followed, only two yearly chart-toppers got the nod: "Raiders of the Lost Ark" and "E.T.: The Extra-Terrestrial."[543]

"Jaws" may be an all-time great but is not nearly harsh enough to be a true shock film by 1975 standards. "The Exorcist" would prove to be the last horror shockbuster for many years, and in the late 1970s really strong violence would be relegated to cheap exploitation. This was part of the synthesis that the cinematic world settled on: You can have your gore, but it had to be quarantined in a realm that was only a bit more socially acceptable than pornography.

For instance, in 1978, "**Faces of Death**" became the new "Mondo Cane." It was a hit pseudo-documentary cataloguing shock material, some real, some faked. There is no lasciviousness in "Faces of Death," just violence. The genuine scenes are of corpses in a morgue, a slaughterhouse, surgery, and some news footage that was too grisly to air. All of this is truly disturbing.

Much of "Faces of Death" is given to faked footage, of animal attacks, a cannibalistic cult, people killing a monkey and eating its brain, etc., etc. These scenes fooled plenty of people, and the debates about what was and wasn't real were probably a lot more fun than the movie itself. I couldn't help but feel my intelligence being insulted during these sequences.

"Faces of Death" was of course widely banned and decried. It still did well in theaters and would later become a favorite videotape rental for teenage boys out for a thrill. Several sequels followed

---

[543] Based on data from thenumbers.com, which counts only earnings from a movie's initial theater run, not re-releases

which I feel no need to see. I don't know if I sound like I'm going through the motions here; I certainly feel like I am. Sigh. "Faces of Death" will do that to you. Like I said in the previous chapter, it feels to me like someone hitting rock bottom after chasing the dragon too long.

I'm much more interested in an enterprising exploitationeer hitting on a new topic for shock material. Doris Wishman is one of the few exploitation directors with an enduring legacy – I mentioned her roughies as being the only ones anyone watches nowadays. In 1978, she tackled transgender identity with the documentary "**Let Me Die a Woman**."

As I'm not transgender, I should not be the arbiter of whether "Let Me Die a Woman" explores its topic with any level of honesty or sensitivity. It does include interviews with real trans people telling their own stories. But those stories are overshadowed by close-ups of actual sex reassignment surgery in which a penis is cut and turned into a vagina. I hope I don't offend any transgender readers when I say that, for a cis man especially, this sight taps into some powerful emotions. If you agree and you want to test your capacity for shock, "Let Me Die a Woman" is a good choice. At the very least, I found it a lot more interesting than "Faces of Death."

Horror Heyday

"Let Me Die a Woman" aside, exploitation became basically synonymous with horror in the late 1970s. Horror movies boomed throughout the late 1970s and 1980s, and were increasingly disdained as disreputable. Films like "Rosemary's Baby," "The Exorcist," and "Don't Look Now" had been seen as artistic triumphs made by internationally acclaimed directors. By the 1980s the genre would be characterized by "low culture" movies for young people like "Friday the 13th."

There are parallels with the genre that blossomed for graphic sexuality, pornography. Both had mainstream hits that established a beachhead for the movies that followed: "Deep Throat" for porn and "The Exorcist" for horror. Both types of movies are relatively inexpensive to make, leading to a flood of titles for devoted fans. These fans were usually male and had a reputation for being undesirable. If you were at a fancy cocktail party in the late 1970s or 1980s, you obviously wouldn't talk about a porn that you saw, but you'd probably keep a horror movie to yourself too.

I'm skipping a few horror movies that are quite important to the genre. "The Hills Have Eyes" (1977) is Wes Craven's disturbing follow-up to "The Last House on the Left." "Halloween" (1978) is a very effective shocker that set the template for the slasher movies that dominated the 1980s. If you like horror, you've probably seen them already. I don't think either tops "The Last House on the Left" or "The Texas Chain Saw Massacre" in terms of raw shocks.

The low-budget independent horror film **"I Spit on Your Grave"** (1978) is a different story. It is a rape-and-revenge movie with an extremely long rape scene committed by a series of perpetrators. Of course, avoid it at all costs if you do not want to see rape.

Any rape scene in a movie runs the risk of titillating people who have rape fantasies. A movie like "Lorna" leans into that, making rape seem like a valid sexual act that the victim will come to enjoy. A movie like "Deliverance" shows rape as the horrific act of violence, not sexuality, that it really is.

I can only speak for myself, as a straight man who has never experienced sexual assault. If you're not interested in my take, I don't blame you – skip the rest of this paragraph. To my eyes, the rape scene of "I Spit on Your Grave" is much more like "Deliverance" than "Lorna." It is certainly much too long – no question there. But to me it felt like a scene of brutal torture which powerfully depicts the true monstrousness and dehumanization inherent in rape. One perpetrator is developmentally disabled, and his friends push him to rape the woman for his first "sexual" experience. I think this can be interpreted as a criticism of the sort of male sexual entitlement that would populate teen sex comedies throughout the 1980s.

"I Spit on Your Grave" only made it to a few drive-in theaters in 1978. In 1980, it finally secured wider distribution and became a flashpoint for popular anger over horror. Roger Ebert gave it zero stars and called it the worst movie of all time. The blowback made it stand out among the many cheap horror movies of the late 1970s that were trying to be the next "The Last House on the Left."

The Germans Are Back

Since "Fellini's Casanova" declared that the shock art film trend had run its course, internationally renowned films mostly stuck with more civilized matters. Many were throwbacks to pre-1960s styles, like the Italian neorealist "The Tree with Wooden Clogs" (1978) and the Akira Kurosawa war epic "Kagemusha" (1980).

The auteurs of the 1970s New German Cinema movement were not shooting for respectability. Rainer Werner Fassbinder was busy cranking out film after film filled with LGBTQ+ characters and deep, soul-crushing cruelty. I don't know if it's his best movie, but "**In a Year with 13 Moons**" (1978) would likely be most shocking to the audiences of the 1970s.

"In a Year with 13 Moons" takes the perspective of a trans woman who suffers one heartrending humiliation after another. For good measure, the movie also features a scene in a slaughterhouse. I felt unsure how to feel about the main character's motivations; a trans person would be a better judge of that. Mostly I was just stunned by how skillfully Fassbinder could pull just the right strings at the right times to make me feel the full weight of a character's complete and utter devastation.

Fassbinder's life would make a good shock film. He was openly gay but got married twice to two different women.[544] Despite spending his nights trolling for sex and drugs, he was maniacally productive with a consistently high level of quality. Fassbinder directed 40 feature films, two TV series, 24 stage plays, four radio plays, and three short films before dying of a drug overdose at age 37.[545]

Germany's 1970s film renaissance was capped off with "**The Tin Drum**" (1979). It was the first German movie to win the Cannes Film Festival Palme d'Or and the first to win the Oscar for Best Foreign Language Film. "The Tin Drum" is a darkly funny magical realist story about a boy who simply refuses to grow older than 3 years old. The movie gets pretty disturbing when he starts having sexual feelings, but I thought this was handled skillfully and non-exploitatively. It certainly did not romanticize underage lust.

In 1997, several Oklahomans had a different view. An Oklahoma City resident checked out a copy of "The Tin Drum" from a library and sent it to the police, saying it violated the state obscenity law's prohibition on depictions of minors having sex. A state district judge agreed. Quickly the police confiscated all copies from video stores. They then used video store records to go door to door tracking down everyone who had rented the movie.[546]

One of the people who had rented "The Tin Drum" happened to be Oklahoma's development director for the American Civil Liberties Union (ACLU). Over his objections, his tape was confiscated by police. City officials threatened to press criminal charges against anyone else with a copy.[547]

---

[544] Juliane Lorenz, Marion Schmid, Herbert Gehr, eds. "Chaos as Usual: Conversations About Rainer Werner Fassbinder," p. 45, 243-246
[545] Susan King, "An L.A. love letter to Rainer Werner Fassbinder". *Los Angeles Times*, May 30, 2012
[546] Sova, p. 291-292
[547] Ibid

The ACLU sued. In 1998 a federal judge ruled that "The Tin Drum" was not child pornography and that the Oklahoman judge and police had acted unconstitutionally. They were also guilty of violating the Video Privacy Protection Act of 1988, which prevents video stores from sharing customer information. Then the police lost a civil case lodged by video store trade groups and had to pay $575,000 to settle another.[548] It had been a long time since local authorities had tried to suppress a movie they found offensive, and this attempt was swatted down pretty hard. Times had certainly changed since the days of the thesis stage of shock-film history.

New Hollywood Shockers Limp to the End Point

The late 1970s did see a few serious New Hollywood dramas that pushed the shock envelope forward. A risk-taking director could still find a controversial topic to build a high-quality hard-R-rated film around.

After establishing himself with the groundbreaking shocker "The Lovers" (1958), director Louis Malle often tackled other controversial topics, such as incest in "Le souffle au cœur" (1971) and Nazi collaboration in "Lacombe, Lucien" (1974). In 1978, he made a period drama about child prostitution called "**Pretty Baby**."

"Pretty Baby" was written by Polly Platt, the ex-wife of Peter Bogdanovich who may have been the more talented of the pair. She based the story on a real-life account of a New Orleans girl whose mother forced her into prostitution in 1917, just before brothels were outlawed. In her *You Must Remember This* podcast, Karina Longworth says that the "Pretty Baby" script is Platt's critique of the powerful men of the 1970s who sexually exploited young girls. The most infamous example of this abuse occurred as "Pretty Baby" was

---

[548] Ibid

being filmed, when "Rosemary's Baby" director Roman Polanski gave a 13-year-old girl quaaludes and raped her.[549]

"Pretty Baby" struck me as a realistic and sensitive examination of sexual exploitation. At age 12, Brooke Shields is perfect as a girl who is matter-of-fact about sex because she grew up in a brothel, but also behaves very much like the kid she is. The shocks of "Pretty Baby" come from watching adults treat a 12-year-old sex worker as normal. I watched in horror as cheery, well-dressed, middle-aged men party at the brothel in anticipation of an auction to take the virginity of Shields' character.

Louis Malle was very careful to not have anything approaching a sex scene in "Pretty Baby." He does eventually show Shields posing nude for a photograph, which I don't think was necessary. It's not that I felt the movie was trying to suggest Shields was sexy in that moment. I thought it was trying to induce a stomach-churning cognitive dissonance at seeing a little girl that other characters were perceiving as a sex object. Still, I'd argue that there is no artistic purpose for a sexualized shot of a child so important that it could justify giving pedophiles something potentially arousing. "Pretty Baby" is the very rare shock movie that I would prefer to see as an edited version.

The public was expecting much worse when they heard the premise of "Pretty Baby," and condemnations flew. The controversy did not translate to big ticket sales, though. Shocks just didn't sell like they had just a few years before.

Maybe the general public would have never flocked to a movie about child prostitution. "Let's try something else," New Hollywood types might have said. Just five years earlier, hard-core pornography was a big theater draw; perhaps a high-quality drama set in the porn world could make a mark.

---

[549] Karina Longworth, "Polly Platt: The Invisible Woman, Pretty Baby and a Playmate Murder," *You Must Remember This*, episode 165

Paul Schrader had a strict religious upbringing in Grand Rapids, Michigan. He didn't see a movie until he was 17. While in college he became obsessed with film, which led him to a career as a critic and then a screenwriter. After spending two weeks living in his car in New York City, coping with insomnia by going to pornographic bookstores and theaters all night, he wrote the script for "Taxi Driver."

Schrader got into directing with the brilliant "Blue Collar" (1978) and then made "**Hardcore**" (1979). "Hardcore" taps into the extremes of Schrader's own life. In the movie, a conservative, religious Michigander, played by George C. Scott, discovers that his missing daughter has appeared in a hard-core porn film. He travels to California to find her and gets immersed in an even scuzzier demimonde than that of "Taxi Driver." This is a world where child pornography is touted as an entry point for aspiring porn producers, and a sadomasochistic porn actor screens a regular supply of snuff films. It's an exaggerated Sodom that feels like it came from a prude purging all of his darkest imaginings, regardless of whether they reflect reality.

When talking about "Hardcore," Schrader said, "Because I didn't participate in the sexual liberation of the '60s … my sexual freedom took this rather aberrant form of an obsession with people who lived the forbidden life."[550] His good friend John Milius said "Schrader was this character who had fallen from his Calvinist grace, and was really enjoying his time in Hell, sampling every part of it. He loved perversion, but all sexuality in some way was a failure for him."[551]

I wanted to be sure to cover a Paul Schrader movie because of his fascination with shock material, which takes the specific character of an outsider eagerly peering in. Sometimes he indulges his fascination a bit gratuitously in my opinion, especially in "Hardcore," but he's no schlockmeister. He makes compelling stories about

---

[550] Quoted in Karina Longworth, "Erotic '80s: 1980: Richard Gere and 'American Gigolo'" *You Must Remember This* podcast, episode 190
[551] Ibid

realistic characters who sometimes immerse themselves in the extremes of sex and violence. I feel some kinship with him as a fellow Midwesterner who grew up puritanical but developed a voyeuristic interest in the forbidden. From what I've read about Schrader, he's been more of a participant in the dark side of life than I have (as have almost everyone alive). But we are both dorky intellectuals who also love staid and sober art films. I like to imagine he might enjoy this book.

Anyway, "Hardcore" was also not a financial success. Shock films in the New Hollywood style just couldn't catch a break anymore. The preferences of baby boomers dominated popular culture, and by the late 1970s they were raising kids in the suburbs. Now they wanted family entertainment, not taboo-breaking drama.

What If Kiddie Porn Were Cutesy?

Instead of honest, adults-only examinations of child prostitution and hardcore pornography, baby boomers apparently wanted child pornography packaged as family entertainment. I might be exaggerating a bit. But I struggle to find other explanations for why "**The Blue Lagoon**" was a major hit in 1980. It's the story of a boy and girl who are marooned on a desert island, grow into teenagers, and fall in love. To me, it felt like a live-action Disney movie interspersed with jarring shots of child characters being naked and having sex. Some of the nudity is presented as being of 14-year-old Brooke Shields, who was being relentlessly sexualized by American culture at large.

After "Pretty Baby" and before "The Blue Lagoon," Shields appeared in suggestive Calvin Klein ads that caused a huge stir. In one TV ad that was pulled after a public outcry, she said "Want to know what comes between me and my Calvins? Nothing."[552] Shields was clearly a major reason for the success of the R-rated "The Blue

---

[552] Stated in "Brooke Shields," Season 14, episode 3; *Inside the Actors Studio*, original airing Sept, 22, 2008

Lagoon." At least some of that reason must have been tied to an implicit promise that she would be shown naked and possibly having sex.

Shields' manager/mother tried to spread the word that a body double, 32-year-old stunt coordinator Kathy Troutt, was used for the graphic nudity in "The Blue Lagoon."[553] That means the movie does not technically qualify as kiddie porn, but it's still very problematic. Plenty of people would not have heard about the body double – many casual movie watchers in 1980 wouldn't have even known what a body double was.

Moreover, the whole point of a body double is to create an illusion that you're seeing a famous actor naked. Most people would have left "The Blue Lagoon" thinking Shields had the body of a 32-year-old woman. That would have made it even easier to sexualize her. Also, Shields still appears in sex scenes, even if certain private body parts are not seen in the shots in which her face is visible. There's really no way to make this OK.

Beyond prurience, I could imagine a young teen enjoying the premise of "The Blue Lagoon." A heterosexual boy with low self-esteem would revel in the fantasy of being the only available option for a beautiful girl. I remember having this sort of non-sexual feeling watching the squeaky-clean 1960 Disney movie "Swiss Family Robinson" when I was 13.

But "The Blue Lagoon" was rated R. Some kids no doubt went to it with their parents, but you have to assume most of the audience was made up of adults. At least some of those adults went to it to be turned on by what they assumed was a naked 14-year-old. Does that mean it would be better if only 12-17 year-olds could see "The Blue Lagoon" because then any arousal would not be like mental

---

[553] Karina Longworth, "Erotic '80s: 1982: Teen Sexploitation, Fast Times at Ridgemont High, Porky's and The Blue Lagoon" *You Must Remember This* podcast, episode 192

statutory rape? Ugh, this is all a very unseemly area that is best avoided entirely.

The poster for "The Blue Lagoon" consists of a photograph of its two teen stars naked from the shoulders up and a ridiculously long piece of text that attempts to justify its existence. It calls the movie a "sensual story of natural love" and says "When their love happens, it is as natural as the sea, and as powerful." In interviews, director Randall Kleiser often used the phrase "natural love." The implication is that because it's natural for teens to fall in love and have sex, it's OK to watch a movie about it.

"Natural" can be a loaded word. People use it to justify any practice that was replaced by the norms of modern civilization. Natural childbirth means eschewing drugs and hospitals. Natural remedies date to before medicine was overtaken by the scientific method. The assumption is that if something is natural, it's automatically better, because it's untainted by the corrupting influence of modern institutions.

Civilization is far from perfect, but there are reasons it developed the way it did. Before drugs and hospitals, women and babies regularly died in childbirth. Before science-based medicine, doctors harmed patients as often as they helped them. Both natural childbirth and natural remedies can be beneficial if used judiciously, but if you use either exclusively, you are putting yourself at great risk. Giving birth at home can be safe only if trained professionals have ruled out complications. Taking an herbal remedy for stomach pain is fine as long as you make sure the pain is not a symptom of cancer or some other serious condition. For almost everything life-threatening, scientists have developed methods that are objectively more effective than the natural ones ever were. Choosing scientific interventions over natural ones is the main reason life expectancies for Americans have shot up from 40 years in 1860 to 78 today.[554]

Many people are still attracted to the idea of doing things because they seem more "natural." The word conjures a long-lost Eden of contented, stress-free, "primitive" life that was "in tune with nature." "The Blue Lagoon" is based on this fantasy, one that is not supported by historical or anthropological evidence. Nature is more complicated than that. Sure, nature can provide the bare necessities without demanding you punch a clock. But it also contains competitors and predators. Distant times could have been better in some ways, but they were even more packed with bloodshed than the current age. Death rates by violence could approach 50% in prehistoric societies.[555] In 2019 the worldwide rate of death from homicide, war and terrorism combined was less than 1%.[556]

People have a tendency to romanticize the past, even the distant past they didn't experience. They have a similarly strong tendency to take for granted the positive aspects of the present and dwell only on its negatives. This is the negativity bias, the foundation of Grumpy Old Man Syndrome, but even people who don't spend their days grumbling about new gadgets can fall prey to it now and again.

Is it "natural" for a boy and a girl who grew up outside civilization to have sex at age 14? I suppose it is. But that's not the issue at hand here; the question is whether it should be in a movie for everyone to see. The advertising for "The Blue Lagoon" suggests that it should, because it's "natural." One of the lessons that has been

---

[554] "Life expectancy (from birth) in the United States, from 1860 to 2020," statista.com, https://www.statista.com/statistics/1040079/life-expectancy-united-states-all-time/

[555] Max Roser, "Data review: ethnographic and archaeological evidence on violent deaths," *Our World in Data*, August 2, 2013, https://ourworldindata.org/ethnographic-and-archaeological-evidence-on-violent-deaths

[556] Max Roser, "Causes of death globally: what do people die from?," *Our World in Data,* December 7, 2021, https://ourworldindata.org/causes-of-death-treemap

incorporated into modern civilization is that it's very dangerous for adults to look at 14-year-olds as sex objects. That results in sexual abuse that shatters lives. Roman Polanski's rape and many others demonstrate this fact.

You won't see movies trying to sell the sight of naked young teens anymore, even if they examine young sexuality. That at least proved to be an aspect of the shock-film antithesis that was corrected. The immediate synthesis was to continue sexualizing teens, but to stick with twenty-somethings playing all parts. More on that later, unfortunately.

And Now for Something Completely Different

Let's clean off the muck of "The Blue Lagoon" with some humor. I haven't covered much comedy so far. Comedy depends on surprises, which can sometimes be violent, but usually not gory. A pratfall can make you laugh, but not if it draws blood. Horror/comedy like "Evil Dead 2" would prove the exception to this rule, but it tended to be more compartmentalized into the horror realm.

Sex and comedy are common bedfellows in the form of cheeky jokes, but they are usually pretty tame ones. Genuine eroticism is taken quite seriously. A laugh is a release of tension, and that's not the kind of release you want in a moment of sexual tension.

One way to shock people into laughter is to satirize sacred cows. "**Monty Python's Life of Brian**" (1979) took on Christianity, and people were not happy about it.

The British troupe Monty Python had already revolutionized comedy with the TV show "Monty Python's Flying Circus" (1969-1974). Made up of five Cambridge and Oxford grads, plus American Terry Gilliam, the group perfected a style that combined erudition and absurdity. In one sketch, game-show contestants got 15 seconds each to summarize Marcel Proust's 4,000-page novel "In Search of Lost Time," once in a swimsuit and once in an evening dress. The troupe went on to make the favorite movie of every nerdy 13-year-old boy (myself included), "Monty Python and the Holy Grail" (1975).

In the documentary series "Monty Python: Almost the Truth – The Lawyer's Cut," troupe member Eric Idle relates the origin of "Life of Brian." He says someone asked him what their next movie would be, and he joked "Jesus Christ: Lust for Glory." He and Terry Gilliam then began to seriously consider the idea. But in researching Jesus' life, they found nothing to ridicule. "[Jesus is] not particularly funny; what he's saying isn't mockable. It's very decent stuff,"[557] said Idle later.

Instead Idle and Gilliam invented a protagonist, Brian, who was born next door to Jesus and was often mistaken for a messiah. The troupe worked out a screenplay that ridicules religious fanaticism and many other targets but doesn't lay a hand on Jesus or the Judeo-Christian god.

A few days before filming was scheduled to begin for "Monty Python's Life of Brian," the chairman of its production company finally read the screenplay. He then panicked and cut off all funding. In desperation, Idle called the richest person he knew, former Beatle George Harrison. Harrison remortgaged his mansion and created Handmade Films to back the movie.[558] Handmade Films would go on to produce many of the most creative and enduring British movies of the 1980s, including "Time Bandits," "Mona Lisa," and "Withnail and I."

Once "Monty Python's Life of Brian" was completed, authorities were frightened. Norway and Ireland banned it outright. It played in most of the U.K. but some town councils banned it, usually sight unseen.

---

[557] Graham Chapman, John Cleese, Terry Gilliam, Eric Idle, et al. "The Pythons Autobiography by The Pythons." p. 349–387
[558] Nicholas Barber, "How George Harrison – and a very naughty boy – saved British cinema". *The Guardian*, April 3, 2019

"Monty Python's Life of Brian" probably would have received a C from NCOMP, but that last vestige of the Legion of Decency had stopped rating movies the year before and would close up shop the year after. Screenings of "Life of Brian" still drew plenty of protests and pickets in the States, almost invariably by people who hadn't seen it.

As with the 1948 Roberto Rossellini movie "The Miracle," the devout heard that a movie tackled Christianity without 100% reverence and assumed the worst. Even in 1979, after every other type of shock content had been exploited ad nauseam, blasphemy remained a third rail. "Monty Python's Life of Brian" was a financial success anyway, and now tops many lists as the greatest comedy of all time.

Comedy in the United States had been overtaken by its own group of elite-educated rabble rousers. In 1970, Harvard graduates Doug Kenney and Henry Beard spun the *Harvard Lampoon* into the humor magazine *National Lampoon*. It delivered shock humor that was harsher than anything anyone had ever seen. One satirical article, "Children's Letters to the Gestapo," included the letter "Dear Mr. Himmler, Thank you very much for the gold star to wear on my jacket. Now I can pretend I am a cowboy sheriff. Best wishes, Naomi Feinberg." My source for the following, the documentary "Drunk Brilliant Stoned Dead" (2015), is a good summary of the full story of the National Lampoon company. "A Futile and Stupid Gesture" (2018) is a fun fictionalized version that I also recommend.

I don't think these movies count as shock films in themselves, but they show how the National Lampoon movement took the same trajectory as shock films did. The magazine was a strong antithesis to the tame, family-friendly humor that preceded it. It trafficked in sex and cruelty, along with, it should be said, the entitled-sociopathic-straight-white-male misogyny and racism that proliferated in the 1960s and 1970s. There was of course blowback from moralists, which came to a head in 1980 when the *National Lampoon* magazine had a joke about a baby in a blender. Christian conservative groups successfully lobbied to get advertisers to drop out. The magazine was dead soon after.

By then the magazine was a small part of the National Lampoon empire. It was already shifting to a synthesis stage, producing entertainment that infused shock humor into more palatable packages for general audiences. "The National Lampoon Radio Hour" (1973-1974) was part of the antithesis, but it laid the track for the syntheses to come. It pulled together the most promising young talent from improv companies: John Belushi, Chevy Chase, Christopher Guest, Bill Murray, Gilda Radner, Harold Ramis, and more. Much of this group formed the foundation of the first cast of "Saturday Night Live." That show was not produced by National Lampoon, which instead pivoted to movies – "Animal House," "Vacation," etc. – that set the course for American comedy. These were the syntheses, like "Jaws," that put shock material into forms that the mainstream could embrace.

One major National Lampoon contributor was left behind when the movement shifted to the synthesis stage. Michael O'Donoghue was known for going the farthest with the magazine's shock humor. He became the initial head writer of "Saturday Night Live" and appeared in its first-ever sketch opposite John Belushi. As revolutionary as "Saturday Night Live" was in the 1970s, it was still network TV, and much of O'Donoghue's brutality had to be sanded down or blocked from air.

NBC gave O'Donoghue his own TV special, and he turned in "**Mr. Mike's Mondo Video**" (1979). As the title suggests, it's a parody of the shock pseudodocumentary genre created by "Mondo Cane." A few of the most disturbing sequences involve throwing cats into a swimming pool and Sid Vicious's violent rendition of "My Way." A highlight for me was a chaotic performance by Root Boy Slim and his band. They don't do anything explicitly shocking, but I felt this sequence perfectly captured a uniquely late-1970s feeling of rock-bottom, bad-drug-trip, hollow devastation. It's a frenzied, addled refusal to accept that the party's over, like a 40-year-old unemployed alcoholic at a dive bar raging to no one about how his old drinking buddies are getting married and moving to the suburbs. Maybe it's just me.

There was no way NBC was going to actually air "Mr. Mike's Mondo Video," so it was padded out and released to theaters instead. Critics hated it and it didn't find much of an audience. It was a mostly failed last-gasp attempt to keep the antithesis going as the country turned to Reagan-era conservatism. Perhaps it's an eccentric choice to represent National Lampoon and its descendants, but I think it's the purest filmic distillation of the movement's shock humor.

The Absolute Rock Bottom

Some might argue that shock film hit its absolute rock bottom with "Faces of Death" or "I Spit on Your Grave." My vote would go to "**Caligula**" (1979). "Caligula" catalogs the most depraved stories about the real-life ancient Roman emperor, which involve incest, anal rape with a fist, bashing a child's head in, and much more. The final cut wasn't pornographic enough for producer Bob Guccione, who had made millions publishing *Penthouse* magazine. So he took the finished film to a new director who cut some talky parts and replaced them with a few hard-core sex scenes.

When I sat down to watch "Caligula," I was on a mission to watch all the most disturbing films in history. Since my late teenage years I had wanted to find where my line was – at what point I'd say "too far." "Caligula" proved to be the line. It was the single most unpleasant movie watching experience of my life, and my stomach is turning right now just thinking about it. After watching a grainy uncut version on YouTube (which hopefully someone has since taken down), I had to go pick up my kids from school. When I got there, I was so upset and discombobulated that I ended up cursing at some other parent who didn't really do anything wrong. I had to sit down and collect myself so that I wouldn't yell at my kids for no reason.

"Caligula" cured me of my obsession with shock films. I'm obviously still interested enough to write a book about them. But my goal changed to seeing all the weirdest movies of all time (per the terrific list on the website 366 Weird Movies) and then to watching as many of the They Shoot Pictures, Don't They? top 1000 as I could. (I like lists.)

It may have been the hard-core sex scenes of "Caligula" that put me over the edge. The scenes themselves are not the problem; it's the context. The very idea that anyone could possibly be in the mood to masturbate after watching so many brutal tortures and humiliations suggested a psychopathy that was too horrific to stomach.

"Caligula" played first in Italy for a weekend, until it was confiscated by police.[559] When footage was sent to the States, Customs officials seized it. A court declared it wasn't obscene and "Caligula" entered the country.[560] In Boston, the film was seized anyway. A judge declared it passed the obscenity test established by *Miller v. California* because it contains the message about absolute power corrupting absolutely.[561] (This is the same message that Pier Paolo Pasolini used to justify "Salò, or 100 Days of Sodom." When a movie is about people abusing each other, you can always tease out some message involving the human capacity for evil.) Bob Guccione was relishing all the free publicity.

In the United States, "Caligula"'s distributor landed on the unusual strategy of renting individual arthouse theaters for the movie rather than leasing it for exhibitors. This ensured that it wouldn't end up in porn theaters.[562] It worked; there proved to be plenty of people who did not want to sit among masturbating strangers but did want to

---

[559] "Guccioni, Rossellini 'Caligula' Seized As 'Flagrantly Obscene'". *Variety*. November 21, 1979. p. 3.
[560] Stephen Vaughn, "Freedom and Entertainment: Rating the Movies in an Age of New Media," p. 74
[561] Stephen Prince, "A New Pot of Gold: Hollywood Under the Electronic Rainbow, 1980–1989." p. 349-350.
[562] Vaughn, p. 74-75

test their ability to withstand this filmic assault that authorities were trying to ban. In a May 8, 2023 episode of the *Unspooled* podcast called "Sex Scenes in Film," guest Dan Savage talks about how going to see "Caligula" was like participating in an extreme sport.

In 2023, a radically reworked version of "Caligula" hit the Cannes Film Festival. This version, dubbed "The Ultimate Cut," drew from 96 hours of alternate footage. It follows Gore Vidal's original screenplay, restoring important plot points that Bob Guccione had sacrificed in favor of hard-core sex scenes. I forced myself to watch "**Caligula: The Ultimate Cut**," and I have to say, I didn't hate it. It's more of a conventional 1970s shock film that displays violent and sexual sadism without wallowing gleefully in it. That makes it a huge improvement over the original. As they say, movies are made in the editing room (especially if you avoid splicing in gratuitous hard-core sex scenes).

The 1979 version of "Caligula" is quite exploitative, but it got plenty of mainstream attention because of its big budget and a star-filled cast of Malcolm McDowell, Helen Mirren, John Gielgud, and Peter O'Toole. Following on the heels of "Caligula" was the no-doubt exploitation film "**Cannibal Holocaust**" (1980). It also has origins in Italy and an English-speaking cast, and also rolls out every atrocity imaginable.

"Cannibal Holocaust"'s main storyline follows a group of callow young filmmakers traveling into the depths of the Amazon to document indigenous tribes. This is presented as found footage recovered after all of them disappeared. "Cannibal Holocaust" is padded out with a professor, played by porn star Robert Kerman, recovering their footage and then screening it for TV executives. Along with the executives, we watch the young documentarians attack the indigenous people in various horrific ways in order to manufacture shocking scenes.

The found footage of "Cannibal Holocaust" is made to be convincing. Director Ruggero Deodato didn't tell people it was real

— he was a more creative ballyhoo artist than that. He spread the rumor that the Italian government thought he'd made a snuff film and charged him with murder, which he then refuted by producing the alleged murder victim alive and well. Deodato also said the actors playing the young documentarians signed a contract to stay out of the public eye for a year so that people would think they were really gone. None of this proved true, but these stories would be retold for decades and add to the movie's taboo mystique.[563]

The more genuine reason that "Cannibal Holocaust" stands out as a rock-bottom shock film is its animal abuse. Real animals are crushed and ripped apart in excruciating ways. One brutalization of a turtle plagued my mind for weeks.

"Cannibal Holocaust" was banned in Italy after a brief run[564] and never made it to screens in most countries. It didn't get to United States theaters until the mid-1980s, when it gained little attention.[565] Ruggero Deodato said it was a big hit in Japan, but it's wise to verify anything he said, and Japanese box-office data before 1997 is spotty at best. The truth is that movie theaters across the world were turning away from extreme shock content.

Home viewing would prove a different story. VCRs came into vogue in the early 1980s and movies like "Cannibal Holocaust" could bypass censorship boards and amass money through rentals. More on that later.

The Synthesis Is Formed

The period of 1977 through 1980 saw a slow and subtle transition in shock film. It's not nearly as clear of a change as Joseph Breen and the Legion of Decency slamming the door to shocks in 1934 or the rating system flinging the doors back open in 1968. Instead of a

---

[563] Nathan Wardinski, "Dissecting 'Cannibal Holocaust,'" p. 11, 184
[564] Don Sumner, "Horror Movie Freak," p. 189
[565] Eric Henderson, "Film Review: Cannibal Holocaust". *Slant Magazine*, 2005

major event remaking the landscape, the late 1970s saw a sorting out of how Americans wanted their shocks.

"Jaws" was the watershed moment for the mainstream, shifting it to family-friendly blockbusters that would include fewer and fewer shocks. Serious, transgressive New Hollywood dramas like "Taxi Driver" dropped in popularity until they died out entirely. Movies that tried to up the shock ante couldn't get R ratings and thus found limited audiences of extreme sensation-seekers.

There were still plenty of mainstream movies with more sex, violence, and curse words than would have been conceivable before 1968. But the rating system gave baby-boomer parents a way to shield their children from them. As for how effective that was … well, at least it shifted the onus onto parents and away from studios and theaters. If their kids saw a movie that was clearly labeled R, parents could get mad at themselves or their kids.

This synthesis would stay relatively stable through the 1980s. Even a turn toward political conservatism in the English-speaking world wouldn't lead to much change.

Chapter 9: The Reagan Era: 1980-1988

Conservatism and the Status Quo

In 1980, Ronald Reagan was elected president. Margaret Thatcher had become prime minister of the United Kingdom the year before, and the two shaped the dominance of conservative politics in the 1980s. This took the form of a new fiscal conservatism, which is largely irrelevant to this book, and a traditional, patriarchal, family-centered social conservatism, which often affects trends in what movies are allowed to show.

But changes in social politics don't map precisely onto the ebbs and flows of shock-film history. The return to social conservatism in the mid-1930s did help Joseph Breen and the Legion of Decency clamp down on the perceived excesses of American movies. But during the conservative 1950s, movie content got naughtier, if slowly.

You'd expect the pendulum to swing back to restricting movie content in the 1980s. It did in the United Kingdom, but not as much in the States. In general, the shock-film synthesis provided a pretty workable peace treaty. The blockbusters were family-friendly, grown-ups could go to R-rated movies if they chose to, and the really strong stuff was unrated and therefore obscure. There was always some movie that conservatives could get upset about, but there weren't any major flashpoints until 1988.

If you didn't share the tastes of conservative heterosexual white males, though, the Reagan Era didn't give you much. This was hardly a big change; powerful straight white guys had never made much space for other voices to begin with. Women, people of color, and queer folk squeezed in some vital contributions to the early antithesis stage of shock-film history, but they were almost entirely silenced once the synthesis began.

The days of "Sweet Sweetback's Baadasssss Song" and "Shaft" were long gone by 1980. Movies centering on Black characters were nearly extinct. In his documentary "Is That Black Enough For You?!?" (2022), Elvis Mitchell blames this on movies like "Saturday Night Fever" co-opting the themes and tropes of early 1970s Black films. In his telling, the expensive flop "The Wiz" (1978) gave Hollywood an excuse to give up on films with predominantly Black casts.

Black directors were unable to break out of little-seen independent movies until Spike Lee at the end of the 1980s. Even Black film actors, with the major exception of Eddie Murphy, were relegated to stereotypes or dull supporting roles that contributed little besides token non-white faces. You may have forgotten, for example, that Ernie Hudson played one of the Ghostbusters. In his semi-autobiographical film "Hollywood Shuffle" (1987), Robert Townshend brilliantly lampoons the limited opportunities for Black people in 1980s movies.

A few female directors did establish careers in the 1980s, but they had to do it the hard way. Penelope Spheeris broke through with the timely punk documentary "The Decline of Western Civilization" (1981). Amy Heckerling and Martha Coolidge pulled the same trick Stephanie Rothman had with "The Student Nurses," turning dumb exploitation premises into surprisingly interesting movies. Heckerling was tasked with cranking out a teen sex comedy and turned in "Fast Times at Ridgemont High" (1982), which deals honestly with teen sexuality from a girl's point of view. Coolidge was hired to capitalize on the hit song "Valley Girl" and the Valleyspeak it popularized. Her 1983 movie of the same name was, to my eyes and those of many others, an affecting romance that took full advantage of Nicolas Cage's charisma. Despite these triumphs, there was no resulting wave of female directors getting their shots.

As for LGBTQ+ representation in 1980s movies – it was not a boon time, to say the least. The 1970s was not great either, honestly. Paul Morrissey and John Waters were the success stories among directors, and they remained in the low-budget independent world long after they had proven their abilities to earn high profit margins. Waters only really crossed over when he toned down the provocation in the PG-rated "Hairspray" (1988). (It still stars Divine and is still pretty great, though.) Morrissey did make one studio film in 1978, "The Hound of the Baskervilles," but it was a flop and he returned to the underground. There wouldn't be another major moment for LGBTQ+ filmmaking until the New Queer Cinema of the early 1990s.

It didn't help that the minor gains earned by the gay liberation movement in the 1970s suffered a severe setback from the AIDS crisis. Throughout the 1980s, AIDS was inaccurately seen as an exclusively gay disease. In fact, its first name was Gay Related Immune Disorder (GRID). Other stigmatizing myths proliferated, such as that you can contract AIDS by touching an infected person. In this climate, the genuine film representations of LGBTQ+ people were vastly outnumbered by demeaning stereotypes.

Ignorance and Exploitation of LGBTQ+ Identities

The 1980s began with a significant film controversy about the depiction of LGBTQ+ people. **"Cruising"** (1980) is the story of a cop who goes undercover in New York's gay leather scene to catch a serial killer. It is partially based on a series of articles about unsolved murders of gay men that were written by journalist and LGBTQ+ activist Arthur Bell.

Director William Friedkin and his team took the story in a direction that Bell did not approve of. As Friedkin began filming "Cruising" in New York City, Bell wrote in the *Village Voice* that the movie "promises to be the most oppressive, ugly, bigoted look at homosexuality ever presented on the screen, the worst possible nightmare of the most uptight straight and a validation of Anita Bryant's hate campaign." He urged "readers — gay, straight, liberal, radical, atheist, communist, or whatever — to give Friedkin and his production crew a terrible time if you spot them in your neighborhood."[566]

The people of New York obliged. They interfered with filming by playing loud music, setting off air horns, and using mirrors to mess up lighting. Gay bars refused to allow the production to use their establishments. To foil a simple shot of star Al Pacino leaving a building, people obstructed his movements and made faces into the camera.[567]

"Cruising" did eventually get made, but the controversy did not sell a ton of tickets. That might not have just been a result of the protests. In the article "Trash and Treasure at the Razzies" on Criterion.com, Mark Asch compares "Cruising" to William Friedkin's Oscar-winning "The French Connection," the number four box-office champ of 1971. Asch says "It is hardly more murky and abrasive than the earlier Best Picture winner, but its unhappier reception indicates how the zeitgeist for which Friedkin had been a standard-bearer had flagged by the dawn of the Reagan eighties."[568] "Cruising" was another attempt to heighten shocks in the gritty New Hollywood style, but by 1980 New Hollywood was dead.

Friedkin all but admitted that he was exploiting the gay leather subculture for shock value, saying that it was "just an exotic background for a murder mystery."[569] This exoticization is the problem with the film, in my opinion and that of many critics. Several shots linger excessively on men having sex in leather bars in the same way that Herschell Gordon Lewis lingered on gory messes in "Blood Feast." Gay sex and murder are of course not equivalent, but you wouldn't know it from the way they are presented in these two movies. As Richard Goldstein wrote in the *Village Voice*, the sex

---

[566] Quoted in Jason Bailey, "Making Sense of 'Cruising'", *Village Voice*, March 21, 2018
[567] Ibid
[568] Mark Asch, "Trash and Treasure at the Razzies" on Criterion.com, March 25, 2024
[569] Quoted in Bailey

scenes in "Cruising" are "designed to resemble a filmmaker's fantasy of dangerous sex."[570]

Speaking as a straight man, I can say that the gay sex scenes of "Cruising" seemed more graphic than any others I've seen in a mainstream film. They stay barely within the bounds of an R rating by obscuring penises and penetration. William Friedkin claimed in an interview that his initial version got an X rating, and he had to cut 40 minutes to get an R. Much of that footage, he says, was unsimulated sex.[571] I find it hard to believe that Friedkin brought many minutes of hard-core gay sex scenes to the MPAA in 1980, but we'll never know for sure because the excised footage was lost.

A much better judge of gay issues than I am, Dan Savage, talks about the problems with "Cruising" in the aforementioned episode of the *Unspooled* podcast called "Sex Scenes in Film." He mentions that in the movie's first murder, someone is tied up without their consent, which is wildly unrealistic. This demonstrates, in his view, how people who are outside a subculture can get it wrong. If Friedkin had just consulted gay men, the film could have felt more authentic.

Savage also says he saw "Cruising" at age 15 and was horrified at the suggestion that all gay sex had to happen in dingy basements. When there are so few representations of a lifestyle in popular media, as was the case for gay identity in 1980, those few carry extra weight. Bigots like the aforementioned anti-LGBTQ+ activist Anita Bryant could point to "Cruising" as epitomizing all gay culture.

Similarly, viewers could get a very skewed and negative impression of transgender people from Brian De Palma's 1980 film "**Dressed to Kill**." De Palma was an enthusiastic purveyor of film shocks, sometimes skirting at the edge of pornography. Probably his best movie, "Carrie" (1976), begins with a scene in a girls' locker room that felt at times to me like a *Playboy* video. At one point, De

---

[570] Quoted in Bailey
[571] Alex Simon, "Cruising with Billy". *Venice*. p. 68–71.

Palma's camera focuses only on the private body parts of Sissy Spacek (or possibly a body double) in a shower, leaving the head out of frame. These sorts of shots seldom have any purpose besides titillation. In this case, we are objectifying a character who is an underage girl (though Spacek was 26 at the time). Maybe there is some small justification in how this objectification relates to what happens next to Spacek's character, but it still felt gratuitous to me.

"Dressed to Kill" also opens with a shower scene in which a woman's head is often out of shot and her body parts are filmed in pornographic close-ups. This is followed by her husband grabbing her genitals from behind and covering her mouth, which makes her scream and writhe as if she is being sexually assaulted. The movie then cuts to them having some rather workmanlike missionary-position sex. The whole sequence begs the question of whether her seemingly horrified screams were meant to be arousing, either to her, her husband, or the viewer. It's a confusing scene that swam uncomfortably close to "endorsement of rape" territory for me. That sequence and other misogynistic content led feminist groups to protest the movie.

<SPOILER ALERT>

"Dressed to Kill" also drew protests over its ludicrous and harmful misrepresentation of transgender identity. It conflates trans people with those who suffer from dissociative identity disorder (DID), which was once known as multiple personality disorder. This nonsensical combination is meant to explain the motivations of a Norman Bates-style killer. De Palma often paid homage to (some might say "ripped off") Alfred Hitchcock, which extended to Hitchcock's often troubling treatment of characters who weren't straight men.

De Palma clearly wasn't interested in what transgender actually is, instead cobbling together the stereotypes from movies that best enable shocks and twists. Granted, not many people understood transgender identity at the time. Women Against Violence in Pornography and Media, one of the groups that arose around the time of "Snuff," decried the portrayal in "Dressed to Kill" but cited the wrong alternative sexuality when it declared in a leaflet that "The distorted image of a psychotic male transvestite [sic] makes all sexual minorities appear sick and dangerous."[572]

</SPOILER ALERT>

Just like with gay men and "Cruising," there were so few media representations of trans people in 1980 that "Dressed to Kill" unfortunately filled a gap in people's knowledge. It reached quite a few people too, as it was a critical and financial success. De Palma went on to make a few more glossy, stylish, and arguably misogynistic shock films before "The Untouchables" put him on a more conventional mainstream track. William Friedkin's style of gritty drama may have been passé, but De Palma's slicker shocks could still sell in the 1980s.

New Horror Heights (or Lows, Depending on Your Perspective)

Grittiness could still sell in horror. The independent producers and directors trying to make the next "The Last House on the Left" or "The Texas Chain Saw Massacre" had little choice but to be gritty. They couldn't afford to make anything look slick.

"Anthropophagus" (1980) and "Maniac" (1980) each caused waves with some graphic scenes, but the best representative of gritty, early-1980s low-budget shock horror is "**The Evil Dead**" (1981). Young Sam Raimi pulled together $90,000, a handful of actors, and a lot of fake blood, and then holed up in an isolated forest cabin to make a movie.

"The Evil Dead" contains a lot of gore and a bizarre sexual assault that went over the line for most censors. In the United States, it was

---

[572] Quoted in "Dressed to Kill protested" *Jump Cut: A Review of Contemporary Media*, no. 23, Oct. 1980, p. 32

rated X, and in the United Kingdom it had to be cut to earn an X. It still made a huge return on a tiny investment and launched the careers of Raimi and star Bruce Campbell.

Gory special effects had certainly improved since the early 1970s. As inexpensive as "The Evil Dead" was, its effects are a step or two above the "actors yelling with red paint on them" fakey-ness of Herschell Gordon Lewis. Still, some attempted scares in "The Evil Dead" got unintentional laughs out of me. Later installments of the "Evil Dead" franchise would court very clearly intentional laughs while also having the money for more convincing gore.

For gore that is very convincing, as well as deeply disturbing, look no further than **"The Thing"** (1982). Early in production, Universal offered producer Rob Cohen $200,000 for creature effects, which was a record high for the studio. Cohen countered with an educated guess of $750,000, which turned out to be low. He and director John Carpenter cut expensive scenes from the script to ensure the best effects possible.[573] For me, it was worth it; "The Thing"'s power comes primarily from how brilliantly it builds toward some of the most inventively grisly sights ever put on film.

Critics often cited the effects as being too disturbing and generally panned "The Thing." Many compared it unfavorably to "The Thing From Another World" (1951), a much tamer adaptation of the same story. David Ansen accused it of "sacrificing everything at the altar of gore."[574] Vincent Canby scorned anyone who might enjoy the special effects and called "The Thing" the "quintessential moron movie of the 80's."[575]

---

[573] Stuart Cohen, "A producer's guide to the Evolution and production of John Carpenter's 'The Thing' – The Budget". The Original Fan blog, June 25, 2013: https://theoriginalfan.blogspot.com/2013/06/the-budget.html
[574] David Ansen, "Frozen Slime". *Newsweek*, June 28, 1982
[575] Vincent Canby, "'The Thing,' Horror And Science Fiction". *The New York Times*, June 25, 1982

Reading these reviews now, I get the impression that these middle-aged folks just couldn't emotionally handle the powerful imagery in "The Thing." It was easy for them to channel that discomfort into the then-common Grumpy-Old-Man refrain against movies that centered on special effects. "Star Wars" and its descendants were replacing the critically beloved New Hollywood dramas in part because they fully embraced fantastical visuals. Within this then-frowned-upon aspect of filmmaking, gore effects occupied the lowest status, rooted as they were in "Blood Feast" and other exploitation movies. Smart people simply did not deign to enjoy a movie because it's gory.

But why shouldn't a movie center on gore? The previous decades proved every other type of shock content can be explored with great artistic validity. Sex on film was a repulsive taboo until Ingmar Bergman and others proved it could be a legitimate subject for a high-quality movie. Many more people thrill to sex scenes than to gore scenes, but that doesn't mean the latter are necessarily illegitimate. Herschell Gordon Lewis may not have been a good enough filmmaker to make gore into art, but John Carpenter was.

Real-Life Horror

It's not a horror movie, but "**Pixote**" (1980) gets my vote for the most horrific movie of the early 1980s. It follows a 10-year-old boy struggling to evade abuse and rape in the most hellish areas of São Paulo and Rio de Janeiro. The movie's documentary-style neorealism heightens the brutality, especially since young star Fernando Ramos da Silva was an amateur actor who really lived on the mean streets being depicted.

"Pixote" was the first Brazilian film in many years to win international acclaim. In the late 1960s and early 1970s a major movement called Cinema Novo had rebelled against the Hollywood-style crowd pleasers of traditional South American film. Cinema Novo combined the intellectualism of the French New Wave and the politically motivated focus on underclass struggles you see in Italian neorealism. It's fascinating stuff but not really concerned with shocks, with the possible exception of the Glauber Rocha film "Antonio des Mortes" (1969). "Pixote" is like a later-era Cinema Novo movie with the strong content of the shock-film synthesis stage.

Young actor Fernando Ramos da Silva became famous, but it didn't last. He got a gig on a soap opera but struggled with his lines because he was illiterate. After being fired, he went to an acting school but quit after two days. Da Silva returned to a life of crime, and in 1987, he was shot and killed by police.[576] There are no happy endings with "Pixote."

The 1981 German film "**Christiane F.**" is another story of a very young person caught in the depths of urban degradation. Christiane leaps into the Berlin night life at 13 years old and becomes a heroin addict and prostitute by 14. The film uses real locations and amateur actors to faithfully re-create the source material, a biography of a girl named Christiane Felscherinow.

Depicting a harrowing true story like Felscherinow's as realistically as possible meant putting underage actors into dangerous situations. The young actors moved among real heroin addicts and sex workers; one of the most disturbing shots of the film simply pans through a line of Berlin street kids who look like they're on the brink of death.

The actress who played Christiane described her most frightening experience during shooting:

> "We shot a scene on Kurfürstenstraße. Christiane, my character, is standing alone waiting for someone to pick her up. It was a long lens shot so the camera team was far away. A car drove up and I was about to get in when I saw, out of the corner of my eye, some of the crew running

---

[576] Alan Riding. "Fernando Ramos da Silva, 19, Star of Brazil's 'Pixote,' Dies". *The New York Times*, August 27, 1987

towards me shouting: 'No! No! No!' And it came to me: this was a real guy, not an actor, trying to pick me up. I almost got into a car with someone who wanted to sleep with a 13-year-old."[577]

Current German law would not allow a film production to put underage actors through what "Christiane F." did. If it were all done to make a cheap exploitation film, I would unambiguously condemn it. But while "Christiane F." has the basic plot of a drug polemic, it felt to me like a well-written neorealist film. I thought it convincingly makes heroin use look like a grimy descent into hell. It both discouraged people from trying it and woke Germans up to the problem of teenage heroin addicts.

"Christiane F." reached a surprising number of people too; it was the most successful West German film of the year in its home country.[578] Some of the credit for that is probably due to David Bowie, who appears in concert in the movie and contributed much of the soundtrack.

Real-Life Horror of a Very Different Kind

Americans were less interested in documenting children enduring urban degradation in 1981. The most horrific non-horror movie made that year in the United States had a very different intent. "**Roar**" tries to be a sweet PG-rated drama about a family that lives on a Tanzanian nature preserve with dozens of lions, tigers, panthers, cougars, etc. The movie is somewhat autobiographical, as it stars and was made by a family that did keep all of these dangerous animals as pets: film producer Noel Marshall, his wife Tippi Hedren, her daughter Melanie Griffith, and their sons Joel,

---

[577] Quoted in Eric Morse, "How we made Christiane F – the shocking cult film about a child heroin addict," The Guardian, April 19, 2021, https://www.theguardian.com/culture/2021/apr/19/how-we-made-christiane-f-the-shocking-cult-film-about-a-child-heroin-addict
[578] "Top 25 Pics in West Germany". *Variety*. Nov. 7, 1984. p. 52.

Jerry, and John Marshall. (Most of the below information is taken from Tippi Hedren's wildly entertaining book "Tippi: A Memoir.")

The inspiration for "Roar" dates back to 1969, when Noel Marshall and Tippi Hedren were on a movie shoot in Mozambique. They were horrified to discover that lions were headed to extinction and sought to film a narrative plea for conservation a la "Born Free."[579]

The couple sought out domesticated lions but learned that there were very few in Africa. In the United States, no individual lion trainer had a large enough pride for their purposes. Lion trainers also did not want their animals mixing with other trainers' animals, because fights were inevitable. So Marshall and Hedren started collecting their own lions in their home, which was in the Sherman Oaks neighborhood of Los Angeles. Their initial goal was a pride of 50.[580]

In 1972, authorities discovered the family's unusual pets and gave them 24 hours to get the big cats out of town. Marshall and Hedren moved everyone to a compound in a remote desert area of California.[581] There the menagerie kept growing until it included "seventy-one lions, twenty-six tigers, ten cougars, nine black panthers, four leopards, two jaguars, one tigon [a lion-tiger hybrid] six black swans, four Canadian [sic] geese, seven flamingos, four cranes, two peacocks, and a marabou stork."[582]

The original plan was for a film budgeted at $3 million, but by 1973 that was looking unrealistic. It cost $4,000 a week just to feed the animals and crew.[583] Noel Marshall was an executive producer of "The Exorcist" and was supposed to receive 15% of its profits, which would have easily covered their costs. But it took years of legal wrangling to see a cent of it because "The Exorcist" writer William

---

[579] Tippi Hedren, "Tippi: A Memoir", p. 142-143
[580] Hedren, p. 150-154
[581] Hedren, p. 189-192
[582] Hedren, p, 442
[583] Tippi Hedren and Theodore Taylor. "The Cats Of Shambala." P. 145

Peter Blatty put his initials on the contract but did not sign it.[584] The family eventually had to sell four homes and 600 acres of land.[585] Tippi Hedren even pawned her wedding ring and a fur coat given to her by Alfred Hitchcock.[586]

Principal photography for "Roar" finally began in 1976. It consisted mainly of filming the animals, hoping to catch them doing something interesting. If you've ever seen big cats at a zoo, you can imagine how much film stock was necessary.

Sometimes Marshall and Hedren would stage a very dangerous scene. One entailed a leopard licking honey off of Hedren's face while its trainers stood too far away to prevent an attack.[587] Another involved a 450-pound lion sitting on Hedren until Marshall pulled it off her.[588]

During the first week of filming, a lion bit Noel Marshall's hand, which became infected. Lions' mouths are packed with bacteria, and bites often result in infections. Production shut down for a week.[589] Soon after Marshall returned to set, another lion bit him. This time he was hospitalized and diagnosed with advanced blood poisoning. Marshall was near death for 12 hours and in the hospital for three weeks.[590] As soon as he could walk, he returned to the compound and resumed filming. Yet another lion bite left eight puncture wounds in his leg and another case of blood poisoning.[591]

---

[584] Hedren, p. 264
[585] Alex Pappademas, "'We'd All Been Bitten, and We Kept Coming Back': 'Roar' Star John Marshall on Making the Most Dangerous Movie of All Time". *Grantland*, April 17, 2015
[586] Hedren, p. 283-284
[587] Hedren, p. 320
[588] Hedren, p. 400
[589] Hedren, p. 305
[590] Hedren, p. 283
[591] Hedren, p. 338

Tippi Hedren's head was bitten by a lion[592] and her ankle was fractured by an elephant, which led to gangrene.[593] A lion attacked Melanie Griffith's head, causing wounds that required 50 sutures. She barely escaped losing an eye.[594] Cinematographer Jan de Bont was scalped by a lion and received 120 stitches to reconstruct his head. Three weeks later, he returned to the shoot.[595]

At least 70 and possibly more than 100 people were injured during the making of "Roar."[596] The only principal player who escaped unscathed was actor Kyalo Mativo, who was born and raised in Kenya and refused to spend any more time around the big cats than was absolutely necessary.[597]

In 1978, a flood destroyed the compound and 28 lions and tigers escaped. Three were killed by police.[598] Filming was delayed for a year. Finally in 1981, after 11 years of production, there was enough footage to release "Roar."

I'd like to provide an inspirational ending to this story of an independent passion project completed at incredible financial and physical cost – something along the lines of what happened with "Sweet Sweetback's Baadasssss Song" or Robert Rodriguez's film "El Mariachi." Instead I have to give you a brutal punchline: "Roar" was not even picked up for distribution in the United States.[599] It screened in a few countries but made back only $2 million of its eventual $17 million budget.[600]

---

[592] Hedren, p. 277
[593] Hedren, p. 323-324. 329
[594] Hedren, p. 334
[595] Hedren, p. 310
[596] David Onda, "The Unbelievable True Stories Behind 'Roar,' the Most Dangerous Film Ever Made". *Xfinity*, July 9, 2015
[597] Hedren, p. 302
[598] Hedren, p. 404-414
[599] Hedren, p. 443
[600] Hedren, p. 447

<SPOILER ALERT>

A big reason "Roar" was unsuccessful is its absolutely ludicrous plot. Its middle third is little besides dangerous animals terrorizing and attacking people. Then, out of nowhere, the big cats snuggle with the family and fall asleep. The movie spins this as proof that they are all big teddy bears who only want love. Cheesy music plays over people laughing and playing with lions and tigers. Everyone is happy and all is resolved.

</SPOILER ALERT>

Throughout "Roar," wild-eyed Noel Marshall gives himself line after line about how manageable and harmless his big cat friends are, often while fighting them off. He seemed to me like a cult leader who believes his own nonsense. Any time this type of person's pronouncements are disproven, he only becomes more convinced of their rightness. Marshall and Hedren were such zealots for human/big cat cohabitation that they endangered the lives of dozens of people, including their children, and still kept the faith. I imagine that if they let any doubt creep into their heads, they would have collapsed under guilt for all they had put everyone through. At the very least, they did not believe in the concept of sunk costs.

The story behind "Roar" entertains me much more than the movie does, which makes me feel a bit guilty. As delusional as the Marshall/Hedren family was, they had a genuinely altruistic aim. They just wanted to convince the world that lions and other wild animals deserve to be protected. Their mistake was one that many people make: assuming that wildlife worthy of protection should also get along well with human beings. Only a handful of animal species cohabitate amicably with homo sapiens, and most of those were bred specifically for that purpose.

I am a big environmentalist, but unlike most, I don't really like being outdoors. (It's harder to watch movies there, for starters.) I think the best way to respect nature is to leave it the hell alone. Maybe human beings don't have to insert themselves and their garbage into every single ecosystem on Earth. Anyway, I just had to squeeze in my own little message.

New and Old in Shock Comedy

In "Tippi: A Memoir," Tippi Hedren claims that American distributors passed on "Roar" because it was not a "sex-and-violence movie." The movie is of course loaded with animal-on-human violence that would traumatize the family audiences they were shooting for. But yes, it has no sex or nudity, which was indeed unusual in the early 1980s.

Everyone was adopting the rules Roger Corman had established in the early 1970s about the number and frequency of naked female breast and butt shots that had to be in each movie. In the documentary "Skin: A History of Nudity in the Movies" (2020), actress Diane Franklin talks about how if a young woman wanted to be in movies in the early 1980s, she had no choice but to disrobe.

"American Gigolo" (1980) made headlines for including a hot naked guy (Richard Gere, specifically), but that was the exception that proved the rule. While directing "Fast Times at Ridgemont High" (1982). Amy Heckerling wanted to show an actor's penis. She had found it unfair that the so-called sexual revolution only allowed female nudity, and wanted to try to change things. The censors told her she couldn't show a penis. She asked how that made any sense, when women were naked in most movies, including "Fast Times at Ridgemont High." The censors said it was because a penis is "aggressive."[601] Again, it's just a matter of the people in power having an irrational visceral reaction, which is of course not a legitimate reason for a double standard.

Especially in comedy films, naked young women became de rigueur. Blake Edwards was a legendary director behind "Breakfast at Tiffany's" and the "Pink Panther" series. His career was

---

[601] "Amy Heckerling," *Gilbert Gottfried's Amazing Colossal Podcast*, Episode 110, July 4, 2016

floundering until his 1979 movie "10," which succeeded in large part because it offered Bo Derek nude. Edwards' next movie "S.O.B." (1981) satirizes the Hollywood of the time by depicting a struggling director who turns his musical into a softcore porn film. In a meta touch, Julie Andrews plays a squeaky-clean movie legend who relents to appearing topless, both within the film-within-the-film and within the film.

Catering to straight men's most toxic desires reached a peak with the biggest surprise hit of 1981, "**Porky's**." Even more than "Animal House," in my opinion, "Porky's" is devoted to championing entitled sociopathic straight white males. All that our heroes care about is having sex with women they have no feelings for, pulling cruel pranks on each other, and defeating other groups of entitled sociopathic straight white males. It's the humor of "punching down" and bullying, and the plot is about who can do so the most brutally.

Considering "Porky's" is about teenage boys in the patriarchal 1950s, perhaps its focus on meaningless sex and pointless fighting isn't totally unrealistic. Regardless, it's hard not to conclude that the makers and fans of "Porky's" were indulging in nostalgia for a time before second-wave feminism when they didn't have to consider that women might have feelings.

I know I should only speak for myself, and for me, it was deeply disturbing to see sociopathy treated as an acceptable norm to be celebrated. The one character in "Porky's" with moral objections is a female teacher who is characterized as an unattractive (and therefore beneath contempt), cartoonish prude. The movie does shoehorn in a subplot about anti-Semitism being wrong, and I guess the bros stand up for each other occasionally. Most of it felt to me like "Caligula" toned down and played for laughs.

I'm resisting the temptation to say you have to be a sociopath to enjoy "Porky's." When watching movies, almost everyone sometimes indulges that lizard-brain sociopath that lies under the systems of empathy and morality. Some people thrill to the exploits of serial killers, and some apparently find abuse and dehumanization hilarious. Serial killers might cause more damage, but at least they get caught in the end and some sort of moral universe is restored. In "Porky's," the monsters win.

"Animal House" didn't make it as an official shock film, but I am including "Porky's" because it's about underage high school students. All the actors are over 18, of course, but I think joking about teenage characters sexually abusing each other is a step beyond doing so with adult characters.

"Porky's" set a template for a new style of teen sex comedies that proliferated throughout the 1980s. The next year, an old style of shock comedy had a last gasp. "**Eating Raoul**" (1982) hearkens back to John Waters' campy low-budget collections of outlandish atrocities. Director Paul Bartel and former Andy Warhol entourage member Mary Woronov star as the Blands, a prudish couple who get into the business of killing swingers and selling their bodies.

"Eating Raoul" is rated R, so it doesn't go to the extremes of early John Waters. And despite having a 1970s shock-comedy tone, it reverses the audience's sympathies. Instead of hedonists giving a middle finger to the squares, it's about squares slaughtering the hedonists. This is most apparent when our heroes casually dispose of a pack of self-satisfied swingers who are having a very 1970s-style hot tub party. The surprise success of "Eating Raoul" in the Reagan Era indicates how passé the sexual revolution was becoming.

As far as I can tell, "Eating Raoul" did not lead to many more John Waters-style comedies. Waters himself was busy shifting to the toned-down (but still delightfully over-the-top) R-rated "Polyester" (1981) and then the PG-rated musical "Hairspray" (1988). Teen sex comedies, for better or for worse (I vote "worse"), filled the gap.

You Can See It at Home

Even the teen sex comedies that didn't hit big in theaters began seeing sizable returns from home rentals. Sales numbers for VCRs exploded in the early 1980s, and video stores cropped up everywhere. People who were too bashful to buy tickets to "Screwballs" could safely watch it in the privacy of their own homes.

More overt pornography also made the switch to videotape. Meanwhile, pay cable stations were bringing uncensored movies and other adults-only content to broadcast TV. People's living rooms became the new centers for shock media.

David Cronenberg's "**Videodrome**" (1983) comments on this new media landscape. James Woods plays a procurer of shock media for an independent and apparently unregulated UHF TV station. The station is always seeking a higher level of transgressive thrill, chasing the dragon just like real-life exploitation movie audiences did in the 1960s and 1970s. The trajectory in the movie also reaches an endpoint with snuff films, through a mysterious transmission from Malaysia. This parallels how the advertising for "Snuff" played up the fact that most of it was filmed in South America. Americans could more easily imagine snuff films being made in a non-wealthy country of non-white people they didn't know much about.

"Videodrome" also features some subversive sex and a creative use of videotapes. I think it's a fascinatingly bizarre exploration of how media can change people, though I did feel it was a little GOMSy in its alarmism over new technology.

I admit that the easy availability of shock media at home was changing some people in the 1980s, especially kids. Every Gen-X person I've met has a story about being traumatized by a movie rental they were too young to see. Often it was something like "Poltergeist" that they presumed would be relatively safe. "Hey, this is a Steven Spielberg movie, it's PG, and it's about a suburban

413

family. I bet it's like 'E.T.' Oh, apparently Spielberg wrote and produced it and the director was some guy named Tobe Hooper. Whoever that is, I'm sure he wouldn't just randomly throw in, say, a scene of a guy ripping apart his own face."

Spielberg's "Indiana Jones and the Temple of Doom" (1984) provided a tipping point. It's not a shock film by the standards of this book, but if I wrote "A History of PG-Rated Shock Films," it would be a surefire inclusion. The violence hits a peak when a man's heart is ripped from his chest, after which he magically heals. He is then lowered into a pit of fire to be tortured forever, an idea that I found more disturbing than the gore.

In the mid-1980s even Disney was inappropriately incorporating horror in their animated films. "The Black Cauldron" (1985) culminates in a character's flesh being ripped from his bones. The movie was a very expensive flop and almost sunk Disney's animation department for good. A stronger line clearly needed to be drawn between content for kids and content for teens.

By the time "The Black Cauldron" came out, a solution had already been found. In the early summer of 1984, parents started a groundswell of complaints about "Indiana Jones and the Temple of Doom" and "Gremlins," another giant hit that Spielberg produced. Spielberg suggested creating a rating between "PG" and "R." The MPAA, no doubt eager to please the man who was instrumental in almost every recent blockbuster, wasted no time in introducing the PG-13 rating on July 1, 1984. The rating reflected a key distinction between what teens and pre-teens can handle. It quickly proved effective in solving the problem with the PG rating.

It was still very easy for kids to watch shock films on VHS. Over in the more strictly regulated movie landscape of the United Kingdom, this problem caused an awful row, as a Brit might say. The British Board of Film Censors had already spent the 1970s blocking many gruesome horror movies from theaters, including classics like "The Texas Chain Saw Massacre." But there was no law against people renting videotapes of banned films. Children were seeing movies at home that adults were not allowed to watch in theaters.

The National Viewers' and Listeners' Association (now known as Mediawatch) successfully compelled British authorities to prosecute purveyors of shocking films under the Obscene Publications Act 1959. This was the law that filmmakers risked violating if they didn't get at least an X rating from the British Board of Film Censors. Local police started seizing videos and prosecuting each one on a case-by-case basis. Often the seizures were based on titles and box art instead of the content of the films.[602] One infamous raid confiscated the Dolly Parton movie "The Best Little Whorehouse in Texas" because its title sounded like a porno.[603]

Soon enough, something closer to order came to the chaos, partially because the distributors of "Cannibal Holocaust" tried to get clever. They thought they could get some free publicity by sending an anonymous letter complaining about their own movie to Mary Whitehouse of the National Viewers' and Listeners' Association.[604] Instead of taking the bait, Whitehouse started a more general campaign against what she called "video nasties."

The British Director of Public Prosecutions released a list of "video nasties" so that video stores could know which titles could get them in trouble. The list changed often and had several different sections that were linked with different penalties. Mainstays of the absolute no-gos included "Blood Feast," "Cannibal Holocaust," "Faces of Death," "Flesh for Frankenstein," "I Spit on Your Grave," "The Last

---

[602] "Video Nasties". BBFC, May 19, 2005
[603] Elizabeth Donnelly, "Free Flick Fridays: The Best Little Whorehouse in Texas," Tribeca Film Festival, January 21, 2010, https://www.tribecafilm.com/news/512c16b01c7d76d9a9000980-free-flick-fridays-the-be
[604] Laurence Phelan, "Film censorship: How moral panic led to a mass ban of 'video nasties'", The Independent, July 11, 2014, https://www.independent.co.uk/arts-entertainment/films/features/film-censorship-how-moral-panic-led-to-a-mass-ban-of-video-nasties-9600998.html

House on the Left," "Snuff," and dozens of others.[605] Of course, being on this list made a movie forbidden fruit for British shock seekers.

The Video Recordings Act 1984 brought videotapes under the auspices of the British Board of Film Censors, which was renamed the British Board of Film Classification. The Act made it illegal to distribute any movie that was not classified by the Board. The Act remains in place, though restrictions on individual films have relaxed over time.

In the United States, the case law we've already covered prevented anything like a national Board of Film Classification or a Video Recordings Act 1984. There was still plenty of anxiety about exposing kids to horror movies. This came to a head over the advertising for "**Silent Night, Deadly Night**" (1984).

"Silent Night, Deadly Night" was not the first exploitation movie about a serial killer dressed as Santa Claus. It just came along at the wrong time, and its marketers made the mistake of buying ad time during family TV shows like "Diff'rent Strokes" and "Little House on the Prairie." The Parent Teacher Association (PTA) launched protests and Siskel and Ebert came down hard on "Silent Night, Deadly Night" in their popular TV show. The movie's distributor ceased all advertising and then pulled it from theaters after only a week.[606]

This was a controversy I remember reaching my non-cinephilic suburban Midwestern family. I was eight years old and still too scared to watch anything stronger than "Scooby-Doo." At a church Christmas event, my older sister took me aside to gently warn me that there was this movie called "Silent Night, Deadly Night" that kids might talk about on the playground. She genuinely wanted me

---

[605] Julian Petley, "Film and Video Censorship in Modern Britain", p. 213
[606] J.A. Kerswell, "Ho-Ho-HOMICIDE: The Silent Night, Deadly Night Controversy". Hysteria Lives! Website, https://www.hysteria-lives.co.uk/silent_night_deadly_night/

to be prepared to deal with it emotionally; this was no mean older-sibling trick.

I finally saw "Silent Night, Deadly Night" recently and of course it's just a boilerplate 1980s slasher film. It's no more or less shocking than a zillion other movies released in 1984. What made it controversial was that it broke the rules established by the shock-film synthesis. You were allowed to have your transgressive shocks, as long as parents can shield their children from them. "Not only did you advertise during family hour – you scared the kids into thinking Santa Claus will murder them. A burnt-up child-molesting janitor with finger knives was bad enough, but a killer Santa? That's the last straw."

Eventually "Silent Night, Deadly Night" would become a hit on video and inspire sequels. The whole fuss was just a bump in the road for horror movies in the United States. At most, marketers learned a valuable lesson about how not to advertise them. Horror kept selling tickets and kids kept watching them on videotape.

Exploitation filmmakers of all kinds quickly learned where the money was. They churned out cheap movies with dashes of gore and nudity that skipped theaters entirely. As long as these "direct-to-video" releases had lurid titles and box art, they could reliably recoup their low budgets. It was just like the old days when Roger Corman and his ilk would produce a poster and title that could turn heads, and then slap together a movie to fit it. And as with these older films, the direct-to-video releases tended to be formulaic and rarely as outré as their titles and promotional art would suggest.

One exploitation outfit that did try to push the envelope of shock was Troma. Picking one Troma movie out of their dozens of similar titles feels like a fool's mission, especially since it would involve watching dozens of Troma movies. I'll just go with "**The Toxic Avenger**" (1984), which established the Troma template. Both its acting and its gore are cartoonishly over-the-top so as to best extract lowbrow laughs and squeals of disgust. At least "The Toxic Avenger" is never dull, which is a rare quality for an exploitation movie.

Troma movies generally strike me as straight white guys' versions of John Waters films. For me at least, that cuts out 90% of the fun. I find it much less satisfying to watch the powerful and privileged types wallow in bad taste. That almost invariably entails some punching down, and indeed "The Toxic Avenger" throws in abuse of half-naked young women and some gay and racial stereotypes.

Maybe Troma pissed off some squares, but that feels less bold in the 1980s when it was a proven money making strategy. In a perhaps ironic way, Troma and other direct-to-video movies are emblematic of the 1980s' turn toward conservatism. During the Reagan Era, even extreme sex and violence was formulaically packaged to cater to straight white guys.

In the wild days of the early 1970s, just after the ratings system was established, John Waters wasn't the only member of a dispossessed group experimenting with the new freedoms, as you may remember. Melvin Van Peebles expressed Black rage with a new, raw power. Stephanie Rothman stuck feminist themes within the strictures of exploitation films. Straight white men quickly learned from these pioneers and made their own shock movies that left out the messages. As always, straight white men's movies were the ones that got the funding and the distribution deals, so they were the ones people saw.

But then the VCR came along in the early 1980s and democratized millions of home screens. It was the first time most people could see a movie outside of a theater or in whatever edited version happened to pop up on a TV channel. You'd hope that the broad opportunities opened up by home viewing could result in a greater diversity of cinematic voices, shocking or non-shocking. In theory at least, smaller markets should crop up to cater to various niches of the movie-watching public. There ought to be a way to supply demand for LGBTQ+ interest, or movies targeted to Black people. The movies shouldn't have to be star-studded studio affairs; they could be low-budget indies about people talking. Mere representation would be revelatory for groups who never see themselves on screen. You see that now with streaming, but barely at all in the monoculture of the 1980s.

The problem was that video stores controlled the supply of titles. VHS tapes of new releases were prohibitively expensive, often around $80-$90 each. This was intentional, so that only video rental stores would buy them.[607] After stores stocked up on blockbusters new and old, their shelf space went mostly to the aforementioned exploitation movies with covers that excited teenage boys.

Your hip college town might have an independent store with a copy of "Sweet Sweetback's Baadasssss Song" or "Pink Flamingos." Even unhip towns were often blessed with an eccentric mom-and-pop outfit that had a seemingly random selection. But by the early 1990s, those had been mostly replaced by Blockbuster Video and other chains. These chains could afford to stock hundreds of copies of the new releases that everyone wanted to see at the same time.[608] Anything that wasn't a new release at the chains was standardized. Everyone got whatever performed best country-wide, which was whatever appealed to straight white America. This was the limited selection that people could rent and eventually buy for $20 per tape.

By the 1990s, most video stores were no longer great sources for culturally diverse films or shock films, unless you count the toned-down exploitation types. Blockbuster's policy of carrying only movies rated R or lower ensured that both John Waters and Troma would not make shelves. It all added up to a less comprehensive or official

---

[607] David Farquhar, "How much did VHS tapes cost in the 80s?", *The Silicon Underground*, https://dfarq.homeip.net/how-much-did-vhs-tapes-cost-in-the-80s/

[608] "The Rise and Fall of Video Rental Stores and Their Lasting Legacy" *Capture.com*, March 2, 2025, https://www.capture.com/blogs/insights/the-rise-and-fall-of-video-rental-stores-and-their-lasting-legacy

prohibition than the UK's, but it still made the true video nasties hard to come across. Kids may have still been watching movies that were inappropriate for them, but grown-ups would struggle to find the ones that pushed their boundaries. (Besides porn, I guess. Video was a boon for porn, even if Blockbuster wouldn't carry it. You get it; I don't need to expound any further.)

Can the Arthouse Still Shock?

While exploitation films flourished by going straight to video in the mid-1980s, films by internationally renowned shock auteurs still needed to establish credibility in theaters. After the controversy over "The Devils" in 1971, Ken Russell stuck with movies that only occasionally offended people. In 1984, he went full-bore shocker again by directing "**Crimes of Passion**."

Kathleen Turner stars as a woman who works as a fashion designer by day and a sex worker by night. It sounds like a premise for a cheap exploitation film, but there's a lot more than that going on. Anthony Perkins goes all-out as a mentally unstable preacher with obvious parallels to Norman Bates.

Along with a critique of religious sexual repression, "Crimes of Passion" offers a great empathy for sex workers. You could argue that the development of Turner's character undermines that message a bit, but for the most part I don't think the movie falls into any of the old sexist clichés. For instance, it makes johns look like unattractive, middle-aged louts instead of the sweet youngsters yearning for experience that you see in a lot of films. Russell declared "Crimes of Passion" was a "film about the exploitation of women, especially at the hands of the macho American male."[609]

As was the case with almost all non-pornographic American film productions of the time, Ken Russell was contractually obligated to deliver a movie that would get at least an R rating. His first cut of

---

[609] Ken Russell. "The talent to abuse". *The Guardian*. September 7, 1985, p. 8.

"Crimes of Passion" got an X from the MPAA. He recut and submitted again, and got another X.[610]

The MPAA was not relishing its role as a killjoy. The head of the ratings board called producer/screenwriter Barry Sandler and told him he should release "Crimes of Passion" with an X to "re-legitimize the X rating."[611] The MPAA didn't like that the X rating had been co-opted by porn. It wanted some way to allow for genuine narratives with strong content. With a well-known director, a newly minted star in Kathleen Turner, and a classic star in Anthony Perkins, "Crimes of Passion" was a great candidate to reestablish that X-rated movies can be respectable. But the movie's studio, New World Pictures, was trying to legitimize itself away from its roots as Roger Corman's exploitation empire. Russell was railroaded into cutting the movie further until it earned an R.

The bowdlerized version of "Crimes of Passion" did not perform well in theaters, but the uncut one did good business on videotape and laserdisc. I'm sure many home viewers had prurient interests in mind. At least they were exposed to Ken Russell's outrageous, operatic style and blatant social commentary. As for Russell himself, he had had enough of the United States and returned to Europe.

Other famous European filmmakers were mostly being polite in the mid-1980s, except one. Jean-Luc Godard was already firmly established as one of history's most important filmmakers. He was the leading light of the 1960s French New Wave, which freed cinema from many rules set in stone by Golden Age Hollywood. For instance, Godard loved to defy the conventions of "invisible editing," in which filmmaking technique never called attention to itself. You were not supposed to risk pulling a viewer out of total immersion in

---

[610] Michael London. "Film Clips: Russell's 'Crimes' Stirs Passion Over Its Rating". Los Angeles Times, September 21, 1984

[611] Ian White, "Barry Sandler Crimes of Passion". *Starburst*. August 22, 2016

the narrative. Godard used techniques like jump cuts that reminded viewers they were watching a film.

Occasionally Godard's movies would have some sex and violence, but he didn't produce a shock film by my definition until "**Hail Mary**" (1985). The movie puts the story of the Virgin Mary in a modern context. Young student Marie has never had sex, always refusing the advances of her boyfriend Joseph. Like the more famous Mary, she becomes pregnant anyway. Most of the movie is told from her perspective, as she weathers doubts about her virginity from Joseph and everyone else. She struggles to remain celibate and to compel Joseph to love her without lust.

Marie's story is contrasted with that of another young woman who does have sex with a man, who then dumps her. It created a surprisingly conservative moral from a dyed-in-the-wool lefty like Godard. But I doubt he was really endorsing this message; I think he was trying to engage with the Virgin Mary story on its own terms. This meant accepting traditional Christian ideals that are no longer so popular, such as virginity being a supreme virtue that brings a woman closer to God.

In 1985, Pope John Paul II had a different perspective, declaring that "Hail Mary" "deeply wounds the religious sentiments of believers."[612] Certainly Godard's Mary shows a lot more full frontal nudity than any other in history. At times I wondered if some of it was gratuitous, but I could never be sure. Godard's films always contain so many shots that might seem irrelevant but actually have some symbolic or thematic purpose.

As with "The Miracle" and "Monty Python's Life of Brian," devout Christians did not debate those sorts of distinctions. They heard a movie was about religion but was not entirely by The Book, and launched into action. Around 1,400 protesters showed up to the premiere of "Hail Mary" at the Sydney Film Festival, and a bomb

---

[612] Quoted in Saul Austerlitz, "The Last Great Godard Film," *Slate*, October 2, 2006

threat evacuated the theater.[613] Smaller protests proliferated, and the movie didn't perform well at the box office. Religion remained a third rail even as movies laid waste to every other taboo.

"**In a Glass Cage**" (1986), for example, concerns pedophilia, torture, Nazis, and brutality against a man confined to an iron lung. It was inspired by the story of Gilles de Rais, a serial killer of children I mentioned before as the subject of the planned follow-up to "Salò, or the 120 Days of Sodom."

The debut feature for Spanish director Agustí Villaronga, "In a Glass Cage" is a precise, cold, and very serious movie, as its subject matter warrants. I'd put it more on the art-film side of the coin than the exploitation side, but others might disagree. In that sense it's a throwback to something like "The Night Porter." And as with that earlier film, I'm not sure that "In a Glass Cage" really understands the very sensitive topics it's exploring. It seems to suggest that being sexually abused as a child can make you gay, which is of course a vicious and untrue stereotype.

"In a Glass Cage" could not get shown in places like Australia and the United Kingdom that had nationwide censorship systems, but got enough attention to launch Villaronga's career. In the history of shock films it's far from monumental, but it does demonstrate that dark, violent art shockers were not extinct in the mid-1980s.

Pure, Distilled Gore

Sigh. I don't think I can justifiably ignore "**Guinea Pig: Devil's Experiment**" (1985). It is a 44-minute Japanese "found footage" movie in which a few men inflict escalating tortures on a young woman. It has no plot and no real characters – just one pointless brutality after another. Even Herschell Gordon Lewis and his imitators felt a need to include some sort of narrative. I suppose we

---

[613] "Australian film and television chronology: 1980s" Australian Screen, an NFSA Website, https://aso.gov.au/chronology/1980s/

can at least credit "Guinea Pig: Devil's Experiment" with dispensing with all pretense about why people are watching.

An opening crawl says that the footage was discovered, but, as with the ending of "Snuff," anyone with a passing knowledge of how movies are made can tell it's all fake. "Guinea Pig: Devil's Experiment" has too much lighting, cuts between too many camera angles, and wastes a lot of time on rather half-hearted demonstrations of age-old stage fighting techniques. The movie does culminate in a torture of a very sensitive body part that is somewhat convincing, until you realize that the victim isn't moving. People don't tend to lie there calmly and silently as their bodies are being destroyed.

"Guinea Pig: Devil's Experiment" was not released to theaters but was surprisingly successful on video in Japan. Many rental places refused to stock it, but then gave in after getting a deluge of requests.[614] Japanese films had long been shocking, especially in terms of sexuality, but "Guinea Pig: Devil's Experiment" marked the beginning of Japanese cinema focusing on over-the-top violence.

A sequel released the same year, "**Guinea Pig: Flower of Flesh and Blood**," is a more professional effort. It avoids the pitfalls of pretending to show genuine found footage by billing itself as a "semi-documentary." I suppose that is technically true in that it contains a few shots of ordinary people walking the streets. The rest is made of fairly convincing gore effects as a man chops up a young woman. (You have to wonder why young women are always the victims. It's reminiscent of roughies.) Again, the way the film is assembled makes it obvious that it's fake.

In 1991, Charlie Sheen, veteran of more than 25 films at the time, did not find this so obvious. He watched a videotape of "Guinea Pig: Flower of Flesh and Blood," concluded it was a real snuff film, and called the authorities. The FBI launched an investigation into the

---

[614] Scott Gabbey, "American Guinea Pig: Bouquet of Guts & Gore 3-Disc Limited Edition" [Pamphlet]

movie, but quickly figured out the truth and dropped the case. The makers of the "Guinea Pig" series released a timely documentary showing how it was done.[615]

Horror with Meaning

All the FBI would've had to do to close the "Guinea Pig: Flower of Flesh and Blood" case was catch a screening of "**Day of the Dead**" (1985). The third in George A. Romero's "Living Dead" series, "Day of the Dead" features some startlingly realistic gore. While the "Guinea Pig" movies always cut between the actor's face and the body parts being mutilated, "Day of the Dead" shows what looks like real actors' heads screaming while their guts are being pulled apart.

More importantly, "Day of the Dead" has a narrative, characters, themes, messages, a grounding in humanity, and all the other things that make movies enjoyable. It is anchored by a strong female protagonist who is repeatedly belittled and underestimated by macho idiots at a compound that is holding out against a zombie apocalypse. I'm going with "Day of the Dead" over the second "Living Dead" movie, "Dawn of the Dead" (1978) because I think the gore in "Day of the Dead" is more shocking. But you can hardly go wrong with either.

Both "Dawn of the Dead" and "Day of the Dead" were too violent for R ratings. "Dawn of the Dead" got an X, and the producers of "Day of the Dead" did not want to commit a ton of money to another X-rated movie. Romero had to dramatically pare back his initial ambition to make "the 'Gone with the Wind' of zombie films."[616] (I have no idea what that could mean, but I'm quite curious.) Rather than make a movie that could get an R, Romero accepted a smaller

---

[615] Barbara Mikkelson, "Snuff Films," Snopes.com; https://www.snopes.com/fact-check/a-pinch-of-snuff/
[616] April Snellings,"The 25 Greatest Zombie Movies of All Time," *Mental Floss*, https://www.mentalfloss.com/article/651804/best-zombie-movies

budget and "Day of the Dead" was released unrated. It didn't do well in theaters, but made plenty of money on videotape.

Critics condemned "Day of the Dead" for being too nihilistic, but they hadn't seen anything yet. First shown in 1986 but not seen widely until 1990, **Henry: Portrait of a Serial Killer**" eventually gained notoriety as one of the grimmest and most disturbing films of all time. Like "The Last House on the Left," it centers on an excruciatingly long scene of sexual violence. Within the film, the characters videotape the horror, and you see their tape in one extended, unyielding shot. It felt to me a thousand times more real than anything in a "Guinea Pig" movie.

"Henry: Portrait of a Serial Killer" does not glorify these sorts of scenes. Henry is not an alluring, clever mastermind, like so many movie serial killers. He is much more like a real-life serial killer: withdrawn, lonely, pathetic, and unable to connect in any meaningful way with other human beings. Much of the movie's power comes from presenting, in a stripped-down, documentary-like style, the true despair of being a monster.

This was not what the producers of "Henry: Portrait of a Serial Killer" expected to get from their investment. They ran a video equipment rental business and gave their former delivery man John McNaughton $110,000 to make the kind of horror movie that flew off of video-store shelves throughout the 1980s.[617] McNaughton knew he couldn't afford the special effects necessary to make a convincing supernatural slasher like Jason Voorhies or Freddy Krueger. Instead he was inspired by a segment of the TV show "20/20" about serial killer Henry Lucas.

After a controversial premiere at the Chicago International Film Festival in 1986, "Henry: Portrait of a Serial Killer" struggled to land

---

[617] "Henry: Portrait of a Serial Killer (1986) Reviews and overview," Moviesand Mania.com, https://moviesandmania.com/2013/03/04/henry-portrait-of-a-serial-killer-1986-horror-movie-overview-cast-plot-reviews-trailer-blu-ray/

distribution. In 1989 Atlantic Entertainment Group took it on, but dropped it after it got an X rating from the MPAA. According to Roger Ebert, the MPAA told McNaughton not to bother recutting and submitting his movie – there was no conceivable version that could get an R.[618] Ebert's rave review was one factor that eventually got a limited release for an unrated cut in 1990. As with all unrated movies, "Henry: Portrait of a Serial Killer" got a huge majority of its viewership from home rentals.

A Shock Film About Shock Film Fans

There are so many things I could cover about one of the top 10 films of all 1980s cinema, "**Blue Velvet**" (1986). (For the record, it ranks 7th among 1980s movies in the 2025 They Shoot Pictures, Don't They? list, after "Raging Bull," "Blade Runner," "Fanny and Alexander," "Shoah," "Do the Right Thing," and "The Shining.") Our introduction to Frank Booth (Dennis Hopper) in Dorothy's (Isabella Rossellini's) apartment is a contender for the most disturbing scene I've ever seen. But I'd like to focus on the protagonist, Jeffrey (Kyle MacLachlan).

Jeffrey is the clean-cut All-American post-war kid to a near-farcical extreme. Kyle MacLachlan plays him perfectly, in my opinion, as a loveable square. Seemingly running counter to that personality type, Jeffrey is thrilled to discover a severed ear in a field. He becomes single-minded in his quest to find out where the ear came from. When he relates this obsession to his squeaky-clean love interest Sandy (Laura Dern), she asks him, "You like mysteries that much?" Jeffrey very earnestly says "Yeah."

We're not talking about an Agatha Christie-style "cozy mystery" here. Sandy is not referring to a mystery about someone being killed bloodlessly in a tasteful manor house, after which a benevolent genius uses their higher mental faculties to unmask the killer and

---

[618] Roger Ebert, "Henry: Portrait of a Serial Killer," Sept. 14, 1990, RogerEbert.com, https://www.rogerebert.com/reviews/henry-portrait-of-a-serial-killer-1990

reassuringly restore law and order. Jeffrey finding a severed ear and then sneaking into a mysterious woman's apartment is more motivated by the thrill of exploring the darkest recesses of human experience. When Sandy speaks on behalf of the movie audience by asking, "I don't know if you're a detective or a pervert," Jeffrey replies "Well, that's for me to know and you to find out."

We find out along with Sandy after Jeffrey gets sucked into the lives of Dorothy and Frank Booth. It proves to be such a nightmare that Jeffrey learns his perversion has limits. He is so shaken that he cries "Why are there people like Frank? Why is there so much trouble in this world?" Far from reveling in evil, he is now upset that it even exists.

I hope I'm not spoiling anything when I say that after his encounter with Frank, Jeffrey is quite satisfied to remain ensconced in cheesily idyllic Americana. The suburban scenes of "Blue Velvet" are drenched in irony to point out the artificiality of that world. But it still looks very preferable to anything involving Frank Booth. Maybe some things are better left pushed under the surface.

Jeffrey may thrill at observing and investigating disturbing events from a distance, but he is not built to experience them first-hand. His character arc is about discovering that he needs his shocks delivered only in a vicarious form, from a safe remove. Jeffrey thus epitomizes a shock-film fan.

Maybe some people would say that this is a wimpy or phony character trait, but, as I've mentioned, I don't. I'd say it's a wise and healthy way to indulge your lizard brain while keeping it from hurting you or anyone else. I think most people are with me too, especially if they have well-developed systems of empathy and morality. I bet you or someone you know loves true-crime podcasts while being very law-abiding. It's pretty much the same thing.

And "Blue Velvet" does not shame Jeffrey for retreating from real-life perversity. That is Frank Booth's domain, and no sane person would want to go there.

What I've heard about "Blue Velvet" director David Lynch makes me believe that he was essentially Jeffrey. He was by all accounts a polite, strait-laced fellow, often downright dorky. In an essay called "David Lynch Keeps His Head," David Foster Wallace writes that Lynch had the kind of fascination with perversity that only a true prude could have. Lynch and Paul Schrader should have hung out. (Lynch did hang out regularly with David Cronenberg at Bob's Big Boy, according to Cronenberg in his "Criterion Closet" video on YouTube.)

Dennis Hopper tells a story that I think encapsulates Lynch's personality in a documentary short that accompanies the Criterion Collection release of "Blue Velvet." One day on the set of "Blue Velvet," Lynch came over to Hopper, pointed to a word in the script, and said "OK, Dennis, when you say this word …" Hopper interrupted him by saying "David, that word is 'fuck.'" Lynch replied, "Right, when you say that word …"

David Lynch, the man who wrote and filmed some of the most disturbingly perverse scenes in cinema history, couldn't bring himself to say "fuck" on the set of his own movie. I imagine that whatever first-hand encounters Lynch had with the real-life dark and twisted world made him very uncomfortable. That didn't stop him from spinning the bizarre, shocking thoughts swimming through his brain into great art.

Return of the Roughie?

Despite not feeling qualified or entitled to do so, I am once again in the position of evaluating scenes about rape. It's my own fault for choosing to write a book about films with sex and violence; sexual violence is bound to come up frequently. I can't give short shrift to such a prevalent and important topic relevant to shock films. As always, the best I can do is give my perspective without ever implying that it is an authoritative or universal view.

So I will have to talk about "**9 ½ Weeks**" (1986). Mickey Rourke plays John, a sexually dominating psychopath who makes his commands with a soft voice and a cute smile. This demeanor fools Elizabeth (Kim Basinger), and likely many viewers, into seeing him as a romantic.

Reviews of "9 ½ Weeks" often call John's relationship with Elizabeth "sadomasochistic," which I think is inaccurate. I'm no expert on BDSM, but I know informed consent is critical to it. John never asks for consent. He just tells Elizabeth what to do and then gets angry when she refuses.

For me, "9 ½ Weeks" starts as an interesting exploration of a woman being swept away by a skillful manipulator. Then at the halfway point it takes a drastic turn into misogynistic trash. John catches Elizabeth snooping through his desk. He insists that she has to be spanked as punishment. She refuses and tries to leave, and he grabs her and rapes her. Toward the end of the rape, she is shown to be enjoying it.

Throughout most of the rest of the movie, Elizabeth continues to be in John's sexual thrall. We see several more scenes of their sex play, each more gratuitous than the last, few of them relevant to the plot. They have sex in a clock tower, Elizabeth strips for John, a street fight inspires more sex, etc. Elizabeth's regular life pales in comparison, but she doesn't show dissatisfaction with John again until he tries to push her into a threesome. This struck me more as her not wanting to "share" him than a reaction to his domination.

In the last half of "9 ½ Weeks," rape has helped the victim fall in love with her rapist. It is an endorsement of rape, just like "Lorna."

I grant that "Blue Velvet" also has shocking sexual violence. But only the most twisted pervert could be turned on by the scene of Frank Booth and Dorothy. It is presented as a horror. In "9 ½ Weeks," John and Elizabeth are filmed like they're in a softcore porno. Many home viewers reportedly watched these scenes accordingly.

A complicating factor of "Blue Velvet" is that Dorothy is shown to enjoy some aspects of Frank's abuse. But I feel this is portrayed as her coping mechanism; she is able to translate pain into pleasure for a few fleeting moments. In every other minute of her day, her psyche is broken.

In "9 ½ Weeks," Elizabeth seems happier after the rape, at least for a while. Eventually she realizes the damage the relationship is doing to her. But even this is portrayed more like a woman trying to quit a typical bad boyfriend than someone escaping an abusive monster.

Some might argue that this is how it really works sometimes. I can't say, but apparently the true story that inspired "9 ½ Weeks" was quite different. The memoir "Nine and a Half Weeks" is about "what is initially a consensual relationship in which the line between desired, negotiated rough play and abuse disappears until the woman becomes the prisoner of the man."[619] Instead of the movie's plot of sadistic domination that Elizabeth enjoys until she decides the negatives outweigh the positives, the original story is a more clear trajectory of a woman trapped in a relationship that begins with legitimate BDSM elements but devolves into abuse.

The first cut of the "9 ½ Weeks" movie was faithful to the memoir, according to Karina Longworth in episode 196 of *You Must Remember This*. The movie fared terribly with test screening audiences who couldn't understand why Elizabeth stayed with John. MGM decided "9 ½ Weeks" would reach a wider audience if it changed from a horror story to a romance. This meant making Elizabeth enjoy almost everything John forced on her.[620] Rape and control dressed up as love was apparently more accessible to mid-1980s moviegoers than consensual BDSM descending into psychosexual domination.

---

[619] Karina Longworth, "Erotic '80s 1986: 9 ½ Weeks, Mickey Rourke," *You Must Remember This* podcast, season 18, episode 196
[620] Ibid

After getting an X rating from the MPAA, "9 ½ Weeks" underwent another re-edit to get to an R. This cut flopped in the States, and it's now impossible to find. The unedited version was a huge hit overseas. Everywhere, it made a lot of money from home rentals.[621]

As "9 ½ Weeks" was being released, Kim Basinger went public with the abusive manipulations Rourke and director Adrian Lyne had put her through during filming. For one scene, Lyne wanted Basinger to look very upset, so he told Rourke to grip her arm tightly until she cried. Basinger wondered why Lyne didn't just tell her what he wanted her to do rather than manufacturing it through Rourke. Lyne was quoted as saying he didn't think Basinger was capable of emoting because "she doesn't read books."[622]

There are obvious parallels to Bernardo Bertolucci and Marlon Brando assaulting Maria Schneider on the set of "Last Tango in Paris." Some directors think that women can't be trusted to do their jobs, so they have to abuse women into doing what is required.

Reportedly Rourke was later inspired to treat his own girlfriend, Carrie Otis, the same way his character treated Basinger's in '9 ½ Weeks." According to Otis, Rourke would make demands and punish her when she did not obey: pushing her, slapping her, or threatening her with a gun. When Rourke asked Otis to marry him, he pulled out a harakiri knife and said he would kill himself if she didn't say yes immediately. Otis barely escaped him with her sanity intact.[623]

I think "9 ½ Weeks" is mostly an indulgence of sadistic misogyny. I want to say it's a roughie with a budget, but that is going too far. The movie at least centers on a female protagonist of some depth in the

---

[621] Douglas Martin, "Zalman King, Creator of Soft-Core Films, Dies at 70". *The New York Times*, February 8, 2012
[622] Quoted in Longworth, season 18, episode 196
[623] Ibid

first half, even if the second half distorts her to cater to psychopathic male fantasies.

"9 ½ Weeks" eventually made so much money on VHS that it inspired a sequel and many copycat "erotic thrillers." The business plan for an erotic thriller became to release an R-rated version in theaters as a sort of loss leader. News stories would spread the word that some sex had to be removed to avoid an X rating. Its theatrical run wouldn't make much money, but an unrated version would do big business for home viewing.

This strategy tapped into the large market of people who wanted pornography but were too bashful to go into the section of the video store behind a beaded curtain or saloon doors. It makes you appreciate internet porn, in a way. Now everyone can be honest about what they want, and Hollywood doesn't have to devote its budgets and resources to turning on shy guys.

Blackface is Back

When roughies set such a low standard, it's not hard for "9 ½ Weeks" to surpass it. Similarly, "**Soul Man**" (1986) is not as awful as a minstrel show, in my view. That is of course the faintest praise possible, and no one needs to see it.

In "Soul Man," a rich white college kid darkens his skin and pretends to be Black to get a scholarship to Harvard Law School. Mostly his persona doesn't change. But in several scenes, for the purposes of "comedy," he acts out different stereotypes of Black people that were prevalent in the 1980s, just as minstrel shows did for stereotypes of earlier eras. He does this to reflect how the racist white characters see him, but that does not make it much less painful to watch.

"Soul Man" sparked widespread criticism, including a rebuke by the Los Angeles chapter of the NAACP. Producer Steve Tisch responded by saying "We never designed the film to be the definitive statement on racial dynamics in the 1980s; our intention was to offer the audience a comedy."[624]

This is of course an idiotic statement; you don't jump into a minefield of racial politics just for shits and giggles. And Tisch's rebuttal does not even do justice to "Soul Man," which is a very low bar for him to trip on. The movie does in fact try to be a statement on racial dynamics, occasionally at least. Some scenes show what it's like to grapple with pervasive racism: police following you until they can find an excuse to arrest you, landlords searching for a reason to evict you, etc. James Earl Jones and Rae Dawn Chong skillfully play realistic characters who embody the maxim that Black people must work twice as hard to get half as far. In the end the protagonist realizes the gravity of his crime (spoiler alert, I guess, but you hopefully weren't going to see it anyway). "Soul Man" is a synthesis of a political message film and a minstrel show that I doubt anyone asked for, but it was a financial success.

Unfortunately, "Soul Man" is mostly about using racism as fodder for hacky comedy. Roger Ebert's review agrees: "This is a genuinely interesting idea, filled with dramatic possibilities, but the movie approaches it on the level of a dim-witted sit-com. Thoughtful scenes are followed by slapstick, emotional moments lead right into farce, and the movie doesn't have an ounce of true moral courage; it sidesteps every single big issue that it raises."[625]

Ebert suggests that in the right hands, the premise for "Soul Man" could have worked. Is this true? Melvin Van Peebles did tread through similar territory in "Watermelon Man." Granted, that movie was critically different in that its white protagonist did not choose to become Black, and was played by a Black man. The latter difference occurred only because of Van Peebles' insistence; maybe the same sort of casting decision could have made "Soul

---

[624] Quoted in John Voland. "NAACP, Black Students Protest Film 'Soul Man'". *Los Angeles Times*. Oct. 29, 1986
[625] Roger Ebert, "Soul Man," October 24, 1986, Rogerebert,com, https://www.rogerebert.com/reviews/soul-man-1986

Man" quite different? I honestly would have loved to see what Van Peebles could have done with the script to "Soul Man." He would not have been available at the time, though, as he had quit filmmaking to work in the totally 1980s job of Wall Street stockbroker.

Later, Spike Lee would bring minstrelsy into a modern context with "Bamboozled." I imagine a Black director could have situated "Soul Man" fully in the Black experience and made it a cutting satire of racism. But in the mid-1980s, there were no Black directors that Hollywood studios wanted to hire. So instead it let a bunch of white people trivialize racism with lame sitcom gags.

Now we have two 1986 movies, "9 ½ Weeks" and "Soul Man," that synthesized realistic drama with the worst detritus of the bad old days, roughies and minstrel shows, respectively. Meanwhile mainstream comedy continued to take after "Porky's" and lionize smug, entitled white guys who womanize and battle other smug, entitled white guys. If not for fun Steven Spielberg blockbusters and the occasional arthouse masterpiece like "Blue Velvet," American cinema in the 1980s would really look to me like a regressive wasteland.

Can Horror Get More Shocking?

Of course, there is always the wild and wonderful world of 1980s horror, which kept finding new material to plumb for shocks. "9 ½ Weeks" might not actually be about BDSM, but "**Hellraiser**" (1987) sure is.

Or maybe it isn't? The people who solve the puzzle box in "Hellraiser" certainly don't know what they are consenting to. Some are jaded hedonists seeking new levels of sensation; others are just fiddling with a toy they found. Either way, they d0 not realize they are inviting Cenobites into their lives. And Cenobites do not honor safewords. They shoot hooks into people and rip the poor saps apart for their own pleasure.

The leader of the Cenobites, who is not named but is universally known as "Pinhead," loves giving speeches almost as much as he loves tearing flesh. In this first "Hellraiser" movie he delivers a barnburner about how Cenobites are interdimensional travelers seeking new levels of carnal sensation. They are at the point where they can't tell the difference between pain and pleasure.

Both the Cenobites and one of the main characters, Frank, are so desensitized by overindulgence that they keep having to heighten their experiences – the old "chasing the dragon" phenomenon. Writer/director Clive Barker was inspired by seeing people get pierced and spill blood in the most extreme nights at a New York BDSM club.[626]

Barker later said he was trying to mix sexuality into horror in a new way. In a traditional slasher, an asexual monster will kill teens after they have sex. Barker saw this as reflecting a sort of reactionary attitude against sexual behavior.[627] The Cenobites attack libertines too, but they do so in a perverse spirit of hypersexuality. They use violence to heighten carnal pleasure, not suppress it.

I still don't know if any of this represents a fair take on BDSM, but practitioners of that lifestyle apparently love "Hellraiser."[628] It's probably my favorite horror movie, for the opposite reason. "Hellraiser" brilliantly taps into the deep-seated revulsion I can't help but have for any kind of self-mortification, if that's the right word. Even tattoos kinda ick me out a bit, to be honest; they make me think of a needle piercing flesh over and over. As always, I am not judging anyone else's choices. I'm just not wired to enjoy physical pain in any context.

I was so shocked by "Hellraiser" that I resolved to see all the movies in the series. I managed to sit through the first eight but haven't gotten up the gumption to go any further. "Hellraiser II" and

---

[626] Phil Hoad, "How we made Hellraiser". *The Guardian*, May 17, 2020
[627] Ibid
[628] Ibid

"Hellraiser III" retained much of the magic of the first one. Even the notorious "Hellraiser IV" had its moments for me. It puts Pinhead on a space station in 2127, which is as silly as it sounds. The original director of "Hellraiser IV," Kevin Yagher, demanded his name be removed, so it's one of those special movies credited to the imaginary Alan Smithee. It also offers young Adam Scott as a debauched French noble in the 1790s, which is at least worth looking up on YouTube. Unfortunately, after the wackiness of "Hellraiser IV," the series gets much more predictable and dull, as far as I've seen.

The first "Hellraiser" is universally considered hard-core horror, so I'm not the only one elevating its shock level above the pack. It's also extremely gory. The original cut got an X rating, so they trimmed a bit of the nastiest gore to squeak by with an R.[629] It's worth a shot if you're desensitized to conventional horror and need a stronger fix.

Another subject to mine for hard-core horror is war atrocities. The Hong Kong movie "**Men Behind the Sun**" (1988) is a sincere effort to dramatize the crimes of the Imperial Japanese Army's Unit 731, which tested biological weapons on Chinese and Russian prisoners during the Second Sino-Japanese War (1937-1945). Whatever the intentions behind it, "Men Behind the Sun" tends to get classified as an exploitation film, because it rather artlessly strings together a series of brutal tortures onto a very thin plot.

Two of the sequences in "Men Behind the Sun" made it especially controversial. One is allegedly real footage of a young boy's corpse undergoing an autopsy,[630] which is genuinely disturbing. The other purports to show a room full of rats eating a cat. This looked to me like a poor bedraggled kitty being loved to death by rats, which is

---

[629] Ibid

[630] Donato Totaro, "T.F. Mous: The Man Behind the Sun, part 1, The Horror of Camp 731," OffScreen.com, https://offscreen.com/view/tf_mous?/9901/offscreen_columns/ManBehind1.html

still upsetting but not a "Cannibal Holocaust"-level travesty. Director Tun-Fei Mou said the cat was slathered with fake blood and honey, which the rats were licking.[631]

The Hong Kong New Wave had been in full swing since 1979. It was a relatively free-wheeling cinematic world, certainly more so than anything in mainland China. But it still worked under some governmental censorship restrictions until 1988. That year a new rating system opened the door for truly transgressive material. "Men Behind the Sun" was the first to get the new Level III rating, which meant no one under 18 was allowed to rent it, buy it, or see it in a movie theater. Many more outré Level III Hong Kong movies would follow.

The backlash to "Men Behind the Sun" in 1988 was severe. According to Tun-Fei Mou, it was screened commercially only once in Japan, after which a right-wing party threatened to burn down any theater showing it again.[632] "Men Behind the Sun" was banned in most other countries and never released in the United States. If it had come out in the mid-1970s antithesis stage of shock-film history, it could have done well at drive-ins. But the synthesis stage was unfriendly to any grubby, beyond-the-pale exploitation movie, even one that was trying to expose historical crimes.

Over in West Germany, the government was clamping down on extreme cinema. Starting in 1984, violent scenes were routinely cut out of horror movies for both theater and home viewing. Some films, including "The Texas Chain Saw Massacre" and "The Evil Dead," were banned outright.[633]

---

[631] J.L. Carrozza, "Black Sunshine: Conversations With T.F. Mou", documentary
[632] Totaro, "T.F. Mous: The Man Behind the Sun, part 1, The Horror of Camp 731"
[633] David Kerekes, "Sex, Murder, Art: The Films of Jörg Buttgereit," p. 35-50

Rebelling against these restrictions, independent filmmaker Jörg Buttgereit created "**Nekromantik**" (1988). It mines new territory by being the first feature film, to my knowledge, to center on necrophilia. With almost no budget, Buttgereit stages a few very disturbing scenes, including a climax that is so over-the-top that it almost made me not regret seeing the movie.

This ending and a couple of other moments of "Nekromantik" have a gonzo horror-comedy tone that I think should have been sustained throughout. Instead, these precious few interesting scenes are surrounded by what I found to be dreary, incompetent filler. One stretch I thought was especially tedious is devoted to the protagonist catching a horror movie in a theater. This scene contains loads of footage from an earlier, failed Buttgereit effort. It was obviously spliced in to pad "Nekromantik" out to feature length. Maybe "Nekromantik" could have been worthwhile as a short film. Indeed, it was chopped down and combined with an edited version of "Nekromantik 2" for its release in Japan.

An obscure independent New Zealand filmmaker named Peter Jackson could have done a much better job with "Nekromantik." By 1988, he had already mastered no-budget gonzo horror-comedy with "Bad Taste" (1987). It's a shocking movie, but it looks like "E.T." compared to his follow-up, "**Meet the Feebles**" (1989).

"Meet the Feebles" is a parody of "The Muppet Show" in which puppets shoot drugs, film pornos, and kill each other with impunity. It also throws in some racist puppet depictions of Vietnamese people. It's very creative and well-assembled, as you'd expect from Peter Jackson, but it went over my personal line.

"Meet the Feebles" is one of those works that people smirkingly call "equal-opportunity offenders" with "something to offend everyone." I hate when people say that. That just means that sometimes it "punches down," i.e. ridicules the less powerful the way a bully would. Beyond the jokes that are racist, sexist, etc., "Meet the Feebles" literalizes punching down when its evil boss character vaporizes a weak, fearful underling just to demonstrate the effectiveness of some dangerous goo. Somehow this was the shot that plagued my mind like the turtle brutalization in "Cannibal Holocaust" had.

It's possible that I could have rolled with "Meet the Feebles" if it had actors instead of puppets. It reminded me of my reaction to the cute cartoon characters having sex in "Fritz the Cat." There are a few things that I simply do not want to see, and one of them is adults-only subjects inserted into children's domains. I doubt that's just me.

The Last Third Rail of Cinema

In 1988, many people did not want to see Jesus Christ being anything like a real person, and they did not want anyone else to see it either. "**The Last Temptation of Christ**" caused a massive controversy.

In previous movies about Biblical times, Jesus Christ is almost always a supporting character, if he appears at all. This is odd when you consider that he is certainly the star of the religion named after him. In these movies, Jesus is always a perfectly warm, calm, loving presence. He has no inner conflict and deflects any outer conflict with a smile, kind words, and self-sacrifice. As such, he can't make for much of a protagonist. He can't be challenged, face real obstacles, fight, grow, or even change. There's no drama there. Viewers can aspire to be like him but not identify with him.

"The Last Temptation of Christ" is the story of a Jesus with struggles and flaws. His job is to nail people to crosses. The movie shows him imagining sexual experiences, but not indulging. He feels a genuine calling to serve God, but he struggles with doubt and fear. Once he does attract a following, he is unsure how to lead them. It is a realistic story of inner torment in the New-Hollywood style that you would expect from its director, Martin Scorsese.

Willem Defoe portrays Jesus with a furrowed brow and a troubled frown instead of a calm gaze and a beatific smile. In his review, Gene Siskel said "Defoe draws out the humanity in Christ without denying the divinity." This latter point is important; "The Last Temptation of Christ" does not contradict the basic story of Jesus Christ. A sequence at the end might seem like a major departure at first, but you have to stick with it.

That sequence eventually became the centerpiece of the blowback to "The Last Temptation of Christ." But the very idea of making a movie out of the 1948 novel of the same name was always very controversial. When Paramount began planning production in 1983, hundreds of protestors gathered outside the offices of parent company Gulf and Western every day for a month. Paramount received letter after letter from fundamentalists "expressing outrage that an artist would be 'allowed' to make such a film."[634] Most of them believed the rumors that the movie would contain hard-core sex scenes and that Jesus would be shown to be gay. Paramount dropped the project.[635]

Universal took it on in 1987 and hired a Christian marketing consultant to sell "The Last Temptation of Christ" to religious groups. The consultant was so offended by the film's content that he quit and joined the growing protests. As production wrapped up, the leader of one Christian group got all theaters in San Antonio to sign a contract stating they would not screen "The Last Temptation of Christ." Another offered to pay Universal back for all production costs if he could get all the film stock and burn it. Hundreds of congregants of a Los Angeles church picketed outside the studios and then outside the house of Lew Wasserman, chair of parent company MCA. Their signs said things like "Wasserman Fans Anti-Semitism" but they got their signals crossed when they chanted "Jewish money! Jewish money!"[636]

---

[634] Quoted in Sova, p. 174-175
[635] Sova, p. 175
[636] Ibid

One high-profile Christian leader after another urged their followers to boycott all MCA products, and many demanded that Universal cancel "The Last Temptation of Christ." NCOMP had given its last movie rating in 1978, but the United States Catholic Church still found a way to rate the movie "O" for "morally offensive." The day before its release date, 25,000 members of various religious groups came together to protest at Universal Studios.[637]

Meanwhile, Martin Scorsese was getting death threats. Remembering what happened to Pier Paolo Pasolini, he kept bodyguards by his side for years.[638]

Several major American theater chains that collectively owned thousands of screens refused to book "The Last Temptation of Christ." It was banned in New Orleans, Oklahoma City, and Santa Ana, California.[639] Many countries blocked or edited it, including Mexico, South Africa, Greece, and Singapore.[640] None of this prevented "The Last Temptation of Christ" from playing in many places, earning a sizable profit, and gaining plenty of acclaim both from critics and more open-minded religious leaders.

By the time people started seeing "The Last Temptation of Christ," it represented a major front in America's culture wars. In her book "Sex, Sin, and Blasphemy: A Guide to America's Censorship Wars," Marjorie Heins writes about how the film came along just as high-profile sex scandals were rocking the world of televangelists. She says that for fundamentalist leaders the campaign was "not just a protest against cinematic transgression but a struggle for the survival of their coalition and for its members' 'Vision' for America."[641]

---

[637] Sova, p. 175
[638] Ibid
[639] Sova, p. 177
[640] Alexander Larman, "'It has the power to destroy souls': the undervalued Scorsese epic that almost got him killed," The Telegraph, January 10, 2024
[641] Quoted in Sova, p. 176

The UK Gets in on the Fun

The very next year, the United Kingdom had its own, smaller-scale controversy about a blasphemous movie. "**Visions of Ecstasy**" (1989) is a dialogue-free experimental short in which St. Teresa of Avila writhes sexually after giving herself stigmata, then while caressing another woman, and finally with Christ on the cross. The British Board of Film Classification considered demanding that offending scenes be removed, but that would have cut the 19-minute movie in half. Instead, it chose to just ban the film outright.[642]

Most movies banned by The British Board of Film Classification are in danger of being legally prosecuted under the Obscene Publications Act 1959. "Visions of Ecstasy," though, was deemed prosecutable for "blasphemous libel," which was part of English common law. There's no actual libel in blasphemous libel – Halsbury's Laws of England defines it as publishing "contemptuous, reviling, scurrilous or ludicrous matter relating to God, Jesus Christ, the Bible or the formularies of the Church of England." So it's just about saying things that might offend Christians, not telling disprovable lies.

The director of "Visions of Ecstasy," Nigel Wingrove, appealed the Board's decision and lost. The film's distributor then went over the United Kingdom's head, taking the case to the European Court of Human Rights. Now instead of "Visions of Ecstasy" being on trial, British blasphemous libel law was.

While the case was pending, then-prime minister John Major was so offended that he told his colleagues that if the court ruled in the film's favor, he would derogate from the provisions of the European Convention on Human Rights. This would have been a huge international incident; not on the level of Brexit, but in the same ballpark. Foreign Secretary Douglas Hurd reminded Major that such

---

[642] "Visions Of Ecstasy gets UK rating after 23 year ban" BBC.com, January 31, 2012, https://www.bbc.com/news/entertainment-arts-16809977

an act was impossible "except in cases of war or threats to the life of the nation." It turned out to be moot, as the European Court of Human Rights ruled that blasphemous libel was consistent with the rights of freedom of expression.[643] Blasphemous libel was repealed in the United Kingdom in 2008 and "Visions of Ecstasy" got an 18 rating in 2012.

Let's Wrap This Chapter Up

The major American conservative campaign against "The Last Temptation of Christ" was the first of its kind in the 1980s. Nothing else comes close; among the movies we've covered, the brief flap over "Silent Night, Deadly Night" is the only other controversy that penetrated the mainstream, suburban, non-cinephilic world that John Hughes movies portrayed and kids like me lived in. And that fuss quickly dissipated after the movie was yanked from theaters.

Sometimes a sex film like "9 ½ Weeks" would cause a bit of a stir, or something like "Cruising" or "Soul Man" would provoke traditionally liberal groups. Otherwise, extreme shocks were successfully quarantined in the horror and art/foreign film realms during this period. For the most part, parents were able to keep their kids away from all the nasty stuff without too much effort. They worried about horror, and sometimes the movies that themselves were syntheses – "Indiana Jones and the Temple of Doom," "Gremlins," "Poltergeist," etc. – took things too far. Adding a PG-13 rating tamped down those problems, as people relied on the rating system to divide the monoculture into more manageable slices.

Thus "The Last Temptation of Christ" represented the only major time since the inauguration of Ronald Reagan that the system of the shock-film synthesis broke down. The years following its release would bring a few more incursions of shock material into the mainstream, which contributed to the conservative backlash. "The

---

[643] Caroline Davis, Owen Bowcott, and Patrick Greenfield. "Files show John Major's aides viewed emails as passing fad". December 28, 2018. *The Guardian*.

Last Temptation of Christ" is thus a harbinger of things to come in the next chapter.

Honestly, though, this does not provide as clear of a dividing line as I'd like for the end of this chapter. "The Miracle" was a perfect chapter-ender because the Supreme Court's ruling about it constituted the first major victory of the antithesis over the thesis. The true enforcement of the Production Code in 1934, the initiation of the rating system in 1968 – these are clear turning points in the shock-film story. "The Last Temptation of Christ" represents something more like a slight adjustment.

This is not as satisfying for the narrative I'm spinning, but that's just how the synthesis stage of shock film goes. Before this stage, we had something close to a three-act story arc going. Freedom is the protagonist in my history, with censorship as the antagonist. Freedom was the underdog in the first act and was gaining ground until Joseph Breen and the Legion of Decency turned the tide in 1934. The Code Era was a drag for me to write (but hopefully not for you to read – though if it was, I get it) because there was little or no conflict; censorship was dominating. But then there was some good rising action from 1948 through 1968. Freedom then won the war and was dominant in the early-to-mid 1970s, sometimes excessively so. That part made for an awfully long denouement, but at least it gave us some wild movies to talk about.

This chapter has been more of a laundry list of shocking movies, most of which followed the synthesis-stage rule of staying out of sight of mainstream families. This doesn't provide a lot of narrative movement.

I'm not thrilled about that, but I also don't want to distort reality to make for a more enjoyable read. The world is under no obligation to arrange itself according to the dramatic structures that human beings happen to find most pleasing. The three-act structure works so well on our emotions not because it reflects how the world works but because we are wired to revel in stories with clear conflicts and resolutions. A one-act play or short film can set up a conflict and then resolve it without all the ups and downs of three acts. But the three-act structure has become the dominant storytelling form of our time because all those ups and downs ratchet up the intensity of the central conflict.

Unfortunately, the three-act structure doesn't explain real life as well as systems like Hegelian dialectics do. It's not like dialectics are devoid of drama: When the antithesis defeats the thesis, you do get a nice resolution of conflict. A lesser conflict is then started when the antithesis reveals its flaws and the thesis fights back. But next the synthesis mixes the thesis and antithesis, the protagonist and antagonist. I can't think of any fictional narrative in which the bad guys and good guys spend the last third melding together and figuring out how to coexist.

Sadly, the human brain is much more stimulated by tales of conflicts won and lost than by stories of accommodation and compromise. This is why many more people watch sports than live streams of legislative hearings. The latter is a thousand times more relevant to our lives, but we can't help ourselves: Our minds wander when no one's fighting.

I'd argue that this is a flaw of human nature that we should continually work to counteract in every realm besides entertainment. One of the major lessons of history is that accommodation and compromise make for much happier, healthier societies than constant conflict does. This is why stable democracies are generally more desirable than autocracies in which power regularly changes hands through murders and wars. Government works best when it's boring. As the old saying goes, the greatest curse is "may you live in interesting times."

The problem is that people get so much more involved when the times are interesting. I worry sometimes that immersing ourselves in so much conflict-based entertainment has trained us to seek conflict in politics at all times, even when it's counterproductive. As I write this in 2025, I wonder whether many Americans' lust for drama has overwhelmed their reverence for the founding principles of the nation.

This is beyond the scope of a book about boobs and blood in movies. The point I should be making is that I'm ending this chapter here because it's already plenty long, and the synthesis stage of shock-film history shifts subtly after "The Last Temptation of Christ." That will have to be good enough.

Chapter 10: A Slight Swing Back Toward Freedom

NC-17-Rated

During the Reagan administration from 1981-1989, conservatism reigned in the United States and the shock-film synthesis stage held. The antithesis stage of 1969-1976 had tested out all content and messages that had been forbidden by the Production Code. After the late 1970s sorted out the synthesis stage, most of the previously forbidden elements were integrated into mainstream filmmaking and divided among the categories provided by movie ratings.

Some material didn't fit into this system, though. Movies with extreme violence ("Day of the Dead," "Henry: Portrait of a Serial Killer") and strong sexual content ("Crimes of Passion," "9 ½ Weeks") could either undergo severe cuts or appear only in the few theaters willing to show unrated or X-rated movies. These releases wouldn't make much money. Videotape provided a second life that eventually brought profits for some of these films.

But that's not what self-respecting non-exploitation filmmakers want to do. They want reviews in the papers, a big premiere, awards buzz, and other signs of cultural impact. They didn't go to film school to make the filling that is sold by a lurid VHS cover.

If they're arty cineastes like Peter Greenaway, who orchestrates every shot as if it's a Baroque painting, they don't want all their meticulous craftsmanship broadcast on a tiny TV with a built-in VCR. Greenaway's **The Cook, The Thief, His Wife, and Her Lover**" (1989) was made to be experienced on big screens so it can overwhelm and disgust crowds of urban sophisticates.

Peter Greenaway's movies are not for everyone. They are unique combinations of high art and extreme transgression. A delicate classical composition will play over an ornate, dazzlingly art-directed long shot of two people screwing on piles of meat. A child dressed as a Renaissance cherub will sing with a gorgeous dubbed operatic soprano voice while urinating into a pool full of people. Greenaway's target audience is the very small intersection in a Venn diagram of cinematic shock seekers and art historians.

In 1984, the MPAA had wanted "Crimes of Passion" to revert the meaning of the X rating away from pornography and back to its original intent, of art meant only for adults. While "Crimes of Passion" is indeed a valid artistic achievement, by my estimation and that of others, it feels schlocky compared to "The Cook, The Thief, His Wife, and Her Lover." Greenaway's unabashedly artsy style makes his films difficult to interpret as smut. No one would go to all that trouble just to give straight guys boners.

"The Cook, The Thief, His Wife, and Her Lover" could not get an R rating without cutting out its heart. It was released unrated and generated tremendous buzz for such an artsy movie. Cineastes wanted to see it but had trouble finding showings.

Around the same time, "Henry: Portrait of a Serial Killer" finally hit screens – too few of them, because it was also unrated. Again, cineastes were annoyed. The MPAA jumped at the chance to right the wrong it had made when it didn't copyright the X rating. In 1990 it created a new rating, NC-17, to cover non-pornographic movies that should only be shown to adults.

Much the same way critics gushed about the possibilities for adults-only art after seeing the X-rated "Last Tango in Paris," the new NC-17 rating was heralded as a great opportunity for opening up movie content. It didn't work out that way. Many theaters refused to screen movies with NC-17 ratings, Blockbuster Video wouldn't stock them, and TV stations wouldn't run ads for them.

This reaction to NC-17 movies defeated 99% of the purpose of the new rating. Very few movies have been released with an NC-17 rating since. It has remained in place because of inertia and the occasional movie that is helped by it. Older non-pornographic X-rated films like "Beyond the Valley of the Dolls," "Pink Flamingos," "Last Tango in Paris," and "The Evil Dead" were more appropriately re-rated NC-17.

I think the rating system was so ingrained in people's minds by 1990 that they couldn't help but think of NC-17 as pornographic, or at least well beyond the pale of what most adults want to see in a movie theater. The R rating had already expanded beyond its 1968 mandate to encompass gore, sex scenes, all the cursing your heart could desire – what else could there be? Most people didn't want to find out.

A major problem is that the line between a hard R and NC-17 is a mostly fuzzy one. Sexual penetration and erect penises make for easy decisions, but apart from that, you're stuck with judgement calls based on differences in degree, not kind. It's hard to know exactly which sexual or violent acts will make the MPAA review board say "too far." Many filmmakers have been surprised when their movie got an NC-17, and then followed the review board's recommendations to cut it down to an R. Others added scenes they knew were beyond the pale, so the board could demand they cut those and feel it did its job – meanwhile a few other scenes slipped through that may not have otherwise. It's the same set of games that filmmakers and the ratings board played with the X rating.

The 1989 Pedro Almodóvar film "Tie Me Up! Tie Me Down!" was one of the first to get an NC-17 rating in the States. It was a mainstream smash hit in Almodóvar's native Spain, and to my eyes seems like an non-shock film by 1989 standards. The MPAA ratings board was triggered by its sexuality, with one quick shot of a bath toy pleasuring a woman probably pushing it over the top.

The 2006 Kirby Dick documentary "This Film Is Not Yet Rated" explores the biases and hypocrisies of the MPAA ratings board. The film shows how a shot of a woman masturbating will bring a more severe rating than a man doing the same. Gay sex is treated more harshly than hetero sex. There is very little violence that is strong enough to push a movie to NC-17. Independent movies tend to get higher ratings than comparable studio films.

An upshot for this book is that the NC-17 rating doesn't make my job of determining what constitutes a shock film much easier. It can certainly help, but mostly I'll just have to keep plodding ahead going by my subjective judgement and whatever public controversies arise.

Do the Right Thing

Speaking of public controversies, "**Do the Right Thing**" created a major one in 1989. It has violence and sexuality but nothing that could come close to warranting an NC-17 rating. If not for the cursing, it perhaps could have qualified for a PG-13.

That would never have happened in reality, because "Do the Right Thing" delivers the message-based shock of telling Reagan-era America what it didn't want to hear. It is a tremendously powerful movie that rips open the facade that 1980s conservatism had maintained to obscure systemic racism. Black people were thrilled to see a realistic demonstration of how simmering racial tension can explode into tragedy. Some white people were also blown away; others were just terrified.

To say I was among the former group of blown-away white people is an understatement. I saw "Do the Right Thing" when I was 14 years old and it changed my life in a major way. It not only turned me into a film buff; it also got me obsessed with Black history, left-wing politics, and even music – I became a lifelong hip-hop fan and "Fight the Power" is still my favorite song. "Do the Right Thing" remains my all-time favorite movie.

The white people who were terrified created the controversy. "Do the Right Thing" director Spike Lee later cited three New York critics, David Denby, Joe Klein, and Jack Kroll, for sparking rampant fearmongering that the movie would incite Black people to riot. Their implication was that Black people would be unable to control themselves after watching a work of fiction. Lee minced no words, saying, "These reviews were absolute racism. Racism."[644]

In American history, the rare uprisings by primarily Black people were sparked by slavery, assassinations, killings by police, and other real-life injustices – not movies. (Meanwhile, race-based uprisings by white people, like the Tulsa massacre of 1921, have been incited by Black people exercising their rights as human beings.) Still, there is a long history of white people worrying that artistic statements can "put ideas in their heads," as if Black adults were children who need to be shielded from content that might upset them.

I'm reminded of the Ohio censorship board's suppression of the film version of "Native Son." Its justification didn't mention riots, but you can read between the lines of its legalese about how the movie "contributes to racial misunderstanding, presenting situations undesirable to the mutual interests of both races ... undermining confidence that justice can be carried out [and presenting] racial frictions at a time when all groups should be united against everything that is subversive."[645]

The fuss over "Do the Right Thing" put pressure on Universal Pictures president Tom Pollock to cancel its release or at least postpone it until some heat blew over. Spike Lee later noted that Pollock had just received death threats over "The Last Temptation of Christ." Pollock stood firm, and "Do the Right Thing" hit American

---

[644] Quoted in Susan King, "'Universal Was Not Afraid': Spike Lee Reflects on the Fearmongering That First Met 'Do the Right Thing,'" *The Hollywood Reporter*, https://www.hollywoodreporter.com/movies/movie-news/do-right-thing-spike-lee-reflects-fearmongering-first-met-1989-film-1220715/
[645] de Grazia and Newman, p. 242

theaters on June 30, 1989. There were no resulting riots or violent incidents of any kind.[646]

<SPOILER ALERT>

Really, it was white people who were the most triggered by "Do the Right Thing." Their anxiety was channeled into a few stock criticisms. These came out at a press conference about the movie at the Cannes Film Festival, which is available on its Criterion Collection DVD.

The most common loaded question Spike Lee faced was "Why did Mookie throw the trash can into Sal's?" At the press conference, Lee responded that while white people invariably asked him this, Black people never did. He also wondered aloud why white people latched onto this moment instead of the death of Radio Raheem at the hands of a policeman. The former is property damage, while the latter is homicide.

I'm sure Spike Lee knows why many white people were so upset about this moment, but at the press conference he didn't take it further. As a white person who has talked to a lot of white people about "Do the Right Thing," I think I know why. Even some of the most seemingly liberal-minded white people can have a latent mindset of being on the white "team." They might have Black friends, they might avoid saying or doing racist things, but they still instinctively identify with white people and regard Black people as a potentially dangerous "other." They spend "Do the Right Thing" quietly siding with at least two of the three white characters, Sal, Vito, and Pino, who spend their days on an almost entirely Black street. Mookie, as an employee of Sal's and friend of Vito's, was sort of on their "team." He's seen as "one of the good ones" among the Black characters. When Mookie throws the trash can, these

---

[646] King, "'Universal Was Not Afraid': Spike Lee Reflects on the Fearmongering That First Met 'Do the Right Thing'"

white people feel the betrayal of him "switching sides" at a critical moment.

The movie does not suggest that destroying Sal's was the right thing to do, as many white people concluded in their fits of pique. One brilliance of "Do the Right Thing" is that the title is ironic. It demonstrates how doing the right thing gets very muddled within the complex reality of American racism. The cop is clearly at fault for the death of Radio Raheem, but how do you get justice for that? Especially in 1989, you don't. There will be no consequences, and you could be killed the same way at any time. The resulting anger and frustration can sometimes boil over and find another outlet, which is seldom the right one. "Do the Right Thing" is not the simple morality play that many white people wanted it to be; it's a realistic and complex depiction of how systemic racism can lead to tragedy.

</SPOILER ALERT>

I could spend the rest of this chapter talking about "Do the Right Thing," but I should cut myself off here. For the purposes of this book, it's important as the first movie in many years to deliver to large groups of white people the message-based shock of an unrestrained, unapologetic, confrontational Black perspective. "Do the Right Thing" was preceded in this by the music of Public Enemy, NWA, Boogie Down Productions, and other rap acts. It would be followed by films like "Boyz N the Hood," "Malcolm X," "Menace II Society," and more. The early 1990s would be a boom time for honest Black political expression through art.

New Queer Cinema

Soon after "Do the Right Thing" broke through Reagan-era conservatism to give the United States an unfiltered Black voice, LGBTQ+ filmmaking burst in with its own movement. New Queer Cinema got its first widespread attention with the documentary **"Paris Is Burning"** (1990 in Canada, 1991 in the States).

"Paris Is Burning" documents the New York City drag ball culture for people of color. The scene arose as an alternative to the drag competitions shown in "The Queen" (1968), which tended to favor white blondes. "Paris Is Burning" reveals a world populated by a vibrant set of chosen families made up of people who have been discarded by society and usually by their birth families. At the balls they find both affirming community and tough competition.

Drag balls are shown to be a wildly creative environment. You might be surprised to see much of recent slang, like "shade," "slay," "read," "realness," etc., pop up in "Paris Is Burning." In the early 1990s, its voguing dance style made the biggest splash, especially after Madonna brought it to a huge audience with her song "Vogue."

"Paris Is Burning" also offers fully sympathetic depictions of transgender people, which were exceedingly rare before it. In fiction films, trans characters were usually shown as predatory freaks to be exposed and laughed out of the room, as in "Crocodile Dundee" and "Soapdish." The best you could hope for was the occasional likeable side character whose identity is presented as at least somewhat ironic, like John Lithgow's football-star-turned-woman in "The World According to Garp."

There's no joke about being trans in "Paris Is Burning." We see one trans woman pursue her dream to be a model. Another frolics on the beach in celebration of her recent top surgery. A main participant meets a very tragic end after someone discovers she is trans. Transgender rights have a long way to go at this writing, but the honest portrayals in "Paris Is Burning" deserve some credit for pushing them forward.

Because it was a documentary, "Paris Is Burning" could go farther in giving conservative America information it didn't want to know. The Todd Haynes drama "**Poison**" (1991) caused a bigger stink even though it treaded territory that had been covered by Rainier Werner Fassbinder, Paul Morrissey, Kenneth Anger, etc. Granted, there's little chance that Senator Jesse Helms and American Family

Association leader Donald Wildmon knew about any of those filmmakers when they fussed over "Poison" winning the Grand Jury Prize at the 1991 Sundance Film Festival. Wildmon said it features "explicit porno scenes of homosexuals involved in anal sex,"[647] which is not true.

"Poison" does explore gay desire in a prison story inspired by the writings of Jean Genet. There are sex scenes but they don't reach the level of pornography. People like Donald Wildmon would not make such distinctions, of course; to them any gay sexuality is automatically pornographic.

"Poison" also weaves in two other very different stories to make for a fascinating and unusual viewing experience. It launched Todd Haynes' career, but it wasn't his first film controversy. In 1988 he made "Superstar: The Karen Carpenter Story," a 43-minute biopic of Karen Carpenter with Barbie dolls enacting all the roles. It was never released in any form because it was obstructed by a lineup of powerful copyright holders: Karen's brother and bandmate Richard, A&M Records, and the Mattel toy company. For many years "Superstar: The Karen Carpenter Story" was nearly impossible to see, but thanks to the internet, I bet you can find it.

Even "Poison" was barely seen in 1991, earning less than a million dollars in box-office returns. It didn't have the high profile that usually provokes mainstream blowback. Helms, Wildmon, et al. were primed to be triggered by movies after "The Last Temptation of Christ" put the medium under conservative crosshairs once again. Also, "Poison" was partially funded by the National Endowment for the Arts, which was under fire for supporting the photography of Robert Mapplethorpe. Conservatives were trolling for all sorts of data points in their campaign against the erosion of the Reagan-era

---

[647] Michael Koresky, "On the Margins: Todd Haynes's Poison," Criterion.com, https://www.criterion.com/current/posts/7418-on-the-margins-todd-hayness-poison

bulwark that suppressed voices that weren't straight, white, and male.

New Queer Cinema was hardly forestalled by this minor skirmish. Haynes, Derek Jarman, Gregg Araki, Gus Van Sant, Cheryl Dunye, and others made more independent triumphs. In a few years openly LGBTQ+ protagonists showed up in mainstream movies like "Philadelphia," "Heavenly Creatures," "The Adventures of Priscilla, Queen of the Desert," "To Wong Foo, Thanks for Everything, Julie Newmar," "The Birdcage," "Bound," etc. Queer representation in movies has ebbed and flowed since, in both quantity and quality, but I'm confident in declaring that New Queer Cinema provided the critical turning point away from the previous status quo of coding, ridicule, and demonization.

What About Women?

So the early 1990s saw major movements of Black and queer filmmakers after around 15 years of repression (or 95, if you don't count the early 1970s as significant enough). Was there a similar wave of movies that shocked straight white men with the unrestrained perspectives of women?

The female directors I mentioned before as breaking through in the 1980s – Martha Coolidge, Amy Heckerling, and Penelope Spheeris – kept working into the 1990s, which is an achievement in itself in Hollywood. But If any of them wanted to make no-holds-barred feminist movies, none got the chance. They were subsumed into the Hollywood system and expected to turn out conventional product. On an episode of "Gilbert Gottfried's Amazing Colossal Podcast," Heckerling talks about how women don't get second chances, so she had to strategically choose safe projects.[648]

It's not a bad thing that women were integrated into the Hollywood system, especially if that was their goal. They weren't pigeonholed

---

[648] "Amy Heckerling," *Gilbert Gottfried's Amazing Colossal Podcast*, Episode 110, July 4, 2016

into films about women the way Black and LGBTQ+ directors were for their identities. Female directors were given conventional scripts that otherwise would have gone to white men. On the downside, we didn't get as many movies that unabashedly promoted female points of view like we did for Black and LGBTQ+ ones.

Some women did gain enough clout from directing big successes to force through major movies with female protagonists, which were rare in the 1990s. After writing and directing "Look Who's Talking" (1989) and its sequel, Amy Heckerling was able to get backing for "Clueless" (1996), which proved to be another huge hit. Penny Marshall cashed in her chips from the $100-million-grossers "Big" (1988) and "Awakenings" (1990) to make "A League of Their Own" (1992), which brought in $134 million. Hollywood execs were shocked that profitable films could feature actresses in the top two or three names of their call sheets. Otherwise, "Clueless" and "A League of Their Own" are more important and influential than shocking.

The one mainstream movie from this era that could qualify as delivering a message-based shock of feminist rage was directed by a man but written by a woman: **Thelma & Louise**" (1991). As you may know, Geena Davis and Susan Sarandon star as friends who fight back against sexual harassment and would-be rapists and end up on the lam.

You can tell that "Thelma & Louise" had a shocking message for its time by the controversy it generated. Many men complained that all its male characters were evil,[649] as if there were some dearth of positive representation of straight men in popular culture. This claim was also demonstrably false: Harvey Keitel plays a sympathetic cop and Sarandon's character had a good husband. I'm betting these petulant male moviegoers had simply never empathized with complex female protagonists before and didn't know how. As

---

[649] June Sawyers, "Callie Khouri Answers Critics of 'Thelma and Louise'" *Chicago Tribune*. July 7, 1991

screenwriter Callie Khouri shot back, "If [critics are] feeling threatened, [they're] identifying with the wrong character."[650]

Khouri also said that she wrote the script as "a conscious effort to counter" the typical Hollywood roles for women as "bimbos, whores and nagging wives."[651] The characters of Thelma and Louise broke from the saint/sex worker dichotomy by being full-fledged human beings with feelings and opinions, some of which men might not enjoy hearing. And maybe these triggered men were unsettled by being shown that sexual harassment and assault are unwelcome behaviors.

It had long been revolutionary just to center a major movie on a female friendship. In the documentary "Sois belle et tais-toi) (Be Pretty and Shut Up)" (filmed in 1976 and released in 1981), Jane Fonda says the characters she played almost never had any female friends at all. The one film in which her character did have a friendship with a woman prompted a producer to corner her with his concern that it came across as a lesbian relationship. Fonda says there was not even a hint of such a thing; this man just couldn't conceive of two attractive women having a connection that wasn't sexual.

There were some clearly feminist films in the 1990s indie/art film realm. "Daughters of the Dust" (1991), "Orlando" (1992), and "The Piano" (1993) are all fascinating period pieces about women who refuse to conform to gender roles in one way or another. The most strident one I've found from this era is "**Female Perversions**" (1996). Its title is intentionally provocative but easily misinterpreted. It is explained by a quote that runs at the end:

> "For a woman ... to explore and express the fullness of her sexuality, her ambitions, her emotional and intellectual capacities, her social duties, her tender virtues, would entail

---

[650] Quoted in Larry Rohter, "The Third Woman of 'Thelma and Louise'". *The New York Times*. June 5, 1991
[651] Ibid

who knows what risks and who knows what truly revolutionary alteration to the social conditions that demean and constrain her. Or she may go on trying to fit herself into the order of the world and thereby consign herself forever to the bondage of some stereotype of normal femininity – a perversion, if you will."

-Louise J. Kaplan, "Female Perversions: The Temptations of Madame Bovary"

This quote sums up "Female Perversions" pretty well. Tilda Swinton stars as a woman whose goal in life is to become a judge. Within the patriarchy, this requires her to be a brilliant lawyer as well as look sexy while shrugging off leers, act tough but not threatening to men, smile just the right amount, etc., etc. Her plight is contrasted with several other women struggling in other ways with the "bondage of some stereotype of normal femininity."

"Female Perversions" has so much to say that sometimes it can feel a bit like a Ph.D. thesis. But that just means it is jam-packed with messages that could offend oblivious latent misogynists. I also found it quite moving at parts, and of course Tilda Swinton is terrific. I'd love to see it experience a resurgence, and I'd be very curious if it would trigger some straight men today.

Return of the Shock Auteurs

Let's head back to 1989, when one artsy shock auteur made a triumphant comeback from a long hiatus. Alejandro Jodorowsky, director of the bizarre midnight movies "El Topo" and "The Holy Mountain," turned out "**Santa Sangre**."

Compared to the chaos of "El Topo" and "The Holy Mountain," "Santa Sangre" is relatively controlled. It has a mostly straightforward narrative and can be categorized as horror, assuming that anything Jodorowsky does can fit comfortably into any genre. In his review, Roger Ebert praised it for standing out among what he called the "countless Dead Teenager Movies" of the 1980s:

> "Of course the movie is rated NC-17. I believe more horror films should be made for adults, so that they are free to deal with true malevolence in the world, instead of retailing the pornography of violence without consequences."[652]

"Santa Sangre" was not a hit anywhere and only made it to a handful of theaters in the United States. Jodorowsky made one more movie in 1994, "The Rainbow Thief," which was only released in France. He would not get another film until a resurgence of interest in his career in the 2010s. I and many other people became fascinated with him, and with weird movies in general, after seeing the 2013 documentary "Jodorowsky's Dune."

Even if Alejandro Jodorowsky doesn't sound like your cup of tea, you should watch "Jodorowsky's Dune." It's packed with wild stories. I'll spoil only a few.

After the success of "The Holy Mountain" internationally and on the American midnight-movie circuit in 1973, Jodorowsky was tapped to go big-time with an adaptation of the Frank Herbert novel "Dune." He blew through $2 million of the $9.5 million budget in a pre-production process that lasted two and a half years.

Jodorowsky had big, bold ideas. For instance, he was determined to hire Salvador Dali to play the emperor. Dali demanded a rate of $100,000 per hour (about $615,000 in 2025 dollars). Jodorowsky accepted, provided he could film Dali for just one hour, with a robotic lookalike playing the rest of the role. Dali agreed to this plan as long as the robotic lookalike would end up in his museum. He also insisted that his character's throne be a toilet made of intersecting dolphins.

---

[652] Roger Ebert, "Santa Sangre," rogerebert.com, August 31, 2003, https://www.rogerebert.com/reviews/great-movie-santa-sangre-1989

Jodorowsky was dead-set on the movie being 10-14 hours long. This hurt attempts to raise more funding, and the project collapsed in 1976. Jodorowsky was a wildly creative artist, but he was not exactly a pragmatic man. He switched to making graphic novels, a medium in which his imagination could run wild within a budget.

All the creativity of the pre-production for Jodorowsky's "Dune" didn't go to waste. It was captured in a massive book of 3,000-plus storyboards created by Jodorowsky and French artist Jean "Moebius" Giraud. Allegedly, George Lucas pulled ideas from this book to make "Star Wars." Creature designs by H.R. Giger later became the xenomorph in "Alien." Several other successful science-fiction franchises were also inspired by this movie project that never produced a single frame of film.

The rights to adapt "Dune" eventually passed to another shock-prone weirdo director making his own foray into blockbuster territory: David Lynch. His 1984 "Dune" is acknowledged as the nadir of his career, by him and critics. Lynch returned to bizarre dramas that he could maintain full creative control of.

After the success of "Blue Velvet," Lynch cranked up the sex and violence a titch in "**Wild at Heart**" (1990). It's more schlocky in an ironic way than "Blue Velvet," lacking the moments of sincerity and humanity of that all-time classic. Lynch later said "Wild at Heart" was all about how the world is so crazy and violent nowadays.[653] That sounds to me like the trite, oversimplified pessimism of a Grumpy Old Man who watches too much cable news. Straight white male baby boomers are particularly prone to this sort of nostalgia-based gloom and doom, as their baseline is the delusion that the 1950s was as idyllic for everyone as it was for them.

To be fair, violent crime was at an all-time high in the early 1990s. As I mentioned before, rates would tail off in the mid-1990s for

---

[653] Zach Schonfeld, "A Love Story in Hell': David Lynch on Wild at Heart," *Vulture*, Jan. 31, 2025. https://www.vulture.com/article/a-love-story-in-hell-david-lynch-on-wild-at-heart.html

reasons that had nothing to do with movies. I admit that I'm easily triggered after hearing the old "everything is crazy nowadays!" gripe repeated ad nauseam by people who are living well in relatively easy and stable times.

"Wild at Heart" also pushes my personal buttons by being centered on two thoroughly clichéd 1950s archetypes: The characters played by Nicolas Cage and Laura Dern were based on Elvis Presley and Marilyn Monroe. That is, the characters were based on the stage-managed public personas of Presley and Monroe. The real lives of those icons were much more complicated.

"Wild at Heart" could be my least favorite David Lynch movie, though I'd say it's still worth seeing for a few brilliant scenes. The judges at the Cannes Film Festival loved it so much they gave it the Palme D'Or. This was a controversial choice even among cinephiles. When the award was announced at Cannes, the cheers were almost drowned out by a chorus of boos led by Roger Ebert.[654] Ebert had dragged "Blue Velvet" over the coals in an infamous review. His review of "Wild at Heart" wasn't as savage, but he still wrote, "There is something repulsive and manipulative about it, and even its best scenes have the flavor of a kid in the school yard, trying to show you pictures you don't feel like looking at."[655]

At several points in "Wild at Heart" I was actually reminded of the Roger Ebert/Russ Meyer collaboration "Beyond the Valley of the Dolls." Both are ironic melodramas with brutal violence. Perhaps the more graphic violence of "Wild at Heart" pushed Ebert out of his comfort zone.

The first cut of "Wild at Heart" went too far for everyone, apparently. Test audiences were so disturbed by a graphic torture scene that Lynch worried "there wouldn't have been anybody in the theater"

---

[654] "David Lynch's New Peak," *Newsweek*, Jun 03, 1990. https://www.newsweek.com/david-lynchs-new-peak-206160
[655] Roger Ebert, "Wild at Heart," August 17, 1990, RogerEbert.com, https://www.rogerebert.com/reviews/wild-at-heart-1990

after it.[656] He cut that scene down, but the MPAA still wanted to give "Wild at Heart" an X rating. (This was just before NC-17 went into effect.) Lynch was contractually obligated to deliver an R-rated movie. He minimized the gore in one scene and "Wild at Heart" got an R.[657]

David Lynch later said "If you look at the films that came out after 'Wild at Heart,' something about it — it sort of opened a door to a certain kind of cinema. And it had to do with the craziness in the world. And a certain attitude in the craziness."[658] There might be something to that, at least in terms of cinematic trends. The shock-film synthesis of the 1980s was loosening up a bit, allowing more extreme material to get in front of more eyeballs.

Shocks Return to the Mainstream

In the 1980s, Academy Award nominees had to be high-toned and inoffensive. To get a Best Picture Oscar you must make an epic drama about historical events ("Chariots of Fire," "Gandhi," "Amadeus," "The Last Emperor") or a smaller-scale interpersonal drama ("Ordinary People, "Terms of Endearment," "Out of Africa," "Rain Man," "Driving Miss Daisy"). Maybe a war movie ("Platoon") can sneak in if it reminds baby boomers of late-New-Hollywood-era classics "The Deer Hunter" and "Apocalypse Now."

Oscar-bait films always debut at the end of the calendar year so they're fresh in the minds of voters. The summer months are devoted to big family-friendly spectacles. The beginning of each year is a dumping ground for movies that are neither Oscar-worthy dramas nor potential blockbusters.

The horror film "**The Silence of the Lambs**" hit theaters in January and February of 1991 and broke all the molds. Only two movies earned more money in the U.S. and Canada all year: "Terminator II:

---

[656] Quoted in Schonfeld
[657] Roger Ebert, "Wild at Heart"
[658] Quoted in Schonfeld"

Judgment Day" and "Robin Hood: Prince of Thieves."[659] "JFK," released in December 1991, is an epic drama about historical events that fits the profile of a Best Picture winner. Instead, "The Silence of the Lambs" won not only Best Picture, but also Best Director, Best Actor, Best Actress, and Best Adapted Screenplay. Only two other movies in history managed such a sweep: "It Happened One Night" and "One Flew Over the Cuckoo's Nest."

I'm sure the studio suits who planned the release dates for 1991 just thought "It's horror, so the dead of winter is fine." After "The Silence of the Lambs" became a mainstream phenomenon, people insisted on calling it a "thriller." That's a snobby cop-out. "The Silence of the Lambs" might be so good it crosses over to people who don't normally like horror, but it's still hard-core horror to a tee. It's about not one, but two serial killers. One of them makes a suit of women's skin while the other poses a freshly killed corpse like a crucifix with its intestines hanging out. This is the kind of thing that nearly got "Hellraiser" an X rating.

"The Silence of the Lambs" is classier, deeper, and more grounded in reality than "Hellraiser," of course. A better analogue for "The Silence of the Lambs" as a whole is probably "The Exorcist," which was also a major commercial success and Best Picture nominee. It had been so long since "Rosemary's Baby," "The Exorcist," and "Don't Look Now" that people forgot horror movies can be critically beloved and dramatically engaging artistic achievements.

Extreme violence wasn't confined to horror in the late 1980s and early 1990s. Dutch-born director Paul Verhoeven had already made several American movies with violence so graphic that they tested the borderline between R and X ratings. "Robocop" (1987) and "Total Recall" (1990) are much gorier than typical sci-fi fare. If you wanted to add either to your shock film list I wouldn't object.

---

[659] "North America (US and Canada) Domestic Movie Chart for 1991," TheNumbers.com, North America (US and Canada) Domestic Movie Chart for 1991

America being America, Verhoeven didn't cause a big domestic controversy until he threw sex into the mix. "**Basic Instinct**" (1992) is about a bisexual woman, played by Sharon Stone, who apparently gets off on killing men while having sex with them. It's in the "erotic thriller" tradition established by "9 ½ Weeks," except that I imagine many shy guys watching "Basic Instinct" alone on videotape had to be quick on the draw with the pause button before sex scenes got too nasty.

"Basic Instinct" indulges in many homophobic stereotypes. Many were upset that the all-too-rare LGBTQ+ character in a 1990s film was a murderous psychopath. The co-president of the Los Angeles chapter of the Gay & Lesbian Alliance Against Defamation (GLAAD), Jehan Agrama, said, "The linking of evil with lesbians is no coincidence. In Hollywood, lesbian and gay has been shorthand for menacing, deviant and dangerous."[660] Protests by LGBTQ+ groups during filming in San Francisco got so disruptive that "Basic Instinct" producer Alan Marshall tried to make citizen's arrests of several protestors.[661] Later several people rushed the stage during Sharon Stone's monologue when she hosted "Saturday Night Live."

"Basic Instinct" also taps into the old straight-guy fetish that lesbians and female bisexuals are especially sexually promiscuous. This arises from the misconception that they are men in female bodies. Indeed, the movie contains several slurs along those lines.

There's also plenty of misogyny in "Basic Instinct." A rape scene led the president of the Los Angeles chapter of the National Organization of Women, Tammy Bruce, to publicly state that the film

---

[660] "Protests set for 'Basic Instinct' opening", UPI, March 20, 1992 https://www.upi.com/Archives/1992/03/20/Protests-set-for-Basic-Instinct-opening/8548701067600/
[661] Ibid

promoted the idea "that women like violence, women like to be used, women like to be raped."[662]

Several pornographic shots of Sharon Stone were included in "Basic Instinct" without her knowledge or consent. During the filming of the famous scene in the police interrogation room, she was assured that shadows would obscure her genitalia. At a test screening she discovered that her vulva was visible. She slapped Verhoeven and walked out.[663] I'm not aware of another R-rated movie in which a woman's vulva is exposed.

This scene became one of the most famous in film history, and not just because of the explicit nudity. Sharon Stone's charisma overpowers the array of domineering men trying to stare her down. I found her performance to be a major bright spot amidst the exploitative muck of "Basic Instinct." Her character is honest about and unashamed of her sexual appetite and conquests, which Stone plays with a sly, unflappable defiance. She isn't the "sexy baby" type who feigns ignorance of her effect on men; she knows it and makes sure you know she knows. She is like a Mae West with fewer one-liners and more graphic language. In 1992, this was a bold move. At the time, almost all of American culture was busy shaming Madonna for daring to reveal that women can be as openly proud of their sexual adventures as men can.

"Basic Instinct" was another movie that underwent some judicious trimming to secure an R rating, but what was left probably should have still gotten an X or NC-17. "**Bad Lieutenant**" (1992) just went with the NC-17. This decision got plenty of media attention but few screenings and not much box office. "Bad Lieutenant" was edited

---

[662] Quoted in Scott Harris and Miles Corwin. "Opposition to Film 'Basic Instinct' Rises : Entertainment: A coalition of women's and gay rights activists fears the movie's depiction of bisexuals and lesbians will result in increased violence against women". Los Angeles Times, March 21, 1992
[663] "A Conversation with Sharon Stone" DVD extra, Basic Instinct: Ultimate Edition DVD

down to an R-rated version for Blockbuster Video, and this is the version you will see on most streaming sites.

"Bad Lieutenant" does not show sexual penetration or erect penises, so it is a very rare movie that got an NC-17 for unsimulated drug use, violence, nudity, simulated sex acts, blasphemy, and all the other factors that require judgement calls. The most shocking aspect for me was more conceptual, specifically the philosophies of co-writer and actor Zoë Lund. I read up on her and discovered she was very open about and even proud of her addiction to heroin. In interviews and her own writing she comes across as an intelligent and reasonable person. I had the very discomfiting feeling of almost being swayed by her views on heroin legalization. Lund died of an overdose at age 37.

A High Rating That Worked

"Bad Lieutenant" was not successful enough commercially or critically to spark a wave of movies released with an NC-17 rating. Getting the highest rating in the American system simply shrunk a movie's potential audience too severely.

Hong Kong's Category III rating worked much better. This is the rating that was created in 1988 and first given to "Men Behind the Sun." It covered content that spanned hard-R and NC-17 territory in the States. Despite Category III meaning a movie was strictly forbidden for children, just like NC-17, getting the rating was not an automatic box-office kiss of death. By at least one account, more than half of Hong Kong movies in the early 1990s were rated Category III.[664]

Sex comedies had long been a staple of Hong Kong cinema, but Category III allowed them to flourish and become more extreme. In the book "Once Upon a Time in China: A Guide to Hong Kong, Taiwanese, and Mainland Chinese Cinema," Jeff Yang writes that

---

[664] Jeff Yang, "Once Upon a Time in China: A Guide to Hong Kong, Taiwanese, and Mainland Chinese Cinema," p. 104

even though this genre essentially became soft-core pornography in the 1990s, it didn't occupy the same sort of strictly separated, underground cinematic universe that Western pornography did:

> "Unlike so-called adult films in the West, Cat III films are essentially mainstream; although they are still seen as a cinematic ghetto, they lack the stigma that damns its performers as 'porn stars,' as opposed to real stars. Category III films screen in many of the same theaters as standard action films, dramas, and comedies, and sometimes rake in higher box office takes. And otherwise reputable actors — at least some of them — occasionally descend into the world of Cat III and re-emerge, largely unscathed." (p. 102)

"**Sex and Zen**" (1991) epitomizes the 1990s Category III movie. Being loosely based on centuries-old literature gives it a veneer of respectability, as with Pasolini's Life Trilogy. Unlike Pasolini's films, though, "Sex and Zen" is loaded with flawless bodies in gratuitous sex scenes that are long enough to qualify as pornographic. It's like if a producer of Cinemax-style softcore got a big budget and made an "American Pie"-esque sex/shock comedy. The only apparent restriction that "Sex and Zen" works under is never showing a penis – well, not if it's attached to a human body, anyway. Severed penises do make appearances.

It was also possible for a Hong Kong movie to get a Category III rating for violence alone. If any movie could do so, "**Riki-Oh: The Story of Ricky**" (1991) would be the one. It very faithfully translates the ultraviolence of the Japanese manga "Riki-Oh" to the screen. Perhaps the most cartoonishly over-the-top gore in cinema history alternates with scenes that were apparently intended as sincere heart-tuggers. Watching "Riki-Oh: The Story of Ricky" is a mind-blowing experience in which at any moment you could witness a character's mind being blown to pieces by a single punch.

Peter Jackson's Last, Best Shock Film

Another candidate for the goriest movie of all time is "**Braindead**" (1992), which was called "**Dead Alive**" in North America to distinguish it from "Brain Dead" (1990). "Braindead"/"Dead Alive" is Peter Jackson's version of a zombie film, complete with undead copulation, a lawn mower used for slaughter, and a gonzo climax that left me delirious.

Censors were split on "Braindead"/"Dead Alive." Many countries banned it or cut out the most grisly parts. Germany banned all versions, cut or uncut. Surprisingly, the British Board of Film Classification was positively delighted by the movie. The Board's notes call it "one of the funniest splatter movies ever made" that "is played for belly laughs rather than screams." The Board came close to giving "Braindead"/"Dead Alive" a 15 certificate, which is close to a PG-13, but in the end realized it had to get an 18.[665]

It's an interesting perspective. I suppose the difference between "Braindead"/"Dead Alive" and the cartoon gore of, say, the Black Knight sequence in "Monty Python and the Holy Grail" is one of degree, not kind. It's as if the Brits know a thing or two about humor that other countries' censors might miss.

"Braindead"/"Dead Alive" didn't find an audience in theaters but later became a cult hit on VHS. Peter Jackson left shock horror/comedy behind and has not looked back.

More Adventures at the Borderline Between R and NC-17

In the States, conservatives kept grumbling about shock media of all kinds into the mid-1990s. Most of the ire was directed at music, in a large-scale movement that began in 1985 when Tipper Gore

---

[665] "Education/Case Studies: Braindead," BBFC.co.uk, https://www.bbfc.co.uk/education/case-studies/braindead

founded the Parents Music Resource Center (PMRC). She was triggered by a Prince song, but much of the fuss was over heavy metal and alleged satanist messaging. In the 1990s the main focus turned to rap and metal acts like 2 Live Crew and Ice-T's group Body Count. Some movies were pulled into the fight just for old times' sake.

In 1995, presidential candidate Bob Dole gave a speech lambasting contemporary music, television, and movies. He criticized film producers and distributors for releasing "nightmares of depravity."[666] One of Dole's targets was "**Natural Born Killers**," which had come out the year before to some controversy.

"Natural Born Killers" is Oliver Stone's subtle-as-a-sledgehammer message film about the media's culpability in turning real-life violent criminals into celebrities. I feel like its thesis is a bit surface-level, which I wouldn't mind if it weren't delivered with that self-important "I'm making a huge important statement here, you dumb sheeple!" attitude that Oliver Stone is known for.

"Natural Born Killers" is still fascinating for its assaultive visuals, which use many quick cuts and deliberately clashing film styles. This approach makes the movie's violence feel more shocking to me.

I was most disturbed by a scene in which Rodney Dangerfield plays a father who sexually abuses his daughter Mallory, played by Juliette Lewis. It's presented as a sitcom called "I Love Mallory," complete with a laugh track that erupts as Dangerfield does horrific things. Again, it's not exactly subtle messaging ("Wait, sitcoms don't reflect harsh realities of American family life? Say it ain't so, Oliver!"), but I found it effective in delivering a punch to the gut.

At this point in film history, a totally realistic New-Hollywood-style version of the same scene wouldn't hit as hard. The scene gains

---

[666] Quoted in Richard Lacayo, "Bob Dole's Violent Reaction," *Time*, June 12, 1995

more power by violating the tropes of a sitcom, a genre our brains are trained to think of as safe. This demonstrates that even after everything that can shock people has already been done, you can still evoke that feeling of deeply disturbed surprise by delivering it in a creative way.

Bob Dole didn't go into detail about why "Natural Born Killers" was on his shit list. He also didn't provide a real solution for the alleged wave of society-destroying media. He specifically stated he wasn't calling for censorship, saying that instead producers and distributors should practice better self-restraint.[667] In a fervently capitalist country like the United States (of which Dole was leading its most fervently capitalist sector, the Republican Party), asking corporations to voluntarily stop profitable projects because some people disapprove of them is beyond unrealistic. It's such a non-solution that you have to assume Dole was just pandering to worried parents.

In a *Time* magazine article about Dole's speech, Richard Lacayo attempts to analyze the worried parents of the 1990s, who were of course the same baby boomers who had reveled in shock media during the 1970s:

> "The complications set in during the '90s, when the boomers who were once pop culture's most dedicated consumers became the decision makers at media companies – but also the parents of the next generation. Pulled one way by their lifelong instinct for whatever is sensational, unsanitized or unofficial, they find themselves dragged in the other direction by their emerging second thoughts as citizens and parents."

I'd argue that Lacayo is a decade late in his analysis, as baby boomers had the same inner conflict in the 1980s. The difference was that they found it easier in the 1980s to shield their children from shock content because the kids were too young to make many of their own decisions. In the 1990s, Generation X was old enough

---

[667] Ibid

to own the freedom and purchasing power to turn shocking movies and music into mainstream hits.

Naughty albums got Parental Advisory labels and alternate clean versions, but nothing much happened to crack down on movies in the 1990s. The NC-17 rating was already keeping a lid on the most extreme material, "Natural Born Killers" notwithstanding. In the mid-1990s it wasn't easy to push the envelope any further.

I suppose you could try to make an NC-17 movie mainstream, like Paul Verhoeven did with "**Showgirls**" (1995). Its shock level is comparable to that of "Natural Born Killers," with less violence but more nudity and simulated sex. In the United States, that will get you a higher rating every time. Still, a few judicious cuts, especially to a very disturbing rape scene, could have ensured an R. A version later produced for Blockbuster Video lost only 3 minutes.

Paul Verhoeven had no intention of compromising for the theater release, though. He was still smarting from having to do that with "Basic Instinct." He used the power he had built up through a string of big money makers to shoot for the first NC-17 blockbuster.

"Showgirls"'s rating severely restricted its advertising but it got a ton of free publicity. The biggest news story was that its Vegas stripper protagonist was played by Elizabeth Berkley, who was famous for starring in the squeaky-clean kids' sitcom "Saved by the Bell." The buzz, and likely some behind-the-scenes strong-arming, convinced many theaters to screen "Showgirls," making it the first NC-17 movie to get a wide American release. This was a breakthrough that no movie rated higher than R had been able to achieve in more than 20 years.

"Showgirls" remains the last wide-release NC-17 movie at this writing because it did not make back its budget in theaters. It's possible that this was one time in which any publicity was not good publicity. "Showgirls" and Berkley became widespread laughingstocks in a mid-1990s America that spent much of its time tee-heeing about sex. Anyone who expressed interest in going to see "Showgirls" was opening themselves up to ridicule, especially if they were a heterosexual male. (For the record, I was too much of a snooty cinephile to be interested.) The status quo held.

If a goal of "Showgirls" was to legitimize the NC-17 rating, it was probably the wrong movie for the job. A more serious, less ostentatiously sleazy test case could have rallied the liberal-minded urban cineastes to the cause. I'm imagining something like a prestige Oscar-bait historical drama that has some valid reason for showing an erect penis, like if Harvey Keitel had been fully aroused in "The Piano." With "Showgirls," it was very easy for people to look at its rating, its premise, its bad-taste Las Vegas setting, and its "sullying" of a child TV star and conclude it was just big-budget porn. Predictably, it did tremendous business on videotape, proving once again that strong sexual content sells best for home viewing.

"Showgirls" is more campy than "Basic Instinct," which made tons of money, but I don't think it's much worse. At least it has less homophobia. What "Showgirls" lacks is an actress with the powerful charisma of Sharon Stone; Berkley tries her hardest but just can't meet that high standard, in my opinion.

Let's Try That Famous 1990s Indie Scene

The big-budget film world was pretty implacable by the mid-1990s, but you could still find ways to shock people within the decade's independent film boom. I was one of the young Gen-X cinephiles using their freedom and purchasing power to wrest popular culture away from baby boomers at long last. We wanted media that didn't feel like slick corporate product that our parents had cranked out to sell merchandise tie-ins. We put on our thrift-store flannel shirts, stuck tapes of garage bands into our car stereos, and drove to shabby independent theaters to see odd little passion projects.

Our parents weren't dumb, so they quickly figured out how to sell us designer flannels, major-label grunge rock, and "indie" films backed by huge studios. Oh well. At least they were pandering to our tastes rather than indulging their own for once.

The Quentin Tarantino films "Reservoir Dogs" (1992) and especially "Pulp Fiction" (1994) epitomized the indie film boom. Both have their shocks, but I think we can dig deeper. What could make baby boomers really upset in the 1990s?

Religion and LGBTQ+ issues were still hot-button items that the mainstream didn't want to interrogate with much depth. "**Priest**" (1994) tackles both in a sober, humanist story of a conservative Catholic priest who has a secret male lover.

I rarely cry at movies, though I always want to. If a movie squeezes at least a couple of tears out of me, I rate it at least 4.5 out of 5 on Letterboxd. Any film that triggers genuine weeping gets an automatic 5 stars. I was bawling at the end of "Priest," so it joined the rarified air of "Do the Right Thing" and precious few others in my 5-star club.

Whether "Priest" or any of my other favorites are genuinely among the greatest of all time is a separate issue. As I said in the first chapter, I think it's a fool's errand for one person to try to judge movies by some pseudo-objective standard of greatness. All we can do as individuals is declare our favorites. Then someone else can compile thousands of people's lists of favorites to rank the all-time best, as the They Shoot Pictures, Don't They? website does.

"Priest" is not going to show up on any rankings of the all-time greatest movies, I realize. It pushes my personal buttons by realistically portraying a victim of societal bigotry who gains at least some grace and acceptance. It's similar to "Victim," the 1961 Dirk Bogarde "message film" that dramatized the evils of the criminalization of homosexuality. "Priest" ups the ante by also criticizing the Catholic Church's vows of celibacy and historical persecution of LGBTQ+ people. The movie is not a simplistic hit job, though, as it also shows how, in the right hands, the church can propagate its more fundamental principles of compassion and forgiveness.

With any "message film," if you don't like the message, you're going to grasp for other reasons why the movie is terrible. Roger Ebert gave "Priest" one star largely because it misrepresents the rules of confessionals to add extra elements of drama and critique.[668] He's probably right about that one plot point, but I can't see how that is enough to invalidate the many things that "Priest" does well. It strikes me that the movie's criticisms of Catholic dogma sent Ebert off the deep end, just like with "The Devils."

Ebert was far from alone. The Catholic League for Religious and Civil Rights and a pro-life organization called the American Life League threatened a boycott of all products by Disney, which was then the parent company of "Priest" distributor Miramax. The organizations released a statement calling the movie "smut," "blasphemous" and "sacrilegious."[669]

The "smut" label is homophobic nonsense – "Priest" has just one brief non-explicit gay sex scene and one makeout session that gets interrupted before it can go too far. The same scenes with a heterosexual couple would make for an average R-rated movie. "Blasphemous" and "sacrilegious" are words meaning "this cannot be criticized," which is not only an invalid concept in a free society but also a harmful one. No criticism means no oversight, and no oversight creates free space for abuses to proliferate unchecked.

This is best exemplified by the now well-established facts about child sexual abuse by Catholic priests. The facts are now well-established only because enough brave victims went public with their stories. In the face of intense resistance, these people kept

---

[668] Roger Ebert, "Priest," April 7, 1995, rogerebert.com, https://www.rogerebert.com/reviews/priest-1995
[669] Greg Evans, "'Priest' foes pass over Miramax, boycott Disney," *Variety*, April 3, 1995, https://variety.com/1995/film/features/priest-foes-pass-over-miramax-boycott-disney-99127850/

being blasphemous and sacrilegious in criticizing the Catholic Church. Because they did, genuine progress has been made.

If such horrors can happen in an institution like the Catholic Church that was founded on precepts of humility, love, and peace, they can happen anywhere. Nothing, no matter how important it may be to millions of people, should ever be shielded from criticism.

In the mid-1990s, another area you could still plumb for shocks outside the mainstream is teen sex. Well, actually, that had been done ad nauseam by "Porky's" and the vast trough of R-rated teen sex comedies that followed. Those were cartoonish depictions of teen boys peeping on, assaulting, and otherwise violating teen girls without suffering any real consequences. You also never see how the girls are affected by any of this treatment. They are portrayed as mere bodies to be conquered and then discarded.

"**Kids**" (1995) got an NC-17 rating (but was released unrated) for delivering an honest, realistic picture of teenage sexual behavior. Telly is a 16-year-old boy whose goal is to have sex with as many virgins as he can, a character type that wouldn't be out of place in a "Porky's" movie. The difference is that Telly targets 12- and 13-year-old girls and does not know that he is HIV-positive. Also, "Kids" does not have gratuitous nudity or play sexual assault for laughs.

The girls of "Kids" are not objectified and have genuine personalities and inner lives. The heart of the movie is the character Jennie, played by Chloë Sevigny. She discovers she became HIV-positive from one sexual encounter with Telly and spends the movie trying to find him and tell him before he spreads the virus further.

"Kids" is a very grim cautionary tale about out-of-control teens destroying their lives. It actually promotes a downright conservative message that the film shares with "Mom and Dad" and the other old sex hygiene exploitation films. "Kids" is not nearly as didactic and cheesy as those old movies, which gives it a stronger impact. It also gains a lot of power by being filmed like a documentary, even though it is almost entirely scripted.

"Kids" is one of the rare movies, like "Henry: Portrait of a Serial Killer," that the MPAA declared could not be cut down to an R. The focus on teen sex was just too much. There is no small irony that "Porky's," et al., had no trouble getting R ratings using the same focus to promote more noxious and harmful messaging, not to mention much more titillation.

"**Crash**" (1996) is another movie that had no chance of getting anything but an NC-17. It's about people who are sexually aroused by violent car crashes, and there's not a heck of a lot going on besides that. It's not some sort of fetish porn film, though. If it were I doubt it would sell, since it's about a fetish that probably almost no one actually has. (I say this at the risk of kink-shaming because I don't actually want to Google it.)

David Cronenberg directed "Crash" with his signature cold, cerebral style. That, combined with the heavy focus on an eroticism that nobody finds erotic, made me feel like I was a detached alien observer while watching it, trying to analyze the bizarre human phenomenon of sexual arousal.

In that spirit, let's try to break down what "Crash" might say about those two main pillars of shock film, sex and violence. The film combines them in a unique way. Most films feature both of course, but they usually separate the sex and violence into different scenes. If they combine them, it's in the form of sexual violence, which brings with it a whole host of other issues. There is no sexual violence in "Crash": The women and the men are all willing and enthusiastic participants.

The premise of car-crash fetishists is not totally dadaistic because both sex and violence entail the fundamental feeling of excitation. By "excitation" I mean just the set of physiological responses – racing mind, increased heart rate, clenching stomach – that puts the human body on alert, ready to take quick and decisive action. It's called "arousal" in the below circumplex model of emotion [670] that I also included in the first chapter. But that word connotes sexual arousal, which is only part of the story. So let's stick with "excitation."

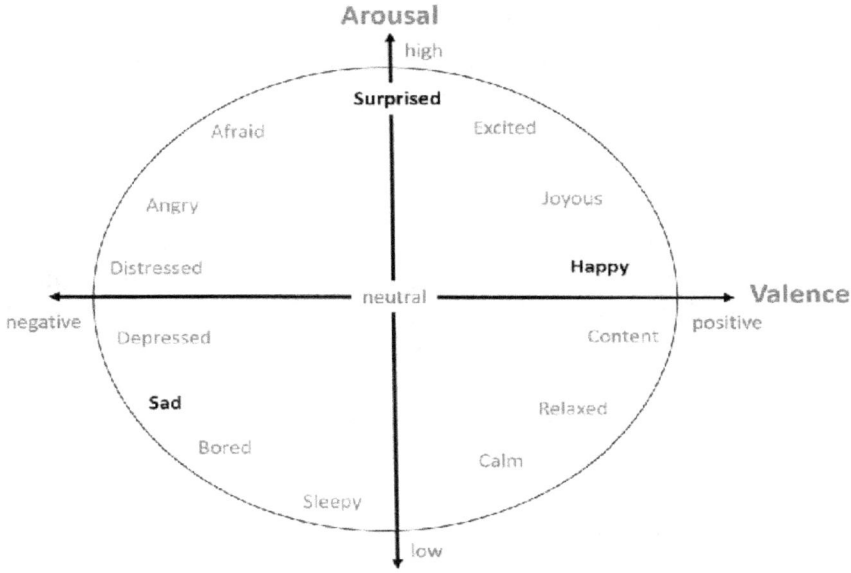

Excitation is a relatively involuntary reaction; you can't really tell yourself to not have your heart race and stomach clench after seeing something alarming. Almost everyone is going to feel comparable levels of excitation when they're shown something violent or sexual. Excitation is a lizard-brain reaction.

Valence, meanwhile, is more variable and subjective. That's the spectrum I traveled on as I grew into adulthood. The extreme excitation of watching shock films didn't change, but the valence moved from negative to positive. Valence involves the systems of

---

[670] Reproduced from "Independence and bipolarity in the structure of current affect," by L. Feldman Barrett and J.A. Russell, 1998, *Journal of Personality and Social Psychology*, 74(4), p. 970. Copyright 1998 by the American Psychological Association.

empathy and morality, plus other mechanisms like the ability to separate fantasy from reality.

That only describes what happened to me in the realm of movie watching as I became a teenager. Real-life sex, in some forms at least, moved from the negative to the positive end of the spectrum, as it should. But any real-life violence remains as firmly on the negative side now as it was when I was a kid. (Even football is too violent for me – I feel it in my bones when someone sustains a hard hit.)

Part of what makes real-life violence upsetting is the victimization: A stronger or just more lucky person injures a weaker or more unlucky person. In real life, this is almost never a rightful action, so my systems of empathy and morality place the reaction on the negative side of the valence spectrum. This varies by person; if you're more of a "might makes right" type than I am, you will feel differently about witnessing real violence.

But what if the violence was the result of an accident, with no guilty perpetrator? Then, in theory at least, you could experience the excitation of witnessing violence without your morality labeling it as negative.

Empathy is a trickier issue, as it's very hard to not empathize with the pain someone feels after being injured (unless you're a psychopath). But what if you've already fetishized pain in a pseudo-BDSM sort of way? Then could you heighten sexual arousal with that voyeuristic fetishized pain, free of any aggression or subjugation?

That's the theory, anyway. It makes enough sense in theory to make "Crash" a comprehensible film. But even that's only because we are watching a film, and our systems of morality and empathy are giving our lizard brains a lot more leeway. Any real-life encounter with car-crash fetishists would be nothing but horrifying, I feel. They could only be pure psychopaths who lack any morality or empathy at all.

The problem with my theory, I think, is that the violence of auto accidents isn't really similar to the kind of pain that people seek in BDSM practices, in which you consent to very specific actions that are not life-threatening. Anything can happen in a car accident, up to and including death.

Anyway, let's move from a very specific focus on shock material to a more scattershot one. "**Gummo**" (1997) is "Kids" screenwriter Harmony Korine's showcase of atrocities, including teenagers harvesting dead cats, sexual exploitation of a developmentally disabled person, and more. It all hearkens back to 1970s antithesis-stage peak shock films like "Sweet Movie" and "Salò or the 100 Days of Sodom" in being more a compilation of button-pushing scenes than anything concerned with plot or character. In style, it is most like "Salò," using mostly non-professional, unpretty actors and a grubby, realistic look to make it feel like a documentary.

Harmony Korine would pretend to be a dopey drugged-up slacker in appearances on "Late Night with David Letterman," but he was actually the sort of brilliant cinephilic prodigy you have to be to direct your first feature at age 24. When Korine was a teen, he would watch 3 or 4 movies every day.[671] Eventually he became desensitized to most films.[672] Then he saw the Werner Herzog film "Even Dwarves Started Small" (1970) and was inspired to become a filmmaker.[673] I considered "Even Dwarves Started Small" for this book but ruled it out because it exploits ableism for most of its shocks; its cast is made entirely of little people. It still has some genuinely disturbing sights, like one of a crucified monkey that Korine cites as being the most impactful for him.[674]

---

[671] "Gummo's Whammo", November 1999, Harmony-Korine.com. https://web.archive.org/web/20210107120925/http://www.harmony-korine.com/paper/int/hk/whammo.html
[672] "A Conversation with Harmony Korine, Director of 'Gummo'", Indiewire, October 6, 1997. https://www.indiewire.com/features/general/a-conversation-with-harmony-korine-director-of-gummo-83415/
[673] "Gummo's Whammo", Harmony-Korine.com.
[674] Ibid

I get the impression that Korine wanted to continue in the tradition of the Viennese Actionists and revel in shock for shock's sake. Less charitably, you could say he was like the exploitation filmmakers of the 1960s and 1970s who were chasing the dragon of heightening shocks. Maybe the two aren't that different.

The film reviewers of 1997 did not want to revisit peak antithesis-stage shock material. Several condescendingly addressed Korine directly like they were scolding a naughty little boy. In the *Austin Chronicle*, Russell Smith wrote "Yo, Harmony, the battle to legitimize shocking themes, surrealistic whimsy, and unapologetically scabrous content in film has already been fought and won by generations of your artistic betters: Luis Buñuel, Werner Herzog, Todd Haynes, even David Lynch. To honestly build upon that legacy calls for you, the director, to bring some fresh intellectual or conceptual goods to the table."[675]

Smith presumed that a filmmaker's only permissible option is to build on the legacy of films made before. Apparently, no one is allowed to try out an older approach and see what happens. Or at least, you can't attempt an out-and-out shock film now that the synthesis stage is firmly established and we've incorporated formerly forbidden material into films with plots and characters grounded in humanity.

Personally, I don't see why you can't at least attempt to heighten film shocks further, as long as you're not hurting anyone. Granted, you won't find much of an audience for that perspective many years into the synthesis stage. I think "Gummo" succeeds in its goal of capturing the feeling of a 1970s peak antithesis-stage film, but I wouldn't recommend it to anyone who isn't a fiend for the stuff.

The documentary "**Sick: The Life and Death of Bob Flanagan, Supermasochist**" (1997) is more than just an exercise in shocks, but the shocks do overwhelm the rest of the story, for me at least.

---

[675] Russell Smith, "Gummo," *Austin Chronicle*, Nov. 28, 1997, https://www.austinchronicle.com/screens/gummo-11916245/

Bob Flanagan was a performance artist who mutilated his own body at museum shows and in short videos.

His work gains more depth when you learn that he had cystic fibrosis, a brutal genetic disease that caused him extreme pain his entire life. Both of his sisters died of cystic fibrosis, one at birth and one at age 21. The documentary paints Flanagan's extreme masochism as a coping mechanism that enabled him to relish pain instead of being oppressed by it. Thus he was able to live a relatively full life until his death at age 43, which was about as long as someone with cystic fibrosis could hope to live at the time.

I gained some admiration for Flanagan while watching "Sick: The Life and Death of Bob Flanagan, Supermasochist," but man, those self-mutilations were tough to get through. The movie includes Flanagan's most disturbing video clip, which one-ups the biggest shocker of "Maîtresse." There's no point in me spoiling anything further; you know by now if you want to see the movie.

The Internet Disrupts

Since the 1920s, movies had occupied the center of mass entertainment in the United States and most of the rest of the developed world. Radio and television staked out their own territories, but cinema remained at the top tier. Making or starring in a successful radio or TV show would certainly be a big deal, but being involved in an all-time great film was the clearest path to immortality.

In the 1990s, the internet began laying the groundwork to disrupt film's primacy. First it had to reach enough people. The percentage of Americans with internet access grew from less than 1% in 1990 to 43% in 2000. When the iPhone was introduced in 2007 the rate would peak at 75%, where it would stay relatively stable until climbing further starting in 2016.[676]

The internet's first major disruption to movies, predictably, was in pornography. As soon as the World Wide Web got powerful enough to share video clips, short pornographic ones proliferated. Suddenly you didn't have to undergo the embarrassment of renting a porno tape, much less slink into whatever X-rated theaters might still exist. Porn fans flocked to the internet, and the convenience and privacy afforded by the new medium brought in many new users. Some of the latter were the bashful adults who had been getting their kicks from erotic thrillers, but many were kids.

Whatever distress remained from Bob Dole and co.'s feeble protests about film content was redirected to the internet, and then some. Forget about whatever outré movie a few people might come across in a big-city downtown theater; here was a way for every kid in the country to access hard-core pornography. Even child pornography was easily accessible until activists forced changes in the laws – see the documentary "Call Me Lucky" (2015) for an inspiring account of this campaign.

For the purposes of shock-film history, internet pornography's earliest effect was to obviate much of the need for erotic thrillers, direct-to-video exploitation, and other non-explicit sources of titillation. The internet could cater to all masturbatory tastes, including those who preferred the likes of "Showgirls" to something like "Deep Throat." Even T&A comedies became briefly passé when it became easy to download pictures of Cindy Margolis in your living room.

Losing the entire masturbator audience to the internet left Hollywood without much left to do in the way of shock film. Everything had been thoroughly explored after the breakdown of Reagan-era conservatism opened up pretty much every avenue. Violence

---

[676] "Internet users for the United States," Federal Reserve Bank of Saint Louis, https://fred.stlouisfed.org/series/ITNETUSERP2USA

couldn't get much more extreme after "The Silence of the Lambs" and "Natural Born Killers" became mainstream hits. Any message was fair game: By 1997, New Queer Cinema and films with unfiltered, confrontational Black perspectives were well-established. Maybe you could be sacrilegious, but that has always been an occasional thing that doesn't have box office appeal in and of itself.

In dialectical terms, the synthesis of the 1980s had become the new thesis. Then an antithesis of greater freedom in messages and content forced a slightly different new synthesis in the mid-1990s. This new synthesis was so comprehensive, encompassing everything that just about any audience could want to see in a movie, that it became difficult to imagine where shock film could go next. It would take very creative artists to come up with something in the late 1990s and beyond. We'll meet a few in the next chapter.

Chapter 11: The Shock Auteurs

The mid-1990s marks the last gasp of shock film history's narrative arc. Afterwards there were still shockers, some of which would fit within definable movements. But the battle of freedom vs. repression that defined shock films since the 1890s was over. The dialectic process had swung back and forth and ended on freedom.

This central narrative had already been pretty weak for 15-20 years, I realize. Many sections in the previous two chapters of this book, such as the one on 1990s indie films, are more like laundry lists of movies than anything pushing the story forward. I'm marking the mid-1990s as the point at which the narrative finally sputtered to a complete stop, but I probably could have put it out of its misery earlier. I just wanted to cover what I think is an interesting mini-dialectic in the 1980s and early 1990s.

This final chapter of the book is more like a typical history of an artistic medium. I'll review interesting artists and movements, but there won't be some central conflict driving the plot forward. Individual movies might occasionally spark consternation, but not a concerted campaign against the entire medium of film.

It's like with painting: Vincent Van Gogh broke new ground and was unappreciated in his lifetime, but it's not like he had to fight censors or other less blatant forms of societal repression. Sometimes an innovation in painting caused controversy, like with Henri Matisse and les Fauves. But even that was more of a fight within the artistic community than some sort of national political issue. I don't think anyone came out of the 1905 Salon d'Automne screaming "Won't someone think of the children?", but I admit I'm no expert.

With shock films now being more like any other artistic medium, innovations came primarily from art cinema. Exploitation had nowhere else to go; it had been many years since you could just throw sex and violence on a screen and make it feel like something new. The mainstream wasn't much different. Everything easy had been done, and then maybe done a bit less for a while, and then done again. Now you had to be really creative to shake things up.

The Godfather of the 21st-Century European Shock Auteurs

The sophisticated auteur who brought shock film into a new stage was the Austrian director Michael Haneke. He had made several cold, brutal films before "**Funny Games**" (1997), but that one has had the most staying power of his pre-2000 work. The movie's plot, about a family at a remote cabin who meet some inscrutable psychopaths, is more accessible than those of his other 1990s films.

"Funny Games" may have the premise of a conventional horror movie, but it is more powerful in execution because it refuses to follow genre tropes. A typical shocker will build suspense up to a quick and bloody shot that makes both characters and the audiences scream. Think of a teenager nervously stumbling through a dark, scary basement. This builds tension. Then pow! A monster attacks, and the teenager either gets killed or escapes. The tension thus gets a quick, satisfying release. We then move on to the next sequence.

Michael Haneke doesn't do quick, satisfying releases of tension. He puts you in a state of extreme anxiety and prolongs it as much as possible. First a slow-paced, realistic story will lull you into a false sense of security, perhaps even some boredom. Little hints give you the vague feeling that something terrible will happen, but you have no idea what. Suddenly a spasm of violence will erupt almost out of nowhere. It's seldom gory, instead gaining power from a long shot that Haneke will hold for what feels like hours.

"**The Piano Teacher**" (2001) puts sexual repression and BDSM under Haneke's clinical, unsparing lens. A middle-aged woman tries to bring about the sex life she believes she wants, but every attempt goes horribly wrong. It might sound like the premise of a wacky sex comedy, but "The Piano Teacher" is anything but.

I'm trying to think of a single funny moment in a Michael Haneke movie and coming up empty. Maybe a character tells an amusing story at some point, but there's no humor within the filmmaking. You won't see any cheesy special effects, jokey pop-culture references, or lines that are too clever to be genuine. The last adjective anyone would use for a Haneke film is "campy." His completely serious and earnest approach represented a welcome departure from the smirking irony that overwhelmed every entertainment medium in the 1990s and beyond.

Haneke's style of stripped-down, documentary-like realism makes his shocking moments more impactful. There probably won't even be a musical cue in the sound design to warn you that a shock is coming. Haneke doesn't allow anything that could pull the viewer out of total immersion in a tense and very real-feeling situation.

Shockfathers

The Dogme 95 movement sought the same sort of verisimilitude by establishing ironclad protocols for making movies as realistic as possible. Founding Danish directors Lars von Trier and Thomas Vinterberg forbade any music that wasn't diegetic, i.e. being played within the narrative and heard by the characters. All filming had to be done with handheld cameras in real locations. They couldn't even use props or lighting that didn't already exist in the "set," although I hesitate to even use that word because it implies a location that was created for film production.

The earliest Dogme 95 films violated a few of these stringent rules, but not many. The first one, "Festen," aka "The Celebration," (1998) is one of my all-time favorite movies, and explores a very disturbing area. For shock value, Dogme #2, **Idioterne**, aka **"The Idiots,"** (1998) probably tops it. "Idioterne" has a brief shot of sexual penetration within an orgy scene, but the main shocker is the premise: It's about a group of young people who pretend to be developmentally disabled in public as a way of freeing themselves from bourgeois proprieties.

Even if "Idioterne" doesn't exactly endorse these characters' ableist nonsense, it's quite problematic. The movie was controversial upon release, but only within the cinephile circles that it reached. At its screening at the Cannes Film Festival, Mark Kermode, the critic who re-inserted the "Rape of Christ" sequence into "The Devils," screamed "Il es merde! Il es merde!" (i.e. "This is shit!") until he was thrown out.[677] Cannes-watchers heard about it, but it otherwise wasn't a big news story.

This is a main characteristic of shock movies in this era: They are not going to crack the front page of many newspapers. On the plus side, no filmmaker had to contend with any Bob Doles, much less Joseph Breens. You can shock a limited audience, gain a name for yourself, and then do it again.

The director of "Idioterne," Lars von Trier, would do just that. All his films are shockers in one way or another. "Breaking the Waves" (1996) and "Dancer in the Dark" (2003) use less blatantly provocative premises than that of "Idioterne" to tell much more shattering and meaningful stories, in my opinion and probably most people's. His later films would verge far from Dogme 95 principles to find new ways to disturb audiences. If Michael Haneke is the godfather of 21st-century European art shock film, von Trier is the father.

Then again, Gaspar Noé might also have a claim to the title. In 1998, he made "**I Stand Alone**," a sequel of sorts to his 1991 short "Carne." Both profile a rageful middle-aged butcher whose paroxysms of violence keep knocking him farther and farther into ruin. "I Stand Alone" is like a French "Taxi Driver" with about half the action and ten times the internal monologue. The butcher's thoughts are disturbingly realistic, roiling in fury and justifying his psychotic behavior with half-baked nihilism. (Is there another kind?) But man, the movie has a lot of that. "I Stand Alone" probably would've worked better as a book.

---

[677] Mark Kermode, "Why I hate Cannes". BBC News, May 13, 2002

When it's not just showing the butcher walking and fuming, "I Stand Alone" offers incest, graphic violence, and shots of sexual penetration from a porn film that illustrate one of the butcher's musings but probably aren't totally necessary. It earns its shock-movie bona fides but isn't central to the canon, in my view. Noé's films would get more interesting.

Mothershockers

This European shock-film movement also had a female director leading the charge. You may remember that back in 1976, Catherine Breillat was tasked with making an "Emmanuelle" knock-off about a woman's journey of sexual self-discovery. Breillat took the producer at his word and gave him "A Real Young Girl," which is an honest and uncensored portrayal of a young girl coming of age. This was not what the producer wanted at all; he was expecting a fantasy packed with masturbatory material for straight men. So "A Real Young Girl" didn't see the light of day until Breillat took another stab at the theme with the more sophisticated "**Romance**" (1999).

"Emmanuelle" and its many imitators are male directors' wet dreams about women's journeys of sexual self-discovery. They always include many couplings, with at least one lesbian one, and lots of naked female breasts. "Romance" is at least one example of how a woman might portray a woman's sex life. It's the story of a woman who isn't attracted to other women, so you aren't going to get a lesbian scene or a lot of naked female breasts. This woman does like erect penises, so you will see some of those.

Those shots provoked howls of protest that "Romance" was pornography. As we've seen, seeing penises in any state on screen sends men into a tizzy, even if they're Supreme Court justices who are trying to kill off censorship. Erect penises are especially frightening, and their presence in a movie is an automatic signifier of pornography. But why? Why is one erect penis automatically pornographic while acres of female flesh is not? Is it just because straight men want to see naked women but not erect penises?

Breillat did hire an Italian pornographic actor for one part. She needed a man who could maintain an erection for a long time surrounded by a film crew, which is a rare skill that male porn actors have. Otherwise, his character seemed no different than the rest to me.

"Romance" certainly doesn't look or feel like a porno. It follows the grand French art-film tradition of tastefully dressed, stone-faced people inflating their personal thoughts and feelings into bold philosophical pronouncements. When it isn't over-generalizing, "Romance" offers plenty of interesting insights, complex characters, and realistic dialogue. I did not find it exploitative; all the sex scenes felt relevant to the protagonist's struggles to achieve a satisfying sex life.

A major obstacle for the protagonist of "Romance" is that her boyfriend won't have sex with her. Several times she tries unsuccessfully to induce an erection with her hands and mouth. If you can get past the shock of seeing a woman manipulate a man's penis in a tasteful French art film, it feels only natural to see it in this context. This is at the root of their conflict, after all.

Breillat could have framed the shots so they didn't show penises, which could have secured an R rating and its equivalents in other countries. But this plot point is about whether or not a man can get an erection. If the erection or lack thereof were obscured or just out of frame, it could have felt false. It would be just like the old movie cliché in which a contrived arrangement of sheets obscures a woman's breasts when she is naked in bed. An edited version of "Romance" for American audiences apparently did force these sorts of contrivances, but the film was shown mostly uncut throughout most of the rest of the world.

A man's ability to get an erection is not a topic that movies often cover. If they do, it's usually in a sadly comedic scene after a man's implied failure to do so, in which the woman consoles him by saying "it happens to everybody." Or, conversely, maybe a woman yells at a man for not performing in bed, which signifies that she is an evil harpy. Both versions cater to male insecurities: If you can't get it up, it's not your fault, and if the woman is upset, she's evil. But what about a woman's real feelings about erectile dysfunction? What if she said something besides what men wanted to hear?

In a larger sense, "Romance" poses an important question: Why can't movies show sex as sometimes messy, difficult, and complex? Despite sex being in almost every movie for grown-ups, it is almost invariably portrayed just one way: as a perfectly choreographed act in which participants totally lose themselves in some mix of overwhelming thrill and expression of love. Anyone who's had sex knows that it often doesn't work out that way. Few filmmakers beyond Catherine Breillat ever explore that.

Critic Kenneth Turan was one of many who translated their shock over "Romance" into a complaint that it overcomplicates sex. In response, academic Linda Williams wrote:

> "Breillat's film insists, Kenneth Turan notwithstanding, that hard-core, arousing sex can coexist with philosophy, sexual politics, and contradictory emotions. To Turan it would seem that anything more than arousing sex is pure pretension and an automatic turn-off. But what kind of moving-image art do we condemn ourselves to if sex must be so compartmentalized? I would argue that the even greater pretension may be the very idea that sex is mindless."[678]

In the same article, Linda Williams points out how Breillat revived "In the Realm of the Senses" director Nagisa Ôshima's mission of breaking down the wall between narrative film and pornography. She noted that Americans in particular have trouble with this idea:

> "In the U.S. we have grown so used to the separation of pornography from art that we tend to assume – sometimes

---

[678] Linda Williams, "Cinema and the Sex Act," *Cinéaste*, Vol. 27, No. 1 (Winter 2001), p. 20-25

rather hypocritically – that any arousal response is antithetical to art and any emotionally complex art antithetical to arousal."[679]

Casting a pall over all of these interesting arguments about "Romance" are the accusations made by star Caroline Ducey in 2024. In her autobiography, Ducey says she consented to some of the sexual activity but not all. One scene went well beyond what she expected. Even the ones she consented to were traumatic for her, and she would have withdrawn consent if she felt she could have.[680] Catherine Breillat's rebuttal to Ducey's accusations was inadequate, to say the least.

Catherine Breillat may have succeeded in making a woman's version of a movie about sex, but it appears she used the same abusive tactics that men like Bernardo Bertolucci did to do so. I hope that in the current age of intimacy coordinators, directors can make intelligent films about sexuality without committing crimes against actors.

If a filmmaker needs a hardcore scene, they can always hire porn actors to do it. For the film version of her novel, "**Baise-moi**," aka "**Fuck Me**" (2000), Virginie Despentes employed two French pornographic actresses to star and took on another to co-direct. This and many hard-core sex scenes compelled many people to call "Baise-moi" pornography.

Some of the sex scenes of "Baise-moi" felt gratuitous to me, but they are not so long that their only purposes could be masturbatory fodder. They don't consist mainly of close-ups of genitals or conform to the other signifiers of pornography that Donald Richie details in

---

[679] Ibid

[680] Par Manon Marcillat, "Dans son essai, Caroline Ducey accuse Catherine Breillat d'avoir organisé son viol sur le tournage du film Romance," *Konbini*, Sept. 4, 2024, https://www.konbini.com/popculture/dans-son-essai-caroline-ducey-accuse-catherine-breillat-davoir-organise-son-viol-sur-le-tournage-du-film-romance/

reference to "In the Realm of the Senses."[681] As we've discussed, a feature-length porno is just a string of extended (and tedious, if you're not masturbating) sex scenes interspersed with filler. "Baise-moi" is structured more like a conventional narrative. I'd classify it under exploitation, a genre also known for gratuitous sex scenes, as well as violence and more plot than a porn film. The protagonists of "Baise-moi" murder a lot of people and proceed along a genuine story arc, if a rather thin one.

Then again, exploitation films are cynical money-making schemes carefully constructed to go up to the line but not cross it. You give the moviegoers some cheap thrills while avoiding anything that could get you a high rating that will block your movie from most theaters. You certainly don't include hard-core sex scenes, which is a surefire way to get it stuck in the underground obscurity of pornography.

National classification boards didn't know what to do with "Baise-moi." In Ontario, "Baise-moi" was banned from theaters for being pornographic. The film's producers rather reasonably requested it then be classified as a pornographic film and distributed on video. That idea was also shot down because the board deemed "Baise-moi" too violent to qualify as pornography. Eventually a slightly edited version got an R rating.[682] No one even tried to get it rated in the United States, where it made only a handful of independent theaters.

In its native France, "Baise-moi" was initially rated 16, then the highest rating besides X. A right-wing group sued to get it rated X, which in France is usually meant for hard-core sex but can also encompass extreme violence. The case came before the French

---

[681] Donald Richie, "In the Realm of the Senses: Some Notes on Oshima and Pornography," Criterion.com,
April 30, 2009: https://www.criterion.com/current/posts/1108-in-the-realm-of-the-senses-some-notes-on-oshima-and-pornography
[682] Siobhan Devine, "My Tango With Porn" (2003), Canadian Broadcasting Corporation.

version of the Supreme Court, Conseil d'État, which ruled the movie's 16 rating illegal. This gave "Baise-moi" an X rating, an effective ban from theaters. It thus became France's first banned film since "The Texas Chain Saw Massacre" in 1977.[683]

Vocal supporters of "Baise-moi," including Catherine Breillat and Jean-Luc Godard, succeeded in getting it back before the censorship board. In 2002, "Baise-moi" was re-rated 18, a new rating that allowed it to return to theaters.[684] The episode opened up the already lax French censorship laws even further. Later French films would take advantage of this.[685]

The unclassifiable nature of "Baise-moi" is one of the most interesting things about it. The other is that it's about two female friends on a hedonistic spree of murder and sex instead of a heterosexual couple, like in "Natural Born Killers" and "Bonnie and Clyde." The women of "Baise-moi" are even more aggressive and psychopathic than the protagonists of those movies. They need little provocation to kill people, mostly men who disappoint or offend them.

"Baise-moi" is sometimes described as a "rape-and-revenge" movie like "I Spit on Your Grave," but it doesn't really follow that plot. Be forewarned that an early scene of "Baise-moi" does show two women being raped by three men. One of these women, Manu, is one of the protagonists. Her story is initially told in parallel with that of a sex worker named Nadine. Manu and Nadine soon join up to

---

[683] Francoise Meaux Saint Marc, "Baise-Moi banned from French cinemas," *Screen Daily*, July 3, 2000, https://www.screendaily.com/baise-moi-banned-from-french-cinemas/402866.article

[684] Miriam Balanescu, "'I never imagined it would be banned': The ultra-violent, sexually explicit French thriller now being reappraised," BBC.com, July 8, 2025, https://www.bbc.com/culture/article/20250707-the-banned-french-thriller-now-being-reappraised

[685] Geoffrey Macnab, 'The rape had to be disgusting to be useful' *The Guardian*, August 1, 2002, https://www.theguardian.com/film/2002/aug/02/artsfeatures.festivals

wreak havoc on almost everyone they meet, but do not specifically target the rapists.

The writer and co-director of "Baise-moi," Virginie Despentes, was raped by three men when she was 17. Later she became a sex worker.[686] It's hard not to wonder if early scenes of "Baise-moi" are somewhat autobiographical for Despentes, and if the later crime spree represents a wish fulfillment of cathartic violence. This presumption at least makes "Baise-moi" more meaningful than most exploitation. I'd still approach it like you would any exploitation film: Expect some of it to be shocking in a bad way, and all of it to look pretty shoddy.

The New French Extremity

"Baise-moi" would later be lumped in with a movement that was dubbed "The New French Extremity." It would give the world a new, updated version of the shock art film trend of 1969-1976. Critic James Quandt thought he was taking the movement down when he coined the name "The New French Extremity" in a 2004 essay. He decried that "[i]mages and subjects once the provenance of splatter films, exploitation flicks, and porn – gang rapes, bashings and slashings and blindings, hard-ons and vulvas, cannibalism, sadomasochism and incest, fucking and fisting, sluices of cum and gore – proliferate in the high-art environs of [French] cinema …"[687]

The movement's label as high art was stamped for good when Claire Denis joined the party with her film "**Trouble Every Day**" (2001). Denis' "Beau travail" (1998) had already established her as one of the world's most important filmmakers. "Beau travail" ranks 52nd on the 2025 They Shoot Pictures, Don't They? list of greatest

---

[686] Angelique Chrisafis, "Virginie Despentes: 'What is going on in men's heads when women's pleasure has become a problem?'" *The Guardian*. August 31, 2018

[687] James Quandt, "Flesh & Blood: Sex and Violence in Recent French Cinema," Art Forum, https://www.artforum.com/features/flesh-blood-sex-and-violence-in-recent-french-cinema-168041/

movies ever, second among all movies released in the 1990s. (If you're curious, number one is Abbas Kiarostami's "Close-Up" (1990).) "Trouble Every Day" isn't in that league, but I doubt few would dispute that it's about as artful as a movie about cannibalism can be. I found Béatrice Dalle to be perfect as a hedonistic literal man-eater. If Dalle herself admitted to eating human flesh (which she has[688]), I'd believe her.

Catherine Breillat returned in 2001 with her most celebrated film, "**Fat Girl**." Two teenage sisters explore their burgeoning sexuality while on a family vacation. One is thin and beautiful, while the other is overweight. The thin girl attracts immediate attention, which the overweight girl can only watch with resentment and longing. Neither sister has a happy fate, to say the least. "Fat Girl" is a painfully realistic film that puts forth the idea that most heterosexual intercourse involving teenage girls takes some form of sexual violence.

I'd say the epitomal New French Extremity film is "**In My Skin**" (2002). Writer/director Marina de Van also stars as a woman who suffers an accidental gash on her leg and then becomes fascinated with self-mutilation. In true turn-of-the-millenium shock-auteur form, the movie centers on excruciatingly long takes of her bloody solo pleasure sessions. The shocking imagery is not underlined by any music or quick editing, which would have only detracted from immersion in the extreme tension. Strict realism once again makes shocks more potent.

If "In My Skin" were just about scenes of self-harm, it would be an exploitation film, but there's a lot more to it than that. Marina de Van has downplayed any feminist messaging,[689] but I don't believe

---

[688] Olivia Blair, "French actress Béatrice Dalle reveals she once ate a dead man's ear," *The Independent*, February 3, 2016, https://www.independent.co.uk/news/people/french-actress-beatrice-dalle-reveals-she-once-ate-a-dead-man-s-ear-a6851346.html
[689] Tim Palmer, "Brutal Intimacy: Analyzing Contemporary French Cinema," 2011, p. 78-88

authorial intent is paramount. I and many other people have found a feminist theme of a woman saying "fuck you" to a world that cares more about protecting her body than her psyche.

With all of these New French Extremity films directed by women, you have to wonder, could a man make a shocking movie? Is there something about masculinity that makes it too difficult? For starters, how could a man find the right balance between work and family?

I'm being facetious, of course, but Gaspar Noé's "**Irréversible**" (2002) makes me wonder if just women should be in charge of this particular movement. "Irréversible"'s centerpiece is a nine-minute-long rape scene, all captured in one shot. The rest of the film is a very unnerving art film constructed in a fascinating way, but that one scene overshadowed the rest, for me at least.

Sexual violence is a frequent subject of New French Extremity films. But much the same way films about racism against African Americans are best left to Black directors, I think women should be in charge of films about rape. It is a very specific trauma that most men are not in a position to comprehend, much less depict, unless they listen to women and work to internalize what women say. Remember that the Production Code banned many subjects but not rape, and Joseph Breen thought it could be a justified punishment for a woman's misbehavior. It took many decades of women speaking out before men even started to understand how destructive rape is.

However, in the case of "Irréversible," the actress who played the victim, Monica Bellucci, was the de facto director of the rape scene, per Gaspar Noé's telling at least. He says Bellucci took inspiration from "I Spit on Your Grave" and "Deliverance,"[690] two movies I previously credited with accurately depicting rape as an act of psychopathic violence, not sexuality. She improvised the scene

---

[690] Nigel W. Smith, "From the iW Vaults | Gaspar Noe Talks 'Irreversible'," *IndieWire*, July 12, 2011, https://www.indiewire.com/features/general/from-the-iw-vaults-gaspar-noe-talks-irreversible-53317/

along with the actor playing the rapist, and she reportedly had complete control of what he did. Noé just held the camera with no idea what would happen.[691] I can't be sure until I hear Bellucci's account, but by all available evidence, Gaspar Noé arranged a scene of sexual violence the right way, unlike Catherine Breillat or many previous male directors.

You could argue that "Irréversible"'s rape scene is so disturbing because it reveals, through its unflinching realism, how horrific rape truly is. I still worry more about men with rape fantasies finding the "Irréversible" scene arousing than those of "I Spit on Your Grave" and "Deliverance." Maybe that's just a subjective call. Either way, "Irréversible" is an important part of shock-film history, but be sure to skip it if it sounds like too much.

Sex Triumphs Over Censorship

There are many other New French Extremity films we could cover, but let's widen our scope. Several films around the world followed "Romance"'s example and incorporated strong sexuality into serious dramas. One, "**Y tu mamá también**" (2001), did it so successfully that it changed a national censorship system.

"Y tu mamá también" is not as graphic as "Romance" or other contemporary films, but it would have gotten an NC-17 rating in the United States if it were rated. Since it wasn't, it had only a limited American release. It still became the all-time second-highest-grossing Spanish-language film in the U.S. through 2001.[692] "Y tu mamá también" was successful everywhere else it was shown. It thus did more than "Romance" or any other film of the era to legitimize strong sexual content in serious drama, to an extent not seen since the 1970s.

---

[691] Geoffrey Macnab, 'The rape had to be disgusting to be useful'
[692] "All-Time Top Grossing Spanish-Language Films in the U.S." *Cinema Tropical*. September 29, 2013. https://www.cinematropical.com/cinema-tropical/all-time-top-grossing-spanish-language-films-in-the-us

In its country of origin, Mexico, "Y tu mamá también" set a new record for opening-weekend box office[693] and then reached second in the country's all-time highest domestic grossers.[694] Director/writer Alfonso Cuarón and writer Carlos Cuarón used the clout they had earned from creating one of the most successful films in Mexican history to challenge the country's governmental censorship system. They sued the Mexican Directorate of Radio, Television, and Cinema (RTC) for giving "Y tu mamá también" a C, which barred it from anyone under 18. The Cuarón brothers argued that the rating violated parents' rights to choose what their children see. The case didn't completely take down the RTC, but it led to a relaxation of Mexican censorship standards.[695]

Japan's Shock Auteurs

Japan is a shock-movie powerhouse that we haven't visited for a while. In 1999, Japan's premier shock auteur, Takashi Miike, established his reputation with his magnum opus "**Audition**."

"Audition" provides one of filmdom's greatest and most drastic tone shifts. It starts as a rather sedate romantic comedy about a sad-sack widower who stages an audition for a female film role that doesn't actually exist. He's really looking for a new wife. It's the sort of deceit that could plausibly drive a conventional romantic comedy even though it's a sociopathic violation of trust that would never fly in real life.

It doesn't fly in "Audition" either. The widower chooses a beautiful young woman whose secrets fall far outside the realm of quirky rom-

---

[693] David Rooney, "Romance woos Venice; 'Dust' busts". *Variety*. Sept. 4, 2001. https://variety.com/2001/film/news/romance-woes-venice-dust-busts-1117852211/

[694] "Las 15 películas mexicanas más taquilleras de la historia". *Forbes Mexico*. July 19, 2013, https://forbes.com.mx/las-15-peliculas-mexicanas-mas-taquilleras-de-la-historia/

[695] Jason Wood. "The Faber Book of Mexican Cinema," 2006

com character traits. I won't spoil "Audition" any more than I already have, but I will warn you that it requires a strong stomach.

An even stronger test of your tolerance level can be found in Miike's ultraviolet "**Ichi the Killer**" (2001). Tadanobu Asano plays a gang leader whose considerable advantage over his rivals is that he is a Bob Flanagan-level supermasochist. It doesn't accomplish much to hurt an enemy who loves being hurt. Beyond the torture that Asano's character sustains, "Ichi the Killer" comes up with some very creative gore.

"**Visitor Q**" (2001) is probably Miike's most shock-packed film, which seems to be largely the point. It's a low-budget movie made in part to explore the then-new technology of digital video. Miike took the opportunity to go hog-wild: "Visitor Q" almost feels like an experimental film compiling every perversity Miike could think of, including some that probably only exist in his head. A tone of dark comedy helps it go down, but "Visitor Q" was honestly a bit much for me, especially the parts about incest. I don't recommend it to anyone who isn't already a Miike fan.

While "Ichi the Killer" was controversial in Japan, as it was gory even by the country's very high standards, "Visitor Q" did not cause as much fuss. That's largely because "Visitor Q" was barely in theaters. It snuck into video stores and catered to a small audience of shockseekers, not unlike the "Guinea Pig" and "Faces of Death" series. Like those movies, "Visitor Q" was made so cheaply that video rentals helped it recoup just fine.

None of Takashi Miike's movies caused as much controversy in Japan as Kinji Fukasaku's "**Battle Royale**" (2000), the story of junior high school students forced to fight to the death. To me it felt like an earlier, cheesier version of "The Hunger Games" (2012). A few scenes of "Battle Royale" hinted at a gonzo horror-comedy that would have been more fun for me. Perhaps that's a bit unkind; Fukasaku was inspired by his own childhood traumas during World War II, so this was not funny stuff for him.

"Battle Royale" is rather gory, but nothing compared to an average Takashi Miike film. The issue among Japanese censors was that it was teenagers committing and suffering the slaughter. It got a R15+ rating, which bars children under 16. This was an unusually high rating for violence alone.[696] Fukasaku protested and submitted an appeal.[697]

Then members of the National Diet, Japan's Congress, raised the stakes considerably. They claimed that "Battle Royale" harmed teenagers and used it to attack the entire censorship system, which was self-regulating like the United States'. This brought the danger of government regulation into view. Fukasaku dropped his appeal and backed away slowly.[698]

A national debate about film violence followed. Conservatives blamed movies for a rash of teen violence.[699] Fukasaku encouraged kids to sneak in to see "Battle Royale."[700] The movie attracted enough paying customers to become a huge hit in Japan and elsewhere.[701] It was not released in the United States because it had been only a year since the Columbine school massacre.

I can't explain why "Battle Royale" was such a hot potato and "The Hunger Games" was a massive mainstream success 12 years later. Japan and the United States are very different cultures, but Japan is usually more tolerant of on-screen violence, not less. "The Hunger Games" was released in Japan and did adequate business with little

---

[696] "Battle Royale," *Variety*, Jan 22, 2001, https://variety.com/2001/film/reviews/battle-royale-2-1200466268/
[697] Jasper Sharp and Tom Mes, "Kinji Fukasaku," MidnightEye.com, http://www.midnighteye.com/interviews/kinji-fukasaku/
[698] Ibid
[699] Ilya Garger, "Royale Terror," *Time*, June 30, 2003, https://web.archive.org/web/20070305133056/http://www.time.com/time/magazine/article/0,9171,501030707-461891,00.html
[700] Neda Ulaby, "'Battle,' 'Games': Cold Brutality A Common Theme," NPR.org, March 21, 2012, https://www.npr.org/2012/03/21/148991013/battle-games-cold-brutality-a-common-theme
[701] Garger, "Royale Terror"

controversy beyond its striking similarity to "Battle Royale." "Battle Royale" is gorier, but the sticking point was the message-based shock of teens shooting each other. That was reason enough to keep it out of American theaters in 2000. Real school shootings have tragically not let up in the United States since then. I would hate to conclude that people had become inured to the idea of teen-on-teen violence. I wish I had a better explanation, but I don't.

Searching for American Shock Auteurs

Well, I guess we should return to the ostensible main country of this book, the United States. True American shock auteurs might be hard to come by at the turn of the millennium, but Todd Solondz qualifies. His best film by my estimation, "**Happiness**" (1998), is a very dark comedy with several intertwining stories, including one about a pedophile who is attracted to his own son. It's the first in a series of Solondz movies, followed by "**Storytelling**" (2001) and "**Palindromes**" (2004), that delve into topics that you don't expect to see in any movie, much less a comedy.

In 1999, "American Pie" initiated a surge of shock comedy movies, but it and its many imitators never approached the cringe-inducingness of a Todd Solondz film. I think Solondz is a master of a deadpan tone that makes the most painful possible scenarios funny. His style is certainly not for everyone. Try "Happiness" if you're curious, but don't feel bad about turning it off if it's not your speed.

A much more popular and influential source of shock comedy was the TV show "South Park." In the mid-1990s it rose from a widely circulated VHS tape made by a few weirdos from Colorado to the flagship show of Comedy Central.

"South Park" exploited a strange rule of TV censorship: You can get away with more if you use animation or puppets instead of real people. I find this rule baffling because of the association between the mediums of animation and puppets and children's entertainment. For me, and I suspect most people, watching puppets or animated characters have sex and slaughter each other is significantly more shocking than watching real people do the same. Making your animated characters children only ups the shock level further, but "South Park" got that past the censors too. It could be illegal to have real underage actors do many of the things that the "South Park" kids do.

The kids hit the big screen in 1999 with **South Park: Bigger, Longer and Uncut.**" Being an R-rated movie allowed it to show characters doing one of the few things they couldn't do on TV: curse. This exposed another quirk of TV censorship. You can show a bunch of cute animals ripping each other apart and then having sex with each other's corpses, as a "South Park" episode does. But when a human character comes across this horrific blood orgy, he can't say "fuck." TV was like independent movies in the 1960s, when the New York censorship board came down on Shirley Clarke's "The Connection" not for its depiction of heroin abuse but because its characters say "shit." Cursing is the hill censors will die on just because they're easier to police; you either hear a bad word or you don't. Every other type of shock content exists in a spectrum that requires difficult judgment calls.

This bizarre set of standards is parodied by "South Park: Bigger, Longer and Uncut." In it, the favorite TV show of the "South Park" kids, "Terrance & Phillip," spins off into a movie version that is loaded with curse words. The kids see it and start cursing, and their parents overreact wildly. Having made their point, creators Trey Stone and Matt Parker didn't bother with another "South Park" movie for theaters. They could do whatever else they wanted on TV.

Calling Trey Stone and Matt Parker shock "auteurs" sounds like the kind of grandiose thing they would parody, but it's not inaccurate. They had other shock films you'll probably like if you're a "South Park" fan, like the NC-17-rated "Orgazmo" and 2004's "Team America: World Police," which features marionettes cycling through subversive sexual practices.

Was David Fincher a shock auteur, at least early in his career? "Seven" (1995) is a descendant of "The Silence of the Lambs," with similarly creative grisliness. It didn't cause much controversy, though, while "**Fight Club**" (1999) did. As you probably know, "Fight Club" is about young men who are frustrated with dull, commodified, "feminized" (from their perspective) late-1990s America and decide the answer is to beat each other up. Their movement then branches out to punishing innocent people who don't share their perspective.

Never mind that late-1990s America was actually a golden age of relative worldwide peace, economic strength, cushy living standards, and societal privilege for young white men. These guys don't feel powerful enough, so they want to hurt someone. It brings to my mind another 1990s touchstone, "The Simpsons," when Bleeding Gums Murphy tells Lisa Simpson, "You know, you play [the blues] pretty well for someone with no real problems." The movie doesn't end up endorsing the fight club's ethos, but it does make it look attractive, at least initially.

I admit that I was one of the young men who were seduced by "Fight Club." When I was 23 I saw it in the theater and was so blown away that I brought some friends to see it the next day. I wasn't thinking too hard about it beyond reveling in its sort of punk-rock "fuck the grown-up world" spirit. Even then, I was hardly some dudebro fuming about masculinity being threatened: I preferred hanging out with women and was put off by most everything, from football to car culture, that is infused with macho posturing. But "Fight Club" somehow tapped into some latent lizard-brain toxic masculinity in me. Tyler Durden, played by Brad Pitt, is an avatar of that masculine lizard brain's ideal identity, which is the movie's point.

Now with the benefit of age and hindsight, I have a lot of ambivalence about "Fight Club." It didn't inspire me to become some men's rights activist, but I can see how it could for some. There are similarities between Tyler Durden's gang and various recent movements of angry young white men with no real problems: incels, alt-right, Proud Boys, etc. These whiny packs of spoiled brats rage as if their civil rights are being violated because they've been told to be more considerate to others (and because they're scared of non-white and queer people, and because they can't get dates with the gorgeous women they feel entitled to – their petty grievances are legion). As much as I despise these groups, I suppose I can empathize with the sociopathic impulses that they are dumb enough to indulge.

The terrorist attacks of September 11, 2001 made the infantile gripes of disaffected young white men seem especially trivial. Somehow, though, their quibbles made a resurgence in later decades and arguably animate an entire major political party as I write this. Now "Fight Club" carries with it the shock of being remarkably prescient.

In 1999, the message-based shock of "Fight Club" was strong enough to cause a lot of discussion. The British Board of Film Classification fielded claims that the film includes "dangerously instructive information" and could "encourage anti-social (behavior)."[702] The Board dismissed these concerns, stating "The film as a whole is — quite clearly — critical and sharply parodic of the amateur fascism which in part it portrays."[703] The Board still imposed a few cuts to some sadistic violence, which was very rare at the time for a mainstream Hollywood movie, especially one like "Fight Club" that is not especially gory.[704]

There are some parallels between "Fight Club" and "**American Psycho**" (2000). Both are satires about charismatic, violent young white men. Patrick Bateman, the protagonist of "American Psycho," is much more clearly a villain than Tyler Durden. Bateman is both a

---

[702] Adam Dawtry, "U.K. to cut 'Club';" Variety, Nov, 8, 1999, https://variety.com/1999/film/news/u-k-to-cut-club-1117757863/
[703] Quoted in ibid
[704] Ibid

serial killer and an overprivileged, shallow finance bro; you would be hard-pressed to create a more detestable combination.

Movies had been overloaded with serial killers since "The Silence of the Lambs." "American Psycho" takes the trope to a new level of subversion by making a serial killer the clear protagonist. There are no major good-guy characters trying to bring him to justice. We're just left with his story arc of petty jealousies and brutal murders, most of them against women.

When a character is positioned so unambiguously as a protagonist, audiences are primed to identify with him. This gets complicated when the character does terrible things almost exclusively, as Patrick Bateman does. Then the character either becomes an anti-hero or you just despise him and the movie.

Psychopaths make terrific villains but it's hard to even make them anti-heroes, much less heroes. Because psychopaths can't feel empathy or love, their emotional lives are very limited. They basically have four emotional states: excited, angry, afraid, and bored. They seldom learn or change, except to become more skilled at manipulating others. Maybe you can allow your lizard brain to identify with a psychopath a bit if they are punishing someone you hate. It's hard to make a feature-length story about just that. Only after "American Psycho" did people figure out how to make psychopathic protagonists, most successfully in the TV shows "Dexter" and "Hannibal."

"American Psycho" would be a "Guinea Pig" movie with a plot and a budget if it weren't also a satire of 1980s-style capitalism. Satire functions through irony, which means the surface-level story is not the point. Still, for any satire, some people will get hung up on the surface-level story. If that story is as repellent as Patrick Bateman's, many people will reject the movie even if they process the satire. I think the tension created by all these factors is a message-based shock of some kind, even if I'm not sure what exactly the message would be.

"Fight Club" and "American Psycho" are special cases. They hit on the very rare message-based shocks that could offend people at the turn of the millennium. The more tried-and-true sources of content-based shock were mostly tapped out.

John Waters demonstrated that the well had run dry with his 2000 film "Cecil B. Demented." It offers some of the celebration of scuzzy subversion that you want from John Waters, but doesn't go far beyond the norm of a typical Quentin Tarantino or Kevin Smith movie. And even that, I feel, is overwhelmed by the movie's pervasive bitterness about American mainstream film. Amidst "Cecil B. Demented"'s thicket of GOMS-y rants about movies like "Patch Adams" and meddling notes from film executives, it offers one line that clearly voices John Waters' take on the state of American shock film: "Your Hollywood system stole our sex and co-opted our violence so there's nothing left for our kind of movies!"

I love you, John, but at a time like this, it's best to turn to the kids for new ideas. "**Jackass: The Movie**" (2002) is a compilation of real stunts and pranks that were too raw for the already brutal MTV show "Jackass." It represented a radical departure from shock films that came before. Does it fit among the documentaries? Maybe technically, because there are no actors. But "Jackass: The Movie" doesn't have even the thin veneer of dispensing information that the mondo films do. Documentaries like "Sick: The Life and Death of Bob Flanagan, Supermasochist" tell an interesting story rather than educating viewers, but there's no story in "Jackass: The Movie" either. It's just alarming acts that escalate in intensity the same way "Sweet Movie" and "Salò" do, except for laughs.

The "Jackass" boys invented a new type of shock film that only they really have license to perform on a large scale. Any other movie centering on dangerous stunts and pranks is bound to seem derivative. Their popular success, and their ownership of a subgenre, has led to many sequels and variations on the theme. As with the mondo movies, if you like the first one, you have plenty more to delve into.

I like to think John Waters would enjoy the balls-out bravado of the "Jackass" films. He at least appreciated "Jackass" star Johnny Knoxville enough to cast him as a sex god in his next effort, "**A Dirty Shame**" (2004). Unlike Waters' previous six movies, "A Dirty Shame" was rated NC-17. According to him, when he asked the MPAA what he should cut to get it down to an R, he was told that partway through watching his movie, the ratings board "stopped taking notes."[705]

I sympathize with the board. "A Dirty Shame" has a story, after a fashion, but its main purpose is to compile silly double entendres and unusual sexual practices that John Waters discovered on the internet. It has no explicit sex or erect penises, which must have only made the ratings board's job more difficult. What do you cut? The trees made to look like penises and vaginas? Is that worse than the police officer whose fetish is dressing up like a baby? Or the guy whose kink is leaving "double deckers"? I'm sure the board just threw up their hands and said "Fuck it – it's NC-17."

I found "A Dirty Shame" to be a big load of campy fun, though I did occasionally wish the plot hinged on more than just people getting hit on the head at random times. Oh well, who cares? This ain't a Catherine Breillat film. If you like John Waters, watch it and have a good time.

Real Sex 2

Meanwhile, some American directors were trying to make Catherine Breillat films. Soon after "Romance" and other serious European films showed real sex in a forthright, non-exploitative way, "Kids" director Larry Clark and screenwriter Harmony Korine did the same in "**Ken Park**" (2002). Like "Kids," "Ken Park" is about sexually active teens with tragic lives. "Ken Park" is significantly more graphic, with clearly unsimulated shots of masturbation, fellatio, etc.

---

[705] Kirby Dick, "This Film Is Not Yet Rated," documentary, 2006

While "Kids" was able to find screens in the United States despite its rating, "Ken Park" found none at all. A movie has to be really good for American distributors to shoulder the added work and risk necessary for an unrated or NC-17 release. "Ken Park" simply didn't clear that bar, according to potential distributors and most everyone else. Larry Clark blamed the non-release on troubles clearing music, but that is a hurdle that producers will always clear if it's worth the expense.

I thought the four parallel stories of "Ken Park" offered very realistic dialogue and acting, but also plots that varied wildly in plausibility. One involving a psychotic boy named Tate felt to me like a John Waters short film with the campiness removed (which would of course defeat the purpose). "Ken Park" was screened in several countries but didn't make much of a mark.

Vincent Gallo thought he should be the next to take a stab at putting real sex in an American art film. Gallo is an independent filmmaker who saw some success with "Buffalo '66" (1998). His 2003 film "**The Brown Bunny**" quickly became infamous for a scene in which he is fellated by his then-girlfriend Chloë Sevigny.

"The Brown Bunny" also generated some attention because it sparked a feud between Gallo and Roger Ebert. Ebert saw an early cut of "The Brown Bunny" at the Cannes Film Festival and called it the worst film in the festival's history. Gallo's clever response was to call Ebert a "fat pig." Then Gallo edited "The Brown Bunny" down into a version that Ebert awarded three stars out of four.[706]

As suggested by his reaction to Ebert's initial criticism, Gallo might not have owned the maturity to make a "Romance"-style breakthrough for real sexual content. I personally find him insufferably pretentious. If you've ever been in a college film class, you've probably had to deal with a Vincent Gallo type. He's the guy

---

[706] Roger Ebert, "Revised editing releases a much improved 'Brown Bunny'" RogerEbert.com, Sept. 3, 2004, https://www.rogerebert.com/reviews/the-brown-bunny-2004

who has nothing but scorn for any mainstream movie because he has shaped his identity around being the only person who can truly understand art cinema. Even if you try to tell him what you like about Godard films, he will scoff or change the subject because he wants to be the only one with valid opinions.

The Gallo-type filmbro makes movies in which he casts himself as a brooding outcast who's just too deep and sensitive for this stupid and cruel world. This alleged depth and sensitivity is often used to justify his character using and discarding women, who throw themselves at him for no clear reason. Filmbro movies tend to be slow and tedious because the director thinks every second he captures is a profound meditation on human existence (especially long close-ups of his own face trying to look soulful).

Even the Ebert-approved version of "The Brown Bunny" qualifies as a filmbro movie by my estimation. It does have an interesting ending that I think rescues it from being solely an exercise in self-absorption. Regardless, "The Brown Bunny" is no "Romance." Vincent Gallo was the wrong director to attempt the herculean task of legitimizing unsimulated sex in American art film.

John Cameron Mitchell was a better candidate. In 2000 he had an arthouse hit with "Hedwig and the Angry Inch," which stars himself as a gender-queer rock singer whose angry inch is the result of a botched gender reassignment surgery. Its subject matter in the context of 2000 would make it a fine choice for the shock-film canon, but Mitchell's "**Shortbus**" (2006) is certainly more transgressive. "Shortbus" weaves together several stories of people working through their sexual problems. This involves showing much more explicit sex than in "Ken Park," "The Brown Bunny," or probably any non-porn movie in history.

I found "Shortbus" to be interesting and occasionally moving, certainly my favorite of the movies in this section. It still didn't strike me as a must-see, and didn't attract a big following. Maybe that was because the actors, while competent, didn't quite exude the charisma of typical movie leads. That might just be a professional hazard of making a movie with lots of unsimulated sex. Your pool of willing actors will be limited.

For whatever reason, "Shortbus" also did not launch an era of sexually explicit serious drama in the United States. The status quo held, and unrated/NC-17 movies remained rare and unprofitable.

Hard-Core Horror Returns

Perhaps Americans should just let the French directors handle the combinations of real sex and art film. The French are the experts in both after all. We Americans should stick to what we know: horrific violence.

American auteurs had better luck emulating the extreme gore of The New French Extremity. I suppose extreme gore never left low-budget American direct-to-video horror movies, but I doubt I have anything interesting to say about any of those. Much the same way I don't see much point in cataloging the atrocities of every "Faces of Death" or "Guinea Pig" sequel, I think I can ignore the likes of "August Underground" (2001) which is apparently just a series of bloody murders in a found-footage style. I say "apparently" because I have not seen it. At this point, I think I've earned the right of refusal for the really obscure stuff.

I'm more interested in extreme gore in movies that make some larger cultural impact and/or have at least a bit of artistic merit. "**Saw**" (2004) certainly qualifies for the former. Distributor Lionsgate planned to release it direct to video but rolled the dice on a theater release after it did well at the Sundance Film Festival.[707] Everyone was surprised when "Saw" became one of the most profitable movies of all time. Gorier sequels followed, as well as video games, theme park rides, and more.

---

[707] Franz Lidz, "As the 'Saw' turns". *The Virginian-Pilot*. October 25, 2009

If you've seen "Saw" you'll see Lionsgate's see-saw, i.e, why the distributor vacillated between theater-release plans and the "Faces of Death/"Guinea Pig" dumping ground of direct-to-video movies for teenage boys testing their boundaries. "Saw" is significantly better made than those cynical compilations of shocks, but it's still low-budget, grimy, and focused on creative forms of torture.

I was on the fence while watching "Saw" until its evil mastermind Jigsaw revealed his motivation, which I found so dumb that I was dumbfounded. If you can't think of anything better, just have him be a sadist wreaking revenge. That's plenty.

Regardless of its merits, "Saw" was a necessary shot in the arm for American horror. Slasher films had been mired in self-parody even before they were literally parodied (and celebrated) by "Scream" in 1996. After "Saw," the roughest end of the horror spectrum was dominated by a subgenre dubbed "torture porn." I don't like that term, as it denotes a masturbatory element that would make it even worse than it is. Let's go with "torture horror."

It might not be as devoted to torture as the "Saw" movies are, but "**Hostel**" (2005) is my pick for the epitomal torture horror movie. "Hostel" has the advantage of some genuinely disturbing ideas underlying all the eye violence and entrails-spilling. In the middle of the movie, a new character explains to the protagonist why people are dying, and it hit me harder than the extreme gore.

Unlike "Saw," "Hostel" and its sequel made their director, Eli Roth, a poster boy for torture horror. He also hearkens back to the era of peak/rock-bottom-era shock films. His first feature, "Cabin Fever" (2002), is a spin on the "Evil Dead" formula, which is not unusual for a young director trying to make a cheap horror movie. A homage to "Cannibal Holocaust," like Roth's "The Green Inferno" (2013), is much less common. Roth's films are R-rated, so they don't go as far as their inspirations. They are still very gory and sometimes as problematic as the peak-era shock films.

I don't know if Rob Zombie's movies qualify as torture horror exactly, but he is a horror auteur who probably deserves mention. His film "**The Devil's Rejects**" (2005) is like "The Texas Chain Saw Massacre" from the perspective of the psychopathic family. I think it effectively creates a singular mood of extreme depravity and despair, using a lot more artistry than I expected.

There's something about "The Devil's Rejects" that just feels like it's a step beyond a typical R-rated horror movie, even if it's hard to pinpoint exactly what. The MPAA ratings board felt the same way, giving it an NC-17 seven times before finally seeing a version it could pass with an R. Rob Zombie said the board just couldn't handle the overall tone of the movie,[708] which I get.

Getting Political

Maybe I'm giving too much credit to "Saw" for bringing extreme gore back to American theaters; after all, it did come out months after "**The Passion of the Christ**" (2004). I doubt many Christians would appreciate the story of the crucifixion being lumped in with torture horror, but "The Passion of the Christ" does feature close-ups of Jesus' flesh being scourged by the Romans, among other surprisingly graphic scenes.

The gore alone isn't enough to label "The Passion of the Christ" a shock film; it's also the context of seeing it in a faithful, traditional Christian story that was embraced by conservatives and earned a ton of money. Simply turning a straightforward Bible story into a major movie of any kind almost constituted a message-based shock in 2004. It had been many decades since "The Ten Commandments" (1956) and other big-budget Biblical epics became mainstream hits.

"The Passion of the Christ" caused controversy for other messages. Jewish characters, apart from Jesus and his disciples, do not come

---

[708] Edward Douglas, "Killin' Time with Rob Zombie," *Coming Soon!* July 20, 2005

across well. The focus on Jesus' suffering instead of his messages of peace and love also sparked plenty of discussion. These elements are inherent to what the movie is adapting, the Passion Play, a centuries-old tradition in many Christian denominations. Questioning the morality of the Passion Play was tantamount to a public challenge to many people's deeply held beliefs. Devout Christians defensively rallied around "The Passion of the Christ" and it became another battle line in the longstanding American culture war.

"**Brokeback Mountain**" (2005) did not set out to be a liberal response to "The Passion of the Christ," but it's not hard to spin it as one. "Brokeback Mountain" is also in a genre, the western, that conservative baby boomers cherished and was much more popular in the 1950s and 1960s. The Grumpy Old Men of 2005 did not appreciate how the film subverted genre conventions by showing the two tough, taciturn cowboys fall in love.

At the time, there were very few LGBTQ+ protagonists in mainstream movies, much less ones that took on avatars of American masculinity. It still felt bold to have uncloseted characters in "Will & Grace" who conformed to more stereotypical roles. Merely suggesting that queerness could exist outside of liberal enclaves, as "Brokeback Mountain" does, made many homophobes very angry and frightened (which is of course the same thing with homophobia, or indeed any other fear of something that doesn't have any actual effect on your life).

I would bet "Brokeback Mountain" accomplished more than any other movie in fostering empathy for gay men in the United States. It had two very sympathetic, multi-faceted protagonists who broke dramatically from stereotypes. More crucially, it was able to preach beyond the choir, as it were, earning $83 million domestically[709] and a Best Picture nomination. (More controversy ensued when it lost the Best Picture Oscar to "Crash" (2005), a film that makes less bold

---

[709] "Brokeback Mountain," *Box Office Mojo*: https://www.boxofficemojo.com/release/rl1833534977/

stances against bigotry in ways that many, including me, find much clunkier.)

"Brokeback Mountain" also came along at a critical time. In 2004, 31% of Americans approved of same-sex marriage and 60% of Americans opposed it.[710] By 2009, the tide had turned and a majority were in favor,[711] and a 2023 poll found that 73% approved of same-sex marriage.[712].

I don't want to overstate the effect "Brokeback Mountain" could have had in this dramatic societal change. The much greater impact came from the thousands of ordinary LGBTQ+ people who were out, proud, and willing to engage with homophobes. They used the most effective method for counteracting bigotry, which psychologists call the "mere exposure effect." This entails exposing prejudiced people to actual members of the group that they are biased against. Getting to know people who are LGBTQ+, or Black, or immigrants, or whatever identity you are irrationally frightened of will almost inevitably soften your feelings, elicit empathy, and help you construct more morally sound principles.

Watching movie characters is a poor substitute for meeting real people, but movies can provide an entry point if done well. A realistic and well-rounded character can foster at least some empathy for a member of a feared group. Roger Ebert often said that movies were "empathy machines" that promote understanding of people you might never meet in person. That can open you up to having real-world interactions.

It's important to qualify Ebert's "empathy machine" idea with the caveat that it only applies to well-made, three-dimensional film

---

[710] "About the Surveys," Pew Research Center, October 6, 2010: https://www.pewresearch.org/politics/2010/10/06/about-the-surveys-64/
[711] "Changing Views on Social Issues: Allemande Left. Allemande Right" (PDF). *ABC News*. April 30, 2009:
https://abcnews.go.com/images/PollingUnit/1089a6HotButtonIssues.pdf
[712] Theia Chatelle, "Is the Respect for Marriage Act a Win for the Right?". *The Nation*. January 16, 2023:

representations. Stereotyped and one-dimensional characters, like most LGBTQ+ ones in mainstream movies before "Brokeback Mountain," reinforce bigotry rather than empathy. Those sorts of characters were becoming less common by 2005, but progress was slow. "Brokeback Mountain" represented a big leap forward that shocked the 60% of Americans who still thought LGBTQ+ people should be barred from marriage.

On the content-based shock side, "Brokeback Mountain" also contains the first gay sex scene that many people had ever seen on screen. In the episode of the podcast "Unspooled" that I've mentioned before, Dan Savage says he and his husband laugh about how unrealistic this scene is.[713] Again, consulting with gay men could have made it more authentic. Still, the scene deserves credit for desensitizing many oversensitive heteros to witnessing a victimless act that consenting adults do every day.

I'd like to investigate this further, if I may. I remember hearing comedian Artie Lange do a bit about how shocking it was to see two men have sex in "Brokeback Mountain." It wasn't much of a bit: He was basically trying to speak on behalf of all working-class tough guys from The Bronx (or maybe Queens? Or New Jersey? I'm sure an East Coaster would be aware of huge differences between all of these that escape me) in insisting the movie should come with a warning label saying "Two Dudes Fuck." Artie Lange is hardly some prudish ascetic; he built much of his public persona on his struggles with drugs and other forms of debauchery.

Regardless of whether it was a hilarious bit, I think Lange did voice what a lot of men felt. So why would jaded hedonists like Artie Lange be so disturbed by a non-explicit gay sex scene? Is it just the scene's subversion of traditional masculinity, showing manly men being sexual with each other? Or is it that these Bronx/Queens/New Jersey tough guys are so programmed into presuming every sex scene should turn them on that their minds can't process one that

---

[713] "Sex Scenes in Film," *Unspooled* podcast, May 8, 2023

doesn't? Or maybe it does turn them on a bit, and that causes the distress?

I don't have any answers beyond my own experience. I remember being shocked by the sex scene in "Brokeback Mountain," but getting over it pretty quickly. Now more explicit scenes like the ones in "Un chant d'amour" or "Poison" don't affect me as much. You can call it desensitization, which is technically accurate even though that word denotes a regrettable loss of feeling instead of a welcome one. I'm perfectly happy to be undisturbed by gay sex.

It's really like getting past an irrational fear. Growing up in the 1980s, I somehow ingested some vague trepidation about gay sex. I guess, by definition, it was homophobia. That fear dissipated after my brain fully incorporated the knowledge that no one is hurt by it. This process was helped along by seeing film representations that show it's no more perverse or scary than hetero sex. But the real change resulted from becoming friends with out and proud gay men.

Mysterious Skin

For centuries, gay sex was lumped into the category of "sexual perversion" that the Production Code Administration made a strict taboo. This resulted in a bizarre dichotomy in most people's minds: A man is either on the "normal" side and wants to have sex with women, or he belongs to the "evil" side of having sex with everyone and everything else.

Because gay sex was categorized within sexual perversion, homophobes would conflate it with the genuinely harmful perversion of child sexual abuse. In their ignorant, fear-addled brains, grown men having sex with each other opens the door to men raping boys. A huge majority of child sexual abuse cases are of straight men raping girls,[714] but malevolent stereotypes are hard to shake when they're powered by irrational fear.

By the 2000s, movies finally started making the proper distinction. Censors began treating LGBTQ+ sex at least somewhat similarly to how they treated hetero sex, but they still justly forbade showing child sexual abuse or sexualized children of any kind. As we've seen, this was not always firmly established. Remember that in the 1930s, any scene of adults having sex would get participants thrown in jail, but the makers of "Child Bride" got away with gratuitous shots of a 12-year-old girl swimming naked.

If you want to make a movie exposing the true horrors of child sexual abuse, you must be very careful. You can show how victims remain warped by the trauma when they are young adults, which **"Mysterious Skin"** (2004) does extremely well, in my view. The film also treads into dangerous territory by depicting the formative incidents of child sexual abuse.

Director Gregg Araki found creative and non-exploitative ways to stage these scenes. Voice-overs explain what is happening while we see child actors looking terrified. Those shots are intercut with ones of the adult abuser doing or saying something horrific. Araki claimed that the underage actors only got a few pages of the script and were never aware that the story had anything to do with sexual abuse.[715] Having seen the movie, I believe him.

These scenes are still uniquely terrifying. The threat of seeing something truly and rightfully taboo created a tension in me that sublimated into even deeper empathy for the victims' trauma. None of it would be watchable if the script did not feel fully authentic to how pedophiles really operate. It could all collapse with a single

---

[714] David Finkelhor, Anne Shattuck, Heather A. Turner, and Sherry L. Hamby, "The lifetime prevalence of child sexual abuse and sexual assault assessed in late adolescence," *Journal of Adolescent Health*, September 2014; 55(3):329-33

[715] Director and actors' commentary track on DVD release

snarky, overwritten line, which Araki's previous films happened to have in spades. (I'm not a fan of those.) To his credit, Araki stuck with the realism necessary for this topic. I was very reluctant to see "Mysterious Skin," but I came away thinking it was a masterpiece.

"Mysterious Skin" does not show any genitalia, so its studio hoped for an R rating. Because of the pedophilia and many scenes of adult gay sex, including one that could only be seen as a rape, the ratings board would not budge from NC-17.

A pressure group called the Australian Family Association wanted "Mysterious Skin" outlawed in Australia. Of course, the organization had not seen it and was going only by the film's synopsis. A spokesman for the Australian Family Association said ""Being able to get hold legally of a DVD where they can play the scene over and over again, showing the adult baseball coach fellating an eight-year-old boy ... could prove very helpful to some pedophiles."[716]

If this spokesman had actually watched the scene in question, he would know that it indicates what is happening in a very oblique way, mostly through voice-over. You certainly do not see any fellating. While I acknowledge, as always, that any rape scene has the potential to arouse a would-be rapist, I find it very difficult to imagine that this or any scene in "Mysterious Skin" could prove "very helpful" to any pedophile. A majority of the Australian Office of Film and Literature Classification agreed, and the movie remained legal.

When faced with any deeply disturbing activity, people experience a very understandable impulse to shut down any discourse about it. It can just feel too painful to think about. But that's playing into the perpetrators' hands. Suppressing discourse only allows the evil activity to keep operating in obscurity. You have to be brave enough to confront horrors if you want to stop them.

---

[716] Quoted in "Pedophilia theme sparks film ban call," *The Sydney Morning Herald*, July 19, 2005

The child sexual abuse scenes of "Mysterious Skin" are set in the 1980s, when there was little public discussion about pedophilia. Since then, people have become more aware of the dangers due to activist campaigns and major news stories about pedophilic Boy Scout leaders, Catholic priests, etc. Parents nowadays are much less likely to not know where their children are at any moment. An adult would not be trusted to spend so much time alone with an underage child they weren't related to. And most importantly, children are educated about the risks.

Pedophilia has not been eradicated – in fact, the internet may have counteracted much of the progress by creating a distribution network, and thus a larger market, for creators of child pornography. But at least a pedophile will likely find it more difficult to "groom" a child the way the abuser in "Mysterious Skin" does.

Because of its rating, few people have seen "Mysterious Skin." I'm convinced that if more people did, the world would be better at preventing child sexual abuse.

The Next Breakthrough in Shock Comedy

There is no respectful way to transition from "Mysterious Skin" to **"Borat: Cultural Learnings of America for Make Benefit Glorious Nation of Kazakhstan**" (2006), so I won't try. I bet you have seen "Borat" or at least know what it's about. Comedian Sacha Baron Cohen pretends to be Kazakh journalist Borat to provoke real people. It takes after a long tradition of prank TV shows, except that Cohen never drops the act to let his victims in on the joke. He captures them reacting in terrible ways and then puts it on screen for the world to see. And Cohen pushes much farther into shock material than any TV show ever could.

It's already shocking enough to watch a large naked man masturbate, causing another naked man to attack him and then chase him through a hotel – all in an R-rated movie, no less. The fact that the hotel is full of actual attendees of a marketing convention, and the actors could easily end up in jail for what they are doing, at least doubles the shock, and therefore the laughs.

The shock is compounded further by the fact that "Borat" was embraced by mainstream America. Just like the "Jackass" boys, Cohen created his own subgenre of shock comedy that no one could copy without appearing derivative. He would use it to make "Brüno" and a "Borat" sequel, both of which are almost as good, and almost as shocking, in my opinion.

Hungary Man

It's time to return to the game of content-based shock one-upsmanship that I've decided was being played by nations from across the world. In 2006, Hungary threw in a surprise bid called **"Taxidermia."**

"Taxidermia" tells three stories from a line of Hungarian men. The first is about a pathetic orderly whose masturbatory fantasies are shown in explicit detail. The second wallows in the grotesque life of an Olympic-level speed-eater. The third lays out a very grim story of a taxidermist who can't help but come across as creepy. The graphic masturbation in the first story qualifies "Taxidermia" as a shocker, but the last shot of the film really clinches it.

"Taxidermia" is meant as a dark comedy, with some of the laughs coming from intentional weirdness. (In case you were wondering, speed eating was never actually an Olympic sport.) I found most of it too dark to even be darkly funny, but I was often impressed with the creativity and filmmaking skill at play.

"Taxidermia" was well-reviewed and Hungary submitted it for the Best Foreign Language Film Academy Award. It did not make the final cut, but it would have been fun if it had. The Academy tends to select Best Foreign Language Film nominees with the same "Oscar bait" profiles as Best Picture nominees: serious, respectable historical dramas that wouldn't feel out of place on "Masterpiece

Theater." Choosing "Taxidermia" would have been a bit like if "Borat" had taken the "hip indie" slot among 2006 Best Picture nominees instead of "Little Miss Sunshine" and then competed with "The Departed," "Babel," "Letters from Iwo Jima," and "The Queen." "Taxidermia" showing up in the Oscars could have at least enlivened a category that too few Americans pay attention to.

The French Up the Stakes

France didn't have time to respond to "Taxidermia" in this international shock arms race that I'm conjuring so I can give this chapter at least some connective tissue. The French were busy countering the U.S.'s torture horror trend. They saw "Saw" and "Hostel" and raised with "**Inside**" (2007) and "**Martyrs**" (2008).

"Inside" is sort of a more upscale, women-centric "Saw." It packs in all the nastiest gore conceivable – if there's one body part that you really don't want to see mutilated, the chances are good that you will see it being mutilated in "Inside." I found the reveal of the killer's motivations kind of lame, but at least it was better than the one in "Saw."

Meanwhile "Martyrs," like "Hostel," has a story that shook me to my core. Writer/director Pascal Laugier reportedly was inspired by "Hostel" to make a movie about pain. He was mired in a severe depressive episode with some suicidal ideation.[717] All this, plus Laugier's Catholic upbringing, combined to produce probably the bleakest movie I've ever seen. I won't spoil it any more except to warn you that even if you get through the torture scenes, you will still have some crushing existential dread to look forward to. I think it's a terrific film, but proceed with caution.

---

[717] Mike Sprague, "This Day in Horror History: Pascal Laugier's MARTYRS Was Released in France in 2008" DreadCentral.com, Sept. 3, 2020, https://www.dreadcentral.com/news/339874/this-day-in-horror-history-pascal-laugiers-martyrs-was-released-in-france-in-2008/

Your Turn, Japan

The United States and France have thrown in their latest testaments to brutality; what can Japan come up with next? How about a movie called "**Tokyo Gore Police**" (2008)?

As the title implies, "Tokyo Gore Police" is not trying to be a sophisticated work of art. It's trying to pack as much gross weirdness as it can into something resembling a movie. Sometimes it would throw out a wacky bit of nonsense that would strike me as funny, but most of "Tokyo Gore Police" just made me feel ill. There are no puppets, but otherwise I was reminded of the way "Meet the Feebles" was mostly about laughing at cruelty, regardless of whether it involves punching up or punching down.

I might not have even brought up "Tokyo Gore Police" if it hadn't been so successful in Japan that it popularized a set of films that some have called "splatterpunk." It's a term that is better known for a type of horror literature, but it fits "Tokyo Gore Police," "Meatball Machine" (2005), "The Machine Girl" (2008), and other low-budget Japanese combinations of over-the-top gore and a sort of weird bio-mechanical body horror first seen in the 1989 movie "Tetsuo: The Iron Man." I'm hoping that by squeezing "Tokyo Gore Police" into this book I have fulfilled my duty and don't need to see any more splatterpunk.

Doc Shocks

Let's cleanse our palates with something respectable, like a documentary. "**Dear Zachary: A Letter to a Son About His Father**" (2008) does not set out to be a shock film, unlike almost every other movie in this chapter. It is director Kurt Kuenne's heartfelt tribute to his late friend Andrew Bagby.

The story takes a very shocking turn. I don't want to oversell it, but its reveal could be the most shattering moment I've ever seen in a movie. Then by some miracle, the ending finds some measure of redemption and warmth that I'm tearing up just thinking about. Watching "Dear Zachary" was one of the most emotionally overwhelming experiences of my life.

That's not what people have traditionally expected from documentaries. Before around the turn of the millennium they were seen as dry, intellectual chores to endure for your own good. Even the ones that gained wide popular appeal, like Ken Burns' series about the Civil War, aim more to educate viewers about an important topic than to push them through an emotionally wrenching story arc. Most of the genuine documentaries I've covered in this book, including "Le sang des bêtes," "Night and Fog" and "The House Is Black," don't really have any kind of narrative at all. They deliver powerful sights in service of a message about some real-life issue.

No one turns on "Dear Zachary" because of the societal importance of Andrew Bagby, who was known only for the events detailed in the film. It belongs in a different subgenre of documentaries about people who might make news reports but not history books. "Sick: The Life and Death of Bob Flanagan, Supermasochist" is another example. Errol Morris is the master of these sorts of documentaries: I perhaps could have included his film "Mr. Death: The Rise and Fall of Fred A. Leuchter, Jr." (1999), a character study of a very strange man who made some shockingly awful choices. "Marwencol" (2010) is another personal favorite; do not judge it by Robert Zemeckis' cutesy-fied bastardization of the same story, "Welcome to Marwen" (2018). "Crumb" (1994) is one of my top 5 favorite movies ever.

These narrative, non-educational documentaries are experiencing a golden age as I write this. Most take the form of mini-series on streaming services about true crime or cults: "The Jinx," "Making a Murderer," "Wild Wild Country," "Tiger King," etc. They reliably deliver shocks that can feel more intense because they involve real people undergoing real events. These series can be trashy, but since they tell true stories, they can impart some truths about human psychology and societal problems (except maybe "Tiger

King.") Even if people aren't learning about the Civil War, I think it's a great trend.

Upset by the Dutch

If international notoriety were a main criterion of the scoring system for my shock-movie Olympic event, the Netherlands would come from nowhere to win the gold medal by producing "**The Human Centipede**" (2009). I bet 100 people know its premise for every one who's actually seen it. It is of course about a mad doctor who stitches three people together, mouth to anus.

When I heard about "The Human Centipede," it brought back the feeling I had as a child, of being powerfully repulsed in a wholly negative way by a movie. I didn't even want to hear jokes about the movie's premise. This was well after I'd watched "Sick: The Life and Death of Bob Flanagan, Supermasochist" and many other films with sights you "can't unsee," in the parlance of internet wags. After I got a little more tolerant of the premise of "The Human Centipede," I read a synopsis of "The Human Centipede 2: Full Sequence," and that bad old feeling returned.

One night during my disturbing-film-watching phase that also introduced me to "The Last House on the Left," "Hellraiser," and, in the end, "Caligula," I had a few drinks and psyched myself up to face "The Human Centipede." It felt like I was taking a big step in getting past an irrational fear, like an arachnophobe touching a spider.

I was surprised to discover that "The Human Centipede" is a rather serious, straightforward horror film and not the blatantly provocative gross-out-fest that I expected. (That would prove to be the approach taken by the sequel.) It has more message-based shock, in the form of its premise, than content-based shock. And the actor playing the mad doctor, Dieter Laser, is truly terrifying. If you're a horror fan, give "The Human Centipede" a try. Even if you don't like it, you can at least brag that you've seen it when people bring it up. (And don't bother with the sequel, which is little more than a feature-length "Guinea Pig" movie.)

Back to the European Shock Auteurs

I guess "The Human Centipede" director Tom Six is technically a shock auteur. But because that word is French, I feel like I should reserve it for the fancy-pants high-status art-film types. Lars von Trier is a full-fledged auteur of international renown/notoriety. After co-founding the Dogme 95 movement and directing its second film, "Idioterne," aka "The Idiots," he pushed far outside its strictures to make several other intensely painful movies.

"**Antichrist**" (2009) is about as un-Dogme-95 as a film can be without starring the Transformers. It is loaded with bizarre imagery and several major shock shots. One self-mutilation is so horrific that it may well overwhelm the rest of the film. It's a body part I'd never even considered seeing destroyed in a film before. Beyond that, the power of its impact derives from the climax it provides in a character's swelling psychosis.

In an interview about "Antichrist," von Trier's take was "it's not so horrific ... we didn't try so hard to do shocks, and that is maybe why it is not a horror film."[718] It sure seemed like a horror movie to me, but maybe he's going by some technical definition that the movie doesn't fulfill. Nothing in the article indicates what the hell he's talking about when he says they didn't try to "do shocks." Maybe he's saying that the shocks came about organically and weren't of the contrived "cat scare" type that fill horror movies?

It's clear at least that "Antichrist" did not arise from a desire to crank out a simple horror movie. Von Trier wrote and directed the film while he was mired in a depressive episode so deep he was often unable to work. Per his typical m.o., he channeled all his pain

---

[718] Quoted in Macaulay, Scott (2009). "Civilization and its discontents". *Filmmaker*. 18 (Fall).

through a female character, played in "Antichrist" by Charlotte Gainsbourg.

Von Trier frequently forces his female protagonists through such extreme gauntlets of suffering that to many viewers he comes across as a sadistic, misogynistic puppetmaster. At the minimum, he exploits the presumption that women are more vulnerable to wring more pathos out of their ordeals. "Dogville" (2003) seems to have little other purpose I can see.

On the other hand, von Trier puts sympathetic, complex female characters at the centers of his films, giving actresses the kind of meaty roles that usually go to men. Gainsbourg won the Best Actress Award at the Cannes Film Festival for her work in "Antichrist." Björk and Kirsten Dunst won the same award for their performances in the von Trier films "Dancer in the Dark" and "Melancholia," respectively. Emily Watson probably would have won the Best Actress Oscar for "Breaking the Waves" in 1996 if Frances McDormand hadn't defined the Platonic ideal of a Minnesotan that year in "Fargo."

In the same interview about "Antichrist" that I cited before, von Trier deflects any suggestion that he might hate women by saying,

> "Okay. I have lots of respect [for women]. Sometimes I hate a certain woman. You can hate certain women. But, you know, hating women altogether doesn't make sense. I don't know if this is right, but I believe that I somehow portray myself better in women maybe because I always was the tiny guy in the school who couldn't fight, who couldn't do anything. So maybe it's kind of my big female side that is being portrayed. I don't know. But the men in these same films are always idiots for some reason, which is also a side of me that I understand. The men are typically representing civilization, in some form, and women are then representing

nature. And this is very banal, but somehow it makes sense for me. It works well for me."[719]

<SPOILER ALERT>

"Antichrist" complicates this dynamic further when Gainsbourg's character is consumed by a twisted, violent misogyny that she has been secretly exploring all along. So if von Trier routinely expresses his so-called "big female side" through his female character, and in this movie his female character wants to hurt women, including herself, it's easy to conclude that he's acting out some latent misogyny.

I don't think it's as cut-and-dried as that, though. Von Trier may also have been acting out the self-hatred he felt during his deep depressive state, in particular his hatred of his "big female side." Speaking as someone who has been through some depressive episodes of my own, I can attest that despising your own sensitivity is a big part of it. You fantasize about destroying that side of yourself just for the relief of feeling numb.

Conceptualizing your own sensitivity as feminine is sexist, but it's not like von Trier invented that from whole cloth. It's woven throughout Western culture. Von Trier may not work to counteract this old stereotype, but at least he uses it to create empathy for this femininity/nature/sensitivity matrix in most of his movies.

In "Antichrist," though, the woman, and nature, for that matter, eventually become villainous. It was clearer in his previous films that the brutality was caused by his "idiot men representing civilization." The woman's husband, played by Willem Defoe, is idiotic in some ways, but in the end he is the hero. So "Antichrist" is problematic, which adds message-based shock value to its already potent content-based shocks.

---

[719] Quoted in ibid

</SPOILER ALERT>

2009 also served as an international coming-out party for another elite shock auteur, Yorgos Lanthimos. His second feature, **"Dogtooth,"** portrays a bizarre family in which the parents have never let their teenaged boy and two teenaged girls leave their property. The parents attempt to block out every hint of the outside world, even making up new definitions of words for things their kids are not allowed to see; e.g., they define "sea" as "armchair" and "motorway" as "strong wind."

The one outside influence the parents permit is a woman they hire to come to the house and have sex with their son. This reveal is all the more shocking in the context of this radically conservative and overprotective family, but it's not a complete non sequitur. I could buy that an arch-conservative family would want to make sure that their son is able to release his sexual urges but not consider that their daughters might as well. This proves to be their downfall, as the daughters explore sexuality in any form that is available to them, and then rebel in other ways.

If you loved the Yorgos Lanthimos films "The Favourite" (2018) and/or "Poor Things" (2023), you might not actually like "Dogtooth" all that much. "Dogtooth" is more spare in every way, with ordinary settings and blank-faced, under-emoting characters. It's more in line with "The Lobster" (2009) and "The Killing of a Sacred Deer" (2017), except without charismatic movie stars. I recommend "Dogtooth" to anyone who liked the odd, cold tone of those two movies. If you've only seen "The Favourite" and/or "Poor Things," maybe start with "The Lobster" and then decide if you're up for "Dogtooth."

What About the Internet?

Meanwhile, as we cinephiles compare tones of Yorgos Lanthimos movies, the rest of the world is online. As I mentioned at the end of the last chapter, 75% of Americans had internet access by 2007. They had long been going to the Web for almost everything, including every kind of pornography, from models in bikinis to hard-core and beyond.

"Beyond" in this case includes "2 Girls 1 Cup," a scat-fetish porn film that became an internet phenomenon in 2007. The phenomenon wasn't about the actual movie as much as it was about watching reaction videos of people gagging with disgust while it played off-camera. Everyone got into the act, including celebrities like Wyclef Jean and Joe Rogan. After *Esquire* magazine made George Clooney watch it, he said, "It's like the rodeo -- see how long you can last.".[720]

I didn't put "2 Girls 1 Cup" in bold type because I haven't seen it. I decided that I don't have to because it's more of an Internet meme than a movie. Maybe that's a shaky rationalization, but I'm sorry y'all, I'm hitting a wall here.

Soon after the internet was overtaken by pornography of all kinds came shock-for-shock's-sake gore of the "Faces of Death"/"Guinea Pig" variety. Rotten.com, Ogrish.com, Goatse.cx, and others collected especially grisly and disturbing images and consistently landed in legal trouble. As video streaming technology got better and better, up sprung "Faces of Death"-style compilations of video-based shocks, like "Snuff R73" and "MDPOPE: Most Disturbed Person on Planet Earth," and a Reddit community called r/watchpeopledie. I'm just going by what I've heard here; I have not seen any of these apart from a few glimpses of Rotten.com 20 years ago. Again, I'm classifying it all as Internet stuff, not movies, so I don't have to deal with it.

The Internet co-opted all kinds of extreme shock content, as it did for most everything. If you really want to be shocked by some specific thing, you can find it somewhere online. It might take some

---

[720] A.J. Jacobs, "The 9:10 to Crazyland." *Esquire*, March 17, 2018, https://web.archive.org/web/20090415222259/http://www.esquire.com/features/george-clooney-2-girls-1-cup-0408-3

digging depending on what it is. As long as it involves consenting adults, that's your business. I'll have to pass.

When I write things like that, I wonder if I sound like the Grumpy Old Men of the 1910s who were shaken by movies because they didn't grow up with them. I was 18 when I first logged onto the internet and I'm on it all the time, but it still doesn't really feel like my world. That's largely because I avoid social media. In my experience, social media makes it too easy for lizard brains to break free from systems of morality and empathy and start hurting people. Maybe someday some young digital native can write their own shock-media history that is full of memes. I feel like I've done plenty.

The Last Movie

In that spirit, I decided to break from my longstanding rule and watch only the censored version of the final shock film of this book, "**A Serbian Film**" (2010). It's about an aging porn star who gets roped into performing for an evil film production company that makes snuff films, child pornography, and every other filmable atrocity. Several minutes of footage were removed to get "A Serbian Film" down to the NC-17-rated version I saw.

The unrated "A Serbian Film" is not banned in the United States but it is illegal in many countries. A court banned it in Spain just before its debut at a film festival. After it was shown at an adults-only screening at a different film festival, the festival director was arrested for exhibiting child pornography. The prosecutor was tipped off by a Catholic organization that had heard about a scene referred to as "newborn porn." The case was later dropped, but it had a chilling effect on other attempts to exhibit "A Serbian Film."[721]

The unrated version is not easy to find streaming but you can buy a DVD of it. Along with all the internet stuff I mentioned in the previous section, the prospect of having to buy and watch the unrated "A

---

[721] Eric Pape, "So Scandalous a Prosecutor Took Notice". *The New York Times*. May 12, 2011

Serbian Film" proved a tipping point for me in writing this book. I had heard about the "newborn porn" scene. Of course an actual newborn is not raped, but do I even want to see what this could mean? And do I want to pay money to own a DVD of it? Even if I found some way to justify it to myself, would I end up on some sort of government watchlist for buying this movie? I decided I'd rather just designate the NC-17 cut as a stopping point for this book than watch the unrated one.

The NC-17 version of "A Serbian Film" apparently lost most of the "newborn porn" scene. Other scenes of sexual violence remain very graphic. The movie's story is mostly in service of the shock scenes, I feel. It reminded me of Mario Bava describing how his giallo film "A Bay of Blood" came to be: He and screenwriter Dardano Sacchetti came up with a basic premise and then conjured up 13 creatively gory kills. Then they wrote a story that would accommodate all those kills. In terms of storytelling technique, this is putting the cart before the horse. But Bava knew that the exploitation films he was making were mere delivery systems for shock scenes. I think "A Serbian Film" has a more sensical plot than "A Bay of Blood," but not by a ton.

In response to the controversy "A Serbian Film" generated, its filmmakers tossed out a lot of furious justifications, mostly about it being a revolt against political correctness. This is the excuse people always hide behind after they've offended people, but there might be more to it in this case. To these filmmakers, "political correctness" denoted an artistic atmosphere specific to Serbia at the time, in which financiers from elsewhere in Europe only supported films that were inoffensive and/or focused on contrition for the country's role in the Balkan Wars.[722]

Few viewers outside Serbia will understand this context, of course. Even if they did, I doubt many would think it justifies "A Serbian

---

[722] Velimir Grgić, "Ovdje će te cijeniti jedino kad crkneš," TPortal.hr, March 12, 2009, https://www.tportal.hr/magazin/clanak/ovdje-ce-te-cijeniti-jedino-kad-crknes-20090310

Film" going so far with so many different horrific vignettes. In the end, it's just a grim and mostly straight-faced exploitation film with relatively high production values.

"A Serbian Film" should probably win the shock Olympics of this chapter, and maybe the whole book. Congrats, I guess? Sigh. "A Serbian Film" has deflated this whole enterprise for me.

Besides the obvious nausea induced by the shock scenes, I think "A Serbian Film" also taps into my fear of the justly forbidden underworld of illegal sexual abuse that hides in the depths of the internet. The movie's evil film production company isn't explicitly cited as based on the internet, but it's a fair assumption that that's where they would find customers.

Maybe this hints at a passing of the torch. As the only feature film I'm aware of that had to be cut to get down to an NC-17, "A Serbian Film" could elucidate the boundary between what can be shown on film and what can happen in the mostly lawless world of the dark web. I don't think any subsequent theatrical film went as far into forbidden territory. "A Serbian Film" could represent the last, flailing death throes of shock film as the internet finally took full control of the market for shock material.

That's probably a bit dramatic. People declaring the end of any cultural movement almost always sound hyperbolic in retrospect. Baby boomers were wailing "Rock is dead!" in the early 1980s, well over 20 years before it actually settled into the niche musical genre akin to jazz that it is now.

Still, I can't help but think that shock films after 2010 are a little like rock hits after around 2005: rare and derivative. There are a few movies I know I would cover if I had to: "Human Centipede 2 (Full Sequence)" (2011), "The ABCs of Death" (2012), "Blue Is the Warmest Color" (2013), "mother!" (2017), etc. I could probably make a laundry list of these movies, relate the controversies surrounding them, connect them to previous shock films, etc. That wouldn't be worthless. I just doubt I'll be able to tease out any overarching narratives from them, not that this chapter had many of those.

So I'm done. I'm going out with a whimper, appropriately. I've seen so many shocking films that I want to cower in a corner for a few years. Maybe I'll watch nothing but Muppet movies until I feel better. Clearly all the sex, violence, blasphemy, cursing, etc. I've seen has warped my soul. Why won't someone do something about these movies? Won't someone think of the children? And what about the immigrants? And illiterates?

Afterword

This book is like a scrappy, no-budget independent film. I worked on it whenever I had a spare moment with only a few friends helping out. Maybe a few people will see the end result, but only one in a million of this type becomes a hit. Oh well. It was still a lot of fun to make.

I didn't even attempt to get funding or distribution, i.e. go through the regular publishing system. The prospect of doing so scares me so much that if that were the only option, I wouldn't write at all. Publishing is one of those industries that depends on "networking," i.e., being born into or forcing yourself into the same social circles as the people in power, and then exploiting those relationships for personal gain. I write precisely because I'm too shy to do those sorts of things. If I were extroverted enough to schmooze with strangers, I'd just tell them the stuff knocking around in my head and then feel no need to write it all down.

Even if by some miracle I was able to network successfully, I'd then have to go through the gauntlet of begging and scrounging for an agent, then begging and scrounging for a publisher, and then enduring the criticisms of an editor. My psyche is simply not strong enough to endure all that.

I understand why the publishing industry has to do some form of gatekeeping. There may be a large demand for books, but there is a much, much larger supply of people trying to write them. You have to winnow down the vast pool of authors somehow. I just know myself well enough to know that the extrovert-centric gatekeeping processes the publishing industry uses would probably wreck my already fragile mental health.

There is a danger that if this book sells any copies at all, some established writer could steal the premise, write their own version, and get it published for real. That might sound paranoid, but I'm pretty sure it happened with my last self-published book, "The

Baseball Hall of Fame Corrected." As I was writing it, I emailed some questions and my first few chapters to an established writer named Jay Jaffe and got no response. This was one of my feeble attempts at networking. A few years later Jaffe published a suspiciously similar book, "The Cooperstown Casebook," to much greater success than my version. Even if something similar happens with this book, that still sounds better to me than networking.

So please look at this book as you would a no-budget indie. It might reflect my personal idiosyncrasies. There may be mistakes, either factual or grammatical in this case, that would have been caught by professionals. This definitely describes "The Baseball Hall of Fame Corrected." I've learned from that experience – this one also has fewer digressions and many, many fewer dumb jokes – but it was a positive one overall.

As with my previous book, I'm up for any feedback that will help me write a better second edition. Send any thoughts to chrisekeedei@yahoo.com. But be nice. Whatever you have to say, you can say it with kindness. The internet allows everyone to unleash their inner lizard-brain sociopath from their systems of empathy and morality, but remember that you're talking to a human being, not watching a movie.

List of Official Shock Films

Chapter 2: The Silent Era, 1895-1929

Title	Year	Judgement	Director	Country
Carmencita	1894	watch it; it's very short	Dickson, William K.L.	USA
The Execution of Mary Stuart	1895	watch it; it's very short	Clark, Alfred	USA
House of the Devil	1896	watch it; it's very short	Méliès, Georges	France
Le Coucher de la Mariée	1896	mostly lost; watch it; it's very short	Kirchner, Albert	France
The May Irwin Kiss	1896	watch it; it's very short	Heise, William	USA
After the Ball	1897	watch it; it's very short	Méliès, Georges	France
Orange Blossoms	1897	lost	?	USA
Electrocuting an Elephant	1903	eh, if you're intrigued	Porter, Edwin S.	USA
The Great Train Robbery	1903	watch it; it's very short	Porter, Edwin S.	USA
Night Riders	1908	lost	?	USA
The James Boys of Missouri	1908	lost	Anderson, Gilbert M. 'Broncho Billy'	USA
Hypocrites	1915	eh, if you're intrigued	Weber, Lois	USA
The Birth of a Nation	1915	skip it	Griffith, D.W.	USA

Title	Year	Status	Director	Country
Inspiration	1916	lost	Platt, George Foster	USA
Intolerance	1916	watch it	Griffith, D.W.	USA
Birth Control	1917	lost	Sanger, Margaret	USA
Cleopatra	1917	lost	Edwards, J. Gordon	USA
Spirit of '76	1917	lost	Siegmann, George	USA
Fit to Fight	1918	lost	Griffith, Edward H./ Lewis Milestone	USA
Anders als die Andern	1919	watch it	Oswald, Richard	Germany
Häxan	1922	watch it	Christensen, Benjamin	Sweden
Flaming Youth	1923	mostly lost; eh, if you're intrigued	Dillon, John Francis	USA
Battleship Potemkin	1925	watch it	Eisenstein, Sergei	USSR
Strike	1925	watch it	Eisenstein, Sergei	USSR
Bed and Sofa	1927	watch it	Room, Abram	USSR
Is Your Daughter Safe?	1927	lost	King, Louis/Leon Lee	USA
Pandora's Box	1929	watch it	Pabst, G.W.	Germany
Un chien andalou	1929	watch it	Buñuel, Luis/Salvador Dali	France
L'Age d'or	1930	watch it	Buñuel, Luis	France

Chapter 3: The Pre-Code Era, 1929-1934

Title	Year	Judgement	Director	Country
The Cock-Eyed World	1929	skip it	Walsh, Raoul	USA
Barnacle Bill	1930	watch it	Fleischer, Dave/ Rudy Zamora	USA
Hell's Angels	1930	eh, if you're intrigued	Hughes, Howard/ Edmund Goulding/ James Whale	USA
Ingagi	1930	skip it	Campbell, William	USA
Morocco	1930	watch it	von Sternberg, Josef	USA
The Blue Angel	1930	watch it	von Sternberg, Josef	Germany
The Divorcee	1930	watch it	Leonard, Robert Z.	USA
Frankenstein	1931	watch it	Whale, James	USA
M	1931	watch it	Lang, Fritz	Germany
Mädchen in Uniform	1931	watch it	Sagan, Leontine/ Carl Froelich	USA
Night Nurse	1931	watch it	Wellman, William A.	USA
The Public Enemy	1931	watch it	Wellman, William A.	USA
Freaks	1932	watch it	Browning, Tod	USA
Island of Lost Souls	1932	watch it	Kenton, Erle C.	USA

Land Without Bread	1932	eh, if you're intrigued	Buñuel, Luis	Spain
Merrily We Go to Hell	1932	watch it	Arzner, Dorothy	USA
One Hour With You	1932	watch it	Lubitsch, Ernst	USA
Red-Headed Woman	1932	watch it	Conway, Jack	USA
Scarface	1932	watch it	Hawks, Howard/ Richard Rosson	USA
The Sign of the Cross	1932	eh, if you're intrigued	DeMille, Cecil B.	USA
Ann Vickers	1933	eh, if you're intrigued	Cromwell, John	USA
Baby Face	1933	watch it	Green, Alfred E.	USA
Convention City	1933	lost	Mayo, Archie	USA
Design for Living	1933	watch it	Lubitsch, Ernst	USA
Ecstasy	1933	watch it	Machaty, Gustav	Czechoslovakia
Elysia (Valley of the Nude)	1933	skip it	Harbaugh, Carl	USA
I'm No Angel	1933	watch it	Ruggles, Wesley	USA
Queen Christina	1933	eh, if you're intrigued	Mamoulian, Rouben	USA
She Done Him Wrong	1933	watch it	Sherman, Lowell	USA

Title	Year	Judgement	Director	Country
The Story of Temple Drake	1933	watch it	Roberts, Stephen	USA
Cleopatra	1934	eh, if you're intrigued	DeMille, Cecil B.	USA
Murder at the Vanities	1934	skip it	Leisen, Mitchell	USA
The Scarlet Empress	1934	watch it	von Sternberg, Josef	USA

Chapter 4: The Code Era, 1934-1948

Title	Year	Judgement	Director	Country
Maniac	1934	watch it	Esper, Dwain	USA
The Goddess	1934	watch it	Wu Yonggang	China
Lash of the Penitentes	1936	skip it	Price Roland/Harry Revier	USA
Marihuana	1936	eh, if you're intrigued	Esper, Dwain	USA
Child Bride	1938	skip it	Revier, Harry	USA
La Bête humaine	1938	watch it	Renoir, Jean	France
Olympia	1938	eh, if you're intrigued	Riefenstahl, Leni	Germany
The Birth of a Baby	1938	eh, if you're intrigued	?	USA
The Outlaw	1943	skip it	Hughes, Howard/ Howard Hawks	USA
Mom and Dad	1945	watch it	Beaudine, William	USA
Song of the South	1946	skip it	Foster, Harve/ Wilfred Jackson	USA

Title	Year	Judgement	Director	Country
Fireworks	1947	watch it	Anger, Kenneth	USA
Monsieur Verdoux	1947	watch it	Chaplin, Charles	USA
Germany, Year Zero	1948	watch it	Rossellini, Roberto	Italy
The Miracle (part of L'Amore")	1948	watch it	Rossellini, Roberto	Italy
Forbidden Films	2014	watch it	Moeller, Felix	Germany
Sex Madness Revealed	2018	watch it	Kirk, Tim	USA

Chapter 5: The Transitional Era, Part 1, 1949-1959

Title	Year	Judgement	Director	Country
Le sang des bêtes	1949	watch it	Franju, Georges	France
Un chant d'amour	1950	watch it	Genet, Jean	France
La ronde	1951	watch it	Ophüls, Max	France
Native Son	1951	eh, if you're intrigued	Chenal, Pierre	USA
Olivia	1951	watch it	Audry, Jacqueline	France
Pool of London	1951	watch it	Dearden, Basil	UK
Summer with Monika	1952	watch it	Bergman, Ingmar	Sweden
Glen or Glenda	1953	watch it	Wood, Ed	USA

Title	Year	Judgement	Director	Country
Niagara	1953	eh, if you're intrigued	Hathaway, Henry	USA
The French Line	1953	skip it	Bacon, Lloyd	USA
The Moon Is Blue	1953	eh, if you're intrigued	Preminger, Otto	USA
Garden of Eden	1954	skip it	Nosseck, Max	USA
Lady Chatterley's Lover	1955	watch it	Allégret, Marc	France
Night and Fog	1955	watch it	Resnais, Alain	France
Teaserama	1955	skip it	Klaw, Irving	USA
The Man with the Golden Arm	1955	watch it	Preminger, Otto	USA
And God Created Woman	1956	eh, if you're intrigued	Vadim, Roger	France
Baby Doll	1956	eh, if you're intrigued	Kazan, Elia	USA
The Lovers	1958	watch it	Malle, Louis	France
Anatomy of a Murder	1959	watch it	Preminger, Otto	USA
Suddenly, Last Summer	1959	eh, if you're intrigued	Mankiewicz, Joseph L.	USA
The Immoral Mr. Teas	1959	eh, if you're intrigued	Meyer, Russ	USA
Window Water Baby Moving	1959	watch it	Brakhage, Stan	USA

Chapter 6: The Transitional Era, Part 2, 1960-1968

Title	Year	Judgement	Director	Country

Black Sunday	1960	eh, if you're intrigued	Bava, Mario	Italy
La Dolce Vita	1960	watch it	Fellini, Federico	Italy
Les yeux sans visage	1960	watch it	Franju, Georges	France
Peeping Tom	1960	watch it	Powell, Michael	UK
Psycho	1960	watch it	Hitchcock, Alfred	USA
The Children's Hour	1961	eh, if you're intrigued	Wyler, William	USA
The Connection	1961	watch it	Clarke, Shirley	USA
Victim	1961	watch it	Dearden, Basil	UK
Viridiana	1961	watch it	Buñuel, Luis	Spain
Lolita	1962	eh, if you're intrigued	Kubrick, Stanley	UK
Mondo Cane	1962	eh, if you're intrigued	Cavara, Paolo/ Gualtiero Jacopetti/ Franco Prosperi	Italy
Blood Feast	1963	skip it	Lewis, Herschell Gordon	USA
Flaming Creatures	1963	eh, if you're intrigued	Smith, Jack	USA
La ricotta (part of "Ro.Go.Pa.G.")	1963	watch it	Pasolini, Pier Paolo	Italy
Promises … Promises	1963	skip it	Donovan, King	USA
Scorpio Rising	1963	watch it	Anger, Kenneth	USA
The House Is Black	1963	watch it	Farrokhzad, Forugh	Iran

Title	Year	Rating	Director	Country
The Silence	1963	eh, if you're intrigued	Bergman, Ingmar	Sweden
491	1964	eh, if you're intrigued	Sjöman, Vilgot	Sweden
2,000 Maniacs!	1964	eh, if you're intrigued	Lewis, Herschell Gordon	USA
Blood and Black Lace	1964	watch it	Bava, Mario	Italy
Kiss Me, Stupid	1964	eh, if you're intrigued	Wilder, Billy	USA
Lorna	1964	skip it	Meyer, Russ	USA
Loving Couples	1964	watch it	Zetterling, Mai	Sweden
Mama and Papa	1964	eh, if you're intrigued	Kren, Kurt	Austria
The Pawnbroker	1964	watch it	Lumet, Sidney	USA
Bad Girls Go to Hell	1965	eh, if you're intrigued	Wishman, Doris	USA
The Defilers	1965	skip it	Frost, Lee/David F. Friedman	USA
Blow-Up	1966	eh, if you're intrigued	Antonioni, Michelangelo	Italy
Chelsea Girls	1966	skip it	Warhol, Andy	USA
Night Games	1966	watch it	Zetterling, Mai	Sweden
Persona	1966	watch it	Bergman, Ingmar	Sweden
The Nun	1966	watch it	Rivette, Jacques	France
The Pornographers	1966	watch it	Imamura Shôhei	Japan
The Wild Angels	1966	skip it	Corman, Roger	USA
Who's Afraid of Virginia Woolf?	1966	watch it	Nichols, Mike	USA

Belle de Jour	1967	watch it	Buñuel, Luis	France
Bonnie and Clyde	1967	watch it	Penn, Arthur	USA
The Fox	1967	eh, if you're intrigued	Rydell, Mark	Canada
The Trip	1967	watch it	Corman, Roger	USA
Titicut Follies	1967	watch it	Wiseman, Frederick	USA
Ulysses	1967	eh, if you're intrigued	Strick, Joseph	UK
Flesh	1968	watch it	Morrissey, Paul	USA
Night of the Living Dead	1968	watch it	Romero, George A.	USA
Rosemary's Baby	1968	watch it	Polanski, Roman	USA
Targets	1968	watch it	Bogdanovich, Peter	USA
The Killing of Sister George	1968	eh, if you're intrigued	Aldrich, Robert	USA
The Queen	1968	watch it	Simon, Frank	USA
Therese and Isabelle	1968	eh, if you're intrigued	Metzger, Radley	Netherlands
Vixen!	1968	eh, if you're intrigued	Meyer, Russ	USA

Chapter 7: The New Freedoms, 1969-1977

Title	Year	Judgement	Director	Country
I Am Curious (Yellow)	1967	eh, if you're intrigued	Sjöman, Vilgot	Sweden

Title	Year	Recommendation	Director	Country
A Thousand and One Nights	1969	eh, if you're intrigued	Yamamoto, Eiichi	Japan
Age of Consent	1969	skip it	Powell, Michael	UK
Blue Movie	1969	skip it	Warhol, Andy	USA
Easy Rider	1969	watch it	Hopper, Dennis	USA
Fellini Satyricon	1969	watch it	Fellini, Federico	Italy
Funeral Parade of Roses	1969	watch it	Matsumoto, Toshio	Japan
Porcile	1969	watch it	Pasolini, Pier Paolo	Italy
The Damned	1969	watch it	Visconti, Luchino	Italy
The Wild Bunch	1969	watch it	Peckinpah, Sam	USA
Beyond the Valley of the Dolls	1970	watch it	Meyer, Russ	USA
El Topo	1970	eh, if you're intrigued	Jodorowsky, Alejandro	Mexico
Multiple Maniacs	1970	watch it	Waters, John	USA
Myra Breckinridge	1970	eh, if you're intrigued	Sarne, Michael	USA
Solder Blue	1970	eh, if you're intrigued	Nelson, Ralph	USA
The Boys in the Band	1970	watch it	Friedkin, William	USA
The Student Nurses	1970	eh, if you're intrigued	Rothman, Stephanie	USA
Watermelon Man	1970	eh, if you're intrigued	Van Peebles, Melvin	USA
Trash	1970	watch it	Morrissey, Paul	USA

Zabriskie Point	1970	watch it	Antonioni, Michelangelo	USA
A Clockwork Orange	1971	watch it, but beware	Kubrick, Stanley	UK
Shaft	1971	watch it	Parks Jr., Gordon	USA
Straw Dogs	1971	watch it, but beware	Peckinpah, Sam	USA
Sweet Sweetback's Baadasssss Song	1971	watch it, but beware	Van Peebles, Melvin	USA
The Act of Seeing with One's Own Eyes	1971	eh, if you're intrigued	Brakhage, Stan	USA
The Decameron	1971	watch it	Pasolini, Pier Paolo	Italy
The Devils	1971	watch it, but beware	Russell, Ken	UK
Viva la Muerte	1971	eh, if you're intrigued	Arrabal, Fernando	France
W.R.: Mysteries of the Organism	1971	watch it	Makavejev, Dusan	Yugoslavia
Wake in Fright	1971	watch it	Kotcheff, Ted	Australia
Behind the Green Door	1972	eh, if you're intrigued	Mitchell, Artie/ Jim Mitchell	USA
Deep Throat	1972	skip it	Damiano, Gerard	USA
Deliverance	1972	watch it	Boorman, John	USA
Frenzy	1972	eh, if you're intrigued	Hitchcock, Alfred	UK

Fritz the Cat	1972	eh, if you're intrigued	Bakshi, Ralph	USA
Last Tango in Paris	1972	skip it	Bertolucci, Bernardo	France
Pink Flamingos	1972	watch it, but beware	Waters, John	USA
The Canterbury Tales	1972	watch it	Pasolini, Pier Paolo	Italy
The Last House on the Left	1972	watch it, but beware	Craven, Wes	USA
Belladonna of Sadness	1973	watch it	Yamamoto, Eiichi	Japan
Flesh for Frankenstein	1973	watch it	Morrissey, Paul	USA
I Will Walk Like a Crazy Horse	1973	eh, if you're intrigued	Arrabal, Fernando	France
The Devil in Miss Jones	1973	eh, if you're intrigued	Damiano, Gerard	USA
The Exorcist	1973	watch it	Friedkin, William	USA
The Holy Mountain	1973	watch it	Jodorowsky, Alejandro	Mexico
Thriller: A Cruel Picture	1973	eh, if you're intrigued	Vibenius, Bo Arne	Sweden
Arabian Nights	1974	watch it	Pasolini, Pier Paolo	Italy
Emmanuelle	1974	skip it	Jaeckin, Just	France
Female Trouble	1974	watch it	Waters, John	USA
Sweet Movie	1974	eh, if you're intrigued, but beware	Makavejev, Dusan	France

The Night Porter	1974	eh, if you're intrigued	Cavani, Liliana	Italy
The Street Fighter	1974	watch it	Ozawa Shigehiro	Japan
The Texas Chain Saw Massacre	1974	watch it	Hooper, Tobe	USA
Vase de Noces	1974	skip it	Zéno, Thierry	Belgium
Coonskin	1975	skip it	Bakshi, Ralph	USA
Ilsa, She Wolf of the SS	1975	skip it	Edmonds, Don	Canada
Salo, or the 120 Days of Sodom	1975	watch it, but beware	Pasolini, Pier Paolo	Italy
The Beast	1975	skip it	Borowczyk, Walerian	France
A Real Young Girl	1976	watch it	Breillat, Catherine	France
Fellini's Casanova	1976	watch it	Fellini, Federico	Italy
In the Realm of the Senses	1976	watch it	Ôshima, Nagisa	Japan
Maîtresse	1976	watch it	Schroeder, Barbet	France
Snuff	1976	skip it	Findlay, Michael/ Horacio Fredriksson/ Simon Nuchtern	USA
Taxi Driver	1976	watch it	Scorsese, Martin	USA
Desperate Living	1977	watch it	Waters, John	USA

Chapter 8: Post-Peak Synthesis, 1978-1980

Title	Year	Judgement	Director	Country
Faces of Death	1978	skip it	Schwartz, John Alan	USA
I Spit on Your Grave	1978	eh, if you're intrigued, but beware	Zarchi, Meir	USA
In a Year with 13 Moons	1978	watch it	Fassbinder, Rainer Warner	West Germany
Let Me Die a Woman	1978	eh, if you're intrigued, but beware	Wishman, Doris	USA
Pretty Baby	1978	watch it	Malle, Louis	USA
Caligula	1979	skip it	Brass, Tinto	Italy
Hardcore	1979	watch it	Schrader, Paul	USA
Monty Python's Life of Brian	1979	watch it	Jones, Terry	UK
Mr. Mike's Mondo Video	1979	eh, if you're intrigued	O'Donoghue, Michael	USA
The Tin Drum	1979	watch it	Schlöndorff, Volker	West Germany
Cannibal Holocaust	1980	eh, if you're intrigued, but beware	Deodato, Ruggero	Italy
The Blue Lagoon	1980	skip it	Kleiser, Randal	USA
Caligula: The Ultimate Cut	2023	watch it	Brass, Tinto	Italy

Chapter 9: The Reagan Era, 1980-1989

Title	Year	Judgement	Director	Country
Cruising	1980	eh, if you're intrigued	Friedkin, William	USA
Dressed to Kill	1980	eh, if you're intrigued	De Palma, Brian	USA
Pixote	1980	watch it	Babenco, Hector	Brazil
Christiane F.	1981	watch it	Edel, Uli	West Germany
Porky's	1981	skip it	Clark, Bob	Canada
Roar	1981	watch it	Marshall, Noel	USA
The Evil Dead	1981	watch it	Raimi, Sam	USA
Eating Raoul	1982	watch it	Bartel, Paul	USA
The Thing	1982	watch it	Carpenter, John	USA
Videodrome	1983	watch it	Cronenberg, David	Canada
Crimes of Passion	1984	watch it	Russell, Ken	USA
Silent Night, Deadly Night	1984	eh, if you're intrigued	Sellier Jr., Charles E.	USA
The Toxic Avenger	1984	eh, if you're intrigued	Herz, Michael/ Lloyd Kaufman	USA
Day of the Dead	1985	watch it	Romero, George A.	USA
Guinea Pig: Devil's Experiment	1985	skip it	Ogura Satoru	Japan

Title	Year	Judgement	Director	Country
Guinea Pig: Flower of Flesh and Blood	1985	skip it	Hino Hideshi	Japan
Hail Mary	1985	watch it	Godard, Jean-Luc	France
9 ½ Weeks	1986	skip it	Lyne, Adrian	USA
Blue Velvet	1986	watch it	Lynch, David	USA
Henry: Portrait of a Serial Killer	1986	watch it	McNaughton, John	USA
In a Glass Cage	1986	watch it	Villaronga, Agusti	Spain
Soul Man	1986	skip it	Miner, Steve	USA
Hellraiser	1987	watch it	Barker, Clive	UK
Men Behind the Sun	1988	eh, if you're intrigued, but beware	Mou Tun-Fei	Japan
Nekromantik	1988	skip it	Buttgereit, Jörg	West Germany
The Last Temptation of Christ	1988	watch it	Scorsese, Martin	USA
Meet the Feebles	1989	skip it	Jackson, Peter	New Zealand
Visions of Ecstasy	1989	eh, if you're intrigued	Wingrove, Nigel	UK

Chapter 10: A Slight Swing Back Toward Freedom, 1989-1997

Title	Year	Judgement	Director	Country
Do the Right Thing	1989	watch it	Lee, Spike	USA

Title	Year	Recommendation	Director	Country
Santa Sangre	1989	watch it	Jodorowsky, Alejandro	Mexico
The Cook, The Thief, His Wife, and Her Lover	1989	watch it	Greenaway, Peter	UK
Paris Is Burning	1990	watch it	Livingston, Jennie	USA
Wild at Heart	1990	eh, if you're intrigued	Lynch, David	USA
Poison	1991	watch it	Haynes, Todd	USA
Riki-Oh: The Story of Ricky	1991	watch it	Lam Nai-choi	Hong Kong
Sex and Zen	1991	eh, if you're intrigued	Mak Michael	Hong Kong
The Silence of the Lambs	1991	watch it	Demme, Johnathan	USA
Thelma & Louise	1991	watch it	Scott, Ridley	USA
Bad Lieutenant	1992	watch it	Ferrara, Abel	USA
Basic Instinct	1992	eh, if you're intrigued	Verhoeven, Paul	USA
Braindead	1992	watch it	Jackson, Peter	New Zealand
Natural Born Killers	1994	watch it	Stone, Oliver	USA
Priest	1994	watch it	Bird, Antonia	UK
Kids	1995	watch it	Clark, Larry	USA
Showgirls	1995	eh, if you're intrigued	Verhoeven, Paul	USA
Crash	1996	watch it	Cronenberg, David	Canada
Female Perversions	1996	watch it	Streitfeld, Susan	USA

Title	Year	Judgement	Director	Country
Gummo	1997	eh, if you're intrigued, but beware	Korine, Harmony	USA
Sick: The Life and Death of Bob Flanagan, Supermasochist	1997	eh, if you're intrigued, but beware	Dick, Kirby	USA

Chapter 11: The Shock Auteurs, 1997-2010

Title	Year	Judgement	Director	Country
Funny Games	1997	watch it	Haneke, Michael	Austria
Happiness	1998	watch it	Solondz, Todd	USA
I Stand Alone	1998	eh, if you're intrigued	Noé, Gaspar	France
Idioterne	1998	watch it	von Trier, Lars	Denmark
Audition	1999	watch it	Miike, Takashi	Japan
Fight Club	1999	watch it	Fincher, David	USA
Romance	1999	watch it	Breillat, Catherine	France
South Park: Bigger, Longer and Uncut	1999	watch it	Parker, Matt/Trey Stone	USA
American Psycho	2000	watch it	Harron, Mary	USA
Baise-moi	2000	eh, if you're intrigued	Despentes, Virginie/ Coralie Trinh Thi	France

Title	Year	Recommendation	Director	Country
Battle Royale	2000	eh, if you're intrigued	Fukasaku, Kinji	Japan
Fat Girl	2001	watch it	Breillat, Catherine	France
Ichi the Killer	2001	watch it, but beware	Miike, Takashi	Japan
Storytelling	2001	watch it	Solondz, Todd	USA
The Piano Teacher	2001	watch it	Haneke, Michael	France
Trouble Every Day	2001	watch it	Denis, Claire	France
Visitor Q	2001	eh, if you're intrigued, but beware	Miike, Takashi	Japan
Y tu mamá también	2001	watch it	Cuarón, Alfonso	Mexico
In My Skin	2002	watch it	de Van, Marina	France
Irréversible	2002	watch it, but beware	Noé, Gaspar	France
Jackass: The Movie	2002	watch it	Tremaine, Jeff	USA
Ken Park	2002	eh, if you're intrigued	Clark, Larry	USA
The Brown Bunny	2003	eh, if you're intrigued	Gallo, Vincent	USA
A Dirty Shame	2004	watch it	Waters, John	USA
Mysterious Skin	2004	watch it	Araki, Gregg	USA
Palindromes	2004	watch it	Solondz, Todd	USA
Saw	2004	eh, if you're intrigued	Wan, James	USA

The Passion of the Christ	2004	watch it	Gibson, Mel	USA
Brokeback Mountain	2005	watch it	Lee, Ang	USA
Hostel	2005	watch it	Roth, Eli	USA
The Devil's Rejects	2005	watch it	Zombie, Rob	USA
Borat	2006	watch it	Charles, Larry	USA
Shortbus	2006	watch it	Mitchell, John Cameron	USA
Taxidermia	2006	watch it	Pálfi, György	Hungary
Inside	2007	watch it, but beware	Bustillo, Alexandre/ Julien Maury	France
Dear Zachary: A Letter to a Son About His Father	2008	watch it	Kuenne, Kurt	USA
Martyrs	2008	watch it, but beware	Laugier, Pascal	France
Tokyo Gore Police	2008	skip it	Nishimura Yoshihiro	Japan
Antichrist	2009	watch it, but beware	von Trier, Lars	Denmark
Dogtooth	2009	watch it	Lanthimos, Yorgos	Greece
Human Centipede, The	2009	eh, if you're intrigued	Six, Tom	Netherlands
Serbian Film, A (NC-17 version)	2010	eh, if you're intrigued, but beware	Spasojevic, Srdjan	Serbia

Shock Film Stats

Country	Shock films	Country	Shock films
USA	183	Hong Kong	2
France	36	Netherlands	2
Italy	20	New Zealand	2
Japan	14	Australia	1
UK	14	Belgium	1
Sweden	9	Brazil	1
Germany	6	China	1
Canada	5	Czechoslovakia	1
Mexico	4	Greece	1
West Germany	4	Hungary	1
Spain	3	Iran	1
USSR	3	Serbia	1
Austria	2	Yugoslavia	1
Denmark	2	**Total**	**321**

My judgement	Shock films
eh, if you're intrigued	68
eh, if you're intrigued, but beware	9
lost	10
mostly lost; eh, if you're intrigued	1
mostly lost; watch it; it's very short	1
skip it	39
watch it	175
watch it, but beware	12
watch it; it's very short	6

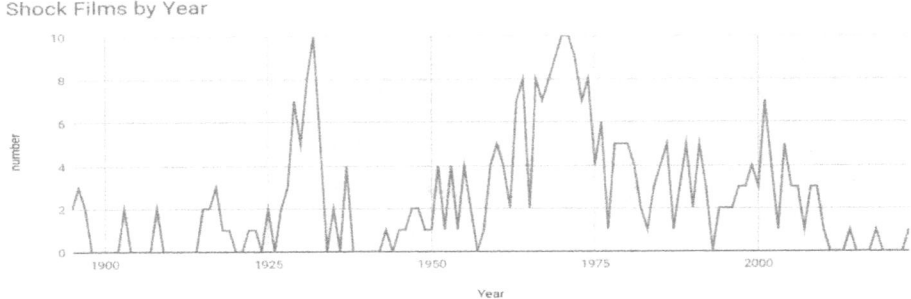

Shock Films by Year

Directors with More than Two Shock Films

Director	Shock films
Pasolini, Pier Paolo	6
Buñuel, Luis	5
Waters, John	5
Meyer, Russ	4
Bergman, Ingmar	3
Breillat, Catherine	3
Fellini, Federico	3
Friedkin, William	3
Hughes, Howard	3
Jodorowsky, Alejandro	3
Miike, Takashi	3
Morrissey, Paul	3
Preminger, Otto	3
Solondz, Todd	3
von Sternberg, Josef	3

Number of times the word "shock" is used in this book (including this one): 794

Index

10, 411
12 Angry Men, 251
1919 Black Sox, 62
2 Girls 1 Cup, 531
2 Live Crew, 471
2,000 Maniacs!, 240, 292
20th Century Fox, 303
366 Weird Movies, 391
491, 256, 257
9 ½ Weeks, 430, 431, 432, 433, 435, 444, 448, 466
A&M Records, 456
ABCs of Death, The, 534
Abduction from the Seraglio, The, 90
Abe, Sada, 365
Academy Award, 73, 93, 186, 195, 196, 224, 232, 237, 251, 267, 268, 269, 277, 278, 284, 293, 336, 374, 378, 398, 464, 465, 474, 515, 522, 523
Accattone, 234
ACLU. See American Civil Liberties Union
Act of Seeing with One's Own Eyes, The, 316, 317
Adult Film Association of America, 340, 356
Adventures of Priscilla, Queen of the Desert, The, 457
After the Ball, 31
Age of Consent, 296
Agrama, Jehan, 466
AIDS crisis, 397
Albee, Edward, 266
Aldrich, Robert, 278
Alfred Hitchcock Presents, 216
Algren, Nelson, 193
Alien, 462
All About Eve, 204
Allied Artists, 252
Almodóvar, Pedro, 450
Alvin Purple, 116, 315
Amadeus, 464
Amazon, 244
American Civil Liberties Union (ACLU), 378
American College of Surgeons, 151
American Committee on Maternal Welfare, Inc., 151
American Family Association, 456
American Film Institute, 48
American Gigolo, 410
American International Pictures, 190, 220, 262
American Nazi Party, 246
American Pie, 469, 503
American Psycho, 106, 506, 507, 508
American Releasing. See American International Pictures
American Society for the Prevention of Cruelty to Animals, The, 33
Anatomy of a Murder, 205, 206, 208, 209, 214
And God Created Woman, 199, 200, 202, 230, 279
Anders als die Andern, 57, 58, 59, 148, 226, 227

561

Anderson, Carolyn, 274
Anderson, Wes, 265
Andersson, Harriet, 198
Andrews, Julie, 411
Anger, Kenneth, 167, 245, 246, 455
Animal House, 389, 411, 412
Animerama, 295, 345
Ann Vickers, 97, 98, 99, 100
Anschütz, Ottmar, 25, 28
Ansen, David, 402
Anthropophagus, 401
Antichrist, 527, 528, 529
Anti-Jewish Youth Group, 83
Antonio des Mortes, 404
Antonioni, Michaelangelo, 270, 297
Apartment, The, 254
Apocalypse Now, 464
Arabian Nights, 324, 368
Araki, Gregg, 457, 519, 520
Arbuckle, Roscoe "Fatty", 61, 62, 65
Argento, Dario, 220
Arkin, Alan, 306
Arkoff, Sam Z., 190
Arrabal, Fernando, 311, 312, 313
Arran, Lord, 227
Arrival of a Train, The, 29
Arzner, Dorothy, 95, 96
Asano, Tadanobu, 501
Asch, Mark, 398
Atrocities: The 100 Deadliest Episodes in Human History, 169
Audition, 500
August Underground, 512
Austin Chronicle, 482
Australian Family Association, 520
Australian New Wave, 315

Australian Office of Film and Literature Classification, 520
Awakenings, 458
Awful Truth, The, 138
Baadasssss!, 309
Babar, 88
Babb, Kroger, 163, 164, 198
Babel, 523
Baby Doll, 196, 197, 198, 254
Baby Face, 120, 121, 128, 135
Bad Girls Go to Hell, 244
Bad Lieutenant, 467, 468
Bad Taste, 439
Bagby, Andrew, 524, 525
Baise-moi, 493, 494, 495, 496
Baker, Josephine, 67
Bakshi, Ralph, 345, 346, 347
Balkan Wars, 533
Bambi, 162
Bamboozled, 435
Banda della Magliana, 327
Bank Dick, The, 75
Banned Films: Movies, Censors, and the First Amendment, 34, 45, 338
Bara, Theda, 51, 60, 63
Barbie, 456
Bardot, Brigitte, 199, 200
Barker, Clive, 436
Barnacle Bill, 103
Bartel, Paul, 412
Baseball Hall of Fame, 66
Baseball Hall of Fame Corrected, The, 537
Basic Instinct, 466, 467, 473, 474
Basinger, Kim, 430, 432
Battle Royale, 501, 502

Battleship Potemkin, 71, 370
Bava, Mario, 220, 533
Bay of Blood, A, 533
Be Pretty and Shut Up. *See* Sois belle et tais toi
Beard, Henry, 388
Beast, The, 362, 363, 364
Beatty, Warren, 268, 269, 340, 341
Beau travail, 496
Bed and Sofa, 72, 117
Bedtime for the Bride. *See* Le Coucher de la Mariée
Behind the Green Door, 335, 336
bel Geddes, Barbara, 177
Bell, Arthur, 397
Belladonna of Sadness, 295
Belle de Jour, 277
Belle of the Nineties, 133
Bellucci, Monica, 498, 499
Belshazzar, 48
Belushi, John, 389
Beneath the Valley of the Supervixens, 306
Ben-Hur, 224
Bergman, Ingmar, 198, 212, 230, 255, 256, 257, 270, 279, 349, 403
Berkeley, Busby, 131
Berkley, Elizabeth, 473
Berle, Milton, 192
Berlin Film Festival, 251
Bernstein, Carl, 334
Bertolucci, Bernardo, 330, 331, 332, 432, 493
Best Dressed Woman in Paris, The, 95
Best Little Whorehouse in Texas, The, 415
Betty Boop, 103, 295

Beyond the Valley of the Dolls, 305, 306, 450, 463
Bible, The, 22, 235, 443, 514
Bicycle Thieves, 171, 172, 184, 185, 186, 187, 194, 208, 230, 232
Big, 458
Big Doll House, The, 300
Bird with the Crystal Plumage, The, 220
Birdcage, The, 457
Birdwell, Russell, 154, 155, 156
Birth Control, 49, 50, 57, 148, 245
Birth of a Baby, The, 151, 152, 154, 162, 211
Birth of a Nation, The, 44, 45, 46, 47, 48, 49, 58, 74, 148, 165, 166, 167, 240, 338
Biskind, Peter, 261, 269, 373
Björk, 528
Black Cauldron, The, 414
Black Panthers, 310
Black Sunday, 220, 239
Blade Runner, 427
Blatty, William Peter, 407
Blaxploitation, 307, 309, 310, 311, 346
Blockbuster Video, 419, 420, 449, 468, 473
Blondell, Joan, 115
Blood and Black Lace, 220
Blood Feast, 239, 240, 292, 398, 403, 415
Blood for Dracula, 347
Blood of the Beasts, 175, 219, 316
Blot, The, 40
Blow-Up, 261, 262, 265, 270, 297

Blue Angel, The, 102, 103, 121
Blue Collar, 381
Blue Is the Warmest Color, 534
Blue Lagoon, The, 382, 383, 384, 385, 386
Blue Movie, 290
Blue Velvet, 427, 428, 429, 430, 431, 435, 462, 463
Bob's Big Boy, 429
Boccaccio, 323
Body Count, 471
Body of a Female, 242
Bogarde, Dirk, 225, 226, 227, 361, 475
Bogdanovich, Peter, 262, 264, 265, 342, 379
Bold! Daring! Shocking! True!, 53, 79, 88, 143
Bonnie and Clyde, 19, 268, 269, 291, 495
Boogie Down Productions, 454
Borat, 521, 522, 523
Born Free, 406
Borowczyk, Walerian, 362, 363, 364
Bottle Rocket, 265
Boudu Saved From Drowning, 240
Bound, 457
Bow, Clara, 72
Bowen, Michael, 244
Bowie, David, 405
Boy Scouts of America, 521
Boys in the Band, The, 302
Boyz N the Hood, 454
Bradley, James A., 25
Brain Dead, 470
Braindead, 470

Brakhage, Stan, 211, 212, 315, 316
Brando, Marlon, 116, 195, 196, 330, 331, 332, 432
Breakfast at Tiffany's, 410
Breaking the Waves, 489, 528
Breathless, 230
Breen, Joseph, 129, 130, 131, 132, 133, 134, 135, 137, 138, 140, 142, 143, 156, 160, 168, 171, 172, 184, 185, 186, 187, 193, 194, 197, 208, 224, 393, 395, 445, 489, 498
Breillat, Catherine, 15, 364, 490, 491, 492, 493, 495, 497, 499, 509
Brennan, Justice William, 200, 288, 338
Breton, André, 82
Brexit, 443
Bridegroom's Dilemma, The. See Le Coucher de la Mariée
British Board of Film Censors, The, 111, 114, 227, 229, 237, 271, 272, 281, 318, 327, 352, 367, 414, 415, 416, 443, 470, 506
Broadcast News, 265
Broeck, Ten, 25
Brokeback Mountain, 515, 516, 517, 518
Brooks, Louise, 80
Brown Bunny, The, 510, 511
Browning, Tod, 112, 114
Bruce, Tammy, 466
Brüno, 522
Bryant, Anita, 397, 399
Buck and the Preacher, 310
Buetel, Jack, 160
Buffalo '66, 510

Buñuel, Juan Luis, 82
Buñuel, Luis, 81, 82, 83, 84, 122, 123, 175, 233, 234, 249, 257, 277, 329, 482
Bureau of Narcotics, 194
Burgess, Anthony, 320, 321
Burns, Ken, 525
Burstyn, Joseph, 171, 173
Burton, Richard, 266
Burton, Tim, 190
Buttgereit, Jörg, 439
Cabin Fever, 513
Cabinet of Dr. Caligari, The, 56
Cage, Nicolas, 396, 463
Cagney, Jimmy, 107
California Supreme Court, 246
Caligula, 390, 391, 392, 411, 526
Call Me Lucky, 484
Calvin Klein, 382
Cambridge University, 386
Cambridge, Godfrey, 307
Campbell, Bruce, 402
Camps of the Dead, 192
Canby, Vincent, 361, 402
Cannes Film Festival, 170, 233, 237, 272, 378, 392, 453, 463, 489, 510, 528
Cannibal Holocaust, 392, 393, 415, 438, 440, 513
Canterbury Tales, The, 324, 368
Capone, Al, 107
Captain Phillips, 150
Carlin, George, 223
Carlisle, Kitty, 132
Carmencita, 25
Carnal Knowledge, 339
Carne, 489
Carpenter, John, 402, 403

Carpenter, Karen, 456
Carrie, 399
Carson, Johnny, 289
Casablanca, 140
Casanova, Giacomo, 368, 369
Castle, William, 285
Catherine the Great, 135
Catholic Church, 27, 83, 84, 89, 97, 118, 119, 129, 130, 132, 136, 157, 197, 233, 235, 236, 267, 319, 324, 442, 475, 477, 521, 523, 532
Catholic League for Religious and Civil Rights, The, 476
Caught, 177
Cecil B. Demented, 508
Celebration, The. See Festen
Censored Hollywood, 223
Chaplin, Charlie, 61, 168, 169
Chariots of Fire, 464
Chase, Chevy, 389
Chelsea Girls, 261, 280, 290
Chevalier, Maurice, 115, 116
Chiba, Sonny, 348
Chicago Board of Censors, The, 51
Chicago City Council, 36
Child Bride, 145, 149, 240, 354, 519
Children's Hour, The, 225, 228, 277
Children's Hour, The (play), 138, 224
China's Film Censorship Law of 1930, 147
Chong, Rae Dawn, 434
Christensen, Benjamin, 67
Christiane F., 404, 405
Christie, Agatha, 427
Church of England, 443

565

Cinema Journal, 159
Cinema Novo, 403
Cinemax, 342
circumplex model of emotion, 14, 479
Circus Maximus, 118
Citizen Kane, 60, 140, 257
Citti, Sergio, 326
Civil War, 70, 75, 165, 240, 525, 526
Clansman, The, 44, 46
Clark, Larry, 509, 510
Clark, Tom C., 173
Clarke, Shirley, 221, 222, 223, 246, 504
Claudine, 310
Cleopatra (1917), 51
Cleopatra (1934), 134, 135
Cleopatra (1963), 250, 266
Cleopatra (1970), 295
Clockwork Orange, A, 320, 321, 322, 334, 362
Clooney, George, 531
Close-Up, 239, 497
Clueless, 458
Cock-Eyed World, The, 86, 87, 89
Cocteau, Jean, 82
Cohen, Rob, 402
Cohen, Sacha Baron, 521
Colbert, Claudette, 118, 119, 134, 135
Columbia, 95, 199, 306, 307, 308, 344
Columbine school massacre, 502
Comedy Central, 503
Communist Party of Spain, 122
Compensating moral values, 91, 92, 93, 99, 100, 107, 109, 114, 119, 120, 133, 135, 262, 351
Confessions of a Driving Instructor, 116
Congress of Racial Equality (CORE), The, 346
Connection, The, 221, 222, 223, 504
Conseil d'État, 495
Convention City, 130
Cook, David A., 35, 47
Cook, The Thief, His Wife, and Her Lover, The, 448, 449
Cooley High, 310
Coolidge, Martha, 396, 457
Coonskin, 346, 347
Cooper, Gary, 102
Cooperstown Casebook, The, 537
Coppola, Francis Ford, 269
Corman, Roger, 154, 190, 220, 262, 270, 283, 298, 299, 300, 410, 417, 421
Cotton Comes to Harlem, 307
Crafts, Wilbur F., 60
Crash (2005), 515
Crash (2006), 478, 480
Craven, Wes, 349, 376
Crawford, Joan, 94, 121
Creature from the Black Lagoon, 218
Crime of Monsieur Lange, The, 150
Crimes of Passion, 420, 421, 448, 449
Criterion, 112, 175, 225, 318, 336, 398, 429, 453
Criterion Reflections, 323
Crocodile Dundee, 455
Cronenberg, David, 413, 429, 478

Crowther, Bosley, 165
Cruising, 397, 398, 399, 401, 444
Crumb, 525
Crumb, R., 345
Cuarón, Alfonso, 500
Cuarón, Carlos, 500
Cukor, George, 304
Cultural Revolution, 71
Cummins, Samuel, 125
Cunningham, Sean S., 349
da Silva, Fernando Ramos, 403, 404
da Vinci, Leonardo, 233
Dali, Salvador, 81, 82, 83, 257, 461
Dalle, Béatrice, 497
Dallesandro, Joe, 280, 300, 301
Dame in the Kimono, 76, 183, 214
Dames, 131
Damned, The, 297, 354
Dancer in the Dark, 489, 528
Dangerfield, Rodney, 471
Daughters of the Dust, 459
Davis, Geena, 458
Davis, Ossie, 307
Dawn of the Dead, 425
Day of the Dead, 425, 426, 448
de Bont, Jan, 408
de Grazia, Edward, 34, 35, 45, 64, 338, 339
De Laurentiis, Dino, 368, 369
De Niro, Robert, 109, 287
de Noailles, Marie-Laurie and Charles, 83, 84
De Palma, Brian, 287, 399, 400, 401
de Sade, Marquis, 325, 326
De Sica, Vittorio, 171, 232

de Van, Marina, 497
Dead Alive. *See* "Braindead"
Dear Zachary: A Letter to a Son About His Father, 524, 525
Death in Venice, 226
Death Trilogy, 325
Decameron, The, 323, 324, 368
Decline of Western Civilization, The, 396
Deep Throat, 333, 334, 335, 336, 338, 340, 341, 344, 357, 376, 484
Deer Hunter, The, 464
Defilers, The, 242, 243, 244, 262
Defoe, Willem, 441, 529
Deliverance, 323, 376, 498, 499
DeMille, Cecil B., 118, 134
Denby, David, 451
Denis, Claire, 258, 496
Deodato, Ruggero, 392, 393
Departed, The, 523
Department of Justice, 45, 297, 298
Depp, Johnny, 190
Dern, Bruce, 270
Dern, Laura, 427, 463
Dershowitz, Alan, 341
des Rais, Gilles, 326
Design for Living, 117, 121
Despentes, Virginie, 493, 496
Desperate Decision. *See* Revenge at Daybreak
Desperate Living, 329
Devil and Miss Jones, The, 335
Devil in Miss Jones, The, 335, 336, 357
Devil's Rejects, The, 514

Devils of Loudun, The, 317
Devils, The, 317, 318, 319, 329, 420, 476, 489
Devo, 112
Dexter, 150, 507
Diamond Lil, 128
Diary of Anne Frank, The, 253
Dick, Kirby, 450
Diderot, Denis, 258, 259
Dietrich, Marlene, 102, 103, 121, 135
Diff'rent Strokes, 416
Different From the Others. See Anders als die Andern
Director's Guild, 308
Dirty Shame, A, 509
Disney, 162, 164, 165, 166, 295, 344, 382, 383, 414, 476
Distant Journey, 193
District of Court of Appeal of California, The, 176
Divine, 40, 301, 397
Divine Comedy, The, 40
Divorcee, The, 92, 93, 102, 119, 129
Dixon, Jr., Thomas J., 44, 46
Do the Right Thing, 427, 451, 452, 453, 454, 475
Dogme 95, 488, 489, 527
Dogtooth, 530
Dogville, 528
Doherty, Thomas, 106
Dole, Bob, 471, 472, 484, 489
Don't Look Now, 333, 375, 465
Don'ts and Be Carefuls, 76, 79, 80, 86, 89, 110, 119, 159
Dougherty, Cardinal Dennis, 132

Douglas, Justice William O., 177, 178, 203, 241, 289
Douglass, Frederick, 74
Dr. Mabuse, the Gambler, 67
Dracula (1931), 110, 112, 218
Dracula (1958), 218
Drag, The, 127
Dressed to Kill, 399, 400, 401
Dreyfuss, Richard, 340
Driving Miss Daisy, 464
Drunk Brilliant Stoned Dead, 388
Ducey, Caroline, 493
Dune, 461, 462
Dunst, Kirsten, 528
Dunye, Cheryl, 457
E.T.: The Extra-Terrestrial, 374, 414, 439
earrings of Madame de ..., The, 177
East of Eden, 196
Easy Rider, 292, 293, 298
Easy Riders, Raging Bulls, 261, 269, 373
Eat, 290
Eating Raoul, 412
Ebert, Roger, 13, 240, 280, 291, 305, 306, 319, 329, 344, 361, 377, 416, 427, 434, 460, 463, 476, 510, 511, 516
Echoes of the Jazz Age, 68
Ecstasy, 123, 124, 125, 201
Ed Wood, 190
Edison, Thomas, 25, 26, 28, 32, 33
Edwards, Blake, 410
Eisenstein, Sergei, 71
Ekeroth, Daniel, 256
El Mariachi, 408

El Topo, 312, 313, 320, 328, 329, 460
Electrocuting an Elephant, 32, 33, 52
Elgin Theater, 312
Elysia, 126, 127, 142, 190
Emmanuelle, 342, 343, 344, 345, 363, 364, 490
Empire, 260, 290
Empire State Building, 260, 290
Enforcement Act of 1871, 46
Ephron, Nora, 129
Esper, Dwain, 114, 142, 143, 144, 153, 154
Espionage Act of 1917, 52
Esquire, 531
European Convention on Human Rights, 443
European Court of Human Rights, 443, 444
Even Dwarves Started Small, 481
Evil Dead 2, 386
Evil Dead, The, 401, 402, 438, 450, 513
Execution of Mary Stuart, The, 26, 53
Exorcist, The, 23, 217, 350, 351, 374, 375, 376, 406, 465
Exterminating Angel, The, 234
Eyes Without a Face. *See* Les yeux sans visage
Facebook, 47
Faces of Death, 374, 375, 390, 415, 501, 512, 513, 531
fallacy of composition, 141
Fando & Lis, 312
Fanny and Alexander, 427

Fanny Hill. *See* Memoirs of a Woman of Pleasure
Fantasia, 162
Fantasm, 315
Fargo, 528
Farrokhzad, Forugh, 238
Fascism on a Thread: The Strange Story of Nazisploitation Cinema, 354
Fashions for Women, 95
Fassbinder, Rainer Werner, 377, 378, 455
Fast Times at Ridgemont High, 396, 410
Fat Girl, 497
Faulkner, William, 99
Faust, 227
Fauves, les, 486
Favourite, The, 530
Federal Bureau of Investigation, 20, 169, 297, 424, 425
Federal Council of Churches of Christ, 132
Federal Trade Commission, 88
Fellini Satyricon, 296, 323, 368
Fellini, Federico, 172, 232, 270, 296, 354, 368, 369
Fellini's Casanova, 368, 369, 377
Felscherinow, Christiane, 404
Female Perversions, 459, 460
Female Perversions: The Temptations of Madame Bovary, 460
Female Trouble, 329
Ferman, James, 345
Festen, 488
Fetchit, Stepin, 75

Fields, W.C., 75
Fight Club, 505, 506, 508
Fight the Power, 451
Film as a Subversive Art, 81
Film Comment, 247
Film Culture, 247
Filmsite.org, 162
Fincher, David, 505
Fireworks, 167, 245
First Amendment, 34, 42, 173, 203, 242, 289
Fit to Fight, 53, 54, 55, 57, 90, 142, 150
Fit to Win. *See* **Fit to Fight**
Fitzgerald, F. Scott, 68
Five Fingers of Death, 347
Flaming Creatures, 246, 247, 248, 260, 276
Flaming Youth, 68, 69
Flanagan, Bob, 482, 483, 501
Flesh, 280, 281, 347
Flesh for Frankenstein, 347
Fletcher, Louise, 341
Focus on D.W. Griffith, 44
Fonda, Jane, 459
Fonda, Peter, 270, 293
Forbes, Elliot, 162
Forbidden Films, 148, 149
Forbidden Love, 114, 142
Ford, John, 166
Fortas, Judge Abe, 248
Foucault, Michel, 323
Fountainhead, The, 159, 335
Fox, The, 277, 279
Foxy Brown, 311
Francis, Coleman, 189
Franco, Francisco, 83
Franju, Georges, 175, 219, 316
Frankenstein, 110, 111, 112, 140, 218, 415
Franklin, Diane, 410

Freakonomics, 20
Freaks, 112, 113, 114, 142
French Board of Censors, 84
French Connection, The, 398
French Line, The, 186, 187, 188, 191, 195
French Ministry of Information, 258
French New Wave, 230, 258, 259, 268, 309, 403, 421
French Revolution, 372
Frenzy, 322
Freud, Sigmund, 18, 81, 258, 314
Friday the 13th, 349, 375
Friedkin, William, 397, 398, 399, 401
Friedman, David F., 164
Fritz the Cat, 345, 346, 347, 440
Fuck. *See* Blue Movie
Fuck Me. *See* **Baise-moi**
Fukasaku, Kinji, 501, 502
Funeral Parade of Roses, 294
Funny Games, 487
Futile and Stupid Gesture, A, 388
Gabin, Jean, 150
Gainsbourg, Charlotte, 528, 529
Gallo, Vincent, 510, 511
Gandhi, 464
Garbo, Greta, 96
Garden of Eden, 190
Garland, Judy, 101
Gaslight, 304
Gay & Lesbian Alliance Against Defamation (GLAAD), 466
Gein, Ed, 216, 322, 352

Genet, Jean, 175, 176, 242, 248, 456
Gentlemen Prefer Blondes, 187
George, Susan, 320
Gere, Richard, 410
Germany, Year Zero, 170, 171
Ghostbusters, 396
Gielgud, John, 392
Giger, H.R., 462
Gilbert Gottfried's Amazing Colossal Podcast, 457
Gilliam, Terry, 386, 387
Ginsberg v. New York, 285
Giraud, Jean "Moebius", 462
Girl Can't Help It, The, 250
Glen or Glenda, 189
Goatse.cx, 531
Godard, Jean Luc, 230, 268, 421, 422, 495, 511
Goddess, The, 146, 147
Godfather, The, 295, 374
Goebbels, Joseph, 147
Gold Diggers of 1933, 131
Golden Globes, 278
Goldstein, Robert, 52
GOMS. *See* Grumpy Old Man Syndrome
Gone with the Wind, 138, 140, 154, 155, 425
Google, 478
Gore, Tipper, 470
Gospel According to St. Matthew, The, 235, 236, 326
Goto: The Island of Love, 363
Graduate, The, 269, 374
Grand Illusion, The, 150
Grant, Cary, 95
Great Big Book of Horrible Things, The. *See* Atrocities: The 100 Deadliest Episodes in Human History
Great Depression, 87, 91, 111, 127, 130, 143
Great Train Robbery, The, 34, 37
Green Inferno, The, 513
Greenaway, Peter, 448, 449
Greetings, 287, 294
Gremlins, 414, 444
Griffith, D.W., 39, 44, 47, 48, 69, 102, 165
Griffith, Melanie, 405, 408
Grumpy Old Man Syndrome, 65, 66, 69, 72, 90, 176, 231, 242, 289, 326, 385, 403, 413, 462, 508, 515, 532
Guccione, Bob, 390, 391, 392
Guerrero, Ed, 166
Guess Who's Coming to Dinner, 308
Guest, Christopher, 389
Guinea Pig: Devil's Experiment, 423, 424, 425, 426, 501, 507, 512, 513, 527, 531
Guinea Pig: Flower of Flesh and Blood, 424, 425
Gulf and Western, 441
Gummo, 481, 482
Habe, Hans, 170
Hail Mary, 422
Haines, William, 121
Hairspray, 397, 412
Halloween, 376
Halsbury's Laws of England, 443
Handmade Films, 387
Haneke, Michael, 487, 488, 489
Hanks, Tom, 150

Hannibal, 507
Happiness, 503
Hardcore, 381, 382
Harding, Warren G., 63
Hardy, Oliver, 304
Harlow, Jean, 101, 107, 119, 127, 128, 226
Harrison, George, 387
Hartman, Saidiya, 69
Harvard Lampoon, 388
Harvard University, 388, 433
Hawks, Howard, 108, 155
Häxan, 23, 67, 68, 110
Haynes, Todd, 455, 456, 457, 482
Hays Code, 51
Hays Formula, 69
Hays Office, 73, 74, 76, 79, 91, 98, 108, 109, 111, 117, 118, 125, 127, 128, 129, 131, 132, 137
Hays, Will, 63, 64, 69, 76, 80, 86, 87, 89, 99, 107, 108, 118, 127, 128, 130, 132, 182
Hearst, William Randolph, 60, 61, 64
Heavenly Creatures, 457
Heckerling, Amy, 396, 410, 457, 458
Hedren, Tippi, 405, 406, 407, 408, 409, 410
Hedwig and the Angry Inch, 511
Heffner, Richard, 351
Hegel, Georg Wilhelm Friedrich, 372
Hegelian dialectics, 372, 446
Heins, Marjorie, 442
Hell's Angels, 100, 101, 102
Hellman, Lillian, 138, 224, 225

Hellraiser, 435, 436, 437, 465, 526
Hellraiser II, 436
Hellraiser III, 437
Hellraiser IV, 437
Helms, Jesse, 455, 456
Henry: Portrait of a Serial Killer, 426, 448, 449, 478
Hepburn, Audrey, 224, 225
Hepburn, Katherine, 204
Herbert, Frank, 461
Hercules, 156
Hereditary, 41
Herschell Gordon Lewis: The Godfather of Gore, 239
Herzog, Werner, 481, 482
Hills Have Eyes, The, 376
Himmler, Heinrich, 388
Hirschfeld, Dr. Magnus, 58
History of Narrative Film, A, 35, 47, 56
History of Sexuality, The, 323
History of the American People, 45
Hitchcock, Alfred, 205, 215, 216, 217, 255, 322, 323, 400, 407
Hitler, Adolf, 54, 84, 147, 149
Hoberman, J., 247
Hogan's Heroes, 354
Holiday Inn, 74
Hollywood and the Holocaust, 253
Hollywood Babylon, 60, 167
Hollywood Shuffle, 396
Holocaust, The, 192, 193, 251, 253, 354
Holy Mountain, The, 313, 460, 461
Homer, 22
Hong Kong New Wave, 438
Hooper, Tobe, 352, 414

Hoover, J. Edgar, 297
Hopper, Dennis, 270, 293, 427, 429
Horrible Dr. Hichcock, The, 221
Hostel, 513, 523
Hound of the Baskervilles, The, 397
House Is Black, The, 238, 275, 525
House of the Devil, 31
House on Haunted Hill, 284
How to Eat Your Watermelon in White Company (And Enjoy It), 310
Howard Hughes, 100, 154, 161
Hudson, Ernie, 396
Hughes, Howard, 100, 101, 108, 154, 155, 156, 157, 158, 161, 177, 186, 187, 193, 195
Hughes, John, 444
Hula, 72
Human Centipede 2: Full Sequence, The, 526, 534
Human Centipede, The, 526, 527
Humphrey, Daniel, 323
Hunger Games, The, 501, 502
Hurd, Douglas, 443
Huxley, Aldous, 317
Hypocrites, 39, 40, 41
I Am Curious (Yellow), 287, 288, 289, 290, 291, 338
I Drink Your Blood, 348
I Spit on Your Grave, 376, 377, 390, 415, 495, 498, 499
I Stand Alone, 489, 490
I Vitelloni, 368
I Will Walk Like a Crazy Horse, 313
I'm No Angel, 128, 129, 134
Ice-T, 471
Ichi the Killer, 501
Idioterne, 488, 489, 527
Idiots, The. *See* Idioterne
Idle, Eric, 387
If They Move ... Kill Em!, 291
Ilsa: She Wolf of the SS, 353, 354, 361
Imamura, Shohei, 259
Immediate Experience, The, 12
Immoral Mr. Teas, The, 209, 210, 239
Imperial Japanese Army's Unit 731, 437
In a Glass Cage, 423
In a Year with 13 Moons, 377
In My Skin, 497
In Search of Lost Time, 386
In the Realm of the Senses, 365, 366, 367, 368, 492, 494
Indiana Jones and the Temple of Doom, 414, 444
Indiana, Robert, 290
Ingagi, 87, 88, 89, 142, 144, 356
Innocence Unprotected, 314
Inside, 523
Inside Deep Throat, 334
Inspiration, 40, 41
Internet Archive, 164
Interstate Circuit v. Dallas, 285
Intolerance, 47, 48, 49
Invasion of the Body Snatchers, 218
Irréversible, 498, 499

Is That Black Enough For You?!?, 396
Is Your Daughter Safe?, 73, 74, 76, 142
Island of Lost Souls, 111, 112
It Ain't No Sin, 133
It Follows, 41
It Happened One Night, 465
Italian neorealism, 169, 170, 171, 232, 297, 324, 325, 377, 404, 405
Jackass, 508, 509, 522
Jackass: The Movie, 508
Jackson, Peter, 279, 439, 470
Jaffe, Jay, 537
Jagger, Mick, 320
James Boys in Missouri, The, 23, 36, 37, 50
Jannings, Emil, 102
Japanese New Wave, 259
Jarman, Derek, 175, 457
Jason Joy, 108
Jaws, 350, 373, 374, 389, 394
Jazz Singer, The, 74, 76
Jean, Wyclef, 531
Jeremy, Ron, 333
Jesus Christ, 47, 76, 119, 144, 172, 234, 318, 319, 387, 440, 441, 443, 489, 514
JFK, 465
Jinx, The, 525
Jodorowsky, Alejandro, 311, 312, 313, 460, 461, 462
Jodorowsky's Dune, 461
Johnson, Eithne, 357, 358
Johnson, Jack, 298
Johnson, Lyndon, 338
Jones, James Earl, 434
Jorgensen, Christine, 188

Journal of Film and Video, 355, 357
Joy, Jason, 74, 80, 86, 91, 108, 118, 131
Joyce, James, 98, 271
Jud Suss, 148
Kael, Pauline, 330
Kagemusha, 377
Kaplan, Louise J., 460
Karloff, Boris, 111, 283
Kazan, Elia, 195, 196, 197, 212
Keitel, Harvey, 458, 474
Ken Park, 509, 510, 511
Kennedy, John F., 269
Kenney, Doug, 388
Kerman, Robert, 392
Kermode, Mark, 318, 329, 489
Kerr, Deborah, 204
Khouri, Callie, 459
Kiarostami, Abbas, 497
Kids, 477, 478, 481, 509, 510
Killing of a Sacred Deer, The, 530
Killing of Sister George, The, 278, 294
Killing of the Unicorn, The, 264, 342
Killing, The, 228
King Jr., Martin Luther, 264, 287, 297
King Kong, 88
Kino Lorber, 40
Kinsey, Alfred, 163, 181
Kiss, 183
Kiss Me, Stupid, 254
Klein, Allan, 312
Klein, Joe, 451
Knoxville, Johnny, 509
Kodak, 212
Koresky, Michael, 225

Korine, Harmony, 481, 482, 509
Kren, Kurt, 249
Kristel, Sylvia, 344
Kroll, Jack, 451
Ku Klux Klan, 43, 44, 45, 148
Kubrick, Stanley, 228, 229, 321, 322
Kuenne, Kurt, 524
Kuleshov, Lev, 70
Kurosawa, Akira, 259, 377
L'Age d'Or, 83, 84, 114, 122, 249
La Bête humaine, 150
La Dolce Vita, 232, 233, 296, 370
La ricotta, 234, 235, 296
La ronde, 176, 177, 181, 202
La Strada, 232
La Vérité, 41
LaBeija, Crystal, 282
Lacayo, Richard, 472
Lacombe, Lucien, 379
Lady Chatterley's Lover, 201, 202, 203, 223, 228, 271, 277
Lady Sings the Blues, 310
Lamarr, Hedy, 123, 124, 125
Land Without Bread, 122, 123, 175
Landis, Judge Kenesaw Mountain, 62
Lang, Fritz, 67, 104, 106
Lange, Artie, 517
Lanthimos, Yorgos, 530
Las Hurdes, 123, See **Land Without Bread**
Laser, Dieter, 526
Lash of the Penitentes, 144, 145
Last Call, 59
Last Emperor, The, 464
Last House on the Left, The, 348, 349, 350, 352, 376, 377, 401, 416, 426, 526
Last Supper, The, 233
Last Tango in Paris, 330, 331, 332, 333, 337, 360, 365, 432, 449, 450
Last Temptation of Christ, The, 440, 441, 442, 444, 445, 447, 452, 456
Late Night with David Letterman, 481
Laughton, Charles, 111
Laugier, Pascal, 523
Laure, Carole, 359, 360
Laurel, Stan, 304
Law and Order, 205
Law and Order: SVU, 205
Lawrence, D.H., 202, 271, 277, 317
Le Corbusier, 82
Le Coucher de la Mariée, 29, 30, 31
Le sang des bêtes. See Blood of the Beasts
Le souffle au cœur, 379
League of Patriots, 83
League of Their Own, A, 458
Leave it to Beaver, 66
Lee, Canada, 180
Lee, Spike, 396, 435, 451, 452, 453
Lefebvre, Jules Joseph, 41
Leff, Leonard J., 76, 183, 202, 214, 253
Legion of Decency, 125, 130, 131, 132, 137, 150, 157, 163, 171, 172, 174, 183, 186, 193, 194, 196, 197, 198, 199, 200, 202, 208, 214, 229, 232, 242, 252, 253, 254, 262, 267, 284,

321, 350, 388, 393, 395, 442, 445
Lemmon, Jack, 306
Lenin, 70
Lennon, John, 312
Les yeux sans visage, 219, 239
Let Me Die a Woman, 375
Letter from Birmingham Jail, 264
Letterboxd, 149, 475
Letters from Iwo Jima, 523
Lewis, Herschell Gordon, 97, 239, 240, 283, 292, 300, 347, 348, 355, 398, 402, 403, 423
Lewis, Juliette, 471
Lewis, Sinclair, 97
Library of Congress, 36
Life Trilogy, 324, 469
Lincoln, Abrahan, 165
Lindsay, John, 333
Little Caesar, 107
Little House on the Prairie, 416
Little Miss Sunshine, 523
Live and Let Die, 336
Living Corpse, The, 21
Loayza, Beatrice, 178
Lobster, The, 530
Lola Montes, 177
Lolita, 228, 229, 231
Long Day's Journey Into Night, 251
Longing for Women, 96
Longworth, Karina, 51, 60, 154, 156, 165, 166, 265, 379, 431
Look Who's Talking, 458
Lord of the Rings, The, 347
Lord, Father Daniel, 76, 89, 93, 119, 129, 132

Loren, Sophia, 232
Lorna, 240, 241, 242, 280, 313, 320, 329, 376, 430
Lorre, Peter, 105, 204
Los Angeles Zoo, 88
Louis XIII, 319
Love Express: The Disappearance of Walerian Borowczyk, 362, 363, 364
Love Me Tonight, 116
Lovelace, 334
Lovelace, Linda, 334
Lovers, The, 200, 201, 379
Loving Couples, 257
Lubitsch, Ernst, 117
Lucas, George, 426, 462
Lugosi, Bela, 189
Lumet, Sidney, 251
Lumière, Auguste and Louis, 28, 29, 31, 32
Lund, Zoë, 468
Lupino, Ida, 160
Lynch, David, 429, 462, 463, 464, 482
Lyne, Adrian, 432
Lynn, Vicki, 191, 192
M (1930), 105, 106
M (1951), 106, 177
M*A*S*H*, 184
MacDonald, Jeanette, 116
Machatý, Gustav, 123
Machine Girl, The, 524
Mack, The, 311
MacLachlan, Kyle, 427
MacLaine, Shirley, 224, 225, 340
Mad Max, 315
Mädchen in Uniform, 104, 178, 279
Madonna, 92, 455, 467

Madonna/whore dichotomy. *See* Saint/sex worker dichotomy
Maîtresse, 367, 368, 483
Major, John, 443
Makavejev, Dušan, 314, 359, 360
Making a Murderer, 525
Malcolm X, 454
Malle, Louis, 200, 379, 380
Maltese Falcon, The, 204
Maltin, Leonard, 304
Mama and Papa, 249
Mamma Roma, 234
Man Is Not a Bird, 314
Man Ray, 83
Man with the Golden Arm, The, 194, 195, 198, 205, 208, 222
Man with the Golden Arm, The (novel), 193, 194
Maniac (1934), 142, 143, 149, 153, 189, 191
Maniac (1980), 401
Mankiewicz, Joseph L., 204
Mann Act, 297
Mann Theaters, 356
Mansfield, Jayne, 184, 250
Mapplethorpe, Robert, 456
Margolis, Cindy, 484
Marihuana, 143, 144, 153, 193
Maris, Roger, 66
Mark of the Devil, 348
Marnie, 322
Marshall, Alan, 466
Marshall, Noel, 405, 406, 407, 409
Marshall, Penny, 458
Martyrs, 523
Marwencol, 525
Mary, Queen of Scots, 26

Maryland Supreme Court, 289
Massachusetts Supreme Court, 275
Matisse, Henri, 486
Mativo, Kyalo, 408
Mattel, 456
May Irwin Kiss, The, 26, 27, 33, 46, 52, 53
MCA, 441, 442
McDaniel, Hattie, 165
McDormand, Frances, 528
McDowell, Malcolm, 392
McGranery, James P., 169
McKenna, Justice Joseph, 42
McKinley, William, 28
McNamara, Maggie, 184, 185
McNaughton, John, 426, 427
MDPOPE: Most Disturbed Person on Planet Earth, 531
Meatball Machine, 524
Mediawatch, 415
Meet the Feebles, 439, 440, 524
Melancholia, 528
Méliès, Georges, 31, 32, 34
Memoirs of a Woman of Pleasure, 288
Memoirs v. Massachusetts, 288
Men Behind the Sun, 437, 438, 468
Menace II Society, 454
Merrily We Go to Hell, 94, 95
Mexican Directorate of Radio, Television, and Cinema (RTC), 500
Meyer, Russ, 209, 239, 240, 280, 300, 305, 306, 319, 463

MGM, 89, 91, 92, 112, 113, 114, 121, 142, 179, 311, 431
Middle Ages, 323, 324
Midnight Cowboy, 293, 294, 302
Midnight Frolics, 191
Miike, Takashi, 500, 501, 502
Milius, John, 381
Miller v. California, 339, 391
Miller, Frank, 223
Miracle, The, 23, 172, 173, 174, 175, 176, 177, 179, 181, 183, 188, 191, 201, 203, 388, 422, 445
Miramax, 476
Miró, Joan, 83
Mirren, Helen, 296, 392
Miss All-America Camp Beauty Contest, 281
Mitchell, Elvis, 396
Mitchell, John Cameron, 511
Mizoguchi, Kenji, 259
Mom and Dad, 161, 162, 163, 164, 175, 181, 198, 237, 249, 477
Moment of Innocence, A, 239
Mona Lisa, 387
Mondo Cane, 236, 237, 238, 239, 316, 354, 374, 389
Mondo Cane 2, 237
Mondo Trasho, 301
Monet, Claude, 260
Monika, the Story of a Bad Girl. *See* Summer with Monika
Monroe, Marilyn, 13, 183, 184, 250, 463
Monsieur Verdoux, 168, 169
Monty Python and the Holy Grail, 387, 470

Monty Python: Almost the Truth – The Lawyer's Cut, 387
Monty Python's Flying Circus, 386
Monty Python's Life of Brian, 386, 387, 388, 422
Moon Is Blue, The, 184, 185, 186, 187, 188, 193, 205, 208
Moreau, Jeanne, 111, 200
Morgan, Marion, 96
Morgan, Robin, 357
Morgenthau, Robert M., 356
Morocco, 102, 103
Morris, Chester, 119, 120
Morris, Errol, 525
Morrissey, Paul, 175, 261, 280, 300, 301, 347, 396, 397, 455
mother!, 534
Motion Picture Producers and Distributors of America, 63, 69, 128, 158, 173, 194, 195, 197, 210, 216, 221, 229, 230, 252, 265, 266, 267, 285, 287, 294, 309, 351, 352, 399, 414, 421, 427, 432, 449, 450, 464, 478, 509, 514
Mou Tun-Fei, 438
Mozart, Wolfgang Amadeus, 90
MPAA. *See* Motion Picture Producers and Distributors of America
Mr. Death: The Rise and Fall of Fred A. Leuchter, Jr., 525
Mr. Mike's Mondo Video, 389, 390
Mr. Skin, 134, 200
Muehl, Otto, 359, 360

Multiple Maniacs, 301
Muni, Paul, 109
Munson, Audrey, 40
Muppets, The, 348, 439, 535
Murder at the Vanities, 131, 132
Murphy, Eddie, 396
Murray, Bill, 389
Mussolini, Benito, 124
Mutual Film Corporation v. Industrial Commission of Ohio, 42, 43, 50, 51, 64, 173
My Fair Lady, 304
My Lai massacre, 292
My Way, 389
Myra Breckinridge, 303, 304, 305
Mysterious Skin, 518, 519, 520, 521
National Association for the Advancement of Colored People, The (NAACP), 45, 165, 433
National Association of Broadcasters, The, 271
National Board of Censorship of Motion Pictures, The, 38, 39, 40, 44
National Catholic Office for Motion Pictures. *See* Legion of Decency
National Constitution Center, 139
National Endowment for Arts, 456
National Lampoon, 388, 389, 390
National Lampoon Radio Hour, The, 389
National Organization of Women, 466
National Viewers' and Listeners' Association. *See* Mediawatch
Native Son, 179, 180, 181, 203, 452
Natural Born Killers, 471, 472, 473, 485, 495
Nazisploitation, 354, 361
NCOMP. *See* Legion of Decency
Nekromantik, 439
Nekromantik 2, 439
New Andy Warhol Garrick Theater, 290
New French Extremity, The, 496, 497, 498, 499, 512
New German Cinema, 377
New Hollywood, 150, 268, 269, 293, 373, 379, 380, 382, 394, 398, 403, 464
New Queer Cinema, 397, 454, 457, 485
New World Pictures, 298, 421
New York Appellate Division, 152
New York Board of Censors, 172
New York Board of Directors, 133
New York City License Commissioner, 50
New York Film Festival, 273, 274
New York Society for the Prevention of Vice, 127
New York Supreme Court, 173
New York Times, 51, 163, 228, 312, 325, 361
New Yorker, The, 180
Newman, Paul, 68

579

Newman, Roger K., 34, 35, 45, 64, 338, 339
Niagara, 183, 184, 188, 250
Nichols, Mike, 266, 341
Nicholson, Jack, 270, 293, 340, 341
Nicholson, Jim, 190
Night After Night, 127
Night and Fog, 192, 193, 238, 525
Night Games, 257, 258
Night Nurse, 115
Night of the Living Dead, 283, 284, 349
Night Porter, The, 361, 423
Night Riders, 36, 37
Nightmare on Elm Street, A, 13
Nights of Cabiria, 232
Nine and Half Weeks, 431
Nissen, Greta, 101
Nixon, Richard, 305, 338
No Exit, 335
Noé, Gaspar, 489, 490, 498, 499
Nosferatu, 110
Not Quite Hollywood: The Wild, Untold Story of Ozploitation!, 315
Nun, The, 258, 259
NWA, 454
O'Donoghue, Michael, 389
O'Toole, Peter, 392
Obscene Publications Act 1959, 318, 415, 443
Octopus, The. *See* Is Your Daughter Safe?
Ogrish.com, 531
Ohio Constitution, 43, 174
Ohio Supreme Court, 280
Okrent, Daniel, 59
Olivia, 178, 279

Olympia, 149
Olympic Games, 149, 522, 526, 534
On the Waterfront, 196
Onassis, Jacqueline Kennedy, 289
Once Upon a Time in China: A Guide to Hong Kong, Taiwanese, and Mainland Chinese Cinema, 468
One Flew Over the Cuckoo's Nest, 465
One Hour with You, 116, 117
One Thousand and One Nights, 295
One-Armed Swordsman, The, 347
Ophüls, Max, 176, 177
Orange Blossoms, 31, 32
Ordinary People, 464
Orgazmo, 504
Orlando, 459
Oscar. *See* Academy Award
Ôshima, Nagisa, 365, 366, 492
Oswald, Richard, 58
Oswalt, Patton, 153, 154
Otis, Carrie, 432
Out of Africa, 464
Outlaw, The, 154, 155, 156, 157, 158, 159, 160, 161, 172, 184, 185, 187, 344
Outrage, 160
Oxford Dictionary of World Cinema, 176
Oxford University, 386
Ozu, Yasujirō, 259
Pacino, Al, 109, 398
Page, Bettie, 191
Palindromes, 503
Palm Beach Story, The, 75
Palme, Olof, 287

Pandora's Box, 80, 81, 102
Panic Movement, 311, 312, 313
Paper Moon, 336
Paragraph 175 of Germany's Penal Code, 57
Paramount, 95, 99, 115, 116, 127, 128, 133, 135, 216, 347, 441
Parent Teacher Association (PTA), 416
Parents Music Resource Center (PMRC), 471
Paris Is Burning, 282, 454, 455
Parker, Matt, 504
Parks, Gordon, 307, 310, 311
Parrish, Larry, 339, 340
Parton, Dolly, 415
Pasolini, Pier Paolo, 234, 235, 236, 296, 323, 324, 325, 326, 327, 354, 368, 391, 442, 469
Passion of the Christ, The, 514, 515
Patch Adams, 508
Pathé, 64
Paths of Glory, 228
Pawnbroker, The, 251, 252, 253, 265, 267
Peckinpah, Sam, 291, 320
Peeping Tom, 217, 218, 219, 220, 283, 296
Pelosi, Pino, 326, 327
Penn, Arthur, 268
Penthouse, 390
Pépé le Moko, 150
Perkins, Anthony, 420, 421
Persona, 257, 370
Pervert's Guide to Cinema, The, 16, 30
Pesci, Joe, 109

Peter III, 135
Phantom of the Opera, The, 110
Philadelphia, 457
Philadelphia Story, The, 304
Philosophy of History, 372
Piano Teacher, The, 487
Piano, The, 459, 474
Picasso, Pablo, 82
Picnic at Hanging Rock, 315
Pierce, David, 36
Pig Fucking Movie, The. *See* **Vase de Noces**
Pigsty. *See* Porcile
Pink Flamingos, 312, 328, 329, 350, 362, 419, 450
Pink Panther, 410
Pinky, 179
Pinocchio, 162
Pitt, Brad, 505
Pixote, 403, 404
Planned Parenthood, 49
Plaster Caster, Cynthia, 314
Plato, 168
Platoon, 464
Platt, George Foster, 40
Platt, Polly, 265, 379
Playboy, 13, 181, 250, 264, 285, 300, 399
Plimpton, George, 281
Poe, Edgar Allan, 283
Poison, 455, 456, 518
Poitier, Sidney, 178, 308
Polanski, Roman, 284, 380, 386
Pollock, Tom, 452
Poltergeist, 13, 413, 444
Polyester, 412
Pool of London, 178, 179
Poor Things, 530
Pope John Paul II, 422
Pope John XXIII, 234, 236

Porcile, 296
Porky's, 411, 412, 435, 477, 478
Porno chic, 334, 336, 341
Pornographers, The, 260, 294
Porter, Edwin S., 34
Possessed, 94, 100
Powell. Michael, 217, 218, 296
Pre-Code Hollywood, 106
Preminger, Otto, 185, 193, 194, 195, 205, 206, 208, 212, 215, 224
Presley, Elvis, 463
Pretty Baby, 379, 380, 382
Priest, 475, 476
Prince, 471
Production Code, 51, 89, 91, 92, 97, 100, 119, 125, 137, 138, 144, 146, 150, 156, 159, 171, 172, 178, 181, 183, 184, 185, 186, 188, 191, 193, 194, 195, 197, 198, 199, 204, 205, 210, 212, 214, 215, 216, 224, 251, 252, 259, 265, 266, 268, 286, 350, 445, 448, 498
Production Code Administration, 132, 133, 152, 156, 157, 158, 159, 171, 174, 183, 184, 185, 186, 188, 194, 197, 198, 200, 202, 203, 204, 206, 208, 215, 216, 217, 224, 225, 227, 228, 229, 232, 242, 250, 252, 253, 254, 266, 267, 335, 518
Progressive Era, 34, 35
Prohibition, 34, 59, 60, 92, 106

Projansky, Sarah, 159
Promises ... Promises, 250, 251
Prostitution, 57
Prostitution II, 57
Proud Boys, 506
Proust, Marcel, 386
Prucnal, Anna, 360
Psycho, 214, 215, 216, 217, 218, 219, 220, 239, 283, 322, 370
Public Enemy (musical group), 454
Public Enemy, The, 107
Pulp Fiction, 291, 475
Quandt, James, 496
Queen Christina, 96, 97
Queen, The (1968), 281, 282, 455
Queen, The (2006), 523
Quigley, Martin, 129
Radner, Gilda, 389
Raging Bull, 427
Raiders of the Lost Ark, 374
Raimi, Sam, 401, 402
Rain Man, 464
Rainbow Thief, The, 461
Ramis, Harold, 389
Rampling, Charlotte, 361
Rank Organization, The, 226
Rapf, Harry, 113
Rappe, Virginia, 61, 65
Rarefilmm.com, 175
Raucher, Herman, 306, 307
Reagan, Ronald, 390, 395, 398, 412, 418, 444, 448, 451, 454, 456, 484
Real Young Girl, A, 364, 365, 490
Reddit, 531
Redford, Robert, 369

Red-Headed Woman, 119, 120, 121, 128
Reefer Madness, 143, 144, 193
Reems, Harry, 340, 341
Regulating Prostitution in China, 146
Reich, Wilhelm, 314, 359
Reid, Wallace, 68
Remick, Elizabeth J., 146
Renoir, Jean, 150, 240
Report of the Commission on Obscenity and Pornography, The, 338
Reservoir Dogs, 475
Revenge at Daybreak, 241
Revier, Harry, 145
Revolt of Mamie Stover, The, 187
Revolutionary War, 52
Richelieu, Cardinal, 317, 319
Richie, Donald, 336, 365, 366, 367, 493
Riefenstahl, Leni, 149
Riki-Oh: The Story of Ricky, 469
River, The, 150
Rivette, Jacques, 258, 259
RKO, 99, 186, 187
Ro.Go.Pa.G., 234
Roar, 405, 406, 407, 408, 409, 410
Robin Hood, 344, 345
Robin Hood: Prince of Thieves, 465
Robocop, 465
Rocha, Glauber, 404
Rocky Horror Picture Show, The, 312
Rodriguez, Robert, 408
Rogan, Joe, 531
Romance, 364, 490, 491, 492, 493, 499, 509, 510, 511
Romancing the Stone, 292
Rome, Open City, 170, 171
Romero, George A, 425
Roosevelt, Eleanor, 104, 152
Root Boy Slim, 389
Rope, 205
Rosemary's Baby, 284, 285, 348, 350, 375, 380, 465
Rossellini, Isabella, 427
Rossellini, Roberto, 170, 172, 212, 232, 388
Roth v. United States, 209, 210
Roth, Eli, 109, 513
Roth, Samuel, 209
Rothman, Stephanie, 299, 300, 310, 396, 418
Rotten.com, 531
Roundtree, Richard, 311
Rourke, Mickey, 430, 432
Rules of the Game, The, 150
Ru-Paul's Drag Race, 282
Russell, James, 14
Russell, Jane, 154, 155, 156, 157, 158, 159, 160, 161, 181, 183, 184, 186, 187, 191, 195
Russell, Ken, 317, 318, 319, 320, 420, 421
Russian Civil War, 70
Russian Revolution, The, 70
S.O.B., 411
Sacchetti, Dardano, 533
Saint Joseph, 172
Saint/sex worker dichotomy, 93, 119, 459
Salò, or the 120 Days of Sodom, 325, 326, 327,

328, 350, 354, 369, 391, 423, 481, 508
Salon d'Automne, 486
Salvation Army, 81
Sanctuary, 99
Sand Creek massacre, 292
Sandler, Barry, 421
Sanger, Margaret, 49, 50, 57
Santa Sangre, 460, 461
Sapphic Underground, 278
Sarandon, Susan, 458
Sarne, Michael, 303, 304
Sartre, Jean-Paul, 335
Sátántangó, 260
Saturday Night Fever, 396
Saturday Night Live, 389, 466
Satyricon, The, 296
Savage, Dan, 392, 399, 517
Saved by the Bel, 473
Saw, 512, 513, 514, 523
Scarface, 108, 109, 120, 154
Scarlet Empress, The, 135
Schaefer, Eric, 53, 79, 88, 143, 357, 358
Schenk, Justice Gilbert V., 152
Schlock! The Secret History of American Movies, 242, 244
Schneider, Maria, 330, 331, 332, 360, 432
Schrader, Paul, 381, 382, 429
Scooby-Doo, 13, 416
Scorpio Rising, 245, 246, 247
Scorsese, Martin, 269, 440, 442
Scott, Adam, 437
Scott, Evelyn, 96
Scott, George C., 381
Scream, 513
Screwballs, 413
Seberg, Jean, 297

Second Sino-Japanese War, 437
September 11, 2001, 506
Serbian Film, A, 532, 533, 534
Servant, The, 226
Seven Words You Can Never Say on Television, 223
Seventh Seal, The, 255
Sevigny, Chloë, 477, 510
Sex and Zen, 469
Sex Madness, 153
Sex Madness Revealed, 153, 162
Sex, Sin, and Blasphemy: A Guide to America's Censorship Wars, 442
Sexual Behavior in the Human Female, 163
Sexual Behavior in the Human Male, 163
Sexual Offences Act, 226
Sexual revolution, 244, 264, 342, 410, 412
Shackleton, Allen, 355, 356, 357
Shaft, 310, 311, 396
Shakespeare, William, 21, 90
Shaw Brothers, 347
She Done Him Wrong, 128, 129, 134, 140, 141
Shechtman, Anna, 180
Sheen, Charlie, 424
Shepherd, Cybill, 265, 370
Shields, Brooke, 380, 382, 383
Shining, The, 14, 427
Shoah, 427
Shock Value: How a Few Eccentric Outsiders Gave Us Nightmares, Conquered

Hollywood, and Invented Modern Horror, 322, 350
Shoot the Piano Player, 231
Shortbus, 511, 512
Showgirls, 473, 474, 484
Shurlock, Geoffrey, 188, 203, 254
Sick: The Life and Death of Bob Flanagan, Supermasochist, 482, 483, 508, 525, 526
Sight and Sound, 10
Sign of the Cross, The, 118, 119, 134
Silence of the Lambs, The, 14, 216, 322, 464, 465, 485, 505, 507
Silence, The, 255, 256
Silent Night, Deadly Night, 416, 417, 444
Simmons, Jerold L., 76, 183, 202, 214
Simpsons, The, 65, 505
Sin in Soft Focus: Pre-Code Hollywood, 100, 129
Sinatra, Frank, 194
Siskel, Gene, 416, 441
Six, Tom, 527
Skin: A History of Nudity in the Movies, 410
Skinner, B.F., 321
Sleep, 290
Smallwood, Christine, 112
Smiles of a Summer Night, 255
Smith, Kevin, 508
Smith, Russell, 482
Smithee, Alan, 437
Snopes, 355
Snuff, 355, 356, 357, 358, 401, 413, 416, 424
Snuff R73, 531

Soapdish, 455
Society for the Development of the National Industry, 28
Socrates, 372
Sois belle et tais-toi, 459
Soldier Blue, 292, 347, 348
Solondz, Todd, 503
Some Like it Hot, 254
Song of the South, 162, 164, 165, 166, 179, 181, 346
Sontag, Susan, 247
Soul Man, 433, 434, 435, 444
South Park, 503, 504
South Park: Bigger, Longer and Uncut, 504
Space Jam: A New Legacy, 362
Spacek, Sissy, 400
Spanish Civil War, 233
Sparre, Ebba, 97
Spartacus, 217, 228
Spellman, Cardinal Francis, 197
Spheeris, Penelope, 396, 457
Spielberg, Steven, 413, 414, 435
Spirit of '76, 52
Spook Who Sat by the Door, The, 310
Spruce Goose, The, 156, 157
St. Teresa of Avila, 443
Stalin, 70, 71
Stanley v. Georgia, 289, 338
Stanwyck, Barbara, 115, 120, 127, 135
Star Trek, 19
Star Wars, 350, 373, 374, 403, 462
Stars and Stripes, 183
Steckler, Ray Dennis, 189
Steiger, Rod, 251
Steinem, Gloria, 94

Stewart, Jimmy, 17, 206
Stewart, Justice Potter, 30, 201, 203
Stone, Oliver, 471
Stone, Sharon, 466, 467, 471, 474
Stone, Trey, 504
Stonewall riots, 302
Storm, Tempest, 191
Story of Temple Drake, The, 99, 100
Storytelling, 503
Stratten, Dorothy, 264
Straw Dogs, 319, 320, 322
Street Fighter, The, 348
Streetcar Named Desire, A, 116, 160, 196, 197, 198
Strick, Joseph, 272
Strike, 71
Student Nurses, The, 299, 300, 396
Studio Relations Board, 99, 131, 132
Studio Relations Committee, 80
Sturges, Preston, 75
Suddenly, Last Summer, 204, 205, 224
Summer with Monika, 198, 199, 200, 255
Sun Shines Bright, The, 166, 179
Sundance Film Festival, 456, 512
Super Fly, 311
Superman III, 13
Superstar: The Karen Carpenter Story, 456
Supervixens, 306
Supreme Court of Illinois, 37
Supreme Court of Ohio, The, 181

Surrealism, 81, 82, 83, 123, 175, 257, 311, 313, 360, 363, 482
Sutherland, Donald, 369
Swann, William Dorsey, 282
Swedish Sensationsfilms, 256
Sweet Marijuana, 132
Sweet Movie, 359, 360, 361, 369, 481, 508
Sweet Sweetback's Baadasssss Song, 308, 309, 310, 311, 396, 408, 419
Swing Time, 74
Swinton, Tilda, 460
Swiss Family Robinson, 383
Sydney Film Festival, 422
Tanguy, Yves, 83
Tarantino, Quentin, 475, 508
Targets, 283, 284
Tarr, Bela, 260
Tasmanian Devil, 110
Tauro, Justice G. Joseph, 338
Taxi Driver, 370, 371, 381, 394, 489
Taxidermia, 522, 523
Taylor, Elizabeth, 204, 250, 266
Tea And Sympathy, 204
Team America: World Police, 504
Teaserama, 191
Temple, Shirley, 99, 100, 258, 305
Ten Commandments, The, 514
Teorema, 296
Terminator II: Judgment Day, 465
Terms of Endearment, 464
Tetsuo: The Iron Man, 524

Texas Chain Saw Massacre, The, 216, 322, 351, 352, 376, 401, 414, 438, 495, 514
Tezuka, Osamu, 295
Thalberg, Irving, 89, 91, 92, 112, 114
Thatcher, Margaret, 395
Thelma & Louise, 458
Therese and Isabelle, 279, 280
These Three, 138, 224, 225
They Shoot Pictures, Don't They?, 10, 255, 325, 370, 391, 427, 475, 496
Thing From Another World, The, 402
Thing, The, 402, 403
Thirty Years' War, 97
Thomas, Olive, 60
Thousand and One Nights, A, 295
Thriller: A Cruel Picture, 353, 361
Through a Glass Darkly, 255
Tie Me Up! Tie Me Down!, 450
Tierra Sin Pan. See **Land Without Bread**
Tiger King, 525
TikTok, 36
Time, 472
Time Bandits, 387
Tin Drum, The, 378, 379
Tingler, The, 284
Tippi: A Memoir, 406, 410
Tisch, Steve, 433, 434
Titicut Follies, 273, 274, 275, 276, 281
Titus Andronicus, 90

To Wong Foo, Thanks for Everything, Julie Newmar, 457
Tokyo Gore Police, 524
Tolstoy, Leo, 21, 22, 107, 279
Tonight Show, The, 289
Tony Award, 266
Torture horror, 513, 514, 523
Torture porn. See Torture horror
Total Recall, 465
Townshend, Robert, 396
Toxic Avenger, The, 417, 418
Traffic in Souls, 53
Trainspotting, 194
Transformers, 527
Trash, 300, 347
Trash Trilogy, 329
Tree with Wooden Clogs, The, 377
Trip, The, 270, 271, 293, 311
Triumph of the Will, 149
Troma, 417, 418, 419
Trouble Every Day, 496
Troutt, Kathy, 383
Truffaut, Francois, 231, 268
Tulsa massacre of 1921, 452
Turan, Kenneth, 492
Turner, Kathleen, 420, 421
Tweed, Shannon, 342
U.S. Public Health Service, 152
U.S. Supreme Court, 30, 42, 51, 66, 106, 163, 173, 176, 177, 179, 181, 186, 191, 200, 203, 209, 212, 227, 231, 241, 248, 275, 285, 288, 289, 291, 339, 445, 490, 495
Ulysses, 98, 272
Ulysses (film), 271, 272, 273

Un chant d'amour, 175, 176, 242, 248, 276, 288, 518
Un chien andalou, 81, 82, 83, 84, 175, 257
United Artists, 168, 185, 194, 293, 317, 318
United Nations General Assembly, 305
United Negro Congress, The, 165
United Presbyterian Church, 107
United States Customs Bureau, 124, 256, 288, 391
United States Treasury Department, 194
United States v. One Book Called Ulysses, 98, 271
United States v. Paramount, 163, 171, 172
Universal, 402, 441, 442, 452
University of California, Berkeley, 358
University of Utah, 159
Unspooled, 392, 399, 517
Untouchables, The, 401
Up!, 306
Uptown Saturday Night, 310
Vacation, 389
Valenti, Jack, 267, 285, 351
Valley Girl, 396
Valley of the Dolls, 305
Valley of the Nude. *See* Elysia
Van Gogh, Vincent, 486
Van Peebles, Mario, 309
Van Peebles, Melvin, 306, 307, 308, 309, 310, 311, 418, 434
Van Sant, Gus, 329, 457
Variety, 114, 187, 336
Vase de Noces, 359

Vengeance!, 347
Venice Film Festival, 124, 257
Verhoeven, Paul, 465, 466, 467, 473
Vertigo, 17
Vertov, Dziga, 70
Veterans of Foreign Wars, 107
Vibenius, Bo Arne, 353
Vicious, Sid, 389
Victim, 225, 226, 227, 245, 475
Vidal, Gore, 303, 392
Video nasties, 415, 420
Video Privacy Protection Act of 1988, 379
Video Recordings Act 1984, 416
Videodrome, 413
Vieira, Mark A., 100, 129
Viennese Actionists, 249, 312, 359, 360, 370, 482
Village Voice, 397, 398
Villaronga, Agustí, 423
Virgin Mary, 93, 233, 422
Virgin Spring, The, 230, 255, 349
Viridiana, 233, 234
Visconti, Luchino, 297, 354
Visions of Ecstasy, 443, 444
Visitor Q, 501
Viva la Muerte, 313
Viva Maria!, 285
Vixen!, 280, 305
Vizzard, Jack, 168
Vogel, Amos, 81
Vogue, 455
von Krusen, Agnes, 257
von Sternberg, Joseph, 102, 103, 135
von Trier, Lars, 488, 489, 527, 528, 529

W.R.: Mysteries of the Organism, 314, 359
Wake in Fright, 315
Wallace, David Foster, 429
Warhol, Andy, 175, 247, 260, 261, 280, 281, 290, 300, 412
Warner Brothers, 63, 110, 266, 267, 269, 318, 321, 350, 351
Warshow, Robert, 12
Washington, George, 143
Wasserman, Lew, 441
Watergate, 334, 351
Watermelon Man, 307, 434
Waters, John, 240, 246, 280, 301, 304, 328, 329, 330, 362, 396, 397, 412, 418, 419, 508, 509, 510
Watson, Emily, 528
Wayward Lives, Beautiful Experiments: Intimate Histories of Social Upheaval, 69
Weber, Lois, 39, 40, 41
Wedding Trough. See **Vase de Noces**
Weddle, David, 291
Weimar Republic, 80
Weiss, George, 188, 189
Welch, Raquel, 304
Welcome to Marwen, 525
Welles, Orson, 179
West, Mae, 127, 128, 129, 133, 134, 198, 280, 304, 467
Whale, James, 111
White, Chief Justice Edward Douglass, 43, 231
White, Matthew, 169
Whitehouse, Mary, 415
Whitman, Charles, 283

Whitman, Walt, 239
Who's Afraid of Virginia Woolf?, 266, 267, 268
Wikipedia, 244
Wild Angels, The, 263, 264, 265, 266, 270
Wild at Heart, 462, 463, 464
Wild Bunch, The, 291, 292, 320, 321, 334
Wild Strawberries, 255
Wild Wild Country, 525
Wilder, Billy, 253, 254
Wildmon, Donald, 456
Will & Grace, 515
Will Success Spoil Rock Hunter?, 250
Williams, Linda, 358, 492
Williams, Tennessee, 196, 197, 204
Wilson, Woodrow, 44, 45
Window Water Baby Moving, 211, 316, 317
Wingrove, Nigel, 443
Wings, 72
Winter Light, 255
Wiseman, Frederick, 273, 274, 275
Wishman, Doris, 244, 375
Withnail and I, 387
Wiz, The, 396
Wizard of Oz, The, 140
Wizards, 347
Woman Rebel, The, 49
Women Against Violence Against Women (WAVAW), 357
Women Against Violence in Pornography and Media (WAVPM), 357, 400
Women In Love, 317
Women of the World, 237
Women's Film Classics, 40

589

Wood, Ed, 188, 189, 190, 303
Woodlawn, Holly, 301
Woods, James, 413
Woodward, Bob, 334
Workers Leaving the Lumière Factory, 28
World According to Garp, The, 455
World War I, 52, 54, 56, 69, 70, 100
World War II, 48, 84, 106, 109, 140, 146, 156, 164, 169, 181, 192, 204, 223, 230, 279, 325, 501
Woronov, Mary, 412
Wright, Richard, 179, 180, 181
Wu Yonggang, 147
Wyler, William, 224, 225, 255

Y tu mamá también, 499, 500
Yagher, Kevin, 437
Yang, Jeff, 468
You Must Remember This, 51, 60, 154, 156, 165, 166, 265, 379, 431
Young Widow, 158
YouTube, 26, 27, 40, 88, 123, 153, 175, 249, 276, 278, 320, 390, 437
Zabrecky, Rob, 153
Zabriskie Point, 297, 298, 340
Zemeckis, Robert, 525
Zetterling, Mai, 257
Zinoman, Jason, 284, 322, 350
Zizek, Slavoj, 16, 17, 18, 30
Zombie, Rob, 514

Acknowledgements

Thank you to Sean Shore, Erin Dykhuizen, Matt Pietz, and Joe Pettigrew for reading all or some of the manuscript.

www.ingramcontent.com/pod-product-compliance
Lightning Source LLC
Chambersburg PA
CBHW052005070526
44584CB00016B/1629